29.95

D1088247

The American Encyclopedia of

SOCCER

The American Encyclopedia of

SOCCER

An Associated Features Book

Edited by
ZANDER HOLLANDER

Everest House  Publishers

New York

PHOTO CREDITS

American Soccer League: 274, 278. Bermuda News Bureau: 506. Bettman Archive: 11,14,16,22,23,264,500,502. Mickey Cochrane Collection: 66T,76. Dallas Morning News: (Gary Barnett) 283,289,292,297; (John Rhodes) 296. Harry Fairfield Collection: 30,36. Harrison Funk: 508. Billy Gonsalves Collection: 262,266,512. Ray Gouldsberry: 300,303. Phil Hailer: 305. Jack Hynes Collection: 267,268,271,272,510. North American Soccer League: 323T. Richard Pilling: 2,280,307,312,315,321,322,326. Bill Smith: 323B. Patrick Surrena: 275. Tampa Tribune Times: (Britt Laughlin) 133; (Mack Goethe) 201B,200. George Tiedemann: 8,298,304B,308B,319T,320,350. UPI: 199B,302,304T,308T,314,330,476,485,487,488,489,490,491,493,494, 496,497,503,504. Don Yonker Collection: 159; (Carlo J. Zilliani) 162.

Dallas Tornado: 309. Detroit Express: 318. Fort Lauderdale Strikers: (Steve Merzer) 313. Kansas City Spurs: 287. Los Angeles Aztecs: 335. Minnesota Kicks: 319B. New England Tea Men: (Thomas Croke) 317. New York Apollo: (Bruce Bennett) 277. New York Cosmos: 291; (Paul Bereswill) 294; 311,327. Toronto Falcons: 261.

Air Force: (Thomas E. Simondi) 150. Akron: 151. Alderson-Broaddus: 153. American: 107,154. Army: 155. Babson: (Alan Steacy) 156. Ball State: 157. Baltimore: 122. Bates: 158, 173. Brown: (Robinson Collection) 96; 115,121,163. Brandeis: 54. Bucknell: 165. California-Berkeley: 166. California-UCLA: 167. CCNY: 74; (L. Karabaic) 171. Central Florida: 169. Clemson: 172. Columbia: 33,101; (Michael Verderame) 174. Connecticut: 49,58,175. Dartmouth: 177. Davis &

Elkins: 102,178. Denver: (Tim Imel) 179. Drew: 180. Drexel: 71,75T,181. Duke: 68. East Stroudsburg State: 111. Elizabethtown: 183. Fairleigh Dickinson: 185,215B. Florida International: 186. Fredonia State: 187. Furman: 188. George Mason: (Alexandra Gerry) 189. George Washington: 190. Goshen: 191. Grove City: 192. Hartford: 81B. Hartwick: (Tipple-Helmer Studio) 103T,106; 127,194T. Harvard: (Walter Fleischer) 42; 75B; (David Duhme) 84; 100,109,117; (Bob Alexander) 194B; 195. Haverford: 28,196. Hobart: 198. Howard: 80; (Dick Darcey) 110; (James Wallhermfechtel) 118B; 199T. Indiana: 125; (Paul Peck) 131; 201T. Ithaca: 89L,202. James Madison: 114. LaSalle: 79T,205. Lock Haven State: 103B. Long Island U.: (Alan Tepper) 91; 93,95T,207. MacMurray: 209T. Maine: 209B. Maryland: 59,98,211. Michigan State: 77BL-BR,79B,83B,86,94,213T. Middlebury: 82,92,95B,213B. Missouri-St. Louis: 214,215T. Morris Harvey: 216. Navy: 83T,85B,217. New Hampshire: (Ed Wisneski) 218. New Jersey Tech: (Handy-Boesser) 219. North Carolina: 221. Old Dominion: 223. Oneonta State: (Garth Stam Collection) 224. Penn State: 61,126,225. Pennsylvania: 50,64,66B,108,123,226. Pfeiffer: 227. Plymouth State: 228. Princeton: 18,27,40. Quincy: 90,113,116,229,230. Randolf-Macon: (Brace Duncan) 231. Rockford: 233. Rollins: 234. San Francisco: 120; (Rodney Lee) 124,128; 130. Sangamon State: (Ron Ackerman) 238T. San Jose State: 89R,97,238B. Seattle Pacific: 239. Seton Hall: (George Van) 62T. Simon Fraser: 241T. Slippery Rock: 241B. Southern Illinois-Edwardsville: 129,242. Springfield: 51. Stanford: 244T; (Robert Byers) 244B. St. Louis: 85T,88,104,105,112, 134,344. Syracuse: (Dennis McDonald) 246. Temple: 62B,67,77T. Trinity: 72,248. Vermont: 99. Wesleyan: 252. Wheaton: (Alan Walter Whitelock) 69; (Lincoln Beals) 73; 255. Williams: 81T,256. Wooster: 118T,258.

CONTENTS

THE PROFESSIONALS

PREFACE

Soccer has been on the American scene in one form or another for more than a hundred years, and our libraries have housed a modest number of soccer books. But most of them, like the sport, came from Europe. As the game in the United States experienced its dramatic boom in the 1970s, it became apparent that there was a singular need for a total work that would tell the story of soccer, American style.

The search for material for *The American Encyclopedia of Soccer* would eventually span the country—from the archives of Haverford and the University of Pennsylvania, to a college president in Indiana who had coached soccer, to a ninety-year-old former newspaperman in Pittsburgh, to a fireman in New York who was once a leading professional player.

The college president, Dr. Robert Baptista, of Taylor University, made available his doctoral dissertation on the history of intercollegiate soccer in the United States, and Cornelius (Mickey) Cochrane, veteran coach at Bowling Green and a soccer historian, provided his masters thesis on intercollegiate soccer data. The Spalding and National Collegiate Athletic Association guides were also useful sources.

Donald Yonker, a coach for thirty years at Drexel in Philadelphia and editor of the *Soccer Journal* published by the National Soccer Coaches Association, was invaluable in his counsel and as a contributor to the encyclopedia (especially in the chapter, The College Game Comes of Age). The other contributing writers include Pete Alfano of *Newsday* (Origin of the Game, The Immigrant Sport in America), Jim Smith of *Newsday* (The American Soccer League), Temple Pouncey of the Dallas *Morning News* (The North American Soccer League), and author and TV commentator Paul Gardner (World Cup, Glossary).

Statistics are a vital part of the encyclopedia, and it took massive research by Mal Karwoski of the North American Soccer League to compile the All-Time NASL Player Register (more than 2,000 players).

The editor acknowledges with appreciation the varied support services of Howard Blatt, Jim Poris and Eric Compton, and the cooperation of Commissioner Phil Woosnam, Ted Howard, Chuck Adams, and Joan Murtha of the NASL, and Jim Trecker, former NASL director of public relations now with the Washington Diplomats. The all-time records of the NASL are reprinted with permission.

A special word of appreciation for the designer, Gerry Burstein of SOHO Studio.

There were countless others who gave an answer, a suggestion, a prop, or a photo that helped make the encyclopedia a reality. They include Jack Hynes, the fireman who was a star in the American Soccer League; Harry Fairfield, the nonagenarian from Pittsburgh, and Marion Rudden, whose stepfather was Billy Gonsalves, called by many "the Babe Ruth of Soccer."

Also Kurt Lamm, Julius Alonso, and Walt Chyzowych of the United States Soccer Federation; Otto Radich, Haskell Cohen, and Marty Berman of the ASL; referees Harry Rodgers, Don Byron, and the late Jim Walder; Jack Waters, NCAA; Abe Goteiner, formerly NAIA; George Killian, National Junior College Athletic Association; Charlie Scott, Herb Hartnett, and Seth Roland, Pennsylvania; Walter Bahr, Penn State; Whitey Burnham, Dartmouth; Joe Bean, Wheaton; Bob DiGrazia, California at Berkeley; Bob Durkin, New Paltz; Fred Hartrick, Buffalo State College; Bob Guelker, Southern Illinois-Edwards-

ville; Joe Baum, Michigan State; Sam Foulds, Edner Breton, Gene Chyzowych, Phil Fox, Enzo Magnozzi, Erwin Single, Archie Stark, Lynn Smith, Colin Jose, Aaron Elson, Frank Kelly, Lee Stowbridge, and Chip Young.

To list them all individually would take a book, but let it be said that the sports information directors at the colleges and the club publicity men in the NASL and ASL made important contributions. So did Phyllis Hollander of Associated Features.

ZANDER HOLLANDER

INTRODUCTION

Have you ever wondered what people in the late 1960s might have thought about the potential for soccer in North America in the 1980s? Could they have imagined the amazing development of the sport from a game that was played on a local basis mainly by immigrant groups to a sport whose popularity has now attracted a major segment of our society?

In a relatively brief period, soccer has witnessed major changes and is now as widely accepted as other sports due to the efforts of thousands of volunteers committed to its development as an exciting activity for boys and girls across North America. With so many youngsters now playing soccer on a regular basis from the age of six, I am confident that the quality of play at all levels will be as good as anywhere in the world in the next decade.

Soccer, a sport that is easy to understand, provides a high level of fitness for its participants and has an extremely low incidence of injury. It has gained its broad acceptance as a result of great strides made on both the professional and youth levels.

Of course, the arrival of Pelé with the New York Cosmos in 1975 was the biggest factor in establishing the appeal and credibility of the sport. Until then, there had been doubt, often expressed by worldwide media, as to whether soccer could become popular in a nation that has so many other well-established home-grown pastimes. Pelé changed the face of soccer in not only the United States but in Canada as well.

The media, the public, major corporations and their advertising agencies responded, to be sure, but it was one man, Pelé, who filled the major stadiums and was responsible for the soccer boom. He is, as everyone in the soccer world knows, an exceptional individual who, on and off the field, has lived up to his status as a superstar.

Other international superstars, such as Franz Beckenbauer and Johan Cruyff, followed Pelé and are leaving their mark on the sport in North America. Surely the valuable experience gained by young Americans and Canadians playing with and against such outstanding performers will accelerate their development and improve their play. And although we at the professional level have yet to feel the full impact of improved programs for high school and youth players, it will not take long because colleges around the nation are reflecting a higher standard.

There is every indication that soccer will soon be taking its place alongside collegiate football and basketball as a sport capable of attracting large audiences and producing an abundance of top-quality talent for the pros.

An added dimension is that soccer offers the opportunity for intense international competition or, alternately, friendly exchange programs at all levels. Already, thousands of players have traveled overseas to enjoy the opportunity of playing soccer and experiencing a different way of life. Some of them will grow up to become accomplished professionals and will represent their nations in World Cup competition.

Eventually we look to the ultimate privilege of hosting the most prestigious tournament—the World Cup. Over one billion television viewers watched the final of the 1978 World Cup, making it the most widely watched sporting event. Staging the finals of the World Cup in the United States will enable Americans to gain a first-hand appreciation of the impact of soccer around the world.

Longtime followers and those with recent interest should take this opportunity to become familiar with the accomplishments of those who have played a major role in the U.S. development of the sport. Zander Hollander and his contributors to THE AMERICAN ENCYCLOPEDIA OF SOCCER have produced a comprehensive text which fills a void in defining America's historic role in the game. It will provide an insight into the enormous potential of soccer in North America.

PHIL WOOSNAM
Commissioner
North American Soccer League

This rendering of a game between England and ▶
Scotland is dated March 6, 1875. Early matches were
often wild affairs, and any number could play.

THE EARLY YEARS

Group II. No. 358   SEPTEMBER, 1915   PRICE 10 CENTS

SPALDING'S

ATHLETIC LIBRARY

Auxiliary Series

Spalding's Official College Soccer Foot Ball Guide

Published under the Auspices of the
National Collegiate Athletic Association

Edited by

GEORGE W. ORTON

University of Pennsylvania

1915

AMERICAN SPORTS PUBLISHING CO.
21 Warren Street, New York

1

Origin of the Game

While the beginnings of such North American pastimes as baseball, basketball, and hockey can be pinpointed with a minimum of debate, the same cannot be said of soccer. Where did soccer (or football, as it is known throughout most of the world) originate?

Was man's introduction to the sport a result of kicking stones in an idle moment or booting a ball filled with hair or perhaps kicking the skull of a detested Dane, as Englishmen are wont to believe?

Did soccer have its birthplace in ancient China—one of the mysteries of the Orient? Can Greece, Rome or Florence take the credit? Maybe the first goal was scored in England as some boy booted the Danish skull past a defender.

History is filled with speculation, and in this case too there is no indisputable answer. In truth, soccer—in its crude form—probably had a hundred inventors, all doing what seemed to come naturally. For kicking an object comes as easily as walking, and how many of us have innocently walked down a street or country road, leisurely kicking a pebble until it was directed too far off course?

There are some historians who believe the sport is enhanced because of its undetermined origins. N.L. Jackson noted how trivial the origin of a game was when it was not popular with the masses. But allow a game to rise to the level of a national pastime, Jackson adds, and a pedigree must be forthcoming.

Some have credited China with being the birth-place of soccer. Historians document the writings of Chinese in 80 B.C. who wrote of the popular activities of the day, which included cock fighting, dog racing, playing stringed instruments, and playing football.

The poet Li Yu, who lived in the first century A.D., described the scene during a Chinese football game. Others also have described in detail the Chinese game. There was just one goal, formed with two bamboo poles, thirty or more feet high, adorned with colored silks, and having an opening of more than one foot in diameter. Players took turns trying to kick a ball through the opening. Points were scored for each success.

There are others, however, who find little support for soccer's origins in the Orient. Nothing in China's art or literature supports the claim. And no one has attempted to trace the origin of soccer in China to the present game and its flowering throughout the world.

The same uncertainties exist for those who believe soccer had its start in Greece and Rome. Although sport was pursued as religiously then as it is today, the Greeks and Romans limited their use of the legs to running.

In Greece and Rome, three types of balls were used in games. The harpastum was a small ball filled with hair. It was used in a game played with the hands. The pila trigonalis was stuffed with hair but was larger. Three players formed a triangle and threw this ball back and forth as quickly as possible. Can anyone envision the National Pila Trigonalis League? The follis was a large ball

Reproduction of a painting of soccer on the public square in Florence, Italy, around 1500.

filled with hair and similar to a modern-day soccer ball.

Harpastum and follis were believed to be games from which modern soccer was derived. Harpastum originally was called phaeninda. Participants tossed the ball to one another while others tried to intercept it or tackle the player who caught it. Some historians believe it was closer to rugby than to soccer because the harpastum was never kicked.

Romans played a game called follis in which the objective was to toss the ball in the air and to keep it up by using the hands. There was no indication the feet were used, unless the Romans were kicking one another. In Florence, calcio was the biggest team sport. There were twenty-seven players on a side and the idea was to pass, kick, or carry the ball across the goal. Imagine fifty-four players on the field at the same time. Envision the mayhem which ensued. Calcio was thought by some to be a term synonymous with mob violence.

Like the beginnings of our solar system, soccer had a definite origin. It remains unknown, however. What historians do agree on is that the sport found a home and began to develop in England.

Now about that Danish skull. According to English folklore, sometime between 1050 and 1075, workmen digging in an old battlefield came across the skull. Still smarting from the Danish occupation of the period, the workmen took out their animosity on the skull of their former enemy and in the process discovered the first soccer ball.

A tall tale, perhaps, for although the Danish occupation of England is well documented, how were these workmen to know it was a Danish skull they were booting across the field? No matter how hardheaded the Dane might have been, how long could the skull have stayed in one piece? Finally, why is there no specific date to mark this occasion, which otherwise is described so vividly? Well, it's a good story anyway.

Football's first mention in English literature

appeared in William Fitzstephen's history of London, written in 1174. Again, as in Rome, Greece, and Florence, the games described were ones in which the players were allowed to use their hands when advancing the ball. It would be farfetched to call these games the forerunner of soccer.

During the twelfth and thirteenth centuries, a game was played throughout England which was comparable to football but also seemed like a form of permissive violence. Again, the idea was basic: attempt to advance the ball to the opponent's goal. Using strategy and/or force, the two sides hungrily went at one another.

As described by historians, this game took place in the marketplace. It was a bloody affair with broken limbs a regular occurrence. Games matched town against town, married men against bachelors, parish against parish. Roads, trees, shrubs, and buildings were used as boundaries and goals.

Needless to say, the sport did nothing to further the image of the English gentleman. It made dueling at sunrise seem safer and more humanitarian. This game bore no link to soccer. At times, the sport was an excuse for men to fight with one another, flailing away with their fists and throwing elbows with more purpose than a basketball center.

Average citizens recoiled at such events. They often took refuge in their homes or shops as a game of mob football continued at their front door. Toward the end of the Middle Ages, mob football had become a nuisance at best. Personal injury and property damage made it difficult to classify this activity as a sport.

Also, football was competing against archery, and archers were needed to defend the kingdom. How could they if they were busy recovering from a broken leg suffered on the football field? A long-awaited backlash was felt in 1314, during the reign of Edward II. Nicholas Farndon, the Mayor of London, issued an edict which banned football in that city.

Yet football continued to be played in spite of the opposition. During the reign of Edward III and Richard II, proclamations were issued banning football as well as other sports such as tennis and dice.

Despite these efforts, the game flourished. It also was confined to a preestablished field. No longer did shopkeepers have to fear a half-dozen combatants would come tumbling through their window. Rules governing the conduct of play were adopted. Toward the latter part of the fifteenth century, a football game was described as one in which the ball was propelled not by the hands or by carrying it, but by striking it with the feet.

In the following century, the sport no longer was the pastime of only the workingman. Football made its appearance on college campuses. In 1580, though, the vice-chancellor of Cambridge decreed that scholars could play football against fellow schoolmates, but not against scholars from other campuses. Thus, football at Cambridge was an intramural sport.

The vice-chancellor was fighting a losing battle. By 1620, intercollegiate games were being played at Cambridge. Sir Symonds D'Ewes wrote in his diary of finishing supper on March 29, 1620, then venturing to the field behind Queens College to engage in some "hot foot-ball playing." Symonds also wrote of how he participated in a match between St. John's College and Trinity College.

Criticism had not waned, however. Throughout the seventeenth and eighteenth centuries groups tried to ban football in England. Like modern-day opposition to football and boxing, the outcry was the loudest following a soccer-related death.

In 1709, in the parish of Great Ness, one such death occurred. Richard Venable, a servant, died after colliding with two opponents in a game of football.

Controversy existed on religious grounds as well. Sunday football was discouraged by various groups, and the Puritans did much to curtail it on the sabbath. Their effort met with limited success. In fact, football seemed to have a divine stamp of approval after people read the St. James Journal on December 1, 1722.

It seemed that a hurricane struck a village near Eastlow during an hour when parishioners usually were in church. But there was a football game in progress. While the parishioners watched the game, the hurricane toppled the church steeple. Because it was empty, many lives were saved. The journal never did explain why a football game was being played in a hurricane, however.

Perhaps it was because the game remained one of violence and brute force despite the rules changes made prior to the nineteenth century.

IS FOOT-BALL BRUTAL?

It won't be when the Pneumatic Foot-Ball Suit of the future comes into use.

Cartoonist Opper, a precursor of Rube Goldberg, had the solution for safer football.

And even a hurricane could be taken in stride. There were more accounts of how frustrated players lashed out at one another by kicking shins instead of the ball. An unknown Frenchman, who was repulsed at the sight of the game, was alleged to have said, "Well, if this is play, then me for France when they begin to fight."

Football had been attacked by kings, legislation failed to have any lasting impact, and the church made it forbidden. It was a disorganized and bloody, violent sport, but it survived. In fact, it soon began to thrive.

In the 1800s, the sport of mob football gradually declined, then disappeared from the English scene. In its new form, football was introduced in the public schools where it became more regulated and refined. Rules replaced rowdyism. Order overcame chaos. But soon the game was at its crossroads.

Would it continue as a kicking game, or should the use of the hands be permitted? It seemed to depend on where the game was played. At the schools where the playgrounds were smaller, the kicking game was dominant. Charterhouse and Westminster regularly participated in the kicking game.

Rugby School, however, had more wide open spaces. And while the kicking game was dominant here too, a monument on the campus attests to the event which split English football into two distinct games. The inscription on the monument commemorates the exploit of William Webb Eliis, who disregarded the rules one day, took the ball in his arms and ran with it in the manner of Jim Brown, O. J. Simpson, and Earl Campbell.

Thus, the games of soccer and rugby emerged from the same egg and began to compete. Westminster and Charterhouse championed the kicking game, while Rugby promoted the game in which the hands were allowed to be used.

In 1863, a milestone was reached when Charterhouse and Westminster played the first interschool football game in history. Westminster won, 2-0.

As English boys graduated and went to college, they brought with them a variety of football games, each with minor rules changes and some with major changes. In 1846, a group of Cambridge University students—all who played the kicking game—attempted to draw up a uniform set of rules. The Cambridge Rules did not gain widespread acceptance, but it marked the beginning of an effort to devise a universal set of rules for the sport of football.

In lieu of a common game, soccer and rugby continued to compete for most favored status. From the playgrounds to the college campuses to the towns and country, each district had its own game. Confusion was its middle name. In 1863, an attempt was made to resolve the differences. Representatives from the schools and various football clubs were invited to a meeting at Freemasons' Tavern in London.

It was held on October 26, 1863, and it marked the birth of The Football Association. It also marked the irreparable split in football. J. C. Thring, a Westminster graduate, drew up the Cambridge Rules and the rules for The Simplest Game. The new game, however, was essentially soccer and met with disapproval from the rugby adherents.

The rugby group did have two new rules added to the tentative set already drawn up. Rules IX and X would have allowed a player to run with the ball and his opponent to tackle him. A long and heated debate ensued.

The fate of football was in the balance. Finally, the Cambridge advocates won out and rules IX and X were eliminated. The motion was carried, and the rugby features of the game were removed.

The rugby group was infuriated, and led by the Blackheath Club, they immediately withdrew from The Football Association. Thus, hope of one, universal game of football in England had faded. From December 8, 1863, two games of football have thrived in England. They are known as rugby and soccer.

2

The Immigrant Sport
Comes to America

The English colonists who settled in America brought with them customs and traditions established over a period of hundreds of years. They also brought their diversions, and football was one of them. It would be the stuff of mythology, however, to report that the result of the first game was carved into Plymouth Rock or that the colonists at Jamestown interrupted their tobacco farming for the game of the week.

It would be a romantic notion to presume that a football game between settlers and Indians spiced the celebration on Thanksgiving Day. But football, indeed, made its appearance in America during the seventeenth and eighteenth centuries. Historians agree that a form of the game was played in Virginia as early as 1609.

As is the case with the sport in general, it is nearly impossible to fix a date for its inception in the colonies. Yet history well documents the growth and development of football in the United States. And the early game as played in the colonies, mimicked the rough-'n'-tumble brawls that created such a stir in the homeland. Rules—where anyone bothered to make some—were of local origin and subject to change.

Descriptions of those early games should be familiar by now. There were two sides with any number of players to a side. The teams kicked an inflated bladder or skin toward the goal. The ball could not be carried or thrown. But the effort to score points using only the feet led to innumerable bruised shins, mangled toes, and broken legs.

Games were few and far between. Observers thought them to be disorganized. Audiences cheered the combatants, but little progress seemed to be made. And there were reports that some games of football were closer to rugby as the players tossed the ball to one another. More than any rule stipulation, this might be credited to just plain frustration. The players could not keep their hands idle.

Wherever the game was played, it met with disapproval from the authorities. As in England, football was played on the street as often as on a grassy field. The mayhem which ensued forced authorities in Boston, for instance, to issue an edict in 1657.

In brief, the statement banned football from the streets of town and instituted a penalty of twenty shillings for any offenders. Anyone who has had a baseball come crashing through a front window or has had a rubber ball lodged in the drain on the roof probably wishes the law were in effect today.

All the edicts that might be written, however, could not slow the spread of football in the colonies. The sport gained credence when it made its appearance on the school campuses. As early as

◄ *W.M. Boyd's painting of the first intercollegiate game, between Rutgers and Princeton, on November 6, 1869.*

1800, the sport had made its presence felt on college campuses in the East. Although it was a vigorous activity, it seemed to be an outlet for students who had a demanding academic workload. Football was a diversion, and no one attempted to organize it or to establish a single set of rules at this time.

At Yale, one of the first colleges where football was played, there are accounts of students playing at football on a field, kicking the ball with no apparent goal. At best, college authorities tolerated the game. Privately, they frowned on this activity and thought it was detrimental to the students' studies.

At Princeton, their version of football was called ballown. Players advanced the ball by using their fists. Eventually, the kicking aspect was incorporated into the game. At Harvard, football was more organized. On the first Monday of the fall semester, sophomores and freshmen met in a game to determine class supremacy. More serious-minded juniors and seniors refrained from such activities.

By the mid-1800s, though, it was apparent that football was being interpreted by students the same way it was by those ruffians who so riled the townspeople of Boston. College officials no longer felt they could ignore the violence associated with matches. In 1837, football was banned at Columbia by school president William A. Duer. At Harvard, the annual interclass game was played on what became known as Bloody Monday.

At Yale, Amherst, and Brown, football was no more civilized than anywhere else. Observers were critical of the pushing, shoving, kicking, and outright punching that marred matches.

Regular contests between freshmen and sophomores became a regular occurrence at Yale. Eyewitnesses described these games as open riots, which must have borne little semblance to the modern form of football. Students fought with one another as much as they devoted time to advancing the ball. The sport was merely becoming a means of sanctioning assault.

Following the game of 1858, which was particularly violent, the faculty—supported by New Haven officials—voted to prohibit students from playing football. City authorities banned the game from city streets and public squares. Although

there were law breakers, prohibition effectively killed football at Yale for nearly a decade.

In a humorous account, John Langdon Sibley, a librarian at Harvard, documented the game between the freshmen and sophomores on Bloody Monday, August 31, 1846. After classes were held that day, the annual game was held. "The football is thrown among them," Sibley wrote, "and the object of each class is to kick the other and 'bark their shins' as much as possible."

Other Harvard graduates told of how the game had become an excuse for gang fights among the players. The ball—a leather case filled with paper, leaves, and rags—attracted little attention following the opening kickoff.

The sport was being watched by Harvard faculty members. They saw class football degenerate even further. By 1860, the game had become a brawl and action finally was taken. In the year that Abraham Lincoln took office as president and the Civil War was about to start, the Harvard faculty informed the freshmen class that following the annual game that year, football would be prohibited.

There was no mutiny among the students, though. Instead, they displayed their sense of whimsy by staging a mock funeral for football. On September 3, 1860, the game of football was laid to rest in an impressive ceremony on the campus. There was a coffin and a football was placed inside. A grave was dug. There was a tombstone which listed football's age as sixty years. Of course, what would a funeral be without a eulogy? A student delivered a moving speech.

The student orator said, " . . . the wise men who make big laws around a little table have stretched out their arms to protect your eyes and noses. For us there is naught but sorrow, the sweet association and the tender memories of eyes bunged up, of noses wonderfully distended and of battered shins, and the many chance blows anteriorly and posteriorly received and delivered. . . . "

While football was played intermittently at other colleges, it had entered its dormant stage at Columbia, Yale, and Harvard. If the sport were to progress, it would have to do so in the streets where it originated. There was no more fitting place than Boston.

At this time, a game was born that was a variation of the football that was played in colleges. It was called the Boston Game and it would have an impact on the college game. Youngsters attending secondary school adopted the Boston Game and played it extensively. The game gave birth to the first organized football club in America.

Early in the 1860s, the Oneida Football Club was formed and stocked with players from various Boston schools such as the Epes Sargent Dixwell Private Latin School, the Boston Public Latin School, and the Boston English High School. From 1862 through 1865, this team enjoyed great success.

It became, in a sense, the first football dynasty in the United States. During these years, the Oneida club was undefeated. More impressively, it was unscored upon. Even in the low-scoring, modern-day version of soccer, this is an accomplishment that would impress coaches all over the world.

The boys from Oneida had their own identifying mark which distinguished them from their opponents. Although in this day and age of gaudy uniforms with a rainbow of colors the Oneida red handkerchief would hardly seem flamboyant, it was considered bold at the time. The boys wore the red silk handkerchief in pirate fashion around their heads.

Indeed, it seemed like piracy, the way the Oneida Club easily dismantled most opponents. Playing the Boston Game, there were sixteen players to a side. Features of soccer and rugby were included.

In the history of the Oneida Club, an interesting description of the Boston Game was included. It gave the first evidence that strategy was being employed in playing football. No longer was the result dependent solely on random kicking of the ball.

Gerrit S. Miller, the team captain, diagramed the formation which assigned the sixteen players to specific areas of the field. Miller wrote: "As the football was in almost constant motion after the kickoff, our men were placed on the field where they would be most likely to catch or meet the ball when kicked by our opponents, in order that we might return it without delay toward their goal."

In another account, written by team member James D'Wolf Lovett, the action is described. Lovett enthusiastically tells of how one teammate maneuvered the ball deftly between defenders—an early-day Pelé, perhaps.

"What fun it was to see Arthur Beebe, with body bent close to the ground, patting the ball with his hands, this way and that, steering it clear of the ravening wolves who were pursuing and rapidly hemming him in, until . . . he deftly tossed the ball over the surrounding heads into the ready hands of an alert partner. . . . "

In any sport, coaches yearn for someone who will give up the ball. The Boston Game had succeeded in making football a science and it seemed only natural that these high school players would continue their education in college. It was only a matter of time before the Boston Game found a place at Cambridge, home of Harvard.

Although football's flame had burned to an ember, the sport did not die out completely in the 1860s. Rutgers College students regularly participated in a simple kicking game which seemed like the offspring of the game that had its start at Princeton.

These two schools were just twenty-five miles apart and had developed a fierce rivalry over possession of a revolutionary war cannon which periodically would be stolen by students from one school and then the other. The rivalry manifested itself on the athletic field in 1866 when Princeton trounced Rutgers, 40-2, in their first cricket match. Rutgers sought revenge, and football presented an excellent way of getting it.

In early fall of 1869, Rutgers started its football program. Sophomore William J. Leggett was named the first captain. It wasn't long before Rutgers issued its challenge to Nassau Hall, which is what Princeton was known as in those years. Three football games were proposed. Princeton agreed and quickly fielded its own team. William S. Gummere was the captain. And on Saturday, November 6, in New Brunswick, Rutgers and Princeton met for a football contest.

The Princeton team arrived on the Rutgers campus accompanied by a group of students who had come to provide some verbal support. The field would not be mistaken for one of the modern-

This Winslow Homer etching of the annual match between the sophomores and the freshmen at Harvard dates back to 1857.

day stadia that are monuments to themselves. It was a vacant lot on College Avenue surrounded by a board fence which served as a grandstand for spectators. There was no admission fee, and the fans sang college songs and rooted for their teams.

The rules were discussed before the game by the captains, and minor changes were made. The ball could be batted with the hand, but no one was allowed to carry it. A point was scored by knocking the ball through the goal posts.

Of that, historians are sure. However, there are disagreements concerning several factors. William Demarest, who attended the game and later became president of Rutgers, noted there was no crossbar, and a goal was allowed no matter how high the ball when it passed between the posts. Other accounts, quoting participants in the game, insist there was a crossbar.

There were twenty-five players to a side, and the Rutgers team wore scarlet caps to distinguish itself from Princeton. The winner would be the first team to score six goals. The first goal in intercollegiate football history was scored by Rutgers, although Demarest's account does not state whether Stephen G. Gano or George R. Dixon scored that goal. Presumably, one assisted the other.

Throughout the game, Rutgers was in control. The Scarlet Knights led, 2-0, and seemed on the verge of a rout when one of the players inadvertently kicked the ball into his own goal, giving Princeton hope. During the game several players collided with the board fence, toppling a section of the fence and tossing spectators to the ground. This was the closest the fans got to audience participation. Their downfall did not temper what had become an exciting game. Princeton would not quit and tied the score at 4-4. But Rutgers was the stronger team and scored the next two goals to win, 6-4. Although the game the teams played was not football or soccer as Americans know it, adherents to both sports look upon this meeting as the first intercollegiate contest.

The traditional engagement between the classes was prohibited following a brawl in 1860.

There still were two games to be played in the series, and Rutgers' celebration was short-lived. The following week the teams met at Princeton, and even then the home-field advantage was imposing. However, it was for a different reason. The rules of the second match were changed to conform to the game Princetonians played. It permitted a free kick when the ball was caught in the air. Princeton players had developed this technique for advancing the ball. Their free kicks occurred close to the Rutgers goal and they were mostly on target.

In contrast to the evenly fought match the week before, this one was a rout. Princeton won, 8-0. Unfortunately, the third game—scheduled for New Brunswick—was cancelled because of difficulty scheduling a starting time and because of faculty opposition. Yes, football still had its hardcore opponents.

Despite the success of these two matches, despite the enthusiasm which greeted them, and the sportsmanship displayed, the future of football still was in the balance as the new decade began. In 1870, Rutgers ventured twice to Princeton and lost. Authorities at Nassau Hall would not permit their team to play away from home.

Rutgers grew weary of losing to Princeton, especially when it did not have an opportunity to turn the tables at home. So the Scarlet looked around for new competition and found Columbia eager to play.

Student support at Columbia overshadowed what school spirit existed at Rutgers and Princeton. The student body unanimously elected Stuyvesant Fish as captain of the Columbia team, the first team in school history.

Fish organized and served as coach for a twenty-man team which he led to Rutgers on November 20, 1870. Enthusiasm, though, was no substitute for experience. Rutgers won the game, 6-3.

While the sport the teams played that day was a form of football, it was not quite the same game that was played at Princeton. There were two goalkeepers on a side, playing simultaneously, which would make professional hockey goalies envious. The ball was a light rubber sphere which could be batted with the fist or kicked.

Once again, violence surfaced as players kicked at one another, jumped on each other's stomachs, and hammered away with their fists. No substitutions were allowed, and the only way a player could leave was if he were carried off the field.

There were, of course, as there are today, idle moments when the goaltender has enough time to sit back and light a cigar. Indeed, one of the Columbia keepers did precisely that, according to one report of the game. Much to his surprise, the Rutgers team quickly gained possession of the ball and broke in on the Columbia goal. The resourceful goalkeeper merely shoved the lighted cigar into his opponents' faces.

It is easy to see, then, why faculty members at various colleges opposed football. But while there was no record of intercollegiate games in 1871, football again was flourishing on several campuses. At Harvard, the Boston Game was the variation being played, as a group of students who learned that game formed the Harvard University Foot-Ball Club. The purpose of the club was to promote the game within the college itself. There was little thought given to playing other universities.

David S. Schaff, who was weaned on football in England, established an informal program at Yale. Princeton advocates organized the Football Association and agreed to a definite set of rules in 1871.

But this intramural competition was bound to outgrow the ivy-covered walls of these institutions. In 1872, Rutgers, Columbia, Yale, Princeton, and Stevens resumed intercollegiate matches. These schools played a kicking game of the soccer type. In spite of local differences in rules, everyone agreed that the ball could not be picked up with the hands, thrown, or carried.

Total agreement was impossible. This time Harvard was the dissenter, opting for the popular Boston Game. Football remained an intramural sport at Cambridge. The advocates there believed that participants should be allowed to run with the ball, to throw it, and to tackle the opponent.

Football was growing, and in the interest of uniformity, Harvard, Yale, Rutgers, Princeton, and Columbia were invited to a meeting to determine

rules and to form an intercollegiate association. It took place in October of 1873. Only Yale, Rutgers, and Princeton were represented. The delegates from Columbia failed to appear, while Harvard refused to send someone.

The Cambridge decision was not a hasty one. Following the invitation, all the football players at Harvard were called together to discuss the proposed convention. Although each school had its own version of football, only Harvard permitted use of the hands, impeding an opponent, and passing. The other schools played a kicking game similar to present-day soccer.

The Harvard men were proud and insistent that their game was the better one. They concluded it was more important to maintain the Boston Game than to enter intercollegiate competition. In their statement, they noted that attending the convention would mean being outvoted, 4-1, and becoming morally obligated to follow the majority and drop the Boston Game. Simply, they did not like the odds.

The delegates representing Yale, Rutgers, and Princeton decided not to form a league. They did, however, adopt uniform rules similar to those of English Association Football. The two most significant rules were Rules V and VII. They stated that no player was allowed to throw or carry the ball, and that no tripping, holding, or pushing an adversary was allowed.

At this point, soccer might have become the dominant sport on American campuses in the fall. The game that evolved from the crude contests played by colonists in Virginia might have become the national pastime a long time ago. All that was needed for this to take place was for Harvard to step into line. Instead, soccer was to struggle.

There was little question that the absence of Harvard weakened the kicking game. After Columbia, Princeton, Yale, and Rutgers inaugurated intercollegiate competition on the association level in 1873, contests decreased in following years. The most important game of the period was played by renegade Harvard.

It occurred in 1874, and it altered the course of American intercollegiate football. Harvard, remember, had to look long and hard to find opponents once its natural rivals formed their own association. In the spring of 1874, Harvard's search took it north to Canada, where a series of football matches against McGill University in Montreal were proposed.

After some discussion, it was agreed to play two games at Harvard. One would be played under Harvard rules—the Boston Game—while the other would be played according to McGill's rules. The latter game was not received well at Harvard. Basically, McGill played rugby, which was considered by the *Harvard Advocate* as unscientific and unsuitable to colleges.

On May 14, 1874, the first game was played. From the opening moments, Harvard was in control, displaying the fine points of the Boston Game that were foreign to the McGill team. Harvard won easily.

The following day was expected to result in a reversal as the rugby rules seemed more suited to McGill. Surely, the Canadian team would toy with Harvard as the Crimson had with them. But the Cambridge boys were fast learners and quickly picked up the nuances of rugby. They played McGill to a scoreless tie. Not only that, but the snooty stand taken by the *Harvard Advocate* was forgotten. Harvard liked the rugby game. The *Advocate,* reversing its field eloquently and without any pangs of conscience, stated: "Football will be a popular game here in the future. The rugby game is in much better favor than the somewhat sleepy game now played by our men."

What, someone may ask, happened to the hallowed Boston Game? The game that came before everything else? The game that made Harvard an outsider in the intercollegiate association? Well, the Boston Game was abandoned like an orphan the following fall when a return match with McGill was held. Harvard was the first to suggest the game be played under rugby rules.

The game was played in Montreal, further complicating Harvard's task. But playing as if they had been born to the game, the Crimson athletes dominated throughout and won convincingly, 3-0.

Rugby had made the Boston Game seem sleep inducing by comparison. It gained steadily in popularity at Harvard. Meanwhile, the association kicking game had been spinning its wheels. Princeton continually fielded strong teams, but interest waned at schools such as Yale, Columbia, Stevens, Pennsylvania, and Rutgers.

In 1875, a natural rivalry proved to be a stronger bond than the association. Yale yielded to the urge to compete against Harvard. The universities agreed to a football game in Springfield, Massachusetts. It was played according to a newly defined set of rules, which basically incorporated the best features of rugby into the game. This match sounded the death knell for American intercollegiate soccer for the remainder of the 1800s.

Concessions made to Yale in this eventful game included the ruling that goals alone and not touchdowns would count in the scoring. The concessions to Harvard included provisions that the ball could be handled, thrown, and carried, and that the hands could be used to hold an opponent. Playing its game, Harvard won easily, 4-0.

Yale backers, however, were favorably impressed. Walter Camp noted he was most interested when watching the Harvard players running with the ball, seemingly doing what they pleased.

The 1875 contest between Yale and Harvard convinced most fans that rugby was the collegiate game of the future. Yale completed its soccer schedule that season against Columbia and Wesleyan, but in the following season, rugby replaced soccer at Yale. There were those at Princeton who pushed for the installation of rugby at the expense of soccer, but at Nassau Hall, there were mitigating circumstances.

Princeton had not lost a soccer game since the inaugural against Rutgers in 1869. Obviously, it was quite pleased with the kicking game. But, with the exception of a victory against Yale in 1873, most of Princeton's victories had been at the expense of Rutgers, Columbia, Stevens, the smaller colleges. Attempts to schedule Yale and Harvard were unsuccessful. Now they would be impossible with the growing attraction of rugby.

Early in the fall semester of 1876, a group of students determined that rugby was by far the superior game and that Princeton should join with the other colleges in promoting this exciting new variation of football. Student and alumni opposed this at first, stung by the notion that their beloved kicking game was inferior.

Gradually, though, support for rugby grew. At a mass meeting in early November, the rugby faction won out in a close vote. A committee was formed to contact other schools to form a rugby league. Representatives from Columbia, Harvard, and Princeton met in Springfield, Massachusetts, on November 23, 1876, where they formed the Intercollegiate Football Association.

Following the meeting, there was some confusion as to when rugby would become the official intercollegiate game. Yale, for instance, did not join the association until 1877. Yet it cancelled all its soccer matches to practice rugby.

Columbia compromised by playing both sports during the 1876 season. Princeton completed another undefeated soccer season before turning its attention to rugby. Few of the Princeton players had ever played the game, and fewer had even seen a rugby ball. They acquired one only four days before their game against Yale. They did not know how to kick the ball until they watched Yale practice the day before the game.

Princeton was to learn some lessons that season. It was beaten by Yale and Harvard. But the Princetonians loved the new game. They participated in a full rugby schedule the following season.

Thus, Princeton, the bastion of power in soccer, had abandoned the kicking game for rugby. Soccer was in ashes and a revival would not occur for some time. In fact, from 1877 to 1902, there was no record of intercollegiate soccer in the United States. It seemed the game was gone for good.

THE COLLEGES

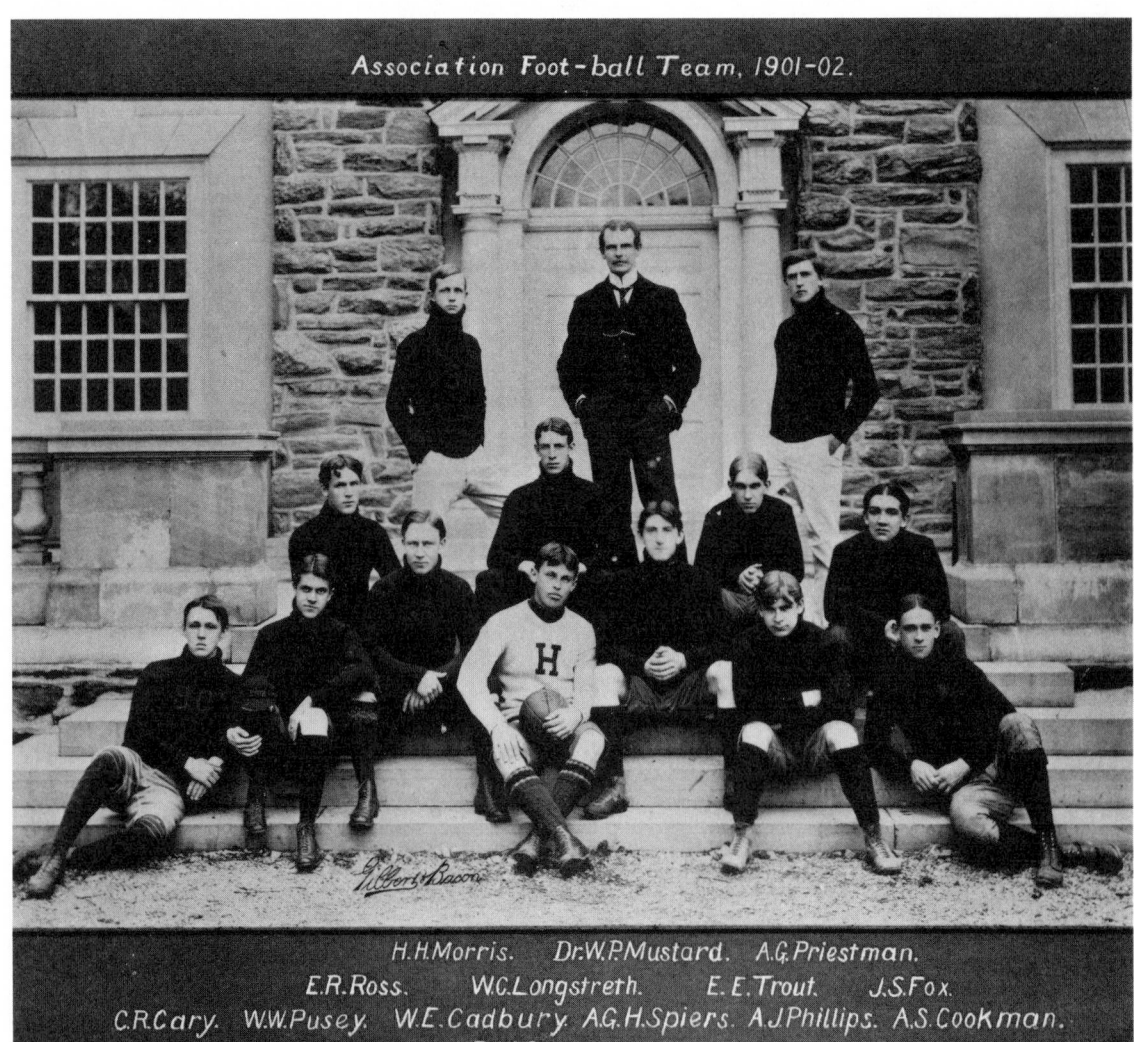

Association Foot-ball Team, 1901-02.

H.H.Morris.   Dr.W.P.Mustard.   A.G.Priestman.
E.R.Ross.   W.C.Longstreth.   E.E.Trout.   J.S.Fox.
C.R.Cary.   W.W.Pusey.   W.E.Cadbury. A.G.H.Spiers. A.J.Phillips. A.S.Cookman.
R.M.Gummere.   CAPTAIN.

Richard Gummere editorialized on behalf of soccer in the Haverford school paper and then captained the school's initial team in 1902. One of the club's better players was a Latin professor named W.P. Mustard, who was appointed coach.

3
Return to the Campus
(1900-1925)

Like a fickle lover, American colleges had spurned soccer at the close of the nineteenth century. Rugby was their new flame, and the kicking game disappeared as if it never had existed. But the Englishmen whose ancestors had settled this country still enjoyed playing the sport. Soccer clubs were formed, primarily in New York and Philadelphia, and the game continued to be played.

Make no mistake, this was a private affair. Soccer was not making any impact on the American sporting scene. It seemed destined to remain a quaint tradition of the British.

Late in 1900, however, C. P. Hurditch, a soccer zealot, convinced those at the Belmont Cricket Club in Philadelphia to add soccer to the agenda of winter sports. The game was a hit. And once the club members had become more than novices at it, they followed their natural competitive urge and sought an outside opponent. They soon were accommodated.

It seemed that rugby also had met with disfavor in some circles. At Girard College, a secondary school in Philadelphia, the faculty had banned rugby. Students turned to soccer as an alternative and they felt capable of meeting the Belmont Club. A match was arranged.

At first sight, it appeared to be a mismatch. The players on the Belmont Club were older, stronger, and seemingly more rugged. The Girard students were youngsters, most of whom had little need for a razor in the morning. The spectators at the cricket club envisioned a rout.

Soccer, however, is not a sport which relies necessarily on brawn. The Girard boys were agile and quick. Their use of technique and finesse confused the cricket club team. Belmont eventually won, but the game was intriguing enough to arouse interest elsewhere.

Hurditch, who captained the Belmont team, received offers for games from other cricket clubs which had not yet started soccer programs. The sport that had been reduced to ashes was beginning to flame again.

In a year's time, soccer was flourishing on the club level. It did not go unnoticed. An editorial in the student newspaper at Haverford College favored introduction of the game at that school. In the editorial, soccer was extolled as an alternative for athletically minded students who had little to do once the cricket and tennis season ended. Rugby claimed the crème de la crème of the Haverford student body, leaving eighty or ninety students spectating or taking cross-country walks.

Soccer would keep them in excellent physical condition. It would not compete for athletes with rugby, which still would get the best players the school could offer. The student editor who wrote this plea was Richard M. Gummere, who had learned soccer as a schoolboy in England. He later had broadened his interest in the game at a Swiss school. In America, he would become a spreader of the gospel.

The editorial brought an immediate and favorable student response. Soon, a soccer team was

While American colleges turned to rugby at the close of the 19th century, the sport of soccer flourished on the club level because of teams like the 18th Ward from Lawrenceville, Pennsylvania. One of the first teams formed in its district, the 18th Ward was the Western Pennsylvania champion in 1887. Back row (left to right): George Grove, Tom Badger, Ben Grove, officials John and Joseph Waters, Charles White, Hugh Holden and the trainer. Middle row: Sam Taylor, Bob Adams. Front row: Thomas Longmore, Alfred Grove, Joseph Wardle, Thomas Taylor and Ted Adams.

formed, practice matches were held, and an eight-game schedule was drawn up for the winter of 1902.

Haverford's first soccer season began on January 4, 1902, with a victory over the Germantown Cricket Club. Gummere was captain of the team which boasted a faculty member as one of its better players. He was W. P. Mustard, a Latin professor. Rugby players who had completed their season also were on the team.

Mustard, though, drew most of the attention. He brought what was described as an air of dignity to the team. He had come to watch practice one day and booted a few balls back on the field after they had gone out-of-bounds. Gummere's eyes lit up like a neon sign. This was no stranger to the game.

Actually, Mustard had been an all-Canada player in rugby and soccer. Also, he had run the quarter-mile in forty-nine seconds while an undergraduate at the University of Toronto. The Haverford team did not waste any time fitting this modest man for a uniform.

Duly impressed, Gummere appointed Mustard the coach. Haverford went on to a championship season. The team played only five of its eight games, however. Because soccer was played in the dead of winter, inclement conditions often cancelled games. Of the five games played, Haverford won four. This included a 1–0 upset of the Belmont Cricket Club in the final game of the season.

The victory was accomplished on a field slickened by ice, but it did not diminish its importance for Haverford—especially since it avenged an earlier 7–0 defeat to Belmont. The victory gave Haverford claim to the unofficial championship of the cricket club league. It seems the college had not yet gained recognition as a member of the league.

The Haverford team did not receive an earlier version of a ticker tape parade when it returned home, however. As successful as he had been in a short period of time, Gummere could not convince the student body that varsity letters were due the soccer players.

He went before the Student Association and succeeded in having the question brought before the entire student body. The students rejected the request for varsity letters. The soccer team was congratulated for its fine record, but total recognition was withheld because it had not played any other college teams.

Gummere's appeal was more symbolic than real. Many players on the team had earned letters in rugby or tennis or cricket. But after having failed to win the Philadelphia Cricket Club League championship outright because it was not a member, the soccer team now was being rebuked at home too. Perhaps it would have been different had the students realized their team was the first recognized American college soccer team of the twentieth century.

Soccer proved to be no fad at Haverford. With the exception of 1918, a war year, soccer has been a staple at the Philadelphia school. Although Gummere and others had graduated, an Association Football Association was formally established on campus in November, 1902. Application was made to the Philadelphia Cricket Club League, and Haverford was assigned to the second division.

Although the school seemed further advanced than this, soccer was on the upswing among club teams. Haverford would have to prove itself.

To strengthen its hand, Haverford's schedule was made to accommodate rugby players whose season ended first. Following a successful debut in the second division in 1903, the school was moved up to the first division the following year. In 1905,

Haverford won three of its four games, thus claiming the Manheim Cup, awarded annually to the champion of the cricket club league.

The student newspaper used this occasion to once again champion the sport of soccer. It also scolded the students for not supporting the team. The newspaper called for other colleges to join Haverford in making soccer an intercollegiate sport.

The power of the press once again was demonstrated. Richard Gummere, who was now taking graduate studies at Harvard, had helped revive soccer at that school in 1904. After taking note of the editorial in the Haverford newspaper, the Harvard team arranged a two-game series with Haverford to be played in April. The first game was scheduled for Cambridge; the second for Philadelphia.

A glowing story in the *Haverfordian* recounted how Haverford won both games in close and exciting fashion. They were billed as the first intercollegiate association football games in the United States.

Thus, after a twenty-five–year absence, intercollegiate soccer was reborn. It had lost out in its bid for survival against rugby, but gradually the colleges had accepted it again. With Haverford, the little Main Line Philadelphia school, leading the way, Columbia, Cornell, and Pennsylvania were soon fielding teams.

During this early period, rugby was undergoing close scrutiny. It had become a roughhouse sport, and in an effort to eliminate this aspect of it, a White House conference was called by President Theodore Roosevelt in 1905. A modification of the sport—and possible elimination of rugby from the intercollegiate program—was discussed.

It was in that same year that another group of pilgrims landed in America. They had come to spread the word of soccer. The Pilgrims were a team composed of outstanding players from the best amateur teams in England. They came to the United States to help promote soccer. With feelings running high against rugby, their two-month tour was timed perfectly. The Pilgrims traveled from St. Louis to Boston, playing club teams which also had several collegiate players in their lineups.

The only complete college team the Pilgrims played was the University of Pennsylvania. The game showed just how much the college boys had to learn. The Pilgrims won by the one-sided score of 10–0. The tour was an immense success. The Pilgrims had not discouraged Americans, but only had made them appreciate the finer points of soccer.

In 1906—with intercollegiate soccer just beginning to wet its feet—another touring team came to North America. The Corinthians, an English club team, toured Canada and the United States. The Corinthians, like the Pilgrims before them, were too advanced for their American competition. Yet an English reporter traveling with the team wrote of the formidable opposition offered by some college teams, most notably Haverford.

The reporter praised the sportsmanlike spirit which prevailed. The Corinthians could afford to be charitable. They defeated Haverford, 6–0.

A few days later, the Corinthians defeated a combined Harvard-Princeton team, 11–1. Once again, this demonstration of the finer points of soccer had helped educate Americans. It made it less difficult to promote the game. Historians predicted that Americans would now improve, having seen soccer played at its best.

Now the time was ripe for formation of an intercollegiate league, and again it was Haverford that took the initiative. James Babbitt, director of the college's physical education department, invited representatives from soccer playing colleges to an organizational meeting. In contrast to similar meetings held in the past, this one was fruitful. The Intercollegiate Association Football League was formed with Columbia, Cornell, Harvard, Haverford, and Pennsylvania as members.

Haverford had the honor of being the league's first champion. In the course of the season, it traveled by train to Ithaca, New York, to play a Cornell team whose players were of many nationalities. One account of the meeting stated that the Haverford players spent part of the train ride from Philadelphia learning to pronounce the names of their opponents.

Once on the field, Haverford knew the language. It won, 3–1. In a report of the game in the *Haverfordian,* one goal was described as having rolled through the legs of Cornell's Scottish halfback, then through those of the Dutch fullback, and finally past the outstretched hands of the Greek goaltender.

Yale and Princeton were admitted to the Intercollegiate Association Football League in 1907. By then, a proposal was made to change the soccer season from winter to fall. Soccer practice generally started in December following the rugby season. Games began in January and ran into the spring months. Those games often were hampered by snow, sleet, ice, rain, and mud, and poor conditions usually were the rule rather than the exception.

At the annual league meeting, the move to change the schedule was voted down, however, because some schools were unwilling to challenge rugby football for attention. Soccer continued to be played during the winter and spring. In 1907–08, Yale tied Haverford for the league title. In 1908–09, Columbia began the first year of a two-year reign.

Off campus, the year 1909 was marked by the return of the Pilgrims, the English team that had been an inspiration four years earlier. They arrived by sea for a twenty-two–game tour on September 30 in New York, boasting what team captain Fred Milnes said was an even stronger team than the one which swept through the States in 1905. It seemed that way, too, as they handily won their first three games, beating teams by a combined score of 31–0.

By November 4, however, the competition had become more formidable and the long tour began taking its toll on the Pilgrims. It was on this day that the Hibernians of Philadelphia shocked the soccer world by posting a 1–0 upset. The goal was scored by Andy Brown in the second half when the Pilgrims—playing with the wind at their backs—were expected to take command.

A few days later, the Pilgrims met stern opposition once more when the Fall City Rovers played them to a 1–1 tie. On November 13, the Rovers proved the tie was not a fluke.

The Rovers defeated the Pilgrims, 2–1, scoring two clean goals while the losers' goal came on a penalty kick. They won despite a furious second-half assault in which the Pilgrims had their reputations as well as the game at stake. The Rovers won despite losing fullback Thomas Bagley, one of their better players.

By the conclusion of the tour, the Pilgrims had won sixteen games, lost two, and tied four. They had outscored the opposition, 123–13. But for the

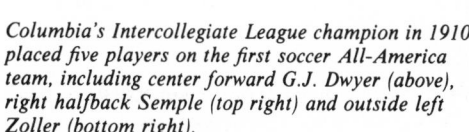

Columbia's Intercollegiate League champion in 1910 placed five players on the first soccer All-America team, including center forward G.J. Dwyer (above), right halfback Semple (top right) and outside left Zoller (bottom right).

first time they had been beaten and this was something for Americans to boast about.

On the collegiate front, there were significant strides as well. For one, soccer expanded westward to California. It was in 1910 that soccer found a home in Palo Alto on the Stanford campus and in Berkeley at the main campus of the University of California. Teams at both schools were composed mostly of foreign players. They competed against local club teams, but in their one meeting, Stanford lost to California, 1–0.

Following that 1909–10 season, in which

Columbia was the repeat champion of the Intercollegiate Association Football League, the first All-America soccer team was chosen by the captains of the teams in the IAFL. Columbia placed five players on the first team: goaltender C. B. Spencer, right halfback Semple, center forward G. J. Dwyer, inside left C. E. Dwyer and outside left Zoller.

In today's world, coaches are plentiful, although good ones are difficult to find. In 1910, however, not many men were qualified to skillfully handle the coaching duties. Often, the lifespan of soccer at any school depended on how long the coach remained. Douglas Stewart was one of the early coaching legends of the kicking game.

Stewart had learned the sport in his native Scotland and had played with some of the best amateur teams in England and Canada. He came to Philadelphia in the early 1900s and wasted little time establishing himself on the local soccer scene. He trained several amateur clubs and helped to form the soccer referees' association in 1904.

Stewart had watched the game be reborn in the Philadelphia Cricket Club League, and he was most willing to help it through its growing pains at the University of Pennsylvania. His first season was not a memorable one as Penn won only three of ten games. But during the next twenty-five years, his teams would dominate intercollegiate soccer. Between 1914 and 1925, Penn won six Intercollegiate Association Football League championships.

In this period, the Penn junior varsity captured four Pennsylvania League titles. Stewart's enthusiasm was infectious. Soccer became a cult at Penn, and he was its high priest.

His success can be attributed to his knowledge of the finer points of soccer, which were still foreign to many Americans. Stewart also was known as a despot who struck fear into his players' hearts. He was a former soldier who subscribed to the popular metaphor of sports as war. He was the officer, and his players were the enlisted men.

Stewart called everyone by his last name. He was known to strike a player across the legs with his walking stick for assorted soccer crimes. Because his program was so widespread, Stewart was aided by assistant coaches and a battery of student managers. The managers were required to bring him a typed report of each day's practice by eight o'clock the same evening. In another life, he might have been Vince Lombardi.

Often, Stewart's practices would begin under the direction of an assistant. Soon, however, he would leave his office, walking stick in hand, and head to the soccer field. He was critical of his players. Yet, despite his tyrannical nature, Stewart's program gained the admiration of his players, friends and the opposition in his thirty-three years at Penn.

His talents were not confined to the soccer field

either. Stewart was a clerk for a blind patent attorney. He did much of the legal work and was known informally as a lawyer. He never, however, received a degree in law.

His organizational talents were effective in helping to form the United States Football Association, the governing body of professional and amateur soccer in the U.S. Stewart served on numerous committees on the local and national level. And in 1948, the Soccer Coaches Association recognized his achievements and presented him with an award for having done the most for soccer.

This was not all. For twenty-seven years, the Scotsman was the editorial voice of the annual *Soccer Guide*. In addition to listing the playing rules and a resume of the past season, the guide contained a number of instructional articles for players, referees, and coaches. He also chose the All-Intercollegiate team from 1920 through 1925.

Stewart served as a member of the National Collegiate Athletic Association Rules Committee and was the final word on many rules interpretations. He tutored soccer enthusiasts around the country. Perhaps more than any single person, he helped advance soccer as an intercollegiate sport in America.

Other coaching legends followed Stewart, and several of them began their lengthy careers during the first twenty-five years of the twentieth century. Allison W. Marsh began his forty-two years as a coach in 1916 at Ohio State. In 1920, he moved to Amherst, where he stayed until 1957. Hugh G. McCurdy, who coached into the 1960s, took over his first Wesleyan team in 1922.

Robert H. Dunn spent forty-one years coaching at Swarthmore, fielding his first team in 1920. Thomas J. Dent led Dartmouth from 1924 to 1959, and Navy coach Thomas G. Taylor began his twenty-seven–year reign at the academy in 1919.

Coaches such as these helped solidify soccer at various campuses—most of which were in the East. And there were some new additions as Pratt, St. Olaf, and Emporia State took up the game in the years following 1910. Stanford and California continued the pioneer spirit out West. Progress at other schools was slow, however. In 1911, there was to be an awakening in rural Pennsylvania that would shift the balance of power not only in the state, but on the national level. It was in that year that soccer came to Penn State University.

Athletic director W. Nelson Golden was interested in starting soccer at Penn State, so he contacted Westtown Academy, located near Philadelphia, hoping it would supply a coach. Westtown competed on even terms with a number of college teams. One of its best players was Walter Savery, who was recommended for the Penn State job. He served as student coach and captain of the team from 1911 to 1913.

Quakers from Philadelphia who had attended Westtown or George School composed the first Penn State teams. James G. White, a college trustee, donated the then ample sum of one hundred dollars to help finance the Penn State team's trip to Philadelphia where it arrived during the Christmas vacation to play Westtown and second-string teams from Haverford and Penn.

White continued to supply financial assistance in subsequent years as Penn State journeyed to Philadelphia to play all its games. These trips were not always successful. In 1913, Penn State lost two of three games. Savery's absence was blamed for the poor showing. Penn State's dominance of intercollegiate soccer was still a decade or so away.

In 1911, Haverford returned to the top in the Intercollegiate Association Football League, posting a 3–1–1 record. Harvard had a similiar record, but Haverford was awarded first place because it averaged more goals. It also defeated Harvard, 4–0, in the teams' only meeting. Princeton, which was not yet in the league, had a 3–3 record playing club, collegiate, and high school teams.

A sour note was sounded by C. Wreford Brown, president of the Corinthian Football Club of England. In a 1911 tour of the U.S. and Canada, the Corinthians lost only one game. They routed the six American teams they played, prompting Brown to say he was disappointed that soccer was not growing faster in the States. He acknowledged, however, that the quality of play continued to improve.

In 1912, soccer became an Olympic sport. In the summer games held in Sweden, England defeated Denmark, 4–2, to win the gold medal.

In the U.S., Yale went unbeaten in five games to win the Intercollegiate League title. The Bull-

dogs played an aggressive style, led by inside left A. A. Gay. Goaltender Dickinson and right full-back Dickey of Yale also were named to the All-American team.

Harvard moved into the top spot in 1914, winning five of six games. It was a disputed championship which resulted in a rules change. Although Pennsylvania finished unbeaten, with two ties and the same number of points as Harvard, it was relegated to second place because of Harvard's slightly better goal average. This, despite the fact that Penn also accounted for Harvard's only defeat. It was determined that in the future a play-off would break a tie in the standings.

There was a more serious crisis in 1914 as the world stood on the brink of war. Still, all looked bright for soccer in the United States. The number of schools playing soccer nearly doubled. Nine new teams, most of them from the midwest, were formed. The *Soccer Guide* boasted that no sport in America was making more rapid strides than soccer.

Four of the new entrants were in Ohio. Ohio State, Baldwin-Wallace, Ohio Wesleyan, and Wooster were the pioneers. Again, foreign students accounted for most of the players and most of the support for the movement.

In Minnesota, St. Olaf joined St. Thomas and the University of Minnesota in an informal soccer league. The University of Minnesota won all four of its games and decided to quit while it was ahead. Its soccer team was disbanded.

These early years revealed a pattern of sporadic growth in college soccer. In his annual report to the National Collegiate Athletic Association, James Babbit explained that this was a result of one or more men working individually rather than a grass roots appeal for the sport. Soccer could live or die at any institution depending on whether one man or a group of students pushed for its acceptance, whether they remained zealots or eventually departed. Soccer still was lacking a solid foundation.

In 1914, for example, St. Thomas fielded a team when Father Murray arrived from Ireland and rallied enough students to play the game. When he left, no one was able to step in and the sport died.

At Lafayette that same year there was a hap-

Immediately prior to World War I, the colleges were experiencing a steady growth while club teams such as the 1913–14 Pittsburgh Rovers were the backbone of the game.

pier result. David Freeman, a member of the music department and an Englishman by birth, sponsored the school's first intercollegiate team. Only four men, two of them Freeman's sons, had any knowledge of the game. But with their support and encouragement, the others learned rapidly, and soccer soon became established at Lafayette.

A roadblock to soccer's growth finally was removed in 1914. The sport was changed to the fall months, despite its potential conflicts with rugby, track, and baseball. Richard M. Gummere, the former team captain who had returned to Haverford as a Latin professor, expressed an opinion that soccer no longer posed a threat to rugby football and could coexist with it during the same season. Initially, it was to be an experiment, but the fall season proved to be a smashing success and it gained permanent adoption.

To be sure, there were continued setbacks dur-

ing this period. As quickly as it came, soccer was forgotten in Minnesota, passing like a comet. At Columbia, the sport was dropped because of a lack of a playing field.

For these minuses there were pluses, however. Soccer emerged at Dartmouth College and also made its first appearance in the state of Oregon. Colin V. Dymet, a journalism professor and former soccer captain at the University of Toronto, introduced the game at the University of Oregon. A year later, it spread to Oregon State, then to an agricultural college. R. K. Hicks, professor of Romance languages and former soccer captain of the Emmanuel College team at Oxford University, instructed thirty players in the fundamentals of soccer at Dartmouth. After playing on the intramural level for one season, the school entered intercollegiate competition in 1915.

The Midwest still was an erratic area. As soccer bloomed at one school, it wilted and died at anoth-

er. At Baldwin-Wallace, American converts to the kicking game needed some convincing. After one season, the game was being extolled for its conditioning qualities.

Haverford had climbed back on top of the Intercollegiate League in 1915. Pennsylvania won the title in 1916 with a 5–1 record. Haverford captured the 1917 championship.

By 1917, soccer was feeling its oats. The game was firmly established in the East and was making progress in California, Oregon, and the Midwest. The *Soccer Guide* confidently predicted that the future of soccer was assured. It said that ten years from this point, if advances continued to be made, all the colleges in the country would be playing soccer.

Meanwhile, on the club level, soccer had long since been successful, and it continued to grow. Forty teams—some from as far west as Chicago—took part in the first National Challenge Cup competition in 1914. The championship game was played before ten thousand fans in Pawtucket, Rhode Island, but it was strictly a New York affair. The Brooklyn Field Club defeated the Brooklyn Celtic Field Club, 2–1.

In the American Football Association Cup competition, the Bethlehem, Pennsylvania, Field Club team made the most of its first year in the league by winning the championship.

The United States entry into World War I on April 16, 1917, had its effect, of course. The sport's boosters pointed out how soccer could thrive because of its conditioning program. The game did not require much in the way of equipment either, so it was inexpensive. Only seven schools, however, fielded teams in 1918. For the first time in the history of the Intercollegiate Association Football League, the schedule was not completed.

Soccer supporters were concerned because the game did not have a storied tradition at the college level and had been maintained by the enthusiasm of the players. The war summoned these enthusiasts, leaving the campuses abandoned.

But these same collegians were introducing soccer to the soldiers, and when the armistice was signed in November 1918, soccer, and other American sports, were revived. There was a boom in the East where fourteen schools resumed or initiated soccer programs. Some devotees predicted

the game would soon be second only to baseball in the hearts of Americans.

One problem soccer faced was the lack of spectator appeal. It seemed to be a participant sport, thoroughly enjoyed by the competitors but considered slow and boring by the people watching. In 1924, when the National Collegiate Athletic Association Football Committee considered plans to heighten the action, the major complaint was that not enough goals were being scored.

The committee's task was to increase goal production and reduce the number of tie games. A questionnaire was mailed to two hundred people actively associated with American soccer, but only twenty-five responded.

The NCAA committee called a conference of college, secondary school, and league representatives to discuss rules changes. The meeting took place at the University Club in Philadelphia on December 13, 1924. Twenty-five delegates attended, but nothing was accomplished. The feeling was that soccer was an international game whose rules should not be tampered with unilaterally.

The movement, however, did have international appeal. At the crux of the matter was the offside rule which required three opponents to be positioned between an offensive man and the goal line before the attacking player could receive a pass. In 1925, the international rules were revised, requiring only two players, not three, to be in defensive position. The colleges adopted the rule change, too. Thus the balance between offense and defense was restored and the game became a faster, more high-scoring contest.

In some soccer hotbeds, the rules change would not have been needed. Thousands of spectators were common at Yale, Princeton, Cornell, and Pennsylvania during the early 1920s.

Penn, in fact, was the first postwar Intercollegiate League champion, winning the title in 1919. Penn and Princeton accounted for nine of the eleven players chosen by Douglas Stewart to the All-Intercollegiate team.

In 1920, Penn and Princeton tied for the league championship and met in a play-off at Princeton before the biggest crowd the school ever had for soccer. After four overtimes, darkness halted play, and the score was tied at 3–3. Another play-off was scheduled for Philadelphia, and this time

Penn won, defeating Princeton before six thousands fans at the Merion Cricket Club.

Penn and Princeton monopolized the championship through 1925. Penn won it in 1923 and 1924, while Princeton finished on top in 1921, 1922, and 1925. Attendance continued to rise. In 1922, eight thousand fans were at Franklin Field in Philadelphia to witness a Penn-Princeton match. The streets were empty as it seemed everyone was at the game. Cornell drew nearly six thousand for a match against Penn in Ithaca that year. By 1924, Penn faced Cornell and Haverford in front of capacity crowds. And these were highly partisan crowds, capable of cheering wildly. They were fueled by noisy bands and energetic cheerleaders.

On the West Coast, interest also ran high, although Stanford and California were the only two intercollegiate teams. A crowd of thirty thousand was reported to have witnessed one of their meetings, and this stunned the eastern establishment. It seems, however, the match was the preliminary to the football game scheduled between the schools, and many people had arrived early. Still, it gave soccer an opportunity for more exposure and the sport won new converts.

Although the crowds had grown, they did not match those drawn by football. And by the mid-1920s, soccer had stagnated again. Instead of sharing the football field as a preliminary event, soccer fields were built, giving the sport its total independence but also creating conflicts. Teams no longer played second fiddle on the schedule to football teams, but they did not have the same appeal on their own turf.

By the end of the 1925 season, there was a growing dissatisfaction with the Intercollegiate Association Football League. For twenty years, a handful of schools had competed for the championship. As more and more colleges fielded soccer teams, they clamored for admittance to this exclusive league. No longer was it taken for granted that the Intercollegiate League champion was the best team in the country.

Changes were forthcoming. The evolution of soccer in America would be striking in the next twenty-five years. By 1924, the U.S. even fielded an Olympic soccer team. Although there were no collegiate players on the team, the U.S. defeated Estonia, 1–0, before losing, 3–0, to Uruguay in its second game in Paris.

Princeton's Poe Field was the site of spirited Middle Atlantic League action during the 1930s. Princeton joined with Cornell, Haverford, Lehigh, Pennsylvania and Swarthmore to form the new conference in 1932.

4

Outward Bound
(1926-1945)

In the spring of 1926, with more than twenty eastern colleges playing soccer, it was apparent that these schools also deserved to be part of a league. Six colleges remained in the Intercollegiate Association Football League, and it seemed impractical to enlarge the league by so many teams.

The six schools met in the spring and decided to discontinue league competition and to form a new organization called the Intercollegiate Soccer Football Association of America. Pennsylvania was permanently awarded the old league trophy. Thus, soccer now was on a steady course toward expansion. The new association was open to any college regardless of its location. Its objectives were to advance the game and to maintain a uniformity of rules among all the colleges and universities in the United States.

Two types of membership were available. They were associate and active, with the active membership open to any college which played at least four other association members during the season. But with soccer expanding and being played from coast to coast, this new equality raised one significant problem: how would the intercollegiate championship be determined?

Travel was not as advanced as it is today, and it was beyond the budgets of most schools to take extended trips. There was a possibility several teams would claim the championship, all with a legitimate stake in it.

In an effort to resolve the problem, the Intercollegiate Soccer Football Association decided to poll its members and to let the coaches vote for the champion. That first vote in 1926 showed equal support for Haverford, Princeton, and Penn State. All three were named champions which pleased no one.

While lip service had been paid the schools in the West, California was snubbed in 1926 even though it was undefeated. Neither California nor Stanford was eligible to win the title in the California Intercollegiate Soccer Conference which was formed following the 1926 season. It seems that these two schools, which pioneered soccer on the West Coast, were considered to be too strong for the league. Other teams in the California league included San Mateo Junior College, San Jose State, and freshmen teams from California and Stanford. It was not until 1930 that varsity teams from the latter pair replaced the freshmen teams in the conference.

Between 1926 and 1930, there was little dispute over the Intercollegiate Soccer Football Association champion. Princeton was named champion in 1927, followed by Yale in 1928 and Penn State in 1929.

In 1928, a United States soccer team made its second appearance in the Olympic Games. Again, there was no collegiate representation on the U.S. team which was trounced by Argentina, 11–2, at Amsterdam.

Another dilemma occurred in 1930, however, when Harvard (8–1), Yale (8–1), and Pennsylvania (9–2) completed the season with nearly identical records. Harvard defeated Penn, 6–1, but lost to Yale, 1–0. Yale lost to Penn, 5–2.

John Carr coached Harvard from 1929 through 1940.

Pennsylvania lost to the Philadelphia Cricket Club League team in addition to Harvard. A playoff seemed to be the best solution, but it could not be arranged. The association once again declared all three teams champions, seemingly the best answer given the circumstances.

However, it also helped focus attention on the problem of determining league champions. It was not in the best interests of the game for its best team to be given this honor by virtue of an election. It was as ludicrous as settling football's Super Bowl champion with the toss of a coin.

In short order, the problem was partially solved when the Middle Atlantic Intercollegiate Soccer League was organized and began to play in the fall of 1932. Cornell, Haverford, Lehigh, Pennsylvania, Princeton, and Swarthmore played a full

schedule with Pennsylvania winning the title. In addition to winning the Thayer Cup—awarded to the new league's champion—Penn was named cochampion, with Navy, of the Intercollegiate Soccer Football Association.

The success of the Middle Atlantic League encouraged other colleges to form sectional conferences. New York City area schools, for instance, formed the Metropolitan Intercollegiate Soccer Conference. Ten other schools formed the New England Intercollegiate Soccer League.

By 1935, several leagues were in existence, and more than seventy-five schools were participating in college soccer. The Intercollegiate Soccer Football Association had continued to name champions through the early 1930s. Penn had won in 1931; Penn and Navy in 1932; Penn and Penn

State in 1933; Cornell in 1934; and Yale won in 1935. At this point, however, the association stopped naming champions.

Despite the aims of the association, it was difficult for the western colleges to earn much acclaim. In 1931, for instance, when Penn was named champion, Stanford had perhaps its best team in a decade. It finished with a 7–0–2 record in the California league. But Stanford's accomplishments were to be lost across the three thousand miles separating the Atlantic and Pacific oceans. In fact, Easterners were enraptured with another team from Pennsylvania at this time.

Even though Penn State had gone unbeaten between 1919 and 1925, winning twenty-nine consecutive games, its era of true greatness and domination was yet to begin. From 1926 through 1941, Penn State would be the scourge of collegiate soccer.

Following the 1925 season, Penn State coach R.G. Leonard informed athletic director Hugo Bezdek that he was leaving and that a replacement should be found. Bezdek had been impressed by the playing manager of the Altoona (Pennsylvania) railroad shops team which had played Penn State during the season. The player-manager's name was Bill Jeffrey. Bezdek contacted Altoona and arranged to borrow Jeffrey for the 1926 season.

At the time, neither man would envision that a three-month leave of absence would become a twenty-seven year stay at Penn State. Bill Jeffrey would become one of the most celebrated college soccer coaches of all time.

There were other lengthy coaching tenures during this period. Longevity was not to be Jeffrey's exclusive claim to fame. William P. Leaness coached at Temple for thirty-two years, beginning in 1930. That same year Lawrence E. Briggs of Massachusetts began his thirty-two year reign. In 1928, Earle C. Waters began the first of his twenty-nine years at West Chester. Donald C. Baker of Ursinus coached at that school for thirty years, starting in 1932.

There were others. Because soccer was still a relatively new sport, coaches were not routinely dismissed for having a losing season or for not achieving the level of success expected of them. Jeffrey was in a class by himself, however, even among this close-knit fraternity of coaches.

He was born in 1892 in Edinburgh, Scotland. He excelled in soccer as a youngster, and as a teenager he was recognized as a star in semipro circles. Several professional teams eagerly sought his services. He was a minor and needed parental approval before he could turn professional. His mother, though, would not consent. She had been disturbed by an injury Jeffrey had suffered while playing the game.

His mother realized that he soon would be of legal age and entitled to turn professional without parental consent. So she contacted her brother in the United States and arranged for Jeffrey to live with him. Bill Jeffrey joined his uncle in Altoona and went to work as a mechanic in a railroad shop. His mother was satisfied that his soccer days were behind him.

Jeffrey arrived in Altoona in 1912 and soon became engrossed in his work. But a number of foreigners were working in those railroad shops and they shared a common interest: in their native land, soccer was the national pastime. They would talk of the sport, and, in time, talk turned to action. Why not a game of soccer against other shop teams? Thus, six months after his mother had sent him to the United States to escape soccer, Jeffrey had become an integral part of the railroad shop team.

For thirteen years, Jeffrey played against shop, mill, and mine teams from Homestead, Braddock, and Bethlehem. In 1925, as player-manager, he took his team to Penn State, where they were to face college boys on the campus sheltered by the Nittany Mountains.

It was in State College that Jeffrey met Hugo Bezdek. When he returned the next season, it was as the school's coach. In his first year, Penn State was unbeaten and once tied (5–0–1). This was nothing new at a school that was synonymous with unbeaten seasons. But unlike the five previous coaches who arrived and departed as if State College were a train station, Jeffrey possessed a dynamic quality that few coaches have.

At the end of his three-month stay, Jeffrey was preparing to return to Altoona. Bezdek knew, though, that he could not allow this coach to leave. The athletic director arranged a job for Jeffrey as an instructor in the Industrial Engineering Department. He insisted that Jeffrey remain. With the security of full-time employment, Jef-

frey accepted the offer to continue as the soccer coach. He did not leave until he retired in 1952.

Under him, Penn State compiled the greatest record in the history of intercollegiate soccer. During Jeffrey's twenty-seven year stint, the Nittany Lions compiled a 151–23–27 record, playing one of the toughest schedules of any team. From 1933 through 1940, Penn State was unbeaten, a streak which lasted sixty-four games.

In 1935, not only was Penn State unbeaten and untied, but also unscored-upon. The previous year, Penn State outscored its opponents, 38–5, never allowing more than one goal a game. In 1934, Bill McEwan, a center forward, was outstanding, scoring 20 goals. He was only a sophomore. In 1935, he was the leading scorer in collegiate soccer.

And in 1935, goaltender Ray Bell completed three years with the varsity, having allowed a total of three goals.

It was not until 1944—a war year—that Jeffrey experienced a losing season at Penn State. That year the Lions dropped four of seven games, including two at home—to Army and Navy. They were the first defeats the Lions suffered at home since 1932.

Jeffrey brought a conservative style to State College. While most college teams attempted to spice the game with long passes and an aggressive offense designed for crowd appeal, Penn State was more methodical. Jeffrey was a tireless worker and he expected as much from his players. He stressed fundamentals and conditioning. He refined the talents of some of his players; others learned how to play the game for the first time under his guidance.

Jeffrey tried to impress upon his players that strength was not necessarily the most important factor in a soccer game. Cleverness—the ability to outthink an opponent—was more valuable. His players often were fundamentally superior to opposing players, making up for any occasional lack of talent.

Jeffrey believed that one of the best ways to teach soccer was to demonstrate the techniques himself. At practices, he often wore tennis shoes rather than conventional soccer shoes so he could more aptly demonstrate that the toe should never be used when kicking the ball. He would join the team in a scrimmage from time to time, playing the center forward position that had earned him

his reputation when he was a teenager. Jeffrey played on the second team so as to demonstrate these points against the varsity. Rarely would any of his players encounter a more accomplished player.

Unlike Douglas Stewart, the great Pennsylvania coach of an earlier era, Jeffrey was not as autocratic. Whereas Stewart was a stern taskmaster, Jeffrey often displayed a sense of humor. He was quoted as telling his players that "as a Scotchman, take small steps and let the ball do the work."

In 1936, he introduced soccer-volleyball at Penn State. Much of his success stems from teaching this simple game which effectively taught the elements of ball control. Jeffrey referred to it as the "main cog in the machine that built great Nittany soccer teams."

Because of the school's immense success, and because he was a native son, Jeffrey's team was invited to tour Scotland in 1934. Penn State would play against several of the best amateur teams in Scotland. Jeffrey viewed the invitation as an opportunity to go home and for his players to gain valuable experience.

Penn State supplied the equipment. Each of the players had to raise $250 to cover his traveling expenses. The team sailed from New York on August 11, 1934, on the S.S. *Caledonia*.

The six-week tour indeed was an exciting experience. There were banquets, receptions, and parties in the team's honor. Jack Fletcher, the Penn State captain, was so infatuated with a Scottish girl he met that he married her. Yes, the Nittany Lions were treated royally.

On the soccer field, it was another matter. Penn State lost all eight games it played. Despite averaging four goals, the Lions allowed eight per game. The short passing game that Jeffrey coached back in Pennsylvania was played to perfection by the Scots. More importantly, however, Penn State picked up the insight that Jeffrey hoped it would. Because it was the following fall that the Lions had their phenomenal unbeaten, untied, and unscored-on season.

The 1935 season which stands a model for intercollegiate soccer performance was tarnished, however, because Penn State was not named the intercollegiate champion. Yale, which won twelve consecutive games, was accorded the honor. It seems that the association had frowned upon the fact that Jeffrey had played in some of the games on Penn State's tour of Scotland. Because of injuries to his team—which numbered only fourteen men—Jeffrey felt compelled to suit up against his countrymen. It was also felt he was becoming frustrated with the one-sided defeats.

Because of his great success, Jeffrey was encouraged to write a book. In 1935, *The Boys With the Educated Feet* was published. To this day it serves as a practical guide for soccer players and coaches in the United States.

In 1941, after all his years as a soccer coach and instructor. in industrial engineering, Jeffrey earned his B.S. degree in physical education from Penn State.

Despite what many may have been led to believe, soccer was played with winning results at schools other than Penn State during the 1930s. In 1934 and 1935, for example, Cornell fielded two of its better teams, winning the Middle Atlantic Intercollegiate championship in 1934 and tying Penn for the title the following season.

In the New England Intercollegiate League, Yale had its unbeaten season in 1935, placing four players among the league's top ten scorers. In 1936, Princeton won the Middle Atlantic title while Brown had its best season, winning all six of its league games. Maregeson and Read of Brown were the top two scorers in the league, totaling nineteen goals. Jackson, their teammate, was fifth with five more goals.

Princeton repeated as the Middle Atlantic titlist in 1937. It finished 5–0. Springfield also won all five of its games to win the New England crown, even though Brown was 6–0–2. Those two ties enabled Brown to finish with more points, but cost it the championship. In 1938, Haverford, which pioneered the rebirth of soccer in the twentieth century, climbed on top of the Middle Atlantic League while Harvard swept seven games to reign in New England. Mendell of Harvard had nine goals to lead the league.

Soccer also was finding new horizons out West. For a number of years following World War I, Stanford and California were the only collegiate teams playing soccer on the Pacific Coast. Mostly, they played amateur teams from the Bay Area. This was in addition to their annual game.

Some of these annual matches between Stan-

ford and California were reminiscent of the rowdy games of the sport's past. Speaking of the 1925 game which ended in a 2–2 tie, the California coach said that the Stanford games were always very rough and that teamwork and skill were thrown to the winds. The casualty list from that game included a broken leg, five broken ribs, and three cracked heads.

Only four other western schools had joined the soccer movement by 1940. They were San Francisco, UCLA, San Jose, and San Francisco State. During the mid-thirties, San Francisco and California dominated the West Coast scene.

In 1934, San Francisco finished 7–0–1, while California, which still played several games against club teams, was 9–2–3. In 1935, when Penn State was unbeaten, untied and unscored on; when Yale also was unbeaten in twelve games, San Francisco was 17–0–1. California had an 8–2–1 record.

San Francisco slipped a bit in 1936 and 1937. California was the best on the Pacific Coast, going unbeaten in six games in 1936 and finishing 11–1–2 the following year. In 1938, California had a 14–0–4 record. San Francisco had returned to prominence, winning eight of twelve games and tying two.

In the southern part of the country, soccer also was on the upswing. Navy fielded the first southern team in 1918, then returned to intercollegiate competition in 1921, following World War I.

The University of Florida became the second school in the region to field a soccer team when it played a three-game schedule against local high school teams in 1922.

Over the next four years, Florida compiled what on the surface seemed like an impressive record. It won twenty-three games, lost only one, and tied two. However, Florida was playing its matches against teams called Alachua, Eustis, Duval, Live Oak, and Umatilla. In 1925, the Gators lost their first match when they were beaten by Groveland.

A short time after that game, coach Harry Metcalf died and the team cancelled the remainder of its 1925 schedule. Soccer disappeared at Florida and was not played at the school for more than twenty-five years.

By 1939, however, there were fifteen collegiate teams playing in the South. The growth was centered in Maryland where seven schools took up the kicking game. They were led by Western Maryland and Towson State. Maryland's proximity to Philadelphia and the East Coast schools enabled the state's teams to find an abundance of competition. In the deep South, though, soccer's growth pattern was much slower. The game enjoyed only temporary success at schools such as Clemson, Davidson, Christian Brothers, Hampton, and High Point.

Midwestern universities also were handicapped by a lack of competition. Michigan formed a team in 1920 but dropped the sport the following year because it could find competition only at the club level in Detroit. Ohio State tried in 1923 and also failed to establish a team.

In 1927, Ohio State gave it another try and was joined by Illinois. The first meeting between the teams preceded the annual football game. On a field adjacent to Ohio Stadium, the first Big Ten soccer match was played with Ohio State winning, 2–0. A barrier seemingly had been torn down in the Midwest, and soccer was expected to flower.

As the 1928 season approached, there was a great deal of enthusiasm at Ohio State and Illinois. The three games between the two were won by Illinois. The school's athletic council was so pleased with its team's effort that twelve major I letters were awarded, and gold championship balls were presented to those players who participated in more than half the playing time.

Illinois looked ahead to possible intersectional play. At Ohio State, that prospect had become reality. With their victory over Illinois in 1927 solidifying their claim to the mythical, if abbreviated, Midwest title, the Buckeyes challenged Princeton to a match. Princeton had been unbeaten in 1927 and was awarded the intercollegiate league championship.

Ohio State traveled east for the confrontation as the 1928 season unfolded. It was billed as the battle of champions, but it was far from a battle. Princeton won handily, 6–0, even though it was embarking on what was to be a dreadful year for a school which had known so much soccer success. Princeton finished 3–4–1 that year.

Although soccer seemed entrenched at both Big Ten schools, the problem of finding satisfactory opponents was becoming acute. Other conference schools did not start soccer programs.

Finally, a discouraged Ohio State dropped soccer after the 1931 season. Illinois, which had to travel nineteen hundred miles to fulfill its 1934 schedule, followed the Ohio State lead in 1935. The two titans of the Midwest had been unable to survive while waiting for their sister schools to accept soccer.

Midwestern soccer did not die out entirely during the 1930s. Oberlin College in Ohio and Wheaton in Illinois carried on their intercollegiate programs without interruption. In 1927, C. W. Savage, the Oberlin Athletic Director, asked George E. Willbond, an Englishman employed by the college, to give soccer instructions in the service class program. Savage wanted to broaden the scope and to improve the quality of the physical education program. Willbond agreed to help.

He had played soccer in his youth and still was active in semipro leagues. His teachings were effective and helped soccer mature on the intramural level. After the completion of the 1928 intramural competition, an all-star team was selected to play an exhibition match against outside competition. In following years, this practice evolved into an intercollegiate schedule which followed intramural play.

Outstanding players from the class teams were brought together following the intramural season to play under Willbond. Soccer acquired varsity status in 1930 at Oberlin but the practice of choosing teams from its class programs continued. The small school found adequate competition without having to venture beyond Ohio's borders.

The method was different at Wheaton College. Early in the 1930s, young men who had played soccer on missionary fields or in prep schools gathered for informal games on the college campus. It was not long before they approached the athletic director of Wheaton, Edward A. Coray, with a request to begin an intercollegiate soccer program.

Coray did not give immediate approval. He knew there were few schools in the Midwest playing soccer. He knew that it might be difficult arranging a schedule. He instructed the eager students to look into the matter to see if a workable schedule might be arranged.

By the autumn of 1935, the students had found several willing opponents. They also had found a coach in Jim McKellin, a soccer enthusiast from the East who was working at Wheaton. Coray endorsed the plan and in 1935 Wheaton embarked on its first season of soccer.

Wheaton played seven games, winning four and losing three. Two of the losses were to Illinois. The following season saw a reduced schedule as Illinois had dropped the sport and opponents were difficult to find. Wheaton won all three games it played, facing the likes of Mooseheart, Oak Park, and the Swedish American Club of Rockford. Growing confidence in its game prompted Wheaton to contact eastern schools for possible matches in 1937. A five-game trip was arranged.

In the fall of 1937, following three games in its own region, Wheaton embarked on the first extended intersectional trip in intercollegiate soccer history. The players traveled by auto and stayed with friends and alumni. During its ten-day journey, Wheaton played West Chester, Princeton, Army, St. John's, and Oberlin. It won two games and gained a world of experience, so it was agreed they would return the following year. Until the start of World War II, Wheaton made an annual eastern tour, playing the bulk of its schedule on visiting fields. Because of economics, the trips were confined to a ten-day period.

It was apparent that a winning record was not the school's priority on these excursions. Only in 1938–when Wheaton defeated Oberlin, Western Maryland, and Franklin & Marshall—did they return home with a winning record. It was this continued effort—along with that of Oberlin—to keep soccer alive in the Midwest, which spurred Wheaton on.

Those looking at the recent history of soccer would notice several factors in its growth just prior to World War II. The sport often became popular at a school because of the involvement of foreign students. Sometimes, it was brought to the campus by students who had played the sport in high school. Once in a while, soccer flourished because of the persistence of one man.

Even at schools which did not have an intercollegiate program, soccer was very much a part of campus life. In 1922, Ohio State reported that 475 students were playing on thirty-one intramural teams. At Navy, 460 midshipmen—more than a quarter of the entire corps—were playing soccer on an interclass level. Cornell boasted of twenty

teams in an intrafraternity league and ten in the intercollegiate leagues, not counting freshmen and varsity teams.

By 1930, there were reports of at least four hundred intramural college teams playing soccer. A pattern of forming teams to participate on the intercollegiate level was born in this fashion. For example, in 1934, Rochester students were so taken by the sport as played on the intramural level, that they arranged a game with Hamilton College. Rochester thus entered the intercollegiate ranks. Bucknell's team evolved from the intramural level, as did Grove City's team, which was selected from the best among the intramural players. It was much in the same manner that Oberlin chose its team.

These programs developed at the grass-roots level. Other schools depended on the influx of foreign students to support soccer. Worcester Tech was playing the kicking game as early as 1921, because of a large immigrant population in Worcester. Renssalaer listed students from Colombia, Cuba, Germany, Greece, and Panama on its roster in 1935. Foreign students helped soccer gain a foothold at Howard University.

To this day, there is a communications problem on teams with a mix of ethnic representation. Back in the days when Stanford was becoming formidable, its soccer team had eleven nations represented. The players got along well, it was reported, but communication often was difficult. On the field, players often converse with hand signs.

The makeup of some college teams was fascinating. MIT had athletes from England, South America, South Africa, Norway, China, and Russia on its squad. MIT had difficulty arranging practice sessions. Teamwork was nearly impossible. And despite the fact this ethnic mix made for a group of individually superb players, MIT rarely had success on the field.

Fathers of soccer were everywhere, touching campuses that otherwise would not have had a spark of interest in the kicking game. At Lock Haven, Blake Hammond, an Episcopal clergyman and former soccer player at Lehigh, volunteered his services for an infant soccer program. He coached the Lock Haven team until the sport was dropped during World War II.

Frank Dotterweich, a former high school and

Merritt Baldwin of Connecticut was an All-New England selection in 1941.

club player, organized a team at Johns Hopkins which gained varsity status in 1935. Dotterweich was the coach. Hugh G. McCurdy introduced soccer to his Wesleyan gym classes in 1922. By the end of the fall, Wesleyan played its first intercollegiate match, against Amherst. And McCurdy began a long reign as the Wesleyan coach.

Fitchburg State and Bridgewater State—both in Massachusetts—developed soccer programs through the effort of its director of athletics. Frank Crosier, a graduate of Springfield College, served as director at both colleges. He initiated soccer on each campus, appointing student-coaches to handle the teams. He sat back and watched as Fitchburg and Bridgewater met.

For whatever reason—no matter who provided the incentive—soccer was a thriving sport as the 1930s ended. More than eighty college teams were playing it on a varsity basis. The sport was firmly entrenched in the East and was making strides in the South and West.

Night soccer made its first collegiate appearance in 1939 at West Chester in Pennsylvania when it hosted a game against Salisbury Teachers College. A large audience watched the match played on a field lighted by floodlights.

The United States still was competing in the Olympic Games. There was no soccer tournament in the 1932 games at Los Angeles, but the 1936 Olympics in Berlin signaled the return of the

Douglas Stewart set the highest goals for his players at Pennsylvania during his nearly 40-year reign. From his 1941 team (left to right): E. Graham Gibbons, Stewart McCracken, Harvey Genden, David Johnston and captain Arthur Caturani.

Co-captain Mort Thau was a standout player on Springfield's 1942 team.

game. The Americans were beaten by Italy, 1—0. Once again, there were no college players on the United States team.

In 1941, the National Soccer Coaches Association was formed. Prior to this, there was no board of coaches. John Brock of Springfield was the first president of the group. He was succeeded in 1942 by Earle Waters, the West Chester coach who held the post for three years.

Despite the progress soccer was making, there still were voices of protest to be heard. Ironically, one voice belonged to Douglas Stewart, who coached those great Pennsylvania teams and who edited the *Soccer Guide*. Stewart felt that the quality of soccer was suffering during this period of growth. He was a purist and the game disturbed him.

Through his outlet in the *Soccer Guide,* Stewart criticized coaching inadequacies and unskilled performances by players. He wrote: "Their [the players] brains do not work, and while they may get some muscular exercise they get very lit-

tle of the mental exercise which the game requires."

He had a similiar scorn for coaches, also vented in the pages of the *Soccer Guide:* " . . . there is still a great number of teams who are appallingly ignorant of anything approaching ball control and who rely entirely on their speed and strength to make up for their deficiency in skill. . . . The necessity for greater concentration on primary instruction in the fundamentals of playing the game, that is, properly kicking the ball and properly trapping the ball, is still glaringly apparent."

Stewart would constantly tell the coaches to encourage players to use both feet instead of one. He attacked high school coaches for not properly instructing players in the fundamentals of the game, and for not preparing them for the rugged physical conditioning that is needed in college soccer. Stewart suggested that many players arriving in college were starting from scratch. Referees—as officials in any sport—did not escape the wrath

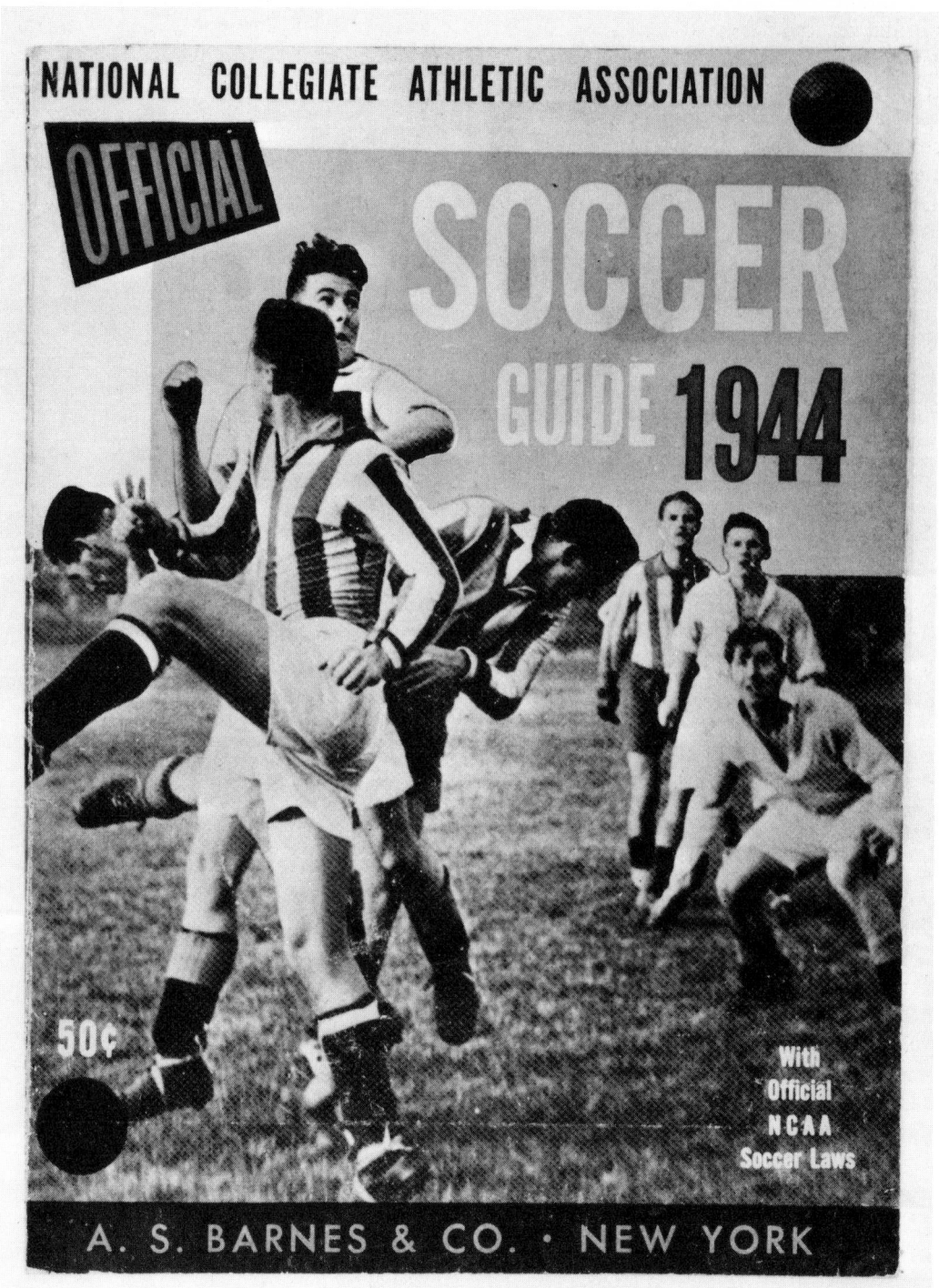

of coaches and players. Stewart also assailed them, claiming many were not well-versed in the rules or did not know them at all.

Perhaps Stewart's outrage was to be expected. Rarely have observers of one era of sport admitted the sport and the athletes who played it had progressed to a higher level. And it is true that when a sport expands as quickly as soccer did, the quality of play deteriorates. Stewart should have been pleased, however, that the struggling game he knew had grown so quickly and was a part of the American college scene.

Soccer would have to endure another crisis, however, one more staggering blow to its existence. In 1940 and 1941, when war raged in Europe, the game, and life in general, continued without change in America. In the fall of 1941, eighty teams completed their intercollegiate schedules. But in December of the year, the Japanese attacked Pearl Harbor and America entered the second World War. Fielding a soccer team became a problem for many collegiate soccer coaches.

5

The College Game Comes of Age (1946–1978)

World War II left its mark on every front. College athletic programs were reduced across the country. Soccer, often looked upon as a minor sport, was dropped completely by many schools. Where the sport was retained—there were only forty-two active teams by 1945—there was little intersectional play, since only essential travel was permitted in the fuel-rationed economy.

While this break in continuity may have interfered with and slowed development in other home-grown sports, it proved a benefit to American soccer due to several significant factors.

First, many more young men were opting for a college education. Most of this increase was in those magnet schools that had been chosen to house military preservice training units, where participation in such training was financially underwritten by the government. A large part of these programs were directed toward physical conditioning, and it was natural for administrators to look for a stamina-building, competitive team sport to meet this need.

Second, thanks to Commander Tom Hamilton, who headed four navy preflight schools, and the influence of Tom Taylor, soccer coach at the Naval Academy, soccer was chosen. Hamilton selected Earle C. Waters, coach at West Chester State College, to organize and staff the pilot program at the University of North Carolina in Chapel Hill.

Waters, a veteran of World War I and the first president of the National Soccer Coaches Association, founded in 1941, threw himself enthusiastically into the program. He looked upon the opportunity as a means to further his favorite sport and to educate a whole new segment of players and coaching personnel in the values of the game.

Several other well-known college coaches were connected with preflight programs elsewhere. Walter McCloud, secretary of the coaches' organization and coach at Trinity, and John Squires, coach at the University of Connecticut, provided some soccer input, but it was in Waters' program at UNC that most of the inspiration originated for the strong postwar surge.

In those years, the men who would participate in and guide the destiny of the postwar game were exposed to the international aspect of soccer for the first time. They came to grips with soccer on its own terms, and it was an eye-opening experience.

A Dutch team, made up of youths from the Netherlands, trained with the Marines at Camp Lejeune in North Carolina and provided competition for preflight indoctrinees at Chapel Hill.

Some navy personnel, whose convoys to South America put in at Belem—or, more frequently, at Recife—witnessed the high standard of club play in Brazil.

When they began to collect in numbers, enemy prisoners of war staged their own versions of the competition that was a favorite pastime in their homeland. American soldiers and sailors were amazed by the ball-handling wizardry of the dusty, little Italians in the camps in North Africa and the precise play of captured Germans.

Toward the close of hostilities, military staffs began to guide their men slowly back toward normal life. It was then that Ralph Rosner, an American referee, achieved a notable first when he was called upon to officiate several prestigious games in Italy between sides of touring English professionals and military-type, prewar stars.

During the postwar era, soccer outgrew the unimaginative tactics of its first quarter-century in America and began a period of uninterrupted flow toward the refinement that would bring respectability to the college game.

1946

The young men who trooped back into American colleges after the war were not to be denied their enthusiasm for soccer. The maturity that had been gained abroad provided the spark for the formation of college soccer clubs where there had been no previous programs and for the revival of the game at many schools which had been forced to drop sports during the war years. The return of a contingent of men who played soccer either before or during military service led to a strong rebirth of the game that saw forty-four schools either begin or resume fielding teams in 1946.

One such school, Springfield College, which had discontinued its entire athletic program during the war, fielded a side that went through its eight-game season undefeated and received the Outstanding Team Award from the Intercollegiate Soccer Football Association of America.

On that undefeated team were many who were to leave their mark on the game. Whitey Burnham and Irv Schmid went on to become college coaches at Dartmouth and Springfield, respectively. Art Bridgman became part of the college renaissance in California. Australian Lloyd McDonald, John Hogan, and Don Molten all later coached secondary school teams to outstanding records.

There were other distinguished teams and players. Temple University was second to Springfield with a 6–1–0 log. Dartmouth, Princeton, and Penn State showed only one loss. The University of Pennsylvania won the Middle Atlantic League; Swarthmore topped the Middle Atlantic Conference.

Charles Matlack, who would later bring the

game to Earlham College, was among the leading scorers on the Haverford team of the Middle Atlantic Conference. Bill van Breda Kolff, of basketball fame, was an All-American in soccer for Princeton. Within the year, Al Laverson, Temple All-American, and Rolf Valtin, Swarthmore striker, became the first amateurs to go directly from college soccer competition into professional play.

In California, coach Julius Schroeder's University of California team took the title in the newly formed Northern California Soccer Conference. This conference was a most encouraging development, because college soccer had all but died on the West Coast, with the exception of the University of California-Berkeley, which had continued to play in the second division of the San Francisco Amateur League.

The University of North Carolina—previously with only club status—fielded its first varsity eleven, and Wheaton College played three games each against Morton Junior College and the University of Chicago and lost only to its own alumni.

But most of the attention-catching action came at the close of the season when records were announced, all-star players were cited, and the first ISFAA All-Star College Game was staged in New York City.

The ISFAA North-South Game, a 1-0 victory for the South, was remarkable to the press for its speed and skill level. The two teams were coached by Tom Dent, Dartmouth (North), and Bill Jeffrey, Penn State (South). A single goal—scored by Evan Jones of Haverford—proved the winning margin in the hard-fought match.

If this first of the postwar soccer seasons began quietly, it finished on a strong note when the decision was reached to use the postseason game as an initial tryout for the United States team in the 1948 Olympic Games. Further plans were laid for more college tryouts prior to the final selections in the spring of 1948. For the first time, the college soccer player was considering his chances of playing for his country in international competition.

1947

This season was to be the last for scholarly Dr. John Brock, coach of Springfield College. Son of an immigrant Scottish couple, Dr. Brock had had a marked effect on the college game. And his players rewarded him with a fitting valedictory—a second straight undefeated season and a repeat No. 1 national ranking.

There was a maturity in this Springfield team that reflected the fact that many of the players were physical education students whose education had been interrupted by the war. Others had been led into the field—a specialty at Springfield—by way of the conditioning programs in the various service arms they had just left. Indeed, some had been exposed to instructors who were Springfield graduates and Brock disciples.

But with team travel reestablished, teams from previously sterile areas were being heard from, and notice was served on New England and the East that a competitive leveling process would spread across the nation in a few short years.

Washington College came up with an 8–0–0 season in the strong Mason-Dixon Conference, upsetting the Baltimore conclave of Loyola, Johns Hopkins, and the University of Baltimore. The University of Pennsylvania won the Middle Atlantic League, and Rutgers and Bucknell deadlocked in a 2–2 final game to share the Middle Atlantic Conference crown.

Oberlin, one of only a handful of colleges playing the game in the Midwest, recorded a 7–1–0 season against intersectional opposition in Pennsylvania, Illinois, and Indiana. On the West Coast, Julius Schroeder's University of California eleven finished with an 11–2–4 mark, competing against reborn sides at UCLA, University of San Francisco, San Francisco State, California Aggies, and Stanford.

It was in this year, too, that the first of the junior colleges established regular competition in the sport. San Francisco Community College held the University of California to a narrow 3–2 victory, which was prophetic of the impressive junior college teams that were to come.

During the latter part of 1947, the Eastern Intercollegiate Soccer League was formed, comprised of teams from Army, Brown, Cornell, Dartmouth, Harvard, Navy, Pennsylvania, Princeton, and Yale.

It was also the "Year of the Clinic." Uniquely designed to aid players and coaches, three clinics were held in New York City and two in the Delaware Valley by the Philadelphia and Vicinity Coaching Association.

The press helped as well. Joe Mackie of the *Springfield Union*, George Collins of the *Boston Globe*, Milt Miller of *PM*, Bill Graham of the *Brooklyn Eagle*, and George Butz of the *Philadelphia Inquirer* formed a postwar coterie of sportswriters dedicated to the spread of college soccer. They had something to write about, too, as for the first time college soccer players were accepted as bona fide candidates for the United States Olympic team.

Rolf Valtin, Swarthmore's inside forward, joined Walt Bahr and Ben McLaughlin, two former Temple standouts, on the playing squad. Valtin was the only undergraduate to break through the strong club bloc and earn a spot on the United States team at the 1948 Olympic Games in London.

But, in the series of trial games against amateur competition, other collegians proved themselves, too. Carmen Moutinho and John Hogan, Springfield's two All-Americans, and Cornell's Derl Derr were strong contenders from New England. Haverford's Andy Lucine and Gettysburg's Charles Meschter represented the Middle Atlantic states. Loyola's Nick Kropfielder and Bill Linz, Maryland's Jim Belt, and Frank Nelson, Gus Johnson, and Dave Boak, all of North Carolina, formed a surprisingly strong contingent from the South. The University of Pennsylvania's giant center half, Irv Antoni, Seton Hall's Bill Sheppell, and Navy goalkeeper Al Schaufelberger all made it to the final tryouts.

1948

The close of the 1948 season saw the University of Connecticut atop the world of collegiate soccer with a perfect 11–0–0 record. Under Springfield grad Jack Squires, the Huskies won the New England championship and numbered among their regular-season victories a 3–2 triumph over Springfield, which had been unbeaten since 1940 (with time out for wartime).

Navy and Cornell were ranked second and third in the nation respectively, while Swarthmore College was chosen as the outstanding team in the Middle Atlantic Conference. Temple, an indepen-

Connecticut finished 11–0 and was named best in the nation. Front row (left to right): Lawrence Dubuc, Jan Olms, Carlos Fetterolf, Stuart Johnson, Norman Pratt, Merritt Baldwin, Paul Salling. Second row: Frank Malinconico, Donald Berger, Marvin Kirschman, Charles Ritchie, Thomas Nevers, Frank Rohloff and Herbert Tschummi. Back row: manager John Osterhoudt, John Tedford, Milton Nichols, Donald Grant, James Blozie, George Cleveland and coach John Squires.

dent which finished the year at 7–1–0, was cited as the top club in eastern Pennsylvania. Bill Jeffrey's Penn State booters started to write one of the hottest postwar success stories by defeating Temple and earning recognition as the best team in western Pennsylvania.

At most Midwest colleges, soccer was still nonvarsity. There were flourishing clubs at Indiana, Michigan State, and Purdue, but in Ohio, only Kenyon and Oberlin—the latter a consistently excellent side—had recognized varsities. Even in the St. Louis area, a strong soccer community, there was no college play.

In Chicago, where the University of Chicago, Morton Junior College, and Wheaton College had established good postwar programs, the standard did approach that of eastern schools. Wheaton was the only team to defeat Oberlin in 1948.

Oberlin had mastered Chicago and played a strong Western Pennsylvania contingent of Slippery Rock, Allegheny, and Carnegie Tech, showing the potential to play with the best.

North Carolina University won the Southern Conference. On the West Coast, University of San Francisco ended the reign of University of California to win the Northern California. One of the strong players for the Dons was their All-America fullback, Steve Negoesco, who would later lead the team to national prominence as coach.

Henri Salaun, a national champion in squash rackets, was an outstanding inside forward at Wesleyan in New England. Brockport's Ted Bondi and Navy's Al Schaufelberger were top-level goalkeepers.

The All-America team was still predominantly native born and heavily laced with older, mature, war veterans. If not as democratic as might have been desired, the selection process represented an honest attempt by the small committee of the National Soccer Coaches Association to arrive at a group representative of all parts of the country.

If there was dissatisfaction with this method, help was on the way. In December—too late for use in the current campaign—T. Fred Holloway, coach at Cortland, published his *Statistical Method of All-America Selection*. This index system took the politics out of All-America determination and, with little change, is used in the sport today.

In 1948, promotion was uppermost in the minds of the leaders in the game, and they struggled to reach for the stars in a burst of official action. Early in the year, the NSCA voted honorary membership to popular movie actor Victor McLaglen, who lent his name and support to an amateur team in Hollywood.

With the young coaches looking for ways to Americanize the sport and to attract the public, the rules makers were change conscious and the result was not always beneficial. The New England Intercollegiate League, chafing under some spotty officiating, opted for a one-hand throw-in. The innovation, happily, was not written into law. But much discussion developed around this matter

and over the legality of "charging the keeper," and the door was set ajar for the anomalies that eventually did appear in the intercollegiate game. All of this was to take the United States farther from the world standard of play than was deserved by the quality players then inhabiting the campuses.

The U.S. Olympic team met with a depressing fate in its match with Italy. Approximately ten minutes into a game played in driving rain on a mud-soaked field, the Americans lost one of their players to serious injury and were then forced to play with only ten men the rest of the way. The Italians posted a 9–0 victory, scoring six times in the final thirteen minutes against their exhausted U. S. opponents.

1949

The nation's first college Soccer Bowl, held in St. Louis on New Year's Day, 1950, brought together designated national cochampions Penn State and the University of San Francisco, both of which had compiled perfect 8–0–0 records in 1949.

Time was running out in the Nittany Lions' fourteen-game unbeaten string, as USF, on the strength of two goals by Dick Baptista, carried a

Maryland, an early power in the South, went 8–2 and won the Southern Conference title.

2–1 lead into the final stages. But, with only ten seconds remaining, a San Francisco fullback was called for a handball. Penn State's Harry Little scored his second goal of the game on a penalty kick to knot the game at 2–2. That's the way it ended, as the two coaches agreed that the game should not go into overtime.

So when it was all over, little had been decided. But the game did bring the cross-country intersectional meeting into the realm of reality and gave a large boost to the growth of the sport in the Midwest and West. Pete Rozelle, then sports information director at USF and now Commissioner of the National Football League, wrote in the *NCAA Soccer Guide* that the fine showing " . . . did much to foster the game along the Pacific slope."

At the close of the season, the New England champion was little Amherst College. Cornell, with German student Gunter Meng to complement All-American Derl Derr, won the Eastern Intercollegiate; Swarthmore returned to the head of the Middle Atlantic Conference; Navy was ranked first in the South.

In New York City, Brooklyn College, with Gerald Mahrer and Clement Grillo making All-American, began a several-year domination of the metropolitan colleges. And some of that urban strength spread over into North Jersey where Seton Hall, led by Jim Hannah and Marty Kelly, came up with another fine season.

For the first time, Fred Holloway's selection method was used to determine the All-America team, and coaches endorsed its objectivity with enthusiasm. On the first team were players from nine different colleges. Twenty-seven schools were represented overall, a significant distribution from among the slightly over one hundred known colleges with soccer varsities.

Holding firm to the idea that any postseason all-star game would be promotionally valuable, the NSCAA and ISFAA jointly staged a match in April between a New York State amateur selection and members of the 1948 All-America team. The collegians returned a satisfying 2–2 draw against players from the German-American and Metropolitan League clubs.

A second publicity coup was pulled off in the early fall when a team from the University of Havana played five games with representative eastern squads. The Cubans displayed a mastery of ball control in defeating Maryland State, Harvard, and Rensselaer Poly. They lost to Tom Dent's Dartmouth Indians, 2–0, before managing to bounce back at the University of Connecticut with a 1–0 victory.

1950

A second Soccer Bowl was played at the same site the following year, but it did not decide the mythical national championship. Since San Francisco, West Coast champion once again, was unable to make the long trip to St. Louis, Penn State, beaten once during the season, was forced to meet Purdue, the second-place team in the Midwestern Conference and a substitute for champion Wheaton.

The Nittany Lions' 3–1 triumph strengthened the East's claim of soccer superiority over the Midwest, but it left unresolved the relative strength of San Francisco. When West Chester was named national champion, there was dissatisfaction in the West.

Earle Waters' West Chester eleven had been knocking on the door for several seasons and was not to be denied in 1950. With impressive wins over Penn State (the Nittany Lions' only loss), Southern Conference champion Maryland, Mason-Dixon champion University of Baltimore, and the University of Pennsylvania, West Chester compiled a spotless 8–0–0 mark.

Elsewhere, Yale took the New England title; Army topped the Eastern Intercollegiate for the first time and Haverford College, with U.S. Olympic coach James Mills in charge, won the Middle Atlantic Conference. The Metropolitan Conference went to Brooklyn, and Seton Hall and Temple were recognized as leaders in New Jersey and Eastern Pennsylvania, respectively. Lock Haven State broke into the championship circle by winning the Pennsylvania Teachers' College League.

Drexel Tech's Bob Linde led the nation in scoring with seventeen goals in nine games. Though modest by today's standards, the record was to stand for some years. Linde, a specialist in penalty kicking, scored twelve goals in as many attempts from the spot and totaled forty-five goals during a

Penn State coaching legend Bill Jeffrey is surrounded by members of his 1950 Soccer Bowl team (clockwise from lower left): Clarence Buss, Ron Emig, Ron Coleman and Harry Little.

four-year career. Still, Linde was only an honorable mention All-American in 1950.

It may seem strange that there are years when soccer players of proven excellence are not included on the All-American team. Much effort was made to have national representation, but communication between areas and especially among leaders in the game—many of whom were part-time coaches—was not reliable, and good players were missed. Thus, in 1950, no player from the West was listed, though there were certainly many of merit.

Three schools placed two players each. Ted Bondi, the Brockport goalkeeper, headlined the mythical team as a three-time All-American. He was joined by teammate Dick Mothorpe, a strong fullback. Seton Hall placed their fearsome midfield pair of Jim Hannah and Bill Sheppell, and West Chester did a double with Ralph Stern, a native New Yorker at left halfback, and Lou Dollarton, an outstanding winger from the sandlots of Philadelphia.

Speedy George Andreadis, a member of the Brooklyn College Sports Hall of Fame, teamed with Penn State's Harry Little to make a potent right side attacking unit. Dartmouth fullback Jackson Hall, who became a serious contender for the 1952 Olympic team, rounded out the defense, while Cornell's Derl Derr and RPI's Venezuelan, Gustavo Gomez, provided center-of-the-line scoring punch.

There were additional outstanding players. Brooklyn's Gerald Mahrer would later star for his country in the Maccabiah Games of 1953, and Amherst's Howie Burnett further established his credentials for a second straight year. Penn State's Joe Lane scored seven goals against Bucknell.

Jim Hannah was one of two All-Americans at Seton Hall. The other was Bill Sheppell.

Temple's Jack Dunn scored a goal as the North defeated the South, 3–2, in the All-Star Game.

Penn State, led by its irrepressible coach, Bill Jeffrey, was invited by the State Department to make a goodwill tour of Iran. Certainly it would have been difficult to conceal the fact that this event was politically motivated.

Oil-rich Iran was being wooed by the USSR, but by way of a carefully manipulated invitation from the Iranian Football Association to Dr. Milton Eisenhower, President at Penn State, this college soccer team contributed to the course of world events. Everywhere the Nittany Lions went in Iran they were showered with flowers and toasted as heroes. Niel See, manager of the team, wrote, "There is a bit of Bill Jeffrey's philosophy which, I think, covers the diplomatic angle of our tour very nicely. As Bill has said, 'People have to learn to play together before they can work together.' "

Prior to World War II, college soccer had rules virtually identical to the international standard. In 1950, in an effort to speed up the American game, the throw-in from touch was dropped from college rules and replaced by an indirect free kick, inspiring the wrath of traditionalists.

1951

In 1951, the University of San Francisco scored forty-seven goals while winning all twelve of its regular-season games. The Dons, selected as hosts of the Soccer Bowl against 7–0–1 Temple, carried a forty-game winning streak over four seasons into the showdown before ten thousand—the largest crowd, at the time, in college soccer history—at Kezar Stadium in San Francisco.

Temple, the first college team to use the airways for such a long journey, was determined to make its trip worthwhile. With Ed Tatoian scoring twice in the opening twelve minutes, and goalkeeper Vic Napolitano shutting down the vaunted Dons' attack, Dr. Pete Leaness' Owls posted a 2–0 upset victory and were named national champions.

The 1951 game would mark the end of the Soccer Bowl contests. For the next seven years, the national champion was selected without the benefit of a postseason intersectional struggle and for those seven years only the East was represented in the winner's circle.

But there was evidence that the balance of power was shifting from traditional eastern dominance toward more even distribution. The two earlier Bowl games had stimulated great enthusiasm for the sport in the Midwest. At the end of the 1951 season, five first-team All-Americans were from midwestern schools.

Oberlin, under coach Ben Collins, put together an 8–0–0 record and captured three spots, the first time any college had so dominated. Goalkeeper Dick Miller, center half Bob Palmer, and inside forward Pete Bellows were the choices. Tom Morrell, a fullback from Indiana, and Tom Kennan, an Earlham right wing, were their schools' initial All-Americans.

Jim Hannah was performing stylishly for Seton Hall at halfback. Tony Orbacker was outstanding in the same position at Brockport State. Swarthmore's George Place and West Chester's Tony Puglisi were outstanding forwards, and George Andreadis led the offense at Brooklyn College.

A crowd of five thousand attended a North-South All-Star Game in December at LaSalle College in Philadelphia. The North jumped to a 2–0 lead on a pair of Howie Burnett goals before Baltimore's Larry Surock and Temple's Jack Dunn knotted the score. A goal by Seton Hall's Joe Polinski late in the game gave the North a 3–2 victory.

Quality players such as Burnett, Dunn, Surock, Dartmouth's Jackson Hall, and USF's Olufryomi Osibogun and Jim Diaz failed to earn first-team All-American status. But the Coaches' Association, aware of the controversial aspects of its selection system, printed an explanatory note in the *NCAA Soccer Guide*, pointing out the difficulty in estimating All-America ability and the fact that there was no distinction made between those selected first and those selected fifth.

The University of Chicago won the young Midwestern Collegiate Soccer Conference. Yale duplicated its New England title win of 1950; Army triumphed in the Eastern Intercollegiate; Baltimore again took the Mason-Dixon, and Maryland won the Southern Conference.

There were four perfect regular-season records. Besides Oberlin and USF, Brockport and RPI showed clean slates. RPI allowed only three goals during the season and defeated all its opponents by at least two goals.

Pennsylvania, practicing here, was one of four Ivy League teams that provided players for an all-star team that toured Bermuda.

1952

While foreign players were leaving their mark almost everywhere else, little Franklin & Marshall College used homegrown talent like goalkeeper Walt Lenz and forward Carl Yoder to outscore opponents, 33–4 in nine games, win the Middle Atlantic Conference title, and earn designation as the nation's best team.

Though it was still years before athletic scholarships were to become a controlling factor, many teams turned to foreign-born collegians who were brought to campus, in many cases by the International Relief Organization.

Howard University, under James Chambers, was already fielding an almost completely foreign-born side. Washington, DC schools such as Catholic University, American University, George Washington, and Georgetown all profited from the enrollment of sons of diplomatic families. Brooklyn College was a little United Nations and RPI awarded a letter to Albert Grundland, a senior from Uruguay, who served as team translator for a year.

Dartmouth won the New England crown. Jim Bly's Duke Blue Devils cracked the grip of Maryland to win the Southern Conference. Baltimore continued to lead the Mason-Dixon, and Army was undefeated in the Ivy League. Earlham College, newcomer to the Midwestern Conference, topped the traditionally strong sides at Wheaton, Purdue, and Chicago.

Dartmouth's Jackson Hall and Harvard's Charles Ufford, who was also a nationally ranked squash rackets champion, gave the Ivy League two of the outstanding defenders in the country. Temple's Jack Dunn and West Chester's Tony Puglisi were both high-scoring forwards. With Franklin & Marshall's Yoder, Penn's Joe Devaney and Duke's Dave Strauch, there was a scoring potential of eighty-plus goals on the All-America forward line selected this year.

There were developments on a variety of fronts.

Temple's Dunn and Baltimore's Larry Surock made the U.S. Olympic team, but the Americans were eliminated by Italy, 8–0, in the preliminary round.

The Ivy League invaded Bermuda with an all-star aggregation of players from Cornell, Dartmouth, Yale, and Penn. Wally Hughes, a Bermudian and a member of the Cornell varsity, promoted the tour, and the Americans wound up with a respectable 2–3 record against superior opposition.

The first Sarasota (Florida) Soccer Forum, organized by Navy's Glenn Warner, took place. And a soccer clinic was held in Nuremberg for U.S. servicemen stationed in occupied Germany.

There was a significant rules change, too. The offsides violation was made to apply on the kick-in, restoring a semblance of order and helping to control the bruised shins and hard body contact in front of the net that had resulted from the 1950 substitution of the indirect free kick for the throw-in.

1953

At the beginning of the season, Temple coach Pete Leaness, not normally given to extravagant statements, predicted that his Owls would go undefeated. Temple did not disappoint, winning all nine of its games against major competition and earning the title of the nation's best club. The Owls' record of scoring six-plus goals per game against Haverford, Drexel, Army, Penn State, and Rutgers, all leaders in their respective leagues, was impressive.

The individual statistics were striking as well. Inside forward Jack Dunn led the team in scoring with twenty goals—a collegiate record. Ed Tatoian and Frank Fanucci tallied thirteen and twelve, respectively, while Lefty Didricksen, who was also a standout in basketball and baseball, notched ten.

Of all the Temple Owls, however, none approached All-American center halfback Len Oliver in technical grace and efficiency of play. By any standard he would have been impressive; by those of the early 1950s only superlatives suffice. He was a world above the others on the college level.

There was excellent talent at other schools, too. Vincent Palmieri, at Cortland, was a formidable halfback. Gabor Czako, a Hungarian student at Penn, was a fine forward. On the West Coast, San Francisco had standouts in goalkeeper Bill Cox and outside right Manny Ortiz. East Stroudsburg

In his first year as coach, Mickey Cochrane (left) produced the Mason-Dixon champion at Johns Hopkins. Two of his stars were Jim Hutchins (center) and David Hack.

Gabor Czako was an All-American at Pennsylvania.

State fashioned a good season, thanks to a stingy defense anchored by fullback Fred Gahres.

It was no surprise that the University of Maryland won the first title in the new Atlantic Coast Conference, since the Terrapins were a perennial power in the South. But it was unusual to find Johns Hopkins as the top team in the Mason-Dixon and it represented a considerable achievement by the Blue Jays and their young coach, Mickey Cochrane, who was in his first college post.

Haverford won the MAC; Springfield took the New England title; City College of New York triumphed in the Metropolitan New York Inter-City League; Purdue, with a strong foreign-born flavor, headed the Midwestern Conference and USF was rated best in the West. Cortland, Army, and Oberlin, none showing more than one setback, were also among the leaders.

Schools that were previously unheard of in soccer placed their athletes among the elite chosen to the All-America team. Allegheny, Roanoke, Albany State, Johns Hopkins, Delaware, San Francisco State, and Earlham proved that no one school had a lock on the top talent. Talented secondary school players were traveling farther to matriculate in the colleges of their choice.

One major coaching change took place in 1953 when Bill Jeffrey resigned at Penn State to accept a similar post in Puerto Rico. After a twenty-six-year tenure of unparalleled success, Jeffrey gave over the reins of the Nittany Lions to his former player, Ken Hosterman. College soccer would miss the influence of this gentle Scot.

The Sunshine Bowl Game, the keynote event of the second annual Florida Forum, attracted many of the better college players, and there was feeling among the organizers of the event that it had outgrown the facilities available at Sarasota. They planned to move the 1954 meeting to St. Petersburg when the city promised a promotion that would reflect a big-time interest in college soccer.

1954

Early in the year, Dick Schmelzer, editor of the *NCAA Soccer Guide*, counted 125 college teams in thirty-one states, a number which had more than doubled in the span of two years.

Five teams ended the season with perfect slates. Oberlin, under young coach Cliff Stevenson, carried its victory streak to forty-one straight. Dartmouth, perfect in eight games, was the New England champion, and Brockport State, a nine-game winner, was first in New York. Not to be outdone, CCNY, with Gus Naclerio pumping in a school-record number of goals, went through its eight-game schedule without a loss.

The Intercollegiate Association, however, recognizing a strength of schedule not common to all—it included eight of the strongest teams in the East—named 8–0–0 Penn State the best in the nation.

All-American midfielder Len Oliver helped Temple to an 8–1–1 mark.

Hector Riquezes made All-American at Duke.

Washington College won the Middle Atlantic Conference over Haverford. Though the University of Maryland and the University of Baltimore continued to dominate the Atlantic Coast Conference and the Mason-Dixon, Howard University was regarded as the strongest independent in the South.

In the Midwest Conference, Earlham survived an opening-game draw with Indiana to prove best. It clawed its way to the top by posting four successive shutout wins over conference opponents.

In California, a new league had been formed by the colleges in the southern area. UCLA, Cal Tech, California Poly, and Pomona-Claremont had to play a double round-robin to form a functional schedule. UCLA topped the field in this first running, but bowed to San Francisco, repeat northern winner, in a playoff.

Temple's exceptional midfielder, Len Oliver, and high-scoring Jack Dunn carried the Owls through another fine season, marred only by a loss to Penn State and a tie with Haverford. Undoubtedly it was the strong duo of John Pinezich and Dick Packer who helped the Nittany Lions to their unblemished season. Included in their victories was a 5–1 conquest of Army, which this year was anchored by Francis Adams.

Something of a mild sensation occurred on the West Coast when two players helped focus attention on a two-year school, San Francisco City College. Rudolpho Molina and Fred Samora engineered the 5–4 SFCC victory that snapped the

University of San Francisco's fifty-six game conference winning streak.

There was a flair for offensive soccer in all sections. The University of Pennsylvania showed only a 5–5–1 record, but tallied a record forty-six goals, providing evidence of a trend in college soccer.

Duke had a mediocre season, but it was distinguished by the play of left fullback Hector Riquezes.

1955

The season produced only two major colleges with perfect playing records, and the awards committee showed no hesitation in selecting them—

Brockport and Penn State—as national cochampions.

A postseason playoff tournament, won by West Chester, was a hastily formed attempt to arrive at a worthy eastern champion which could then meet a team from the West for the true national championship. Though the competition was short-lived—it could not always attract the major sectional winners due to institutional restrictions (neither Penn State nor Brockport competed)—it did prove to be the germ of the idea which flowered at the end of the decade into the NCAA Tournament.

There were now 171 colleges playing the game. It is possible to fault this statistic and scale it upward, for there was now much unreported club activity in the Midwest, the South, and the Rocky

Wheaton's Cliff McCrath was All-Midwestern Collegiate Conference as a sophomore.

Mountains that would shortly achieve full varsity recognition.

San Jose and Santa Clara appeared for the first time in the Northern California Conference, which was won by USF. The University of Southern California joined the Southern California Conference, which belonged for the first time to Cal Poly. There was no state playoff in California because a suitable site could not be agreed upon, so USF and Cal Poly shared state honors.

Other colleges fielded teams for the first time. Queens College and Pratt Institute played in the Metropolitan League, which was again won by CCNY. Akron and Dayton fielded their first varsity teams. The thoroughly restructured Southern Conference, with additional members, showed Washington and Lee as its champion.

Sectional winners were Harvard in New England, Drexel Tech in the Middle Atlantic, and Baltimore in the South. The University of Pennsylvania, 10–1, lost only to Yale. Colgate lost only to the two national cochampions.

The Atlantic Coast Conference title again went to Maryland, but Frostburg State was counted best among southern independents. Indiana, though beaten by Ohio State, won its first midwestern title.

Western Maryland, profiting from a strong cadre of Baltimore players and led by captain Dennis Harmon, unseated the University of Baltimore to win the Mason–Dixon.

Dick Packer was the strength of the Penn State offense, while Walter Schmidt served the same function for Brockport. Brockport also featured strong backs in Bill Hughes and Peter Hinchey.

Oleh Karawan was denting the nets consistently for University of Illinois Chicago Circle, a new team in the Midwest. West Chester's Sergio Rey and Temple's Bob Simpson were excellent backs who had learned their fundamentals in the metropolitan junior leagues of New York City and Philadelphia, respectively.

Education in the game continued as well. In the early spring, Bill Jeffrey came away from the beaches of Puerto Rico for a U.S. Army Special Services clinic in Germany. Ross Smith, former coach and director of physical education at Cornell, joined him. Ed Bullock, former coach at Williams, headed up another clinic session in Vermont. In Ohio, Ohio State's Skip Knuttgen and

Oberlin's Cliff Stevenson spearheaded the formation of the Ohio Soccer Coaches Association.

1956

College players were becoming increasingly prominent on major amateur club sides during the off-season.

Andy Hritz, an All-American from the University of Pennsylvania and Temple, during the 1940s, and John Pinezich, a former Penn State winger, were playing in the New York German-American League for the German Hungarians and Eintracht, respectively.

Gerald Mahrer, of Brooklyn College and Blue Star, and Al Laverson, of Temple and Elizabeth, S.C., had represented the United States in the Maccabiah Games of 1953. Temple's Walt Bahr and Ben McLaughlin played in the 1950 World Cup in Brazil alongside Harry Keough, who would later lead St. Louis University to five NCAA titles between 1967 and 1973.

Three former collegians—Jack Dunn, Larry Surock, and Bill Sheppell—were members of the 1952 Olympic team and the 1956 Olympic eleven was anchored by another college trio: Dick Packer, finishing a brilliant career at Penn State; Ron Coder, another All-American and the captain of the 1950 Penn State squad; and the University of Rochester's Zenon Snylyk. The U.S. Olympians were beaten in the first round by eventual finalist Yugoslavia, 9–1.

Trinity College, owner of an 8–0–0 record as the New England titlist, was named the nation's outstanding team by the awards committee of the Intercollegiate Soccer Football Association. Brown University, with English and Canadian professional Joe Kennaway as coach, was runner-up in New England. Drexel Tech took the Middle Atlantic Conference, and Catholic University, which had threatened for several seasons, won the Mason–Dixon.

Maryland once again topped the ACC, while Navy was the best independent in the South. Yale won the Ivy crown and the University of Illinois took top honors in the Midwest. Michigan State, showing early strength, fielded its first varsity, tying Illinois and winning five other games. USF,

High-scoring Tony Washofsky (above) and Ossie Jethon were Drexel's "twin bombers."

All-American center forward Doug Raynard co-captained Trinity to designation as the nation's top team.

with its usual preponderance of foreign players, was the class in the West.

CCNY posted a clear record to win its league title, and was 9–1–1 overall. Little Grove City finished unbeaten and untied.

Excellent forwards could be found on many campuses. Trinity's Douglas Reynard, Western Maryland's Denny Harmon, USF's Joe Njokuobi, Illinois' Oleh Karawan, Yale's Mike Cooke, and the twin bombers of Drexel, Tony Washofsky and Ozzie Jethon, were all scorers of note.

Bill Hughes again manned the defenses for Brockport. Paul Coward defended for Purdue, while Ray Wilson, West Chester's standout halfback, and Earlham's Newlin Otto were early examples of the attacking midfielder. Big Henry Litchfuss, a gifted center half, was the first player

from Towson State College to make the All-American team.

The top goalkeepers were Wheaton's Mike Easterling, Drexel's Dave Whitney, and East Stroudsburg's Tom D'Armi.

Glenn Warner reluctantly announced the discontinuation of the Florida Forum due to lack of interest. However, as a direct result of the sessions and the Forum's showpiece event, the Sunshine Bowl, soccer competition had begun in the state. Alan Moore, a former Springfield player, had founded a successful club at University of Florida, and both Stetson University and Rollins College had started varsity play. Rollins was coached by the president of the school, Dr. Hugh McKean.

1957

Although launched without fanfare, the birth of a student soccer club at St. Louis University was a significant happening in 1957. The club was headed by Bob Guelker, then soccer coach at Seminary High School. Guelker, a St. Louis graduate, was responsible for the development of a massive soccer movement in the diocesan school system and Catholic Youth Council. From these foundations, the university would reap a rich harvest.

Additional college teams were appearing— Danbury State and New Haven University in the East, University of California at Riverside and at Davis in the West, and Carleton College, MacMurray, Greenville, and Benedictine in the Midwest. Kentucky registered in with the University of Louisville and Berea College.

In New England, Springfield fashioned another title-winning season with a 9–0–0 record. However, in New York, CCNY went the Maroon one better and closed with the Metropolitan League crown and a 10–0–0 log.

So the awards committee was again faced with a problem in diplomacy. The members solved it by declaring national cochampions. They might have been a bit more generous and included Catholic University, which sported a 10–0–0 mark, won the Mason-Dixon crown for a second year and claimed among its victims Roanoke, Towson, Loyola, and Baltimore, all tough opponents. The Cardinals of player-coach Hicabi Emekli did claim one indisputable achievement: Their sev-

Wheaton coach Bob Baptista (second from right) huddles with his stars: goalkeeper Mike Easterling, Cliff McCrath and Bob Adolph (left to right).

enty-one goals was a college record. It was an indication of the offensive character of the college game in that period.

Swarthmore won the Middle Atlantic Conference, Princeton took the Ivy League and Washington and Lee triumphed in the new Southern Conference. In Florida, Rollins and Stetson had been joined by Jacksonville and Florida Southern to form the Florida Collegiate Conference. After winning the first-year championship, the Rollins booters were treated to a postseason trip to Bermuda where they played games with representative sides.

Penn State and West Chester were rated the strongest independents in Pennsylvania; Dayton showed the way among the colleges in Ohio. Purdue, after a loss to Earlham, fought off the rest of its competitors to win the Midwest Conference. The start of league play in the Rocky Mountain Conference found Colorado Mines and Air Force Academy tying at the end of the campaign.

Once again, the Terrapins of Maryland won the Atlantic Coast Conference and the Dons of San Francisco finished atop the Pacific Coast. Cal Tech was the top team in southern California.

For a second year, Mike Easterling was impressive in the net for Wheaton, making hard work for the scorers in the Midwest Conference. Ethiopian Telahun Bekele was one of these who had helped bring success to Purdue. Brothers Newlin and Richard Otto were outstanding halfbacks at Earlham. Cliff McCrath was a prominent center half and Easterling's teammate at Wheaton.

Penn State and West Chester State College still continued to produce fine forwards. Per Torgensen of the Nittany Lions and Tom Fleck of the Rams were excellent linkmen and could read a game with the best. Sergei Retinov almost singlehandedly ripped through Swarthmore's opponents in the MAC. And one of the most penetrating forwards of the year was Gerry Husted of Franklin & Marshall.

1958

In the spring the final tryouts for the Pan American Games and the 1960 Olympic Games were held, and current or former college players made up one-quarter of the men screened. Trinity's Alex Guild and Cornell's Ron Maierhoffer were leading undergraduate candidates. There were, in addition, glowing accounts of the play of George Endler and Bill O'Brien of the St. Louis Universi-

Members of CCNY's 11–0–1 squad hailed from all over the globe: (left to right) Bruno Wachter, John Paranos, Gabor Schlisser and Billy Sund.

ty club team. Temple's Bob Crompton and Michigan State's Ted Saunders were in contention up to the final determination.

The college season had its own stars. Earlham's Newlin Otto and MSU's Alberto Sarria headlined the midwestern players. John Jennings, a strong fullback from Washington College, and Navy center half John Meehan were outstanding against their opponents in the South. Dick Williams was a class goalkeeper who gave the University of Pennsylvania the top defensive record in the Ivy League.

Drexel Tech, coached by Don Yonker, was named national champion, largely through the efforts of a set of outstanding forwards and a solid defense headed by fullback Bob Muschek. Drex-

el's record was 12–0–0. USF, which outscored opponents by a count of 67–2 in its eight games, and UCLA, which won thirteen straight, were the other candidates for the title of the nation's top club.

Drexel scored an astonishing seventy-six goals en route to winning the Middle Atlantic title, with the firepower coming from a variety of sources. Igor Lissy was the national leader with twenty-six goals, while All-Americans Stan Dlugosz and Oswald Jethon logged twenty-two and twenty-one, respectively. Gulyas Simon, an Hungarian expatriate, provided stability.

Trinity's Alex Guild scored twenty-one times in eight games to set a national goals-per-game record of 2.6. Al Miller was an outstanding inside forward at East Stroudsburg State. After graduation, Miller would coach at New Paltz in the State University of New York (SUNY) loop and then move to Hartwick College where his teams would become national title contenders in a few short years. He'd then become the first American-born coach in the North American Soccer League.

Elsewhere, UCLA, winner of the Southern California Conference and second to Drexel in the scoring race, was led by Remo Tabello, Mohamed Ganie, and Ed Lopresto.

The University of Connecticut finished at 10–1–0 and won the New England Conference, holding off challenges from 9–1–0 Harvard and 6–1–0 Trinity. Harvard did gain a measure of success by capturing the Ivy League title.

One forward who wore the Crimson that season for Harvard was Karim Aga Khan. Descendant of the adopted son of Mohammed, he would graduate from Harvard and, in due course, assume the hereditary title of his family—the Aga Khan.

The future Aga Khan played soccer at Harvard.

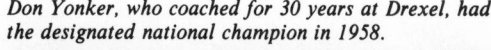

Don Yonker, who coached for 30 years at Drexel, had the designated national champion in 1958.

CCNY was forced to share the Metropolitan title. Pratt Institute, playing the first fifteen-game season of record, matched the Beavers in a mid-season game to secure a piece of its first title in the league. Maryland won the ACC, the University of Baltimore took the Mason–Dixon, and the Dons of USF were again undefeated in northern California.

Howard University was the leading independent in the South, and Florida Southern displaced Rollins College to win the intercollegiate conference in that state. Earlham topped the Midwest Conference and Akron was the class of the young Ohio Association. The Rocky Mountain League showed Colorado Mines taking the play away from Air Force Academy.

There were highlights off the field. Navy coach Glenn Warner and his committee reorganized the Florida Forum. Jack Squires, coach at Connecticut, was appointed to formulate a national plan for staging the first NCAA Soccer Tournament slated for 1959.

Ceremonies marking an historic occasion—Maryland at West Chester State in a first-round game of the first NCAA tournament. Left to right: George Mohl, official; Charles Scott, NCAA committee; Don Minnegan, NCAA committee (obscured): Harry Rodgers, official; Doyle Royal, Maryland coach; Dr. LaRue Frain, West Chester president; Mel Lorback, West Chester coach; Bob Dunn, NCAA committee; Mickey Cochrane, NCAA committee; and Ray Kraft, official.

1959

The first NCAA Soccer Tournament, organized by Connecticut's John Squires, was greeted with enthusiasm in all sections of the country. It meant that for the first time each area would be able to send its best team to compete for the national championship.

The 1959 field featured representatives from the East and one each from the Midwest and West, with the four surviving teams meeting at the University of Connecticut during Thanksgiving week.

Bridgeport University edged Colgate, West Chester State held off the gunners from previously unbeaten ACC champion Maryland, and CCNY squeaked by Little Three champion Williams to gain the final four along with St. Louis University in its first varsity season.

For the Billikens, it was a storybook climb. They were chosen by lot to represent the Midwest in the tournament. The Eastern Division of the Midwestern Conference was won by Gene Kenny's Michigan State team. But its record of 7–2–0 could not match those of the three once-beaten cowinners in the Western Division—St. Louis, Wheaton, and Illinois.

After Bob Guelker's Billikens won the toss, they proceeded to outclass the better-known sides one by one. The University of San Francisco, representing the West, traveled to St. Louis to absorb a 4–0 defeat. Then, at Storrs, Connecticut, largely on the strength of magnificent attacking center half John Dueker, St. Louis overwhelmed CCNY, 6–2, and mastered Bridgeport in the final, 5–2.

The colleges generally were heartened by this evidence that a team of American college students could match teams that were loaded with foreign-born players. From that time, schoolboy players in St. Louis became the target for the recruiter-coach, and the sport entered a new era where recruiting would become a major factor in determining team success.

The National Association of Intercollegiate Athletics Tournament was also born in 1959, due to the organizational efforts of Slippery Rock

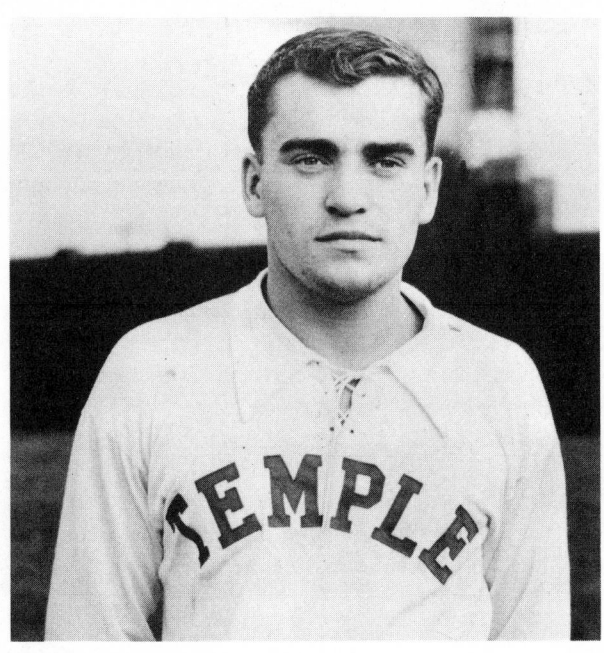

Walt Chyzowych, who would later become the U.S. National coach, starred for Temple.

Cecil Heron (left) and Erich Streder were All-Americans at Michigan State.

coach Jim Egli. The first one was invitational and only eastern teams participated. New Bedford Tech and Howard, independents from New England and the South, respectively; Metropolitan League champ Pratt Institute, and MAC titlist Elizabethtown College were on hand, with Pratt taking close decisions over New Bedford and Elizabethtown to top the field.

Harvard repeated its triumph in the Ivy League, and the first run of the New York Intercollegiate (later the SUNY Conference) saw Cortland emerge as the winner. In Florida, Jacksonville won a close race over Rollins College. Air Force Academy took the Rocky Mountain League; Akron continued its domination in Ohio.

In California, San Francisco Community College soundly whipped USF, but was not eligible for the four-year college tournament. In Mason–Dixon competition the title was won by newcomer Lynchburg College. George Varga, a Western Maryland forward, set a new individual scoring record by averaging over three goals per game in an eleven-game season.

Walter Chyzowych was a high-scoring forward at Temple. He would later coach the United States Soccer Federation. Cecil Heron and Eric Streder, forwards at Michigan State, were terrorizing opposing goalkeepers in the Midwest.

Trinity's Alex Guild and Cornell's Ron Maierhofer, both of whom had played on the U.S. team which finished second to Argentina in the Pan American Games the summer before, were still very much in evidence. Springfield's Terry Jackson, who would later coach at Moravian and Wesleyan, and CCNY's Lester Solney, who would become coach of his alma mater, were fullbacks of note.

On other fronts, there was a major promotional step taken in the Midwest, when the Michigan State–Wheaton game was televised to an audience estimated at 225,000.

The gospel was spreading.

1960

It was a season for upsets, apart from the NCAA title-winning repeat performance by St. Louis University, which nipped West Chester, 1–0, in

the semis and then edged ACC champion Maryland, 4–3, in the final.

The pattern of surprises loomed early in the year when Fairleigh-Dickinson took the measure of St. Louis when the Bills made a trip East. Of the eight finalists in the NCAA tournament, only Rutgers, Brooklyn, the Metropolitan League champ, and Cortland, champion of the New York Intercollegiate, were unbeaten. Rutgers bowed to Drexel in the MAC title game, and all three lost in the NCAA quarterfinals.

University of Connecticut was beaten by Bridgeport while winning the New England Sampson Trophy. West Chester, regarded as the strongest team in the MAC, had been held to a draw by Pitt. Maryland was beaten by Army and tied by Navy. California, which had won the Northern California League, was nipped by its nemesis, USF.

Though Drexel Tech won the MAC title in a postseason playoff with Rutgers, it showed a regular-season loss to Elizabethtown. Princeton took the Ivy crown, but bowed to Yale. Baltimore University won the Mason–Dixon, but lost by a two-goal margin to West Chester. Trenton State College won the New Jersey State College title, but was defeated by several nonleague opponents.

Newark College of Engineering was tops among eastern independents until the final day of the NAIA Tournament. There, the Elizabethtown Blue Jays battled Mal Simon's Highlanders on even terms through three overtimes and until darkness forced a halt to the game. The two shared the NAIA crown. Tabor College returned home to Kansas winner of the consolation match over Fitchburg.

UCLA was phenomenal. The Bruins swept all of their opponents in the Southern California League and showed but one tie in a thirteen-game season during which they scored a total of one hundred goals.

Scrappy Tom Scanlon, a LaSalle College halfback, was his school's first All-American. Elusive Bill Charlton, inside forward at Temple, and Igor Lissy, Drexel's high-scoring captain, were at the height of their careers. Rutgers' Herb Schmidt, who combined height, strength, speed, and splendid technique, was the center forward of the year. Schmidt was also an All-American in lacrosse and would later coach both sports at Penn State.

1961

Halfback Tom Scanlon was LaSalle's first All-American.

It was easy to see that the college soccer tournament had become an important factor in promoting soccer. One reason was the upset of St. Louis University by West Chester State in the 1961 NCAA championship game.

It was a major achievement. The year before, a St. Louis graduate had remarked that with the material available in the city, "there was no reason they could not continue to win the championship forever."

Behind strong performances by goalkeeper John Juenger, backs Dale Bievenour and Jerry Yeagley and center forward Don Williams, West Chester pinned a 2–0 championship-game loss on the Billikens before sixty-five hundred spectators in the St. Louis Public Schools Stadium, marking the first time St. Louis had ever been shut out and the Billikens' first loss on their home pitch.

St. Louis, paced by Bob Malone and Gerry Balassi, had gained the final by establishing suprema-

Led by All-American Reiner Kemeling, Michigan State went 8–1, losing only to NCAA runner-up St. Louis.

An event that took place which opened even wider vistas for soccer was the founding of the International Soccer League by William D. Cox, a graduate of Yale.

In major sports stadia in and around New York, the soccer buff could see Burnley, champion of the English First Division, play the French team, Nice. He could enjoy the sharp, short-passing game of Red Star of Belgrade against Rapid-Austria and the exciting Bangu, from Rio, playing the stubborn Scots of Kilmarnock. It was not only fun watching, it was a learning experience that would add to the quality of the college game.

The U.S. Olympic team was defeated by Mexico, 2–0, in Mexico City and 3–1 in Los Angeles and was not among the sixteen teams that made it to Rome in 1960.

Howard finished the year at 9–0–1 to capture its first NAIA championship. Back row (left to right): Cecil Durham, Vincent Lasse, Eden Reeves, Robert Chee-Mooke, Patrick Noel and Vincent Lewis. Second row: Errol Williams, Hugh Wilson, Ernest Ikpe, Joseph Sanguinetti, Martin Padareth-Singh, Aloysius Charles, Victor Henry and manager Cleveland Howard. Front row: Alexander Romeo, Milton Swaby, Carlos Paul, Carlton Hinds, Noel Carr, Michael Phillips, Winston Alexis and coach Ted Chambers.

cy in the Midwest and then topping Rutgers and USF in quarterfinal and semifinal games. Coached by Mel Lorback, West Chester, the top eastern power, had dropped Maryland, ACC champion, and blanked Bridgeport, the New England representative. Ted Chambers guided Howard University to a sweep of the NAIA Tournament, held at Lock Haven State College. Newark College of Engineering finished second.

The first NCAA College Division Tournament—the Atlantic Coast Regional—was held at Adelphi College, where Baltimore, chosen to represent the South because of its outstanding record, outplayed Brooklyn College.

The first Junior College Soccer Championship was won by Dean Junior College, from Franklin, Massachusetts, over host Orange County Community, from Middletown, New York. This proj-

ect was the result of efforts by coach Chris Chachis of Orange County.

In California, the first preseason tournament was initiated. Bob DiGrazia's University of California entry beat San Francisco Community College and, as a result, was touted as a sure repeater for the northern California crown. But pesky, two-year SFCC had other ideas and it won the regular-season campaign, with USF finishing second and again qualifying for NCAA tournament play. In southern California, UCLA was the leader; only a draw with Cal Tech marred its season.

Williams won the Sampson Cup of the New England Conference, with Trinity runner-up. Washington headed the Mason–Dixon. Drexel Tech repeated as champion of the MAC, and Brockport took the New York Intercollegiate crown. The University of Miami roared to the top

1962

Stung by the West Chester tournament victory of 1961, St. Louis University ran through the 1962 season undefeated—there was a tie with the Notre Dame club—and found itself in the NCAA final against Atlantic Coast Conference champion Maryland in a rematch of the 1960 championship contest.

With the Billikens trailing, 3–2, All-American outside right Gerry Balassi scored his third goal of the game at 13:28 of the final period and four minutes later fed a perfect corner kick to fullback Joe Hennessey, who headed home the winner. Balassi's hat trick and assist earned him recognition as the Most Valuable Player.

All-American Alvord (Skip) Rutherford helped Williams win the Sampson Cup as New England's top team.

Fullback Wolfried Mielert made All-New England and led Hartford to victory over Elizabethtown in the NCAA Atlantic Coast Regional final.

of the Florida Intercollegiate in its first year of competition. Air Force won the Rocky Mountain League and Fairleigh-Dickinson was champion in the Garden State. Harvard was the best of the Ivies. This was due, largely, to Nigerian Olympian Chris Ohiri who, though only a sophomore, overturned all previous scoring records in that league.

Many teams were within striking distance of the leaders at the close of the campaign, indicating competitive balance. In almost every case this was due to outstanding individual players. Besides those who appeared in the tournament games, Williams' Alvord Rutherford and the University of California's Kun Choo were notable. Inside forward Magid Kria was the major factor in Washington University's excellent 10–1–1 showing. Others who figured: Michigan State's Reiner Kemeling, Navy's Neil Fagan, Brooklyn's Helmut Poje, San Francisco's Gerald Li, Rutgers' Herb Schmidt, and Bridgeport's Armand Dikranian.

Two other familiar colleges were in the final four: Springfield, representing New England, and Michigan State, which bowed twice to arch-rival St. Louis, once during the season and again in the tournament.

In the NCAA Atlantic Coast Regional, the University of Hartford blanked MAC champion Elizabethtown in the title game. Grove City and Lynchburg, the Mason–Dixon leader, rounded out that field.

An additional college division postseason fixture had been established for the smaller schools of the western areas. It had the curious title of Mideast Regional. In this first tournament Denison College had to survive two grueling overtime battles to gain the trophy. Denison outlasted top-seeded Wheaton on a fifty-yard goal by fullback Bill Marks and then posted a six-overtime triumph over Oberlin in the final on a score by Mike Snyder.

In the NAIA, held on the Earlham campus, East Stroudsburg, coming in with a 12–1–0 record, beat Pratt, the New York Metropolitan titlist.

The New England Intercollegiate Soccer League now boasted thirty members. But it was one of the smallest of these—Williams College—that showed its heels to the rest of the field and became the first to carry off the title two years running. On the way Williams beat both Harvard, cochamp of the Ivy League with the University of Pennsylvania, and powerful Springfield.

Fitchburg won the New England State College crown and Cortland unseated Brockport in the New York Intercollegiate. In the Ivy competition, Harvard and Penn produced the leading scorers. Exhibiting flair and magnetism, Harvard's Chris Ohiri had all of college soccer buzzing about his play. Ohiri's ten goals set an Ivy record, even though he missed half of the season due to an injury that was to handicap him for the remainder of his career. German-born Arno Witt of Charley Scott's Penn team was runner-up with seven goals.

Ohio University, led by Ed Hemminger, crushed Akron, 9–3, for a convincing win in the Ohio Soccer Association, and the University of Miami underlined the effect of its city as a port of entry for South Americans when it dominated the colleges in Florida.

Air Force Academy had to share the Rocky Mountain title with Denver University. New

Middlebury's Keith Van Winkle (right) was a first-team All-American and his brother Davis made honorable mention.

Fullerton State in California, was a fine back. Akron's Fritz Kungl, Michigan State's Reiner Kemeling and St. Louis' Bill Veith were the leading halfbacks in the Midwest. Middlebury's Keith Van Winkle and West Chester's Don Williams were splendid forwards. Karl Kaeser, a midfield performer for Navy, was noted for his strength and endurance. Michigan State's Rubens Filizola played a key role in the Spartans' abortive drive for the Midwest title.

On the international scene, several former college All-Americans participated in the Conseil International du Sport Militaire (CISM) Championship in Turkey. Ithaca's Sandor Szabo, Brockport's Walt Schmidt and Bridgeport's Hans Zucker were on the U.S. team.

Michigan State failed to win the Midwest, but Rubens Filizola achieved All-American honors.

Navy had an All-American in midfielder Karl Kaeser.

names entered the record books in California as Stanford won the northern competition and Pomona-Claremont unseated five-time champ UCLA in the southern end of the state. Leading Claremont to its 12–0–1 season was Korhan Berzeg, who racked up thirty-three goals.

There was an elite cut of players in all sections. Dartmouth's Dave Smoyer was a spectacular goalkeeper; Cortland's Paul Fardy, later coach at

Harvard's Chris Ohiri (white) challenges Brown's Fred Akuffo. The two teams tied for Ivy honors.

1963

Studies conducted by a committee headed by Trenton State's Mel Schmid convinced the NCAA Rules Committee that a return to the international standard was needed. So, it was no surprise when chairman Hugh McCurdy of Wesleyan announced that in 1963 college pitches would be marked with the rectangular penalty area and that a ball in touch would be returned by a throw-in.

The news was received with acclaim. With another Olympic year upcoming, college players would be able to compete on an equal basis in the trials with amateurs who played according to international rules.

The changes made little difference in St. Louis. The Billikens won the NCAA championship again

with a 7–3 semifinal triumph over ACC champion Maryland and a 3–0 final over previously unbeaten Navy.

St. Louis was not, however, without scars. Michigan State, captained by halfback Sam Donnelly, defeated the Billikins to win its first Midwest title after five years of effort. In addition, USF, making its perennial bid for national recognition, carried St. Louis to overtime before bowing, 3–2, in an intersectional playoff.

Harvard won the New England title outright, but again had to share Ivy honors, this time with Brown. In postseason play, Brown was strong enough to beat Springfield in an NCAA elimination, but was, in turn, defeated by Army. The Cadets advanced to the final round of four before being eliminated by Navy.

There was a nip-and-tuck affair between Akron

St. Louis coach Bob Guelker (center) made it two NCAA titles in a row, thanks to the efforts of Pat McBride (rear left), Carl Gentile (rear right), Don Ceresia (front left) and Dan Leahy (front right).

and Ohio Wesleyan, with the former capturing the Ohio crown. That might have just strengthened the resolve of the latter, however, as Ohio Wesleyan came on strong in the NCAA Mideast tournament, turning back Akron, Wheaton, and Lake Forest.

Colorado University won the Rocky Mountain League, and Cortland repeated in New York but had a close call against Huntley Parker's Brockport squad.

Baltimore took the Atlantic Coast NCAA Tournament but was not able to master Lynchburg in the Mason–Dixon. The 0–0 playoff in that league resulted in cochamps for the year. The MAC was again won by Elizabethtown. But the Blue Jays went down to Baltimore in Atlantic Coast play.

There were other outstanding teams. Fairleigh Dickinson, West Chester, and Drexel in the East, and Howard University in the South, made it to the NCAA championship tournament. San Jose, Adelphi, LIU, and Bridgeport were also contenders.

Myron Hura was an All-American midfielder for Navy.

The NAIA Tourney, held in Frostburg, Maryland, was plagued by bad weather, forcing the organizers to cancel the final game and declare Earlham and Castleton State cotitlists.

Miami again rolled over Florida competition, never scoring fewer than five goals per game—that is, until it met touring NCAA champion St. Louis and suffered a six-goal setback.

In California, Stanford finished atop the Northern League, but had to forfeit to the University of San Francisco when it was discovered the Cardinals had played an ineligible player. UCLA beat defender Pomona-Claremont to top the southern section.

Harvard's Nigerian Olympic athlete, Chris Ohiri, again set an Ivy scoring mark. He matched the effort of Penn's Bob Finney, as they each closed the season with eleven goals.

Bridgeport's acrobatic Roger Curylo was goalkeeper of the year with a stellar performance between the sticks. St. Louis' Tom Hennessey and Brooklyn's Helmut Poje, along with Trenton State's Lee Cook, were solid backs, rarely beaten by the opposition. Navy's Myron Hura and USF's Fernando Lopez-Contreras were the strongest midfield players in the South and West, respectively. St. Louis' Pat McBride and Carl Gentile were forwards of note, while San Jose's Dave Kingsley gave defenses fits on the West Coast.

In New England, Middlebury's Keith Van Winkle was the man to mark, while in New York, Pratt's Walt Schmotolocha rewrote the record book in the Metropolitan League. Al Hershey, a midfielder-striker for the Elizabethtown Blue Jays, captured scoring honors in the MAC, and Winston Alexis, Howard's center forward, combined a deftness of touch with explosive speed which made him virtually unmarkable.

1964

The technical gap between the native-born player and the overseas athlete was closing, as indicated by the earlier successes of St. Louis University in the NCAA tournament. Elizabethtown College, in 1960, and East Stroudsburg, in 1962, both manned largely by native sons, had shown a similar pattern when they won their respective NAIA titles.

Michigan State turned back Army in an NCAA semifinal on a pair of goals by Peyton Fuller.

In 1964, as if to underscore this fact, Navy, led by Paul Daulerio, stopped a slick Michigan State University eleven, 1–0, in the NCAA final at Providence, Rhode Island.

Conditions at the Brown University pitch could hardly have been worse. The Navy-MSU game was played on an icy turf and in subfreezing temperatures. But with everything to the advantage of the better ball-handling side, the Glenn Warner-coached Navy eleven protected the margin provided by Jim Lewis late in the fourth period for its first perfect season and the national title.

It was the first major championship for any service academy, and the Middies had the added satisfaction of ousting St. Louis in the semifinal to avenge their defeat of the year before. Navy halfback Myron Hura was named defensive MVP, and Michigan State's Sydney Alozie was tabbed the best offensive player.

Three of the NCAA's four finalists came in with undefeated records, and Army had lost only to Navy. It might have been an all-services final except for a close MSU semifinal win over the Cadets. Peyton Fuller's two goals for the Spartans were matched by Army's John Boretti and Jose Gonzales. Then, against the run of the play in the overtime, Alozie got loose and scored the clincher with a spectacular shot into the upper right corner of the net.

The Coast Guard Academy won the Atlantic Coast Regional Tournament when it eked out a 1–0 result over Washington and Lee. The Midwest Tournament was won by Wheaton over Akron.

There was a third successive tie in Ivy competition. This time Dartmouth and Brown were the shareholders, with the former making its initial appearance at the top.

Trinity's 7–1–0 record topped the New England Intercollegiate. Norwich, a participant in the Atlantic Coast NCAA, was runner-up. Castleton State again led the New England Teachers Circuit.

The New York Intercollegiate went to powerful Cortland, which then suffered a tough overtime loss to Army in the qualifying round for the NCAA Tournament. The Metropolitan League was won by Long Island University for the first time. Gary Rosenthal's Blackbirds were started on a streak that would carry them to national prominence.

San Jose, with Al Korbus leading the offense, won the Northern California League and was the western representative in the NCAA Tournament. Denver, the best of the Rocky Mountain group, beat San Jose, Western titlist, but was again ineligible for postseason honors and Colorado College was the replacement in the tournament. Colorado lost to Air Force in its regional game, and the Falcons then were eliminated by San Jose.

The NAIA Tournament provided further evidence of successful American-born squads, as largely homegrown Trenton State College triumphed over a Lincoln University team that was dominated by foreigners.

In the regional Olympic eliminations in Mexico City, the United States finished a respectable third. St. Louis' Pat McBride and Carl Gentile, Temple's Len Oliver, and LaSalle's Bobby Watson were the backbone of the youngest team ever to represent the country in international play.

Through the efforts of Larry Briggs, University of Massachusetts coach, and Middlebury's Joe Morrone, the National Intercollegiate Soccer Officials Association was formed. An executive committee of outstanding referees—Jim Walder as president, Harry Rodgers as vice president and Bill Rosenthal as secretary-treasurer—would move to standardize officiating methods throughout the country.

1965

St. Louis University, again the champion, was 14–0–0 when it was all over. The Bills featured Pat McBride and Carl Gentile in an offense that completely dominated the University Division NCAA postseason classic from the quarterfinals on. They defeated University of San Francisco handily, then swept by Navy in spite of the Middies' All-American Myron Hura.

The Bills experienced the most difficulty with neighboring Michigan State when the two Midwest powers met for the first time in the finals. MSU, with proven strikers Peyton Fuller and Guy Busch, was again beaten in the finals, by the same 1–0 score inflicted upon it by Navy in 1964. The margin of victory was a goal scored on a penalty kick by Carl Gentile. The Spartans' Nick Krat and the Bills' Jack Gilsinn were voted the best defenders, while Pat McBride was the offensive MVP of the tournament.

Trenton State showed top form in the NAIA Tournament. With All-American Lee Cook, Ed Zimbicki, and Wayne Huston leading the way, Trenton State topped Earlham, the Midwest College Division standard-bearer, in Rockhurst, Missouri.

The Atlantic Coast Tournament, held at Rensselaer Poly, was won by New Paltz, coach Al Miller's first major title victory. New Paltz also captured the SUNY crown. Bill Doon and Joe Facciolli were solid backs and Nigerian Solomon Iyasere and Italian-born Gino Ventriglia were

Carl Gentile is St. Louis' all-time leading goal scorer with 67 in three seasons.

effective forwards at New Paltz, which lost only to East Stroudsburg.

East Stroudsburg made its mark, reaching the NCAA quarterfinals, where it bowed to Michigan State in overtime.

Denison gained the Ohio crown over Oberlin on goal average and then won the Mideast NCAA title over host Lake Forest. Bowdoin made news by winning the first running of the Maine Intercollegiate. Massachusetts, Vermont, and Connecticut shared the Yankee Conference crown. Brown and Middlebury—the latter led by high-scoring forward Dave Nicholson—shared the University Division of the now two-sectioned New England Conference. Al King's Worcester Tech won the College Division race. Brown, with Amer-

ican-born cocaptains in John Krupski and Phil McGuire, captured the Ivy League title with a perfect 7–0–0 record.

Army, the top New York independent, again made the final four in St. Louis. Long Island University, led by center forward Dov Markus, won top honors in the Metropolitan League, but was eliminated from the postseason tournament by Army in the regionals. Elizabethtown and Temple met for the Middle Atlantic Conference title—the Blue Jays winning, 3–1. The University of Maryland won the Atlantic Coast Conference and Baltimore took the Mason–Dixon. Air Force topped the Rocky Mountain schools, but Denver's club team had the better record. The Pioneers romped through a seven-game slate without permitting a

Ithaca's Janos Benedek (left) and San Jose State's Lew Fraser earned All-American honors.

goal. USF, relying heavily on forward Fernando Lopez-Contreras, won in northern California. The southern sector, with all colleges now adhering strictly to intercollegiate standards, was won by Loyola of Los Angeles.

There were other top performers, even if their schools were not in the championship circle. Harvard's Charles Njoku was the Ivy scoring leader; Boston University's George Karalexis was an exceptional forward, as was San Jose's versatile Jim Fraser on the West Coast; Drexel backs Gene Calaphatis and Lou Maertin were fine defensive players; Temple forwards Charley Ducilli and Lou Meehl would later team up again on the Philadelphia Atoms in the NASL. In the South, Jack Writer scored a record four goals in one game for the University of North Carolina, and Ken Swomley, playing at Mount St. Mary's College, made an unprecedented fourth appearance on the South all-star team.

1966

The arena for championship play in 1966 was the Far West. The turf in Memorial Stadium at the University of California was soggy from a week of rain, but this proved no deterrent to the University of San Francisco when it took the field for the NCAA final against Long Island University.

Both teams experienced close calls in the rugged qualifying rounds before reaching the moment of truth. USF posted a narrow 2–1 victory in a first-round game with Julie Menendez's San Jose State squad and then outlasted defending champion St. Louis, 2–1, in four overtimes. LIU squeaked past favored Michigan State in the semifinals by the narrowest of margins, winning on an odd corner kick after a 2–2, three-overtime contest.

Balance was a problem on the slippery grass in the final, but the Dons were not to be denied. They led on a goal by Sandor Hites after only nine minutes. LIU never caught up and USF put together a convincing 5–2 conquest before fifty-five hundred spectators. Rudolphus Dekkers and Lother Ospiander also scored for the Dons, but Hites, the offensive MVP, had a hat trick.

Goalkeeper Mike Ivanow proved to be the difference in the key games, stopping critical thrusts by both San Jose and St. Louis on USF's way to the top. He would earn U.S. international honors while still a collegian and be an early NASL draft choice upon graduation.

LIU had stars who had brought the Blackbirds supremacy in the East and the Metropolitan League championship. Carlo Tramontozzi, later the coach at St. Francis College, Dov Markus and Marcello Luni combined to post a fearsome attack. Reinhold Jabusch was an All-American choice at center back.

Quincy College, with Ed Comacho the outstanding player, won the annual NAIA Tournament over Belmont Abbey of South Carolina.

The NCAA Atlantic Coast postseason classic

ended in a draw between Hartwick, a New York independent, and Elizabethtown, winner of the Middle Atlantic Conference. The Blue Jays had to beat Temple University for the MAC crown, which they did in spite of the Owls' perpetual-motion center half, John Boles, one of the strongest players at this position in the modern era.

Wheaton College won the Mideast Regional over Wooster. Wheaton's 11–0–3 season log was its best since 1946, but it had to share the championship of the new Indiana–Illinois League with Earlham.

In the East, Brown won both the New England and the Ivy League crowns. Winger Victor

Reinhold (Ron) Jabusch, who would later coach at Hunter and Pratt, was an All-American with Long Island University's Metropolitan League champion.

◀ *Ed Camacho was voted Most Valuable Player of the NAIA tournament after leading Quincy to another crown.*

All-American John Garrison helped perpetuate a proud soccer tradition at Middlebury.

DeJong was a big plus in the Bruin offense. Curiously, Brown had an opening-game loss to Wesleyan, making for a bleak season outlook. But the Ephmen also beat Williams, runner-up to Brown in the NEISL, to make the Bruins' title possible. Worcester Tech and Norwich tied for first place in the College Division race.

Vermont won the Yankee Conference; Bowdoin and Barrington took the Maine Intercollegiate and Colonial Conferences, respectively. Oswego State hung on after beating defending champ New Paltz early and recorded its first SUNY title.

Two outstanding players in the SUNY Conference were brothers Peter and Don Prozik of Buf-

falo and Brockport, respectively, and their confrontations in important league games made for interesting battles. Another leading performer was Middlebury goalkeeper John Garrison.

Akron won the Ohio Collegiate Soccer Association. Wooster's Mo Rajabi was named Player of the Year. Colorado College won the Rocky Mountain League, besting Air Force. It's an interesting fact that Nassau Community College won the Junior College Tournament over Florissant Valley of St. Louis to balance the major tournament titles geographically—the NCAA went to USF, in the West; the NAIA fell to Quincy in the Midwest, and the JUCO belonged to Nassau in the East.

1967

Thanks to the weather, St. Louis and Michigan State had to settle for coownership of the NCAA crown in a season that also saw Quincy College score a record 120 goals and repeat its title triumph in the NAIA.

The semifinal and final rounds of the NCAA were played at Washington University in St. Louis, and they featured four quality sides. Michigan State, with a .927 playing percentage, led the Midwest University Division. But the Spartans were constantly pursued by St. Louis, which earned its way to the tourney finals defeating Rocky Mountain champion Colorado College, West Coast Intercollegiate titlist San Jose, and a determined Navy team which was the best in the South. In fact, the Middies led St. Louis on corner kicks in a 0–0 deadlock before a rebound off the chest of the Navy keeper was converted into the

winning goal by Walt Werner in the last minute of play.

Michigan State had advanced by way of a comfortable semifinal win over Long Island University, the Metropolitan League champion, and thus the stage was set for another meeting between the old rivals. They had played earlier in the season to a 3–3 tie. But St. Louis had lost two games in the season and the Spartans were undefeated, allowing only eleven goals while scoring seventy-three.

MSU coach Gene Kenney was looking to All-American back Peter Hens and to an array of goal-scorers that included Trevor Harris, Guy Busch, Ernie Tuchscherer, and Gary McBrady for the punch that would bring the crown, at last, to the college from East Lansing.

But the weather dictated otherwise and, for the first time, the national final had to be abandoned when the pitch became unplayable because of tor-

Long Island University coach Joe Machnik gets a hug from Dov Markus, the first Hermann Trophy winner, after 1967 NCAA quarterfinal win.

Michigan State was forced to settle for a co-titlist role when weather forced cancellation of the final against St. Louis. Back row (left to right): John Zensen, Ed Skotarek, Alex Skotarek, Tom Belloli, Bert Jacobsen, Denny Boles, Ken Hamann and Terry Sanders. Second row: coach Gene Kenney, Gary McBrady, Trevor Harris, Nick Archer, Peter Hens, Guy Busch, Bill Myerson, Tom Kreft, Barry Tiemann and assistant coach Terry Bidiak. Front row: freshman coach Kev O'Connell, Rich Nelke, Tony Keyes, Joe Baum, Orhan Enuston, Ernie Tuchscherer and Dave Trace.

rential rain, bone-chilling cold, and impossible playing conditions.

From the start, ball control was almost impossible. Players were going to the ground on almost every play when, with time running out for the period, the Spartans' McBrady took a shot that hit the bar and caromed away from St. Louis keeper Jim Conley. Both Conley and MSU's Guy Busch went for the loose ball. Busch, in an all-out effort, crashed into the goalpost and serious injury was feared. It was then that officials from both colleges and the NCAA decided that the chance of further injury was too great. The game was stopped and cochampions were declared.

Wheaton College took the Mideast Regional by defeating Kenyon; Tufts won the Atlantic Coast Regional. Brown University repeated in both the New England and the Ivy League, and Vermont did the same in the Yankee Conference. Maryland again won the Atlantic Coast Conference,

and Elizabethtown again defeated Temple for the Middle Atlantic. Trenton State recaptured the New Jersey Teachers League, RPI won the Independent Conference in New York, and Akron topped the Ohio Conference.

Dayton's Pat Obiaya scored a state-record thirty-five goals. Temple's Jacob Meehl and Bob Peffle and Brown's Pat Migliore were excellent midfielders; St. Louis' Walt Werner, San Jose's Henry Camacho, and San Francisco's Sandor Hites, the hero in the 1966 NCAA Tournament, were dangerous forwards. Camacho scored all three goals for San Jose in a 4–3 loss to St. Louis in the West-Midwest NCAA quarterfinal.

Brown's Victor DeJong and Elizabethtown's Rick Wenger were two incisive wings; Bob Ludwig of Philadelphia Textile and Mike Villa of Quincy were high-scoring forwards, Villa setting a national record with forty-four goals. Akron's Joe Queiroga and Springfield's Jim Quigley were

Giedris Klivecka (left), who would become a dentist, and his brother Rimantis (Ray), who would later coach the New York Cosmos, teamed up at Long Island University.

John Marks won All-American laurels at Middlebury.

Pat Migliore helped Brown successfully defend its Ivy and Yankee crowns.

sticky halfbacks who gave opposing forwards little room. Dov Markus of Long Island University was the first recipient of the *Sporting News* Robert R. Hermann Award, named for the Chairman of the Board of the California Surf, presented annually to the College Player of the Year.

Bates unseated Bowdoin in Maine. Westfield State dislodged Castleton in the New England Teachers Conference. Amherst won the Little Three, and Buffalo outclassed the field for its first title in the ten-college SUNY competition. Little St. Andrews College won the Dixie Conference on a strong 11–3–2 season, paced by Yank Albers, the leading scorer in the South. Earlham won the Illinois–Indiana; Case Tech took the President's Athletic and the Missouri–Kansas competition saw St. Benedict's and Rockhurst deadlock at the end of the season.

Three former collegians were prominent in the launching of the National Professional Soccer League in 1967. Pat McBride and Carl Gentile had been stalwarts on a succession of championship teams at the University of St. Louis, and they quickly made a place for themselves on the St. Louis Stars. The third, powerful Willy Roy, was a graduate of the University of Illinois. In his first professional season, playing for Chicago, he would be named Rookie of the Year.

1968

The University Division NCAA Tournament was held in Atlanta, with Emory University and Georgia Tech as cohosts. Both had club sides, and W. Clyde Partin, the athletic director at Emory, had

San Jose State's Manuel Hernandez led his team to the Final Four and won the Hermann Award.

Giancarlo Brandoni (left) and Alvaro Bitencourt played key roles as co-captains of Maryland's 14–0–1 co-national champions.

been active in the Intercollegiate Association and was eager to promote soccer in the South.

Michigan State, University of Maryland, Brown, and San Jose State were the final four. Three were experienced and one, Brown, was new to the NCAA Tournament. Now that the Ivies had relaxed the rule restricting members from postseason play, Brown, burning to prove itself, had seized the opportunity.

It was apparent the Bruins were capable as they blew by Fairleigh Dickinson and Army in the prelims. Even in the semifinal with MSU, they held a 16–6 shots-on-goal edge in the first half. But they fell, 2–0, to the sharpshooting of Michigan State's Ernie Tuchscherer and Alex Skotarek.

Doyle Royal's University of Maryland team had an exciting come-from-behind 4–3 win over San Jose. Hermann Award winner Manuel Hernandez, with help from Fred Nourzad, put San Jose ahead and after teammate Henry Camacho scored unassisted, it looked dark for the Terra-

pins. But at the end of a quick counter, Maryland's Rocco Morelli put in the first of his four goals to insure the Atlantic Coast champion a place in the final. Nourzad had netted two goals for San Jose, but Morelli's effort—a tournament record—made the difference.

The final was less exciting. Maryland drew first blood on a goal by Alvaro Bitencourt, but MSU's high-scoring Tony Keyes tied the game in the third period. Then, Jerry Chareczko put the Terps ahead with a blistering shot into the back of the net. With four minutes left, the Spartans' Frank Morant tied it up again. Two overtimes failed to produce a score and the teams settled for a deadlock and cochampionship status.

There were notable close encounters. Michigan State had lost to Akron, the first time the Zips defeated the Spartans. Gene Kenney's forces had to prove the first meeting was a mistake in order to qualify for the NCAA tournament. Maryland had to eliminate a St. Louis team led by Al Trost and also up-and-coming Hartwick to reach the same level.

San Jose had stumbled over University of British Columbia during the season. The Canadians were coached by Joe Johnson, formerly an inside forward for the Glasgow Rangers. The team was a mixed bag of recently emigrated Britons and high-level Canadians. The University of North Carolina, with Brazilian Lou Bush heading the offense, was tabbed a regional NCAA candidate, but went out to Maryland. The Air Force Academy was led by keeper Gene Kraay. Thanks to his performance, the Falcons were stubborn victims of San Jose, 1–0, in a quarterfinal.

Brockport and RPI were the respective champions in the SUNY and Independent Conference. In New England, Springfield, which topped Division I, won the Atlantic Coast NCAA tournament, while Norwich led the College Division. Rhode Island crowded Vermont into an unfamiliar tie in the Yankee Conference. George Washington surfaced on top of the Southern Conference. The University of Baltimore won the Mason–Dixon and Roanoke led in Virginia. The University of South Florida claimed independent honors in that state. Wheaton College did win the Mideast NCAA Tournament, but its challengers were new: Cleveland State and University of Illi-

Goalkeeper Ed Hubbard helped carry Vermont to co-ownership of the Yankee Conference crown.

Harvard's Pete Bogovich uses his head in game against Cornell.

nois, Chicago Circle. The NAIA was won by Davis & Elkins over defending champ Quincy in overtime.

There was a fine goalkeeper in the Ivy League—Yale's Steve Greenberg, whose father, Hank, had been one of the great sluggers in major league baseball. Shep Messing stood out in goal for NYU, and Joe Lyles, coach at Washington and Lee, was high on John Scott Fechnay, whose high school prepping had been in Spain.

Teams were still dependent on the superstar. Wooster's Pierre Radja and Ohio University's Ihor Mishewycz were voted outstanding players in the state. Other top names were Andy Roboostoff at USF; Alex Papadakis, Hartwick; Walt Nisterenko, University of West Virginia; Casey Bahr, Navy; and Bill Muse, Springfield.

On the international front, some teams traveled to Europe to play against comparable age groups, but usually superior players. In early summer, Ed Athey took Washington College to England, Scandinavia, Switzerland, and Spain, while Joe Morrone's Middlebury College team went to Germany, Scandinavia, the USSR, Poland, and France.

1969

Highlights of the year included the successful expansion of Pat Damore's New York rating system into a nationwide promotional asset, the first staging of a version of a postseason Senior Bowl in Ohio—the brainchild of Toledo's Jim Sarno—and reports of effective varsity activity in the North-west.

There was the rebirth of the Florida Intercollegiate Conference, dormant for the past four years. In Washington, DC, Ted Chambers invited Stu Parry's Akron team to provide the opposition to Howard University in a game that was truly international—thirty nations were represented by players on the two sides.

The national rating system was primarily intended for communication among coaches. But thanks to Damore, the athletic director at Fredonia State, his board and fellow coaches, it grew to be an effective promotional factor in this first season. If the media was cool to the publication of weekly rankings, most acknowledged the final Top Ten ranking.

So, when second-ranked Harvard, 13–0–0 and

Columbia All-American Len Renery (right) was the only Ivy League player to gain first-team national honors.

Every loose ball created a stir as Eastern Illinois subdued Davis & Elkins (white), 1–0, in the NAIA final.

the New England and Ivy titlist, and top-ranked St. Louis, leader in the Midwest at 8–0–0, met in the NCAA semifinal at San Jose, spectators and fans everywhere were predicting the winner would be the eventual champion. There was great excitement as each squad strove to retain its unbeaten status. After the teams played to a 1–1 first-half tie, the St. Louis quick-passing style proved one goal better. The Bills' Mike Seerey and Al Trost, the season's Hermann Award winner, notched scores to overcome a Solomon Gomez–to–Charles Thomas second-period goal for Harvard, as St. Louis prevailed, 3–2.

St. Louis did emerge winner of the four-team match-up—its seventh title in an eleven-year history of the tournament—posting a relatively unexciting 4–0 win over USF. The Dons had advanced at the expense of Maryland.

St. Louis' Trost and Pat Leahy were named the outstanding players in the tournament. They had support from Seerey, Jim Leeker, Gary Rensing, and keeper Don Copple. By all accounts, it was the best NCAA classic to date, a financial success for the first time, with crowds ranging from five to eight thousand.

The NAIA tournament was won by Eastern Illinois. Of only two losses suffered in its sixteen-game season, one was to JUCO champ Florissant Valley Community College.

Wheaton and Elizabethtown—the latter with a fine defender in Karim Yassim—won their Regional NCAA meetings, downing Kenyon and Springfield, respectively.

Bucknell University was a new winner in the Middle Atlantic. Undefeated Philadelphia Textile—with Bob Durham, Barry Barto, and Gordon

An All-American trio of Timo Liekoski, Tony Elia and Alec Papadakis (left to right) signalled the emergence of Hartwick as a national power.

Cholmondeley—and Washington College shared first place in the college division when no play-off could be arranged. Adelphi won its first Division I Metropolitan title, and the University of Virginia had the whole South talking when a draw with Maryland gave it the title in the Atlantic Coast Conference.

No less heady was the achievement of University of San Francisco. In order to reach the NCAA tournament venue, the Dons had to beat Chico State, a San Diego team led by center back Pete Goosens, and a Mannie Hernandez-paced San Jose, champion of the West Coast Intercollegiate, which had beaten the Dons by two goals in an earlier game.

There was a quartet of excellent players at Hartwick: Alex Papadakis, Tony Elia, Timo Liekoski and Terry Fisher. The latter pair would follow coach Al Miller into professional coaching.

Wooster's Pierre Radja repeated as the best defender in Ohio, while Jim McMillan of Cleveland State took honors as the top forward. Columbia right half Len Renery, Dartmouth center back Charley Silcox, and Brown striker Herm Sebazza were leading performers in the Ivy League.

In the Rockies, Colorado College depended on Bob Nitka and Stan Griswold for a first-place fin-ish in an All-Big Eight Tournament. But Hank Eichin's Air Force, with keeper Gene Kraay still guarding the net, was the class team of the Rocky Mountain League. Another excellent netminder, Ray Remstedt of Wyoming, kept his team in contention most of the season.

In the South, an individual record was set in Mason–Dixon competition when Western Maryland's Ron Athey scored three goals in less than three minutes in a game against Mount St. Mary's.

Bruce Parkhill brought attention to little Lock Haven State as a first-team All-American goalkeeper.

◄ *Denny Hadican celebrates after scoring the lone goal in St. Louis' 1–0 NCAA final triumph over UCLA.*

1970

"The best college soccer team I've ever seen anywhere, any time" was the way Hartwick coach Al Miller described the 1970 St. Louis University squad after the Billikens had outplayed talented UCLA, 1–0, in the NCAA Tournament finals.

Indeed this St. Louis team was special. Harry Keough, the St. Louis coach, had started the season wondering how to preserve his team's national championship, protect a winning streak of thirteen games, and retain leadership of the Midwest with a squad that had only four seniors. That he was successful is a tribute to his coaching and to the vast "witches' kitchen" of soccer out of which his players came.

UCLA, Hartwick, and Howard University were the other three finalists. There were players in the NCAA from Canada, Ethiopia, Trinidad, Great Britain, Nigeria, Greece, Italy, Mexico, and other lands. But none of them played for native-stocked St. Louis, a team that was not dominated by any one player.

Howard bowed to the tremendous forward line of UCLA in the first semifinal, 4–3. But this single game was enough to mark Howard's Keith Aqui as the oustanding offensive player of the tournament.

Hartwick lost to St. Louis, 1–0, when U.S. Olympian and Hermann Award repeater Al Trost kept his balance past three defenders and unleashed a hard shot at goalkeeper Norm Wingert. Wingert blocked the bullet into a melee of bodies at the bottom of which was St. Louis' Mike Seerey. But Seerey got his left foot on the ball and it sailed into an open net.

St. Louis wouldn't have been there if it hadn't been for an earlier victory over Southern Illinois-Edwardsville. The Cougars were tourney hosts, and eager for a place in the final. The difference was a fluke goal that bounced into the cage off the head of the Billikens' Dan Counce.

Mark Demling and Denny Hadican were, along with Trost and Seerey, the St. Louis heroes in the championship game. Demling had to deal with an awesome opposing line of Solomon Terfa and Shoa Agonafer, members of the Ethiopian Olympic team, Fesseha Emanuel of Trinidad, and Bernardo Ortiz of Colombia.

St. Louis' Al Trost was NCAA tournament MVP and winner of the Hermann Award.

Hartwick's 14–1 NCAA semifinalists included many players who went on to coaching and playing careers in the pros. Back row (left to right): assistant coach Bill Muse, Brendan Keenan, Tony Elia, Felipe Dulanto, Ray Flanigan, Roman Gurgacz, Frank van der Sommen, Timo Liekoski, Frank Chillemi, Colm Keenan, Bill Bettison and coach Al Miller. Front row: manager Dan Marsh, Phil Russo, Ed Hill, Alec Papadakis, Terry Fisher, Norm Wingert, Ed Austin, John Gibson, Rick Clark, Bruce Cowan and manager Joe Fornera.

That Demling and his teammates were able to contain these players should not have been surprising. In September, Keough had brought his team east where it won handily over St. Joseph's and Rider. Other subsequent victims were the University of South Florida, the University of British Columbia, Rockhurst, Indiana, and Eastern Illinois, the defending NAIA champion with its Canadian trio of Gerardo Pagnani, Tony Durante, and Carmelo Rago. Earlier in the year the Billikens beat the professional St. Louis Stars, 4–2.

Davis & Elkins returned to the top of the NAIA when it outlasted Quincy in the final. Wheaton ran its string of NCAA Mideast titles to five, and Brockport won a tough overtime game over Springfield to give it the medal spot in the Atlantic Coast Tournament.

Davidson was new champion in the Southern Conference, as its Icelandic center half, Gudmundar Karlsson, provided defensive consistency.

On the West Coast, San Jose was again a winner. Manuel Hernandez, returning from a year's absence, and Tony Suffle provided most of the firepower. USF wasn't far off the mark, however, as Hans Friessen and Alex Roboostoff were also heavy scorers. Only a tie with Santa Clara kept the Dons from sharing the league crown with San Jose.

Jean Tassy and Randy Smith, the latter of basketball fame, were playing at Buffalo State. Art Demling and John Houska led the defense and offense of a strong Michigan State team. Brown had Frank Van der Sommen in goal. Both Philadelphia Textile, MAC College Division winner, and Pennsylvania, second to Harvard in the Ivies, had players who would mark them for the top ten for several more years. Textile featured striker

Bob Durham and sweeper Gordon Cholmondeley, while Penn boasted a splendid trio in Stan Startzell, Bob Watkins and Tom Lieberman. Zach Papanikolaou scored thirty-six goals for the University of Wisconsin-Green Bay.

1971

Exactly ten years after winning the NAIA title, Howard University snapped defending champion St. Louis' forty-four–game winning streak in the final of the NCAA Tournament and became the first school ever to win both championships.

The dramatic showdown took place in Miami's Orange Bowl as part of the Holiday Festival after both finalists had survived grueling semifinal matches decided by a goal late in the game. Mike Seerey, another in a series of five consecutive Hermann Award winners from St. Louis, boomed a long, left-footed bullet past USF goalkeeper Bill Rapp to give the Bills' their 3–2 semifinal win, while Howard's Ian Bain slipped a ball past Harvard's Shep Messing to give his team a 1–0 conquest.

The final game featured scoring plays that introduced many to the magnetism of the game. With only four minutes gone, Seerey converted a Howard miscue into the first St. Louis score. It took only three minutes for Howard to reply through Alvin Henderson, who did his scoring the hard way—from flat on his back! After the Billiken scoring pair of Seerey and Denny Hadican put together a score, Howard's Mori Diane pushed

Pelé (center) took time out from touring with Santos of Brazil to visit with six admiring American University players (left to right): Jeff Wood, Ken Davidson, Charlie Dexter, Ira Kamens, Chris Kalvritrinos and Dennis Church.

◀ *It was crowded everywhere, including the Harvard net, as Penn defeated the Crimson, 5–2, before 12,000 spectators, a record college audience.*

one past goalkeeper Al Steck to make it 2–2. In the second half Howard scored quickly on a Henderson rocket and then protected its lead to the end. Much credit for the 3–2 victory must be given to goalkeeper Sam Tettah, from Ghana, who turned away at least six last-period St. Louis shots.

Harvard's talented mix was headed by sophomore Felix Adedeji. The Crimson were an undisputed No. 1 in New England. But Harvard lost the Ivy title to Penn as the Crimson suffered its only regular-season defeat before twelve thousand at Franklin Field. Adedeji was not fit in that game, and the Harvard defense could not contain the Quakers' Stan Startzell, Steve Baumann and Larry Houston.

Penn was beaten, in turn, by Penn State for a spot in the NCAA Tournament. With Andy Rymarczuk, Chris Bahr, and Rick Allen, the Nittany Lions had a fine run until they were stopped by Howard in the quarterfinal. Brockport won the Atlantic Coast NCAA crown and shared the SUNY title with Oneonta State. Lehigh came up with its first title in the University Division of the Middle Atlantic. Wheaton won its sixth straight Mideast NCAA Tournament, an unbreakable record since this was the last year for this prototypical College Division tourney. Hartwick was voted No. 1 in New York State, as midfielder Colm Keenan and forward Ed Austin paved the way to an 11–2–1 finish that included a victory over Long Island University, Metropolitan League Division I champion.

Bolstered by a 3–1–1 preseason trip to Arab communities in East Jerusalem and the West Bank, Quincy rode an airtight defense anchored by Al Harte to an NAIA championship. Its victim was Davis & Elkins. Dennis Wit and Jim Loftus brought Loyola the Mason–Dixon championship. Dartmouth challenged the other Ivies with Frank Gallo, a versatile St. Louis product. Cornell had talented Vic Huerta at forward. Army's two standouts were Chip Ciupak and Randy Nelson,

Shep Messing, a transfer from NYU, shone in the nets to lead Harvard to a spot in the NCAA semifinals.

the latter the son of former All-American Frank Nelson, from the University of North Carolina.

Joe Fink and Herb Austin were high-scoring forwards at NYU, and later both would play in the NASL. East Stroudsburg and Madison College each produced a goalkeeper who would enter the professional ranks upon graduation—Bob Rigby and Alan Mayer, respectively.

Familiar names from the past several years were in the cadre that Bob Guelker and Julie Menendez were training for the 1972 Olympic Games in Munich: USF's Mike Ivanow, Harvard's Messing, San Jose's Manuel Hernandez and Jim Zylker, SIU's John Carenza, and Navy's Casey Bahr. In addition, there were Al Trost, Mike Seerey, Joe Hamm, and Dan Counce, all from St. Louis.

Keith Aqui of Howard's NCAA champions was one of two All-Americans from his school (the other was Alvin Henderson).

1972

The NCAA effected two changes for the new season—a switch to two 45–minute halves from four 22–minute quarters, and a College Division tournament of national scope.

The new tournament took the place of several regional tournaments and offered more schools an opportunity to compete in postseason play. It was designed the same as the University Division playoff, with twenty-four teams playing in single-game elimination competition.

The first runoff was to spawn a mild and short-lived controversy concerning the relative strength of the champions in the two divisions. The University of St. Louis again won the NCAA University

Division—its ninth crown in fourteen years—over UCLA, 4–2. In spite of this, St. Louis' Harry Keough termed the season "almost a disaster" on the basis of a final record of 15–2–3. This was a disappointment for a team so loaded with Olympic and college talent.

SIU-Edwardsville was 11–0–3 with one of the three ties coming against St. Louis, when SIU's Tom Galati, Chris Carenza, and John Stremlau

Bob Rigby, who would later star in the NASL, takes ▶ matters firmly in hand, leading East Stroudsburg State to a 3–0 NCAA playoff victory over Baltimore.

Quincy's Al Harte became the first player ever to be selected as a first-team All-American three successive years.

had matched the Bills' best. When SIU prevailed in the College Division tournament, SIU rooters were quick to make comparisons.

From an objective standpoint, the efforts of both clubs were admirable. Besides fighting off the challenge of UCLA's Fesseha Wolde-Emmanuel, Shoa Agonafer, Solomon Terfa, and Tekeda Alemu, the Bills had to hold off Howard University in a semifinal match that was complicated by a late NCAA declaration of ineligibility of several key figures. Ian Bain played the game of his life for Howard, but St. Louis gained momentum as the game wore on and won in overtime, 2–1.

Cornell, a surprise qualifier at the expense of

◀ *St. Louis' Denny Hadican hoists his fist in celebration of his goal during the Billikens' 4–2 NCAA championship triumph over UCLA in Miami's Orange Bowl.*

Army, LIU and Harvard, all leaders in the northeast, tested UCLA in the other semi and emerged as a 1–0 loser. Cornell goalkeeper Bruce Arena earned the defensive MVP award, while St. Louis' Dan Counce gained the offensive honor.

SIU won the College Division at the expense of Oneonta State, 1–0, spoiling the first tournament experience of Garth Stamm's Red Devils, whose 16–2–1 record ranked with the best in the nation; they shared the SUNY title with Brockport and Cortland. Oneonta offered a mix led by Britishers Dave North and Farrukh Quraishi, and a speedy Latin, Carlos Camacho.

Both St. Louis, led by two-time Hermann Award winner Mike Seerey, and SIU offered striking examples of wholly native-born sides winning over teams with a strong infusion of foreign athletes. The title was Keough's fourth at the helm of a St. Louis eleven. SIU coach Bob Guelker, who had coached national champions five

Goalkeeper Alan Mayer, who would later defend NASL nets, earned recognition at James Madison.

times at St. Louis, added an unequaled sixth major title.

The NAIA found its champion in the West. Westmont College, the Southern California titlist, had to survive matches with Fredonia State, Davis & Elkins, and defending champ Quincy.

Al Harte, of Quincy, was the first player to be selected first-team All-America three successive years. Greenville College notched fifty-seven goals in thirteen games, with Loren Aandahl, its Norwegian striker, notching twenty-three of the total. But that performance was second best to Americo Araujo of Southern Massachusetts State, who had a high of thirty-five.

Brown won the University Division in New England, but was unable to dislodge Penn from the top of the Ivy tree. Already showing excellent forward and midfield strength, the Quakers had bolstered their defense with Bill Straub. His match-up with Harvard's Chris Papagianis was a highlight of the Ivy season as the teams stalemated.

Bob Smith, who would make the successful jump from the college to the pro ranks, was play-ing at Rider College. St. Joseph's, though beaten by Drexel in MAC league play, rallied to win the Middle Atlantic University Division. Brooklyn College triumphed in the Metropolitan League.

1973

SIU-Edwardsville was determined to show that its 1972 College Division title was deserved. For starters, the Cougars moved up to the major division and they made their claim creditable by playing a record ten games without allowing a goal.

But then they met St. Louis. The Billikens

Even high-scoring Ferdinand Treusacher (white) ▶ couldn't prevent Brown from suffering semifinal elimination at the hands of champion St. Louis, 3–1.

slipped a goal past the SIU defense anchored by Tom Galati and triumphed, 1–0, in the only regular-season meeting between the two teams. With John Stremlau, Tim Twellman, and Steve Cacciatore scoring almost at will, SIU continued its phenomenal run for another two games before it came down to play-off time to determine the regional representative in the NCAA Tournament.

The Cougars met St. Louis once again in Busch Stadium before twenty-thousand fans and suffered their second loss and elimination, 3–0. The indomitable Billikens stormed past Brown, which was led by Guyanese goalkeeper Mike Hampden and high-scoring Ferdinand Treusacher, 3–1, on goals by Hermann Award winner Dan Counce, Bob Matteson, and Bruce Rudroff. In the other semifinal, UCLA beat Clemson, 2–1, on goals by Efren Herrera and Tekeda Alemu.

The final was almost anticlimactic—it represented a familiar disappointment for Dennis Storer, UCLA coach. He had been this route before, each time to face St. Louis, the colossus of college soccer. This time, the Bruins led at the half on a goal by winger Firooz Fowzi. But, even though keeper Fred Decker turned aside numerous dangerous thrusts, the UCLA defense was beaten twice by Counce, St. Louis winning its tenth title, 2–1.

The Division II championship went to the University of Missouri-St. Louis, with a 3–0 decision over Fullerton State. UMSL had a tougher time in its semifinal victory over Adelphi, in which the hero was freshman John McKenna. On a pass from Kevin Missey, McKenna scored on a topspin shot that Adelphi keeper Gene DuChateau thought was over the net. But there was no mistake in the final when Missey netted two and teammate Mark LeGrand another to beat Dennis Checkett's Fullerton eleven, 3–0.

Quincy had problems throughout the season, but solved them in time to win the NAIA over Rockhurst for its fourth national crown.

Individual scoring honors went to Drew's Dean Rosow, North Texas State's Iseed Khoury, and Greenville's Loren Aandahl, each of whom netted thirty-six goals. Clemson, with Henry Abadi

Despite an up-and-down regular season, Quincy won its fourth NAIA title, turning back Rockhurst. Back row (left to right): manager Paul Herrman, coach Jack MacKenzie, Andy Probst, Frank Camacho, Neil Fredrickson, Larry Franzoi, Larry Carron, Frank Vinciguerra, associate coach Frank Longo and assistant coach John Schneider. Second row: Jim Eagen, Bill Fann, Jim Pollihan, John Green, Mark Mathis, Sam Bick, Rich Zielder and Paul Greeling. Front row: Steve Brightman, Matt Weiss and Ed Renaud.

Harvard forward Felix Adedeji does a balancing act during a four-goal performance in an 8–4 victory over Amherst.

(thirty-two goals), easily won the Atlantic Coast Conference title and totaled ninety-six goals.

Penn pushed Brown in the Ivy League, thanks to two forwards John Borozzi and Santiago Formosa; Penn State fielded another offensive threat to join Chris Bahr in Randy Garber, a junior college All-America transfer from Mercer County Community College. Philadelphia Textile featured Bermudians Dale Russell and Elson Seale to complement Gordon Cholmondeley in the defense.

Two-time All-American Mickey Whelan and keeper Con Davis were top players at Davis & Elkins, where Tim Murphy added support. At West Virginia, Jack Cardozo scored twenty-eight goals in front of strong fullback Manny Matos. Bill Soussi matched that total at Belmont Abbey. Seattle Pacific's Ken Covell was the highest scorer on the West Coast, with twenty-one goals. Cleveland State's defense of Bud Lewis and Stave

Cabalku limited the opposition to seven goals. Delaware's Chip Smallwood and West Chester's George Claypoole were tough defenders in the East, and Temple's Enver Diker was a standout playmaker.

1974

As it turned out, the Midwest's domination in 1973 was a last hurrah. In 1974, except for Quincy, which remained atop the NAIA, there was a geographical shift in title laurels.

Howard won the Division I NCAA by outlasting St. Louis—an uncommon feat for any opponent—in a brilliantly played final in Busch Stadium. The Billikens, led by Don Aubuchon and Don Droege, scored first, and it looked as if St. Louis would win its third straight NCAA crown. But Howard's Ayomi Bamiro tied things in the

All-American Tom Kazembe of Wooster, a Malawi native, scored six goals in a game against Baldwin-Wallace.

Howard capped a 19–0 season with a come-from-behind 2–1 victory over St. Louis in the NCAA final.

final period—on an assist from Ian Bain—and Ken Ilodigwe added the winning goal in a fourth overtime as Howard ended its season with a perfect record of nineteen victories.

This was one year that St. Louis was fortunate to be among the final four. It had to struggle to beat UCLA in the semifinals, finding the Bruins' Sergio Velazquez hard to contain. The Bills had been beaten by SIU-Edwardsville during the season—a first for the Cougars—and forced into a rematch to secure qualification, but they won the second game, 2–1.

Howard had come into the tournament at 17–0–0. Only Clemson and Federal City had been able to limit the Bisons to one goal. They had seven freshmen on the team, hardly a portent of a title. But these players were not ordinary freshmen. Howard posted a 2–1 victory over Hartwick in the semifinals, despite the efforts of Glenn Myernick. Hartwick was able to parlay the abilities of Myernick, Duncan McDonald, and keeper Von Eron into a third-place finish over UCLA.

Adelphi, the winner in Division II, had an excellent goalkeeper in Gene DuChateau and a fine back in Nimrod Dreyfus. The Panthers went to the University of Missouri-St. Louis campus, hoping for another shot at the Rivermen who had knocked them out the year before. En route to the final, they had to beat Babson and Springfield, and, in the semifinals, had to stand up to the guns of Federal City, whose Herb Gordon came into the tournament with twenty-four goals.

Adelphi's opponent in the final was a complete surprise. After a lackluster 8–3–5 season, Seattle Pacific had come on strong. The Falcons upset Hayward and Fullerton in the Far West play-offs. In their semifinal with Eastern Illinois, they were outshot, 22–12, and trailed on corner kicks late in the fourth period. But Jose Reyes made Seattle Pacific the winner on a goal scored from an indirect free kick.

Division III play, at Wheaton, was marred by bitter cold and a field that had to be plowed to be serviceable. Brockport, seeded last in its qualifying round, had nevertheless disposed of Binghamton, the SUNY champ, and Trenton State, the New Jersey State College king. In the final, it met Swarthmore, another underdog. Swarthmore had beaten Lynchburg, the Dixie League leader, and Lock Haven, a strong Pennsylvania Conference side.

Defensive-minded Swarthmore had a strong offensive threat in McWelling Todman. His single goal was enough to knock out MacMurray in the semifinals and he gave Will Stetson's charges a short-lived lead in the final. But Steve Klaasen and Nelson Cupello tallied for Brockport and Cupello then put the game out of reach with an additional penalty kick.

This year, the Eastern College Athletic Conference began its own version of the invitational tournament. The first—the Metropolitan New York–New Jersey ECAC—was won by William Paterson State over Marist.

Oneonta's Farrukh Quraishi was voted the Hermann Award winner. But it was apparent that a new youth force was making a significant impact on the game. Besides those first-year men who had carried Howard and Adelphi to the top, many other freshmen assumed the spotlight. They included Matt Bahr, the younger brother of Chris, at Penn State; Pete Hulval, the University of Arkansas' 6–6 defender; Loyola goalkeeper John Houska; SIU's Greg Makowski; Philadelphia Textile's Adrian Brooks; Indiana's Angelo DiBernardo; Akron's Lou Nanchoff; and Quincy's Emilio John. The Ivy League legalized freshman play, and Princeton's Paul Milone showed promise. The average age of the college teams was going down.

1975

Many observers noted that results were no longer predictable. More teams were reaching a high level in playing skills and tactics, resulting in equalized competition. The pattern ran through all the major races.

The University of San Francisco won the Division I crown over host SIU-Edwardsville, 4–0. This time the weather was perfect, and the Dons profited. Mal Roche assisted on two goals—head shots by Greg McKeown and Vic Arbelaez. A goal was scored by Paul Korn, the Dons' leading marksman, and then Roche started a play that ended with an Andy Atuegbu bomb into the back of the net.

San Francisco coach Steve Negoesco stood head and shoulders above the rest after leading the Dons to NCAA crown.

Tim Twellman, an SIU striker, mentioned lack of preparation and overconfidence in his analysis of the crushing defeat. His first contention was not likely in the case of a team coached by Bob Guelker and there was little reason for overconfidence. The Dons were 20–1–2 coming in and the Cougars, 14–3–0. If the teams were reasonably equal in technical ability, USF enjoyed a subtle edge in strategy.

Brown, relying on a rugged defense centered around Hermann Award winner Steve Ralbovsky and the sharpshooting of forward Fred Pereira, beat the heavily favored foreign legion of Howard to take third place.

In the Division II tourney, played in Seattle, Baltimore, the least publicized of the four finalists, crushed Wisconsin-Green Bay in the semis and then beat Seattle Pacific in the final game.

The Super Bees had no offensive stars like Nezi Hasanoglu, Green Bay's Turkish striker, or Adelphi's Ron Atanasio, and had no keeper of the ability of Adelphi Olympian Gene DuChateau. They had no one who approached Jose Reyes and Terry White of coach Cliff McCrath's Seattle Pacific team. But Baltimore's plan of controlling the midfield and supporting a sticky defense won it a national championship.

Babson, a team of like pattern, captured Division III, defeating Brockport on the losers' pitch. The victory was a team effort, engineered independent of a superstar. A Jim Baumann–led Ohio Wesleyan team won third over Johns Hopkins, which got a fine defensive effort from back Frank Olzewski.

The NAIA trophy was returned to Quincy College. Led by Sam Bick and Jim Pollihan, Quincy was able to meet the challenge of Simon Fraser, Canadians on the way up.

During the season, Philadelphia Textile beat a touring USF squad, 4–2—the Dons' only loss—by using a tenacious man-for-man marking against a travel-worn collection of brilliant athletes. USF had just come off a victory over St. Louis and might have been overconfident, but the play of John Nusum, Adrian Brooks, and Brooks Cryder was a factor in the Textile triumph.

Babson won the College Division race in New England with a 17–0–1 record—its lone draw coming against local rival Brandeis, the Greater Boston titlist. Babson goalkeeper Shane Kennedy fashioned a string of 13 shutouts en route to the Division III crown.

Outstanding players abounded—likely draft choices for the North American Soccer League—such as Baltimore's Pete Caringi and Dale Roth, South Florida's Fergus Hopper, Akron's George Nanchoff, Philadelphia Textile's Dave MacWilliams, SIU's Greg Villa, and St. Louis' Ty Keough.

Hartwick was playing a young Bill Gazonas, and East Coast Conference champion Temple showed the promising Bill Sautter. There was another Salvemini at University of California—Dan—following in the footsteps of brother Len of Air Force and Olympic fame. Emilio Romero scored twenty goals at Metro State College to lead the Rocky Mountain schools. Versatile Charley Lineweaver was at Binghamton in the SUNY Conference.

Scranton University had broken Elizabethtown's grip in the MAC. Bowdoin topped the small, but high-level CBB group. Oneonta won the SUNY, and Slippery Rock led the field in Western Pennsylvania. Madison, Clemson, Lynchburg, Eckerd, Morehead State, and Appalachian State all produced the type of champion-

Brown's Steve Ralbovsky received the Hermann Award as Player of the Year.

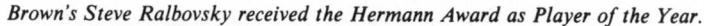

All-American Dale Roth, displaying his skills against Old Dominion, led Baltimore to the NCAA II crown.

Tim Mazzetti was a high-scoring soccer player at Penn before he would make the jump from bartender to professional football placekicker with the Atlanta Falcons.

Misak Pirinjian (left) helped San Francisco post a 20–2–3 record and another national championship.

ship-quality player that marked college soccer as the prime U.S. source for the professional recruiter.

1976

The changing of the guard among midwestern soccer powers took place in 1976 as Indiana relegated traditional powers St. Louis and SIU to the backseat with an undefeated romp through the regular season and an 18–1–1 record overall.

Paced by Angelo DiBernardo, Charlie Fajkus, and Dave Shelton, the defensive MVP of the tournament, Jerry Yeagley's team marched all the way to the NCAA finals where it met San Francisco, led by keeper Pete Arnautoff, midfielder John Brooks, and attackers Andy Atuegbu and Tony Gray. But, in the Bicentennial Year tournament, held at Pennsylvania's Franklin Field, the Dons turned back Indiana, 1–0, on a goal by Atuegbu to win the NCAA I title despite losing two games and tying three during the regular season. The Dons defeated Clemson in one semifinal,

while Hartwick was ousted by Indiana in the other semi. A combination of Hermann Award winner Glenn Myernick, Keith Van Eron, Bill Gazonas, and Tom Maresca enabled Hartwick to defeat Clemson for third place.

In Seattle, Loyola, featuring sparkling play by striker Ian Reid and keeper John Houska, won the Division II crown over Joe Machnik's New Haven team, led by goalkeeper Rick Kissell. Chico State and Missouri–St. Louis finished third and fourth.

The NCAA Division III tournament, held on the Babson campus, was won by Brandeis over Bob Cupelo–led Brockport. The Judges had an almost unstoppable forward in Cleveland Lewis, who was named MVP. Elizabethtown College bested MacMurray for third.

True to the warning it posted in 1975, Simon Fraser outscored Rockhurst to win the NAIA after an unbelievable fourteen-overtime semifinal with defending champion Quincy. The latter, under Jack MacKenzie, had enough to finish third, ahead of Davis & Elkins.

In a National Christian College play-off, a field

Sophomore Angelo DiBernardo (left) led Indiana to the NCAA final.

Penn State's version of All in the Family: coach Walter Bahr (right) with sons Matt (top left) and Chris.

of forty-eight was narrowed down to a final which saw Bryan College triumph over Grace. King's College defeated Le Tourneau for the consolation spot.

Many players made the year memorable. The top scorer at St. Louis was Don Huber, while SIU-Edwardsville countered with Greg Villa. Akron keeper Paul Dueker looked out at an incisive offense that kept opposing teams honest. The Zips earned the Ohio title, nosing out Cleveland State, which had outstanding strikers in Bob Hritz and John Tyma. Connecticut, sparked by Paul Hunter, who would be an early-round draft choice of the pros, topped the New England universities. Brown won its fourth consecutive Ivy title with striker Peter Van Beek. Rhode Island displayed big Dan McCrudden, whose head goal forced the Rhode Island–Connecticut NCAA qualifying game into overtime.

Soccer-playing brothers have always been a feature on college campuses. To cite a few, there have been the Jeremenkos (Mike and Al at Drexel); the Bahrs (Casey at Navy, Chris and Matt at Penn State); the Proziks (Don at Brockport and Pete at Buffalo State); the Rosuls (Roman and Alex at Cleveland State); and the Carenzas (John and Chris at SIU).

Then there were the Brooks brothers—not the sartorial duo, but the soccer Brookses. John played in the West, at USF, and his older brother Adrian played at Philadelphia Textile. In 1976, All-American Adrian was the best man on the field in a losing cause, as Textile was defeated by Clemson in an NCAA tournament showdown. So, unfortunately, the brothers never got to play against each other.

1977

In recognition of the growing popularity of the game, the NCAA restructured its tournaments. Two new areas were created by subdividing the existing six. Hereafter, there would be rankings in eight regions, and selections for postseason play would no longer be clouded by the sometimes suspect "at large" category and the awkward first-round bye.

As if to underscore the new setup, the tournaments provided significant results. Hartwick, a

Freshman goalkeeper Aly Anderson sparked Hartwick to the 1977 NCAA title (above) and coach Jim Lennox collected the hardware to prove it.

New York independent, defeated defending champion San Francisco, 2–1 for the NCAA I title. The upstate New Yorkers did it on goals by Art Napolitano and Steve Long at Berkeley's Memorial Stadium.

USF was thus thwarted in its attempt at three straight crowns, as Hartwick put its best feet forward with an array that included Hermann Award winner Billy Gazonas, Duncan McDonald, goalkeeper Aly Anderson, and Tom Maresca.

Brown, New England University Division champ, and SIU-Edwardsville were surprise qualifiers. Brown upset Clemson, which was previously unbeaten and untied. SIU, led by All-American Greg Makowski, had to survive ten overtimes in regional games with St. Louis, Indiana, and Cleveland State, the latter two the highest-ranked teams in the Midwest. SIU, with its homegrown squad, lost to San Francisco in the semifinal and beat Brown for third.

In the Division II tournament, held in Miami, Alabama A & M stopped Seattle Pacific's third final-game bid for the title. The game stats clearly favored Cliff McCrath's Falcons. But the westerners failed to convert a penalty kick that would have tied the game, and A & M held on for a 2–1 triumph as Ken Okafor tallied the winning goal. Joe Machnik's New Haven University entry, the best in the New England College Division, finished third ahead of Wisconsin-Green Bay.

In Division III, another unheralded team took the title. Pretournament guessers favored host Babson, or at least, powerful Cortland State, the SUNY winner. When the two met in the semifinal, it was predicted that the survivor of that match would be the titlist. But Lock Haven State, wearing the Pennsylvania Conference crown, fashioned a 3–1 semifinal victory over Wooster, tops in the Ohio Conference, and then upset Cortland, 1–0.

The NAIA produced a more typical result. Quincy College was the winner for the fourth time in five years. Keene State was runner-up, Davis & Elkins third, and Erskine fourth.

◀ *Fidelus (Andy) Atuegbu, offensive MVP of the tournament in 1975 and 1976, led San Francisco to a 25–4–1 record, but couldn't lift the Dons to a third straight title.*

There were other isolated, yet notable achievements. Spring Arbor College logged an astounding 18–0–0 season record. It might have furthered that except for a restriction which prevented its participation in postseason NAIA play. Forward Tony Crescitelli of North Adams State College scored thirty-four goals to lead that department in New England. Emilio Romero, at Metro State in the Rocky Mountain League, tallied a record-breaking forty-one. Metro ran second to Air Force, champion of the league.

In the Northern Illinois Conference, John Bergh, Rockford's left wing, a gymnast, became one of the longest throw-in specialists when he unveiled his unique "handspring" style. The Uni-

Southern Illinois-Edwardsville's Greg Makowski attained All-American honors for the second consecutive year.

Roar Andersen, making his move against Indiana's Rudy Glenn during the 1978 NCAA final, and his San Francisco teammates made it three NCAA titles in four years.

versity of Rhode Island, with Joe Kanzler in goal, won the Yankee Conference with an unblemished league record. Cornell finally took the Ivy championship outright, and St. Lawrence headed the Independent Conference in New York.

Philadelphia Textile remained the class team in Pennsylvania, New Jersey, and Delaware, defeating both Penn and Penn State in Division I qualifying games. But though it played at home, the John Nusum–Adrian Brooks–Dave MacWilliams side was unable to knock determined Hartwick out of contention. The University of Maryland-Baltimore County, with sweeper Mark Woodward, again won the Mason–Dixon, while Appalachian State took the Southern Conference. In the Far West Conference, Chico State finished ahead of San Francisco State, and in the Northwest Conference, Simon Fraser beat the University of Washington and Seattle Pacific.

1978

This time it would be different. At least that's what Indiana coach Jerry Yeagley must have been thinking as he entered the NCAA final rematch against San Francisco. Determined to avenge its loss to the Dons in 1976, Indiana, led by Angelo DiBernardo, Hermann Award winner, and Charlie Fajkus, had proven virtually unstoppable en route to the NCAA I finals in Tampa. The Big Red even owned an early season triumph over the Dons which established them as a favorite in the final.

But All-America defender Bjorn Dahl and his teammates surprised the Hoosiers, posting a 2–0 victory to give USF its third national title in four years.

Earlier in the season, Indiana had whipped powerful San Jose, in addition to USF, to win the

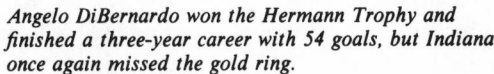

Angelo DiBernardo won the Hermann Trophy and finished a three-year career with 54 goals, but Indiana once again missed the gold ring.

Shriners' Classic in San Francisco, and it won the crown in its own Big Red Tournament over a field that included SIU-Edwardsville, Penn State, and defending NCAA Division I champion Hartwick.

During the season, Hartwick lost to both SIU and Indiana but relied on its experience for a fourth-place finish in the Empire State rankings behind St. Francis, Columbia, and Adelphi, all championship teams.

A spirited Seattle Pacific team triumphed over 1977 nemesis Alabama A & M to take the NCAA Division II crown. The finalists were followed by Eastern Illinois and Southern Connecticut, newcomers on the tournament circuit whose presence indicated a healthy national development.

Lock Haven State repeated in Division III. To do so, it had to defeat another newcomer, Washington University.

Quincy College again outplayed the NAIA field and won the tournament final over host University of Alabama-Huntsville, with Rockhurst finishing third.

Messiah won the National Christian College crown, with John Wesley and Tabor shouldering aside the usual block of southern contenders. Bryan College, 1977 champion, managed a fourth-place finish.

The University of Connecticut, ranked No. 1 in the New England region, was closely pressed by both Brown and Southern Connecticut. In New York, St. Francis had the help of All-American keeper Dragan Radovich and turned back both Columbia and Adelphi. Philadelphia Textile, showing talent and speed in the twin threats of Adrian Brooks and striker Dave MacWilliams, tore through the opposition. Textile met its toughest test in an overtime game against Loyola of Baltimore, ranked No. 1 in the Mid-Atlantic region. Loyola's Peter Notaro and his teammates showed quality play throughout a season that ended with a defeat at the hands of Alabama A & M in the Division II tournament.

Clemson, repeat winner in the Atlantic Coast Conference, was ranked first in the South; Indiana headed the Mideast; and Quincy had the satisfaction of topping both SIU-Edwardsville and St. Louis in the final poll in the Midwest. There was no question about Far West rankings. Top honors

went to USF, with Seattle Pacific garnering second over Simon Fraser, winner of the Northwest Conference, Loyola's Notaro scored the opening goal in the East-West Senior Bowl Game at Orlando. But it was Papa Jobe, from Evansville, who scored two goals and was voted the outstanding offensive player in the West's 4–3 victory. Defensive honors went to Ron Schneider of Adelphi.

Others who figured in the scoring in this game read like a *Who's Who* in college soccer for the year. William and Mary's Bill Watson scored on an assist from Dave MacWilliams of Philadelphia Textile. Dan McDonnell of Quincy helped Jobe on one of his markers. Indiana's DiBernardo had two assists, one on a Jobe goal and one on a score by Mike McLenaghan of Simon Fraser. Both Larry Mees of Chico State and Tony Crescitelli of North Adams State notched single goals.

Excellent players abounded. St. Louis had three—midfielder Ty Keough, son of coach Harry, and forwards Larry Hulcer and Don Huber. George Gorleku of Eastern Illinois, Rich Chinapoo of LIU, Andy Leeker of Rollins, Trevor Franklin of Keene State, Adolphus Lawson of Southern Connecticut, Mike Kelly of SIU, Dan Salvemini of California-Berkeley, Gaetano Messina of St. Francis, and Barry Nix of Columbia were top college backs.

Temple's George Lesyw, Penn State's Jim Stamatis, Connecticut's Joe Morrone, LIU's Hans-Peter Rietz, Clemson's Christian Nwokocha, Lynchburg's Tim Emmons, and Appalachian State's Thompson Usiyan were dangerous schemers and strikers. Goalkeeper Randy Phillips and back Greg Ryan of Southern Methodist brought recognition to the Southwest for the first time.

Columbia won the Ivy title—its first. Temple University took the East Coast Conference, and Adelphi, King's Point, and St. Peter's won the three divisions of the Metropolitan Conference. The University of Massachusetts won the Northern Region ECAC over Boston University, LIU and Army. Lehigh took the Southern Region over Rider, William and Mary, and Old Dominion. The Metro ECAC was won by Trenton State over Montclair, Mercy, and Kings Point. The Southern Regional saw Slippery Rock get past Franklin &

Adrian Brooks is closely marked by Indiana's Randy Hocking (12), but the Philadelphia Textile star was rarely contained en route to becoming the second pick in the NASL draft.

Marshall, Frostburg, and UMBC. In New England, Colby took the ECAC crown over Connecticut College, Middlebury, and Wesleyan. In upstate New York, St. Lawrence topped Rochester, Hamilton, and Fredonia. Denver won the Rocky Mountain title and, with a win over powerful Simon Fraser, Lewis and Clark won the Northwest NAIA loop.

Recognition proved to be the spur to both players and teams, and if there was less emphasis on conference races, there was more on regional and national rankings.

St. Louis University's Harry Keough and his vast collection of NCAA championship trophies.

6
College Records Section

COLLEGIATE
NATIONAL CHAMPIONSHIP

NCAA DIVISION I
1959—St. Louis 5, Bridgeport 2
1960—St. Louis 3, Maryland 2
1961—West Chester 2, St. Louis 0
1962—St. Louis 4, Maryland 3
1963—St. Louis 3, Navy 0
1964—Navy 1, Michigan State 0
1965—St. Louis 1, Michigan State 0
1966—San Francisco 5, Long Island 2
1967—Michigan State 0, St. Louis 0 (Game called due to inclement weather)
1968—Maryland 2, Michigan State 2 (Game called after two overtimes)
1969—St. Louis 4, San Francisco 0
1970—St. Louis 1, UCLA 0
1971—Howard 3, St. Louis 2 (Howard vacated title for using ineligible player)
1972—St. Louis 4, UCLA 2
1973—St. Louis 2, UCLA 1
1974—Howard 2, St. Louis 1
1975—San Francisco 4, Southern Illinois-Edwardsville 0
1976—San Francisco 1, Indiana 0
1977—Hartwick 2, San Francisco 1
1978—San Francisco 2, Indiana 0

NCAA DIVISION II
1972—Southern Illinois-Edwardsville 1, SUNY-Oneonta 0
1973—Missouri-St. Louis 3, California-Fullerton 0
1974—Adelphi 3, Seattle Pacific 2
1975—Baltimore 3, Seattle Pacific 1
1976—Loyola 2, New Haven 0
1977—Alabama A&M 2, Seattle Pacific 1
1978—Seattle Pacific 1, Alabama A&M 0

NCAA DIVISION III
1974—SUNY-Brockport 3, Swarthmore 1
1975—Babson 1, SUNY-Brockport 0
1976—Brandeis 2, SUNY-Brockport 1
1977—Lock Haven 1, SUNY-Cortland 0
1978—Lock Haven 3, Washington (Mo.) 0

NAIA
1959—Pratt Institute 4, Elizabethtown 3
1960—Elizabethtown 2, Newark Engineering 2 (co-champs)
1961—Howard 3, Newark Engineering 2
1962—East Stroudsburg 4, Pratt Institute 0
1963—Earlham, Castleton State co-champs
1964—Trenton State 3, Lincoln (Pa.) 0
1965—Trenton State 5, Earlham 2
1966—Quincy 6, Trenton State 1
1967—Quincy 3, Rockhurst 1
1968—Davis & Elkins 2, Quincy 1 (5 overtimes)
1969—Eastern Illinois 1, Davis & Elkins 0 (2 overtimes)
1970—Davis & Elkins 2, Quincy 0
1971—Quincy 1, Davis & Elkins 0
1972—Westmont 2, Davis & Elkins 1 (2 overtimes)
1973—Quincy 3, Rockhurst 0
1974—Quincy 6, Davis & Elkins 0
1975—Quincy 1, Simon Fraser 0
1976—Simon Fraser 1, Rockhurst 0
1977—Quincy 2, Keene State 0
1978—Quincy 2, Alabama-Huntsville 0

CONFERENCE CHAMPIONS

Intercollegiate Association
Football League

1904–05—Haverford
1905–06—Haverford
1906–07—Haverford
1907–08—Haverford, Yale
1908–09—Columbia
1909–10—Columbia
1910–11—Haverford
1911–12—Yale
1912–13—Harvard
1913–14—Harvard
1914—Penn
1915—Haverford
1916—Penn

1917—Haverford
1918—No competition
1919—Penn
1920—Penn
1921—Princeton
1922—Princeton
1923—Penn
1924—Penn
1925—Princeton
(League play discontinued, award given to outstanding team)

Intercollegiate
Soccer Football Association

1926—Haverford, Princeton, Penn State
1927—Princeton
1928—Yale
1929—Penn State
1930—Harvard, Penn, Yale
1931—Penn
1932—Penn, Navy
1933—Penn, Penn State
1934—Cornell
1935—Yale
1936—No award
1937—No award
1938—Penn State
1939—Penn State, Princeton
1940—Penn State, Princeton
1941—No award
1942—No award
1943—No award
1944—No award
1945—No award
1946—Springfield
1947—Springfield
1948—Connecticut
1949—San Francisco, Penn State
1950—West Chester State
1951—Temple
1952—Franklin and Marshall
1953—Temple
1954—Penn State
1955—Brockport, Penn State
1956—Trinity
1957—City College of New York, Springfield
1958—Drexel Tech

Middle Atlantic Intercollegiate
Soccer League

1932—Penn
1933—Penn
1934—Cornell
1935—Cornell, Penn
1936—Princeton
1937—Princeton
1938—Haverford
1939—Princeton
1940—Princeton
1941—Cornell
1942—Princeton
1943—No champion
1944—Penn
1945—Haverford
1946—Penn, Princeton
1947—Penn

California Intercollegiate
Soccer Conference

1926—San Mateo Junior College
1927—San Mateo Junior College
1928—San Mateo Junior College
1929—San Mateo Junior College
1930—San Mateo Junior College
1931—Stanford
1932—San Francisco
1933—San Francisco
1934—San Francisco
1935—San Francisco
1936—California
1937—California
1938—California
1939—San Jose State
1940—San Jose State
1941—San Jose State
1942—San Jose State
1943—No champion
1944—No champion
1945—No champion
1946—California
1947—California
1948—San Francisco
1949—San Francisco
1950—San Francisco
1951—San Francisco
1952—San Francisco
1953—San Francisco
1954—San Francisco
1955—San Francisco
1956—San Francisco
1957—San Francisco
1958—San Francisco
1959—San Francisco Community College
1960—California
1961—San Francisco Community College
1962—Stanford
1963—Stanford
1964—San Jose State

West Coast Intercollegiate
Soccer Conference

1965—San Francisco
1966—San Francisco
1967—San Jose State
1968—San Jose State
1969—San Jose State
1970—San Jose State
1971—San Francisco
1972—San Jose State
1973—San Francisco
1974—San Francisco, San Jose State
1975—San Francisco
(League became Pacific Soccer Conference)
1976—San Francisco
1977—San Francisco
1978—San Francisco

New England Intercollegiate
Soccer League

1934—Amherst
1935—Yale

1936—Brown
1937—Springfield
1938—Harvard
1939—Springfield
1940—Wesleyan
1941—Springfield
1942—Springfield, Amherst
1943—No award
1944—No award
1945—Yale
1946—Springfield
1947—Springfield
1948—Connecticut
1949—Amherst
1950—Yale
1951—Yale, Dartmouth
1952—Dartmouth
1953—Springfield
1954—Dartmouth
1955—Harvard
1956—Trinity, Brown
1957—Springfield
1958—Connecticut
1959—Bridgeport
1960—Connecticut
1961—Williams
1962—Williams
1963—Harvard
1964—Trinity
1965—Brown, Middlebury
1966—Brown
1967—Brown
1968—Springfield
1969—Harvard
1970—Harvard
1971—Harvard
1972—Brown
1973—Springfield
1974—Connecticut
1975—Brown
1976—Connecticut
1977—Brown
1978—Connecticut

Penn Intercollegiate
Association Football League

1915—Penn JV
1916—Penn JV
1917—Penn JV
1918—No competition
1919—Swarthmore
1920—Swarthmore
1921—Swarthmore
1922—Lehigh
1923—Penn JV
1924—Haverford
1925—Swarthmore
(League disbanded)

Eastern Intercollegiate
Soccer League

1948—Cornell
1949—Cornell
1950—Army
1951—Army

Ivy League

1952—Army
1953—Dartmouth
1954—Dartmouth
1955—Penn, Harvard
1956—Yale
1957—Princeton
1958—Harvard
1959—Harvard
1960—Princeton
1961—Harvard
1962—Penn, Harvard
1963—Brown, Harvard
1964—Dartmouth, Brown
1965—Brown
1966—Brown
1967—Brown
1968—Brown
1969—Harvard
1970—Harvard
1971—Penn
1972—Penn
1973—Brown
1974—Brown
1975—Brown, Cornell
1976—Brown
1977—Cornell
1978—Columbia

Metropolitan Intercollegiate
Soccer Conference

1949—Brooklyn
1950—Brooklyn
1951—City College of New York
1952—Brooklyn
1953—City College of New York
1954—City College of New York
1955—City College of New York
1956—City College of New York
1957—City College of New York
1958—City College of New York
1959—Pratt
1960—Brooklyn
1961—Brooklyn
1962—Pratt
1963—Adelphi
1964—Long Island U
1965—Long Island U
1966—Long Island U
1967—Long Island U
1968—City College of New York
1969—Adelphi
1970—Adelphi
1971—Long Island U
1972—Long Island U
1973—Adelphi
1974—Adelphi
1975—Adelphi
1976—St. Francis
1977—St. Francis
1978—Adelphi

Atlantic Coast Conference

1954—Maryland
1955—Maryland

1956—Maryland
1957—Maryland
1958—Maryland
1959—Maryland
1960—Maryland
1961—Maryland
1962—Maryland
1963—Maryland
1964—Maryland
1965—Maryland
1966—Maryland
1967—Maryland
1968—Maryland
1969—Virginia
1970—Virginia
1971—Maryland
1972—Clemson
1973—Clemson
1974—Clemson
1975—Clemson
1976—Clemson
1977—Clemson
1978—Clemson

Mid-American Conference

1969—Bowling Green, Kent State
1970—Ohio U
1971—Ohio U
1972—Ohio U
1973—Bowling Green
1974—Miami (O.)
1975—Bowling Green

New York State Athletic Conference

1959—Cortland
1960—Cortland
1961—Brockport
1962—Cortland
1963—Cortland
1964—Cortland
1965—New Paltz
1966—Oswego
1967—Buffalo
1968—Brockport
1969—Brockport
1970—Brockport, Buffalo
1971—Brockport, Oneonta
1972—Cortland, Oneonta, Brockport
1973—Brockport, Oneonta
1974—Binghamton
1975—Oneonta
1976—Brockport
1977—Cortland
1978—Brockport

Rocky Mountain Intercollegiate League

1955—Colorado Mines
1956—Colorado Mines
1957—Air Force, Colorado Mines
1958—Colorado Mines
1959—Air Force
1960—Air Force
1961—Air Force
1962—Air Force, Denver

1963—Colorado U
1964—Denver
1965—Air Force
1966—Colorado College
1967—Colorado College
1968—Air Force
1969—Air Force
1970—Denver
1971—Metropolitan State, Air Force, Denver
1972—Air Force
1973—Air Force
1974—Colorado College
1975—Colorado College
1976—Air Force
1977—Air Force
1978—Denver

Midwestern Conference

1950—Wheaton
1951—Chicago
1952—Earlham
1953—Purdue
1954—Earlham
1955—Indiana
1956—Illinois-Chicago
1957—Purdue
1958—Earlham, Wheaton, Purdue
1959—Michigan State
1960—St. Louis
1961—St. Louis
1962—St. Louis
1963—Michigan State
1964—St. Louis
1965—St. Louis
(League disbanded)

Ohio Collegiate Soccer Association

1958—Akron
1959—Akron
1960—Akron
1961—Akron
1962—Ohio U
1963—Akron
1964—Akron
1965—Denison
1966—Akron
1967—Akron
1968—Akron
1969—Cleveland State
1970—Cleveland State

Southern Conference

1968—George Washington
1969—George Washington
1970—Davidson
1971—Davidson
1972—Appalachian State
1973—Appalachian State
1974—Appalachian State
1975—Appalachian State
1976—William & Mary
1977—Appalachian State
1978—Appalachian State

East Coast Conference

1974—Bucknell
1975—Temple
1976—Temple
1977—West Chester
1978—Temple

Mason-Dixon Conference

1946—Johns Hopkins
1947—Washington College
1948—Loyola
1949—Baltimore
1950—Baltimore
1951—Baltimore
1952—Baltimore
1953—Johns Hopkins
1954—Baltimore
1955—Western Maryland
1956—Catholic, Towson State
1957—Catholic
1958—Baltimore
1959—Lynchburg
1960—Baltimore
1961—Washington College
1962—Lynchburg
1963—Baltimore, Lynchburg
1964—Washington College
1965—Baltimore
1966—Towson State
1967—Roanoke, Loyola
1968—Baltimore
1969—Baltimore
1970—Baltimore
1971—Loyola
1972—Baltimore
1973—Baltimore
1974—Loyola
1975—Loyola
1976—Loyola
1977—Maryland-Baltimore

Texas Intercollegiate League

1973—Southern Methodist
1974—Houston
1975—North Texas State
1976—North Texas State
1977—Southern Methodist
1978—Southern Methodist

Yankee Conference

1965—Vermont, Massachusetts, Connecticut
1966—Vermont
1967—Vermont
1968—Vermont, Rhode Island
1969—Vermont
1970—Massachusetts
1971—Rhode Island, Vermont
1972—Rhode Island
1973—Connecticut
1974—Connecticut
1975—Vermont
1976—Connecticut
1977—Rhode Island
1978—Connecticut

Virginia Intercollegiate Soccer Conference

1969—Virginia
1970—Virginia
1971—Virginia
1972—Madison
1973—Madison
1974—George Mason, Madison
1975—Madison
1976—Lynchburg
1977—Lynchburg
1978—William & Mary

Far Western Conference

1969—Chico State
1970—Chico State
1971—Chico State
1972—San Francisco State, Chico State
1973—California-Davis, Chico State
1974—Chico State
1975—Hayward State
1976—Hayward State
1977—Chico State
1978—San Francisco State

Carolinas Conference

1973—Guilford
1974—High Point
1975—Guilford
1976—High Point
1977—High Point
1978—Atlantic Christian

Massachusetts State Conference

1972—Westfield State
1973—North Adams State
1974—Westfield State
1975—North Adams State
1976—Westfield State
1977—North Adams State
1978—North Adams State

New Jersey State Conference

1970—Trenton State
1971—Montclair State
1972—Montclair State
1973—Kean
1974—Trenton State
1975—William Paterson
1976—Trenton State
1977—William Paterson
1978—Kean

Pennsylvania Conference

1972—East Stroudsburg
1973—East Stroudsburg
1974—Slippery Rock
1975—Shippensburg
1976—East Stroudsburg

1977—Lock Haven
1978—Lock Haven

Kentucky Conference

1973—Berea
1974—Berea
1975—Morehead State
1976—Asbury
1977—Kentucky
1978—Berea

Presidents Athletic Conference

1970—Bethany
1971—Bethany
1972—Bethany
1973—Bethany
1974—Bethany
1975—Allegheny
1976—Bethany
1977—Bethany
1978—Allegheny

Independent College Athletic Conference

1969—Renssalaer
1970—Rensselaer
1971—Rensselaer
1972—Rensselaer
1973—St. Lawrence
1974—St. Lawrence
1975—St. Lawrence
1976—St. Lawrence
1977—St. Lawrence
1978—Rensselaer

Tennessee Conference

1972—Sewanee
1973—Bryan
1974—Bryan
1975—Bryan
1976—Tenn Wesleyan
1977—Tenn Wesleyan
1978—Tenn Wesleyan

Michigan Intercollegiate Conference

1970—Hope
1971—Calvin
1972—Hope
1973—Calvin
1974—Calvin
1975—Calvin
1976—Calvin
1977—Hope
1978—Calvin

Minnesota Intercollegiate Conference

1970—Gustavus Adolphus
1971—Gustavus Adolphus
1972—Gustavus Adolphus
1973—Augsburg
1974—Augsburg
1975—Augsburg
1976—St. John's
1977—St. Thomas
1978—St. Thomas

West Virginia Conference

1972—Davis & Elkins
1973—Davis & Elkins
1974—Davis & Elkins
1975—Davis & Elkins
1976—Davis & Elkins
1977—Davis & Elkins
1978—Davis & Elkins

Northwest Conference

1972—Washington
1973—Washington
1974—Seattle Pacific
1975—Simon Fraser
1976—Washington
1977—Simon Fraser
1978—Central Washington

Midwest Conference

1971—Beloit
1972—Beloit
1973—Knox
1974—Lake Forest
1975—Lake Forest
1976—Lake Forest
1977—Carleton
1978—Carleton

Southern California Soccer Association

1951—Cal Tech
1952—Cal Tech
1953—Cal Tech
1954—UCLA
1955—Cal Poly
1956—UCLA
1957—Cal Tech
1958—UCLA
1959—UCLA
1960—UCLA
1961—UCLA
1962—Pomona
1963—UCLA
1964—UCLA
1965—Loyola
1966—Southern California
1967—UCLA
1968—UCLA
1969—San Diego State
1970—UCLA
1971—UCLA
1972—Westmont
1973—UCLA
1974—UCLA
1975—Fullerton State

Southern California Athletic Conference

1972—Whittier
1973—Pomona-Pitzer
1974—Claremont-Mudd
1975—Pomona-Pitzer
1976—Pomona-Pitzer
1977—Whittier
1978—Claremont-Mudd

Middle Atlantic States Athletic Conference

1934—Stevens
1935—Swarthmore
1936—Swarthmore
1937—Swarthmore
1938—Haverford
1939—Haverford, Swarthmore
1940—Swarthmore, Stevens
1941—Haverford
1942—Haverford
1943—No champion
1944—No champion
1945—Haverford
1946—Swarthmore
1947—Rutgers, Bucknell
1948—Bucknell
1949—Swarthmore
1950—Haverford
1951—Lehigh
1952—Franklin & Marshall
1953—Haverford
1954—Washington College
1955—Drexel Tech
1956—Drexel Tech
1957—Swarthmore
1958—Drexel Tech
1959—Elizabethtown
1960—Drexel Tech
1961—Drexel Tech
1962—Elizabethtown
1963—Elizabethtown
1964—Elizabethtown
1965—Elizabethtown
1966—Elizabethtown
1967—Elizabethtown
1968—Hofstra
1969—Bucknell
1970—West Chester
1971—Lehigh
1972—St. Joseph's
1973—Temple
1974—Philadelphia Textile
1975—Johns Hopkins
1976—Scranton
1977—Scranton
1978—Scranton

COLLEGE ALL-AMERICANS

The first collegiate All-America squad was chosen by the various team captains of the Intercollegiate Association Football League for the 1909–10 sea-son. For the next eight years, team managers also had a say in the selection process. There were no teams chosen in 1918 and 1919.

From 1920–25, Douglas Stewart, University of Pennsylvania soccer coach and editor of the *Soccer Guide*, selected the All-Americans.

Beginning with the 1926 team, a group of coaches from the newly organized Intercollegiate Soccer Football Association picked the All-Americans. For the years 1936–40, there was no single All-American team; the coaches' selections (limited to the eastern seaboard) covered several districts.

In 1941, William Jeffrey of Penn State and Richard Schmelzer of Rensselaer Poly chose the team. Thereafter the National Soccer Coaches Association of America has had the assignment.

In 1947, Fred Holloway of Cortland State devised a system of balloting by coaches and referees that serves as the basis of player selection.

1909–10

Goal	C. B. Spencer, Columbia
Right fullback	Fenn, Pennsylvania
Left fullback	Cushing, Harvard
Right halfback	Semple, Columbia
Center halfback	Crockett, Pennsylvania
Left halfback	Young, Haverford
Outside right	Leland, Harvard
Inside right	Gay, Yale
Center forward	G. J. Dwyer, Columbia
Inside left	C. E. Dwyer, Columbia
Outside left	Zoller, Columbia

1910–11

Goal	Stevenson, Cornell
Right fullback	Bannon, Harvard
Left fullback	Tann, Yale
Right halfback	Taylor, Haverford
Center halfback	Young, Haverford
Left halfback	Kistler, Columbia
Outside right	Byng, Harvard
Inside right	Gay, Yale
Center forward	G. J. Dwyer, Columbia
Inside left	Mellor, Pennsylvania
Outside left	Bentley, Haverford

1911–12

Goal	Dickinson, Yale
Right fullback	Dickey, Yale
Left fullback	Pennell, Pennsylvania
Right halfback	Davis, Cornell
Center halfback	Hildor, Columbia
Left halfback	Smith, Haverford
Outside right	Bentley, Haverford
Inside right	Jones, Pennsylvania
Center forward	McPhee, Pennsylvania
Inside left	Gay, Yale
Outside left	Byng, Harvard

1912–13

Goal	Nichols, Harvard
Right fullback	Barron, Harvard
Left fullback	Dickey, Yale
Right halfback	McCall, Harvard
Center halfback	Elkinton, Haverford
Left halfback	Davis, Cornell
Outside right	Needham, Harvard
Inside right	Watson, Pennsylvania
Center forward	Shanholt, Columbia
Inside left	Stokes, Haverford
Outside left	Zoller, Columbia

1913–14

Goal	Jackson, Princeton
Right fullback	Shepard, Yale
Left fullback	Webster, Pennsylvania
Right halfback	Franke, Harvard
Center halfback	Elkinton, Harvard
Left halfback	Grant, Harvard
Outside right	Tripp, Yale
Inside right	Bell, Pennsylvania
Center forward	Shanholt, Columbia
Inside left	E. Stokes, Haverford
Outside left	Weld, Harvard

(changed to fall season)
1914

Goal	Hopkins, Pennsylvania
Right fullback	Webster, Pennsylvania
Left fullback	Gates, Princeton
Right halfback	Mohr, Pennsylvania
Center halfback	Lynch, Cornell
Left halfback	Dyer, Cornell
Outside right	Baron, Pennsylvania
Inside right	Jennings, Harvard
Center forward	Shanholt, Columbia
Inside left	Cary, Haverford
Outside left	Weld, Harvard

1915

Goal	Jackson, Princeton
Right fullback	Thomas, Cornell
Left fullback	Moore, Princeton
Right halfback	Hoskins, Princeton
Center halfback	Hirst, Pennsylvania
Left halfback	Mohr, Pennsylvania
Outside right	Stokes, Haverford
Inside right	Gates, Princeton
Center forward	Baron, Pennsylvania
Inside left	Cary, Haverford
Outside left	Weld, Harvard

1916

Goal	Cohu, Princeton
Right fullback	Edwards, Pennsylvania
Left fullback	Shipley, Haverford
Right halfback	Wood, Yale
Center halfback	Hoskins, Princeton
Left halfback	Mohr, Pennsylvania
Outside right	Buzby, Haverford
Inside right	Preyer, Princeton

Center forward	Baron, Pennsylvania
Inside left	Cooke, Harvard
Outside left	Tinsman, Pennsylvania

1917

Goal	Osler, Haverford
Right fullback	Iler, Cornell
Left fullback	Shipley, Haverford
Right halfback	Dibble, Cornell
Center halfback	C. Thorpe, Haverford
Left halfback	Barrie, Haverford
Outside right	E. H. Thorpe, Haverford
Inside right	Spencer, Pennsylvania
Center forward	Nassau, Pennsylvania
Inside left	Corson, Haverford
Outside left	Tinsman, Pennsylvania

1918, 1919
No teams chosen due to World War I

1920

Goal	Cooper, Princeton
Right fullback	Darrow, Pennsylvania
Left fullback	Keyes, Princeton
Right halfback	Hunt, Princeton
Center halfback	Binns, Pennsylvania
Left halfback	Muench, Haverford
Outside right	Bingham, Pennsylvania
Inside right	Spencer, Pennsylvania
Center forward	Stinson, Princeton
Inside left	Coburn, Yale
Outside left	Dowlin, Pennsylvania

1921

Goal	Cooper, Princeton
Right fullback	Patton, Pennsylvania
Left fullback	Futes, Cornell
Right halfback	Muench, Haverford
Center halfback	Smart, Princeton
Left halfback	Thompson, Cornell
Outside right	Righter, Cornell
Inside right	Woodbridge, Princeton
Center forward	Elli, Cornell
Inside left	Thomas, Princeton
Outside left	Jewett, Princeton

1922

Goal	Cooper, Princeton
Right fullback	Beard, Pennsylvania
Left fullback	Sullivan, Harvard
Right halfback	Amelia, Pennsylvania
Center halfback	Smart, Princeton
Left halfback	Thompson, Cornell
Outside right	Righter, Cornell
Inside right	Woodbridge, Princeton
Center forward	Heiser, Harvard
Inside left	Thomas, Princeton
Outside left	McElroy, Pennsylvania

1923

Goal	Anderson, Pennsylvania
Right fullback	Garrett, Haverford

Left fullback	Castle, Pennsylvania
Right halfback	Downs, Pennsylvania
Center halfback	Smart, Princeton
Left halfback	Fisher, Yale
Outside right	Ritchie, Haverford
Inside right	Cooper, Princeton
Center forward	Lingelbach, Pennsylvania
Inside left	Boos, Pennsylvania
Outside left	McLaughlin, Pennsylvania

1924

Goal	Colebrook, Princeton
Right fullback	Evans, Haverford
Left fullback	Garrett, Haverford
Right halfback	Zantzinger, Yale
Center halfback	Downs, Pennsylvania
Left halfback	Pattinson, Harvard
Outside right	Stewart, Pennsylvania
Inside right	Boos, Pennsylvania
Center forward	Lingelbach, Pennsylvania
Inside left	Gentle, Pennsylvania
Outside left	Barnouw, Princeton

1925

Goal	Colebrook, Princeton
Right fullback	Milliken, Yale
Left fullback	Fisher, Princeton
Right halfback	McKinnon, Harvard
Center halfback	Zantzinger, Yale
Left halfback	McDonald, Pennsylvania
Outside right	Barnouw, Princeton
Inside right	Boos, Pennsylvania
Center forward	Saunders, Haverford
Inside left	Gentle, Pennsylvania
Outside left	Driggs, Harvard

1926

Goal	Thomas, Harvard
Right fullback	Lippencott, Penn State
Left fullback	Logan, Haverford
Right halfback	McDonald, Pennsylvania
Center halfback	Nevins, Lehigh
Left halfback	Shu, Cornell
Outside right	Pecori, Penn State
Inside right	Squires, Princeton
Center forward	Saunders, Haverford
Inside left	Packard, Princeton
Outside left	Barnouw, Princeton

1927

Goal	Alsop, Haverford
Right fullback	Lingelbach, Pennsylvania
Left fullback	Crocker, Princeton
Right halfback	Frazier, Haverford
Center halfback	Edgerton, Penn State
Left halfback	Strimlau, Penn State
Outside right	Richardson, Haverford
Inside right	Marshall, Penn State
Center forward	Packard, Princeton
Inside left	Estes, Haverford
Outside left	Stewart, Princeton

1928

Goal	Ruddy, Yale
Right fullback	Lingelbach, Pennsylvania
Left fullback	Johnson, Swarthmore
Right halfback	Frazier, Haverford
Center halfback	Sexton, Princeton
Left halfback	Coles, Swarthmore
Outside right	Smith, Yale
Inside right	Bullard, Lehigh
Center forward	Rudy, Swarthmore
Inside left	Marshall, Penn State
Outside left	Olditch, Cornell

1929

Goal	McCune, Penn State
Right fullback	Johnson, Swarthmore
Left fullback	Allen, Penn State
Right halfback	Frazier, Haverford
Center halfback	Robertson, Yale
Left halfback	Shirk, Haverford
Outside right	Lutz, Penn State
Inside right	Bright, Williams
Center forward	Stollmayer, Dartmouth
Inside left	Ashley, Yale
Outside left	Kullman, Pennsylvania

1930

Goal	Funde, Harvard
Right fullback	Hutchinson, Navy
Left fullback	Whiteclans, Yale
Right halfback	Bond, Swarthmore
Center halfback	Bland, Harvard
Left halfback	Donovan, Cornell
Outside right	Kullman, Pennsylvania
Inside right	Brownback, Pennsylvania
Center forward	Anderson, Pennsylvania
Inside left	Freeman, Yale
Outside left	Anderson, Penn State

1931

Goal	McCune, Penn State
Right fullback	Stetson, Swarthmore
Left fullback	Byers, Lehigh
Right halfback	Williams, Lehigh
Center halfback	Daykiu, Penn State
Left halfback	Corry, Navy
Outside right	Anderson, Pennsylvania
Inside right	Cochrane, Princeton
Center forward	Rudy, Swarthmore
Inside left	Longacre, Haverford
Outside left	Kullman, Pennsylvania

1932

Goal	Zinti, Haverford
Right fullback	Black, Syracuse
Left fullback	Parker, Springfield
Right halfback	Bermijillo, Cornell
Center halfback	Daykiu, Penn State
Left halfback	Evans, Penn State
Outside right	Robertson, Springfield
Inside right	Jordan, Yale
Center forward	McEwan, Syracuse
Inside left	Hendrickson, Pennsylvania
Outside left	Troth, Princeton

1933

Goal	Bell, Penn State
Right fullback	Black, Syracuse
Left fullback	Graham, Penn State
Right halfback	Strzepack, Illinois
Center halfback	Fletcher, Penn State
Left halfback	Reilly, Pennsylvania
Outside right	Ritchie, Haverford
Inside right	Finzel, Penn State
Center forward	Roberts, Springfield
Inside left	Bielicki, Penn State
Outside left	Gonzalez, Pennsylvania

1934

Goal	Bell, Penn State
Right fullback	Rees, Springfield
Left fullback	Graham, Penn State
Right halfback	Sutliff, Penn State
Center halfback	Bermijillo, Cornell
Left halfback	Oolsner, Princeton
Outside right	Faust, Pennsylvania
Inside right	Brown, Haverford
Center forward	McEwan, Penn State
Inside left	Bielicki, Penn State
Outside left	Sanderson, Navy

1935

Goal	Stewart, Pennsylvania
Right fullback	Ward, Yale
Left fullback	Robie, Harvard
Right halfback	Dorman, Harvard
Center halfback	Carson, Pennsylvania
Left halfback	Pearson, Swarthmore
Outside right	Coerr, Yale
Inside right	Pond, Yale
Center forward	Scott, Pennsylvania
Inside left	Hollowell, Swarthmore
Outside left	Wood, Harvard

1936
Middle Atlantic District

Goal	Follansbee, Princeton
Right fullback	Beck, Swarthmore
Left fullback	Forbes, Pennsylvania
Right halfback	Seely, Haverford
Center halfback	Pearson, Swarthmore
Left halfback	Lucard, Lehigh
Outside right	Hershey, Cornell
Inside right	Hallowell, Swarthmore
Center forward	Davison, Princeton
Inside left	Morgan, Princeton
Outside left	Sanderson, Navy

New England District

Goal	Corn, Brown
Right fullback	Kay, Springfield
Left fullback	Powell, Harvard
Right halfback	Henry, Brown
Center halfback	Spahr, Springfield
Left halfback	Church, Brown
Outside right	Badger, Yale
Inside right	Schoupel, Amherst
Center forward	Margeson, Brown

Inside left	Lasell, Yale
Outside left	Wood, Harvard

1937
Middle Atlantic District

Goal	Brunhouse, Swarthmore
Right fullback	Johnson, Princeton
Left fullback	Whittier, Haverford
Right halfback	Faust, Pennsylvania
Center halfback	Fletcher, Princeton
Left halfback	Evans, Haverford
Outside right	Darling, Cornell
Inside right	Sylvester, Princeton
Center forward	White, Swarthmore
Inside left	Taylor, Haverford
Outside left	Richardson, Princeton

New England District

Goal	Beiber, Springfield
Right fullback	Deardon, Brown
Left fullback	Raleigh, Yale
Right halfback	Jacobson, Harvard
Center halfback	Jackson, Brown
Left halfback	Keefe, Yale
Outside right	Johanson, Harvard
Inside right	Carter, Yale
Center forward	Munro, Springfield
Inside left	Motley, Harvard
Outside left	Mayer, Springfield

1938
Middle Atlantic District

Goal	Decker, Pennsylvania
Right fullback	Johnson, Princeton
Left fullback	Lewis, Haverford
Right halfback	Watts, Princeton
Center halfback	Faust, Pennsylvania
Left halfback	Evans, Haverford
Outside right	Crosby, Cornell
Inside right	W. Evans, Haverford
Center forward	Mears, Haverford
Inside left	White, Swarthmore
Outside left	Richardson, Princeton

New England District

Goal	Williams, Harvard
Right fullback	Hunt, Amherst
Left fullback	Hardenbaugh, Harvard
Right halfback	Dickinson, Yale
Center halfback	Jacobson, Harvard
Left halfback	Fox, Williams
Outside right	Johnson, Harvard
Inside right	Gray, Springfield
Center forward	McEwen, Worcester Tech
Inside left	Herguth, MIT
Outside left	Mendel, Harvard

1939
Middle Atlantic District

Goal	Robertson, Princeton
Right fullback	McDonald, Pennsylvania
Left fullback	Perry, Cornell
Right halfback	Hostermann, Penn State

Center halfback .... Watts, Princeton
Left halfback .... Russell, Princeton
Outside right .... Hunter, Pennsylvania
Inside right .... Nemchik, Temple
Center forward .... Powell, Princeton
Inside left .... Crothers, Swarthmore
Outside left .... Richardson, Princeton

New England District

Goal .... Coote, Wesleyan
Right fullback .... Gidney, Dartmouth
Left fullback .... Roberts, Springfield
Right halfback .... Babb, Springfield
Center halfback .... Bijur, Brown
Left halfback .... Fox, Williams
Outside right .... Page, Harvard
Inside right .... Gray, Springfield
Center forward .... Munro, Springfield
Inside left .... Erickson, Yale
Outside left .... Mendel, Harvard

Southern District

Goal .... Refo, Navy
Right fullback .... Partridge, Navy
Left fullback .... Grenough, Virginia
Right halfback .... Galbreath, Western Maryland
Center halfback .... Harnsberger, Davidson
Left halfback .... Hart, Towson
Outside right .... Shock, Towson
Inside right .... Briggs, Johns Hopkins
Center forward .... Asan, Duke
Inside left .... Parker, Navy
Outside left .... Ernst, Maryland

1940

Middle Atlantic District

Goal .... Ochs, Cornell
Right fullback .... Ewing, Princeton
Left fullback .... Roberts, Haverford
Right halfback .... Hosterman, Penn State
Center halfback .... Evans, Haverford
Left halfback .... Partridge, Pennsylvania
Outside right .... Robie, Princeton
Inside right .... Galindo, Penn State
Center forward .... Flaccus, Haverford
Inside left .... Plummer, Princeton
Outside left .... Chamberlain, Princeton

New England District

Goal .... Munroe, Dartmouth
Right fullback .... Ives, Harvard
Left fullback .... Josephson, Wesleyan
Right halfback .... Klaman, Massachusetts State
Center halfback .... Edgar, Harvard
Left halfback .... Carton, Yale
Outside right .... Smith, Dartmouth
Inside right .... Waters, Wesleyan
Center forward .... Freeman, Wesleyan
Inside left .... Gray, Springfield
Outside left .... Haines, Yale

Southern District

Goal .... Maisel, Maryland
Right fullback .... Lewis, High Point

Left fullback .... Shockley, Western Maryland
Right halfback .... Keyes, Virginia
Center halfback .... Reedy, Navy
Left halfback .... Hart, Towson
Outside right .... Farrior, Davidson
Inside right .... Davis, Navy
Center forward .... Ernst, Maryland
Inside left .... Shock, Towson
Outside left .... Tomlinson, Western Maryland

1941

Goal .... Heisler, Amherst
Right fullback .... Jarina, Springfield
Left fullback .... Ports, Maryland
Right halfback .... Cope, Swarthmore
Center halfback .... Guckeyson, Army
Left halfback .... Cummings, Yale
Outside right .... Smith, Dartmouth
Inside right .... Galindo, Penn State
Center forward .... Schmidt, Springfield
Inside left .... King, Penn State
Outside left .... Haines, Yale

1942

Goal .... Brewer, Princeton
Right fullback .... Millet, Yale
Left fullback .... Schubert, RPI
Right halfback .... Hartman, Penn State
Center halfback .... Palmer, Princeton
Left halfback .... Cummings, Yale
Outside right .... Lonbana, Penn State
Inside right .... Lorenz, Temple
Center forward .... Hritz, Temple
Inside left .... Gifford, Army
Outside left .... Chamberlain, Princeton

1943

Goal .... Gorsline, Navy
Right fullback .... Jarina, Rensselaer Poly
Left fullback .... Reeves, Navy
Right halfback .... Lilley, Rensselaer Poly
Center halfback .... Chaires, Navy
Left halfback .... Palmer, Rennselaer Poly
Outside right .... J. Lonbana, Penn State
Inside right .... Hritz, Pennsylvania
Center forward .... Calisto, Navy
Inside left .... Sciolla, Army
Outside left .... F. Teran, Rensselaer Poly

1944

Goal .... Graebner, Penn State
Right fullback .... McDonough, Cornell
Left fullback .... Reaves, Navy
Right halfback .... Cobb, Army
Center halfback .... Bahr, Temple
Left halfback .... Van Ingon, Dartmouth
Outside right .... Abbath, Yale
Inside right .... Kirk, Navy
Center forward .... Calisto, Navy
Inside left .... Townsend, Pennsylvania
Outside left .... Roberts, Dartmouth

1945

Goal	Tyree, Army
Right fullback	Crowley, Army
Left fullback	Barlow, Temple
Right halfback	Clayton, Haverford
Center halfback	Benedict, Army
Left halfback	Hamilton, Penn State
Outside right	Matlack, Penn State
Inside right	Ketchum, Pennsylvania
Center forward	A. Calisto, Navy
Inside left	Brice, Yale
Outside left	Ruggieri, Navy

1946

Goal	Tyree, Army
Right fullback	Fancher, Dartmouth
Left fullback	Barlow, Temple
Right halfback	Hartman, Penn State
Center halfback	Van Breda Kolff, Princeton
Left halfback	Laverson, Temple
Outside right	Molnar, Lehigh
Inside right	Hamilton, Penn State
Center forward	Jones, Haverford
Inside left	McLaughlin, Temple
Outside left	Blair, Pennsylvania

1947

Goal	Schaufelberger, Navy
Right fullback	Pederson, Swarthmore
Left fullback	Lambert, Temple
Right halfback	Coulter, Navy
Center halfback	Hogan, Springfield
Left halfback	Peard, Navy
Outside right	Whatford, Brockport
Inside right	Hughes, Temple
Center forward	Jones, Haverford
Inside left	Valtin, Swarthmore
Outside left	Rogers, Princeton

1948

Goal	Bondi, Brockport
Right fullback	Moutinho, Springfield
Left fullback	Lambert, Temple
Right halfback	Brown, Cortland
Center halfback	Hosterman, Penn State
Left halfback	Lucine, Haverford
Outside right	Fetteroff, Connecticut
Inside right	Berman, Cornell
Center forward	Stolzfus, Amherst
Inside left	Belt, Maryland
Outside left	Baldwin, Connecticut

1949

Goal	Theodore Bondi, Brockport
Right fullback	James Blozie, Connecticut
Left fullback	Stephan Negoesco, San Francisco
Right halfback	Donald Dunbar, Amherst
Center halfback	Gerald Mahrer, Brooklyn
Left halfback	Donald Thompson, Brockport
Outside right	Godfrey Nelson, Trinity
Inside right	Harry Little, Penn State
Center forward	Clement Grillo, Brooklyn
Inside left	Walter Lownes, Pennsylvania
Outside left	Louis Dollarton, West Chester

1950

Goal	Theodore Bondi, Brockport
Right fullback	Richard Mothorpe, Brockport
Left fullback	Jackson Hall, Dartmouth
Right halfback	James Hannah, Seton Hall
Center halfback	William Sheppell, Seton Hall
Left halfback	Ralph Stern, West Chester
Outside right	George Andreadis, Brooklyn
Inside right	Harry Little, Penn State
Center forward	Derl Derr, Cornell
Inside left	Gustavo Gomez, Rensselaer
Outside left	Louis Dollarton, West Chester

1951

Goal	Richard Miller, Oberlin
Right fullback	Thomas Morrell, Indiana
Left fullback	Jacques Auguste, Rensselaer
Right halfback	James Hannah, Seton Hall
Center halfback	Robert Palmer, Oberlin
Left halfback	Eugene Orbaker, Brockport
Outside right	Thomas Kennan, Earlham
Inside right	George Place, Swarthmore
Center forward	George Boateng, Cornell
Inside left	Peter Bellows, Oberlin
Outside left	Anthony Puglisi, West Chester

1952

Goal	Will Ferguson, Kenyan
Right fullback	Charles Ufford, Harvard
Left fullback	Jackson Hall, Dartmouth
Right halfback	Joseph Marshall, Springfield
Center halfback	Joseph Moulder, Oberlin
Left halfback	Charles Butt, Springfield
Outside right	Carl Yoder, Franklin & Marshall
Inside right	Jack Dunn, Temple
Center forward	Joseph Devaney, Pennsylvania
Inside left	David Strauch, Duke
Outside left	Anthony Puglisi, West Chester

1953

Goal	William Cox, San Francisco
Right fullback	Jay Gernand, Springfield
Left fullback	Fred Gahres, East Stroudsburg
Right halfback	Vincent Palmieri, Cortland State
Center halfback	Fred James, Duke
Left halfback	Leonard Oliver, Temple
Outside right	Manuel Ortiz, San Francisco
Inside right	Henry Ford, Wesleyan
Center forward	Winfield Carlough, Trinity
Inside left	Neil Mutschler, Trinity
Outside left	Gabor Czako, Pennsylvania

1954

Goal	Bruce Newell, Navy
Right fullback	Robert Siemons, Allegheny
Left fullback	Hector J. Riquezes, Duke
Right halfback	Vincent Palmieri, Cortland State
Center halfback	Norman Thoms, Oberlin
Left halfback	Leonard Oliver, Temple
Outside right	Paul Clark, Wheaton
Inside right	Jack Dunn, Temple
Center forward	Richard Packer, Penn State
Inside left	Francis Adams, Army
Outside left	John Pinezich, Penn State

1955

Goal	James Davins, Bridgeport
Right fullback	Carlos Ossio, California
Left fullback	Robert Simpson, Temple
Right halfback	Dale Conly, Oberlin
Center halfback	Sergio Ray, West Chester
Left halfback	John Hicks, Indiana
Outside right	Richard Malinowski, Baltimore
Inside right	Oleh Karawan, Illinois-Chicago
Center forward	Richard Packer, Penn State
Inside left	David Arnold, Wheaton
Outside left	E. C. Kirk Hall, Amherst

1956

Goal	Michael Easterling, Wheaton
Right fullback	Paul Coward, Purdue
Left fullback	William Hughes, Brockport
Right halfback	Thomas Colmey, Duke
Center halfback	Henry Litchfuss, Towson State
Left halfback	Raymond Wilson, West Chester
Outside right	Kenneth Lindfors, Oberlin
Inside right	Michael Cooke, Yale
Center forward	Douglas Raynard, Trinity
Inside left	Anthony Washofsky, Drexel Tech
Outside left	Oswald Jethon, Drexel Tech

1957

Goal	Michael Easterling, Wheaton
Right fullback	John Nelson, Cornell
Left fullback	Paul Coward, Purdue
Right halfback	Daniel Sullivan, Springfield
Center halfback	John Paranos, CCNY
Left halfback	Newlin Otto, Earlham
Outside right	Gerald Husted, Franklin and Marshall
Inside right	Per Torgenson, Penn State
Center forward	Telahun Bekele, Purdue
Inside left	Thomas Fleck, West Chester
Outside left	Sergei Retivov, Swarthmore

1958

Goal	Richard Williams, Pennsylvania
Right fullback	John Jennings, Washington College
Left fullback	Remo Tabello, UCLA
Right halfback	Mohamad Ganie, UCLA
Center halfback	John Meehan, Navy
Left halfback	Newlin Otto, Earlham
Outside right	Edward Lopresto, UCLA
Inside right	Alberto Sarria, Michigan State
Center forward	Stanley Dlugosz, Drexel Tech
Inside left	Oswald Jethon, Drexel Tech
Outside left	Theodore Zornow, Rochester

1959

Goal	John Santos, Fairleigh-Dickinson
Right fullback	James Gallo, Temple
Left fullback	Bohdan Huryn, Fenn
Right halfback	Peter Hezekiah, Howard
Center halfback	John Dueker, St. Louis
Left halfback	Joseph Cosgrove, Baltimore
Outside right	James Taylor, Colgate
Inside right	Walter Chyzowych, Temple
Center forward	Cecil Heron, Michigan State
Inside left	Erich Streder, Michigan State
Outside left	Adam Pintz, Fenn

1960

Goal	George Politz, Baltimore
Right fullback	Hal Taylor, Haverford
Left fullback	Barry Remley, West Chester
Right halfback	Gyula Kovacsics, Haverford
Center halfback	William Heyen, Brockport State
Left halfback	Tom Scanlon, LaSalle
Outside right	Chris Sweeney, Cortland State
Inside right	Igor Lissy, Drexel Tech
Center forward	Walt Schmidt, Rutgers
Inside left	William Charlton, Temple
Outside left	Jim Taylor, Colgate

1961

Goal	Andre Houtkruyer, City College of New York
Right fullback	Helmut Poje, Brooklyn
Left fullback	Gerald Li, San Francisco State
Right halfback	Neil Fagan, Navy
Center halfback	Reiner Kemeling, Michigan State
Left halfback	Harry Shirk, East Stroudsburg
Outside right	Alvord Rutherford, Williams
Inside right	Magid Kria, Washongton
Center forward	Donald Williams, West Chester
Inside left	Robert Malone, St. Louis
Outside left	Kun Choo, California

1962

Goal	Dave Smoyer, Dartmouth
Right fullback	Paul Fardy, Cortland State
Left fullback	Louis Buck, Pennsylvania
Right halfback	Fritz Kungle, Akron
Center halfback	Reiner Kemeling, Michigan State
Left halfback	Bill Vieth, St. Louis
Outside right	Gerry Balassi, St. Louis
Inside right	Karl Kaeser, Navy
Center forward	Don Williams, West Chester
Inside left	Rubens Filizola, Michigan State
Outside left	Keith Van Winkle, Middlebury

1963

Goal	Roger Curylo, Bridgeport
Right fullback	Thomas Hennessey, St. Louis
Left fullback	Helmut Poje, Brooklyn
Right halfback	Michael Lonergan, Fairleigh-Dickinson
Center halfback	Anthony Martelli, Hartwick
Left halfback	Myron Hura, Navy
Outside right	Christian Ohiri, Harvard
Inside right	Walter Schmotolocha, Pratt
Center forward	Winson Alexis, Howard
Inside left	Al Hershey, Elizabethtown
Outside left	Keith Van Winkle, Middlebury

1964

Goal	Timothy Tarpley, California
Right fullback	J. Davis Webb, Middlebury
Left fullback	Lee Cook, Trenton State
Right halfback	Daniel Goldstein, Fairleigh-Dickinson
Center halfback	Don Ceresia, St. Louis
Left halfback	Roy Eales, Maryland
Outside right	Giedris Klivecka, Long Island
Inside right	Pat McBride, St. Louis
Center forward	Albert Korbus, San Jose State
Inside left	Myron Hura, Navy
Outside left	Payton Fuller, Michigan State

1965

Goal	Timothy Tarpley, California
Right fullback	Peter Prozik, Buffalo State
Left fullback	Lee Cook, Trenton State
Right halfback	John Eastman, Ohio
Center halfback	Nick Krat, Michigan State
Left halfback	Steve Varsa, Catholic
Outside right	Carl Gentile, St. Louis
Inside right	Lewis Fraser, San Jose State
Center forward	Guy Bush, Michigan State
Inside left	Pat McBride, St. Louis
Outside left	Janos Benedek, Ithaca

1966

Goal	John Garrison, Middlebury
Right fullback	Reinhold Jabusch, Long Island
Left fullback	Ulick Bourke, Catholic U
Right halfback	Myron Bakun, Newark
Center halfback	John Boles, Temple
Left halfback	Peter Hens, Michigan State
Outside right	Jack Kinealy, St. Louis
Inside right	Donald Prozik, Brockport State
Center forward	Jaffer Kassamali, Amherst
Inside left	Umit Kesim, Indiana
Outside left	Victor DeJong, Brown

1967

Goal	Ford Brunner, Akron
Right fullback	John Marks, Middlebury
Left fullback	Tom Teach, Navy
Right halfback	Ron McEachen, West Virginia
Center halfback	Patrick Migliore, Brown
Left halfback	Jacob Meehl, Temple
Outside right	Henry Camacho, San Jose
Inside right	Sandor Hites, San Francisco
Center forward	Walter Werner, St. Louis
Inside left	Kirk Apostolidis, San Francisco
Outside left	Trevor Harris, Michigan State

1968

Goal	Mario Jelencovich, Maryland
Right fullback	Bob Peffle, Temple
Left fullback	Tom Williams, Brockport State
Right halfback	Torgier Hague, San Francisco
Center halfback	Giancarlo Brandoni, Maryland
Left halfback	William Smythe, Davis & Elkins
Outside right	Fred Nourzad, San Jose State
Inside right	Tony Keyes, Michigan State
Center forward	Trevor Harris, Michigan State
Inside left	Rilda Ferreira, Davis & Elkins
Outside left	Manuel Hernandez, San Jose State

1969

Goal	Bruce Parkhill, Lock Haven
Right fullback	Don Fowler, Trenton State
Left fullback	Karim Yassim, Elizabethtown
Right halfback	Len Renery, Columbia
Center halfback	Peter Goosens, San Diego State
Left halfback	Tony Elia, Hartwick
Outside right	Abdula Jama, New York U
Inside right	Alec Papadakis, Hartwick

Center forward	Bob Durham, Philadelphia Textile
Inside left	Rasim Tugberk, Maryland
Outside left	Manuel Hernandez, San Jose State

1970

Goal	William Nuttal, Davis & Elkins
Back	Art Demling, Michigan State
Back	Alan Harte, Quincy
Back	Nick Iwanik, Chicago
Back	Gerardo Pagnani, Eastern Illinois
Back	Aladin Rodrigues, San Jose State
Forward	Al Trost, St. Louis
Forward	Stanley Startzell, Pennsylvania
Forward	Alvin Henderson, Howard
Forward	Richard Parkinson, Akron
Forward	Randy Smith, Buffalo State

1971

Goal	Cal Kern, Buffalo State
Back	Gerardo Pagnani, Eastern Illinois
Back	Al Harte, Quincy
Back	William Smyth, Davis & Elkins
Back	Andy Smiles, Ohio
Back	John Schneider, Quincy
Forward	Keith Aqui, Howard
Forward	Alvin Henderson, Howard
Forward	Richard Parkinson, Akron
Forward	John Moore, Brockport State
Forward	Mike Seerey, St. Louis

1972

Goal	Robert Rigby, East Stroudsburg
Back	Alan Harte, Quincy
Back	Gerardo Pagnani, Eastern Illinois
Back	Hans Wango, Daivs & Elkins
Back	Gordon Cholmondeley, Philadelphia Textile
Back	Chris Bahr, Penn State
Forward	Ian Bain, Howard
Forward	Andre Rymarczuk, Penn State
Forward	Chris Papagianis, Harvard
Forward	Eugene Durham, Philadelphia Textile
Forward	Tom Kazembe, Wooster

1973

Goal	Frank Tusinski, Missouri-St. Louis
Back	David D'Errico, Hartwick
Back	Farrukh Quraishi, Oneonta State
Back	Kip Jordan, Cornell
Back	Kevin Missey, Missouri-St. Louis
Back	Ferdinand Treusacher, Brown
Forward	Chris Bahr, Penn State
Forward	Stephan Baumann, Pennsylvania
Forward	Henry Abadi, Clemson
Forward	Dale Russell, Philadelphia Textile
Forward	Tom Kazembe, Wooster

1974

Goal	Peter Mannos, Northern Illinois
Back	Bruce Hudson, St. Louis
Back	Farrukh Quraishi, Oneonta State
Back	Jesse Cox, Loyola (Md)

Back	John Nusum, Philadelphia Textile
Back	Mickey Rooney, Keene State
Forward	Chris Bahr, Penn State
Forward	Dale Russell, Philadelphia Textile
Forward	Fred Pereira, Brown
Forward	Tom Kazembe, Wooster
Forward	Frantz Innocent, Connecticut

1975

Goal	Peter Mannos, Northern Illinois
Back	Dale Roth, Baltimore
Back	Sam Bick, Quincy
Back	Nimrod Dreyfus, Adelphi
Back	Greg Makowski, Southern Illinois-Edwardsville
Back	John Nusum, Philadelphia Textile
Forward	Steve Ralbovsky, Brown
Forward	Dale Russell, Philadelphia Textile
Forward	Carlos Merchan, Fairleigh Dickinson
Forward	Elson Seale, Philadelphia Textile
Forward	George Nanchoff, Akron

1976

Goal	Dragan Radovich, St. Francis (NY)
Back	Greg Makowski, Southern Illinois-Edwardsville
Back	George Gorleku, Eastern Illinois
Back	Paul Hunter, Connecticut
Back	Carl Christensen, Vermont
Back	Glenn Myernick, Hartwick
Forward	George Nanchoff, Akron
Forward	Louis Nanchoff, Akron
Forward	Ty Keough, St. Louis
Forward	Andy Atuegbu, San Francisco
Forward	Fred Pereira, Brown

1977

Goal	Dragan Radovich, St. Francis (NY)
Back	Greg Makowski, Southern Illinois-Edwardsville
Back	John Nusum, Philadelphia Textile
Back	Adrian Brooks, Philadelphia Textile
Back	Herve Guilloid, Fredonia State
Back	Bill Gazonas, Hartwick
Forward	Angelo DiBernardo, Indiana
Forward	Emilio John, Quincy
Forward	Paul Milone, Princeton
Forward	John Maciel, Western Illinois
Forward	Rick Reice, Penn State

1978

Goal	Dragan Radovich, St. Francis (NY)
Back	George Gorleku, Eastern Illinois
Back	Adrian Brooks, Philadelphia Textile
Back	Greg Ryan, Southern Methodist
Back	Ty Keough, St. Louis
Back	Barry Nix, Columbia
Forward	Raymond Ford, Maryland-Baltimore College
Forward	George Lesyw, Temple
Forward	Peter Notaro, Loyola (Md)
Forward	James Stamatis, Penn State
Forward	Ole Mikkelsen, UCLA

COLLEGE PLAYERS OF THE YEAR (HERMANN AWARD)

1967–Dov Markus, Long Island University
1968–Manuel Hernandez, San Jose State
1969–Al Trost, St. Louis
1970–Al Trost, St. Louis
1971–Mike Seerey, St. Louis
1972–Mike Seerey, St. Louis
1973–Don Counce, St. Louis
1974–Farrukh Quraishi, Oneonta State
1975–Steve Ralbovsky, Brown
1976–Glenn Myernick, Hartwick
1977–Billy Gazonas, Hartwick
1978–Angelo DiBernardo, Indiana

NATIONAL JUNIOR COLLEGE ATHLETIC ASSOCIATION

The National Junior College Athletic Association, founded in 1937 with the intention of promoting and supervising a national program of junior college sports, held its first Invitational Soccer Tournament in Middletown, New York, in 1961.

The year following that first national tournament, which was won by Dean Junior College of Franklin, Massachusetts, the NJCAA initiated its all-American teams.

In the years since its inception through 1978, the tournament has been won by Florissant Valley Community College of St. Louis a record five times, including three times in a row from 1969–71.

George Killian is the Executive Director of the NJCAA.

NJCAA Champions
1961–Dean Junior College
1962–Mitchell College
1963–Trenton Junior College
1964–Mitchell College
1965–Monroe Community College
1966–Nassau Community College
1967–Florissant Valley Community College
1968–Mercer County Community College
1969–Florissant Valley Community College
1970–Florissant Valley Community College
1971–Florissant Valley Community College
1972–Meramec Community College
1973–Florissant Valley Community College
1974–Essex Community College
1975–Florissant Valley Community College
1976–St. Louis Community College at Meramec
1977–Ulster County Community College
1978–Ulster County Community College

Air Force's John Zimmerman battles a San Francisco player during the Falcons' 8–2–2 season in 1973.

COLLEGE YEAR-BY-YEAR RECORDS AND COACHES

The following year-by-year records were supplied by the universities and colleges. A variety of circumstances accounts for any omission in a given year. World War I and II, for example, forced some schools to cancel their schedules. In some instances, records were destroyed by fire or otherwise lost to the historians. In other cases, schools suspended intercollegiate competition. Records for schools that were at one time junior or women's colleges are listed only from the dates when they became four-year, male, or coeducational institutions. Colleges that are not listed failed to respond.

AIR FORCE (USAFA)

Air Force Academy, Colorado

Falcons

Silver and Blue

Yr.	W	L	T	Coach
1956	5	1	3	Lt. Anthony Biernacki
1957	8	0	2	Arne Arnesen
1958	7	2	1	Arne Arnesen
1959	6	2	0	Arne Arnesen
1960	4	4	2	Arne Arnesen
1961	6	1	2	Arne Arnesen
1962	7	3	0	Capt. Bob Strickland
1963	4	6	1	Capt. Bob Strickland
1964	7	2	1	Capt. Carmen Annillo
1965	6	5	0	Capt. Carmen Annillo
1966	4	5	1	Capt. Carmen Annillo
1967	4	6	0	Capt. J. Loewenberg
1968	10	3	0	Capt. Hank Eichin
1969	11	3	1	Capt. Hank Eichin
1970	9	6	0	Capt. Hank Eichin
1971	9	8	0	Capt. Hank Eichin

Yr.	W	L	T	Coach
1972	7	4	1	Capt. Hank Eichin
1973	8	2	2	Capt. Hank Eichin
1974	4	5	2	Capt. Jim Thames
1975	9	5	0	Capt. Jim Thames
1976	8	5	0	Capt. Rob Judas
1977	8	4	2	Capt. Rob Judas
1978	7	8	1	Capt. Dan Ulmer

AKRON, UNIVERSITY OF

Akron, Ohio

Zips   **Blue and Gold**

Yr.	W	L	T	Coach
1955	2	4	1	Stu Parry
1956	5	2	1	Stu Parry
1957	3	3	1	Stu Parry
1958	9	1	0	Stu Parry
1959	8	2	0	Stu Parry
1960	10	1	0	Stu Parry
1961	12	2	0	Stu Parry
1962	5	4	1	Stu Parry
1963	10	3	0	Stu Parry
1964	9	3	0	Stu Parry
1965	4	7	0	Stu Parry
1966	10	3	0	Stu Parry
1967	12	3	0	Stu Parry
1968	11	1	0	Stu Parry
1969	8	4	0	Stu Parry
1970	8	5	1	Bill Killen
1971	9	3	3	Bill Killen
1972	9	3	2	Bill Killen
1973	6	5	1	Bill Killen

Yr.	W	L	T	Coach
1974	6	5	1	Robert Dowdy
1975	11	2	1	Robert Dowdy
1976	8	5	0	Robert Dowdy
1977	8	5	0	Robert Dowdy
1978	8	5	0	Robert Dowdy

ALABAMA A & M UNIVERSITY

Normal, Alabama

Bulldogs   **Maroon and White**

Yr.	W	L	T	Coach
1977	19	1	0	Salah Yousif
1978	19	2	1	Salah Yousif

ALBANY STATE UNIVERSITY

Albany, New York

Great Danes   **Purple and Gold**

Yr.	W	L	T	Coach
1950	5	2	0	Joe Garcia
1951	3	4	1	Joe Garcia
1952	6	4	0	Joe Garcia
1953	8	2	0	Joe Garcia
1954	5	3	2	Joe Garcia
1955	2	7	2	Joe Garcia
1956	6	3	0	Joe Garcia
1957	2	7	0	Joe Garcia
1958	5	5	0	Joe Garcia
1959	4	6	0	Joe Garcia
1960	4	4	2	Joe Garcia
1961	8	2	0	Joe Garcia

Stu Parry (right), the first and foremost coach in Akron history with 118 wins in 15 years, confers with 1962 players Frank Abel (left) and Fritz Kungl.

Yr.	W	L	T	Coach
1962	4	6	0	Joe Garcia
1963	3	7	0	Joe Garcia
1964	4	5	1	Joe Garcia
1965	4	6	0	Joe Garcia
1966	5	4	1	Joe Garcia
1967	3	7	0	Joe Garcia
1968	3	6	1	Bill Schieffelin
1969	1	7	3	Bill Schieffelin
1970	3	8	1	Bill Schieffelin
1971	2	9	0	Bill Schieffelin
1972	1	10	1	Bill Schieffelin
1973	8	5	1	Bill Schieffelin
1974	7	5	1	Bill Schieffelin
1975	9	4	1	Bill Schieffelin
1976	8	5	1	Bill Schieffelin
1977	8	5	0	Bill Schieffelin
1978	8	6	2	Bill Schieffelin

ALBION COLLEGE

Albion, Michigan

Britons				Purple and Gold
Yr.	W	L	T	Coach
1967	1	7	0	Bruce Brown
1968	6	3	1	Bruce Brown
1969	8	3	0	Tom Balistrere
1970	5	6	1	Mike Turner
1971	7	3	1	Mike Turner
1972	6	6	0	Mike Turner
1973	7	3	2	Mike Turner
1974	1	9	2	Damon Huffman
1975	8	5	2	Jim Francis
1976	7	8	0	Geoffrey Cocks
1977	4	10	1	Geoffrey Cocks
1978	3	11	1	Geoffrey Cocks

ALBRIGHT COLLEGE

Reading, Pennsylvania

Lions				Cardinal and White
Yr.	W	L	T	Coach
1977	1	8	0	Robert D. Boucher
1978	1	6	2	Robert D. Boucher

ALDERSON-BROADDUS COLLEGE

Philippi, West Virginia

Battlers				Blue and Gold
Yr.	W	L	T	Coach
1965	1	4	1	Darrel Saunders
1966	8	3	0	Darrel Saunders
1967	12	2	1	Darrel Saunders
1968	10	1	4	Darrel Saunders
1969	11	1	1	Darrel Saunders
1970	14	2	0	Darrel Saunders
1971	6	3	0	Lee Cook
1972	11	2	1	Lee Cook
1973	10	2	3	Jay Hoffman
1974	9	5	0	Jay Hoffman
1975	8	5	0	Steve Parker
1976	9	5	1	Steve Parker
1977	8	6	0	Steve Parker
1978	7	6	1	Bob Gray

ALLEGHENY COLLEGE

Meadville, Pennsylvania

Gators				Blue and Gold
Yr.	W	L	T	Coach
1934	1	4	0	
1935	1	3	1	
1936	2	3	1	
1937	2	5	0	
1938	2	3	1	
1939	2	3	1	
1940	3	3	0	
1941	2	2	1	
1942	3	4	0	
1943	—	—	—	
1944	—	—	—	
1945	1	3	1	
1946	4	5	0	
1947	1	8	0	
1948	1	7	2	
1949	2	7	0	
1950	2	6	0	
1951	3	2	0	
1952	1	4	0	
1953	4	4	0	
1954	2	6	0	
1955	2	5	1	
1956	1	5	1	
1957	1	6	0	
1958	1	6	1	
1959	3	5	0	
1960	1	6	1	
1961	0	7	1	
1962	0	6	1	
1963	5	1	1	
1964	4	2	1	
1965	5	3	0	
1966	2	4	2	
1967	2	5	1	
1968	1	7	0	
1969	4	4	0	
1970	2	6	0	
1971	5	2	1	
1972	1	4	3	
1973	7	2	0	Sam Freas
1974	4	3	1	Sam Freas
1975	6	2	1	Sam Freas
1976	5	3	1	Dave Higgins
1977	7	3	1	Thomas Erdos
1978	10	0	1	Thomas Erdos

ALLENTOWN COLLEGE

Center Valley, Pennsylvania

Centaurs				Red and Blue
Yr.	W	L	T	Coach
1969	3	5	0	Gil Lopez
1970	4	5	0	Charles Garcia
1971	3	7	0	Charles Garcia
1972	2	8	0	Charles Carcia
1973	0	10	1	Charles Garcia
1974	0	10	1	Charles Garcia
1975	0	5	0	Charles Garcia
1976	0	6	0	Gerard Weiss
1977	2	6	2	Jose Perna
1978	5	9	0	Jose Perna

Alderson-Broaddus' Gary White (right) scores the goal that defeated Davis & Elkins in a 1968 battle for the West Virginia Intercollegiate Conference crown.

AMERICAN INTERNATIONAL COLLEGE

Springfield, Massachusetts

Yellowjackets				Gold and White
Yr.	W	L	T	Coach
1934	1	3	0	Fred Sibley
1935	5	3	0	Fred Sibley
1936	2	1	1	Bert Watling
1937	2	4	0	Bert Watling
1938	2	4	0	Bert Watling
1939	6	0	1	Bert Watling
1940	1	2	1	Bob MacIntyre
1941	0	1	1	Bob MacIntyre
1942	—	—	—	—
1943	—	—	—	—
1944	—	—	—	—
1945	1	1	0	Newton Dehaney
1953	2	0	0	Peter Jackson
1954	0	2	0	William Callahan
1955	—	—	—	—
1956	—	—	—	—
1957	—	—	—	—
1958	1	1	0	William Callahan
1959	1	0	0	William Callahan
1960	0	6	0	William Callahan
1961	4	4	0	Dudley Bell
1962	4	3	0	Tony Skolnick
1963	5	3	0	Tony Skolnick
1964	2	7	0	Tony Skolnick
1965	4	5	0	Tony Skolnick
1966	4	7	0	Maurice Suher
1967	7	3	1	Maurice Suher
1968	5	5	0	Maurice Suher
1969	5	5	0	Maurice Suher
1970	2	7	4	Maurice Suher
1971	7	4	1	Maurice Suher
1972	1	9	3	Peter Esdale
1973	3	10	2	Peter Esdale
1974	2	10	3	Alex Schmid
1975	4	9	1	Alex Schmid

Yr.	W	L	T	Coach
1976	4	10	0	Alex Schmid
1977	5	7	2	Alex Schmid
1978	3	11	2	Matt Peck

AMERICAN UNIVERSITY

Washington, DC

Eagles				Red, White, and Blue
Yr.	W	L	T	Coach
1949	0	6	0	G. Roberts, J. Bentley
1950	2	5	0	Gil Roberts
1951	—	—	—	—
1952	—	—	—	—
1953	—	—	—	—
1954	0	4	0	Bob Frailey
1955	0	10	0	Ken Hildreth
1956	1	0	0	Bill Lauritzen
1957	3	7	0	Bill Lauritzen
1958	3	10	1	Bill Lauritzen
1959	5	4	1	Bill Lauritzen
1960	1	7	0	Howard Sorrell
1961	2	7	0	Howard Sorrell
1962	4	4	1	Howard Sorrell
1963	2	6	1	Sal Esposito
1964	5	3	2	Sal Esposito
1965	5	9	2	Mon Gee
1966	4	7	1	Larry Nyce
1967	2	9	2	Larry Nyce
1968	2	12	0	Ned Boehm
1969	5	5	1	Ned Boehm
1970	6	5	1	Dick Stinson
1971	4	5	1	John Kerr
1972	5	5	0	Pete Mehlert
1973	8	3	0	Pete Mehlert
1974	4	5	2	Pete Mehlert
1975	6	3	3	Pete Mehlert
1976	6	5	2	Pete Mehlert
1977	9	8	0	Pete Mehlert
1978	10	5	1	Pete Mehlert

A goalkeeper from American University withstands a Lynchburg assault during a 1957 contest.

AMHERST COLLEGE

Amherst, Massachusetts

Lord Jeffs   **Purple and White**

Yr.	W	L	T	Coach
1920	1	2	1	Eli Marsh
1921	3	4	0	Eli Marsh
1922	3	2	0	Eli Marsh
1923	4	2	1	Eli Marsh
1924	3	3	1	Eli Marsh
1925	2	3	3	Eli Marsh
1926	5	2	0	Eli Marsh
1927	6	0	0	Eli Marsh
1928	3	3	1	Eli Marsh
1929	5	0	1	Eli Marsh
1930	6	0	1	Eli Marsh
1931	1	2	2	Eli Marsh
1932	3	2	2	Eli Marsh
1933	5	1	0	Eli Marsh
1934	6	0	1	Eli Marsh
1935	3	2	1	Eli Marsh
1936	2	4	0	Eli Marsh
1937	5	1	0	Eli Marsh
1938	5	2	0	Eli Marsh
1939	4	1	2	Eli Marsh
1940	4	3	0	Eli Marsh
1941	4	0	3	Eli Marsh

Yr.	W	L	T	Coach
1942	6	0	0	Eli Marsh
1943	—	—	—	—
1944	—	—	—	—
1945	2	1	1	Eli Marsh
1946	4	1	1	Eli Marsh
1947	4	2	1	Eli Marsh
1948	4	2	1	Eli Marsh
1949	6	0	1	Eli Marsh
1950	8	1	0	Eli Marsh
1951	8	1	0	Eli Marsh
1952	3	2	3	Eli Marsh
1953	5	3	0	Eli Marsh
1954	3	4	1	Eli Marsh
1955	6	2	0	Eli Marsh
1956	6	2	0	Eli Marsh
1957	3	1	4	Eli Marsh
1958	6	1	1	Steven Rostas
1959	2	5	1	Steven Rostas
1960	6	0	2	Steven Rostas
1961	4	4	0	Steven Rostas
1962	3	3	1	Steven Rostas
1963	3	5	0	Steven Rostas
1964	2	6	0	Steven Rostas
1965	4	4	0	Steven Rostas
1966	5	1	2	Steven Rostas
1967	5	2	1	Steven Rostas
1968	5	1	1	Peter Gooding
1969	3	4	1	Peter Gooding

154

Yr.	W	L	T	Coach
1970	3	5	0	Peter Gooding
1971	2	5	1	Peter Gooding
1972	5	2	3	Peter Gooding
1973	4	6	0	Peter Gooding
1974	5	4	1	Peter Gooding
1975	7	3	0	Peter Gooding
1976	2	8	0	Peter Gooding
1977	2	7	1	Peter Gooding
1978	4	5	1	Peter Gooding

ARMY (USMA)

West Point, New York

Cadets   **Black, Gold, and Gray**

Yr.	W	L	T	Coach
1921	3	2	1	S. C. MacDonald
1922	6	2	0	H. J. Ratican
1923	4	3	1	H. J. Ratican
1924	5	1	1	Ray Marchand
1925	6	1	1	Ray Marchand
1926	3	2	1	Ray Marchand
1927	6	1	1	Ray Marchand
1928	4	2	2	Ray Marchand
1929	2	3	3	Ray Marchand
1930	6	2	0	Ray Marchand
1931	6	1	0	Ray Marchand
1932	6	2	0	Ray Marchand
1933	5	2	1	Ray Marchand
1934	6	2	0	Ray Marchand
1935	5	1	2	Ray Marchand
1936	6	2	0	Ray Marchand
1937	5	1	2	Ray Marchand
1938	7	2	0	Ray Marchand
1939	1	5	1	Ray Marchand
1940	6	2	0	Ray Marchand
1941	6	1	1	Ray Marchand
1942	3	3	2	Ray Marchand
1943	5	2	0	Col. G. L. Roberson
1944	6	2	0	Col. G. F. McAneny
1945	7	1	1	Col. G. F. McAneny
1946	7	2	4	Col. G. F. McAneny
1947	6	5	3	Joe Palone
1948	8	2	0	Joe Palone
1949	2	5	1	Joe Palone
1950	8	1	0	Joe Palone
1951	9	1	0	Joe Palone
1952	8	1	1	Joe Palone
1953	8	1	1	Joe Palone
1954	5	2	2	Joe Palone
1955	2	8	0	John B. Kress
1956	3	5	2	John B. Kress
1957	4	6	0	John B. Kress
1958	4	1	4	Joe Palone
1959	7	1	2	Joe Palone
1960	8	2	0	Joe Palone
1961	5	5	0	Joe Palone
1962	7	3	1	Joe Palone
1963	12	1	0	Joe Palone
1964	10	3	0	Joe Palone
1965	12	1	1	Joe Palone
1966	10	3	2	Joe Palone
1967	9	4	0	Joe Palone
1968	10	3	1	Joe Palone
1969	7	3	2	Joe Palone
1970	9	3	0	Joe Palone
1971	9	4	0	Joe Palone
1972	8	3	1	Joe Palone

Joe Palone posted a 29-year coaching record of 235–76–31 before retiring as Army coach following the 1978 season.

Yr.	W	L	T	Coach
1973	9	2	3	Joe Palone
1974	7	3	2	Joe Palone
1975	10	3	1	Joe Palone
1976	8	4	1	Joe Palone
1977	9	2	2	Joe Palone
1978	11	4	0	Joe Palone

ASBURY COLLEGE

Wilmore, Kentucky

Eagles   **Navy and White**

Yr.	W	L	T	Coach
1971	8	1	1	Alan Smith
1972	8	5	1	Cecil Zweifel
1973	11	2	0	Cecil Zweifel
1974	12	2	1	Cecil Zweifel
1975	12	3	0	Cecil Zweifel
1976	13	1	1	Cecil Zweifel
1977	14	2	2	Cecil Zweifel
1978	8	8	0	Cecil Zweifel

ATLANTIC CHRISTIAN COLLEGE

Wilson, North Carolina

Bulldogs   **Royal blue and White**

Yr.	W	L	T	Coach
1972	1	10	0	David Adkins
1973	2	11	1	David Adkins
1974	3	8	2	David Adkins
1975	6	7	1	David Adkins
1976	11	5	0	David Adkins
1977	9	4	4	David Adkins
1978	12	4	0	David Adkins

Bob Hartwell, four-time New England Coach of the Year, led Babson to a Division III national title in 1975.

AUSTIN COLLEGE

Sherman, Texas

Kangaroos				Crimson and Gold
Yr.	W	L	T	Coach
1975	6	6	1	Tom Cook
1976	6	4	2	Tom Cook
1977	11	4	1	Tom Cook
1978	7	5	2	Tom Cook

AVERETT COLLEGE

Danville, Virginia

Cougars				Blue and Gold
Yr.	W	L	T	Coach
1974	3	1	2	Gary Bannister
1975	3	5	0	Gary Bannister
1976	0	10	0	Vesa Hiltunen
1977	9	4	2	Vesa Hiltunen
1978	7	6	2	Vesa Hiltunen

AVILA COLLEGE

Kansas City, Missouri

The Avalanche				Blue, Gold and White
Yr.	W	L	T	Coach
1977	10	3	2	Pete Tumminia
1978	17	5	0	Pete Tumminia

AZUSA PACIFIC COLLEGE

Azusa, California

Cougars				Orange and Black
Yr.	W	L	T	Coach
1973	9	6	0	John Culp
1974	10	6	0	Larry Delamarter
1975	9	7	0	Larry Delamarter
1976	6	8	2	Larry Delamarter
1977	9	7	0	Dave Irby
1978	14	5	0	Dave Irby

BABSON COLLEGE

Wellesley, Massachusetts

Beavers				Green and White
Yr.	W	L	T	Coach
1967	3	6	0	Bob Hartwell
1968	6	6	0	Bob Hartwell
1969	11	3	0	Bob Hartwell
1970	5	4	0	Bob Hartwell
1971	9	4	0	Bob Hartwell
1972	13	2	0	Bob Hartwell
1973	15	1	0	Bob Hartwell
1974	11	3	0	Bob Hartwell
1975	17	0	0	Bob Hartwell
1976	11	3	0	Bob Hartwell
1977	17	2	0	Bob Hartwell
1978	13	3	0	Bill Rogers

BALL STATE UNIVERSITY

Muncie, Indiana

Cardinals   **Cardinal and White**

Yr.	W	L	T	Coach
1961	6	0	1	Chris Sweeney
1962	7	2	1	Joe Brownholtz
1963	3	5	1	Charles Fairben
1964	3	5	1	Charles Fairben
1965	5	4	0	Neil Schmottlach
1966	3	5	0	Neil Schmottlach
1967	1	9	1	Neil Schmottlach
1968	1	8	1	Neil Schmottlach
1969	1	8	0	Arno Wittig
1970	1	8	1	Arno Wittig
1971	2	7	1	Jerre McManama
1972	3	6	2	Jerre McManama
1973	5	3	2	Jerre McManama
1974	5	3	2	Jerre McManama
1975	8	2	0	Jerre McManama
1976	8	3	0	Jerre McManama
1977	6	7	0	Jerre McManama
1978	6	3	1	Jerre McManama

BALTIMORE, UNIVERSITY OF

Baltimore, Maryland

Super Bees   **Burgundy and Gold**

Yr.	W	L	T	Coach
1948	5	4	1	Cal Elmer
1949	9	0	1	Cal Elmer
1950	7	1	1	Cal Elmer
1951	8	0	1	Cal Elmer
1952	8	1	1	Cal Elmer
1953	7	3	1	Cal Elmer
1954	9	1	0	Cal Elmer
1955	8	2	2	Cal Elmer
1956	10	1	1	Larry Surock
1957	8	1	1	Larry Surock
1958	10	1	0	Bill Beck
1959	8	2	1	Bill Beck
1960	9	1	1	Bill Beck
1961	9	1	1	Bill Beck
1962	8	3	1	Reece Livingston
1963	11	0	3	Reece Livingston
1964	8	1	1	Reece Livingston
1965	11	2	0	Ron Luette

In its first year of competition in 1961, Ball State posted the only unbeaten record in its history under the tutelage of coach Chris Sweeney (third row, right).

Jim Tonrey of Bates makes his move against conference rival Colby.

Yr.	W	L	T	Coach
1966	6	4	0	Ron Luette
1967	7	5	0	Ron Luette
1968	9	4	0	Ron Luette
1969	9	2	1	Ron Luette
1970	11	1	1	George Politz
1971	8	5	2	George Politz
1972	17	4	0	Dick Edell
1973	17	3	2	Dick Edell
1974	13	2	2	Dick Edell
1975	16	2	1	Dick Edell
1976	10	4	1	Tom Lynn
1977	14	5	0	Tom Lynn
1978	9	5	2	Tom Lynn

BATES COLLEGE

Lewiston, Maine

Bobcats				Maroon and Garnet
Yr.	**W**	**L**	**T**	**Coach**
1962	5	3	0	James Somerville
1963	6	3	1	Roy Sigler
1964	8	1	2	Roy Sigler
1965	5	3	4	George Wigton
1966	10	4	0	George Wigton
1967	10	4	0	George Wigton
1968	6	6	0	George Wigton
1969	5	3	4	George Wigton
1970	4	6	1	George Wigton
1971	2	7	2	George Wigton
1972	3	7	0	George Wigton

Yr.	W	L	T	Coach
1973	2	5	5	Davis Van Winkle
1974	2	7	3	Davis Van Winkle
1975	3	6	1	Davis Van Winkle
1976	3	9	0	Davis Van Winkle
1977	4	5	2	Davis Van Winkle
1978	2	9	1	C. Jeffrey Gettler

BELLARMINE COLLEGE

Louisville, Kentucky

Knights				Scarlet and Gray
Yr.	**W**	**L**	**T**	**Coach**
1972	2	6	0	Nick Zehnder
1973	4	8	3	Nick Zehnder
1974	11	7	0	Doug Foland
1975	9	6	2	Doug Foland
1976	11	4	2	Bill Beattie
1977	7	9	1	Bill Beattie
1978	10	7	2	Bill Beattie

BENEDICTINE COLLEGE

Atchison, Kansas

Ravens				Black, White, and Red
Yr.	**W**	**L**	**T**	**Coach**
1960	1	0	0	Richard Wittman
1961	2	0	0	Richard Wittman

Yr.	W	L	T	Coach
1962	5	2	0	Richard Wittman
1963	7	0	0	Bill Samuels
1964	4	3	0	Thomas Colwell
1965	7	3	0	Thomas Colwell
1966	9	2	0	Thomas Colwell
1967	9	2	0	Thomas Colwell
1968	6	2	2	Thomas Colwell
1969	5	4	0	Terrance Hanson
1970	8	5	0	Terrance Hanson
1971	8	6	0	Terrance Hanson
1972	9	6	0	Terrance Hanson
1973	13	2	0	Terrance Hanson
1974	12	4	0	Terrance Hanson
1975	9	5	1	Tom Judge
1976	9	5	0	Tom Judge
1977	8	9	0	Tom Judge
1978	11	7	0	Tom Judge

BENTLEY COLLEGE

Waltham, Massachusetts

Falcons   **Blue and Gold**

Yr.	W	L	T	Coach
1972	8	3	2	Detlev Suderow
1973	3	5	4	Detlev Suderow
1974	6	4	4	Detlev Suderow
1975	9	5	0	Detlev Suderow
1976	4	7	1	Detlev Suderow

Yr.	W	L	T	Coach
1977	7	3	1	Dwight Scandrett
1978	6	5	3	Dwight Scandrett

BEREA COLLEGE

Berea, Kentucky

Hardtoes   **Blue and White**

Yr.	W	L	T	Coach
1958	5	1	0	O. H. Gunkler
1959	1	1	0	O. H. Gunkler
1960	3	2	2	Fuad. S. Abu-Zayyad
1961	7	1	0	Fuad. S. Abu-Zayyad
1962	5	1	0	Don McNeil
1963	5	2	1	David Broderick
1964	5	1	3	David Broderick
1965	7	3	0	David Broderick
1966	4	4	0	Charles Conley
1967	3	5	0	Charles Conley
1968	3	4	1	Lester Abbott
1969	4	4	0	Ed de Rosset
1970	7	3	1	Charles Conley
1971	7	6	1	Robert Pearson
1972	9	4	1	Robert Pearson
1973	13	1	2	Robert Pearson
1974	15	1	0	Robert Pearson
1975	9	4	3	Robert Pearson
1976	6	8	2	Robert Pearson
1977	10	4	4	Robert Pearson
1978	13	4	1	Robert Pearson

Berea coach Bob Pearson, who led the school to Kentucky Conference titles in 1973 and 1974, addresses his 1977 squad.

BERRY COLLEGE

Mount Berry, Georgia

Viking Fury   Silver and Blue

Yr.	W	L	T	Coach
1962	5	2	0	Edmundo Vargas
1963	—	—	—	Edmundo Vargas
1964	7	1	1	Edmundo Vargas
1965	5	3	1	Bill McAdams
1966	8	1	2	Bill McAdams
1967	2	7	2	Bill McAdams
1968	5	9	0	Garland Dickey
1969	4	5	1	Garland Dickey
1970	4	5	1	August deBerdt
1971	3	6	2	Ed Palmer
1972	6	3	1	Dr. Dickey
1973	10	4	1	Larry Taylor
1974	10	3	2	Fred Mathis
1975	15	1	0	Fred Mathis
1976	12	3	0	Fred Mathis
1977	7	5	0	Robert Warming
1978	12	5	0	Robert Warming

BETHANY COLLEGE

Bethany, West Virginia

Bisons   Green and White

Yr.	W	L	T	Coach
1968	4	4	0	John Cunningham
1969	4	3	1	John Cunningham
1970	5	1	2	John Cunningham
1971	7	2	1	John Cunningham
1972	5	2	2	John Cunningham
1973	7	1	1	John Cunningham
1974	6	3	0	John Cunningham
1975	4	4	1	John Cunningham
1976	7	2	0	John Cunningham
1977	9	1	2	John Cunningham
1978	7	4	1	John Cunningham

BETHANY NAZARENE COLLEGE

Bethany, Oklahoma

Redskins   Cardinal and White

Yr.	W	L	T	Coach
1978	7	8	0	Wes Harmon

BETHEL COLLEGE

St. Paul, Minnesota

Royals   Blue and Gold

Yr.	W	L	T	Coach
1973	5	4	0	Juan Salas
1974	7	5	0	Steve Voth
1975	7	6	0	Steve Voth
1976	8	4	1	Steve Voth
1977	7	4	2	Peter Genheimer
1978	4	6	2	Dick Voth

BIOIA COLLEGE

La Mirada, California

Eagles   Red and White

Yr.	W	L	T	Coach
1962	3	10	0	Edward Norman
1963	3	7	0	Edward Norman
1964	5	5	0	Edward Norman
1965	7	1	2	Edward Norman
1966	7	3	0	Edward Norman
1967	7	6	0	Edward Norman
1968	12	3	0	Edward Norman
1969	10	5	0	Edward Norman
1970	9	6	0	Edward Norman
1971	4	4	0	Edward Norman
1972	9	7	0	Edward Norman
1973	11	4	0	Doug Nixon
1974	5	8	0	Doug Nixon
1975	4	11	0	Tim Conrad
1976	12	7	0	Tim Conrad
1977	5	13	0	Tim Conrad
1978	12	10	0	Tim Conrad

BLACKBURN COLLEGE

Carlinville, Illinois

Beavers   Red and Black

Yr.	W	L	T	Coach
1954	2	0	0	Charles Gray
1955	1	0	0	Charles Gray
1956	2	1	0	Charles Gray
1957	2	1	0	Charles Gray
1958	3	2	0	Charles Gray
1959	2	4	0	Charles Gray
1960	1	6	0	Charles Gray
1961	4	3	0	Charles Gray
1962	3	4	0	Charles Gray
1963	5	3	0	Pete Hughes
1964	5	1	1	P. O. Smith
1965	2	5	1	P. O. Smith
1966	2	5	1	P. O. Smith
1967	0	10	1	William Cooper
1968	7	3	1	Nick Mohacsy
1969	8	5	1	Nick Mohacsy
1970	10	3	1	Nick Mohacsy
1971	10	1	1	Nick Mohacsy
1972	8	4	0	Joe Donnelly
1973	5	6	2	Joe Donnelly
1974	9	5	1	Joe Donnelly
1975	6	8	0	Kevin Kelly
1976	8	8	0	Kevin Kelly
1977	2	11	0	Kevin Kelly
1978	3	11	0	Kevin Kelly

BLOOMSBURG STATE COLLEGE

Bloomsburg, Pennsylvania

Huskies   Maroon and Gold

Yr.	W	L	T	Coach
1975	4	5	1	Lou Mingrone
1976	6	5	1	Lou Mingrone
1977	10	3	0	Lou Mingrone
1978	11	1	0	Lou Mingrone

BLUFFTON COLLEGE

Bluffton, Ohio

Beavers   **Navy and White**

Yr.	W	L	T	Coach
1967	4	7	0	Frank Porter
1968	2	9	0	Frank Porter
1969	2	9	1	Frank Porter
1970	2	8	0	Frank Porter
1971	0	9	1	George Frazee
1972	2	6	1	George Frazee
1973	4	5	0	George Frazee
1974	5	4	1	George Frazee
1975	4	5	0	Shiv Gupta
1976	3	5	1	Shiv Gupta
1977	0	8	2	Jim Amstutz
1978	1	9	1	Jim Amstutz

BOWDOIN COLLEGE

Brunswick, Maine

Polar Bears   **White**

Yr.	W	L	T	Coach
1958	1	4	0	Benjamin Levine
1959	5	2	1	Benjamin Levine
1960	4	4	0	B. Bockmann
1961	6	2	0	Charles J. Butt
1962	3	4	1	Charles J. Butt
1963	3	4	2	Charles J. Butt
1964	2	7	0	L. Dodge Fernald
1965	6	2	2	Charles J. Butt
1966	6	4	1	Charles J. Butt
1967	5	6	0	Charles J. Butt
1968	6	3	2	Charles J. Butt
1969	4	5	2	Charles J. Butt
1970	7	3	2	Charles J. Butt
1971	6	6	0	Charles J. Butt
1972	7	5	0	Charles J. Butt
1973	4	4	4	Charles J. Butt
1974	6	4	2	Charles J. Butt
1975	7	5	0	Charles J. Butt
1976	10	2	1	Charles J. Butt
1977	4	2	5	Charles J. Butt
1978	3	6	2	Charles J. Butt

BOSTON COLLEGE

Chestnut Hill, Massachusetts

Eagles   **Maroon and Gold**

Yr.	W	L	T	Coach
1967	7	5	1	Gyorgy Lang
1968	3	9	0	Gyorgy Lang
1969	5	4	3	Gyorgy Lang
1970	4	9	0	Gyorgy Lang
1971	6	8	0	Gyorgy Lang
1972	3	9	2	Ben Brewster
1973	7	6	3	Hans Westerkamp
1974	5	9	2	Hans Westerkamp
1975	4	11	1	Hans Westerkamp
1976	6	8	1	Hans Westerkamp
1977	6	9	1	Ben Brewster
1978	13	5	0	Ben Brewster

BOSTON UNIVERSITY

Boston, Massachusetts

Terriers   **Scarlet and White**

Yr.	W	L	T	Coach
1949	1	3	1	John Anderson
1950	3	3	1	John Anderson
1951	3	5	0	John Anderson
1952	2	8	0	John Anderson
1953	2	8	0	John Anderson
1954	2	5	1	John Anderson
1955	5	3	1	John Anderson
1956	1	7	2	John Anderson
1957	3	5	0	John Anderson
1958	2	7	0	John Anderson
1959	4	5	0	John Anderson
1960	2	8	0	John Anderson
1961	2	6	1	John Anderson
1962	5	4	0	John Anderson
1963	6	2	1	John Anderson
1964	5	5	0	John Anderson
1965	3	5	1	John Anderson
1966	2	7	1	Roy Sigler
1967	4	8	1	Roy Sigler
1968	9	4	0	Roy Sigler
1969	6	5	3	Roy Sigler
1970	8	5	1	Roy Sigler
1971	7	5	2	Roy Sigler
1972	8	7	0	Roy Sigler
1973	4	6	3	Roy Sigler
1974	5	8	1	Ron Cervasio
1975	2	9	3	Ron Cervasio
1976	6	9	0	Ron Cervasio
1977	10	5	2	Ron Cervasio
1978	12	4	3	Ron Cervasio

BOWLING GREEN STATE UNIVERSITY

Bowling Green, Ohio

Falcons   **Orange and Brown**

Yr.	W	L	T	Coach
1965	2	4	0	Mickey Cochrane
1966	3	6	0	Mickey Cochrane
1967	2	7	0	Mickey Cochrane
1968	5	4	0	Mickey Cochrane
1969	7	3	0	Mickey Cochrane
1970	4	5	0	Mickey Cochrane
1971	5	4	0	Mickey Cochrane
1972	7	2	0	Mickey Cochrane
1973	9	2	0	Mickey Cochrane
1974	6	3	0	Mickey Cochrane
1975	6	3	0	Mickey Cochrane
1976	4	7	0	Mickey Cochrane
1977	8	6	0	Mickey Cochrane
1978	9	3	0	Gary Palmisano

BRANDEIS UNIVERSITY

Waltham, Massachusetts

Judges   **Blue and White**

Yr.	W	L	T	Coach
1955	0	5	0	Sam Goulds
1956	—	—	—	—
1957	—	—	—	—
1958	—	—	—	—

Yr.	W	L	T	Coach
1959	—	—	—	
1960	6	1	1	Glenn Howells
1961	4	2	1	Glenn Howells
1962	1	9	0	Heinz Lubass
1963	3	9	0	John Hughes
1964	5	7	2	John Hughes
1965	5	5	2	John Hughes
1966	4	5	2	John Hughes
1967	7	3	1	Alan Grayson
1968	5	4	2	Alan Grayson
1969	2	7	3	Alan Grayson
1970	3	9	0	Bob Gustavson
1971	5	8	0	Bob Gustavson
1972	3	11	0	Bob Gustavson
1973	7	4	1	Michael Coven
1974	6	4	2	Michael Coven
1975	10	1	2	Michael Coven
1976	15	2	0	Michael Coven
1977	11	2	1	Michael Coven
1978	12	3	1	Michael Coven

BRIDGEPORT, UNIVERSITY OF

Bridgeport, Connecticut

Purple Knights   **Purple and White**

Yr.	W	L	T	Coach
1948	0	4	0	Tony Iannone
1949	0	5	1	Tony Iannone
1950	3	2	2	Tony Iannone
1951	—	—	—	—
1952	—	—	—	—
1953	4	4	0	John McKeon
1954	9	1	0	John McKeon
1955	9	1	0	John McKeon
1956	5	3	1	John McKeon
1957	5	3	0	John McKeon
1958	8	2	1	John McKeon
1959	11	1	0	John McKeon
1960	7	1	1	John McKeon
1961	9	3	0	John McKeon
1962	9	1	0	John McKeon
1963	11	3	1	John McKeon
1964	10	2	2	John McKeon
1965	6	4	0	Joe Bean
1966	9	4	0	Joe Bean
1967	10	3	0	Joe Bean
1968	6	4	2	Joe Bean
1969	10	2	1	Fran Bacon
1970	6	6	2	Fran Bacon
1971	11	6	0	Fran Bacon
1972	12	4	0	Fran Bacon
1973	11	4	2	Fran Bacon
1974	7	6	4	Fran Bacon
1975	10	5	1	Fran Bacon
1976	8	6	4	Fran Bacon
1977	6	10	0	Fran Bacon
1978	9	7	3	Fran Bacon

BROCKPORT STATE UNIVERSITY

Brockport, New York

Golden Eagles   **Gold and Green**

Yr.	W	L	T	Coach
1946	3	2	0	Huntley Parker
1947	5	2	0	Huntley Parker
1948	8	0	1	Huntley Parker
1949	8	1	0	Huntley Parker
1950	3	2	3	Huntley Parker
1951	6	0	0	Huntley Parker
1952	5	2	0	Huntley Parker
1953	5	2	0	Huntley Parker
1954	9	0	0	Huntley Parker
1955	10	0	0	Huntley Parker
1956	6	3	1	Huntley Parker
1957	5	4	0	Huntley Parker
1958	5	1	4	Huntley Parker
1959	6	4	0	Huntley Parker
1960	5	2	3	Huntley Parker
1961	9	1	0	Huntley Parker
1962	5	3	2	Huntley Parker
1963	8	4	0	Huntley Parker
1964	4	6	0	Huntley Parker
1965	4	6	0	Huntley Parker
1966	7	2	2	Huntley Parker
1967	6	2	2	Huntley Parker
1968	11	0	0	Huntley Parker
1969	10	2	0	Huntley Parker
1970	11	1	2	Huntley Parker
1971	12	2	0	Bill Hughes
1972	9	4	0	Bill Hughes
1973	10	1	0	Bill Hughes
1974	12	2	2	Walter Kopczuk
1975	11	5	0	Bill Hughes
1976	14	4	1	Walter Kopczuk
1977	7	4	3	Walter Kopczuk
1978	9	3	3	Walter Kopczuk

Huntley Parker (left) receives the National Soccer Coaches Association's 1968 Honor Award from Glassboro State's Sam Porch after leading Brockport State to an 11–0 record.

Under coach Cliff Stevenson, Brown has won seven Ivy League titles outright and shared three others.

BROWN UNIVERSITY

Providence, Rhode Island

Bruins, Bears   Brown, Red, and White

Yr.	W	L	T	Coach
1926	1	2	2	Sam Fletcher
1927	1	6	0	Sam Fletcher
1928	1	5	1	Sam Fletcher
1929	1	3	3	Sam Fletcher
1930	1	3	4	Sam Fletcher
1931	2	2	3	Sam Fletcher
1932	2	3	2	Sam Fletcher
1933	3	2	1	Sam Fletcher
1934	6	1	1	Sam Fletcher
1935	5	3	0	Sam Fletcher
1936	7	0	3	Sam Fletcher
1937	8	1	2	Sam Fletcher
1938	2	8	0	Sam Fletcher
1939	3	5	0	Sam Fletcher
1940	3	4	1	Sam Fletcher
1941	4	3	1	Sam Fletcher
1942	3	5	0	Sam Fletcher
1943	2	6	0	Sam Fletcher
1944	2	6	1	Sam Fletcher
1945	7	2	0	Sam Fletcher
1946	3	4	2	Joseph Kennaway
1947	3	3	1	Joseph Kennaway
1948	5	5	0	Joseph Kennaway
1949	5	3	1	Joseph Kennaway
1950	4	4	1	Joseph Kennaway

Brown's Peter Van Beek (right) battles for possession during a 2–1 New England playoff conquest of Connecticut in 1977.

Yr.	W	L	T	Coach
1951	1	5	1	Joseph Kennaway
1952	2	5	1	Joseph Kennaway
1953	2	6	0	Joseph Kennaway
1954	3	6	0	Joseph Kennaway
1955	3	8	0	Joseph Kennaway
1956	7	3	0	Joseph Kennaway
1957	2	6	1	Joseph Kennaway
1958	2	7	0	Joseph Kennaway
1959	3	5	1	Joseph Kennaway
1960	1	9	0	Cliff Stevenson
1961	6	5	0	Cliff Stevenson
1962	5	5	1	Cliff Stevenson
1963	11	2	1	Cliff Stevenson
1964	7	3	2	Cliff Stevenson
1965	12	1	1	Cliff Stevenson
1966	11	1	0	Cliff Stevenson
1967	13	0	1	Cliff Stevenson
1968	11	4	0	Cliff Stevenson
1969	9	4	2	Cliff Stevenson
1970	10	8	1	Cliff Stevenson
1971	7	6	2	Cliff Stevenson
1972	11	5	0	Cliff Stevenson
1973	12	4	1	Cliff Stevenson
1974	14	2	0	Cliff Stevenson
1975	12	3	2	Cliff Stevenson
1976	11	3	1	Cliff Stevenson
1977	11	6	2	Cliff Stevenson
1978	9	5	1	Cliff Stevenson

BRYAN COLLEGE

Dayton, Tennessee

Lions   Red and Gold

Yr.	W	L	T	Coach
1964	1	4	0	Cleve Oliver
1965	4	4	1	Jack Wells
1966	2	6	4	Jack Wells
1967	4	4	1	Jack Wells
1968	4	5	1	Jim Bath
1969	1	9	0	Jim Bath
1970	2	9	0	Jim Bath
1971	1	10	0	Jim Bath
1972	4	5	1	John Reeser
1973	6	9	1	John Reeser
1974	15	2	1	John Reeser
1975	13	4	1	John Reeser
1976	6	5	3	John Reeser
1977	12	3	1	John Reeser
1978	11	6	1	John Reeser

BUCKNELL UNIVERSITY

Lewisburg, Pennsylvania

Bisons   Orange and Blue

Yr.	W	L	T	Coach
1929	0	2	0	J. B. Hopkins
1930	1	3	1	C. W. Meadowcroft
1931	1	4	0	Charles L. Titus
1932	0	7	1	Kenneth Vandenbree
1933	2	5	1	Joseph Reno
1934	3	2	2	Joseph Reno
1935	2	4	1	Joseph Reno
1936	1	5	1	Joseph Reno
1937	4	3	1	Joseph Reno

Yr.	W	L	T	Coach
1938	2	5	1	Merle Edwards
1939	3	3	2	Merle Edwards
1940	3	3	2	Merle Edwards
1941	3	4	1	Merle Edwards
1942	1	5	1	Merle Edwards
1943	1	4	2	Merle Edwards
1944	3	2	1	Merle Edwards
1945	—	—	—	—
1946	1	7	0	Merle Edwards
1947	3	5	2	Bill Lane
1948	6	3	0	Joseph Diblin
1949	5	4	0	Joseph Diblin
1950	3	5	0	Joseph Diblin
1951	2	5	0	Joseph Diblin
1952	1	7	0	Henry J. Peters
1953	2	4	0	Henry J. Peters
1954	4	4	1	Henry J. Peters
1955	4	4	2	Henry J. Peters
1956	3	3	3	Henry J. Peters
1957	3	6	1	Henry J. Peters
1958	3	7	0	Henry J. Peters
1959	6	4	0	Henry J. Peters
1960	7	3	0	Henry J. Peters
1961	4	6	0	Henry J. Peters
1962	5	3	1	Henry J. Peters
1963	2	9	0	Bill Gold
1964	3	9	0	Henry J. Peters
1965	2	8	2	R. Kirk Randall
1966	2	10	1	R. Kirk Randall
1967	8	4	0	Craig Reynolds
1968	8	4	0	Craig Reynolds
1969	10	1	2	Craig Reynolds
1970	6	3	2	Craig Reynolds
1971	5	6	1	Craig Reynolds
1972	6	6	0	Craig Reynolds
1973	9	3	1	Craig Reynolds
1974	12	1	2	Craig Reynolds
1975	10	4	1	Craig Reynolds
1976	10	4	0	Craig Reynolds
1977	4	5	4	Craig Reynolds
1978	3	7	3	Craig Reynolds

BUFFALO STATE COLLEGE

Buffalo, New York

Bengals   Orange and Black

Yr.	W	L	T	Coach
1935	0	3	0	Hube Cover
1936	2	2	0	Hube Cover
1937	3	4	1	Hube Cover
1938	6	1	1	Hube Cover
1939	0	4	0	Hube Cover
1940	0	5	1	Hube Cover
1941	—	—	—	—
1942	3	4	0	Hube Cover
1943	—	—	—	—
1944	—	—	—	—
1945	—	—	—	—
1946	3	5	0	Hube Cover
1947	3	1	1	Hube Cover
1948	2	5	0	Joe Adessa
1949	4	4	0	Joe Adessa
1950	5	3	0	Joe Adessa
1951	3	3	1	Joe Adessa
1952	6	1	1	Joe Adessa
1953	3	4	1	Joe Adessa
1954	2	5	1	Joe Adessa
1955	2	3	1	Rudy Berger

Scott Strasburg (right) helped Bucknell post a 10–4 record in 1976.

Yr.	W	L	T	Coach
1956	4	3	1	Rudy Berger
1957	2	3	1	Si Manspeaker
1958	2	6	0	Ken Johnson
1959	0	8	1	Ken Johnson
1960	1	7	1	Fred J. Hartrick
1961	3	6	2	Fred J: Hartrick
1962	6	5	0	Fred J. Hartrick
1963	5	6	0	Fred J. Hartrick
1964	5	4	2	Fred J. Hartrick
1965	5	6	0	Fred J. Hartrick
1966	8	3	1	Fred J. Hartrick
1967	12	1	1	Fred J. Hartrick
1968	7	5	0	Fred J. Hartrick
1969	10	2	0	Fred J. Hartrick
1970	13	0	2	Fred J. Hartrick
1971	6	6	0	Fred J. Hartrick
1972	4	8	1	Fred J. Hartrick
1973	8	5	1	Fred J. Hartrick
1974	5	9	0	Fred J. Hartrick
1975	3	8	2	Fred J. Hartrick
1976	6	3	3	Fred J. Hartrick
1977	6	6	1	Fred J. Hartrick
1978	10	4	0	Fred J. Hartrick

BUFFALO STATE UNIVERSITY

Buffalo, New York

Bulls				Blue and White
Yr.	W	L	T	Coach
1972	7	4	0	Bert Jacobsen
1973	5	5	2	Sal Esposito
1974	8	3	1	Sal Esposito
1975	9	3	0	Sal Esposito
1976	5	7	2	Sal Esposito
1977	6	6	1	Sal Esposito
1978	4	10	1	Sal Esposito

CALIFORNIA INSTITUTE OF TECHNOLOGY

Pasadena, California

Beavers				Orange and White
Yr.	W	L	T	Coach
1942	3	5	1	Al Landau
1943	2	2	1	Laurence Liddell
1944	—	—	—	—
1945	—	—	—	—

Yr.	W	L	T	Coach
1946	—	—	—	—
1947	—	—	—	—
1948	1	2	1	Laurence Liddell
1949	1	5	0	James Hill
1950	6	2	0	Bob Huttenback
1951	6	0	1	Roy Jones
1952	5	1	0	Bob Huttenback
1953	7	2	0	Bob Huttenback
1954	3	4	1	Bob Huttenback
1955	3	4	1	Bob Huttenback
1956	0	6	2	Charles Miller
1957	4	1	1	Lee Andrews
1958	3	7	1	Lee Andrews
1959	3	6	3	Lee Andrews
1960	4	5	1	Lee Andrews
1961	5	3	2	Lee Andrews
1962	6	4	0	Lee Andrews
1963	6	2	2	Lee Andrews
1964	8	3	1	Lee Andrews
1965	1	10	1	Lee Andrews
1966	0	9	0	Ronald Kehoe
1967	3	10	1	Ronald Kehoe
1968	3	7	0	Ronald Kehoe
1969	6	5	3	Ronald Kehoe
1970	6	7	1	Geoffrey Morgan
1971	1	11	3	Geoffrey Morgan
1972	1	13	0	Donald Cameron
1973	1	11	3	Donald Cameron
1974	1	13	1	Donald Cameron
1975	3	11	0	Donald Cameron
1976	4	9	2	Donald Cameron
1977	3	11	1	Donald Cameron
1978	3	12	0	Donald Cameron

CALIFORNIA, UNIVERSITY OF (BERKELEY)

Berkeley, California

Bears   **Blue and Gold**

Yr.	W	L	T	Coach
1952	4	5	1	Bob DiGrazia
1953	6	4	0	Bob DiGrazia
1954	4	1	1	Bob DiGrazia
1955	6	2	0	Bob DiGrazia
1956	4	4	2	Bob DiGrazia
1957	5	2	0	Bob DiGrazia
1958	5	1	2	Bob DiGrazia
1959	7	1	1	Bob DiGrazia
1960	8	3	0	Bob DiGrazia
1961	6	2	2	Bob DiGrazia
1962	8	3	0	Bob DiGrazia
1963	6	4	1	Bob DiGrazia
1964	6	5	1	Bob DiGrazia
1965	6	5	2	Bob DiGrazia
1966	8	1	2	Bob DiGrazia
1967	8	1	2	Bob DiGrazia
1968	7	6	0	Bob DiGrazia
1969	6	5	1	Bob DiGrazia
1970	7	6	0	Bob DiGrazia
1971	7	6	0	Bob DiGrazia
1972	7	5	3	Bob DiGrazia
1973	8	6	2	Bob DiGrazia
1974	9	6	4	Bob DiGrazia
1975	12	7	1	Bob DiGrazia
1976	10	7	2	Bob DiGrazia
1977	12	6	2	Bob DiGrazia
1978	10	9	2	Bob DiGrazia

Heady Dan Salvemini anchored the Cal-Berkeley defense in the late 1970s.

Bob DiGrazia, a fixture at Cal-Berkeley, founded the school's soccer program in 1952.

Ole Mikkelsen (left), in action against Whittier, was an All-American at UCLA in 1978.

CALIFORNIA, UNIVERSITY OF (UCLA)

Los Angeles, California

Bruins **Blue and Gold**

Yr.	W	L	T	Coach
1937	4	5	1	Dan Stevenson
1938	3	4	1	Dan Stevenson
1939	1	6	3	Dan Stevenson
1948	2	3	0	Jon Drury
1949	13	1	0	Ed "Jock" Stewart
1950	10	2	0	Ed "Jock" Stewart
1951	4	2	2	Ed "Jock" Stewart
1952	1	2	0	Ed "Jock" Stewart
1953	9	5	0	Ed "Jock" Stewart
1954	7	1	0	Ed "Jock" Stewart
1955	5	3	0	Ed "Jock" Stewart
1956	7	2	1	Ed "Jock" Stewart
1957	7	3	0	Ed "Jock" Stewart
1958	13	0	0	Ed "Jock" Stewart
1959	7	0	1	Ed "Jock" Stewart
1960	10	0	0	Ed "Jock" Stewart
1961	12	0	1	Ed "Jock" Stewart
1962	15	2	1	Ed "Jock" Stewart
1963	18	0	1	Ed "Jock" Stewart
1964	18	1	1	Ed "Jock" Stewart
1965	21	2	2	Ed "Jock" Stewart
1966	17	3	2	Ed "Jock" Stewart
1967	12	1	1	Dennis Storer
1968	12	2	1	Dennis Storer
1969	15	1	0	Dennis Storer
1970	16	1	0	Dennis Storer
1971	18	2	0	Dennis Storer
1972	12	2	3	Dennis Storer
1973	18	1	4	Dennis Storer
1974	15	3	4	Terry Fisher
1975	11	6	2	Steve Gay
1976	13	5	1	Steve Gay
1977	19	5	3	Steve Gay
1978	14	8	1	Steve Gay

CALIFORNIA, UNIVERSITY OF (SANTA BARBARA)

Santa Barbara, California

Gauchos   Blue and Gold

Yr.	W	L	T	Coach
1966	4	5	0	Zolton von Somogyi
1967	3	5	0	Zolton von Somogyi
1968	6	2	2	Zolton von Somogyi
1969	6	4	2	Zolton von Somogyi
1970	4	4	2	Zolton von Somogyi
1971	9	2	0	Zolton von Somogyi
1972	4	4	1	Sandy Geuss
1973	5	9	2	Sandy Geuss
1974	5	6	4	S. Geuss, K. Reeves
1975	8	8	1	Al Meeder
1976	10	6	2	Al Meeder
1977	8	9	1	Al Meeder
1978	16	3	0	Al Meeder

CALVIN COLLEGE

Grand Rapids, Michigan

Knights   Maroon and Gold

Yr.	W	L	T	Coach
1959	4	7	0	Brouwer
1960	4	3	2	Brouwer
1961	3	6	1	Marvin Zuidema
1962	8	3	0	Marvin Zuidema
1963	5	4	1	Marvin Zuidema
1964	2	7	0	Marvin Zuidema
1965	2	9	0	Marvin Zuidema
1966	5	4	3	Marvin Zuidema
1967	6	6	1	Marvin Zuidema
1968	5	4	3	Honderd
1969	3	6	3	Marvin Zuidema
1970	8	3	0	Marvin Zuidema
1971	10	1	1	Marvin Zuidema
1972	8	3	0	Marvin Zuidema
1973	10	2	1	Marvin Zuidema
1974	7	5	1	Marvin Zuidema
1975	8	3	3	Marvin Zuidema
1976	11	1	3	Marvin Zuidema
1977	9	4	1	Marvin Zuidema
1978	11	3	1	Marvin Zuidema

CAMPBELL COLLEGE

Buies Creek, North Carolina

Camels   Orange and Black

Yr.	W	L	T	Coach
1963	2	5	1	James Cole
1964	7	5	0	James Cole
1965	5	7	0	James Cole
1966	8	4	1	James Cole
1967	7	4	1	James Cole
1968	9	2	1	James Cole
1969	16	2	1	James Cole
1970	16	2	1	James Cole
1971	14	1	1	James Cole
1972	11	4	0	James Cole
1973	15	3	0	James Cole
1974	14	2	0	James Cole
1975	13	6	0	James Cole
1976	9	8	1	Darrell Saunders
1977	7	7	1	Wayne Cunningham
1978	2	10	3	Wayne Cunningham

CEDARVILLE COLLEGE

Cedarville, Ohio

Yellow Jackets   Blue and Gold

Yr.	W	L	T	Coach
1963	4	5	0	Lane Moody
1964	5	5	1	Lane Moody
1965	7	2	2	Dennis Olsen
1966	8	4	2	Dennis Olsen
1967	8	5	1	Dennis Olsen
1968	7	3	4	Randall Ross
1969	6	6	1	Randall Ross
1970	7	8	1	Randall Ross
1971	10	4	0	Paul Berry
1972	10	4	1	Paul Berry
1973	10	2	0	Paul Berry
1974	13	6	0	John McGillivray
1975	9	3	2	John McGillivray
1976	10	4	1	John McGillivray
1977	4	10	0	John McGillivray
1978	10	9	1	John McGillivray

CENTRAL CONNECTICUT

New Britain, Connecticut

Blue Devils   Blue and White

Yr.	W	L	T	Coach
1969	5	3	3	John Webster
1970	7	5	0	John Webster
1971	8	4	1	John Webster
1972	4	7	1	John Webster
1973	4	6	2	John Webster
1974	3	4	5	John Webster
1975	5	4	3	John Webster
1976	6	7	0	John Webster
1977	4	8	0	John Webster
1978	4	6	2	John Webster

CENTRAL FLORIDA, UNIVERSITY OF

Orlando, Florida

Knights   Black and Gold

Yr.	W	L	T	Coach
1975	10	4	1	Jim Rudy
1976	15	1	1	Jim Rudy
1977	11	4	0	Jim Rudy
1978	4	8	0	Jim Rudy

CENTRE COLLEGE

Danville, Kentucky

Colonels   Gold and White

Yr.	W	L	T	Coach
1973	3	12	2	Piziak, Brown
1974	2	11	0	Piziak, Brown
1975	5	6	1	Piziak, Brown
1976	7	5	0	Piziak, Brown
1977	3	6	2	Piziak, Brown
1978	6	8	0	Piziak, Brown

Central Florida's all-time scorer, Randy DeShield of Bermuda scored five goals against Biscayne in 1978.

CHICAGO, UNIVERSITY OF

Chicago, Illinois

Maroons — **Maroon and White**

Yr.	W	L	T	Coach
1947	1	5	0	Hermanson
1948	3	3	0	Hermanson
1949	2	4	0	Hermanson
1950	3	3	0	Hermanson
1951	5	0	1	Hermanson
1952	3	2	0	Hermanson
1953	4	3	1	Hermanson
1954	4	5	0	Hermanson
1955	2	7	1	Hermanson
1956	4	5	1	Hermanson
1957	1	5	2	Hermanson
1958	1	5	0	Hermanson
1959	1	5	1	Hermanson

Yr.	W	L	T	Coach
1960	0	6	0	Wangerin
1961	1	7	0	Wangerin
1962	1	8	0	Retel
1963	0	10	0	Retel
1964	1	7	0	Vendl
1965	2	8	0	Vendl
1966	2	9	0	Vendl
1967	6	5	1	Vendl
1968	2	9	1	Vendl
1969	1	10	1	Vendl
1970	6	5	2	Vendl
1971	6	7	0	Vendl
1972	8	6	0	Vendl
1973	7	4	2	Vendl
1974	—	—	—	—
1975	0	10	0	Vendl
1976	0	9	0	De Silva
1977	3	4	0	De Silva
1978	8	2	1	De Silva

CHRISTOPHER NEWPORT COLLEGE

Newport News, Virginia

Captains				Blue and White
Yr.	W	L	T	Coach
1974	2	10	2	William Sneddon
1975	9	5	0	William Sneddon
1976	6	7	0	William Sneddon
1977	10	5	1	Robert Cummings
1978	7	9	1	Robert Cummings

THE CITADEL

Charleston, South Carolina

Bulldogs, Cadets				Blue and White
Yr.	W	L	T	Coach
1967	3	4	0	Frank Frohlich
1968	4	3	1	Frank Frohlich
1969	2	1	0	Frank Frohlich
1970	5	3	1	Frank Frohlich
1971	3	4	0	Frank Frohlich
1972	0	7	1	Eddie Teague
1973	9	4	0	Eddie Teague
1974	9	3	0	Eddie Teague
1975	6	5	1	Eddie Teague
1976	6	6	2	Eddie Teague
1977	11	5	0	Mark Berson
1978	10	4	0	Bill Barfield

CITY COLLEGE OF NEW YORK (CCNY)

New York, New York

Beavers				Lavender and Black
Yr.	W	L	T	Coach
1947	5	3	0	Ira Zasloff
1948	5	1	2	Dick Havel
1949	3	4	1	Dick Havel
1950	4	3	3	Werner Rothschild
1951	3	1	0	Werner Rothschild
1952	4	2	3	Werner Rothschild
1953	7	2	0	George Wolfe
1954	8	1	0	Harry Karlin
1955	8	0	1	Harry Karlin
1956	9	1	1	Harry Karlin
1957	10	0	0	Harry Karlin
1958	11	0	1	Harry Karlin
1959	9	2	1	Harry Karlin
1960	7	3	0	Harry Karlin
1961	7	3	0	Harry Karlin
1962	2	6	2	Harry Karlin
1963	6	4	0	Harry Karlin
1964	6	2	2	Harry Karlin
1965	6	3	1	William Killen
1966	5	4	1	Ray Klivecka
1967	4	4	2	Ray Klivecka
1968	9	3	0	Ray Klivecka
1969	4	7	1	Ray Klivecka
1970	4	5	3	Ray Klivecka
1971	3	9	1	Ray Klivecka
1972	3	9	1	Ray Klivecka
1973	0	13	1	Ray Klivecka
1974	6	6	3	Ray Klivecka
1975	4	8	0	Ray Klivecka
1976	6	4	2	Ray Klivecka
1977	7	7	3	Feliks Fuksman
1978	5	9	2	Feliks Fuksman

CLARK UNIVERSITY

Worcester, Massachusetts

Cougars				Red and White
Yr.	W	L	T	Coach
1922	0	2	1	Whitman
1923	—	—	—	—
1924	—	—	—	—
1925	—	—	—	—
1926	3	2	2	H. Russell
1927	2	3	0	H. Russell
1928	—	—	—	—
1929	—	—	—	—
1930	5	2	1	H. Baker
1931	3	2	2	B. Baker
1932	3	4	1	B. Baker
1933	0	3	3	B. Baker
1934	2	6	0	Bares
1935	—	—	—	—
1936	0	6	1	Waterfield
1937	2	3	2	Joyce
1938	4	3	0	Joyce
1939	3	3	0	Joyce
1940	3	3	0	Bernard
1941	1	4	0	Bernard
1942	1	8	0	Bernard
1943	0	5	0	Bernard
1944	—	—	—	—
1945	—	—	—	—
1946	—	—	—	—
1947	1	3	0	Russ Granger
1948	1	5	1	Russ Granger
1949	1	7	0	R. Lambert
1950	0	8	0	R. Lambert
1951	0	8	0	R. Lambert
1952	—	—	—	—
1953	1	6	0	R. Lambert
1954	2	5	0	R. Lambert
1955	—	—	—	—
1956	2	4	1	R. Lambert
1957	1	5	2	Bill Ferrie
1958	3	7	0	T. McMillan
1959	0	10	0	Bill Ferrie
1960	1	8	0	Bill Ferrie
1961	3	7	0	A. Serra
1962	1	8	0	A. Serra
1963	3	7	0	A. Serra
1964	5	4	1	A. Serra
1965	4	2	4	A. Serra
1966	5	3	2	A. Serra
1967	6	2	2	Fan Gaudette
1968	7	2	1	Fan Gaudette
1969	8	1	2	Fan Gaudette
1970	8	3	0	Fan Gaudette
1971	—	—	—	—
1972	3	8	1	D.H. Amaral
1973	5	7	1	J. Kaufman
1974	3	7	0	P. Hart
1975	2	7	4	R. Surette
1976	6	6	1	Jack Cohen
1977	2	11	0	T. Sotiropoulos
1978	5	7	1	Massod Abolfazli

CLARKSON COLLEGE

Potsdam, New York

Golden Knights				Green and Gold
Yr.	W	L	T	Coach
1974	5	5	2	Chafin
1975	6	7	0	Chafin

John Paranos, an All-American in 1957, helped CCNY post a combined record of 21–0–1 in 1957 and 1958.

Yr.	W	L	T	Coach
1976	6	5	2	Chafin
1977	6	6	1	Chafin
1978	5	7	1	Chafin

CLEMSON UNIVERSITY

Clemson, South Carolina

Tigers				Purple and Orange
Yr.	W	L	T	Coach
1967	6	5	0	I. M. Ibrahim
1968	9	3	1	I. M. Ibrahim
1969	5	6	1	I. M. Ibrahim
1970	8	3	2	I. M. Ibrahim
1971	9	3	1	I. M. Ibrahim
1972	13	1	1	I. M. Ibrahim
1973	16	1	0	I. M. Ibrahim
1974	12	3	0	I. M. Ibrahim
1975	15	3	0	I. M. Ibrahim
1976	20	3	1	I. M. Ibrahim
1977	16	1	0	I. M. Ibrahim
1978	18	1	1	I. M. Ibrahim

CLEVELAND STATE UNIVERSITY

Cleveland, Ohio

Vikings				Green and White
Yr.	W	L	T	Coach
1954	2	2	2	Jack Marshall
1955	4	0	1	Jack Marshall
1956	5	3	0	Jack Marshall
1957	4	2	1	Jack Marshall
1958	7	1	1	Jack Marshall

Yr.	W	L	T	Coach
1959	9	1	0	Jack Marshall
1960	6	4	0	Jack Marshall
1961	2	7	0	Jack Marshall
1962	4	3	2	Jack Marshall
1963	4	5	1	Jack Marshall
1964	4	6	0	Jack Marshall
1965	6	4	0	Jack Marshall
1966	4	5	2	Jack Marshall
1967	5	4	2	William Clarke
1968	13	2	1	William Clarke
1969	10	2	2	William Clarke
1970	8	4	1	William Clarke
1971	7	5	1	William Clarke
1972	8	4	0	Klaas de Boer
1973	6	4	2	Klaas de Boer
1974	9	5	0	Klaas de Boer
1975	10	5	0	Klaas de Boer
1976	8	5	1	Klaas de Boer
1977	14	2	0	Klaas de Boer
1978	10	5	1	Steve Parker

COAST GUARD (USCGA)

New London, Connecticut

Cadets				Blue and White
Yr,	W	L	T	Coach
1939	0	3	0	G. N. Buron
1940	3	3	0	G. N. Buron
1941	3	3	0	G. N. Buron
1942	1	1	0	G. N. Buron
1943	3	3	0	G. N. Buron
1944	4	5	0	G. N. Buron
1945	0	10	0	G. N. Buron

Godwin Ogbueze was the top scorer as Clemson won its sixth straight Atlantic Coast Conference title and went 16–1–1 in 1977.

Yr.	W	L	T	Coach
1946	2	4	0	Mike Connally
1955	0	4	1	Clitto Montorsi
1956	2	4	2	Rudy Lenczyk
1957	0	9	0	Rudy Lenczyk
1958	4	5	0	Rudy Lenczyk
1959	4	5	0	Rudy Lenczyk
1960	3	4	2	G. N. Buron
1961	2	7	1	G. N. Buron
1962	3	8	0	G. N. Buron
1963	7	6	0	Jerry Bechtel
1964	8	5	0	Jerry Bechtel
1965	4	7	0	Jerry Bechtel
1966	2	9	0	Jerry Bechtel
1967	2	8	1	Jerry Bechtel
1968	5	4	3	Brent Smith
1969	3	7	3	Brent Smith
1970	5	6	1	Ray Cieplik
1971	5	6	0	Ray Cieplik
1972	5	7	0	Ray Cieplik
1973	6	6	0	Ray Cieplik
1974	6	4	2	Ray Cieplik
1975	4	7	1	Ray Cieplik
1976	8	4	0	Ray Cieplik
1977	8	4	0	Ray Cieplik
1978	8	4	1	B. Wissman

COLBY COLLEGE

Waterville, Maine

White Mules   **Blue and Gray**

Yr.	W	L	T	Coach
1959	7	0	0	Mike Loebs
1960	7	1	0	Mike Loebs
1961	6	1	1	Mike Loebs
1962	9	2	1	Mike Loebs
1963	10	2	1	John Winkin
1964	9	2	1	John Winkin
1965	8	3	2	Silas Dunklee
1966	5	6	1	Silas Dunklee
1967	3	8	2	Silas Dunklee
1968	5	3	3	Jack Scholz
1969	2	7	3	Jack Scholz
1970	2	9	2	Jack Scholz
1971	3	7	0	Jack Scholz
1972	4	7	1	Jack Scholz
1973	3	3	5	Kenneth Mukai
1974	4	4	3	Kenneth Mukai
1975	2	10	0	Kenneth Mukai
1976	1	11	0	Mark Serdjenian
1977	3	7	2	Mark Serdjenian
1978	11	2	1	Mark Serdjenian

COLGATE UNIVERSITY

Hamilton, New York

Red Raiders   **Maroon and White**

Yr.	W	L	T	Coach
1920	2	1	0	James Balentine
1921	2	4	3	James Balentine
1922	1	2	2	James Balentine
1923	5	0	1	James Balentine
1924	4	3	1	James Balentine
1935	1	3	1	James Dalgety
1936	3	5	0	James Dalgety
1937	1	4	1	James Dalgety
1938	2	6	1	James Dalgety
1939	5	1	1	James Dalgety
1940	3	1	2	James Dalgety
1941	0	6	1	James Dalgety
1942	4	4	0	James Dalgety
1943	0	5	0	James Dalgety
1944	0	6	0	James Dalgety
1945	2	3	1	James Dalgety
1946	5	4	1	James Dalgety
1947	5	3	1	James Dalgety
1948	4	3	0	James Dalgety
1949	4	3	0	James Dalgety
1950	2	5	0	Thomas Dockrell

Yr.	W	L	T	Coach
1951	2	4	0	Mark Randell
1952	2	4	1	Mark Randell
1953	0	4	3	Mark Randell
1954	5	2	0	Mark Randell
1955	8	2	0	Mark Randell
1956	6	3	1	Mark Randell
1957	5	3	1	Mark Randell
1958	3	5	1	Mark Randell
1959	7	1	0	Mark Randell
1960	9	0	0	Mark Randell
1961	6	5	0	Mark Randell
1962	8	2	1	Mark Randell
1963	5	3	1	Mark Randell
1964	8	3	0	Mark Randell
1965	7	5	0	Mark Randell
1966	8	1	0	John Beyer
1967	6	2	1	John Beyer
1968	7	3	0	John Beyer
1969	6	3	2	John Beyer
1970	4	7	1	John Beyer
1971	5	6	0	John Beyer
1972	5	5	0	John Beyer
1973	6	4	2	John Beyer
1974	6	3	3	John Beyer
1975	7	4	1	John Beyer
1976	5	5	0	John Beyer
1977	8	4	1	John Beyer
1978	6	6	1	John Beyer

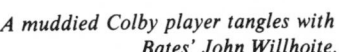

A muddied Colby player tangles with Bates' John Willhoite.

Columbia's all-time leading scorer Shahin Shayan (left) eludes Hartwick's Joey Ryan during the Lions' 3–2 NCAA Regional triumph in 1978.

COLORADO COLLEGE

Colorado Springs, Colorado

Tigers				Black and Gold
Yr.	W	L	T	Coach
1950	5	4	1	Mike Cares
1951	3	5	1	Richard Fox
1952	2	5	1	Bill Boddington
1953	3	3	1	Bill Boddington
1954	5	3	0	Scotty Russell
1955	3	3	0	Paul Bernard
1956	1	3	1	Paul Bernard
1962	2	3	0	Malyshev, Bernard
1963	1	5	0	Malyshev, Bernard
1964	5	1	0	Bill Boddington
1965	5	2	0	Bill Boddington
1966	5	2	0	Horst Richardson
1967	5	2	0	Horst Richardson
1968	5	5	0	Horst Richardson
1969	5	5	1	Horst Richardson
1970	8	5	2	Horst Richardson
1971	3	9	1	Richardson, Boddington
1972	9	3	2	Horst Richardson
1973	6	8	4	Horst Richardson
1974	13	6	1	Horst Richardson
1975	15	3	2	Horst Richardson
1976	15	3	0	Horst Richardson
1977	13	5	0	Horst Richardson
1978	9	7	3	Horst Richardson

COLUMBIA COLLEGE

Columbia, Missouri

Centaurs				Blue and Gold
Yr.	W	L	T	Coach
1974	13	4	2	Dennis Oberg
1975	7	7	1	Dennis Oberg
1976	8	7	1	Dennis Oberg
1977	14	6	0	Dennis Oberg
1978	11	6	0	Dennis Oberg

COLUMBIA UNIVERSITY

New York, New York

Lions				Blue and White
Yr.	W	L	T	Coach
1906	1	1	2	—
1907	1	4	0	—
1908	10	5	1	—
1909	5	0	1	—
1910	10	2	3	—
1911	2	1	2	—
1912	2	4	0	—
1913	6	12	4	—
1914	5	6	2	—
1915	5	1	0	—
1957	1	4	1	—

Yr.	W	L	T	Coach	Yr.	W	L	T	Coach
1958	1	6	2	Joseph Molder	1939	3	6	0	John Squires
1959	2	6	2	Joseph Molder	1940	4	3	1	John Squires
1960	5	7	0	Joseph Molder	1941	6	3	0	John Squires
1961	4	7	2	Joseph Molder	1942	3	6	0	Fischer
1962	6	7	0	Joseph Molder	1943	—	—	—	—
1963	1	6	1	Joseph Molder	1944	—	—	—	—
1964	2	8	1	Joseph Molder	1945	—	—	—	—
1965	4	7	1	Joseph Molder	1946	4	5	0	John Squires
1966	7	4	0	Joseph Molder	1947	7	2	0	John Squires
1967	2	5	2	Joseph Molder	1948	11	0	0	John Squires
1968	6	5	1	Joseph Molder	1949	7	3	1	John Squires
1969	8	3	1	Joseph Molder	1950	3	6	2	John Squires
1970	9	4	0	Jim Rein	1951	5	4	0	John Squires
1971	5	7	0	Jim Rein	1952	5	6	0	John Squires
1972	4	9	0	Jim Rein	1953	5	4	1	John Squires
1973	1	12	1	John Rennie	1954	3	9	0	John Squires
1974	0	10	3	John Rennie	1955	1	9	2	John Squires
1975	3	10	0	John Rennie	1956	4	6	0	John Squires
1976	6	5	3	John Rennie	1957	7	3	1	John Squires
1977	9	4	2	John Rennie	1958	10	1	0	John Squires
1978	13	2	1	John Rennie	1959	4	6	2	John Squires

CONNECTICUT, UNIVERSITY OF

Storrs, Connecticut

Huskies   **Blue and White**

Yr.	W	L	T	Coach
1928	2	2	0	Roy Guyer
1929	0	4	0	Jack Seman
1930	0	6	1	Billie Darrow
1931	1	6	1	Billie Darrow
1932	3	5	0	Jack Dennerly
1933	2	5	0	Jack Dennerly
1934	3	6	0	Jack Dennerly
1935	2	5	0	Jack Dennerly
1936	1	6	0	Jack Dennerly
1937	1	7	0	John Squires
1938	1	7	0	John Squires

Yr.	W	L	T	Coach
1960	11	3	0	John Squires
1961	9	3	0	John Squires
1962	3	9	0	John Squires
1963	4	7	0	John Squires
1964	7	4	2	John Squires
1965	5	6	1	John Squires
1966	8	5	0	John Squires
1967	6	7	0	John Squires
1968	4	6	2	John Squires
1969	3	9	0	Joe Morrone
1970	6	5	2	Joe Morrone
1971	4	11	0	Joe Morrone
1972	8	7	1	Joe Morrone
1973	13	4	2	Joe Morrone
1974	18	2	1	Joe Morrone
1975	16	3	3	Joe Morrone
1976	18	2	2	Joe Morrone
1977	9	11	1	Joe Morrone
1978	19	6	0	Joe Morrone

The 1978 Connecticut squad won the Yankee and New England Conference championships and finished 19–6 under coach Joe Morrone (second row, far left).

CORNELL UNIVERSITY

Ithaca, New York

Big Red   **Red and White**

Yr.	W	L	T	Coach
1910	2	4	0	—
1911	2	5	0	—
1912	1	5	0	—
1913	0	6	1	—
1914	1	1	4	Talbot Hunter
1915	1	1	5	Talbot Hunter
1916	0	5	0	—
1917	0	1	1	—
1918	—	—	—	—
1919	—	—	—	—
1920	2	4	0	—
1921	7	1	0	—
1922	5	1	1	Nicholas Bawlf
1923	1	4	2	Nicholas Bawlf
1924	1	6	0	Nicholas Bawlf
1925	1	3	1	Nicholas Bawlf
1926	3	2	0	Nicholas Bawlf
1927	3	3	0	Nicholas Bawlf
1928	2	5	0	Nicholas Bawlf
1929	1	4	2	Nicholas Bawlf
1930	5	2	0	Nicholas Bawlf
1931	2	4	0	Nicholas Bawlf
1932	3	1	2	Nicholas Bawlf
1933	4	2	0	Nicholas Bawlf
1934	5	0	2	Nicholas Bawlf
1935	5	1	0	Nicholas Bawlf
1936	2	6	0	Nicholas Bawlf
1937	3	5	1	Nicholas Bawlf
1938	0	3	5	Nicholas Bawlf
1939	3	3	2	Nicholas Bawlf
1940	2	4	1	Nicholas Bawlf
1941	5	3	0	Nicholas Bawlf
1942	4	3	1	Nicholas Bawlf
1943	6	1	1	Nicholas Bawlf
1944	6	1	0	Nicholas Bawlf
1945	3	5	1	Nicholas Bawlf
1946	1	6	1	—
1947	2	5	2	Ross Smith
1948	6	0	3	Ross Smith
1949	6	1	1	Ross Smith
1950	4	2	2	Ross Smith
1951	2	2	4	Ross Smith
1952	5	5	0	George Patte
1953	4	2	2	George Patte
1954	5	5	0	George Patte
1955	4	5	0	George Patte
1956	6	1	2	George Patte
1957	5	3	1	George Patte
1958	6	2	1	George Patte
1959	2	7	0	George Patte
1960	4	5	1	George Patte
1961	3	6	1	Bill Pentland
1962	3	5	1	Bill Pentland
1963	0	8	1	Jerry Lace
1964	1	6	2	Jerry Lace
1965	6	4	1	Jerry Lace
1966	0	8	1	Jerry Lace
1967	4	4	1	Jerry Lace
1968	4	6	0	Bill Pentland
1969	4	6	1	Bill Pentland
1970	7	4	1	Bill Pentland
1971	11	4	0	Dan Wood
1972	13	4	0	Dan Wood
1973	8	4	2	Dan Wood

Yr.	W	L	T	Coach
1974	8	4	4	Dan Wood
1975	12	4	0	Dan Wood
1976	9	4	2	Jack Writer
1977	12	3	1	Jack Writer
1978	6	8	0	Jack Writer

CORTLAND STATE UNIVERSITY

Cortland, New York

Red Dragons   **Red and White**

Yr.	W	L	T	Coach
1936	5	3	0	T. F. "Prof" Holloway
1937	4	2	0	T. F. "Prof" Holloway
1938	4	4	0	T. F. "Prof" Holloway
1939	6	1	0	T. F. "Prof" Holloway
1940	3	3	1	T. F. "Prof" Holloway
1941	5	1	0	T. F. "Prof" Holloway
1942	3	3	0	T. F. "Prof" Holloway
1943	—	—	—	—
1944	—	—	—	—
1945	2	3	1	T. F. "Prof" Holloway
1946	5	3	0	T. F. "Prof" Holloway
1947	6	1	1	T. F. "Prof" Holloway
1948	4	2	1	T. F. "Prof" Holloway
1949	6	1	1	T. F. "Prof" Holloway
1950	4	4	0	T. F. "Prof" Holloway
1951	4	4	0	T. F. "Prof" Holloway
1952	7	1	0	T. F. "Prof" Holloway
1953	6	1	0	T. F. "Prof" Holloway
1954	4	3	1	T. F. "Prof" Holloway
1955	5	3	0	T. F. "Prof" Holloway
1956	4	2	1	T. F. "Prof" Holloway
1957	2	4	1	T. F. "Prof" Holloway
1958	3	2	3	T. F. "Prof" Holloway
1959	7	1	0	T. F. "Prof" Holloway
1960	9	1	0	T. F. "Prof" Holloway
1961	7	3	0	T. F. "Prof" Holloway
1962	8	2	1	T. F. "Prof" Holloway
1963	9	1	1	T. F. "Prof" Holloway
1964	9	2	0	T. F. "Prof" Holloway
1965	7	4	1	T. F. "Prof" Holloway
1966	8	3	1	T. F. "Prof" Holloway
1967	5	3	3	T. F. "Prof" Holloway
1968	5	6	0	T. F. "Prof" Holloway
1969	7	3	0	T. F. "Prof" Holloway
1970	5	4	3	T. F. "Prof" Holloway
1971	5	5	2	T. F. "Prof" Holloway
1972	8	5	0	T. F. "Prof" Holloway
1973	9	4	2	Fred Taube
1974	8	2	5	Fred Taube
1975	7	4	1	Fred Taube
1976	11	4	0	Fred Taube
1977	14	5	0	Fred Taube
1978	13	2	3	Fred Taube

DARTMOUTH COLLEGE

Hanover, New Hampshire

Big Green   **Green and White**

Yr.	W	L	T	Coach
1915	1	1	0	—
1916	2	3	1	—
1917	0	2	1	—
1918	—	—	—	—

Tom Dent coached Dartmouth from 1924–59, compiling a 143–111–22 mark.

Yr.	W	L	T	Coach
1941	5	2	0	Thomas Dent
1942	3	2	0	Thomas Dent
1943	4	1	0	Thomas Dent
1944	5	1	0	Thomas Dent
1945	2	3	1	Thomas Dent
1946	7	1	0	Thomas Dent
1947	6	2	0	Thomas Dent
1948	2	5	1	Thomas Dent
1949	4	4	1	Thomas Dent
1950	6	3	0	Thomas Dent
1951	6	1	1	Thomas Dent
1952	7	2	0	Thomas Dent
1953	7	1	0	Thomas Dent
1954	8	0	0	Thomas Dent
1955	6	5	0	Thomas Dent
1956	3	7	0	Thomas Dent
1957	2	6	2	Thomas Dent
1958	4	6	0	Thomas Dent
1959	4	6	0	Thomas Dent
1960	5	6	0	Alden Burnham
1961	5	6	0	Alden Burnham
1962	5	5	1	Alden Burnham
1963	4	6	0	Alden Burnham
1964	7	4	0	Alden Burnham
1965	5	5	0	Alden Burnham
1966	3	6	1	Alden Burnham
1967	2	8	1	Alden Burnham
1968	4	5	2	Alden Burnham
1969	5	6	0	Alden Burnham
1970	3	6	2	George Beim
1971	2	8	1	George Beim
1972	4	7	1	George Beim
1973	2	9	1	George Beim
1974	3	7	1	Thomas Griffith
1975	6	7	0	Thomas Griffith
1976	6	5	2	Thomas Griffith
1977	7	6	2	Thomas Griffith
1978	7	5	3	Thomas Griffith

DAVIDSON COLLEGE

Davidson, North Carolina

Wildcats				Red and Black
Yr.	W	L	T	Coach
1956	1	4	1	Paul Marrotte
1957	4	5	0	Paul Marrotte
1958	6	5	0	Paul Marrotte
1959	7	3	0	Paul Marrotte
1960	8	4	0	Paul Marrotte
1961	6	4	0	Harry Fogleman
1962	6	2	0	Harry Fogleman
1963	9	1	0	Harry Fogleman
1964	7	4	0	Harry Fogleman
1965	8	5	0	Harry Fogleman
1966	5	10	0	Harry Fogleman
1967	5	4	3	Harry Fogleman
1968	4	6	2	Harry Fogleman
1969	4	7	1	Harry Fogleman
1970	10	3	1	Harry Fogleman
1971	11	2	0	Harry Fogleman
1972	7	5	0	Harry Fogleman
1973	5	7	2	Raymond Stone
1974	8	5	3	Raymond Stone
1975	1	10	1	Raymond Stone
1976	3	11	1	Raymond Stone
1977	0	16	0	Karl Kremser
1978	5	10	1	Karl Kremser

Yr.	W	L	T	Coach
1919	1	2	0	W. C. Hulbert
1920	3	1	0	W. C. Hulbert
1921	3	3	0	J. C. Roule
1922	3	3	0	J. C. Roule
1923	1	2	1	J. C. Roule
1924	1	5	0	Thomas Dent
1925	4	1	1	Thomas Dent
1926	2	3	2	Thomas Dent
1927	3	3	0	Thomas Dent
1928	3	4	0	Thomas Dent
1929	4	3	1	Thomas Dent
1930	2	4	2	Thomas Dent
1931	2	3	1	Thomas Dent
1932	3	2	1	Thomas Dent
1933	4	1	1	Thomas Dent
1934	3	4	1	Thomas Dent
1935	4	2	1	Thomas Dent
1936	5	2	0	Thomas Dent
1937	1	5	1	Thomas Dent
1938	6	3	0	Thomas Dent
1939	3	7	0	Thomas Dent
1940	2	1	4	Thomas Dent

Fred Schmalz led Davis & Elkins to an 89–21–5 record and three NAIA national runner-up finishes from 1972–78.

DAVIS & ELKINS COLLEGE

Elkins, West Virginia

Senators   **Scarlet and White**

Yr.	W	L	T	Coach
1961	2	1	1	Hunter Davis
1962	3	5	0	Karl Herman
1963	5	4	0	Karl Herman
1964	3	6	0	Greg Meyers
1965	4	8	2	Jack McDonald
1966	2	10	0	Jack McDonald
1967	3	8	0	Greg Meyers
1968	12	0	3	Greg Meyers
1969	12	1	0	Greg Meyers
1970	13	1	1	Greg Meyers
1971	10	3	3	Charles Smith
1972	12	2	1	Fred Schmalz
1973	13	3	1	Fred Schmalz
1974	13	3	0	Fred Schmalz
1975	8	3	1	Fred Schmalz
1976	16	3	0	Fred Schmalz
1977	14	3	1	Fred Schmalz
1978	13	4	1	Fred Schmalz

DAYTON, UNIVERSITY OF

Dayton, Ohio

Flyers   **Red and Blue**

Yr.	W	L	T	Coach
1956	2	3	0	Pat Smith
1957	6	1	0	Pat Smith
1958	6	2	0	Paul Scheurman
1959	1	8	0	Paul Scheurman

Yr.	W	L	T	Coach
1960	1	5	2	John Wiesler
1961	4	5	0	John Wiesler
1962	1	7	0	John Wiesler
1963	2	5	1	John Wiesler
1964	4	4	0	John Schleppi
1965	7	1	1	John Schleppi
1966	7	1	1	Shaw Emmons
1967	8	2	1	John Schleppi
1968	9	1	1	John Schleppi
1969	7	3	1	Ray O'Hanlon
1970	6	4	1	Ray O'Hanlon
1971	8	2	0	Bob McNamee
1972	10	1	1	Bob McNamee
1973	6	2	2	Bob Richardson
1974	7	3	3	Bob Richardson
1975	11	3	0	Bob Richardson
1976	11	3	0	Bob Richardson
1977	6	9	1	Bob Richardson
1978	5	11	2	Bob Richardson

DELAWARE, UNIVERSITY OF

Newark, Delaware

Fighting Blue Hens   **Blue and Gold**

Yr.	W	L	T	Coach
1926	1	3	0	O'Brien
1927	0	7	1	—
1928	1	6	0	—
1929	4	3	0	—
1930	0	7	0	—
1931	1	4	1	Edward C. Bardo
1932	0	5	1	Edward C. Bardo
1933	3	4	0	Edward C. Bardo
1934	2	4	2	Edward C. Bardo

Yr.	W	L	T	Coach
1935	1	7	0	Edward C. Bardo
1936	4	3	1	A. C. Bowdle
1937	5	1	3	A. C. Bowdle
1938	5	3	2	H. W. Lawrence
1939	4	5	0	H. W. Lawrence
1940	5	3	0	H. W. Lawrence
1941	6	4	0	H. W. Lawrence
1942	3	3	2	H. W. Lawrence
1943	3	3	0	Edmund Prince
1944	0	5	2	Max Kurman
1945	2	5	0	Max Kurman
1946	1	7	0	Max Kurman
1947	2	9	0	Max Kurman
1948	3	6	1	Alden Burnham
1949	1	8	1	Alden Burnham
1950	5	7	0	Alden Burnham
1951	5	5	0	Alden Burnham
1952	2	8	0	Alden Burnham
1953	2	7	0	Alden Burnham
1954	2	6	0	Alden Burnham
1955	2	6	0	Alden Burnham
1956	0	8	1	Alden Burnham
1957	1	8	1	Alden Burnham
1958	1	7	1	Alden Burnham
1959	2	8	0	Alden Burnham
1960	2	9	0	P. Eugene Watson
1961	6	4	1	P. Eugene Watson
1962	1	7	4	P. Eugene Watson
1963	4	8	1	Loren Kline
1964	2	10	0	Loren Kline
1965	7	4	2	Loren Kline
1966	7	5	1	Loren Kline
1967	6	4	2	Loren Kline
1968	10	3	1	Loren Kline
1969	8	5	0	Loren Kline

Yr.	W	L	T	Coach
1970	9	2	2	Loren Kline
1971	8	1	2	Loren Kline
1972	6	5	0	Loren Kline
1973	6	3	3	Loren Kline
1974	6	3	3	Loren Kline
1975	10	2	2	Loren Kline
1976	10	3	2	Loren Kline
1977	8	5	2	Loren Kline
1978	9	4	0	Loren Kline

DENVER, UNIVERSITY OF

Denver, Colorado

Pioneers   **Crimson and Gold**

Yr.	W	L	T	Coach
1961	7	3	0	Edgar Laipenieks
1962	5	2	0	Willy Schaeffler
1963	5	2	1	Willy Schaeffler
1964	8	0	0	Willy Schaeffler
1965	7	0	0	Willy Schaeffler
1966	8	0	0	Willy Schaeffler
1967	8	2	0	Willy Schaeffler
1968	8	3	0	Willy Schaeffler
1969	6	1	0	Willy Schaeffler
1970	11	2	0	Peder Pytte
1971	5	2	2	Peder Pytte
1972	6	2	1	Peder Pytte
1973	2	11	1	Peder Pytte
1974	4	8	1	John Byrden
1975	9	5	0	John Byrden
1976	8	5	2	John Byrden
1977	7	7	0	John Byrden
1978	13	2	1	John Byrden

Goalie Peter Howard had eight shutouts as Denver wound up 13–2–1 in 1978.

Drew's Doug Trott is fully extended during his team's 1969 NAIA playoff win over Trenton.

DE PAUW UNIVERSITY

Greencastle, Indiana

Tigers   **Gold and Black**

Yr.	W	L	T	Coach
1966	0	8	0	Charles Erdmann
1967	5	4	1	Charles Erdmann
1968	6	2	2	Charles Erdmann
1969	2	6	0	Page Cotton
1970	4	6	0	Page Cotton
1971	7	3	1	Page Cotton
1972	5	8	0	Page Cotton
1973	2	7	1	Page Cotton
1974	5	6	1	Page Cotton
1975	4	7	0	Page Cotton
1976	6	5	0	Page Cotton
1977	9	4	1	Page Cotton
1978	8	4	1	Page Cotton

DICKINSON COLLEGE

Carlisle, Pennsylvania

Red Devils   **Red and White**

Yr.	W	L	T	Coach
1964	4	3	1	David Eavenson
1965	6	6	0	David Eavenson
1966	3	9	0	David Eavenson
1967	8	2	2	David Eavenson
1968	6	6	0	David Eavenson

Yr.	W	L	T	Coach
1969	4	6	2	David Eavenson
1970	7	7	0	David Eavenson
1971	4	9	1	David Eavenson
1972	6	6	0	David Eavenson
1973	4	7	3	David Eavenson
1974	8	4	2	David Eavenson
1975	5	7	1	William Nickey
1976	9	5	0	William Nickey
1977	8	7	0	William Nickey
1978	6	8	2	William Nickey

DREW UNIVERSITY

Madison, New Jersey

Rangers   **Green and Gold**

Yr.	W	L	T	Coach
1954	1	4	0	Robert Bannon
1955	5	2	1	Robert Bannon
1956	5	2	1	Robert Bannon
1957	6	3	0	Warren Tappin
1958	5	5	0	Warren Tappin
1959	5	6	0	Warren Tappin
1960	5	4	0	Warren Tappin
1961	5	5	0	Tim Doyle
1962	5	4	0	George Davis
1963	8	4	0	George Davis
1964	11	2	0	George Davis
1965	9	3	0	George Davis
1966	12	2	0	George Davis

Yr.	W	L	T	Coach	Yr.	W	L	T	Coach
1967	8	4	0	George Davis	1953	6	5	2	Don Yonker
1968	4	4	1	George Davis	1954	6	5	1	Don Yonker
1969	12	0	0	John Reeves	1955	10	3	1	Don Yonker
1970	8	3	2	John Reeves	1956	9	2	0	Don Yonker
1971	7	5	2	John Reeves	1957	9	2	0	Don Yonker
1972	10	1	1	John Reeves	1958	12	0	0	Don Yonker
1973	11	2	2	John Reeves	1959	5	4	1	Don Yonker
1974	10	3	3	John Reeves	1960	10	1	0	Don Yonker
1975	10	4	0	John Reeves	1961	8	2	1	Don Yonker
1976	10	3	1	John Reeves	1962	8	2	1	Don Yonker
1977	8	5	3	John Reeves	1963	9	3	0	Don Yonker
1978	8	7	1	John Reeves	1964	9	2	0	Don Yonker
					1965	7	3	0	Don Yonker
					1966	5	4	1	Don Yonker
					1967	4	4	2	Don Yonker
					1968	4	4	2	Don Yonker
					1969	1	10	0	Don Yonker
					1970	2	9	2	Don Yonker
					1971	2	9	2	Don Yonker
					1972	9	5	0	Don Yonker
					1973	3	9	1	Don Yonker
					1974	6	3	4	Don Yonker
					1975	7	4	2	Don Yonker

DREXEL UNIVERSITY

Philadelphia, Pennsylvania

Dragons   **Blue and Gold**

Yr.	W	L	T	Coach					
1947	4	4	1	Don Yonker	1976	6	5	2	Don Yonker
1948	4	3	1	Don Yonker	1977	5	7	1	Johnson Bowie
1949	3	4	1	Don Yonker	1978	6	7	0	Johnson Bowie
1950	5	2	2	Don Yonker					
1951	5	2	2	Don Yonker					
1952	5	4	1	Don Yonker					

Don Yonker (third row, right) and his 12–0 Drexel team were unofficial national champions in 1958.

DUKE UNIVERSITY

Durham, North Carolina

Blue Devils   **Blue and White**

Yr.	W	L	T	Coach
1935	4	1	1	K. C. Gerard
1936	4	0	0	K. C. Gerard
1937	5	0	0	K. C. Gerard
1938	7	1	0	K. C. Gerard
1939	3	3	3	K. C. Gerard
1940	2	5	0	K. C. Gerard
1941	1	6	2	K. C. Gerard
1942	0	3	0	K. C. Gerard
1943	—	—	—	—
1944	1	1	1	—
1945	—	—	—	—
1946	5	1	1	K. C. Gerard
1947	4	2	1	K. C. Gerard
1948	5	1	1	K. C. Gerard
1949	3	4	0	Jim Bly
1950	4	2	1	Jim Bly
1951	5	2	0	Jim Bly
1952	6	1	1	Jim Bly
1953	6	3	0	Jim Bly
1954	4	5	0	Jim Bly
1955	4	4	0	Jim Bly
1956	6	2	0	Jim Bly
1957	4	2	2	Jim Bly
1958	3	5	1	Jim Bly
1959	2	6	0	Jim Bly
1960	5	2	2	Jim Bly
1961	7	3	0	Jim Bly
1962	7	3	0	Jim Bly
1963	3	6	1	Jim Bly
1964	3	6	1	Jim Bly
1965	4	8	0	Jim Bly
1966	4	6	0	Roy Skinner
1967	7	4	0	Roy Skinner
1968	6	4	0	Roy Skinner
1969	7	4	0	Roy Skinner
1970	8	3	0	Roy Skinner
1971	8	3	0	Roy Skinner
1972	7	3	2	Roy Skinner
1973	8	3	0	Roy Skinner
1974	6	4	1	Roy Skinner
1975	4	5	2	Roy Skinner
1976	6	6	0	Roy Skinner
1977	4	8	1	John Wilson
1978	9	7	1	John Wilson

EARLHAM COLLEGE

Richmond, Indiana

Hustlin' Quakers   **Maroon and White**

Yr.	W	L	T	Coach
1949	0	1	0	Tom Brown
1950	1	3	0	Tom Brown
1951	6	1	0	Tom Brown
1952	5	2	2	Tom Brown
1953	4	3	0	Ed Nicholson
1954	7	2	1	Charles Matlack
1955	6	3	0	Charles Matlack
1956	4	2	2	Charles Matlack
1957	6	1	1	Charles Matlack
1958	7	1	1	Charles Matlack
1959	3	6	1	Charles Matlack
1960	4	6	0	Charles Matlack
1961	5	2	3	Charles Matlack

Yr.	W	L	T	Coach
1962	3	6	1	Charles Matlack
1963	9	1	1	Charles Matlack
1964	5	4	1	Charles Matlack
1965	11	2	1	Charles Matlack
1966	9	2	0	Charles Matlack
1967	10	2	0	Charles Matlack
1968	11	2	1	Charles Matlack
1969	10	3	0	Charles Matlack
1970	10	5	0	Charles Matlack
1971	8	4	1	Charles Matlack
1972	14	4	0	Charles Matlack
1973	7	4	1	Charles Matlack
1974	1	7	1	Charles Matlack
1975	0	10	0	Charles Matlack
1976	3	7	1	Charles Matlack
1977	7	7	0	Charles Matlack
1978	8	7	1	Charles Matlack

EAST CAROLINA UNIVERSITY

Greenville, North Carolina

Pirates   **Purple and Gold**

Yr.	W	L	T	Coach
1965	0	5	0	Odell Welborn
1966	2	6	0	Odell Welborn
1967	3	7	0	John Welborn
1968	2	6	1	Jim Grimsley
1969	3	4	1	John Loustedt
1970	3	7	2	John Loustedt
1971	4	7	2	John Loustedt
1972	3	6	0	John Loustedt
1973	3	8	2	Monte Little
1974	7	4	0	Curtis Frye
1975	3	6	2	Curtis Frye
1976	3	11	1	Curtis Frye
1977	2	10	0	Brad Smith
1978	3	11	2	Brad Smith

EAST STROUDSBURG STATE COLLEGE

East Stroudsburg, Pennsylvania

Warriors   **Red and Black**

Yr.	W	L	T	Coach
1930	6	2	0	Howard DeNike
1931	7	0	0	Howard DeNike
1932	5	2	1	Howard DeNike
1933	6	2	0	Howard DeNike
1934	5	2	1	Howard DeNike
1935	2	4	1	Howard DeNike
1936	2	3	1	Charles Vibberts
1937	4	3	0	Charles Vibberts
1938	3	5	1	Charles Vibberts
1939	6	2	1	Howard DeNike
1940	4	1	3	Howard DeNike
1941	4	2	1	Howard DeNike
1942	3	1	1	Howard DeNike
1943	—	—	—	—
1944	5	0	1	Howard DeNike
1945	0	4	2	Howard DeNike
1946	7	0	1	Howard DeNike
1947	1	5	1	Howard DeNike
1948	6	2	1	Howard DeNike
1949	3	3	2	Howard DeNike
1950	5	2	1	Howard DeNike
1951	4	1	1	Howard DeNike
1952	6	0	1	Howard DeNike

Yr.	W	L	T	Coach
1953	5	1	1	Howard DeNike
1954	2	4	1	Howard DeNike
1955	1	3	3	Howard DeNike
1956	6	1	0	John Eiler
1957	3	4	2	John Eiler
1958	5	2	2	John Eiler
1959	5	3	0	John Eiler
1960	5	4	1	John Eiler
1961	10	3	0	John Eiler
1962	11	1	0	John Eiler
1963	7	4	2	John Eiler
1964	12	1	0	John Eiler
1965	11	2	0	John Eiler
1966	5	5	1	John McKeon
1967	5	3	1	John McKeon
1968	4	9	0	John McKeon
1969	9	5	0	John McKeon
1970	5	6	3	John Mckeon
1971	8	3	2	John McKeon
1972	14	3	2	John McKeon
1973	14	4	0	John McKeon
1974	10	4	1	John McKeon
1975	7	7	1	John McKeon
1976	10	6	1	John McKeon
1977	4	11	1	John McKeon
1978	3	9	2	John McKeon

EASTERN ILLINOIS UNIVERSITY

Charleston, Illinois

Panthers				Blue and White
Yr.	W	L	T	Coach
1963	4	1	0	Harold Pinter
1964	2	6	0	Harold Pinter

Yr.	W	L	T	Coach
1965	7	3	0	Fritz Teller
1966	7	3	0	Fritz Teller
1967	5	4	0	Fritz Teller
1968	6	5	0	Fritz Teller
1969	13	2	1	Fritz Teller
1970	7	5	0	Fritz Teller
1971	5	6	3	Fritz Teller
1972	7	3	1	Fritz Teller
1973	7	4	2	Fritz Teller
1974	10	5	0	Fritz Teller
1975	8	4	1	Fritz Teller
1976	8	2	3	Fritz Teller
1977	10	4	1	Schellas Hyndman
1978	15	5	0	Schellas Hyndman

EASTERN MENNONITE COLLEGE

Harrisonburg, Virginia

Royals				Blue and White
Yr.	W	L	T	Coach
1966	2	6	0	Gene Hostetler
1967	6	6	0	Ron Koppenhauer
1968	8	3	0	Ron Koppanhauer
1969	6	6	1	Ron Koppenhauer
1970	4	6	1	Byron Shenk
1971	6	5	1	Byron Shenk
1972	5	7	1	Byron Shenk
1973	4	6	2	Byron Shenk
1974	4	9	2	Byron Shenk
1975	7	5	1	Byron Shenk
1976	11	3	0	Byron Shenk
1977	3	6	2	Byron Shenk
1978	9	5	2	Byron Shenk

Al Hershey (front left), flanked by 1961 Elizabethtown teammates Bob Lash (front right), Jerry Botdorf and Ron Shubert (left to right), was an All-American in 1963.

ELIZABETHTOWN COLLEGE

Elizabethtown, Pennsylvania

Blue Jays				Blue and Gray
Yr.	W	L	T	Coach
1938	1	4	1	Ira R. Herr
1939	3	0	1	Ira R. Herr
1940	3	2	1	Ira R. Herr
1941	1	2	1	Ira R. Herr
1942	2	1	0	Ira R. Herr
1943	—	—	—	—
1944	—	—	—	—
1945	—	—	—	—
1946	—	—	—	—
1947	3	3	0	Ira R. Herr
1948	2	3	0	Ira R. Herr
1949	3	4	0	J. H. Dodd
1950	3	4	1	J. H. Dodd
1951	3	4	1	J. H. Dodd
1952	6	2	0	J. H. Dodd
1953	5	2	1	D. Paul Greene
1954	3	2	3	D. Paul Greene
1955	4	3	2	D. Paul Greene
1956	5	3	1	D. Paul Greene
1957	5	3	1	D. Paul Greene
1958	8	2	0	Ira R. Herr
1959	9	1	2	Ira R. Herr
1960	10	1	1	Ira R. Herr
1961	8	1	1	Dr. Owen Wright
1962	12	2	0	Dr. Owen Wright
1963	12	2	0	Dr. Owen Wright
1964	8	4	0	Dr. Owen Wright
1965	10	4	0	Dr. Owen Wright
1966	14	1	1	Dr. Owen Wright
1967	15	1	1	Dr. Owen Wright
1968	11	2	0	Al Hershey
1969	10	2	3	Dr. Owen Wright
1970	10	4	1	Dr. Owen Wright
1971	12	4	0	Dr. Owen Wright
1972	12	4	0	Dr. Owen Wright
1973	10	3	4	Dr. Owen Wright
1974	6	6	4	Dr. Owen Wright
1975	10	5	0	Dr. Owen Wright
1976	13	7	0	Dr. Owen Wright
1977	10	4	3	Dr. Owen Wright
1978	12	3	3	Dr. Owen Wright

ELON COLLEGE

Elon College, North Carolina

Fightin' Christians				Cardinal and Gold
Yr.	W	L	T	Coach
1975	2	8	0	Charles Harris
1976	6	6	0	Charles Harris
1977	2	10	0	Charles Harris
1978	2	11	1	Stephen Ballard

ERSKINE COLLEGE

Due West, South Carolina

Flying Fleet				Maroon and Gold
Yr.	W	L	T	Coach
1966	1	7	0	Harry Stille
1967	0	8	2	Charles Smith
1968	4	7	1	Charles Smith
1969	12	2	0	Charles Smith

Yr.	W	L	T	Coach
1970	12	1	1	Charles Smith
1971	12	3	0	Darrell Saunders
1972	10	5	0	Darrell Saunders
1973	10	5	2	Darrell Saunders
1974	13	5	0	Steve Parker
1975	10	5	0	Darrell Saunders
1976	12	4	0	Ralph Lundy
1977	14	6	1	Ralph Lundy
1978	11	5	1	Ralph Lundy

EVANSVILLE, UNIVERSITY OF

Evansville, Indiana

Purple Aces				Purple and White
Yr.	W	L	T	Coach
1974	3	8	0	Bill Vieth
1975	6	6	0	Bill Vieth
1976	3	8	0	Bill Vieth
1977	8	7	1	Bob Gaudin
1978	13	6	0	Bob Gaudin

FAIRLEIGH DICKINSON UNIVERSITY

Teaneck, New Jersey

Knights				Blue, Maroon, and White
Yr.	W	L	T	Coach
1955	3	5	0	Bill Hunt
1956	3	4	3	George Glasgow
1957	8	4	3	George Glasgow
1958	10	1	1	George Glasgow
1959	6	2	2	George Glasgow
1960	8	4	1	George Glasgow
1961	8	2	1	George Glasgow
1962	7	2	0	George Glasgow
1963	5	2	3	George Glasgow
1964	9	1	1	George Glasgow
1965	4	5	1	George Glasgow
1966	6	3	0	George Glasgow
1967	9	4	1	George Glasgow
1968	7	5	2	George Glasgow
1969	6	6	0	George Glasgow
1970	4	8	0	Robert Cowell
1971	2	10	1	Robert Cowell
1972	3	10	2	Gerry Clinton
1973	6	6	2	Gerry Clinton
1974	11	2	1	George Glasgow
1975	13	2	0	George Glasgow
1976	10	2	0	George Glasgow
1977	5	5	0	Nick DeJager
1978	6	6	1	Ben Stravato

FITCHBURG STATE COLLEGE

Fitchburg, Massachusetts

Falcons				Green and White
Yr.	W	L	T	Coach
1971	2	9	0	Joseph Farias
1972	2	9	0	Eugene Casassa
1973	2	9	1	Eugene Casassa
1974	4	8	0	Eugene Casassa
1975	5	6	0	Eugene Casassa
1976	2	9	0	Eugene Casassa
1977	8	4	0	Tony Ammendolia
1978	8	4	2	Frederick Vona

Fairleigh Dickinson's Ricky Cataldi is thwarted by Bucknell goalkeeper Ted Peterson during the fourth overtime of a marathon FDU playoff triumph.

FLORIDA INTERNATIONAL UNIVERSITY

Miami, Florida

Sunblazers				Blue and Gold
Yr.	**W**	**L**	**T**	**Coach**
1972	8	4	1	Greg Myers
1973	11	6	2	Greg Myers
1974	8	2	1	Greg Myers
1975	7	4	0	Bill Nuttall
1976	8	4	0	Bill Nuttall
1977	17	2	1	Bill Nuttall
1978	11	6	0	Bill Nuttall

FLORIDA INSTITUTE OF TECHNOLOGY

Jensen Beach, Florida

Spurs				Blue and White
Yr.	**W**	**L**	**T**	**Coach**
1973	8	2	1	Pete Navaretta
1974	7	3	0	Pete Navaretta
1975	9	3	1	Pete Navaretta
1976	10	4	0	Pete Navaretta
1977	8	7	0	Pete Navaretta
1978	7	7	0	Pete Navaretta

FLORIDA SOUTHERN UNIVERSITY

Lakeland, Florida

Moccasins				Scarlet and White
Yr.	**W**	**L**	**T**	**Coach**
1957	1	2	2	Jim Bush
1958	6	1	0	Jim Bush
1959	1	4	2	Jim Bush
1960	2	3	2	Jim Bush
1961	1	5	1	Jim Bush
1962	0	6	3	Jim Bush
1963	5	4	0	Jim Bush
1964	5	4	0	Jim Bush
1965	4	4	1	Jim Bush
1966	5	4	1	Jim Bush
1967	5	2	3	Jim Bush
1968	8	5	0	Jim Bush
1969	5	5	2	Jim Bush
1970	7	7	0	Jim Bush
1971	9	4	0	Jim Bush
1972	10	3	0	Jim Bush
1973	7	4	3	Jim Bush
1974	1	11	0	Jim Bush
1975	7	6	0	Jim Bush
1976	3	7	1	Jim Bush
1977	5	6	1	Jim Bush
1978	8	5	0	Jim Bush

Mark Dryden starred in the nets for Florida International.

FORDHAM UNIVERSITY

Bronx, New York

Rams   Maroon and White

Yr.	W	L	T	Coach
1969	3	9	2	Frank Schnur
1970	5	13	0	Frank Schnur
1971	7	7	3	Frank Schnur
1972	8	5	2	Frank Schnur
1973	11	4	1	Frank Schnur
1974	8	5	0	Frank Schnur
1975	4	9	0	Frank Schnur
1976	7	8	0	Frank Schnur
1977	7	8	1	Frank Schnur
1978	4	9	2	Frank Schnur

FRANKLIN AND MARSHALL COLLEGE

Lancaster, Pennsylvania

Diplomats   Blue and White

Yr.	W	L	T	Coach
1926	1	3	0	P. N. Leinbach
1927	2	3	1	P. N. Leinbach
1928	2	4	0	D. Chambers

Yr.	W	L	T	Coach
1929	1	6	0	W. N. Sipple
1930	5	3	1	John Pyott
1931	2	4	1	Jim Pyott
1932	2	4	1	W. L. Osborn
1933	4	4	1	R. F. Billhart
1934	1	7	1	R. F. Billhart
1935	4	4	0	R. F. Billhart
1936	2	4	2	R. A. Weitzel
1937	2	4	1	R. A. Weitzel
1938	3	4	3	John Pyott
1939	7	5	0	John Pyott
1940	6	4	2	John Pyott
1941	6	3	1	John Pyott
1942	2	3	0	R. H. Harral
1943	—	—	—	—
1944	—	—	—	—
1945	—	—	—	—
1946	2	3	0	George McGinness
1947	5	3	0	Bob Smith
1948	5	6	0	Bob Smith
1949	8	4	0	Bob Smith
1950	8	1	2	Bob Smith
1951	7	3	1	Bob Smith
1952	9	0	0	Bob Smith
1953	7	4	0	Bob Smith

Yr.	W	L	T	Coach
1954	3	6	1	Bob Smith
1955	4	3	2	Bob Smith
1956	3	4	2	Bob Smith
1957	7	2	0	Bob Smith
1958	4	4	0	Bob Smith
1959	3	6	1	Bob Smith
1960	6	3	0	Bob Smith
1961	5	4	1	Bob Smith
1962	10	1	0	Bob Smith
1963	5	3	2	Bob Smith
1964	7	2	2	Nowell Hoover
1965	5	3	2	Nowell Hoover
1966	6	2	2	Nowell Hoover
1967	3	7	0	Nowell Hoover
1968	0	9	1	Nowell Hoover
1969	1	10	1	Nowell Hoover
1970	2	7	0	Nowell Hoover
1971	3	7	0	Nowell Hoover
1972	5	6	1	Al Hershey
1973	8	4	2	Al Hershey
1974	7	4	2	Al Hershey
1975	7	7	0	Al Hershey
1976	7	4	3	Al Hershey
1977	9	6	0	Al Hershey
1978	11	5	3	Al Hershey

FREDONIA STATE UNIVERSITY

Fredonia, New York

Blue Devils   **Blue and White**

Yr.	W	L	T	Coach
1959	2	3	0	Patrick Damore
1960	7	2	0	Patrick Damore
1961	5	3	1	Patrick Damore
1962	2	5	2	Patrick Damore
1963	6	3	0	Patrick Damore
1964	5	2	2	Patrick Damore
1965	5	4	0	Patrick Damore
1966	3	7	1	Patrick Damore
1967	0	8	1	Patrick Damore
1968	1	9	0	Thomas Prevet
1969	2	8	0	Thomas Prevet
1970	4	6	1	Thomas Prevet
1971	8	4	2	Thomas Prevet
1972	12	5	1	Thomas Prevet
1973	12	4	0	Thomas Prevet
1974	9	3	2	Thomas Prevet
1975	17	2	0	James Hoffman
1976	7	5	2	James Hoffman
1977	9	4	2	Thomas Prevet
1978	8	6	1	Thomas Prevet

Fredonia State's Frantz Borno (left) closes in on a Buffalo ballhandler during 1978 action.

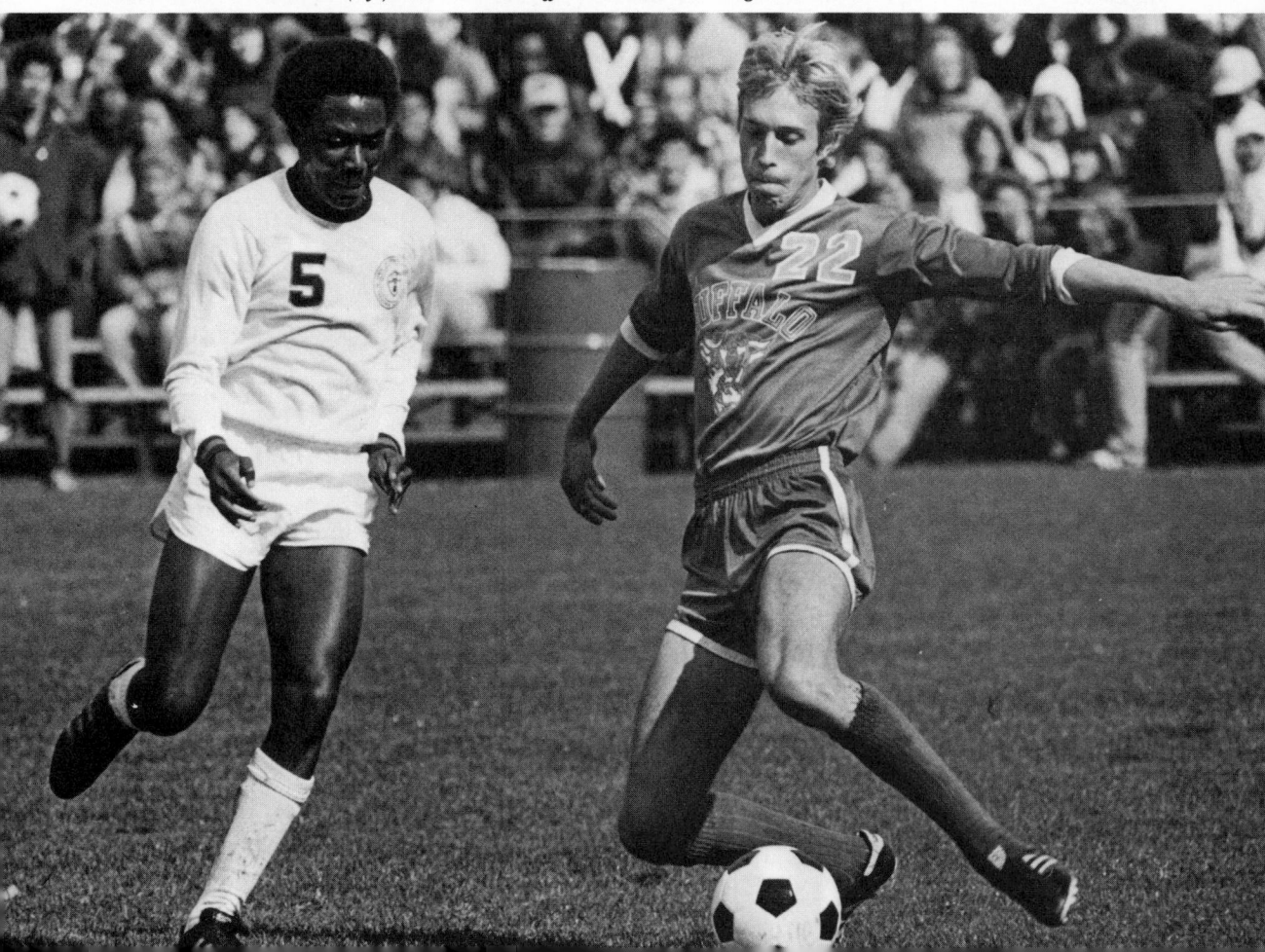

Grounded Furman goalkeeper Stu Magenheimer and teammate Cliff McCormick (dark jersey, nearest ball) do their best against Clemson in a 1976 engagement.

FROSTBURG STATE COLLEGE

Frostburg, Maryland

Bobcats **Black and Gold**

Yr.	W	L	T	Coach
1947	2	4	0	Kenneth Babock
1948	4	3	1	Kenneth Babock
1949	3	3	3	Kenneth Babock
1950	6	3	0	Kenneth Babock
1951	2	3	2	Kenneth Babock
1952	3	2	0	Kenneth Babock
1953	5	1	2	Kenneth Babock
1954	5	2	1	Kenneth Babock
1955	4	1	1	Kenneth Babock
1956	3	3	0	Kenneth Babock
1957	3	5	0	Kenneth Babock
1958	2	4	2	Kenneth Babock
1959	6	1	1	Kenneth Babock
1960	6	3	0	Kenneth Babock
1961	4	3	2	Kenneth Babock
1962	6	3	0	Kenneth Babock
1963	4	5	0	Kenneth Babock
1964	3	5	0	Kenneth Babock
1965	5	4	0	Kenneth Babock
1966	1	8	2	John Barnett
1967	6	8	1	John Barnett
1968	5	7	3	John Barnett

Yr.	W	L	T	Coach
1969	7	4	2	Kenneth Kutler
1970	9	3	1	Kenneth Kutler
1971	8	4	2	Kenneth Kutler
1972	8	4	2	Kenneth Kutler
1973	2	8	2	Kenneth Kutler
1974	8	5	3	Kenneth Kutler
1975	6	6	0	Kenneth Kutler
1976	6	6	1	Kenneth Kutler
1977	9	6	3	Kenneth Kutler
1978	9	2	2	Kenneth Kutler

FURMAN UNIVERSITY

Greenville, South Carolina

Paladins **Purple and White**

Yr.	W	L	T	Coach
1971	1	8	2	Paul Scarpa
1972	4	6	1	Paul Scarpa
1973	4	6	1	Paul Scarpa
1974	3	8	1	Paul Scarpa
1975	6	6	0	Paul Scarpa
1976	0	10	3	Paul Scarpa
1977	5	8	1	Paul Scarpa
1978	7	6	1	Paul Scarpa

GANNON COLLEGE

Erie, Pennsylvania

Golden Knights   Maroon and Gold

Yr.	W	L	T	Coach
1968	2	12	0	—
1969	4	8	0	—
1970	4	9	0	—
1971	5	6	2	—
1972	4	9	0	—
1973	5	7	0	—
1974	4	6	2	Rich Wrobel
1975	5	7	1	Rich Wrobel
1976	5	8	0	Rich Wrobel
1977	3	11	1	Rich Wrobel
1978	3	13	0	Rich Wrobel

Henry Castaneda was an NAIA All-American in 1974 as George Mason finished 11–3–4.

GEORGE MASON UNIVERSITY

Fairfax, Virginia

Patriots   Green and Gold

Yr.	W	L	T	Coach
1968	1	8	0	D. Fecteao
1969	3	10	1	D. Fecteao
1970	4	7	0	L. Cable
1971	9	2	0	H. Laszlo
1972	12	3	1	H. Laszlo
1973	13	5	0	M. Krotee
1974	11	3	4	M. Krotee
1975	3	9	0	M. Krotee
1976	2	9	2	D. Broad
1977	2	11	2	D. Broad
1978	6	6	2	D. Broad

GEORGE WASHINGTON UNIVERSITY

Washington, DC

Colonials   Buff and Blue

Yr.	W	L	T	Coach
1965	3	7	1	Tom White
1966	3	9	0	Tom White
1967	5	7	0	Tom White
1968	6	7	0	Tom White
1969	4	7	0	Tom White
1970	2	6	2	John "Buck" Davidson
1971	4	5	0	John "Buck" Davidson
1972	3	6	2	John "Buck" Davidson
1973	3	6	3	Georges Edeline
1974	8	4	0	Georges Edeline
1975	7	5	0	Georges Edeline
1976	7	3	1	Georges Edeline
1977	10	3	0	Georges Edeline
1978	8	3	2	Georges Edeline

GEORGIA COLLEGE

Milledgeville, Georgia

Colonials   Blue and White

Yr.	W	L	T	Coach
1975	11	3	0	John Kurtz
1976	10	4	1	John Kurtz
1977	8	7	0	John Kurtz
1978	5	8	0	John Kurtz

GEORGIA STATE UNIVERSITY

Atlanta, Georgia

Panthers   Royal Blue and Sky Blue

Yr.	W	L	T	Coach
1968	5	3	1	Costas Alexandrides
1969	6	5	0	Herbert Burgess
1970	10	6	1	Herbert Burgess
1971	12	4	0	Herbert Burgess
1972	12	5	0	Herbert Burgess
1973	7	7	1	Herbert Burgess
1974	8	8	1	Herbert Burgess
1975	11	3	0	Herbert Burgess
1976	9	3	1	Hugh O'Neill
1977	9	4	0	Hugh O'Neill
1978	10	5	0	Hugh O'Neill

Georges Edeline (right rear), flanked by 1967 George Washington teammates Roland Romaine (kneeling), Rudy LaPorta and Fred Ramos (left to right), came back to coach his alma mater in 1973.

GETTYSBURG COLLEGE

Gettysburg, Pennsylvania

Bullets　　　　　　　　　**Orange and Blue**

Yr.	W	L	T	Coach
1930	4	1	1	William Hartshorne
1931	2	5	0	William Hartshorne
1932	0	6	0	William Hartshorne
1933	5	2	0	William Hartshorne
1934	5	3	0	William Hartshorne
1935	3	3	2	William Hartshorne
1936	7	2	0	William Hartshorne
1937	2	6	1	William Hartshorne
1938	2	6	2	William Hartshorne
1939	6	4	1	William Hartshorne
1940	7	2	1	William Hartshorne
1941	2	5	0	William Hartshorne
1942	3	2	1	William Hartshorne
1943	—	—	—	—
1944	—	—	—	—
1945	0	4	0	William Hartshorne
1946	3	4	1	William Hartshorne
1947	2	4	2	William Hartshorne
1948	0	8	1	William Hartshorne
1949	3	5	1	William Hartshorne
1950	5	5	0	William Hartshorne
1951	5	2	1	William Hartshorne
1952	3	5	2	William Hartshorne
1953	4	4	1	William Hartshorne
1954	0	8	1	William Hartshorne
1955	2	8	0	Bob Davies
1956	3	6	2	Bob Davies
1957	9	1	2	Guillermo Barriga

Yr.	W	L	T	Coach
1958	5	6	1	Guillermo Barriga
1959	4	6	1	Louis Hammann
1960	3	7	1	Louis Hammann
1961	8	3	0	Louis Hammann
1962	5	8	0	Louis Hammann
1963	6	7	1	John Loose
1964	4	10	0	John Loose
1965	1	10	1	Louis Hammann
1966	3	8	2	Louis Hammann
1967	3	8	2	Louis Hammann
1968	2	10	1	Bob Smith
1969	4	9	0	Bob Smith
1970	4	8	1	Bob Smith
1971	4	7	1	Bob Smith
1972	5	6	1	Brad Cahill
1973	4	5	3	Brad Cahill
1974	2	8	3	William Rost
1975	4	9	1	William Rost
1976	5	7	1	William Rost
1977	7	7	1	William Rost
1978	7	6	1	William Rost

GLASSBORO STATE COLLEGE

Glassboro, New Jersey

Profs　　　　　　　　　**Brown and Gold**

Yr.	W	L	T	Coach
1955	0	1	0	Sam Porch
1956	1	7	0	Sam Porch
1957	1	6	1	Sam Porch

Yr.	W	L	T	Coach
1958	5	5	0	Sam Porch
1959	6	4	1	Sam Porch
1960	4	5	1	Sam Porch
1961	7	3	0	Sam Porch
1962	6	4	0	Sam Porch
1963	3	6	1	Sam Porch
1964	7	3	0	Sam Porch
1965	8	2	0	Sam Porch
1966	4	5	1	Sam Porch
1967	7	2	1	Sam Porch
1968	3	7	2	Sam Porch
1969	3	7	2	Sam Porch
1970	3	10	0	Sam Porch
1971	4	9	0	Sam Porch
1972	3	7	2	Sam Porch
1973	5	5	4	Sam Porch
1974	6	8	1	Sam Porch
1975	9	4	1	Sam Porch
1976	7	4	3	Dan Gilmore
1977	10	5	1	Dan Gilmore
1978	12	4	1	Dan Gilmore

GOSHEN COLLEGE

Goshen, Indiana

Maple Leafs   **Blue and White**

Yr.	W	L	T	Coach
1958	0	2	0	Art Smucker
1959	0	4	0	Marlin Wenger
1960	1	3	1	Ed Herr
1961	0	3	1	Harold Yoder

Yr.	W	L	T	Coach
1962	0	3	0	Harold Yoder
1963	2	5	0	Byron Shenk
1964	5	5	0	Byron Shenk
1965	9	0	0	Byron Shenk
1966	8	1	1	John Ingold
1967	9	3	0	John Ingold
1968	9	2	0	John Ingold
1969	8	0	1	John Ingold
1970	10	3	0	John Ingold
1971	13	3	0	John Ingold
1972	11	1	0	John Ingold
1973	14	3	0	John Ingold
1974	9	4	0	John Ingold
1975	10	3	1	John Ingold
1976	11	4	0	Dwain Hartzler
1977	12	7	1	Dwain Hartzler
1978	12	3	1	Dwain Hartzler

GREENVILLE COLLEGE

Greenville, Illinois

Panthers   **Orange and Black**

Yr.	W	L	T	Coach
1957	1	1	0	Spencer Mullholand
1958	0	2	0	S. Mullholand, A. Kurdieh
1959	4	2	0	Ali Kurdieh
1960	5	2	0	Ali Kurdieh
1961	3	3	1	J. Strahl, D. Doty
1962	3	6	0	John Strahl
1963	3	6	0	John Strahl

The Goshen soccer team celebrates its fifth-place finish in the 1973 NAIA Tournament.

Yr.	W	L	T	Coach	Yr.	W	L	T	Coach
1964	2	7	0	John Strahl	1945	2	1	2	Bob Thorn
1965	5	4	1	John Strahl	1946	4	2	1	Bob Thorn
1966	4	3	2	J. Strahl, H. Barnes	1947	4	4	1	Bob Thorn
1967	4	4	2	J. Strahl, R. Goldsmith	1948	5	0	3	Bob Thorn
1968	1	8	0	J. Strahl, R. Goldsmith	1949	2	4	2	Bob Thorn
1969	1	10	0	J. Strahl, P. Storer	1950	6	2	0	Bob Thorn
1970	6	6	0	J. Strahl, P. Storer	1951	2	1	3	Bob Thorn
1971	8	4	1	Phil Storer	1952	6	0	0	Bob Thorn
1972	6	7	0	Jim Stuart	1953	6	1	1	Bob Thorn
1973	10	3	2	Jim Stuart	1954	7	1	0	Bob Thorn
1974	4	7	2	Jim Sturat	1955	5	2	1	Bob Thorn
1975	3	10	2	Jim Stuart	1956	7	0	0	Bob Thorn
1976	2	12	2	Jim Stuart	1957	6	2	0	Dan Leviton
1977	10	6	1	Jim Stuart	1958	5	3	0	Dan Leviton
1978	5	10	1	Jim Stuart	1959	4	4	1	Dan Leviton
					1960	1	5	2	Dan Leviton
					1961	2	5	0	Dan Leviton
					1962	6	4	1	Cliff Wettig
					1963	6	3	0	Cliff Wettig
					1964	9	0	0	Cliff Wettig
					1965	8	0	1	Cliff Wettig
					1966	7	1	1	Cliff Wettig
					1967	6	4	0	Cliff Wettig
					1968	7	3	1	Cliff Wettig
					1969	9	2	0	Cliff Wettig
					1970	7	3	0	Cliff Wettig

GROVE CITY COLLEGE

Grove City, Pennsylvania

Wolverines   **Crimson and White**

Yr.	W	L	T	Coach					
1938	1	2	1	Bob Thorn	1971	5	3	1	Russ Trimmer
1939	2	2	0	Bob Thorn	1972	4	4	1	Don Lyle
1940	3	3	0	Bob Thorn	1973	5	5	2	Don Lyle
1941	5	2	0	Bob Thorn	1974	6	4	2	Don Lyle
1942	5	1	0	Bob Thorn	1975	7	5	1	Don Lyle
1943	—	—	—	—					
1944	—	—	—	—					

Bob Thorn, founder of the Grove City soccer program, says farewell to Frank Sbrocco (right), the star of his last Wolverine team in 1956.

Yr.	W	L	T	Coach
1976	10	3	1	Don Lyle
1977	11	3	0	Don Lyle
1978	8	3	1	Don Lyle

GUSTAVUS ADOLPHUS COLLEGE

St. Peter, Minnesota

Golden Gusties   **Black and Gold**

Yr.	W	L	T	Coach
1967	2	1	2	Horst Ludwig
1968	5	0	0	Horst Ludwig
1969	8	0	1	Horst Ludwig
1970	13	1	0	Horst Ludwig
1971	10	2	2	Dan Hanson
1972	9	3	2	Horst Ludwig
1973	6	4	4	Negro Lopez
1974	8	5	3	Dan Hanson
1975	10	3	2	George Demers
1976	7	4	5	George Demers
1977	6	8	4	George Demers
1978	7	4	5	George Demers

HAMPDEN-SYDNEY COLLEGE

Hampden-Sydney, Virginia

Tigers   **Garnet and Gray**

Yr.	W	L	T	Coach
1969	2	3	3	Jim Simms
1970	5	7	1	Jim Simms
1971	4	9	1	Jim Simms
1972	3	8	1	Jim Simms
1973	0	9	5	Jim Simms
1974	4	6	4	Jim Simms
1975	6	9	0	Jim Simms
1976	7	5	0	Jim Simms
1977	4	10	0	Jim Simms
1978	6	7	2	Jim Simms

HARRIS-STOWE STATE COLLEGE

St. Louis, Missouri

Hornets   **Black and Gold**

Yr.	W	L	T	Coach
1961	4	3	0	Diaz
1962	8	2	1	Diaz
1963	—	—	—	—
1964	—	—	—	—
1965	—	—	—	—
1966	6	3	2	Dallas
1967	5	1	2	Dallas
1968	5	3	2	Werstein
1969	10	2	3	Bresnahan
1970	12	7	0	Bresnahan
1971	13	5	0	Bresnahan
1972	10	5	0	Bresnahan
1973	8	4	0	Bresnahan
1974	6	8	5	Bresnahan
1975	5	8	1	D. Maria
1976	11	4	1	Roger Engelhardt
1977	9	5	2	Roger Engelhardt
1978	11	6	1	Roger Engelhardt

HARTFORD, UNIVERSITY OF

West Hartford, Connecticut

Hawks   **Scarlet and White**

Yr.	W	L	T	Coach
1957	3	3	0	A. Peter LoMaglio
1958	3	6	0	A. Peter LoMaglio
1959	3	5	0	A. Peter LoMaglio
1960	5	6	0	A. Peter LoMaglio
1961	1	10	0	A. Peter LoMaglio
1962	9	3	0	A. Peter LoMaglio
1963	6	4	0	A. Peter LoMaglio
1964	4	6	0	A. Peter LoMaglio
1965	0	10	0	A. Peter LoMaglio
1966	0	12	0	A. Peter LoMaglio
1967	1	10	1	A. Peter LoMaglio
1968	0	12	0	A. Peter LoMaglio
1969	0	11	1	Francis Pastor
1970	8	2	1	Peter Sipples
1971	12	1	1	Allan Wilson
1972	11	1	0	Allan Wilson
1973	11	1	2	Allan Wilson
1974	9	3	4	Allan Wilson
1975	7	8	0	Allan Wilson
1976	13	4	0	Allan Wilson
1977	10	6	0	Allan Wilson
1978	11	4	0	Allan Wilson

HARTWICK COLLEGE

Oneonta, New York

Warriors   **Blue and White**

Yr.	W	L	T	Coach
1956	2	3	0	Hal Greig
1957	2	4	0	Hal Greig
1958	5	4	0	Hal Greig
1959	8	1	0	Hal Greig
1960	4	4	0	Dave Hasse
1961	8	1	1	Dave Hasse
1962	10	2	0	Dave Hasse
1963	10	1	0	Dave Hasse
1964	9	2	0	Dave Hasse
1965	4	4	1	Dave Hasse
1966	9	1	1	Dave Hasse
1967	11	1	0	Al Miller
1968	9	3	0	Al Miller
1969	10	2	1	Al Miller
1970	14	1	0	Al Miller
1971	11	2	1	Al Miller
1972	9	3	1	Al Miller
1973	9	2	3	Timo Liekoski
1974	10	4	3	Timo Liekoski
1975	11	3	1	Timo Liekoski
1976	16	1	1	Jim Lennox
1977	16	0	2	Jim Lennox
1978	10	5	1	Jim Lennox

HARVARD UNIVERSITY

Cambridge, Massachusetts

Crimson   **Crimson and White**

Yr.	W	L	T	Coach
1904	1	3	1	—
1905	0	2	0	—
1906	2	1	1	—

Hartwick head coach Al Miller (right) and assistant Bill Muse went on to run the show at Dallas (NASL) and Princeton, respectively.

Harvard celebrates after Morgan Hudson scored a sudden-death overtime goal to defeat Princeton in 1963.

Yr.	W	L	T	Coach	Yr.	W	L	T	Coach
1907	1	2	0	—	1943	—	—	—	—
1908	1	2	2	—	1944	—	—	—	—
1909	—	—	—	—	1945	—	—	—	—
1910	2	3	0	—	1946	2	4	3	James MacDonald
1911	4	2	0	—	1947	7	2	0	James MacDonald
1912	5	0	0	—	1948	8	2	1	J. Bruce Munro
1913	0	1	0	—	1949	6	5	0	J. Bruce Munro
1914	5	1	2	—	1950	6	5	1	J. Bruce Munro
1915	1	6	0	—	1951	2	4	3	J. Bruce Munro
1916	4	2	1	—	1952	5	5	2	J. Bruce Munro
1917	—	—	—	—	1953	4	7	0	J. Bruce Munro
1918	—	—	—	—	1954	8	3	0	J. Bruce Munro
1919	—	—	—	—	1955	10	2	0	J. Bruce Munro
1920	—	—	—	—	1956	3	8	0	J. Bruce Munro
1921	4	4	0	Charles Burgess	1957	6	2	3	J. Bruce Munro
1922	2	6	1	W. R. Welsh	1958	10	2	1	J. Bruce Munro
1923	3	6	0	W. R. Welsh	1959	9	1	3	J. Bruce Munro
1924	4	4	0	Thomas B. White	1960	7	2	1	J. Bruce Munro
1925	0	6	2	Thomas B. White	1961	8	2	1	J. Bruce Munro
1926	4	4	1	Thomas B. White	1962	6	5	0	J. Bruce Munro
1927	4	4	1	John Kershaw	1963	8	2	0	J. Bruce Munro
1928	5	5	2	John Kershaw	1964	6	2	2	J. Bruce Munro
1929	7	2	2	John Carr	1965	7	3	0	J. Bruce Munro
1930	8	1	0	John Carr	1966	8	3	0	J. Bruce Munro
1931	2	3	3	John Carr	1967	7	3	1	J. Bruce Munro
1932	4	1	4	John Carr	1968	6	4	3	J. Bruce Munro
1933	5	1	2	John Carr	1969	14	1	0	J. Bruce Munro
1934	6	1	1	John Carr	1970	12	1	0	J. Bruce Munro
1935	6	2	1	John Carr	1971	13	2	0	J. Bruce Munro
1936	3	3	2	John Carr	1972	10	2	1	J. Bruce Munro
1937	5	2	1	John Carr	1973	3	7	2	George Ford
1938	8	0	1	John Carr	1974	7	4	2	George Ford
1939	5	3	0	John Carr	1975	6	6	1	George Ford
1940	4	3	2	John Carr	1976	5	10	1	George Ford
1941	5	3	1	James MacDonald	1977	6	4	4	George Ford
1942	4	3	2	James MacDonald	1978	5	9	1	George Ford

Peter Bogovich of Harvard's 1970 Ivy champion takes a free kick against Pennsylvania.

Haverford's 1904 team captured the Manheim Cup.

HAVERFORD COLLEGE

Haverford, Pennsylvania

Fords   **Scarlet and Black**

Yr.	W	L	T	Coach
1901	4	1	0	R. M. Gummere
1902	1	1	1	Dr. J. Babbitt
1903	2	1	0	C. C. Morris
1904	5	1	3	R. L. Pearson
1905	8	3	1	—
1906	7	6	1	P. Brown
1907	6	5	2	C. T. Brown
1908	6	2	2	G. H. Deacon
1909	4	3	2	E. W. David
1910	9	6	4	W. J. Young
1911	7	9	2	F. Huish
1912	8	2	3	F. James
1913	6	4	1	J. Thomas
1914	3	5	1	J. Thomas
1915	4	0	2	G. Young
1916	6	2	2	G. Young
1917	—	—	—	—
1918	—	—	—	—
1919	7	7	1	G. Young
1920	7	3	0	D. Oates
1921	6	3	2	D. Oates
1922	4	3	3	J. McPete
1923	8	3	1	J. McPete
1924	7	1	2	J. McPete
1925	7	1	2	J. McPete
1926	8	0	2	J. McPete
1927	6	2	2	J. McPete
1928	6	3	2	J. McPete
1929	6	3	2	J. McPete
1930	5	2	2	J. McPete
1931	6	1	2	J. McPete

Yr.	W	L	T	Coach
1932	2	5	1	J. McPete
1933	4	3	0	J. McPete
1934	4	2	3	J. McPete
1935	0	8	1	J. Gentle
1936	6	4	2	J. Gentle
1937	8	3	0	J. Gentle
1938	8	2	0	J. Gentle
1939	9	5	0	J. Gentle
1940	9	3	0	J. Gentle
1941	7	3	1	E. Redington
1942	8	1	0	R. Mullen
1943	1	3	1	R. Mullen
1944	5	3	2	R. Mullen
1945	8	0	0	R. Mullen
1946	5	4	0	R. Mullen
1947	3	5	1	E. Redington
1948	7	2	1	E. Redington
1949	7	4	0	J. Mills
1950	8	4	1	J. Mills
1951	5	5	1	J. Mills
1952	5	3	3	J. Mills
1953	8	1	0	J. Mills
1954	7	3	2	J. Mills
1955	5	4	1	J. Mills
1956	7	4	0	J. Lester
1957	4	6	0	J. Mills
1958	5	5	1	J. Mills
1959	7	4	0	J. Mills
1960	5	5	0	J. Mills
1961	0	7	3	J. Mills
1962	4	4	1	J. Mills
1963	7	3	0	J. Mills
1964	4	5	2	J. Mills
1965	7	3	0	J. Mills
1966	8	2	1	J. Mills
1967	4	7	0	J. Mills

Yr.	W	L	T	Coach
1968	7	5	1	J. Mills
1969	7	5	1	J. Mills
1970	8	5	3	J. Mills
1971	10	6	0	D. Felsen
1972	7	7	1	D. Felsen
1973	3	11	1	D. Felsen
1974	6	5	4	D. Felsen
1975	11	3	0	D. Felsen
1976	12	4	1	D. Felsen
1977	11	3	0	D. Felsen
1978	9	6	1	S. Jarocki

HAWTHORNE COLLEGE

Antrim, New Hampshire

Highlanders   **Green and White**

Yr.	W	L	T	Coach
1977	12	4	0	Rick Sewell
1978	8	6	0	Bill Miller

HEIDELBERG COLLEGE

Tiffin, Ohio

Student Princes   **Red, Orange, and Black**

Yr.	W	L	T	Coach
1967	2	6	1	R. Scheiber, R. Leaf
1968	2	7	0	Rick Scheiber
1969	1	8	1	Dick Norman
1970	1	6	0	Dick Norman
1971	4	3	2	Dick Norman
1972	1	7	1	Bohdan Kuropas
1973	5	3	1	Bohdan Kuropas
1974	1	8	1	Karl Wittmann
1975	1	10	0	Karl Wittmann
1976	1	7	2	Karl Wittmann
1977	1	9	0	Karl Wittmann
1978	1	8	1	Tom Bartlett

HIGH POINT COLLEGE

High Point, North Carolina

Panthers   **Purple and White**

Yr.	W	L	T	Coach
1929	2	4	1	Edgar Heartley
1930	3	3	2	—
1931	1	5	0	—
1932	2	3	1	—
1933	4	3	0	—
1934	7	0	1	—
1935	4	1	1	—
1936	5	2	0	—
1937	4	1	1	—
1938	5	0	0	—
1939	6	1	0	—
1940	6	0	1	—
1941	5	0	1	—
1971	0	10	0	Chuck Hartman
1972	1	11	0	Ray Alley
1973	3	7	2	Ray Alley
1974	11	1	2	Ray Alley
1975	8	5	1	Ken Chartier
1976	12	6	0	Ken Chartier
1977	9	6	0	Ken Chartier
1978	5	11	0	Woody Gibson

HIRAM COLLEGE

Hiram, Ohio

Terriers   **Red and Blue**

Yr.	W	L	T	Coach
1959	1	1	3	George Sprogis
1960	2	6	0	George Sprogis
1961	3	8	0	George Sprogis
1962	4	7	0	George Sprogis, Bill Donaldson
1963	3	6	1	Bill Donaldson
1964	1	8	0	Bill Donaldson
1965	4	4	0	Bill Donaldson
1966	5	3	0	Bill Donaldson
1967	4	5	0	Reginald Price
1968	3	7	0	Reginald Price
1969	3	7	0	Reginald Price
1970	4	4	1	Peter Brann
1971	2	5	1	Peter Brann
1972	3	6	0	Peter Brann
1973	2	6	0	Peter Brann
1974	2	5	2	Peter Brann
1975	5	2	1	Peter Brann
1976	3	6	0	Peter Brann
1977	2	7	0	Peter Brann
1978	1	8	0	Peter Brann

HOBART COLLEGE

Geneva, New York

Statesmen   **Orange and Purple**

Yr.	W	L	T	Coach
1953	1	2	1	W. Raymond Demuth
1954	4	2	0	W. Raymond Demuth
1955	5	3	0	W. Raymond Demuth
1956	4	3	1	W. Raymond Demuth
1957	2	4	2	W. Raymond Demuth
1958	2	5	1	W. Raymond Demuth
1959	2	5	0	W. Raymond Demuth
1960	6	1	1	W. Raymond Demuth
1961	3	5	0	W. Raymond Demuth
1962	1	6	2	W. Raymond Demuth
1963	5	3	1	W. Raymond Demuth
1964	3	7	0	W. Raymond Demuth
1965	3	6	1	W. Raymond Demuth
1966	4	6	0	W. Raymond Demuth
1967	3	8	0	W. Raymond Demuth
1968	4	5	1	W. Raymond Demuth
1969	3	9	0	W. Raymond Demuth
1970	6	6	0	W. Raymond Demuth
1971	3	8	2	W. Raymond Demuth
1972	9	5	1	W. Raymond Demuth
1973	4	8	1	W. Raymond Demuth
1974	5	8	0	W. Raymond Demuth
1975	6	7	0	W. Raymond Demuth
1976	10	4	0	Jeffrey Warren
1977	9	5	3	Jeffrey Warren
1978	5	8	2	Jeffrey Warren

HOFSTRA UNIVERSITY

Hempstead, New York

Flying Dutchmen   **Blue and Gold**

Yr.	W	L	T	Coach
1955	6	4	1	Paul Lynner
1956	7	5	0	Paul Lynner

Coach Ray Demuth (back row, left) with his first Hobart team in 1953.

Yr.	W	L	T	Coach
1957	5	5	3	Paul Lynner
1958	5	10	0	Paul Lynner
1959	4	7	2	Paul Lynner
1960	5	8	2	Paul Lynner
1961	8	5	1	Paul Lynner
1962	8	3	1	Paul Lynner
1963	3	8	2	Paul Lynner
1964	3	8	2	Paul Lynner
1965	0	17	1	Robert Vanderwarker
1966	2	12	0	Robert Vanderwarker
1967	7	5	2	Robert Vanderwarker
1968	9	0	1	Robert Vanderwarker
1969	9	5	2	Robert Vanderwarker
1970	4	11	0	James Amen
1971	1	14	1	Dan DeStefano
1972	1	11	0	Dan DeStefano
1973	1	14	0	Dan DeStefano
1974	2	12	2	Dan DeStefano
1975	0	14	0	Dan DeStefano
1976	5	5	5	Angelo Anastasio
1977	6	9	0	Angelo Anastasio
1978	8	6	1	Ken Germano

HOPE COLLEGE

Holland, Michigan

Flying Dutchmen   **Blue and Orange**

Yr.	W	L	T	Coach
1963	0	1	0	Phillip Van Eyl
1964	6	1	1	Phillip Van Eyl
1965	4	5	0	Phillip Van Eyl
1966	1	7	0	Phillip Van Eyl
1967	5	5	1	Phillip Van Eyl
1968	6	4	0	William Vanderbilt
1969	3	7	0	William Vanderbilt
1970	7	4	0	Gene Brown

Yr.	W	L	T	Coach
1971	7	6	0	Gene Brown
1972	9	4	0	Gene Brown
1973	3	8	2	Glenn Van Wieren
1974	6	6	1	Glenn Van Wieren
1975	3	8	2	Glenn Van Wieren
1976	7	8	0	Glenn Van Wieren
1977	12	3	0	Glenn Van Wieren
1978	10	4	1	Glenn Van Wieren

HOWARD UNIVERSITY

Washington, D.C.

Bisons   **Blue and White**

Yr.	W	L	T	Coach
1947	5	0	0	James Chambers
1948	6	0	0	James Chambers
1949	10	1	0	James Chambers
1950	3	2	0	James Chambers
1951	2	3	0	James Chambers
1952	2	2	1	James Chambers
1953	5	0	1	James Chambers
1954	6	2	0	James Chambers
1955	3	4	0	James Chambers
1956	3	2	2	James Chambers
1957	4	2	2	James Chambers
1958	10	0	0	James Chambers
1959	8	3	0	James Chambers
1960	7	2	0	James Chambers
1961	9	0	1	James Chambers
1962	7	1	0	James Chambers
1963	7	2	0	James Chambers
1964	7	3	1	George Williams
1965	7	3	0	George Williams
1966	6	4	0	Sydney Hall
1967	6	3	0	Sydney Hall
1968	3	6	2	T. Chambers, E. Ipke

Winston Alexis led Howard in scoring in 1962 and 1963 and was a member of the Bisons' 1961 NAIA championship team.

In the 1974 NCAA championship game, Howard University (whose Calin McLean is on the right) defeated St. Louis, 2–1. The Billikens' Don Aubuchon is heading the ball.

Indiana, which would get as far as the NCAA final, is joyous over its first goal against Philadelphia Textile in 1978 semifinals.

Yr.	W	L	T	Coach
1969	6	6	1	James Chambers
1970	11	1	0	Lincoln Phillips
1971	15	0	0	Lincoln Phillips
1972	14	0	1	Lincoln Phillips
1973	7	1	1	Lincoln Phillips
1974	19	0	0	Lincoln Phillips
1975	11	4	1	Lincoln Phillips
1976	10	4	1	Lincoln Phillips
1977	12	1	0	Lincoln Phillips
1978	9	4	3	Lincoln Phillips

INDIANA UNIVERSITY

Bloomington, Indiana

Hoosiers **Cream and Crimson**

Yr.	W	L	T	Coach
1970	3	8	0	Jerry Yeagley
1971	12	0	0	Jerry Yeagley
1972	11	1	0	Jerry Yeagley
1973	12	2	0	Jerry Yeagley
1974	15	3	0	Jerry Yeagley
1975	13	3	1	Jerry Yeagley
1976	18	1	1	Jerry Yeagley
1977	12	2	1	Jerry Yeagley
1978	23	2	0	Jerry Yeagley

INDIANA UNIVERSITY

Indiana, Pennsylvania

Indians **Maroon and Slate**

Yr.	W	L	T	Coach
1969	8	5	0	Vince Celtnieks
1970	7	4	0	Vince Celtnieks
1971	7	6	0	Vince Celtnieks
1972	4	6	2	Vince Celtnieks
1973	5	5	1	Vince Celtnieks
1974	5	4	4	Vince Celtnieks
1975	5	6	2	Vince Celtnieks
1976	8	2	3	Vince Celtnieks
1977	11	4	0	Vince Celtnieks
1978	5	9	0	Vince Celtnieks

Angelo DiBernardo (left) and Charlie Fajkus carried Indiana to an NCAA Division I runner-up finish in 1978.

Jerry Yeagley founded the Indiana program in 1970 and from 1971–78 no Hoosier team suffered more than three losses in a single season.

Coach Carlton Wood, who led Ithaca to playoff berths in soccer, basketball and baseball, makes a point with Sandor Szabo (center) and All-American Janos Benedek in 1965.

ITHACA COLLEGE

Ithaca, New York

Bombers   **Blue and Gold**

Yr.	W	L	T	Coach
1930	0	1	1	Nick Bawlf
1931	0	3	1	Nick Bawlf
1932	1	3	0	Isadore Yavits
1933	0	3	0	Isadore Yavits
1934	0	4	0	Isadore Yavits
1935	2	2	0	Isadore Yavits
1936	3	1	0	Isadore Yavits
1937	2	3	0	Isadore Yavits
1938	3	2	1	Isadore Yavits
1939	0	5	2	Isadore Yavits
1940	3	2	0	Isadore Yavits
1941	0	6	0	Isadore Yavits
1942	2	3	0	Isadore Yavits
1943	—	—	—	—
1944	—	—	—	—
1945	—	—	—	—
1946	3	1	1	Isadore Yavits
1947	3	3	2	Isadore Yavits
1948	5	3	0	Isadore Yavits
1949	6	1	2	Isadore Yavits
1950	4	4	1	Isadore Yavits
1951	0	8	1	Isadore Yavits

Yr.	W	L	T	Coach
1952	2	6	0	Isadore Yavits
1953	3	5	0	Isadore Yavits
1954	6	2	2	Isadore Yavits
1955	4	5	2	Isadore Yavits
1956	5	4	1	Isadore Yavits
1957	7	3	0	Isadore Yavits
1958	5	5	1	Isadore Yavits
1959	5	4	0	Isadore Yavits
1960	5	5	1	Isadore Yavits
1961	6	3	1	Isadore Yavits
1962	5	6	0	Isadore Yavits
1963	5	6	0	Carlton Wood
1964	9	2	0	Carlton Wood
1965	10	1	1	Carlton Wood
1966	6	2	3	Carlton Wood
1967	7	4	0	Carlton Wood
1968	7	3	1	Carlton Wood
1969	8	4	0	Carlton Wood
1970	7	6	0	Forbes Keith
1971	5	6	1	Forbes Keith
1972	5	6	1	Forbes Keith
1973	7	3	2	Wilfred MacCormack
1974	8	3	2	Wilfred MacCormack
1975	4	9	1	Wilfred MacCormack
1976	2	12	0	Allan MacCormack
1977	7	5	1	Allan MacCormack
1978	3	9	2	Allan MacCormack

JACKSONVILLE UNIVERSITY

Jacksonville, Florida

Dolphins | Green, Gold, and White

Yr.	W	L	T	Coach
1969	14	0	1	Warren Gingras
1970	9	3	1	Warren Gingras
1971	4	7	1	Bill Coulthart
1972	8	6	0	Bill Coulthart
1973	—	—	—	—
1974	3	11	0	Bill Coulthart
1975	4	10	2	Bill Coulthart
1976	6	9	1	Bill Coulthart
1977	12	5	0	Bill Coulthart
1978	13	5	1	Bill Coulthart

JAMES MADISON UNIVERSITY

Harrisonburg, Virginia

Dukes | Purple and Gold

Yr.	W	L	T	Coach
1968	0	6	1	John Rader
1969	1	7	1	John Rader
1970	1	8	1	Bob Vanderwarker
1971	8	4	1	Bob Vanderwarker
1972	13	2	1	Bob Vanderwarker
1973	13	2	1	Bob Vanderwarker
1974	11	3	3	Bob Vanderwarker
1975	11	6	1	Bob Vanderwarker
1976	9	5	2	Bob Vanderwarker
1977	9	6	1	Bob Vanderwarker
1978	11	6	1	Bob Vanderwarker

JOHNS HOPKINS UNIVERSITY

Baltimore, Maryland

Blue Jays | Blue and Black

Yr.	W	L	T	Coach
1935	2	6	0	—
1936	7	1	1	—
1937	5	2	1	—
1938	3	3	2	—
1939	2	5	1	—
1940	3	5	1	—
1941	4	4	1	—
1942	0	6	1	—
1943	4	3	1	—
1944	4	3	1	—
1945	4	2	0	—
1946	4	2	3	George Wackenhut
1947	4	6	0	George Wackenhut
1948	6	3	1	George Wackenhut
1949	1	10	1	George Wackenhut
1950	3	6	0	Fred Smith
1951	2	4	3	Fred Smith
1952	7	3	0	Fred Smith
1953	4	1	0	Cornelius Cochrane
1954	3	4	2	Cornelius Cochrane
1955	2	6	1	Cornelius Cochrane
1956	4	4	1	Cornelius Cochrane
1957	4	5	1	Cornelius Cochrane
1958	5	5	0	Corneliue Cochrane
1959	5	4	1	Cornelius Cochrane
1960	6	4	0	Cornelius Cochrane
1961	3	7	0	Cornelius Cochrane

Yr.	W	L	T	Coach
1962	1	7	1	Cornelius Cochrane
1963	3	5	0	Cornelius Cochrane
1964	4	5	1	Gary Barrette
1965	4	5	1	Gary Barrette
1966	4	6	0	Gary Barrette
1967	6	5	0	Gary Barrette
1968	5	4	1	Gary Barrette
1969	6	2	2	Robert Knauff
1970	3	6	2	Robert Knauff
1971	7	5	0	Robert Oliver
1972	4	8	0	Robert Oliver
1973	6	5	2	Robert Oliver
1974	5	7	2	Robert Oliver
1975	15	3	1	Robert Oliver
1976	5	5	1	Robert Oliver
1977	9	5	0	Robert Oliver
1978	9	7	2	Robert Oliver

JUDSON COLLEGE

Elgin, Illinois

Eagles | Blue and White

Yr.	W	L	T	Coach
1969	4	2	3	—
1970	10	1	0	—
1971	4	9	0	—
1972	8	2	2	—
1973	7	3	2	—
1974	2	8	2	—
1975	10	8	0	—
1976	5	9	0	—
1977	2	10	1	—
1978	7	7	1	—

KEENE STATE COLLEGE

Keene, New Hampshire

Owls | Red and White

Year	W	L	T	Coach
1948	3	4	0	Sumner Joyce
1949	4	3	0	Sumner Joyce
1950	4	1	1	Sumner Joyce
1951	2	4	1	Sumner Joyce
1952	2	2	1	Sumner Joyce
1953	3	2	1	Sumner Joyce
1954	2	5	1	Sumner Joyce
1955	2	6	0	Sumner Joyce
1956	1	6	2	Sumner Joyce
1957	4	5	0	Sumner Joyce
1958	3	6	2	Sumner Joyce
1959	0	10	2	Sumner Joyce
1960	2	10	1	Sumner Joyce
1961	3	9	1	Sumner Joyce
1962	3	7	1	Sumner Joyce
1963	7	5	0	Sumner Joyce
1964	9	2	0	Sumner Joyce
1965	3	6	3	Sumner Joyce
1966	2	10	0	Sumner Joyce
1967	9	4	0	Sumner Joyce
1968	11	4	0	Sumner Joyce
1969	4	7	1	Sumner Joyce
1970	6	6	1	Ron Butcher
1971	19	2	0	Ron Butcher
1972	20	3	1	Ron Butcher
1973	15	1	1	Ron Butcher

Yr.	W	L	T	Coach
1974	17	2	2	Ron Butcher
1975	11	4	3	Ron Butcher
1976	8	5	2	Ron Butcher
1977	17	5	0	Ron Butcher
1978	10	12	1	Ron Butcher

KENT STATE UNIVERSITY

Kent, Ohio

Golden Flashes　　　　　　　　　　Blue and Gold

Yr.	W	L	T	Coach
1965	4	5	1	Rudy Bachna
1966	4	4	2	Rudy Bachna
1967	5	5	0	Rudy Bachna
1968	4	7	1	Rudy Bachna
1969	4	5	1	Rudy Bachna
1970	2	7	1	Rudy Bachna
1971	3	6	1	Garcha A. Singh
1972	8	2	0	Daile Van Patten
1973	0	6	3	Robert Patton
1974	4	7	1	Frank Truitt
1975	6	6	1	Frank Truitt
1976	5	7	2	Frank Truitt
1977	6	6	1	Frank Truitt
1978	6	4	3	Bob Shemory

KENYON COLLEGE

Gambier, Ohio

Lords　　　　　　　　　　Purple and White

Yr.	W	L	T	Coach
1948	0	2	2	Hanfman
1949	0	4	0	Hanfman
1950	3	1	2	Hanfman
1951	3	3	0	Franklin Miller
1952	5	3	1	Franklin Miller
1953	5	2	1	Franklin Miller
1954	4	1	2	Franklin Miller
1955	6	1	0	Thomas Edwards
1956	5	4	1	Thomas Edwards
1957	2	8	0	Ed McArdle
1958	3	3	2	Robert Harrison
1959	2	4	3	Robert Harrison
1960	4	4	0	Robert Harrison
1961	4	5	1	Robert Harrison
1962	5	4	1	Robert Harrison
1963	2	7	1	Robert Harrison
1964	2	8	0	Robert Harrison
1965	1	8	1	Robert Harrison
1966	4	6	0	Robert Harrison
1967	6	3	1	Robert Harrison
1968	5	4	2	Robert Brannum
1969	6	3	1	Robert Brannum
1970	8	3	0	James Zak
1971	6	3	1	James Zak
1972	4	4	2	James Zak
1973	11	2	0	James Zak
1974	6	4	2	James Zak
1975	4	9	0	James Zak
1976	7	6	0	James Zak
1977	5	5	2	James Zak
1978	5	7	1	James Zak

KING'S COLLEGE, THE

Briarcliff Manor, New York

Purple Knights　　　　　　　　　　Purple and White

Yr.	W	L	T	Coach
1964	9	4	0	Pete Hoffman
1965	5	6	0	Pete Hoffman
1966	7	5	0	Norman Wilhelmi
1967	10	2	1	Norman Wilhelmi
1968	9	3	0	Norman Wilhelmi
1969	10	1	1	Norman Wilhelmi
1970	—	—	—	—
1971	9	5	0	Dennis Olson
1972	8	5	3	Dennis Olson
1973	8	6	3	Paul Banta
1974	7	5	6	Paul Banta
1975	8	6	0	Paul Banta
1976	14	6	0	H. C. Miller, Jr.
1977	11	4	3	H. C. Miller, Jr.
1978	18	3	2	H. C. Miller, Jr.

KUTZTOWN STATE COLLEGE

Kutztown, Pennsylvania

Golden Bears　　　　　　　　　　Maroon and Gold

Yr.	W	L	T	Coach
1971	4	3	3	Lee Hill
1972	3	7	1	Lee Hill
1973	7	6	0	Lee Hill
1974	8	6	2	Lee Hill
1975	9	5	2	Lee Hill
1976	5	8	1	Lee Hill
1977	6	7	0	Lee Hill
1978	8	6	0	Lee Hill

LAFAYETTE COLLEGE

Easton, Pennsylvania

Leopards　　　　　　　　　　Maroon and White

Yr.	W	L	T	Coach
1914	1	3	0	—
1915	4	4	2	—
1916	2	3	0	—
1917	0	5	0	—
1918	1	3	0	—
1919	—	—	—	—
1920	8	3	0	Scotty Cutherbertson
1921	1	1	2	Hugh McIlwain
1922	2	2	0	Alex Cuthbertson
1923	1	5	1	D. E. Riddagh
1924	1	4	1	J. Easton, R. Morrison
1925	1	3	2	Fred Pepper
1926	0	5	1	Alex Cuthbertson
1927	3	6	1	D. W. Riddagh
1928	1	7	1	James Easton
1929	4	4	1	James Deardon
1930	0	9	1	James Deardon
1931	1	8	0	Walter Deardon
1932	1	5	0	Harry Snook
1933	1	5	1	James Deardon
1934	2	6	0	James Deardon
1935	2	6	2	Robert Stewart
1936	5	4	2	Frank Fischer
1937	0	7	1	Frank Fischer
1938	0	7	1	Alex Cuthbertson
1939	3	6	0	Alex Cuthbertson

Yr.	W	L	T	Coach
1940	3	6	1	Alex Cuthbertson
1941	3	6	1	Alex Cuthbertson
1942	0	6	0	Alex Cuthbertson
1943	—	—	—	—
1944	—	—	—	—
1945	—	—	—	—
1946	0	10	0	James Deardon
1947	2	8	1	Jack Trotter
1948	4	8	0	Jack Trotter
1949	1	6	3	Jack Trotter
1950	4	8	0	Jack Trotter
1951	3	8	0	Trotter, van Breda Kolff
1952	6	5	1	Bill van Breda Kolff
1953	7	5	1	Bill van Breda Kolff
1954	6	5	1	Bill van Breda Kolff
1955	2	7	2	George Davidson
1956	5	6	1	George Davidson
1957	4	5	0	George Davidson
1958	8	1	1	George Davidson
1959	5	5	0	George Davidson
1960	0	9	1	George Davidson
1961	3	8	0	George Davidson
1962	4	7	0	George Davidson
1963	6	4	1	George Davidson
1964	5	6	0	George Davidson
1965	4	8	0	George Davidson
1966	5	6	0	George Davidson
1967	6	8	0	Herb Schmidt
1968	7	6	1	Gerry Clinton
1969	6	6	1	Gerry Clinton
1970	4	5	3	Gerry Clinton
1971	6	5	2	Gary Williams
1972	3	7	2	Gary Williams
1973	0	10	1	Gary Williams
1974	9	2	2	Gary Williams
1975	6	6	2	Gary Williams
1976	3	7	4	Gary Williams
1977	2	11	1	Jamie McLaughlin
1978	6	6	3	Jamie McLaughlin

LA SALLE COLLEGE

Philadelphia, Pennsylvania

Explorers   **Blue and Gold**

Yr.	W	L	T	Coach
1949	2	4	1	Joe Smith
1950	2	6	0	Joe Smith
1951	1	7	0	Joe Smith
1952	3	5	0	Joe Smith
1953	1	7	2	Joe Smith
1954	3	8	0	Joe Smith
1955	2	6	0	Joe Smith
1956	2	6	0	Joe Smith
1957	4	6	0	Joe Smith
1958	3	6	2	Joe Smith
1959	5	5	1	Joe Smith
1960	5	5	0	Joe Smith
1961	3	7	1	Joe Smith
1962	0	10	1	Joe Smith
1963	1	6	1	Joe Smith
1964	1	8	0	Joe Smith
1965	1	7	0	Joe Smith
1966	0	9	1	Joe Smith
1967	0	9	1	Jack Smith
1968	2	10	0	Jack Smith
1969	5	7	1	Bill Wilkinson
1970	7	5	1	Bill Wilkinson
1971	10	3	2	Bill Wilkinson

LaSalle's John Uelses (right), a world-class pole vaulter, also played soccer for coach Joe Smith in 1963.

Yr.	W	L	T	Coach
1972	9	4	1	Bill Wilkinson
1973	9	5	1	Bill Wilkinson
1974	6	4	4	Bill Wilkinson
1975	6	6	1	Bill Wilkinson
1976	10	4	2	Shelly Chamberlain
1977	9	5	1	Bill Wilkinson
1978	9	5	1	Bill Wilkinson

LEBANON VALLEY COLLEGE

Annville, Pennsylvania

Flying Dutchmen   **Blue and White**

Yr.	W	L	T	Coach
1973	2	7	0	Dr. Jeff Bensing
1974	0	13	0	Dr. Jeff Bensing
1975	0	14	0	Dr. Jeff Bensing
1976	1	13	0	Bruce Correll
1977	2	11	2	Bruce Correll
1978	2	11	0	Bruce Correll

LEHIGH UNIVERSITY

Bethelehem, Pennsylvania

Engineers   Brown and White

Yr.	W	L	T	Coach
1916	3	3	0	James Campbell
1917	3	0	0	James Campbell
1918	2	1	0	James Campbell
1919	1	4	0	A. J. Wilson
1920	1	1	1	J. Murphy
1921	2	3	2	Harry Carpenter
1922	3	4	1	Harry Carpenter
1923	4	3	1	Harry Carpenter
1924	3	5	0	Harry Carpenter
1925	3	4	1	Harry Carpenter
1926	2	6	1	Harry Carpenter
1927	3	8	0	Harry Carpenter
1928	2	8	0	Harry Carpenter
1929	6	4	0	Harry Carpenter
1930	5	4	0	Harry Carpenter
1931	4	3	2	Harry Carpenter
1932	2	2	3	Harry Carpenter
1933	3	7	0	Harry Carpenter
1934	0	10	0	Harry Carpenter
1935	0	9	1	Harry Carpenter
1936	1	9	0	Harry Carpenter
1937	1	5	1	Harry Carpenter
1938	1	6	2	Harry Carpenter
1939	1	7	2	Harry Carpenter
1940	2	7	1	Harry Carpenter
1941	2	8	0	Billy Sheridan
1942	3	4	1	Billy Sheridan
1943	0	5	0	Billy Sheridan
1944	1	5	0	Billy Sheridan
1945	0	3	1	Billy Sheridan
1946	3	6	0	Billy Sheridan
1947	5	4	1	Billy Sheridan
1948	5	5	0	Billy Sheridan
1949	4	2	3	Billy Sheridan
1950	5	5	0	Billy Sheridan
1951	7	3	0	Billy Sheridan
1952	6	4	0	Billy Sheridan
1953	0	8	0	Bill Christian
1954	3	4	2	Bill Christian
1955	3	5	0	Bill Christian
1956	4	3	2	Bill Christian
1957	3	5	0	Bill Christian
1958	8	2	0	Bill Christian
1959	6	3	0	Bill Christian
1960	7	3	0	Bill Christian
1961	4	5	1	Bill Christian
1962	7	2	1	Bill Christian
1963	5	2	3	Bill Christian
1964	7	3	0	Bill Christian
1965	6	3	0	Bill Christian
1966	6	3	1	Bill Christian
1967	3	6	1	Bill Christian
1968	6	3	2	Gerry Leeman
1969	8	4	0	Tom Fleck
1970	6	5	1	Tom Fleck
1971	10	3	1	Tom Fleck
1972	5	8	0	Tom Fleck
1973	8	5	0	Tom Fleck
1974	5	7	2	Tom Fleck
1975	4	8	2	Tom Fleck
1976	6	5	3	Tom Fleck
1977	5	7	1	Tom Fleck
1978	11	2	3	Manny Tavormina

LeMOYNE COLLEGE

Syracuse, New York

Dolphins   Green and Gold

Yr.	W	L	T	Coach
1964	0	8	1	Bob Deger
1965	0	9	0	Bob Deger
1966	0	10	0	Keith Gage
1967	2	7	1	Keith Gage
1968	2	9	1	Keith Gage
1969	4	5	1	Keith Gage
1970	4	7	1	Keith Gage
1971	6	5	0	Keith Gage
1972	3	5	4	Keith Gage
1973	6	4	0	Keith Gage
1974	4	5	3	Keith Gage
1975	9	3	1	Keith Gage
1976	6	4	2	Keith Gage
1977	9	4	1	Keith Gage
1978	7	6	0	Keith Gage

LeTOURNEAU COLLEGE

Longview, Texas

Yellowjackets   Blue and Gold

Yr.	W	L	T	Coach
1976	11	5	3	Stu Brynn
1977	7	10	0	Stu Brynn
1978	6	6	1	Stu Brynn

LIBERTY BAPTIST COLLEGE

Lynchburg, Virginia

Flames   Red, White, and Blue

Yr.	W	L	T	Coach
1975	5	5	0	Ed Dobson
1976	8	7	0	Ed Dobson
1977	8	8	1	Ed Dobson
1978	10	3	1	Ed Dobson

LOCK HAVEN STATE COLLEGE

Lock Haven, Pennsylvania

Bald Eagles   Crimson and White

Yr.	W	L	T	Coach
1956	4	3	1	Dr. Dan Corbin
1957	2	5	0	Dr. Dan Corbin
1958	2	5	1	Dewey Morehouse
1959	3	4	0	Dewey Morehouse
1960	6	4	0	Dewey Morehouse
1961	6	4	0	Dewey Morehouse
1962	4	7	0	Dewey Morehouse
1963	4	5	2	George Lawther
1964	7	2	1	George Lawther
1965	3	6	1	George Lawther
1966	4	3	2	George Lawther
1967	3	7	1	Karl Herrmann
1968	7	2	0	Karl Herrmann
1969	7	4	1	Karl Herrmann
1970	8	2	4	Karl Herrmann
1971	8	3	4	Karl Herrmann
1972	8	3	2	Karl Herrmann

An alumnus and longtime member of the LIU athletic department, Pic Picariello was a favorite of his players.

Yr.	W	L	T	Coach
1973	10	3	0	Karl Herrmann
1974	9	4	2	Karl Herrmann
1975	11	1	1	Karl Herrmann
1976	6	4	2	Mike Parker
1977	9	4	0	Mike Parker
1978	18	2	0	Mike Parker

LONG ISLAND UNIVERSITY

Brooklyn, New York

Blackbirds   **Blue and White**

Yr.	W	L	T	Coach
1933	3	2	1	Yates
1934	2	7	2	Yates
1935	3	3	1	Yates
1936	2	3	0	Picariello
1952	4	3	0	Reno
1953	1	6	0	Picariello
1954	0	7	0	Picariello
1955	2	4	1	Picariello

Yr.	W	L	T	Coach
1956	2	9	1	Picariello
1957	4	7	1	Rosenthal
1958	4	5	1	O'Boyle
1959	0	9	0	Rosenthal
1960	0	8	1	Rosenthal
1961	5	5	0	Rosenthal
1962	8	2	1	Rosenthal
1963	10	3	1	Rosenthal
1964	10	3	1	Rosenthal
1965	11	2	1	Rosenthal
1966	15	2	0	Machnik
1967	14	2	1	Machnik
1968	8	4	1	Machnik
1969	4	7	1	Young
1970	6	7	0	Young
1971	12	2	1	Young
1972	14	1	1	Burke
1973	11	1	3	Burke
1974	9	5	1	Stoopack
1975	6	6	1	Stoopack
1976	10	3	2	Ficken
1977	13	2	2	Ficken
1978	9	4	3	Ficken

LOYOLA COLLEGE

Baltimore, Maryland

Greyhounds				Green and Gray
Yr.	W	L	T	Coach
1946	3	4	0	Bish Baker
1947	6	4	1	Bish Baker
1948	6	1	0	Bish Baker
1949	4	4	0	Bish Baker
1950	5	3	0	Bish Baker
1951	3	3	0	Bish Baker
1952	0	5	1	Lefty Reitz
1953	2	6	0	Lefty Reitz
1954	4	4	2	Tom Lind
1955	3	2	4	Tom Lind
1956	3	7	0	Tom Lind
1957	2	7	0	Tom Lind
1958	2	6	2	Tom Lind
1959	4	5	2	Tom Lind
1960	7	5	0	Tom Lind
1961	4	7	1	Lefty Reitz
1962	9	2	2	Lefty Reitz
1963	3	6	1	Lefty Reitz
1964	2	8	0	Jim Bullington
1965	6	5	0	Jim Bullington
1966	7	6	0	Jim Bullington
1967	12	2	1	Jim Bullington
1968	9	0	2	Jim Bullington
1969	9	2	3	Jim Bullington
1970	11	2	0	Jim Bullington
1971	16	0	0	Jim Bullington
1972	11	3	0	Jim Bullington
1973	11	4	0	Jim Bullington
1974	14	2	2	Jim Bullington
1975	13	4	0	Jim Bullington
1976	21	1	0	Jim Bullington
1977	12	2	0	Jim Bullington
1978	14	4	0	Jim Bullington

LYCOMING COLLEGE

Williamsport, Pennsylvania

Warriors				Blue and Gold
Yr.	W	L	T	Coach
1957	0	4	0	George Lawther
1958	3	7	0	George Lawther
1959	0	8	3	Nelson Phillips
1960	4	6	0	Nelson Phillips
1961	4	5	0	Nelson Phillips
1962	4	5	0	Nelson Phillips
1963	5	6	0	Nelson Phillips
1964	2	10	0	Nelson Phillips
1965	4	6	0	Nelson Phillips
1966	2	8	1	Nelson Phillips
1967	1	9	2	Nelson Phillips
1968	1	10	0	Nelson Phillips
1969	3	7	2	Nelson Phillips
1970	6	5	1	Nelson Phillips
1971	5	5	1	Nelson Phillips
1972	3	7	1	Nelson Phillips
1973	1	8	1	Nelson Phillips
1974	2	6	2	Nelson Phillips
1975	4	6	0	Nelson Phillips
1976	3	8	0	Nelson Phillips
1977	3	10	0	Nelson Phillips
1978	0	12	1	Nelson Phillips

LYNCHBURG COLLEGE

Lynchburg, Virginia

Hornets				Crimson and Gray
Yr.	W	L	T	Coach
1954	2	3	0	Bill Shellenberger
1955	4	5	0	Bill Shellenberger
1956	3	6	1	Bill Shellenberger
1957	6	3	1	Bill Shellenberger
1958	9	3	0	Dale Almond
1959	13	2	1	Bill Shellenberger
1960	14	2	1	Bill Shellenberger
1961	10	6	1	Bill Shellenberger
1962	11	6	2	Bill Shellenberger
1963	12	2	3	Bill Shellenberger
1964	8	8	1	Bill Shellenberger
1965	15	4	0	Bill Shellenberger
1966	12	5	2	Bill Shellenberger
1967	8	8	1	Bill Shellenberger
1968	10	7	0	Bill Shellenberger
1969	11	4	2	Bill Shellenberger
1970	12	3	3	Bill Shellenberger
1971	14	3	1	Bill Shellenberger
1972	15	4	1	Bill Shellenberger
1973	16	3	0	Bill Shellenberger
1974	15	3	1	Bill Shellenberger
1975	16	4	1	Bill Shellenberger
1976	15	3	0	Bill Shellenberger
1977	8	7	0	Bill Shellenberger
1978	11	4	5	Bill Shellenberger

MACMURRAY COLLEGE

Jacksonville, Illinois

Highlanders				Blue and Scarlet
Yr.	W	L	T	Coach
1957	1	2	0	Bill Wall
1958	3	3	0	Bill Wall
1959	3	5	0	Bill Wall
1960	—	—	—	—
1961	6	6	1	Jerry Lace
1962	6	7	2	Jerry Lace
1963	5	5	0	Fred Taube
1964	8	6	0	Fred Taube
1965	5	4	2	Fred Taube
1966	4	4	2	Fred Taube
1967	7	3	0	Fred Taube
1968	5	3	2	Fred Taube
1969	8	2	3	Fred Taube
1970	7	4	1	Bill Serredio
1971	7	4	5	Bob Gay
1972	9	4	2	Bob Gay
1973	7	6	3	Bob Gay
1974	8	8	2	Bob Gay
1975	12	6	0	Bob Gay
1976	12	7	1	Bob Gay
1977	7	8	1	Bob Gay
1978	9	7	0	Pete Glon

MAINE, UNIVERSITY OF

Orono, Maine

Black Bears				Blue and White
Yr.	W	L	T	Coach
1963	0	6	0	Silas Dunklee
1964	1	5	0	Silas Dunklee

The MacMurray bench is all eyes during a contest in 1964.

Josy Byamah was the standout for Maine in 1968.

Yr.	W	L	T	Coach
1965	0	11	0	Tom Reynolds
1966	0	11	0	Bill Livesey
1967	4	6	1	Bill Livesey
1968	2	10	0	Paul Stoyell
1969	4	7	1	Paul Stoyell
1970	7	2	3	Paul Stoyell
1971	7	5	0	Paul Stoyell
1972	7	6	0	Paul Stoyell
1973	7	2	4	Paul Stoyell
1974	5	6	2	Paul Stoyell
1975	5	7	0	Paul Stoyell
1976	4	8	0	Paul Stoyell
1977	5	9	0	Paul Stoyell
1978	4	10	0	Doug Biggs

MAINE, UNIVERSITY OF (PRESQUE ISLE)

Presque Isle, Maine

Owls   Blue and Gold

Yr.	W	L	T	Coach
1964	2	4	0	Johnson
1965	4	2	0	F. J. McGrath
1966	6	1	0	F. J. McGrath
1967	5	2	0	F. J. McGrath
1968	8	1	0	F. J. McGrath
1969	7	2	0	F. J. McGrath
1970	8	3	0	F. J. McGrath
1971	7	6	0	F. J. McGrath
1972	9	4	1	F. J. McGrath
1973	10	3	1	F. J. McGrath
1974	8	3	4	Bill Casavant
1975	13	5	0	F. J. McGrath
1976	12	5	1	F. J. McGrath
1977	17	3	0	F. J. McGrath
1978	4	8	1	F. J. McGrath

MANHATTANVILLE COLLEGE

Purchase, New York

Valiants   Red and White

Yr.	W	L	T	Coach
1973	6	6	0	Tom Kowalski
1974	8	4	0	Bob Casilli
1975	4	8	0	Bob Casilli
1976	3	9	1	Mike Ansbro
1977	5	5	3	Arnold Ramirez
1978	7	6	2	Arnold Ramirez

MARIETTA COLLEGE

Marietta, Ohio

Pioneers   Blue and White

Yr.	W	L	T	Coach
1968	1	6	0	Alan Jones
1969	1	10	0	Donald G. Kelly
1970	2	7	1	J. Phillip Roach
1971	4	6	0	J. Phillip Roach
1972	2	7	1	J. Phillip Roach
1973	5	4	1	J. Phillip Roach
1974	7	3	0	J. Phillip Roach
1975	5	5	0	J. Phillip Roach

Yr.	W	L	T	Coach
1976	5	5	0	J. Phillip Roach
1977	7	3	0	J. Phillip Roach
1978	4	6	0	J. Phillip Roach

MARIST COLLEGE

Poughkeepsie, New York

Red Foxes   Red and White

Yr.	W	L	T	Coach
1963	0	8	0	Dr. Howard Goldman
1964	3	8	0	Dr. Howard Goldman
1965	3	8	0	Dr. Howard Goldman
1966	3	9	0	Dr. Howard Goldman
1967	5	4	3	Dr. Howard Goldman
1968	6	6	1	Dr. Howard Goldman
1969	5	6	1	Dr. Howard Goldman
1970	4	9	1	Dr. Howard Goldman
1971	6	6	1	Dr. Howard Goldman
1972	5	8	2	Dr. Howard Goldman
1973	3	7	4	Dr. Howard Goldman
1974	8	5	2	Dr. Howard Goldman
1975	11	3	0	Dr. Howard Goldman
1976	14	1	1	Dr. Howard Goldman
1977	12	3	1	Dr. Howard Goldman
1978	10	5	0	Dr. Howard Goldman

MARYLAND, UNIVERSITY OF

College Park, Maryland

Terrapins   Red and White

Yr.	W	L	T	Coach
1946	2	1	0	Doyle Royal
1947	6	2	1	Doyle Royal
1948	6	3	1	Doyle Royal
1949	8	2	0	Doyle Royal
1950	8	2	0	Doyle Royal
1951	6	2	0	Doyle Royal
1952	7	1	1	Doyle Royal
1953	8	2	0	Doyle Royal
1954	5	3	2	Doyle Royal
1955	8	2	0	Doyle Royal
1956	9	2	0	Doyle Royal
1957	8	1	1	Doyle Royal
1958	9	0	1	Doyle Royal
1959	8	1	0	Doyle Royal
1960	9	2	1	Doyle Royal
1961	9	1	1	Doyle Royal
1962	10	1	0	Doyle Royal
1963	10	2	0	Doyle Royal
1964	8	3	0	Doyle Royal
1965	6	2	0	Doyle Royal
1966	6	2	0	Doyle Royal
1967	9	2	1	Doyle Royal
1968	14	0	1	Doyle Royal
1969	11	2	2	Doyle Royal
1970	7	5	0	Doyle Royal
1971	7	4	1	Doyle Royal
1972	4	4	2	Doyle Royal
1973	8	4	1	Doyle Royal
1974	5	3	5	Bud Beardmore
1975	6	1	5	Jim Dietsch
1976	7	4	2	Jim Dietsch
1977	9	5	0	Jim Dietsch
1978	5	7	2	Jim Dietsch

Doyle Royal (back row, left) has a special place in his heart for the first of his 28 Maryland squads—the 1946 edition.

MARYLAND, UNIVERSITY OF
(BALTIMORE COUNTY)

Catonsville, Maryland

Retrievers   **Gold and Black**

Yr.	W	L	T	Coach
1969	5	5	2	Tom Rider
1970	7	5	4	Tom Rider
1971	5	7	2	Tom Rider
1972	6	7	1	Tom Rider
1973	8	6	1	Ed Veit
1974	7	5	2	Ed Veit
1975	9	5	1	Ed Veit
1976	6	3	5	Ed Veit
1977	15	2	0	Ed Veit
1978	10	4	2	Ed Veit

MASSACHUSETTS, UNIVERSITY OF

Amherst, Massachusetts

Minutemen   **Maroon and White**

Yr.	W	L	T	Coach
1930	1	4	0	Lawrence E. Briggs
1931	6	0	0	Lawrence E. Briggs
1932	4	1	1	Lawrence E. Briggs
1933	4	3	0	Lawrence E. Briggs
1934	2	2	2	Lawrence E. Briggs
1935	2	4	1	Lawrence E. Briggs
1936	5	3	0	Lawrence E. Briggs

Yr.	W	L	T	Coach
1937	4	2	1	Lawrence E. Briggs
1938	3	2	2	Lawrence E. Briggs
1939	3	4	0	Lawrence E. Briggs
1940	2	3	2	Lawrence E. Briggs
1941	4	2	1	Lawrence E. Briggs
1942	1	4	3	Lawrence E. Briggs
1943	—	—	—	—
1944	—	—	—	—
1945	—	—	—	—
1946	1	6	0	Lawrence E. Briggs
1947	4	5	0	Lawrence E. Briggs
1978	5	4	0	Lawrence E. Briggs
1949	4	5	1	Lawrence E. Briggs
1950	2	7	1	Lawrence E. Briggs
1951	3	6	2	Lawrence E. Briggs
1952	4	6	1	Lawrence E. Briggs
1953	6	5	1	Lawrence E. Briggs
1954	7	5	0	Lawrence E. Briggs
1955	4	4	0	Lawrence E. Briggs
1956	1	4	4	Lawrence E. Briggs
1957	3	4	1	Lawrence E. Briggs
1958	3	6	0	Lawrence E. Briggs
1959	2	7	0	Lawrence E. Briggs
1960	0	10	0	Lawrence E. Briggs
1961	3	6	1	Lawrence E. Briggs
1962	5	5	0	Lawrence E. Briggs
1963	2	7	1	Lawrence E. Briggs
1964	5	4	1	Lawrence E. Briggs
1965	7	3	0	Lawrence E. Briggs
1966	6	3	1	Lawrence E. Briggs
1967	5	5	0	Lawrence E. Briggs
1968	4	6	1	Peter Broaca

Yr.	W	L	T	Coach
1969	6	4	0	Peter Broaca
1970	7	2	2	Peter Broaca
1971	5	3	3	Jack Berryman
1972	5	3	2	Gerry Redmond
1973	6	3	1	Aloysius Rufe
1974	8	3	1	Aloysius Rufe
1975	3	9	2	Aloysius Rufe
1976	5	8	1	Russ Kidd
1977	10	5	0	Russ Kidd
1978	12	5	0	Russ Kidd

MASSACHUSETTS INSTITUTE OF TECHNOLOGY

Cambridge, Massachusetts

Beavers — Red and Gray

Yr.	W	L	T	Coach
1919	2	1	2	—
1920	3	3	1	—
1921	2	4	0	—
1922	2	2	1	—
1923	4	0	1	—
1924	4	3	0	—
1925	2	5	0	—
1926	1	4	3	—
1927	2	5	1	—
1928	2	7	1	—
1929	2	4	2	—
1930	1	7	1	William Welch
1931	3	4	1	Malcolm Goldie
1932	2	5	0	Malcolm Goldie
1933	0	5	0	Malcolm Goldie
1934	1	7	0	Malcolm Goldie
1935	2	4	1	Malcolm Goldie
1936	1	6	0	Malcolm Goldie
1937	1	8	0	Malcolm Goldie
1938	2	6	0	Malcolm Goldie
1939	0	8	1	Malcolm Goldie
1940	0	7	0	Malcolm Goldie
1941	3	4	0	John Craig
1942	1	5	1	John Craig
1943	—	—	—	—
1944	—	—	—	—
1945	4	2	1	John Craig
1946	3	5	1	John Craig
1947	2	6	0	Richard Thomas
1948	4	4	1	Richard Thomas
1949	2	6	1	Richard Thomas
1950	2	6	1	Phil Hardy
1951	1	6	1	Phil Hardy
1952	2	6	1	Ben Martin
1953	4	5	0	Ben Martin
1954	6	1	1	Ben Martin
1955	5	3	1	Ben Martin
1956	3	1	1	Ben Martin
1957	7	1	1	Charles Batterman
1958	5	4	2	Charles Batterman
1959	5	3	2	Charles Batterman
1960	6	4	0	Charles Batterman
1961	6	2	1	Charles Batterman
1962	6	1	1	Charles Batterman
1963	5	4	2	Charles Batterman
1964	4	6	1	Charles Batterman
1965	3	7	0	William Morrison
1966	4	7	0	William Morrison
1967	2	11	0	William Morrison
1968	0	14	0	William Morrison
1969	3	9	0	William Morrison

Yr.	W	L	T	Coach
1970	3	8	1	William Morrison
1971	5	8	0	William Morrison
1972	6	8	0	William Morrison
1973	5	6	2	William Morrison
1974	1	10	2	William Morrison
1975	2	8	1	Walter Alessi
1976	4	7	1	Walter Alessi
1977	7	6	0	Walter Alessi
1978	6	6	1	Walter Alessi

MERCER UNIVERSITY

Macon, Georgia

Bears — Orange and Black

Yr.	W	L	T	Coach
1973	4	4	2	Barry Myers
1974	7	5	0	Barry Myers
1975	3	9	1	Barry Myers
1976	2	6	2	Barry Myers
1977	1	11	1	Vicente Tur-Rojas
1978	0	5	2	Tom Sukaratana

MERCYHURST COLLEGE

Erie, Pennsylvania

Lakers — Blue, Green and White

Yr.	W	L	T	Coach
1976	1	5	2	David Kipp Shimpeno
1977	6	5	0	David Kipp Shimpeno
1978	8	4	1	David Kipp Shimpeno

MIAMI UNIVERSITY

Oxford, Ohio

Redskins — Red and White

Yr.	W	L	T	Coach
1978	2	9	1	Steve D. Cady

MIAMI, UNIVERSITY OF

Coral Gables, Florida

Hurricanes — Orange, Green, and White

Yr.	W	L	T	Coach
1961	6	0	0	Dale Lewis
1962	8	0	0	Dale Lewis
1963	8	1	0	Dale Lewis
1964	3	5	1	Dale Lewis
1965	8	1	0	Dale Lewis
1966	1	5	2	Dale Lewis
1967	3	3	2	Dale Lewis
1968	3	5	1	Dale Lewis
1969	5	4	0	Dale Lewis
1970	7	3	0	Dale Lewis
1971	6	5	0	Dale Lewis
1972	0	10	0	Dale Lewis
1973	3	5	1	Richard Thomas
1974	7	5	1	Richard Thomas
1975	13	2	0	Richard Thomas
1976	5	5	1	Richard Thomas
1977	10	3	2	Richard Thomas
1978	8	5	1	Jamal A. Shurdom

Gene Kenney coached Michigan State to NCAA national co-championships in 1967 and 1968.

Yr.	W	L	T	Coach
1956	2	2	4	Thomas Reynolds
1957	7	1	0	Thomas Reynolds
1958	5	3	0	Joseph Morrone
1959	6	2	0	Joseph Morrone
1960	4	1	3	Joseph Morrone
1961	7	2	1	Joseph Morrone
1962	5	3	0	Joseph Morrone
1963	5	1	2	Joseph Morrone
1964	8	1	0	Joseph Morrone
1965	8	0	1	Joseph Morrone
1966	5	2	2	Joseph Morrone
1967	6	2	1	Joseph Morrone
1968	5	4	1	G. Thomas Lawson
1969	5	4	1	G. Thomas Lawson
1970	6	2	2	G. Thomas Lawson
1971	4	6	0	G. Thomas Lawson
1972	9	0	1	G. Thomas Lawson
1973	10	0	0	G. Thomas Lawson
1974	5	4	1	G. Thomas Lawson
1975	4	4	2	G. Thomas Lawson
1976	8	3	1	Ronald McEachen
1977	7	2	2	Ronald McEachen
1978	4	3	4	Ronald McEachen

J. Davis Webb represented Middlebury on the 1964 All-American team.

MICHIGAN STATE UNIVERSITY

East Lansing, Michigan

Spartans   Green and White

Yr.	W	L	T	Coach
1956	5	0	1	Gene Kenney
1957	6	0	2	Gene Kenney
1958	8	0	0	Gene Kenney
1959	7	2	0	Gene Kenney
1960	8	1	0	Gene Kenney
1961	8	1	0	Gene Kenney
1962	9	2	0	Gene Kenney
1963	9	1	0	Gene Kenney
1964	10	1	2	Gene Kenney
1965	10	2	0	Gene Kenney
1966	10	0	2	Gene Kenney
1967	12	0	2	Gene Kenney
1968	11	1	3	Gene Kenney
1969	7	2	1	Gene Kenney
1970	5	1	3	Payton Fuller
1971	7	2	0	Payton Fuller
1972	4	3	2	Payton Fuller
1973	4	3	3	Payton Fuller
1974	8	1	2	Ed Rutherford
1975	10	2	0	Ed Rutherford
1976	7	4	1	Ed Rutherford
1977	6	7	0	Joe Baum
1978	6	6	2	Joe Baum

MIDDLEBURY COLLEGE

Middlebury, Vermont

Panthers   Blue and White

Yr.	W	L	T	Coach
1954	4	0	2	Frank Punderson
1955	4	3	0	Thomas Reynolds

MIDWESTERN STATE UNIVERSITY

Wichita Falls, Texas

Indians				Maroon and Gold
Yr.	**W**	**L**	**T**	**Coach**
1972	1	8	1	Dr. Mike Flavin
1973	4	9	0	Howard Y. Patterson
1974	10	5	2	Howard Y. Patterson
1975	12	7	0	Howard Y. Patterson
1976	16	6	1	Howard Y. Patterson
1977	17	7	1	Howard Y. Patterson
1978	13	6	1	Howard Y. Patterson

MISSOURI SOUTHERN STATE COLLEGE

Joplin, Missouri

Lions				Green and Gold
Yr.	**W**	**L**	**T**	**Coach**
1972	1	9	3	Hal Bodon
1973	5	8	3	Hal Bodon
1974	14	3	3	Hal Bodon
1975	14	2	0	Hal Bodon
1976	12	6	2	Hal Bodon
1977	10	7	3	Hal Bodon
1978	12	6	1	Hal Bodon

MISSOURI, UNIVERSITY OF (St. LOUIS)

St. Louis, Missouri

Rivermen				Red and Gold
Yr.	**W**	**L**	**T**	**Coach**
1968	4	1	1	Don Dallas
1969	5	2	1	Don Dallas

Don Dallas led Missouri-St. Louis to the NCAA Division II crown in 1973.

Yr.	W	L	T	Coach
1970	5	4	0	Don Dallas
1971	5	3	2	Don Dallas
1972	9	2	0	Don Dallas
1973	11	0	3	Don Dallas
1974	6	5	2	Don Dallas
1975	8	4	3	Don Dallas
1976	9	8	1	Don Dallas
1977	9	5	1	Don Dallas
1978	8	7	1	Don Dallas

MONTCLAIR STATE COLLEGE

Upper Montclair, New Jersey

Indians				Red and White
Yr.	**W**	**L**	**T**	**Coach**
1958	2	8	1	Geza Gazdeg
1959	1	9	1	Geza Gazdeg
1960	7	7	1	Thomas Rillo
1961	6	6	1	Dave Watkins
1962	7	5	1	Dave Watkins
1963	7	4	1	Dave Watkins
1964	9	3	1	Tom Rumsey
1965	3	8	1	John McKeon
1966	4	7	3	Leonard Lucenko
1967	7	5	3	Leonard Lucenko
1968	13	2	0	Leonard Lucenko
1969	13	1	1	Leonard Lucenko
1970	8	3	2	Leonard Lucenko
1971	8	5	1	Leonard Lucenko
1972	11	3	2	Bob Wolfarth
1973	7	3	5	Bob Wolfarth
1974	4	8	3	Bob Wolfarth
1975	7	5	0	Bob Wolfarth
1976	5	6	1	Bob Wolfarth
1977	5	7	2	Bob Wolfarth
1978	5	10	1	Bob Wolfarth

MORAVIAN COLLEGE

Bethlehem, Pennsylvania

Greyhounds				Blue and Gray
Yr.	**W**	**L**	**T**	**Coach**
1963	4	5	1	Terry Jackson
1964	7	3	0	Terry Jackson
1965	8	3	0	Terry Jackson
1966	7	5	0	Terry Jackson
1967	5	6	1	Terry Jackson
1968	9	1	1	John Makuvek
1969	5	6	2	John Makuvek
1970	4	6	3	John makuvek
1971	7	6	1	John Makuvek
1972	7	5	2	John Makuvek
1973	9	3	2	John Makuvek
1974	4	5	4	John Makuvek
1975	5	8	0	John Makuvek
1976	9	5	1	John Makuvek
1977	6	6	1	John Makuvek
1978	11	4	1	John Makuvek

Missouri-St. Louis defender Bill Colletta (right) tangles with a player from NAIA champion Quincy in 1978.

Montclair State's John LaRocca (kneeling) and Rob Gaertner (standing) make a sandwich out of Fairleigh Dickinson's Carlos Merchan.

Andy Loizou shone in the nets for Morris Harvey.

MORRIS HARVEY COLLEGE

Charleston, West Virginia

Golden Eagles Maroon and Gold

Yr.	W	L	T	Coach
1966	2	6	1	Clarke Herdic
1967	2	10	0	Clarke Hedric
1968	6	5	0	Clarke Hedric
1969	7	4	0	Tom Nozica
1970	9	2	0	Tom Nozica
1971	11	1	1	Tom Nozica
1972	6	5	0	Tom Nozica
1973	3	6	2	Tom Nozica
1974	1	10	0	Tom Nozica
1975	2	8	0	Tom Nozica
1976	6	5	0	Tom Nozica
1977	2	8	0	Tom Nozica
1978	2	8	0	Tom Nozica

MOUNT UNION COLLEGE

Alliance, Ohio

Purple Raiders Purple and White

Yr.	W	L	T	Coach
1964	0	7	0	Rafeld, Shellenberger
1965	0	8	0	William Shellenberger
1966	3	7	0	Jack Yoder
1967	0	7	0	Gary Fisher
1968	3	4	2	Gary Fisher
1969	5	2	1	Gary Fisher
1970	7	3	0	Gary Fisher
1971	3	5	1	Gary Fisher

Yr.	W	L	T	Coach
1972	9	2	0	Gary Fisher
1973	8	1	1	Gary Fisher
1974	12	1	0	Gary Fisher
1975	9	1	0	Gary Fisher
1976	9	1	0	Gary Fisher
1977	7	3	1	Gary Fisher
1978	7	3	2	Joe Luxbacher

MUHLENBERG COLLEGE

Allentown, Pennsylvania

Mules Red and Gray

Yr.	W	L	T	Coach
1943	5	2	1	Morgan Schaffer
1944	1	7	0	Morgan Schaffer
1945	2	5	0	Charles Altemose
1946	4	4	1	Charles Altemose
1947	3	2	1	Charles Altemose
1948	2	6	0	Charles Altemose
1949	3	4	2	Charles Altemose
1950	1	7	0	F. Ernest Fellows
1951	0	6	0	F. Ernest Fellows
1952	0	7	2	Samuel Nevins
1953	2	5	0	Samuel Nevins
1954	0	9	0	Samuel Nevins
1955	4	4	1	Samuel Nevins
1956	4	5	1	Samuel Nevins
1957	2	6	0	Samuel Nevins
1958	2	7	1	Rudolph Amelio
1959	0	11	0	Rudolph Amelio
1960	2	6	2	Rudolph Amelio
1961	0	10	0	Rudolph Amelio
1962	0	10	1	Rudolph Amelio

Yr.	W	L	T	Coach
1963	0	12	0	Amelio, L. Hill
1964	7	5	2	Lee Hill
1965	8	4	1	Lee Hill
1966	6	5	1	Lee Hill
1967	10	2	0	Donald Boyer
1968	6	7	1	Ronald Lauchnor
1969	6	4	2	Ronald Lauchnor
1970	11	2	1	Ronald Lauchnor
1971	6	4	2	Ronald Lauchnor
1972	12	2	1	Ronald Lauchnor
1973	12	2	1	Ronald Lauchnor
1974	6	5	1	Ronald Lauchnor
1975	14	2	1	Ronald Lauchnor
1976	9	6	1	Jay Mottola
1977	11	5	1	Jay Mottola
1978	8	8	0	James Trumbo

MUSKINGUM COLLEGE

New Concord, Ohio

Fighting Muskies · **Black and Magenta**

Yr.	W	L	T	Coach
1968	1	2	0	Byron Townsend
1969	2	1	0	Moore
1970	0	7	1	Jim Thieser
1971	1	7	1	Jim Thieser
1972	1	8	1	Doug Riley
1973	1	7	0	Doug Riley
1974	0	8	1	Ken Padfield
1975	4	4	1	Ken Padfield
1976	4	3	2	Ken Padfield
1977	2	8	0	Merrell Crandell
1978	1	6	1	Merrel Crandell

NAVY (USNA)

Annapolis, Maryland

Midshipmen · **Blue and Gold**

Yr.	W	L	T	Coach
1919	1	0	0	Tommy Taylor
1920	2	1	0	Tommy Taylor
1921	2	1	0	Tommy Taylor
1922	3	2	2	Tommy Taylor
1923	2	3	2	Tommy Taylor
1924	4	3	2	Tommy Taylor
1925	4	4	0	Tommy Taylor
1926	5	1	1	Tommy Taylor
1927	3	4	0	Tommy Taylor
1928	4	4	1	Tommy Taylor
1929	4	3	1	Tommy Taylor
1930	6	3	1	Tommy Taylor
1931	4	3	2	Tommy Taylor
1932	6	0	1	Tommy Taylor
1933	5	2	0	Tommy Taylor
1934	2	4	0	Tommy Taylor
1935	4	2	1	Tommy Taylor
1936	4	1	1	Tommy Taylor
1937	4	2	0	Tommy Taylor
1938	3	2	2	Tommy Taylor
1939	2	3	3	Tommy Taylor
1940	4	3	1	Tommy Taylor
1941	5	2	1	Tommy Taylor
1942	6	2	0	Tommy Taylor
1943	6	0	1	Tommy Taylor
1944	6	1	0	Tommy Taylor
1945	7	1	0	Tommy Taylor
1946	7	1	1	Glenn Warner
1947	8	2	0	Glenn Warner
1948	9	1	1	Glenn Warner

Glenn Warner (middle row, second from right) coached Navy to the national championship in 1964.

Yr.	W	L	T	Coach
1949	8	3	0	Glenn Warner
1950	6	4	0	Glenn Warner
1951	5	3	2	Glenn Warner
1952	3	4	3	Glenn Warner
1953	3	5	1	Glenn Warner
1954	4	3	3	Glenn Warner
1955	7	3	1	Glenn Warner
1956	10	2	0	Glenn Warner
1957	5	2	3	Glenn Warner
1958	7	1	3	Glenn Warner
1959	8	3	0	Glenn Warner
1960	7	2	2	Glenn Warner
1961	9	1	1	Glenn Warner
1962	10	1	0	Glenn Warner
1963	12	1	0	Glenn Warner
1964	15	0	0	Glenn Warner
1965	12	1	1	Glenn Warner
1966	10	1	2	Glenn Warner
1967	11	2	0	Glenn Warner
1968	8	2	1	Glenn Warner
1969	8	2	2	Glenn Warner
1970	11	1	1	Glenn Warner
1971	12	1	0	Glenn Warner
1972	5	5	1	Glenn Warner
1973	7	3	1	Glenn Warner
1974	7	3	1	Glenn Warner
1975	9	2	0	Glenn Warner
1976	6	3	3	Fred Myers
1977	7	5	1	Fred Myers
1978	5	4	3	Fred Myers

NEVADA, UNIVERSITY OF (LAS VEGAS)

Las Vegas, Nevada

Rebels				Scarlet and Gray
Yr.	W	L	T	Coach
1974	8	3	3	Tom Khamis
1975	11	5	2	Tom Khamis
1976	13	4	1	Vince Hart
1977	14	6	1	Vince Hart
1978	7	9	0	Vince Hart

NEW HAMPSHIRE, UNIVERSITY OF

Durham, New Hampshire

Wildcats				Blue and White
Yr.	W	L	T	Coach
1922	0	1	0	—
1923	0	0	1	—
1924	0	2	1	—
1925	2	4	0	Henry Swasey
1926	2	2	1	Henry Swasey
1927	3	3	0	Henry Swasey
1964	2	2	0	Walt Weiland
1965	4	5	0	Walt Weiland
1966	4	7	0	Walt Weiland

New Hampshire's Chip Smith (left) and Dartmouth's Roman Lipp are thrashing through the snow during a 1976 contest.

Yr.	W	L	T	Coach
1967	4	7	0	Walt Weiland
1968	6	6	1	Walt Weiland
1969	6	6	0	Peter Fernald
1970	5	4	1	Don Heyliger
1971	6	3	0	Don Heyliger
1972	7	3	3	Don Heyliger
1973	6	5	0	Don Heyliger
1974	4	4	2	Don Heyliger
1975	6	7	0	Don Heyliger
1976	5	6	2	Art Young
1977	3	12	0	Art Young
1978	5	10	1	Bob Kullen

NEW HAVEN, UNIVERSITY OF

West Haven, Connecticut

Chargers   Blue and Gold

Yr.	W	L	T	Coach
1962	12	1	0	Richard Curren
1963	7	3	1	Paul DelGobbo
1964	11	2	1	Paul DelGobbo
1965	10	0	0	Paul DelGobbo
1966	7	2	0	Paul DelGobbo
1967	8	2	2	Donald Wynschenk
1968	5	6	1	Donald Wynschenk
1969	2	10	1	Joseph Machnik
1970	13	5	1	Joseph Machnik
1971	13	4	1	Joseph Machnik
1972	9	2	2	Joseph Machnik
1973	9	4	3	Joseph Machnik
1974	5	9	0	Joseph Machnik
1975	10	5	2	Joseph Machnik
1976	12	6	2	Joseph Machnik

Yr.	W	L	T	Coach
1977	16	2	2	Joseph Machnik
1978	13	2	4	Joseph Machnik

NEW JERSEY INSTITUTE OF TECHNOLOGY

Newark, New Jersey

Highlanders   Scarlet and White

Yr.	W	L	T	Coach
1952	4	3	2	Alec Rae
1953	1	6	0	Alec Rae
1954	3	3	2	Alec Rae
1955	2	4	1	J. Malcolm Simon
1956	2	5	1	J. Malcolm Simon
1957	5	3	0	J. Malcolm Simon
1958	4	1	3	J. Malcolm Simon
1959	6	3	0	J. Malcolm Simon
1960	12	0	1	J. Malcolm Simon
1961	9	1	0	J. Malcolm Simon
1962	5	1	1	J. Malcolm Simon
1963	6	3	0	J. Malcolm Simon
1964	7	3	1	J. Malcolm Simon
1965	7	3	0	J. Malcolm Simon
1966	7	3	0	J. Malcolm Simon
1967	3	5	1	J. Malcolm Simon
1968	5	4	1	J. Malcolm Simon
1969	9	4	0	J. Malcolm Simon
1970	10	4	0	J. Malcolm Simon
1971	12	2	2	Oleg Moiseenko
1972	2	7	3	J. Malcolm Simon
1973	9	6	2	J. Malcolm Simon
1974	10	3	1	J. Malcolm Simon
1975	11	3	0	J. Malcolm Simon
1976	8	5	0	J. Malcolm Simon
1977	10	4	1	J. Malcolm Simon
1978	5	7	2	J. Malcolm Simon

Newark College of Engineering, now known as New Jersey Tech, had a pair of Myrons—1966 All-American Myron Bakun (right) and Myron Worobec.

NEW YORK INSTITUTE OF TECHNOLOGY

Old Westbury, New York

Bears				Blue and Gold
Yr.	W	L	T	Coach
1970	4	4	1	C. Gluck
1971	10	3	2	C. Gluck
1972	8	4	1	C. Gluck
1973	2	12	2	P. Simoneski
1974	2	11	2	L. Markiet
1975	8	5	2	R. Hogan
1976	9	6	0	Philip Santiago
1977	9	6	0	Phillip Santiago
1978	10	6	0	Philip Santiago

NIAGARA UNIVERSITY

Niagara, New York

Purple Eagles				Purple and White
Yr.	W	L	T	Coach
1969	8	4	1	Al Montagna
1970	11	3	0	Al Montagna
1971	7	2	0	Mike Gomez
1972	9	1	2	Mike Gomez
1973	5	4	3	Adrian Humphries
1974	4	7	0	Jean Tassy
1975	7	5	0	Jean Tassy
1976	3	9	0	Jean Tassy
1977	7	3	2	Jean Tassy
1978	8	2	1	Jean Tassy

NORTH ADAMS STATE COLLEGE

North Adams, Massachusetts

Mohawks				Blue and Gold
Yr.	W	L	T	Coach
1968	2	9	0	Gene Lepesque
1969	0	13	0	Gene Lepesque
1970	2	9	0	Bill West
1971	5	7	0	Bill West
1972	7	5	1	Bill West
1973	8	4	2	Tom Baker
1974	6	4	4	Tom Baker
1975	13	1	1	Tom Baker
1976	15	2	0	Tom Baker
1977	15	2	2	Tom Baker
1978	17	2	0	Ron Shewcraft

NORTH CAROLINA STATE

Raleigh, North Carolina

Wolfpack				Red and White
Yr.	W	L	T	Coach
1955	3	5	1	Eric DeGroat
1956	1	7	0	John Kenfield, Jr.
1957	—	—	—	—
1958	5	3	0	Bill Leonhardt
1959	3	6	0	Bill Leonhardt
1960	0	10	1	Bill Leonhardt
1961	2	7	1	Nelvin Cooper
1962	1	9	0	Nelvin Cooper
1963	7	6	0	Nelvin Cooper
1964	7	4	0	Max Rhodes

Yr.	W	L	T	Coach
1965	5	7	0	Max Rhodes
1966	6	3	1	Max Rhodes
1967	5	6	0	Max Rhodes
1968	6	3	1	Max Rhodes
1969	4	8	0	Max Rhodes
1970	5	3	2	Max Rhodes
1971	6	4	2	Max Rhodes
1972	6	3	2	Max Rhodes
1973	5	4	0	Max Rhodes
1974	5	7	0	Max Rhodes
1975	6	3	2	Max Rhodes
1976	7	7	0	Max Rhodes
1977	5	7	1	Max Rhodes
1978	10	4	2	Larry Gross

NORTH CAROLINA, UNIVERSITY OF

Chapel Hill, North Carolina

Tar Heels				Blue and White
Yr.	W	L	T	Coach
1947	6	3	0	Marvin Allen
1948	7	1	2	Marvin Allen
1949	7	3	0	Marvin Allen
1950	5	4	0	Marvin Allen
1951	5	6	0	Al Moore
1952	4	4	1	Al Moore
1953	3	4	1	Marvin Allen
1954	3	4	1	Marvin Allen
1955	4	2	2	Marvin Allen
1956	4	3	0	Marvin Allen
1957	2	3	2	Marvin Allen
1958	8	2	0	Marvin Allen
1959	10	1	0	Marvin Állen
1960	8	3	0	Marvin Allen
1961	8	4	0	Marvin Allen
1962	7	2	0	Marvin Allen
1963	5	3	2	Marvin Allen
1964	5	2	2	Marvin Allen
1965	8	3	0	Marvin Allen
1966	7	2	1	Marvin Allen
1967	10	2	0	Marvin Allen
1968	8	3	0	Marvin Allen
1969	6	4	0	Marvin Allen
1970	5	2	3	Marvin Allen
1971	6	4	1	Marvin Allen
1972	6	3	1	Marvin Allen
1973	8	2	1	Marvin Allen
1974	4	3	4	Marvin Allen
1975	7	4	0	Marvin Allen
1976	9	5	0	Marvin Allen
1977	14	3	1	Anson Dorrance
1978	12	3	4	Anson Dorrance

NORTH CAROLINA, UNIVERSITY OF (CHARLOTTE)

Charlotte, North Carolina

49ers				Green and White
Yr.	W	L	T	Coach
1976	3	9	0	Ike Gardner
1977	6	10	0	Ike Gardner
1978	12	10	1	Ike Gardner

Marvin Allen coached North Carolina from 1938, when soccer was a club sport, through 1976, except for the time he was in the service.

NORTH CAROLINA, UNIVERSITY OF (GREENSBORO)

Greensboro, North Carolina

Spartans				Gold and White
Yr.	**W**	**L**	**T**	**Coach**
1977	5	11	2	G. Bird, Lukaszewski
1978	8	10	1	Geoff Bird

NORTH CAROLINA, UNIVERSITY OF (WILMINGTON)

Wilmington, North Carolina

Seahawks				Green and Gold
Yr.	**W**	**L**	**T**	**Coach**
1965	0	7	0	Charles Sproles
1966	3	6	0	Charles Sproles
1967	4	4	0	Charles Sproles
1968	6	1	2	Charles Sproles
1969	5	7	0	Charles Sproles
1970	5	7	0	Larry Honeycutt
1971	4	5	0	Calvin Lane
1972	5	8	1	Calvin Lane
1973	5	8	3	Calvin Lane
1974	11	7	1	Calvin Lane
1975	13	2	0	Calvin Lane
1976	8	7	0	Calvin Lane

Yr.	W	L	T	Coach
1977	11	4	0	Calvin Lane
1978	11	5	1	Calvin Lane

NORTH TEXAS STATE UNIVERSITY

Denton, Texas

Mean Green				Green and White
Yr.	**W**	**L**	**T**	**Coach**
1976	16	2	1	Simon Sanchez
1977	11	5	0	Simon Sanchez
1978	11	3	5	Simon Sanchez

NORTHERN ILLINOIS UNIVERSITY

DeKalb, Illinois

Huskies				Cardinal and Black
Yr.	**W**	**L**	**T**	**Coach**
1962	0	5	0	Robert Kahler
1963	3	4	0	William Healey
1964	3	4	0	William Healey
1965	0	5	0	William Healey
1966	2	3	0	William Healey
1967	5	1	1	William Healey
1968	8	1	0	William Healey
1969	8	1	0	Dave Bucher
1970	6	3	2	Dave Bucher
1971	7	2	1	Dave Bucher
1972	3	5	2	Dave Bucher
1973	7	2	2	Dave Bucher
1974	5	2	3	Dave Bucher
1975	6	5	0	Dave Bucher
1976	7	3	2	Dave Bucher
1977	7	4	0	Dave Bucher
1978	7	2	3	Dave Bucher

NICHOLS COLLEGE

Dudley, Massachusetts

Bisons				Black and Green
Yr.	**W**	**L**	**T**	**Coach**
1959	6	3	2	Joseph Christopher
1960	11	0	1	Joseph Christopher
1961	7	4	0	Joseph Christopher
1962	3	8	0	Roland Gaudette
1963	12	0	1	Roland Gaudette
1964	9	2	0	Roland Gaudette
1965	12	0	0	Roland Gaudette
1966	8	2	0	Roland Gaudette
1967	4	7	1	Tim Cooney
1968	6	4	2	Tim Cooney
1969	5	5	3	William Steglitz
1970	9	4	1	Lincoln MacDonald
1971	8	5	1	Lincoln MacDonald
1972	9	3	1	Lincoln MacDonald
1973	6	5	3	Lincoln MacDonald
1974	3	7	4	Kurt Durrschmidt
1975	3	10	1	Kurt Durrschmidt
1976	2	11	2	Kurt Durrschmidt
1977	3	10	2	Al Cormier
1978	8	5	2	Al Cormier

NORWICH UNIVERSITY

Northfield, Vermont

Cadets   Maroon and Gold

Yr.	W	L	T	Coach
1959	4	1	2	Robert Axtell
1960	1	7	0	Robert Axtell
1961	5	4	0	Robert Axtell
1962	3	7	0	Roland Lyford
1963	2	5	2	Roland Lyford
1964	7	1	0	Roland Lyford
1965	6	3	0	Roland Lyford
1966	7	1	1	Roland Lyford
1967	7	2	0	Roland Lyford
1968	8	1	1	Roland Lyford
1969	7	3	0	Roland Lyford
1970	5	4	2	Roland Lyford
1971	3	6	2	Chandler Stowell
1972	4	6	1	Chandler Stowell
1973	5	5	1	Chandler Stowell
1974	2	5	4	Chandler Stowell
1975	5	6	1	Chandler Stowell
1976	3	8	2	Chandler Stowell
1977	2	9	1	Chandler Stowell
1978	2	9	1	Tony Mariano

OBERLIN COLLEGE

Oberlin, Ohio

Yeomen   Crimson and Gold

Yr.	W	L	T	Coach
1933	2	2	1	—
1934	3	1	1	—
1935	5	0	1	—
1936	2	2	1	—
1937	1	3	1	G. E. Willbond
1938	1	4	0	G.E. Willbond, C.P. Erdmann
1939	5	1	0	G.E. Willbond, C.P. Erdmann
1940	2	3	0	G.E. Willbond
1941	4	1	1	G.E. Willbond
1942	4	1	0	G.E. Willbond
1943	2	1	0	G.E. Willbond
1944	1	3	3	G.E. Willbond
1945	3	3	0	G.E. Willbond
1946	5	2	1	G.E. Willbond
1947	7	1	0	G.E. Willbond
1948	4	1	2	G.E. Willbond
1949	8	0	1	B.S. Collins
1950	7	1	1	B.S. Collins
1951	8	0	0	B.S. Collins
1952	9	0	1	Clifford Stevenson
1953	9	0	1	Clifford Stevenson
1954	9	0	0	Clifford Stevenson
1955	6	1	1	Clifford Stevenson
1956	4	2	2	Clifford Stevenson
1957	2	6	1	Clifford Stevenson
1958	3	4	1	Clifford Stevenson
1959	6	3	0	Clifford Stevenson
1960	7	2	0	Fredrick Shults
1961	8	1	0	Fredrick Shults
1962	8	3	0	Fredrick Shults
1963	6	3	0	Fredrick Shults
1964	5	3	1	Fredrick Shults
1965	8	2	1	Fredrick Shults
1966	6	2	1	Joe Horn
1967	8	1	0	Fredrick Shults
1968	4	4	1	Fredrick Shults
1969	4	3	3	Fredrick Shults
1970	4	5	1	Fredrick Shults
1971	4	3	2	Fredrick Shults
1972	5	5	0	Fredrick Shults
1973	2	5	3	Fredrick Shults
1974	5	1	3	Fredrick Shults
1975	8	2	0	Fredrick Shults
1976	5	4	2	Fredrick Shults
1977	4	7	1	Fredrick Shults
1978	3	7	1	Fredrick Shults

OHIO DOMINICAN COLLEGE

Columbus, Ohio

Panthers   Black and Gold

Yr.	W	L	T	Coach
1977	0	10	0	Allan Cassals
1978	4	7	0	Andy Pankin

OHIO NORTHERN UNIVERSITY

Ada, Ohio

Polar Bears   Orange and Black

Yr.	W	L	T	Coach
1975	2	8	0	Amar Bhattacharya
1976	8	3	0	Amar Bhattacharya
1977	8	4	0	Amar Bhattacharya
1978	7	3	2	Amar Bhattacharya

OHIO STATE UNIVERSITY

Columbus, Ohio

Buckeyes   Scarlet and Gray

Yr.	W	L	T	Coach
1953	3	6	1	Bruce Bennett
1954	3	6	1	Howard Knuttgen
1955	5	3	1	Howard Knuttgen
1956	7	3	0	Howard Knuttgen
1957	3	6	0	Howard Knuttgen
1958	3	5	1	Walter Ersing
1959	1	8	0	Walter Ersing
1960	3	4	1	Walter Ersing
1961	0	7	1	Walter Ersing
1962	3	5	0	Walter Ersing
1963	2	5	2	Walter Ersing
1964	3	6	0	Walter Ersing
1965	5	4	0	Walter Ersing
1966	3	6	0	Walter Ersing
1967	7	2	0	Walter Ersing
1968	2	7	0	Walter Ersing
1969	2	6	1	Forrest Tyson
1970	2	6	2	Forrest Tyson
1971	4	5	2	Bill Servedio
1972	0	9	2	Bill Servedio
1973	2	3	5	Bill Servedio
1974	6	3	2	Bill Servedio
1975	5	6	2	Bill Servedio
1976	6	6	1	Jerry Bell
1977	10	4	0	Jerry Bell
1978	5	9	2	Jerry Bell

Old Dominion coach Bill Killen drives home a point to Greer McCreedy (left) and Jerry Albino in 1978.

OLD DOMINION UNIVERSITY

Norfolk, Virginia

Monarchs				Blue and White
Yr.	W	L	T	Coach
1969	1	6	1	Ronald Edwards
1970	5	5	0	Steve Cottrell
1971	2	7	0	Steve Cottrell
1972	1	7	1	Guenther Dietz
1973	1	8	1	Guenther Dietz
1974	4	6	1	Guenther Dietz
1975	13	2	0	Guenther Dietz
1976	8	7	0	Guenther Dietz
1977	5	6	2	Guenther Dietz
1978	9	5	1	Bill Killen

OLIVET NAZARENE COLLEGE

Kankakee, Illinois

Tigers				Purple and Gold
Yr.	W	L	T	Coach
1978	3	10	0	Al Lilienthal

ONEONTA STATE UNIVERSITY

Oneonta, New York

Red Dragons				Red and White
Yr.	W	L	T	Coach
1955	2	3	0	Hurley McLean
1956	1	4	1	Hurley McLean
1957	2	5	0	Hurley McLean
1958	8	8	8	Hurley McLean
1959	8	3	0	Hurley McLean
1960	6	3	0	Hurley McLean
1961	7	2	1	Garth Stam
1962	8	3	0	Garth Stam
1963	2	8	0	Garth Stam
1964	2	8	0	Garth Stam
1965	6	6	0	Garth Stam
1966	5	3	3	Garth Stam
1967	9	1	0	Garth Stam
1968	5	4	1	Garth Stam
1969	4	7	0	Garth Stam
1970	9	2	0	Garth Stam
1971	11	0	0	Garth Stam
1972	12	1	0	Garth Stam
1973	11	0	2	Garth Stam

Hurley McLean (bottom right) led the first Oneonta State team into battle in 1955.

Yr.	W	L	T	Coach
1974	10	2	1	Garth Stam
1975	9	1	2	Garth Stam
1976	9	5	2	Garth Stam
1977	11	1	1	Garth Stam
1978	8	6	2	Garth Stam

OSWEGO STATE UNIVERSITY

Oswego, New York

Lakers				Green and Gold
Yr.	W	L	T	Coach
1938	1	2	0	Max Ziel
1939	2	1	0	Max Ziel
1940	1	3	0	Max Ziel
1941	0	2	0	William Stebbins
1942	0	2	0	William Stebbins
1943	—	—	—	—
1944	—	—	—	—
1945	—	—	—	—
1946	1	6	0	James Ashcraft
1947	1	4	2	John Needy
1948	3	3	1	John Needy
1949	3	3	1	Richard Luce
1950	3	3	0	Richard Luce
1951	2	6	2	Richard Luce
1952	0	8	0	Richard Luce
1953	3	4	1	David Campbell
1954	2	6	0	Richard Luce
1955	4	4	0	Richard Luce
1956	2	6	1	Richard Luce

Yr.	W	L	T	Coach
1957	3	4	0	Ernest Luongo
1958	7	1	0	Ernest Luongo
1959	8	3	0	Ernest Luongo
1960	6	3	1	Ernest Luongo
1961	8	2	0	Ernest Luongo
1962	6	2	2	Ernest Luongo
1963	5	5	0	Ernest Luongo
1964	6	3	1	Ernest Luongo
1965	6	4	0	Ernest Luongo
1966	7	2	1	Ernest Luongo
1967	4	4	0	George Crowe
1968	2	5	3	Ken Peterson
1969	2	8	2	Ken Peterson
1970	3	7	3	Ken Peterson
1971	6	6	1	Ken Peterson
1972	4	8	1	Ken Peterson
1973	6	8	0	Ken Peterson
1974	5	8	1	Ken Peterson
1975	6	9	1	Ken Peterson
1976	8	5	2	Ken Peterson
1977	4	9	1	Ken Peterson
1978	5	7	3	Ken Peterson

PACE UNIVERSITY

Pleasantville, New York

Setters				Blue and Gold
Yr.	W	L	T	Coach
1969	5	6	1	—
1970	3	7	0	—

Yr.	W	L	T	Coach
1971	1	11	0	—
1972	—	—	—	—
1973	—	—	—	—
1974	—	—	—	—
1975	0	8	0	Herbert Austin
1976	4	5	0	Herbert Austin
1977	3	6	0	Herbert Austin
1978	1	9	0	Herbert Austin

PACIFIC, UNIVERSITY OF THE

Stockton, California

Tigers   **Black and Orange**

Yr.	W	L	T	Coach
1975	2	9	2	Eddie Araya
1976	0	13	2	Glynn Richard
1977	2	16	1	Glynn Richard
1978	7	11	1	Glynn Richard

PENN STATE COLLEGE (Behrend)

Erie, Pennsylvania

Cubs   **Blue, Red, and White**

Yr.	W	L	T	Coach
1960	0	2	0	James Gallagher
1961	1	2	0	James Gallagher
1962	1	4	0	James Gallagher
1963	3	2	0	Roger Sweeting
1964	1	3	1	Roger Sweeting
1965	2	4	0	Roger Sweeting
1966	0	4	2	Edward Onorato
1967	2	6	0	Edward Onorato
1968	4	3	1	Herbert Lauffer
1969	4	4	2	Herbert Lauffer
1970	5	5	0	Herbert Lauffer
1971	7	4	0	Herbert Lauffer
1972	5	3	1	Herbert Lauffer
1973	4	6	2	Herbert Lauffer
1974	6	5	1	Herbert Lauffer
1975	8	4	0	Herbert Lauffer
1976	8	5	0	Herbert Lauffer
1977	8	6	2	Herbert Lauffer
1978	7	6	2	Herbert Lauffer

PENN STATE UNIVERSITY

University Park, Pennsylvania

Nittany Lions   **Blue and White**

Yr.	W	L	T	Coach
1947	5	2	1	Bill Jeffrey
1948	7	1	1	Bill Jeffrey
1949	8	0	1	Bill Jeffrey
1950	9	1	0	Bill Jeffrey
1951	5	1	2	Bill Jeffrey
1952	7	1	1	Bill Jeffrey
1953	5	2	0	Ken Hosterman
1954	8	0	0	Ken Hosterman
1955	9	0	0	Ken Hosterman
1956	8	2	1	Ken Hosterman
1957	8	1	1	Ken Hosterman
1958	5	4	0	Ken Hosterman
1959	2	7	0	Ken Hosterman
1960	3	6	0	Ken Hosterman

Jim Stamatis was named to the All-American squad after leading Penn State to an 11-5-1 record in 1978.

Yr.	W	L	T	Coach
1961	3	6	0	Ken Hosterman
1962	3	6	0	Ken Hosterman
1963	5	4	0	Ken Hosterman
1964	4	5	0	Ken Hosterman
1965	3	6	0	Ken Hosterman
1966	1	7	2	Ken Hosterman
1967	5	4	1	Ken Hosterman
1968	0	6	3	Herb Schmidt
1969	3	6	0	Herb Schmidt
1970	9	3	0	Herb Schmidt
1971	9	3	1	Herb Schmidt
1972	9	1	2	Herb Schmidt
1973	8	2	3	Herb Schmidt
1974	8	3	1	Walter Bahr
1975	9	5	1	Walter Bahr
1976	10	4	1	Walter Bahr
1977	13	3	0	Walter Bahr
1978	11	5	1	Walter Bahr

Charles Scott captained the 1935 Penn soccer team and then returned to coach the Quakers to 135 wins from 1946–67.

PENNSYLVANIA, UNIVERSITY OF

Philadelphia, Pennsylvania

Quakers				Red and Blue
Yr.	W	L	T	Coach
1905	2	2	0	Douglas Stewart
1906	2	1	1	Douglas Stewart
1907	2	9	0	Douglas Stewart
1908	7	2	4	Douglas Stewart
1909	3	7	1	Douglas Stewart
1910	4	7	3	Douglas Stewart
1911	7	8	3	Douglas Stewart
1912	8	9	3	Douglas Stewart
1913	6	0	4	Douglas Stewart
1914	9	2	1	Douglas Stewart
1915	12	2	2	Douglas Stewart
1916	9	3	1	Douglas Stewart
1917	10	3	0	Douglas Stewart
1918	6	2	2	Douglas Stewart
1919	10	1	0	Douglas Stewart
1920	9	1	2	Douglas Stewart
1921	5	7	0	Douglas Stewart
1922	6	3	3	Douglas Stewart
1923	11	1	0	Douglas Stewart
1924	10	1	0	Douglas Stewart
1925	9	2	0	Douglas Stewart
1926	5	5	0	Douglas Stewart
1927	4	4	1	Douglas Stewart
1928	10	5	1	Douglas Stewart

Yr.	W	L	T	Coach
1929	8	2	1	Douglas Stewart
1930	10	2	0	Douglas Stewart
1931	9	1	1	Douglas Stewart
1932	5	1	2	Douglas Stewart
1933	10	0	0	Douglas Stewart
1934	8	1	0	Douglas Stewart
1935	6	3	1	Douglas Stewart
1936	5	4	1	Douglas Stewart
1937	7	4	0	Douglas Stewart
1938	4	4	2	Douglas Stewart
1939	4	4	3	Douglas Stewart
1940	2	6	1	Douglas Stewart
1941	5	4	3	Douglas Stewart
1942	2	6	0	Douglas Stewart
1943	6	2	0	Charles R. Scott
1944	4	1	0	Arthur M. Binns
1945	3	5	1	Arthur M. Binns
1946	7	2	0	Charles R. Scott
1947	6	3	0	Charles R. Scott
1948	5	3	1	Charles R. Scott
1949	4	6	0	Charles R. Scott
1950	4	6	0	Charles R. Scott
1951	6	4	0	Charles R. Scott
1952	6	3	2	Charles R. Scott
1953	8	3	0	Charles R. Scott
1954	5	5	1	Charles R. Scott
1955	10	1	0	Charles R.Scott
1956	6	4	1	Charles R. Scott
1957	5	5	1	Charles R. Scott
1958	7	2	2	Charles R. Scott
1959	7	2	2	Charles R. Scott
1960	4	5	1	Charles R. Scott
1961	6	4	1	Charles R. Scott
1962	7	1	2	Charles R. Scott
1963	6	4	0	Charles R. Scott
1964	7	2	2	Charles R. Scott
1965	7	3	1	Charles R. Scott
1966	5	5	2	Charles R. Scott
1967	7	1	4	Charles R. Scott
1968	8	3	1	Robert Seddon
1969	11	4	0	Robert Seddon
1970	8	3	2	Robert Seddon
1971	13	2	0	Robert Seddon
1972	14	1	1	Robert Seddon
1973	13	3	0	Robert Seddon
1974	6	6	1	Robert Seddon
1975	10	3	0	Robert Seddon
1976	7	5	1	Robert Seddon
1977	8	5	2	Robert Seddon
1978	5	6	4	Robert Seddon

PFEIFFER COLLEGE

Misenheimer, North Carolina

Falcons				Black and Gold
Yr.	W	L	T	Coach
1957	0	5	0	John Neddy
1958	1	8	1	John Neddy
1959	1	8	0	N. E. Lefko
1960	6	4	0	N. E. Lefko
1961	9	1	1	N. E. Lefko
1962	5	5	0	N. E. Lefko
1963	4	8	0	N. E. Lefko
1964	7	3	0	N. E. Lefko
1965	10	1	0	N. E. Lefko
1966	3	7	2	N. E. Lefko

The fun-loving Pfeiffer team of 1961 went 9–1–1.

Yr.	W	L	T	Coach		Yr.	W	L	T	Coach
1967	4	7	1	N. E. Lefko		1954	3	9	0	John Hughes
1968	4	8	0	N. E. Kefko		1955	2	6	1	John Hughes
1969	3	9	0	N. E. Lefko		1956	6	1	0	Bucky Harris
1970	1	10	1	N. E. Lefko		1957	3	4	2	Bucky Harris
1971	4	7	3	N. E. Lefko		1958	4	2	1	Bucky Harris
1972	3	10	1	N. E. Lefko		1959	4	3	0	Bucky Harris
1973	2	7	2	N. E. Lefko		1960	3	3	0	Bucky Harris
1974	3	8	2	N. E. Lefko		1961	2	4	0	Walt Chyzowych
1975	13	3	0	Bob Parry		1962	6	4	1	Walt Chyzowych
1976	8	5	0	Bob Parry		1963	5	3	1	Walt Chyzowych
1977	12	3	1	Bob Parry		1964	4	5	0	Bill Wilkinson
1978	10	12	1	Bob Parry		1965	5	3	0	Bill Wilkinson
						1966	5	4	1	Walt Chyzowych

PHILADELPHIA TEXTILE

Philadelphia, Pennsylvania

1967	7	5	1	Walt Chyzowych
1968	8	4	1	Walt Chyzowych
1969	13	0	2	Walt Chyzowych
1970	17	1	0	Walt Chyzowych

Rams   **Maroon and White**

Yr.	W	L	T	Coach
1971	8	2	4	Walt Chyzowych
1972	10	2	1	Walt Chyzowych
1953	4	4	1	John Hughes
1973	9	2	2	Walt Chyzowych
1974	17	2	1	Walt Chyzowych

With Pete Simonini posting 14 shutouts, Plymouth State rolled to the best record in its history in 1978—16-1-2.

Yr.	W	L	T	Coach
1975	15	2	0	Walt Chyzowych
1976	13	3	0	Barry Barto
1977	10	3	3	Barry Barto
1978	17	2	0	Barry Barto

PLYMOUTH STATE COLLEGE

Plymouth, New Hampshire

Panthers   **Green and White**

Yr.	W	L	T	Coach
1957	2	4	0	Howard Goldman
1958	6	1	2	Howard Goldman
1959	7	3	0	Howard Goldman
1960	5	5	1	Howard Goldman
1961	5	5	0	Howard Goldman
1962	6	3	3	Howard Goldman
1963	7	3	2	Joe Clark
1964	4	7	1	Doug Wiseman
1965	4	7	1	Doug Wiseman
1966	5	6	1	Doug Wiseman
1967	5	7	1	Doug Wiseman
1968	6	7	1	Doug Wiseman
1969	8	2	0	Gerd Lutter
1970	9	3	0	Gerd Lutter
1971	10	3	1	Gerd Lutter
1972	7	3	2	Gerd Lutter
1973	10	2	2	Gerd Lutter
1974	7	5	1	Gerd Lutter
1975	13	2	2	Gerd Lutter
1976	8	4	3	Gerd Lutter
1977	13	2	4	Gerd Lutter
1978	16	1	2	Gerd Lutter

POTSDAM STATE UNIVERSITY

Potsdam, New York

Bears   **Maroon and White**

Yr.	W	L	T	Coach
1958	2	4	0	Riedel
1959	3	5	0	Bob Serfis
1960	4	5	0	Bob Serfis
1961	5	2	2	Bob Serfis
1962	5	1	3	Bob Serfis
1963	7	2	1	Bob Serfis
1964	3	6	1	Bob Serfis
1965	6	4	0	Bob Serfis
1966	5	4	1	Bob Serfis
1967	4	6	1	Bob Serfis
1968	4	6	1	Bob Serfis
1969	5	5	1	Bob Serfis
1970	5	5	1	Bob Serfis
1971	3	6	1	Bob Serfis
1972	3	6	1	Bob Serfis
1973	7	3	1	Bob Serfis
1974	2	3	3	Bob Serfis
1975	0	7	0	—
1976	0	11	0	Neil Johnson
1977	5	7	0	Jim Kelly
1978	3	8	0	Jim Kelly

PRINCETON UNIVERSITY

Princeton, New Jersey

Tigers   **Orange and Black**

Yr.	W	L	T	Coach
1919	5	2	0	—

Yr.	W	L	T	Coach
1920	8	1	2	—
1921	8	1	1	—
1922	9	2	0	—
1923	4	2	2	—
1924	4	1	2	—
1925	6	0	1	—
1926	5	1	1	—
1927	8	0	0	—
1928	3	4	1	—
1929	4	3	1	—
1930	2	5	1	—
1931	2	5	1	—
1932	3	3	2	—
1933	1	5	1	—
1934	4	2	2	—
1935	4	3	2	—
1936	6	1	1	—
1937	6	2	0	James J. Reed
1938	4	2	2	James J. Reed
1939	9	1	0	James J. Reed
1940	8	0	1	James J. Reed
1941	6	3	1	James J. Reed
1942	8	0	1	James J. Reed
1943	3	2	0	James J. Reed
1944	2	4	0	James J. Reed
1945	3	3	1	James J. Reed
1946	7	1	2	James J. Reed
1947	2	6	2	James J. Reed
1948	2	6	2	James J. Reed
1949	5	3	0	James J. Reed
1950	3	5	0	James J. Reed
1951	4	3	1	James J. Reed
1952	2	6	1	James J. Reed
1953	5	3	1	James J. Reed
1954	6	1	1	James J. Reed
1955	4	3	2	James J. Reed
1956	2	6	1	James J. Reed
1957	8	1	0	James J. Reed
1958	7	2	0	James J. Reed
1959	7	3	0	James J. Reed
1960	8	2	0	James J. Reed
1961	3	3	4	James J. Reed
1962	4	6	0	James J. Reed
1963	7	2	1	James J. Reed
1964	5	4	1	James J. Reed
1965	2	7	1	James J. Reed
1966	0	7	3	James J. Reed
1967	7	5	0	R. Jack Volz
1968	5	6	1	R. Jack Volz
1969	5	6	1	R. Jack Volz
1970	4	6	1	R. Jack Volz
1971	5	4	2	R. Jack Volz
1972	4	6	1	R. Jack Volz
1973	7	2	3	Bill Muse
1974	2	7	3	Bill Muse
1975	3	6	3	Bill Muse
1976	10	4	0	Bill Muse
1977	11	5	0	Bill Muse
1978	9	2	3	Bill Muse

PROVIDENCE COLLEGE

Providence, Rhode Island

Friars   **Black and White**

Yr.	W	L	T	Coach
1968	3	7	1	Bill Doyle

Yr.	W	L	T	Coach
1969	4	7	3	Bill Doyle
1970	11	1	0	Bill Doyle
1971	3	9	0	Bill Doyle
1972	11	2	0	Bill Doyle
1973	6	2	3	Bill Doyle
1974	3	8	1	Bill Doyle
1975	7	4	0	Bill Doyle
1976	9	6	0	Bill Doyle
1977	5	8	1	Bill Doyle
1978	8	4	2	Bill Doyle

QUINCY COLLEGE

Quincy, Illinois

Hawks   **Brown and White**

Yr.	W	L	T	Coach
1964	8	0	0	Frank Longo
1965	9	2	1	Roger Francour
1966	13	0	0	Roger Francour

Quincy's Mike Villa scored a record 10 goals in one game en route to a total of 44 as a senior in 1968.

Jim Pollihan (left), on the move against Philadelphia Textile, played a role in Quincy's three straight NAIA titles (1973–75).

Yr.	W	L	T	Coach		Yr.	W	L	T	Coach
1967	13	2	0	Roger Francour		1957	0	7	0	Hugh Moomaw
1968	11	4	0	Roger Francour		1958	0	8	1	Hugh Moomaw
1969	8	2	2	Jack MacKenzie		1959	2	8	0	A. P. Johnston
1970	15	1	2	Jack MacKenzie		1960	2	7	0	Hugh Moomaw
1971	17	2	0	Jack MacKenzie		1961	1	6	2	Bill Rachaels, Jr.
1972	16	3	0	Jack MacKenzie		1962	1	8	1	Helmut Werner
1973	14	5	1	Jack MacKenzie		1963	3	6	0	Helmut Werner
1974	17	2	1	Jack MacKenzie		1964	7	6	0	Helmut Werner
1975	19	1	1	Jack MacKenzie		1965	8	5	0	Helmut Werner
1976	19	3	1	Jack MacKenzie		1966	7	4	1	Helmut Werner
1977	19	3	0	Jack MacKenzie		1967	7	3	1	Helmut Werner
1978	18	3	1	Jack MacKenzie		1968	7	4	1	Helmut Werner
						1969	9	4	2	Helmut Werner
						1970	7	4	2	Helmut Werner
						1971	7	8	1	Helmut Werner
						1972	9	3	1	Helmut Werner
						1973	4	8	1	Helmut Werner
						1974	7	3	3	Helmut Werner
						1975	11	6	1	Helmut Werner
						1976	14	4	0	Helmut Werner
						1977	11	2	1	Helmut Werner
						1978	10	6	1	Helmut Werner

RANDOLPH-MACON COLLEGE

Ashland, Virginia

Yellow Jackets   **Lemon and Black**

Yr.	W	L	T	Coach
1955	0	2	0	Hugh Moomaw
1956	0	5	0	Hugh Moomaw

Griff Sims made a major contribution as Randolph-Macon posted four straight seasons with 10 or more victories (1975–78).

RENSSELAER POLYTECHNIC INSTITUTE

Troy, New York

Engineers   **Red and White**

Yr.	W	L	T	Coach
1922	1	0	0	R. Boyne
1923	0	3	1	R. Boyne
1924	1	2	1	R. Boyne
1925	1	1	1	R. Boyne
1926	1	2	0	R. Boyne
1927	1	3	0	William Gailey
1928	0	3	1	William Gailey
1929	2	2	0	William Gailey
1930	3	1	0	William Gailey
1931	3	1	0	Richard Schmelzer
1932	0	2	1	Richard Schmelzer
1933	2	2	0	Richard Schmelzer
1934	0	3	1	Richard Schmelzer
1935	2	2	0	Richard Schmelzer

Yr.	W	L	T	Coach
1936	5	1	0	Richard Schmelzer
1937	4	3	0	Richard Schmelzer
1938	4	3	0	Richard Schmelzer
1939	4	1	1	Richard Schmelzer
1940	2	2	2	Richard Schmelzer
1941	4	2	1	Richard Schmelzer
1942	5	0	2	Richard Schmelzer
1943	5	0	0	Richard Schmelzer
1944	2	3	1	William Gailey
1945	4	2	0	William Gailey
1946	2	3	1	Richard Schmelzer
1947	5	3	0	Richard Schmelzer
1948	5	0	2	Richard Schmelzer
1949	3	4	0	William Gailey
1950	5	2	0	William Gailey
1951	7	0	0	William Gailey
1952	3	2	3	William Gailey
1953	3	3	1	Jack Corkery
1954	3	5	0	Jack Corkery

Yr.	W	L	T	Coach
1955	4	4	0	Jack Corkery
1956	4	3	0	Jack Corkery
1957	6	2	0	Jack Corkery
1958	7	1	0	Robert Lueft
1959	4	5	0	Robert Lueft
1960	2	4	3	Robert Lueft
1961	0	9	0	Alan Goodyear
1962	2	7	0	Alan Goodyear
1963	4	4	1	Alan Goodyear
1964	3	6	0	Alan Goodyear
1965	8	2	0	Alan Goodyear
1966	6	3	1	Alan Goodyear
1967	8	2	1	Alan Goodyear
1968	8	2	1	Alan Goodyear
1969	10	2	0	Alan Goodyear
1970	8	4	0	Alan Goodyear
1971	9	2	1	Alan Goodyear
1972	5	6	2	Alan Goodyear
1973	2	9	2	Alan Goodyear
1974	5	7	1	Alan Goodyear
1975	6	7	0	Alan Goodyear
1976	5	6	1	Alan Goodyear
1977	3	10	1	Alan Goodyear
1978	6	7	0	Alan Goodyear

RHODE ISLAND, UNIVERSITY OF

Kingston, Rhode Island

Rams   Blue and White

Yr.	W	L	T	Coach
1960	1	3	0	William Baird
1961	5	6	0	William Biard
1962	5	4	0	Robert Butler
1963	4	6	0	Robert Butler
1964	2	9	0	Robert Butler
1965	2	8	0	Robert Butler
1966	1	8	1	Robert Butler
1967	4	5	0	Robert Butler
1968	7	5	0	Robert Butler
1969	6	5	1	Geza Henni
1970	6	3	2	Geza Henni
1971	7	4	0	Geza Henni
1972	6	5	1	Geza Henni
1973	3	7	3	Geza Henni
1974	6	4	2	Geza Henni
1975	8	3	1	Geza Henni
1976	9	4	0	Geza Henni
1977	10	3	0	Geza Henni
1978	6	4	5	Geza Henni

RICHMOND, UNIVERSITY OF

Richmond, Virginia

Spiders   Red and Blue

Yr.	W	L	T	Coach
1975	0	10	0	—
1976	0	10	0	Bill Horan
1977	4	8	2	Bill Horan
1978	6	9	1	Bill Horan

RIDER COLLEGE

Lawrenceville, New Jersey

Broncs   Purple and Gold

Yr.	W	L	T	Coach
1933	2	2	0	Frank Donlon

Yr.	W	L	T	Coach
1934	2	2	1	Frank Donlon
1935	2	1	0	Frank Donlon
1936	0	2	2	Frank Donlon
1937	2	4	0	Frank Donlon
1938	8	0	0	Frank Donlon
1939	6	0	0	Frank Donlon
1940	9	0	0	Jake Lawrence
1941	7	1	0	Jake Lawrence
1942	2	4	0	Tom Leyden
1943	—	—	—	—
1944	—	—	—	—
1945	—	—	—	—
1946	4	1	1	Frank Donlon
1947	6	2	1	Frank Donlon
1948	2	2	3	Frank Donlon
1949	—	—	—	—
1950	—	—	—	—
1951	—	—	—	—
1952	—	—	—	—
1953	3	4	0	Frank Donlon
1954	4	3	0	Frank Donlon
1955	5	1	1	Frank Donlon
1956	6	2	0	Frank Donlon
1957	6	2	1	Frank Donlon
1958	4	5	1	Frank Donlon
1959	7	1	1	Frank Donlon
1960	5	5	0	Frank Donlon
1961	0	11	0	Glenn Leach
1962	2	9	0	Joe Ritter
1963	3	10	0	Joe Ritter
1964	5	7	0	Joe Ritter
1965	8	3	1	Joe Ritter
1966	10	3	1	Joe Ritter
1967	6	7	1	Joe Ritter
1968	10	3	1	Joe Ritter
1969	4	8	2	Bob Pivovarnick
1970	5	7	3	Bob Pivovarnick
1971	8	5	1	Bob Pivovarnick
1972	8	6	1	Bob Pivovarnick
1973	8	6	1	Bob Pivovarnick
1974	4	8	2	Bob Pivovarnick
1975	10	6	1	Russ Fager
1976	4	9	3	Russ Rager
1977	12	5	1	Russ Rager
1978	9	8	1	Russ Fager

ROCHESTER, UNIVERSITY OF

Rochester, New York

Yellowjackets   Yellow and Blue

Yr.	W	L	T	Coach
1934	0	1	0	Walter Campbell
1935	3	1	0	Walter Campbell
1936	2	2	0	Walter Campbell
1937	2	2	2	Walter Campbell
1938	2	3	1	Walter Campbell
1939	4	3	0	Walter Campbell
1940	3	3	1	Walter Campbell
1941	4	2	1	Walter Campbell
1942	5	2	0	Walter Campbell
1943	2	3	0	Walter Campbell
1944	4	2	0	Walter Campbell
1945	4	1	1	Walter Campbell
1946	4	3	0	Walter Campbell
1947	6	1	0	Walter Campbell
1948	3	3	2	Walter Campbell
1949	2	6	0	Walter Campbell
1950	2	5	0	Walter Campbell
1951	4	3	0	Walter Campbell

Yr.	W	L	T	Coach
1952	1	6	0	Walter Campbell
1953	4	1	2	Walter Campbell
1954	4	2	1	Walter Campbell
1955	4	3	0	Lyle Brown
1956	3	5	0	Lyle Brown
1957	7	0	1	Lyle Brown
1958	7	1	0	Lyle Brown
1959	5	2	1	Lyle Brown
1960	4	3	0	Lyle Brown
1961	6	2	0	Lyle Brown
1962	2	5	1	Lyle Brown
1963	7	2	0	Lyle Brown
1964	5	4	0	Lyle Brown
1965	5	4	1	William Boomer
1966	4	5	1	William Boomer
1967	8	3	0	William Boomer
1968	2	8	1	William Boomer
1969	5	6	0	William Boomer
1970	6	5	1	Gary Brown
1971	5	8	0	Gary Brown
1972	5	6	1	Gary Brown
1973	8	3	3	Tom Connor
1974	7	5	1	Tom Connor
1975	8	7	0	Tom Connor
1976	8	6	1	Tom Connor
1977	3	9	2	Tom Connor
1978	10	6	0	Tom Connor

ROCKFORD COLLEGE

Rockford, Illinois

Regents **Purple and White**

Yr.	W	L	T	Coach
1962	3	0	0	Hans Wolpe
1963	7	3	0	Adrian Parmeter
1964	8	4	0	Charles DeWild
1965	7	4	0	Charles DeWild
1966	4	6	0	Charles DeWild
1967	1	7	2	Howard LaBrant
1968	3	6	1	Howard LaBrant
1969	6	4	0	Hal Henderson
1970	2	9	1	Hal Henderson
1971	4	9	1	Hal Henderson
1972	3	9	0	Stan Greenfield
1973	4	6	2	Stan Greenfield
1974	5	7	1	Stan Greenfield
1975	2	10	1	Stan Greenfield
1976	11	2	0	Fred Bornkamp
1977	7	7	0	Fred Bornkamp
1978	9	4	2	Fred Bornkamp

ROCKHURST COLLEGE

Kansas City, Missouri

Hawks **Blue and White**

Yr.	W	L	T	Coach
1964	7	2	0	Hart
1965	10	2	0	Hart
1966	9	4	0	Hart
1967	10	3	1	Hart
1968	8	5	0	McNally
1969	3	4	2	Hart
1970	6	4	0	Tony Tocco
1971	4	5	0	Tony Tocco
1972	7	6	0	Tony Tocco
1973	11	3	2	Tony Tocco
1974	10	3	1	Tony Tocco

In his first year as coach, 1976, Fred Bornkamp led Rockford to its best season ever—11–2.

Yr.	W	L	T	Coach
1975	18	3	0	Tony Tocco
1976	17	4	1	Tony Tocco
1977	14	4	1	Tony Tocco
1978	17	3	0	Tony Tocco

ROLLINS COLLEGE

Winter Park, Florida

Tars **Royal Blue and Gold**

Yr.	W	L	T	Coach
1956	0	2	3	Hugh F. McKean
1957	5	1	0	Joseph Justice
1958	2	5	0	Joseph Justice
1959	3	2	3	Joseph Justice
1960	5	1	2	Joseph Justice
1961	3	5	0	Joseph Justice
1962	5	2	2	Joseph Justice
1963	4	5	0	Joseph Justice
1964	3	5	0	Joseph Justice
1965	4	7	0	Joseph Justice
1966	5	2	1	Joseph Justice
1967	7	4	3	Joseph Justice
1968	9	1	2	Gordon Howell

Dr. Hugh McKean (right), who coached Rollins'
first soccer team in 1956, was also the school's
president.

Yr.	W	L	T	Coach
1969	10	1	2	Gordon Howell
1970	10	4	0	Gordon Howell
1971	11	5	0	Gordon Howell
1972	9	3	0	Gordon Howell
1973	11	4	0	Gordon Howell
1974	7	5	2	Gordon Howell
1975	10	6	0	Gordon Howell
1976	13	2	0	Gordon Howell
1977	11	3	1	Gordon Howell
1978	14	5	0	Gordon Howell

Yr.	W	L	T	Coach
1967	0	10	0	Russel Sholes
1968	5	7	0	Russel Sholes
1969	5	9	0	Russel Sholes
1970	2	11	0	Russel Sholes
1971	0	8	2	Russel Sholes
1972	2	11	0	Russel Sholes
1973	7	2	2	George A. Phillips
1974	6	4	0	George A. Phillips
1975	7	2	1	George A. Phillips
1976	8	2	0	George A. Phillips
1977	11	5	0	George A. Phillips
1978	8	5	0	George A. Phillips

RUTGERS UNIVERSITY (CAMDEN)

Camden, New Jersey

Pioneers   **Scarlet and Black**

Yr.	W	L	T	Coach
1963	0	9	1	Russel Sholes
1964	0	9	1	Russel Sholes
1965	0	8	0	Russel Sholes
1966	0	9	0	Russel Sholes

RUTGERS UNIVERSITY

New Brunswick, New Jersey

Scarlet Knights   **Scarlet**

Yr.	W	L	T	Coach
1948	1	8	0	George Dochat
1949	3	3	3	George Dochat
1950	5	3	0	George Dochat

Yr.	W	L	T	Coach
1951	5	4	0	George Dochat
1952	1	5	3	George Dochat
1953	5	3	0	George Dochat
1954	3	4	0	George Dochat
1955	8	2	0	George Dochat
1956	4	3	0	George Dochat
1957	9	2	0	George Dochat
1958	4	6	2	George Dochat
1959	7	4	1	George Dochat
1960	11	2	0	George Dochat
1961	12	1	1	George Dochat
1962	8	1	0	George Dochat
1963	2	6	1	George Dochat
1964	7	5	0	George Dochat
1965	8	2	1	George Dochat
1966	8	3	1	George Dochat
1967	5	4	1	George Dochat
1968	4	6	1	George Dochat
1969	1	9	1	George Dochat
1970	2	9	0	George Dochat
1971	3	9	0	Bill Matyas
1972	2	9	0	Bill Matyas
1973	3	6	2	Bill Matyas
1974	2	8	3	Bill Matyas
1975	4	8	0	Kalman Csapo
1976	2	8	1	Kalman Csapo
1977	3	9	2	Kalman Csapo
1978	4	9	1	Kalman Csapo

ST. ANSELM'S COLLEGE

Manchester, New Hampshire

Hawks				Blue and White
Yr.	W	L	T	Coach
1967	2	8	0	John Tierney
1968	3	8	0	John Tierney
1969	7	6	1	John Tierney
1970	10	3	1	John Tierney
1971	9	4	0	John Tierney
1972	6	9	0	John Tierney
1973	1	9	4	John Tierney
1974	2	10	3	John Knowles
1975	5	8	1	Edward Cannon
1976	4	6	4	Edward Cannon
1977	7	6	2	Edward Cannon
1978	7	6	1	Edward Cannon

ST. FRANCIS COLLEGE

Brooklyn, New York

Terriers				Red and Blue
Yr.	W	L	T	Coach
1968	2	8	1	Carlo Tramontozzi
1969	5	6	0	Carlo Tramontozzi
1970	6	5	0	Carlo Tramontozzi
1971	8	5	2	Carlo Tramontozzi
1972	8	5	1	Carlo Tramontozzi
1973	10	4	1	Carlo Tramontozzi
1974	12	1	1	Carlo Tramontozzi
1975	9	4	1	Carlo Tramontozzi
1976	12	2	1	Carlo Tramontozzi
1977	10	2	2	Carlo Tramontozzi
1978	11	3	0	Carlo Tramontozzi

ST. JOHN'S UNIVERSITY

Collegeville, Minnesota

Johnnies				Red and White
Yr.	W	L	T	Coach
1967	3	2	1	Abel Laguna
1968	4	1	0	Abel Laguna
1969	5	1	2	James Vivaldeki
1970	4	2	4	Axel Theimer
1971	4	6	2	Axel Theimer
1972	6	9	0	Axel Theimer
1973	1	6	1	Matt Sikich
1974	13	2	0	Matt Sikich
1975	8	4	2	Matt Sikich
1976	13	2	3	Matt Sikich
1977	8	3	3	Pete Rocheford
1978	5	5	3	Pete Rocheford

ST. LAWRENCE UNIVERSITY

Canton, New York

Saints				Scarlet and Brown
Yr.	W	L	T	Coach
1962	4	1	0	Tom Cartmill
1963	1	7	0	Bob Goodwin
1964	5	3	0	Bob Goodwin
1965	4	6	0	Bob Goodwin
1966	4	6	1	Bob Goodwin
1967	5	5	1	Bob Goodwin
1968	10	1	0	Bob Goodwin
1969	9	2	2	Bob Goodwin
1970	11	1	0	Bob Goodwin
1971	11	1	0	Bob Goodwin
1972	6	3	3	Bob Goodwin
1973	8	3	2	Bob Goodwin
1974	8	2	3	Bob Goodwin
1975	8	6	1	Bob Goodwin
1976	12	2	1	Bob Goodwin
1977	13	2	1	Bob Goodwin
1978	11	4	1	Bob Goodwin

ST. LEO COLLEGE

Saint Leo, Florida

Monarchs				Gold and Green
Yr.	W	L	T	Coach
1968	2	11	0	Bill Ebinger
1969	3	12	1	Bill Ebinger
1970	2	12	0	John Swart
1971	5	6	0	John Swart
1972	8	4	1	John Swart
1973	6	5	2	John Swart
1974	5	6	0	John Swart
1975	0	10	0	John Swart
1976	4	6	0	John Swart
1977	5	4	2	John Swart
1978	1	13	0	John Swart

ST. LOUIS UNIVERSITY

St. Louis, Missouri

Billikens   Blue and White

Yr.	W	L	T	Coach
1959	11	1	0	Bob Guelker
1960	14	1	0	Bob Guelker
1961	13	2	0	Bob Guelker
1962	12	0	1	Bob Guelker
1963	13	1	0	Bob Guelker
1964	11	1	1	Bob Guelker
1965	14	0	0	Bob Guelker
1966	7	4	3	Bob Guelker
1967	8	3	2	Harry Keough
1968	10	1	1	Harry Keough
1969	13	0	0	Harry Keough
1970	14	0	1	Harry Keough
1971	17	1	0	Harry Keough
1972	15	2	3	Harry Keough
1973	15	2	3	Harry Keough
1974	18	3	1	Harry Keough
1975	13	5	2	Harry Keough
1976	14	4	1	Harry Keough
1977	13	5	0	Harry Keough
1978	16	4	1	Harry Keough

ST. MARY'S UNIVERSITY

San Antonio, Texas

Rattlers   Gold and Blue

Yr.	W	L	T	Coach
1966	8	6	0	Rodolfo Bryce
1967	8	1	0	Rodolfo Bryce
1968	10	3	1	Rodolfo Bryce
1969	8	2	1	Dick Ingber
1970	11	1	0	Jaime Villaran
1971	7	1	2	Fred Schouten
1972	4	4	1	Fred Schouten
1973	0	10	0	Chuck Bartush
1974	4	5	1	Dave Stolarski
1975	4	2	2	Dave Stolarski
1976	9	6	0	Dave Stolarski
1977	9	5	3	Dave Stolarski
1978	8	5	2	Dave Stolarski

ST. OLAF COLLEGE

Northfield, Minnesota

Oles   Black and Gold

Yr.	W	L	T	Coach
1970	5	4	1	R. Mellby
1971	3	4	1	R. Mellby
1972	5	2	1	C. Langeland
1973	8	1	0	R. Engebretsen
1974	8	4	2	R. Engebretsen
1975	8	5	1	R. Engebretsen
1976	9	5	1	H. Pensec
1977	7	7	2	H. Pensec
1978	10	7	1	H. Pensec

ST. PETER'S COLLEGE

Jersey City, New Jersey

Peacocks   Blue and White

Yr.	W	L	T	Coach
1959	1	3	2	Ralph Dougan
1960	1	11	0	Ralph Dougan
1961	1	10	0	Ralph Dougan
1962	0	11	0	John Gray
1963	0	10	0	John Gray
1964	1	9	1	Phil Kutt
1965	2	7	2	Phil Kutt
1966	1	11	0	Phil Kutt
1967	0	11	0	Phil Kutt
1968	2	12	0	Tony Verdoni
1969	2	9	1	Tony Verdoni
1970	1	8	3	Mike Granelli
1971	6	9	1	Mike Granelli
1972	8	4	2	Mike Granelli
1973	11	4	0	Mike Granelli
1974	8	5	2	Mike Granelli
1975	10	5	0	Mike Granelli
1976	7	5	1	Mike Granelli
1977	7	5	2	Mike Granelli
1978	13	3	0	Mike Granelli

ST. THOMAS COLLEGE

St. Paul, Minnesota

Toms   Purple and White

Yr.	W	L	T	Coach
1968	4	2	0	James Lindsay
1969	3	6	1	Paul Beggin
1970	9	2	0	Joe Flood
1971	7	2	2	Joe Flood
1972	5	2	5	Joe Flood
1973	11	3	0	Joe Flood
1974	8	7	0	Joe Flood
1975	5	9	1	Joe Flood
1976	12	3	1	Joe Flood
1977	15	3	2	Joe Flood
1978	16	2	2	Joe Flood

SALISBURY STATE COLLEGE

Salisbury, Maryland

Sea Gulls   Maroon and Gold

Yr.	W	L	T	Coach
1934	3	4	2	Benn Maggs
1935	6	6	0	Benn Maggs
1936	7	4	0	Benn Maggs
1937	1	6	0	Benn Maggs
1938	6	4	0	Benn Maggs
1939	1	5	3	Benn Maggs
1940	4	2	0	Benn Maggs
1941	1	2	2	Benn Maggs
1942	2	3	0	Robert Frazier
1943	1	2	1	Helen Jamart
1944	2	2	1	Helen Jamart
1945	7	0	3	Benn Maggs
1946	3	3	1	Benn Maggs
1947	8	1	0	Benn Maggs
1948	6	1	2	Benn Maggs

Yr.	W	L	T	Coach
1949	5	2	2	Benn Maggs
1950	5	1	2	Benn Maggs
1951	5	3	0	Benn Maggs
1952	4	1	1	Benn Maggs
1953	4	2	0	Benn Maggs
1954	3	2	1	Benn Maggs
1955	1	4	0	Benn Maggs
1956	4	2	0	Benn Maggs
1957	1	3	0	Benn Maggs
1958	4	2	1	Benn Maggs
1959	2	3	1	Benn Maggs
1960	2	1	1	Benn Maggs
1961	3	2	2	Benn Maggs
1962	1	4	0	Benn Maggs
1963	1	5	0	Benn Maggs
1964	3	6	0	Benn Maggs
1965	4	6	0	Benn Maggs
1966	7	3	0	Benn Maggs
1967	7	3	1	Benn Maggs
1968	7	2	3	Benn Maggs
1969	7	2	3	Benn Maggs
1970	6	4	1	Benn Maggs
1971	7	4	1	Benn Maggs
1972	5	3	4	Benn Maggs
1973	6	5	2	Benn Maggs
1974	6	6	2	Benn Maggs
1975	3	10	1	Benn Maggs
1976	1	13	1	Keith Conners
1977	3	12	0	Keith Conners
1978	8	7	2	Keith Conners

SAN DIEGO STATE UNIVERSITY

San Diego, California

Aztecs   **Red and Black**

Yr.	W	L	T	Coach
1968	6	2	0	George Logan
1969	9	1	1	George Logan
1970	8	1	1	George Logan
1971	10	3	1	George Logan
1972	6	4	1	George Logan
1973	11	6	3	George Logan
1974	10	1	2	George Logan
1975	10	4	1	George Logan
1976	10	5	1	George Logan
1977	13	4	1	George Logan
1978	13	7	0	George Logan

SAN FRANCISCO STATE UNIVERSITY

San Francisco, California

Gators   **Purple and Gold**

Yr.	W	L	T	Coach
1973	4	5	2	—
1974	4	8	0	—
1975	4	6	2	Art Bridgman
1976	0	12	1	Art Bridgman
1977	9	4	0	Luis Sagastume
1978	10	2	0	Luis Sagastume

SAN FRANCISCO, UNIVERSITY OF

San Francisco, California

Dons   **Green and Gold**

Yr.	W	L	T	Coach
1946	6	3	0	Gus Donoghue
1947	9	2	0	Gus Donoghue
1948	7	1	2	Gus Donoghue
1949	8	0	0	Gus Donoghue
1950	10	0	1	Gus Donoghue
1951	10	1	0	Gus Donoghue
1952	10	0	1	Gus Donoghue
1953	11	0	2	Gus Donoghue
1954	10	1	0	Gus Donoghue
1955	6	0	1	Gus Donoghue
1956	7	0	2	Gus Donoghue
1957	8	0	1	Gus Donoghue
1958	8	0	0	Gus Donoghue
1959	7	2	0	Gus Donoghue
1960	3	2	2	Gus Donoghue
1961	6	2	1	Bob Braghetta
1962	8	2	1	Steve Negoesco
1963	10	1	0	Steve Negoesco
1964	8	2	0	Steve Negoesco
1965	10	1	1	Steve Negoesco
1966	12	0	1	Steve Negoesco
1967	10	1	1	Steve Negoesco
1968	11	3	0	Steve Negoesco
1969	15	2	3	Steve Negoesco
1970	12	1	1	Steve Negoesco
1971	13	3	0	Steve Negoesco
1972	10	5	1	Steve Negoesco
1973	15	1	1	Steve Negoesco
1974	17	3	3	Steve Negoesco
1975	21	1	2	Steve Negoesco
1976	20	2	3	Steve Negoesco
1977	25	4	1	Steve Negoesco
1978	28	1	0	Steve Negoesco

SANGAMON STATE UNIVERSITY

Springfield, Illinois

Prairie Stars   **Blue and White**

Yr.	W	L	T	Coach
1977	13	8	0	Aydin Gonulsen
1978	15	5	1	Aydin Gonulsen

SAN JOSE STATE UNIVERSITY

San Jose, California

Spartans   **Blue, Gold, and White**

Yr.	W	L	T	Coach
1927	1	3	2	A. S. Cakebread
1928	1	6	0	A. S. Cakebread
1929	7	1	2	A. S. Cakebread
1930	3	4	0	A. S. Cakebread
1931	0	8	0	Charles L. Walker
1932	1	6	1	Charles L. Walker
1933	2	4	0	Charles L. Walker
1934	4	5	1	Charles L. Walker
1935	3	6	2	Charles L. Walker
1936	2	7	0	H. C. McDonald
1937	3	5	3	H. C. McDonald

Sangamon State (white) exploded onto the soccer scene, going 15–5–1 in its second varsity season in 1978.

Frank Mangiola was a tower of strength in the nets as San Jose State compiled a 27–6–4 record during his stay from 1965–67.

Yr.	W	L	T	Coach
1938	10	1	4	H. C. McDonald
1939	11	2	2	H. C. McDonald
1940	7	0	1	Gordon Maybury
1941	4	0	3	Gordon Maybury
1942	6	0	0	Roy Diedericksen
1954	0	6	0	Julius Menendez
1955	2	4	1	Julius Menendez
1956	2	5	2	Julius Menendez
1957	2	5	1	Julius Menendez
1958	1	5	1	Julius Menendez
1959	3	4	1	Julius Menendez
1960	4	4	1	Julius Menendez
1961	5	5	0	Julius Menendez
1962	2	6	0	Julius Menendez
1963	7	4	0	Julius Menendez
1964	9	3	2	Julius Menendez
1965	8	3	2	Julius Menendez
1966	9	2	0	Julius Menendez
1967	10	1	2	Julius Menendez
1968	13	2	0	Julius Menendez
1969	13	2	0	Julius Menendez
1970	11	1	2	Julius Menendez
1971	12	3	1	Julius Menendez
1972	14	2	1	Julius Menendez
1973	7	5	3	Julius Menendez
1974	9	3	4	Julius Menendez
1975	9	5	2	Julius Menendez
1976	13	4	1	Julius Menendez
1977	9	8	0	Julius Menendez
1978	19	3	0	Julius Menendez

SANTA CLARA, UNIVERSITY OF

Santa Clara, California

Broncos   **Cardinal and White**

Yr.	W	L	T	Coach
1967	3	4	2	Sal Taormina
1968	6	4	0	Sal Taormina
1969	5	7	2	Sal Taormina
1970	4	4	2	Sal Taormina
1971	5	7	0	Sal Taormina
1972	3	11	2	Dave Chaplik
1973	14	4	3	Dave Chaplik
1974	10	7	3	Dave Chaplik
1975	10	6	4	Dave Chaplik
1976	8	6	4	Dave Chaplik
1977	11	9	2	Dave Chaplik
1978	13	8	2	Dave Chaplik

SCRANTON, UNIVERSITY OF

Scranton, Pennsylvania

Royals   **Purple and White**

Yr.	W	L	T	Coach
1969	2	5	0	John Robertson
1970	0	11	1	John Robertson
1971	3	5	5	John Robertson
1972	4	6	3	John Robertson
1973	5	8	1	Stephen Klingman
1974	11	2	0	Stephen Klingman
1975	11	6	0	Stephen Klingman
1976	15	6	0	Stephen Klingman
1977	13	6	0	Stephen Klingman
1978	14	5	1	Stephen Klingman

SEATTLE UNIVERSITY

Seattle, Washington

Chieftains   **Scarlet and White**

Yr.	W	L	T	Coach
1967	7	2	0	Hugh McArdle
1968	4	3	3	Hugh McArdle
1969	3	4	1	Hugh McArdle
1970	4	2	4	Hugh McArdle
1971	6	2	4	Hugh McArdle
1972	5	6	1	Hugh McArdle
1973	8	2	2	Hugh McArdle
1974	6	6	1	Hugh McArdle
1975	6	6	1	Hugh McArdle
1976	7	7	2	Hugh McArdle
1977	6	9	2	Tom Goff
1978	11	5	1	Tom Goff

SEATTLE PACIFIC UNIVERSITY

Seattle, Washington

Falcons   **Maroon and White**

Yr.	W	L	T	Coach
1968	3	7	1	Arnold Aizstrauts
1969	1	7	0	Arnold Aizstrauts
1970	0	7	3	C. Clifford McCrath
1971	7	3	4	C. Clifford McCrath
1972	9	1	2	C. Clifford McCrath
1973	14	4	1	C. Clifford McCrath
1974	11	4	5	C. Clifford McCrath
1975	14	4	5	C. Clifford McCrath
1976	14	5	1	C. Clifford McCrath
1977	13	6	3	C. Clifford McCrath
1978	18	5	4	C. Clifford McCrath

Seattle Pacific's Cliff McCrath led his team to the NCAA Division II title and was named NSCAA Coach of the Year in 1978.

SETON HALL UNIVERSITY

South Orange, New Jersey

Pirates				Blue and White
Yr.	W	L	T	Coach
1929	0	4	0	—
1938	0	3	1	George Miele
1939	3	2	3	George Miele
1940	0	3	1	George Miele
1941	0	4	0	George Miele
1942	—	—	—	—
1943	—	—	—	—
1944	—	—	—	—
1945	—	—	—	—
1946	0	5	1	Bill Garry
1947	4	2	1	Bill Garry
1948	11	0	3	Bill Garry
1949	10	4	1	Bill Garry
1950	10	0	2	Bill Garry
1951	4	1	0	Bill Garry
1952	5	2	0	Bill Garry
1953	3	1	1	Bill Garry
1954	5	2	0	Bill Garry
1955	0	8	1	Bill Garry
1956	5	5	1	Frank Boccia
1957	8	1	1	Frank Boccia
1958	1	5	1	Nick Menza
1959	4	6	0	Nick Menza
1960	10	3	1	Nick Menza
1961	9	3	0	Nick Menza
1962	10	4	0	Nick Menza
1963	9	3	0	Nick Menza
1964	2	12	0	Nick Menza
1965	1	11	1	Nick Menza
1966	3	10	0	Nick Menza
1967	2	12	0	Nick Menza
1968	2	12	1	Nick Menza
1969	6	9	0	Nick Menza
1970	5	8	2	Nick Menza
1971	8	5	1	Nick Menza
1972	7	7	1	Nick Menza
1973	3	11	1	Nick Menza
1974	8	6	0	Nick Menza
1975	3	8	2	Nick Menza
1976	1	10	0	Nick Menza
1977	1	8	1	Nick Menza
1978	1	10	0	Nick Menza

SHIPPENSBURG STATE COLLEGE

Shippensburg, Pennsylvania

Red Raiders				Red and Blue
Yr.	W	L	T	Coach
1962	0	5	0	Cheng-vin-Cheng
1963	2	5	1	Mohandas Baliga
1964	2	6	0	Keith Hess
1965	4	6	0	Keith Hess
1966	5	4	1	Keith Hess
1967	5	3	2	Keith Hess
1968	0	6	3	Neville Leonard
1969	6	4	0	Tony Puglisi
1970	9	2	2	Tony Puglisi
1971	9	2	3	Tony Puglisi
1972	6	5	0	Tony Puglisi
1973	3	4	2	Tony Puglisi

Yr.	W	L	T	Coach
1974	5	5	2	Tony Puglisi
1975	9	4	0	Tony Puglisi
1976	9	3	1	Tony Puglisi
1977	6	3	1	Tony Puglisi
1978	8	6	0	Craig Hottenstein

SIMON FRASER UNIVERSITY

Burnaby, British Columbia

Clansmen				Red and Blue
Yr.	W	L	T	Coach
1975	8	5	5	John Buchanan
1976	13	3	1	John Buchanan
1977	13	2	3	John Buchanan
1978	20	5	0	John Buchanan

SLIPPERY ROCK STATE COLLEGE

Slippery Rock, Pennsylvania

Rockets				Green and White
Yr.	W	L	T	Coach
1934	5	1	1	Archie Dodds
1935	5	0	1	Archie Dodds
1936	4	0	1	Archie Dodds
1937	4	1	0	Archie Dodds
1938	—	—	—	—
1939	4	2	1	Archie Dodds
1940	5	1	1	Archie Dodds
1946	7	0	2	John Eiler
1947	7	1	1	John Eiler
1948	—	—	—	—
1949	5	2	0	John Eiler
1950	8	0	1	John Eiler
1951	—	—	—	—
1952	5	0	1	John Eiler
1953	5	2	1	John Eiler
1954	2	5	0	John Eiler
1955	2	4	2	John Eiler
1956	1	4	2	Jim Egli
1957	6	1	0	Jim Egli
1958	7	3	0	Jim Egli
1959	6	3	0	Jim Egli
1960	3	5	2	Jim Egli
1961	5	3	2	Jim Egli
1962	4	5	1	Jim Egli
1963	5	4	1	Jim Egli
1964	5	3	2	Jim Egli
1965	9	4	0	Jim Egli
1966	10	3	1	Jim Egli
1967	7	3	2	Jim Egli
1968	8	4	2	Jim Egli
1969	9	7	1	Jim Egli
1970	6	6	4	Jim Egli
1971	7	8	2	Jim Egli
1972	5	9	2	Jim Egli
1973	11	4	1	Jim Egli
1974	17	1	1	Jim Egli
1975	14	3	0	Jim Egli
1976	13	4	0	Jim Egli
1977	9	3	2	Jim Egli
1978	11	4	0	Jim Egli

Mike McLenaghan starred at Simon Fraser and was a first-round draft choice of the NASL's Minnesota Kicks in 1979.

Jim Egli, consulting with Kamal Houari in 1975, has coached Slippery Rock since 1956.

Don Ebert, a Cosmo in 1980, was one of the many home-grown products who have played for Bob Guelker at Southern Illinois-Edwardsville.

SOUTH, UNIVERSITY OF THE

Sewanee, Tennessee

Tigers   **Purple and White**

Yr.	W	L	T	Coach
1968	3	8	1	Tom Griffith
1969	6	5	1	Tom Griffith
1970	8	4	0	Tom Griffith
1971	4	7	1	Mac Petty
1972	6	8	1	Mac Petty
1973	7	5	1	Mac Petty
1974	4	10	0	Mac Petty
1975	1	9	0	Mac Petty
1976	2	9	1	P. R. Walter
1977	0	16	0	P. R. Walter
1978	3	13	0	Aubrey Wilson

SOUTHERN ILLINOIS (EDWARDSVILLE)

Edwardsville, Illinois

Cougars   **Red and White**

Yr.	W	L	T	Coach
1967	3	3	0	Bob Guelker
1968	10	0	0	Bob Guelker
1969	10	1	1	Bob Guelker

Yr.	W	L	T	Coach
1970	9	3	0	Bob Guelker
1971	10	2	1	Bob Guelker
1972	11	0	3	Bob Guelker
1973	11	2	1	Bob Guelker
1974	12	3	0	Bob Guelker
1975	14	4	0	Bob Guelker
1976	12	4	0	Bob Guelker
1977	12	4	1	Bob Guelker
1978	14	3	1	Bob Guelker

SOUTHERN MAINE, UNIVERSITY OF

Gorham, Maine

Huskies   **Blue, White, and Crimson**

Yr.	W	L	T	Coach
1957	1	5	1	R. Costello
1958	3	6	1	R. Costello
1959	8	5	1	R. Costello
1960	6	7	0	R. Costello
1961	8	6	0	R. Costello
1962	5	6	2	R. Costello
1963	10	5	0	R. Costello
1964	8	5	1	R. Costello
1965	7	6	1	R. Costello
1966	4	7	3	R. Costello

Yr.	W	L	T	Coach
1967	3	9	2	R. Costello
1968	4	9	1	J. Bouchard
1969	7	2	2	J. Bouchard
1970	5	3	3	J. Bouchard
1971	6	5	1	J. Bouchard
1972	3	10	1	J. Bouchard
1973	2	10	0	H. Menninger
1974	2	7	3	H. Menninger
1975	9	3	1	H. Menninger
1976	17	2	1	H. Menninger
1977	12	3	1	H. Menninger
1978	9	4	1	H. Menninger

SOUTHERN METHODIST UNIVERSITY

Dallas, Texas

Mustangs   **Red and Blue**

Yr.	W	L	T	Coach
1975	19	3	4	Jim Benedek
1976	12	4	3	Jim Benedek
1977	12	2	6	Jim Benedek
1978	18	1	2	Jim Benedek

SPRINGFIELD COLLEGE

Springfield, Massachusetts

Chiefs   **Maroon and White**

Yr.	W	L	T	Coach
1906	2	1	0	Harry McGuire
1907	3	1	0	Donald North
1908	1	1	0	John Brock
1909	2	0	1	George Affleck
1910	1	2	1	George Affleck
1911	1	2	2	George Affleck
1912	2	2	0	George Affleck
1913	5	1	0	George Affleck
1914	—	—	—	—
1915	—	—	—	—
1916	5	2	0	George Affleck
1917	—	—	—	—
1918	—	—	—	—
1919	4	3	0	George Affleck
1920	3	0	1	George Affleck
1921	7	0	0	George Affleck
1922	3	1	0	George Affleck
1923	5	1	2	George Affleck
1924	5	1	0	George Affleck
1925	7	2	0	George Affleck
1926	4	1	5	George Affleck
1927	5	2	2	George Affleck
1928	6	1	0	George Affleck
1929	5	2	2	John D. Brock
1930	6	3	0	John D. Brock
1931	7	0	0	John D. Brock
1932	6	1	0	John D. Brock
1933	6	1	1	John D. Brock
1934	8	1	1	John D. Brock
1935	4	3	1	John D. Brock
1936	3	2	2	John D. Brock
1937	9	0	0	John D. Brock
1938	7	1	1	John D. Brock
1939	7	1	1	John D. Brock
1940	3	3	1	John D. Brock
1941	6	2	0	John D. Brock
1942	5	0	1	John D. Brock

Yr.	W	L	T	Coach
1943	—	—	—	—
1944	—	—	—	—
1945	—	—	—	—
1946	8	0	0	John D. Brock
1947	9	0	0	John D. Brock
1948	6	1	1	Irvin R. Schmid
1949	7	1	1	Irvin R. Schmid
1950	7	2	0	Irvin R. Schmid
1951	3	4	1	Irvin R. Schmid
1952	6	1	2	Irvin R. Schmid
1953	7	1	1	Irvin R. Schmid
1954	7	2	0	Irvin R. Schmid
1955	6	1	1	Irvin R. Schmid
1956	10	1	1	Irvin R. Schmid
1957	9	0	0	Irvin R. Schmid
1958	7	3	1	Irvin R. Schmid
1959	6	3	1	Irvin R. Schmid
1960	6	3	1	Irvin R. Schmid
1961	6	3	0	Irvin R. Schmid
1962	9	3	1	Irvin R. Schmid
1963	6	3	3	Fred Geisler
1964	7	3	1	Irvin R. Schmid
1965	6	3	4	Irvin R. Schmid
1966	4	7	.1	Irvin R. Schmid
1967	8	4	0	Irvin R. Schmid
1968	13	0	3	Irvin R. Schmid
1969	11	2	1	Irvin R. Schmid
1970	8	3	4	Irvin R. Schmid
1971	7	4	2	Irvin R. Schmid
1972	11	6	0	Irvin R. Schmid
1973	13	4	1	Irvin R. Schmid
1974	10	4	1	Irvin R. Schmid
1975	12	3	3	Irvin R. Schmid
1976	5	8	2	Irvin R. Schmid
1977	5	9	2	Irvin R. Schmid
1978	4	12	1	Irvin R. Schmid

STANFORD UNIVERSITY

Stanford, California

Cardinals   **Cardinal and White**

Yr.	W	L	T	Coach
1911	3	0	0	Harry Maloney
1912	2	0	1	Harry Maloney
1913	1	0	2	Harry Maloney
1914	2	0	0	Harry Maloney
1915	6	2	0	Harry Maloney
1916	6	3	1	Harry Maloney
1917	1	1	0	Harry Maloney
1918	0	2	0	E.R. Knollin
1919	6	2	2	Harry Maloney
1920	1	0	1	Harry Maloney
1921	2	1	0	Harry Maloney
1922	2	0	0	Harry Maloney
1923	8	6	2	Harry Maloney
1924	2	3	2	Harry Maloney
1925	5	1	2	Don Clark
1926	0	1	1	Harry Maloney
1927	1	2	0	Harry Maloney
1928	2	3	0	Harry Maloney
1929	1	3	2	Harry Maloney
1930	4	4	2	Harry Maloney
1931	8	0	2	Harry Maloney
1932	4	2	3	Harry Maloney
1933	4	2	3	Harry Maloney
1934	1	6	0	Harry Maloney
1935	4	5	1	Richard Bullis
1936	3	3	3	Harry Maloney

Fred Priddle led Stanford for more than two decades.

Yr.	W	L	T	Coach
1937	6	3	1	Harry Maloney
1938	5	4	1	Harry Maloney
1939	9	3	1	Harry Maloney
1940	7	2	2	Harry Maloney
1941	5	2	5	Harry Maloney
1942	2	2	3	Harry Maloney
1943	—	—	—	—
1944	—	—	—	—
1945	—	—	—	—
1946	3	2	0	—
1947	1	2	1	David Tappan
1948	3	5	1	John H. Segel
1949	—	—	—	—
1950	2	4	1	Robert Graham
1951	7	4	1	Leo Weinstein
1952	6	2	2	Leo Weinstein
1953	5	3	2	Leo Weinstein
1954	2	3	1	Fred Priddle
1955	4	3	1	Fred Priddle
1956	5	5	0	Fred Priddle
1957	4	4	1	Fred Priddle
1958	3	5	1	Fred Priddle
1959	5	3	0	Fred Priddle
1960	6	3	0	Fred Priddle
1961	4	5	2	Fred Priddle
1962	8	2	0	Fred Priddle
1963	9	2	0	Fred Priddle
1964	10	3	1	Fred Priddle
1965	4	7	0	Fred Priddle
1966	6	4	1	Fred Priddle
1967	3	7	2	Fred Priddle
1968	4	10	0	Fred Priddle

Ted Rafalovich had 28 goals and 23 assists in 1978 as Stanford reeled off a best-ever 16–6 record.

Yr.	W	L	T	Coach
1969	8	7	0	Fred Priddle
1970	10	5	2	Fred Priddle
1971	6	7	3	Fred Priddle
1972	9	7	1	Fred Priddle
1973	10	5	2	Fred Priddle
1974	8	10	3	Fred Priddle
1975	5	12	2	Fred Priddle
1976	10	8	1	Nelson Lodge
1977	10	8	2	Nelson Lodge
1978	16	6	0	Nelson Lodge

STONEHILL COLLEGE

North Easton, Massachusetts

Chieftains   **Blue and Gold**

Yr.	W	L	T	Coach
1972	1	9	2	John Blanchdon
1973	1	9	2	John Blanchdon
1974	2	7	1	John Blanchdon
1975	3	9	1	John Heslin
1976	8	4	1	John Heslin
1977	2	12	2	John Heslin
1978	7	7	1	Richard Shankar

SUSQUEHANNA UNIVERSITY

Selinsgrove, Pennsylvania

Crusaders   **Orange and Maroon**

Yr.	W	L	T	Coach
1960	2	5	0	William Heim
1961	1	8	0	William Heim
1962	1	9	0	John McCahan
1963	5	5	1	James English
1964	4	5	2	James English
1965	5	6	1	Carter Lindberg
1966	2	9	1	Wallace Growney
1967	5	6	1	Neil Potter
1968	5	7	0	Neil Potter
1969	7	4	1	Neil Potter
1970	4	8	1	Neil Potter
1971	3	8	1	Neil Potter
1972	5	5	2	Neil Potter
1973	6	3	4	Neil Potter
1974	6	5	2	William Kepner
1975	5	5	1	Neil Potter
1976	4	7	2	Neil Potter
1977	7	4	2	Neil Potter
1978	8	3	1	Neil Potter

SWARTHMORE COLLEGE

Swarthmore, Pennsylvania

Little Quakers   **Garnet**

Yr.	W	L	T	Coach
1914	0	2	0	—
1915	1	2	0	—
1916	2	2	0	M. A. Addison
1917	1	1	0	LeRoy Mercer
1918	—	—	—	—
1919	3	2	0	R. Perkins
1920	3	3	0	R. H. Dunn
1921	2	2	4	R. H. Dunn
1922	2	3	2	R. H. Dunn
1923	4	3	1	R. H. Dunn

Yr.	W	L	T	Coach
1924	2	4	2	R. H. Dunn
1925	4	2	1	R. H. Dunn
1926	3	5	1	R. H. Dunn
1927	5	3	0	R. H. Dunn
1928	8	0	0	R. H. Dunn
1929	3	3	1	R. H. Dunn
1930	2	6	1	R. H. Dunn
1931	4	3	2	R. H. Dunn
1932	3	3	1	R. H. Dunn
1933	3	4	0	R. H. Dunn
1934	4	4	2	R. H. Dunn
1935	3	3	3	R. H. Dunn
1936	7	2	1	R. H. Dunn
1937	5	2	2	R. H. Dunn
1938	5	2	1	R. H. Dunn
1939	6	2	1	R. H. Dunn
1940	3	3	1	R. H. Dunn
1941	2	6	0	R. H. Dunn
1942	3	3	1	R. H. Dunn
1943	4	4	0	R. H. Dunn
1944	3	4	0	R. H. Dunn
1945	3	5	0	R. H. Dunn
1946	5	4	0	R. H. Dunn
1947	7	1	1	R. H. Dunn
1948	6	1	1	R. H. Dunn
1949	5	3	0	R. H. Dunn
1950	6	2	0	R. H. Dunn
1951	7	2	0	R. H. Dunn
1952	5	1	2	R. H. Dunn
1953	1	5	1	R. H. Dunn
1954	4	4	0	R. H. Dunn
1955	4	4	0	R. H. Dunn
1956	5	2	1	R. H. Dunn
1957	8	1	1	R. H. Dunn
1958	5	4	0	R. H. Dunn
1959	5	4	0	R. H. Dunn
1960	4	5	0	R. H. Dunn
1961	5	3	1	W. J. Stetson
1962	2	7	0	W. J. Stetson
1963	6	3	1	W. J. Stetson
1964	6	3	1	W. J. Stetson
1965	7	2	1	W. J. Stetson
1966	9	0	1	W. J. Stetson
1967	5	5	0	W. J. Stetson
1968	4	6	0	W. J. Stetson
1969	5	4	1	W. J. Stetson
1970	5	6	0	W. J. Stetson
1971	5	6	0	W. J. Stetson
1972	4	6	0	W. J. Stetson
1973	4	4	4	W. J. Stetson
1974	10	3	2	W. J. Stetson
1975	2	9	1	W. J. Stetson
1976	5	6	1	J. F. Leitner
1977	7	4	0	J. F. Leitner
1978	5	9	2	J. F. Leitner

SYRACUSE UNIVERSITY

Syracuse, New York

Orangemen   **Orange**

Yr.	W	L	T	Coach
1920	4	3	2	—
1921	4	4	1	—
1922	—	—	—	—
1923	2	4	4	—
1924	3	4	2	—
1925	2	2	4	—
1926	2	6	0	—

Syracuse's Mark Gompele leaves an Eisenhower player in his wake.

Yr.	W	L	T	Coach	Yr.	W	L	T	Coach
1927	2	4	0	—	1949	2	6	0	—
1928	3	2	1	—	1950	5	2	1	—
1929	2	4	1	—	1951	—	—	—	—
1930	2	2	1	—	1952	5	1	0	—
1931	4	1	1	—	1953	4	2	1	Andrew S. Coccari
1932	4	2	0	—	1954	2	6	0	Andrew S. Coccari
1933	1	5	0	—	1955	0	7	1	Andrew S. Coccari
1934	3	2	0	—	1956	0	9	0	Joe Weber
1935	6	3	0	—	1957	0	9	0	Peter Cataldi
1936	5	1	2	—	1958	1	8	0	Peter Cataldi
1937	5	3	0	—	1959	1	8	0	Peter Cataldi
1938	4	2	2	—	1960	0	8	1	Peter Cataldi
1939	6	1	0	—					
1940	3	5	0	—	1970	0	5	0	Joe Sayer
1941	4	2	1	—	1971	1	7	0	Joe Sayer
1942	1	4	2	—	1972	4	6	1	John Allen
1943	—	—	—	—	1973	3	7	1	John Allen
1944	—	—	—	—	1974	3	7	0	Larry Herzog
1945	—	—	—	—	1975	7	4	0	Bill Goettel
1946	2	4	0	—	1976	6	5	1	Bill Goettel
1947	0	7	0	—	1977	3	11	0	Bill Goettel
1948	3	5	0	—	1978	7	7	1	Bill Goettel

TABOR COLLEGE

Hillsboro, Kansas

Bluejays   **Blue and Gold**

Yr.	W	L	T	Coach
1957	2	3	2	Del Reimer
1958	3	4	2	Del Reimer
1959	8	1	1	Del Reimer
1960	8	1	1	Del Reimer
1961	7	3	1	Del Reimer
1962	4	2	0	Del Reimer
1963	3	4	2	Del Reimer
1964	2	7	0	Del Reimer
1965	6	3	1	Steve Kimery
1966	5	5	0	Steve Kimery
1973	5	0	1	Del Reimer
1974	4	4	1	Del Reimer
1975	6	5	0	Del Reimer
1976	6	6	0	Don Brubaker
1977	4	8	1	Don Brubaker
1978	10	6	1	Don Brubaker

TEMPLE UNIVERSITY

Philadelphia, Pennsylvania

Owls   **Cherry and White**

Yr.	W	L	T	Coach
1926	2	1	0	James Neeley
1927	3	0	2	James Neeley
1928	5	1	1	James Neeley
1929	4	1	0	James Neeley
1930	1	0	4	Pete Leaness
1931	2	4	0	Pete Leaness
1932	5	1	0	Pete Leaness
1933	2	4	2	Pete Leaness
1934	4	3	0	Pete Leaness
1935	4	4	1	Pete Leaness
1936	2	4	2	Pete Leaness
1937	0	5	2	Pete Leaness
1938	3	2	2	Pete Leaness
1939	5	2	1	Pete Leaness
1940	8	1	0	Pete Leaness
1941	5	0	3	Pete Leaness
1942	5	1	2	Pete Leaness
1943	3	2	0	Pete Leaness
1944	4	2	0	Pete Leaness
1945	4	1	0	Pete Leaness
1946	6	0	1	Pete Leaness
1947	8	1	1	Pete Leaness
1948	7	1	0	Pete Leaness
1949	9	1	0	Pete Leaness
1950	6	0	1	Pete Leaness
1951	8	0	1	Pete Leaness
1952	7	2	0	Pete Leaness
1953	9	0	0	Pete Leaness
1954	7	1	1	Pete Leaness
1955	4	3	2	Pete Leaness
1956	6	3	0	Pete Leaness
1957	2	7	1	Pete Leaness
1958	8	4	0	Pete Leaness
1959	9	1	1	Pete Leaness
1960	7	3	0	Pete Leaness
1961	7	2	1	Pete Leaness
1962	11	3	0	Pete Leaness
1963	10	2	1	Pete Leaness
1964	9	2	0	Pete Leaness
1965	12	2	0	Pete Leaness

Yr.	W	L	T	Coach
1966	13	2	1	Pete Leaness
1967	10	2	2	Pete Leaness
1968	8	5	1	Pete Leaness
1969	5	7	1	Pete Leaness
1970	4	7	1	Pete Leaness
1971	6	5	2	Walt Bahr
1972	6	5	3	Walt Bahr
1973	8	2	5	Walt Bahr
1974	10	3	1	John Boles
1975	11	2	0	John Boles
1976	13	1	0	John Boles
1977	11	5	0	John Boles
1978	14	1	2	John Boles

TOWSON STATE UNIVERSITY

Towson, Maryland

Tigers   **Black, Gold, and White**

Yr.	W	L	T	Coach
1921	2	2	0	Harold Callahill
1922	2	0	0	Harold Callahill
1923	7	0	1	Harold Callahill
1924	2	0	0	Harold Callahill
1925	4	1	0	Harold Callahill
1926	7	2	5	Shanks
1927	4	1	1	Donald Minnegan
1928	5	7	3	Donald Minnegan
1929	3	2	1	Donald Minnegan
1930	2	3	0	Donald Minnegan
1931	3	6	0	Donald Minnegan
1932	8	2	0	Donald Minnegan
1933	10	0	1	Donald Minnegan
1934	11	0	0	Donald Minnegan
1935	7	0	2	Donald Minnegan
1936	5	0	2	Donald Minnegan
1937	3	3	3	Donald Minnegan
1938	5	0	1	Donald Minnegan
1939	5	2	2	Donald Minnegan
1940	5	2	1	Donald Minnegan
1947	0	6	0	Jack Hart
1948	0	9	0	Bill Clark
1949	6	3	2	Bill Clark
1950	1	5	1	Bill Clark
1951	5	4	0	Earl Killian
1952	3	3	2	Donald Minnegan
1953	3	4	2	Donald Minnegan
1954	5	2	1	Donald Minnegan
1955	7	1	2	Donald Minnegan
1956	9	0	2	Donald Minnegan
1957	6	3	0	Donald Minnegan
1958	2	7	1	Donald Minnegan
1959	3	5	2	Donald Minnegan
1960	4	2	2	Donald Minnegan
1961	3	4	2	Donald Minnegan
1962	3	4	0	Donald Minnegan
1963	4	4	1	Donald Minnegan
1964	7	2	0	Donald Minnegan
1965	8	2	0	Donald Minnegan
1966	10	1	0	Donald Minnegan
1967	6	5	0	Jack MacDonald
1968	7	5	2	Jack MacDonald
1969	5	7	2	Jack MacDonald
1970	8	5	3	Jack MacDonald
1971	6	7	2	Jack MacDonald
1972	7	7	2	Jack MacDonald
1973	3	10	3	Jack MacDonald
1974	6	8	3	Jack MacDonald

Yr.	W	L	T	Coach
1975	9	7	0	Jack MacDonald
1976	9	6	1	Paul Bell
1977	7	8	1	Paul Bell
1978	7	9	1	Rich Bartos

TRENTON STATE COLLEGE

Trenton, New Jersey

Lions   Blue and Gold

Yr.	W	L	T	Coach
1941	1	3	1	George Ackerman
1942	6	0	0	George Ackerman
1943	—	—	—	—
1944	—	—	—	—
1945	—	—	—	—
1946	2	2	0	Bill Andreas
1947	3	4	0	Bill Andreas
1948	3	3	0	Bill Andreas
1949	5	2	2	Bill Andreas
1950	2	3	3	Bill Andreas
1951	3	4	0	Bill Andreas
1952	3	5	2	Bill Andreas
1953	4	3	2	Bill Andreas
1954	2	6	2	Bill Andreas
1955	7	2	1	Bill Andreas
1956	6	2	2	Bill Andreas
1957	6	3	0	Ed Brink
1958	7	1	2	Ed Brink
1959	6	3	1	Ed Brink
1960	8	4	0	Mel Schmid
1961	4	8	0	Mel Schmid
1962	9	3	0	Mel Schmid
1963	9	4	1	Mel Schmid
1964	12	2	0	Mel Schmid
1965	14	1	0	Mel Schmid
1966	11	3	2	Mel Schmid
1967	11	1	2	Mel Schmid
1968	11	2	0	Mel Schmid
1969	9	5	2	John Chalton
1970	10	3	0	John Chalton
1971	9	3	1	Mel Schmid
1972	9	3	1	W. Huston, N. Bencivengo
1973	2	12	0	Neil Bencivengo
1974	9	3	4	Gary J. Hindley
1975	2	11	1	Gary J. Hindley
1976	8	5	3	Gary J. Hindley
1977	11	7	3	Gary J. Hindley
1978	13	6	1	Gary J. Hindley

TRINITY COLLEGE

Hartford, Connecticut

Bantams   Blue and Gold

Yr.	W	L	T	Coach
1931	3	2	1	G. V. Wright
1932	1	2	1	G. V. Wright
1933	4	1	0	G. V. Wright
1934	3	2	0	Walter McCloud
1935	1	3	0	Walter McCloud
1936	3	2	0	Walter McCloud
1937	1	5	0	Walter McCloud
1938	0	7	0	Walter McCloud
1939	1	6	0	Walter McCloud
1940	3	4	0	Walter McCloud
1941	2	6	0	Walter McCloud

Yr.	W	L	T	Coach
1942	4	1	1	Alvin Reinhardt
1943	—	—	—	—
1944	1	0	0	—
1945	—	—	—	—
1946	1	4	1	J. Bruce Munro
1947	2	4	0	J. Bruce Munro
1948	3	3	1	Harold Shetter
1949	5	1	1	Harold Shetter
1950	6	2	0	Lloyd McDonald
1951	5	2	1	Lloyd McDonald
1952	5	1	2	Roy A. Dath
1953	6	1	1	Roy A Dath
1954	5	2	1	Roy A. Dath
1955	3	3	0	Roy A. Dath
1956	8	0	0	Roy A. Dath
1957	5	2	1	Roy A. Dath
1958	7	1	0	Roy A. Dath
1959	8	1	0	Roy A. Dath
1960	6	3	0	Roy A. Dath
1961	6	3	0	Roy A. Dath
1962	4	2	1	Roy A. Dath
1963	7	1	1	Roy A. Dath
1964	8	1	0	Roy A. Dath
1965	8	1	0	Roy A. Dath

Veteran coach Ray Dath (left) and star pupil Alex "The Flying Scot" Guild (1957–60) were the big names at Trinity.

Yr.	W	L	T	Coach
1966	6	3	0	Roy A. Dath
1967	8	1	0	Roy A. Dath
1968	9	1	0	Roy A. Dath
1969	6	3	1	Roy A. Dath
1970	0	8	1	Roy A. Dath
1971	5	5	0	Roy A. Dath
1972	2	7	1	Roy A. Dath
1973	3	7	0	Roy A. Dath
1974	4	5	3	Roy A. Dath
1975	3	7	2	Roy A. Dath
1976	7	4	1	Robie Shults
1977	7	4	0	Robie Shults
1978	2	7	3	Robie Shults

TUFTS UNIVERSITY

Medford, Massachusetts

Jumbos   **Brown and Blue**

Yr.	W	L	T	Coach
1947	4	5	1	John G. Bohn
1948	1	6	0	John G. Bohn
1949	4	5	0	John G. Bohn
1950	4	7	0	John G. Bohn
1951	6	4	1	John G. Bohn
1952	6	4	1	John G. Bohn
1953	4	5	0	John G. Bohn
1954	6	4	1	John G. Bohn
1955	3	7	0	John G. Bohn
1956	6	3	1	John G. Bohn
1957	5	3	1	John G. Bohn
1958	3	4	2	John G. Bohn
1959	3	6	0	John G. Bohn
1960	4	5	0	Alvin Malthaner
1961	3	6	0	Alvin Malthaner
1962	3	7	0	Alvin Malthaner
1963	2	8	0	Alvin Malthaner
1964	4	6	1	Herb Erickson
1965	2	9	0	Herb Erickson
1966	5	7	0	Herb Erickson
1967	8	4	0	Herb Erickson
1968	6	5	1	Herb Erickson
1969	7	6	0	Herb Erickson
1970	6	5	1	Herb Erickson
1971	10	2	0	Herb Erickson
1972	8	5	1	Herb Erickson
1973	10	2	0	Gerry Clinton
1974	8	5	1	Gerry Clinton
1975	7	6	1	Gerry Clinton
1976	11	3	1	Gerry Clinton
1977	6	5	1	Gerry Clinton
1978	2	8	2	Gerry Clinton

UNITED STATES INTERNATIONAL UNIVERSITY

San Diego, California

Westerners   **Yellow and Blue**

Yr.	W	L	T	Coach
1971	6	5	0	—
1972	5	0	0	—
1973	3	10	3	—
1974	8	7	1	G. Stratopoulos
1975	12	9	0	G. Stratopoulos
1976	15	6	0	K. Ben Marzunk
1977	20	9	0	K. Ben Marzunk
1978	14	5	0	K. Ben Marzunk

UNION COLLEGE

Schenectady, New York

Dutchmen   **Garnet**

Yr.	W	L	T	Coach
1948	0	5	0	Gliech
1949	3	4	1	Gliech
1950	3	5	0	Gliech
1951	3	5	0	Gliech
1952	4	3	0	Gliech
1953	3	4	0	Cliech
1954	1	6	1	Gliech
1955	4	4	0	Gliech
1956	4	4	1	Gliech
1957	3	6	1	Gliech
1958	5	4	0	Cartmell
1959	4	5	0	Witzel
1960	0	7	3	Witzel
1961	1	8	0	Witzel
1962	3	6	0	Witzel
1963	4	5	0	Beaudry
1964	2	7	0	Beaudry
1965	3	7	0	Evans
1966	2	8	1	Evans
1967	4	4	2	Brown
1968	3	8	0	Brown
1969	3	5	1	Brown
1970	2	7	1	McMurray
1971	6	3	1	McMurray
1972	4	5	1	McMurray
1973	5	4	1	Magee
1974	10	2	0	Magee
1975	12	2	0	Magee
1976	4	8	0	Magee
1977	4	7	1	Magee
1978	10	4	0	Magee

UPSALA COLLEGE

East Orange, New Jersey

Vikings   **Blue and Gray**

Yr.	W	L	T	Coach
1963	1	3	1	Fred Wieboldt
1964	4	7	0	Fred Wieboldt
1965	7	4	1	Fred Wieboldt
1966	4	6	2	Fred Wieboldt
1967	2	11	1	Fred Wieboldt
1968	3	10	1	Fred Wieboldt
1969	7	2	1	Fred Wieboldt
1970	4	5	2	Fred Wieboldt
1971	2	9	0	Fred Wieboldt
1972	1	10	0	Fred Wieboldt
1973	3	10	0	Fred Wieboldt
1974	4	9	2	Fred Wieboldt
1975	11	5	1	Fred Wieboldt
1976	11	6	1	Fred Wieboldt
1977	8	9	0	Fred Wieboldt
1978	5	12	0	Fred Wieboldt

URSINUS COLLEGE

Collegeville, Pennsylvania

Bears   **Red, Gold, and Black**

Yr.	W	L	T	Coach
1932	3	1	2	Donald Baker

Yr.	W	L	T	Coach
1933	1	4	2	Donald Baker
1934	3	3	2	Donald Baker
1935	1	6	1	Donald Baker
1936	0	8	0	Donald Baker
1937	4	1	3	Donald Baker
1938	1	2	5	Donald Baker
1939	1	6	1	Donald Baker
1940	2	6	1	Donald Baker
1941	1	7	0	Donald Baker
1942	2	2	0	Donald Baker
1943	2	1	0	Donald Baker
1944	1	4	0	Donald Baker
1945	0	4	1	Donald Baker
1946	0	6	1	Donald Baker
1947	1	7	0	Donald Baker
1948	2	6	0	Donald Baker
1949	1	8	0	Donald Baker
1950	0	8	1	Donald Baker
1951	1	7	0	Donald Baker
1952	2	6	1	Donald Baker
1953	4	5	1	Donald Baker
1954	6	3	0	Donald Baker
1955	3	6	0	Donald Baker
1956	2	5	3	Donald Baker
1957	3	8	0	Donald Baker
1958	3	6	1	Donald Baker
1959	5	6	0	Donald Baker
1960	1	10	0	Donald Baker
1961	4	5	2	Donald Baker
1962	4	7	1	Donald Baker
1963	4	5	2	Donald Baker
1964	4	5	1	Donald Baker
1965	2	8	0	Donald Baker
1966	5	5	1	Donald Baker
1967	3	9	0	Donald Baker
1968	4	8	0	Donald Baker
1969	6	6	1	Donald Baker
1970	5	6	1	Donald Baker
1971	4	7	3	Donald Baker
1972	4	9	2	Walt Manning
1973	6	7	1	Walt Manning
1974	5	9	2	Walt Manning
1975	3	11	0	Walt Manning
1976	1	13	0	Walt Manning
1977	4	10	2	Walt Manning
1978	9	9	0	Walt Manning

VERMONT, UNIVERSITY OF

Burlington, Vermont

Catamounts				Green and Gold
Yr.	W	L	T	Coach
1964	3	4	0	Harold Grieg
1965	7	2	0	Harold Grieg
1966	9	2	0	Harold Grieg
1967	7	2	0	Harold Grieg
1968	6	3	0	Robert Stone
1969	7	1	1	Harold Grieg
1970	1	3	6	Don Soderberg
1971	10	2	0	Don Soderberg
1972	2	10	1	Don Soderberg
1973	5	8	0	Don Soderberg
1974	7	3	3	Don Soderberg
1975	11	3	0	Paul Reinhardt
1976	9	4	0	Paul Reinhardt
1977	12	3	1	Paul Reinhardt
1978	8	5	3	Paul Reinhardt

VIRGINIA MILITARY INSTITUTE

Lexington, Virginia

Keydets				Red, White, and Yellow
Yr.	W	L	T	Coach
1972	1	10	0	Jay Sculley
1973	2	9	0	Jay Sculley
1974	1	8	0	Jay Sculley
1975	3	8	1	Jim Clark
1976	5	7	0	Jim Clark
1977	7	8	0	Jay Sculley
1978	3	13	1	Jay Sculley

VIRGINIA POLYTECHNIC INSTITUTE

Blacksburg, Virginia

Gobblers				Maroon and Orange
Yr.	W	L	T	Coach
1972	2	4	3	George Snead
1973	4	3	3	George Snead
1974	5	6	0	Jerry Cheynet
1975	4	5	1	Jerry Cheynet
1976	4	6	1	Jerry Cheynet
1977	7	4	1	Jerry Cheynet
1978	9	4	2	Jerry Cheynet

VIRGINIA, UNIVERSITY OF

Charlottesville, Virginia

Cavaliers				Orange and Blue
Yr.	W	L	T	Coach
1941	0	6	0	Lawrence Ludwig
1942	4	2	1	Lawrence Ludwig
1943	—	—	—	—
1944	—	—	—	—
1945	—	—	—	—
1946	1	3	1	Lawrence Ludwig
1947	2	2	7	Lawrence Ludwig
1948	3	7	1	Lawrence Ludwig
1949	5	5	0	Lawrence Ludwig
1950	5	5	1	Lawrence Ludwig
1951	1	5	2	W. H. Moomaw
1952	5	2	1	W. H. Moomaw
1953	4	4	1	W. H. Moomaw
1954	5	4	2	Wilson Fewster
1955	3	5	2	Bob Sandell
1956	6	3	0	Bob Sandell
1957	5	2	1	Bob Sandell
1958	5	4	0	Gene Corrigan
1959	4	3	2	Gene Corrigan
1960	2	6	0	Gene Corrigan
1961	7	3	0	Gene Corrigan
1962	3	4	1	Gene Corrigan
1963	5	2	1	Gene Corrigan
1964	4	5	0	Gene Corrigan
1965	4	7	1	Gene Corrigan
1966	0	10	0	Gordon Burris
1967	3	9	0	Gordon Burris
1968	4	5	1	Gordon Burris
1969	9	1	2	Gordon Burris
1970	7	2	1	Gordon Burris
1971	7	5	1	Jim Stephens
1972	8	3	3	Jim Stephens
1973	6	7	0	Jim Stephens
1974	5	4	3	Larry Gross

Yr.	W	L	T	Coach
1975	5	8	0	Larry Gross
1976	8	6	2	Larry Gross
1977	12	6	1	Larry Gross
1978	9	2	2	Bruce Arena

VIRGINIA WESLEYAN COLLEGE

Norfolk, Virginia

Blue Marlins   **Blue and Silver**

Yr.	W	L	T	Coach
1969	1	5	1	Don Forsyth, Howard Mast
1970	1	6	0	Don Forsyth, Howard Mast
1971	5	5	0	Peter Hobard
1972	1	10	1	Horst Seibert
1973	5	7	2	Horst Seibert
1974	8	6	1	Horst Seibert
1975	9	5	0	Horst Seibert
1976	8	6	0	Bill Davis
1977	8	7	1	Bill Davis
1978	12	4	0	Lenny Long

WABASH COLLEGE

Crawfordsville, Indiana

Little Giants   **Scarlet and White**

Yr.	W	L	T	Coach
1967	0	9	0	Phil Daley
1968	0	6	3	Phil Daley
1969	1	7	1	Phil Daley
1970	0	8	1	Doug Landgraf
1971	2	8	1	Doug Landgraf
1972	8	3	0	Doug Landgraf
1973	7	3	2	Doug Landgraf
1974	5	5	1	Doug Landgraf
1975	6	5	0	Doug Landgraf
1976	9	3	1	Doug Landgraf
1977	6	7	1	Doug Landgraf
1978	5	7	1	Doug Landgraf

WAGNER COLLEGE

Staten Island, New York

Seahawks   **Green and White**

Yr.	W	L	T	Coach
1956	1	6	1	Jeff Safford
1957	3	4	1	Jack Hynes
1958	5	7	0	Jack Hynes
1959	8	3	3	Jack Hynes
1960	4	7	0	Jack Hynes
1961	0	13	0	Bill Lied
1962	1	9	1	Bill Lied
1963	4	8	0	Bill Lied
1964	2	9	2	Bill Lied
1965	5	4	0	Bill Lied
1966	4	9	0	Bill Lied
1967	7	6	0	Bill Lied
1968	5	7	0	Bill Lied
1969	3	8	0	Bill Lied
1970	1	10	1	Bill Lied
1971	2	11	0	Bill Lied
1972	1	12	0	Bill Lied
1973	4	7	2	Bill Lied

Yr.	W	L	T	Coach
1974	0	10	1	Bill Bied
1975	1	9	0	Bill Lied
1976	0	8	0	Bill Lied
1977	3	7	0	Bill Lied
1978	3	8	0	Bill Lied

WASHINGTON, UNIVERSITY OF

Seattle, Washington

Huskies   **Purple and Gold**

Yr.	W	L	T	Coach
1971	6	5	1	Mike Ryan
1972	11	0	1	Mike Ryan
1973	17	2	1	Mike Ryan
1974	17	2	4	Mike Ryan
1975	16	4	3	Mike Ryan
1976	13	2	3	Mike Ryan
1977	14	2	1	Mike O'Malley
1978	12	6	2	Mike O'Malley

WASHINGTON UNIVERSITY

St. Louis, Missouri

Bears   **Green and White**

Yr.	W	L	T	Coach
1968	2	7	1	Michael Kessler
1969	4	6	1	Michael Kessler
1970	5	5	1	Michael Kessler
1971	1	7	1	Michael Kessler
1972	6	3	1	Jack Kinealy
1973	4	5	1	Jack Kinealy
1974	9	3	0	Joe Carenza
1975	8	5	1	Joe Carenza
1976	6	6	2	Joe Carenza
1977	12	3	2	Joe Carenza
1978	15	4	0	Joe Carenza

WASHINGTON AND JEFFERSON UNIVERSITY

Washington, Pennsylvania

Presidents   **Red and Black**

Yr.	W	L	T	Coach
1970	4	3	1	Jerry Jennings
1971	1	7	0	Jerry Jennings
1972	2	7	0	Jerry Jennings
1973	4	4	0	Jerry Jennings
1974	4	2	0	Jerry Jennings
1975	3	5	1	Jerry Jennings
1976	2	6	1	Jerry Jennings
1977	2	9	1	Jerry Jennings
1978	0	10	1	Jerry Jennings

WASHINGTON AND LEE UNIVERSITY

Lexington, Virginia

Generals   **Blue and White**

Yr.	W	L	T	Coach
1947	3	0	1	Norman Lord
1948	5	5	0	Norman Lord
1949	2	7	0	Norman Lord
1950	6	2	1	Wilson Fewster
1951	4	3	1	Wilson Fewster
1952	2	7	0	Benjamin Collins

Yr.	W	L	T	Coach	Yr.	W	L	T	Coach
1953	0	8	0	Norman Lord	1931	3	3	1	Hugh G. McCurdy
1954	5	3	2	Charles Herbert	1932	3	1	3	Hugh G. McCurdy
1955	3	6	1	Gene Corrigan	1933	3	4	2	Hugh G. McCurdy
1956	8	4	0	Gene Corrigan	1934	4	4	1	Hugh G. McCurdy
1957	5	4	1	Gene Corrigan	1935	5	4	0	Hugh G. McCurdy
1958	6	3	1	John Poston	1936	6	3	0	Hugh G. McCurdy
1959	5	3	1	Joe Lyles	1937	3	3	3	Hugh G. McCurdy
1960	4	5	0	Joe Lyles	1938	5	1	2	Hugh G. McCurdy
1961	2	7	0	Joe Lyles	1939	6	0	0	Hugh G. McCurdy
1962	6	3	2	Joe Lyles	1940	7	0	1	Hugh G. McCurdy
1963	7	5	0	Joe Lyles	1941	2	4	2	Hugh G. McCurdy
1964	7	2	1	Joe Lyles	1942	5	3	0	Hugh G. McCurdy
1965	7	3	2	Joe Lyles	1943	—	—	—	—
1966	8	3	1	Joe Lyles	1944	1	7	0	Hugh G. McCurdy
1967	9	3	0	Joe Lyles	1945	2	5	0	Hugh G. McCurdy
1968	3	5	1	Joe Lyles	1946	6	1	1	Hugh G. McCurdy
1969	7	4	2	Joe Lyles	1947	4	2	2	Hugh G. McCurdy
1970	3	9	0	Joe Lyles	1948	5	4	0	Hugh G. McCurdy
1971	5	6	0	Joe Lyles	1949	2	2	5	Hugh G. McCurdy
1972	6	2	2	Joe Lyles	1950	4	5	0	Hugh G. McCurdy
1973	7	4	0	Joe Lyles	1951	6	3	1	Hugh G. McCurdy
1974	4	5	3	Joe Lyles	1952	5	3	2	Hugh G. McCurdy
1975	3	10	0	Joe Lyles	1953	7	2	1	Hugh G. McCurdy
1976	3	10	0	Rolf Piranian	1954	4	1	5	Hugh G. McCurdy
1977	6	11	0	Rolf Piranian	1955	6	1	2	Hugh G. McCurdy
1978	3	8	2	Rolf Piranian	1956	4	6	0	Hugh G. McCurdy
					1957	4	5	1	Hugh G. McCurdy
					1958	0	9	1	Hugh G. McCurdy
					1959	3	5	1	Hugh G. McCurdy
					1960	3	6	0	Hugh G. McCurdy
					1961	5	1	4	Hugh G. McCurdy
					1962	8	1	1	Hugh G. McCurdy
					1963	6	3	0	Hugh G. McCurdy
					1964	7	2	0	Stan Plagenhoef
					1965	5	3	1	H. Franklin Irwin
					1966	7	1	1	Stan Plagenhoef
					1967	3	6	1	Don Long
					1968	3	6	1	Terry Jackson
					1969	4	2	4	Terry Jackson
					1970	5	3	2	Terry Jackson
					1971	7	4	0	Terry Jackson

WESLEYAN UNIVERSITY

Middletown, Connecticut

Cardinals　　　　　　　　　　**Red and Black**

Yr.	W	L	T	Coach
1924	1	3	0	Hugh G. McCurdy
1925	2	2	2	Hugh G. McCurdy
1926	2	2	1	Hugh G. McCurdy
1927	3	2	2	Hugh G. McCurdy
1928	2	2	3	Hugh G. McCurdy
1929	2	5	0	Hugh G. McCurdy
1930	3	6	0	Hugh G. McCurdy

Hugh McCurdy (second from right, rear row) reigned for four decades as coach at Wesleyan. This is his 1953 team.

Yr.	W	L	T	Coach
1972	7	5	0	Terry Jackson
1973	9	4	1	Terry Jackson
1974	3	5	4	Terry Jackson
1975	5	7	0	Terry Jackson
1976	5	7	0	Terry Jackson
1977	7	5	1	Terry Jackson
1978	6	6	1	Terry Jackson

WEST CHESTER STATE COLLEGE

West Chester, Pennsylvania

Rams				Purple and Gold
Yr.	W	L	T	Coach
1927	2	3	2	Earle Waters
1928	—	—	—	Earle Waters
1929	2	2	0	Earle Waters
1930	2	2	1	Earle Waters
1931	4	0	1	Earle Waters
1932	5	0	0	Earle Waters
1933	3	0	0	Earle Waters
1934	6	0	0	Earle Waters
1935	5	1	0	Earle Waters
1936	7	0	0	Earle Waters
1937	7	2	0	Earle Waters
1938	9	1	0	Earle Waters
1939	7	1	2	Earle Waters
1940	8	1	2	Earle Waters
1941	7	2	0	Earle Waters
1942	3	1	1	W. Benner, C. Graham
1943	0	5	0	W. Benner, C. Graham
1944	4	3	1	W. Benner, C. Graham
1945	6	2	1	W. Benner, C. Graham
1946	3	5	2	Earle Waters
1947	7	4	0	Earle Waters
1948	6	2	2	Earle Waters
1949	8	2	1	Earle Waters
1950	9	0	0	Earle Waters
1951	8	0	1	Earle Waters
1952	5	2	1	Earle Waters
1953	6	2	0	Earle Waters
1954	8	1	1	Earle Waters
1955	9	1	0	Earle Waters
1956	9	1	2	Earle Waters
1957	8	0	1	Mel Lorback
1958	5	3	1	Mel Lorback
1959	9	1	1	Mel Lorback
1960	10	1	1	Mel Lorback
1961	14	0	0	Mel Lorback
1962	8	3	1	Mel Lorback
1963	10	3	1	Mel Lorback
1964	6	4	2	Mel Lorback
1965	9	3	0	Mel Lorback
1966	7	3	0	Mel Lorback
1967	6	3	3	Mel Lorback
1968	9	3	0	Mel Lorback
1969	10	4	1	Mel Lorback
1970	7	4	2	Mel Lorback
1971	8	5	0	Mel Lorback
1972	4	6	2	Mel Lorback
1973	7	4	3	Mel Lorback
1974	4	6	4	Mel Lorback
1975	3	9	2	Mel Lorback
1976	4	7	1	Mel Lorback
1977	8	6	1	Mel Lorback
1978	5	10	2	Mel Lorback

WEST LIBERTY STATE COLLEGE

West Liberty, West Virginia

Hilltoppers				Gold and Black
Yr.	W	L	T	Coach
1972	3	6	0	Arthur Barbeau
1973	4	6	0	Arthur Barbeau
1974	5	5	0	Arthur Barbeau
1975	3	8	1	Arthur Barbeau
1976	5	7	0	Arthur Barbeau
1977	4	8	0	Arthur Barbeau
1978	4	8	1	Arthur Barbeau

WEST VIRGINIA UNIVERSITY

Morgantown, West Virginia

Mountaineers				Blue and Gold
Yr.	W	L	T	Coach
1961	2	5	3	Jim Markel
1962	8	2	0	Jim Markel
1963	7	3	0	Sam Maurice
1964	8	2	0	Sam Maurice
1965	7	5	1	Greg Myers
1966	13	2	0	Greg Myers
1967	11	1	0	John Stewart
1968	8	1	1	John Stewart
1969	4	5	1	John McGrath
1970	3	8	0	John McGrath
1971	9	3	0	John McGrath
1972	10	3	0	John McGrath
1973	10	2	3	John McGrath
1974	5	4	4	John McGrath
1975	8	5	1	John McGrath
1976	6	6	1	John McGrath
1977	2	9	2	John McGrath
1978	8	6	1	John McGrath

WESTERN CAROLINA UNIVERSITY

Cullowhee, North Carolina

Catamounts				Purple and Gold
Yr.	W	L	T	Coach
1969	1	6	0	Charles Schrader
1970	8	3	0	Charles Schrader
1971	7	3	2	Charles Schrader
1972	9	2	1	Charles Schrader
1973	7	4	2	Charles Schrader
1974	1	10	3	Charles Schrader
1975	4	7	0	Charles Schrader
1976	4	7	1	Charles Schrader
1977	10	6	1	Charles Schrader
1978	6	7	2	Charles Schrader

WESTERN ILLINOIS UNIVERSITY

Macomb, Illinois

Leathernecks				Purple and Gold
Yr.	W	L	T	Coach
1969	6	6	0	John MacKenzie
1970	8	4	1	John MacKenzie
1971	8	6	0	John MacKenzie
1972	4	4	3	John MacKenzie
1973	6	5	1	John MacKenzie
1974	9	4	2	John MacKenzie

Yr.	W	L	T	Coach
1975	8	5	1	John MacKenzie
1976	6	7	2	John MacKenzie
1977	8	5	1	John MacKenzie
1978	6	8	1	John MacKenzie

WESTERN MARYLAND COLLEGE

Westminster, Maryland

Green Terrors   **Green and Gold**

Yr.	W	L	T	Coach
1924	1	1	—	—
1925	4	0	—	Pete Garrett
1926	3	5	—	—
1927	4	4	—	Stauffer
1928	6	1	—	Barney Speir
1929	5	4	—	R. B. Beauchamp
1930	5	3	—	Kermit Longridge
1931	5	4	—	Mike Hernick
1932	5	2	—	Harvey Flater
1933	1	5	—	Harvey Flater
1934	4	5	—	Harvey Flater
1935	8	1	—	Peter Grimm
1936	4	5	—	Elseroad
1937	9	3	—	Jasper Jones
1938	5	8	—	H. B. Wright
1939	4	3	—	Walter Nathan
1940	2	5	—	Walter Nathan
1941	3	4	—	Charles Wallace
1942	2	3	—	Charles Wallace
1943	—	—	—	—
1944	—	—	—	—
1945	—	—	—	—
1946	4	4	—	John B. Jones
1947	4	8	—	John B. Jones
1948	3	9	—	John B. Jones
1949	4	8	—	Phil Uhrig
1950	0	9	—	Henry Corrado
1951	1	9	—	Phil Uhrig
1952	1	7	—	Phil Uhrig
1953	3	6	—	Phil Uhrig
1954	7	2	—	Phil Uhrig
1955	6	3	—	Phil Uhrig
1956	7	2	0	Phil Uhrig
1957	4	8	0	Phil Uhrig
1958	6	6	0	Phil Uhrig
1959	9	1	1	Dennis Harmon
1960	6	4	1	Dennis Harmon
1961	5	5	0	Dennis Harmon
1962	5	3	2	Dennis Harmon
1963	3	4	2	Dennis Harmon
1964	3	6	1	Homer Earll
1965	1	8	1	Homer Earll
1966	0	8	3	Homer Earll
1967	4	6	0	Homer Earll
1968	5	4	1	Homer Earll
1969	6	4	1	Homer Earll
1970	8	4	0	Homer Earll
1971	9	4	0	Homer Earll
1972	5	6	1	Homer Earll
1973	4	5	3	Homer Earll
1974	5	8	0	Homer Earll
1975	4	11	0	Homer Earll
1976	3	8	0	Homer Earll
1977	1	9	1	Homer Earll
1978	3	10	0	Homer Earll

WESTERN MICHIGAN UNIVERSITY

Kalamazoo, Michigan

Broncos   **Brown and Gold**

Yr.	W	L	T	Coach
1971	5	7	0	Pete Esdale
1972	2	10	1	Pete Glon
1973	4	4	5	Pete Glon
1974	7	5	1	Pete Glon
1975	5	5	2	Pete Glon
1976	5	5	2	Pete Glon
1977	6	6	1	Pete Glon
1978	7	2	3	Scott Ferris

WESTERN WASHINGTON UNIVERSITY

Bellingham, Washington

Vikings   **Blue and White**

Yr.	W	L	T	Coach
1978	3	9	0	Bruce Campbell

WESTFIELD STATE COLLEGE

Westfield, Massachusetts

Owls   **Blue and White**

Yr.	W	L	T	Coach
1964	9	2	0	Robert Green
1965	10	3	0	Robert Green
1966	8	4	0	John Kurty
1967	9	5	0	John Kurty
1968	12	2	3	John Kurty
1969	13	2	0	John Kurty
1970	15	1	1	John Kurty
1971	6	5	3	John Kurty
1972	13	2	1	John Kurty
1973	15	3	1	John Kurty
1974	16	4	1	John Kurty
1975	16	3	1	John Kurty
1976	13	3	0	John Kurty
1977	11	4	0	John Kurty
1978	11	4	0	Jim Fonte

WHEATON COLLEGE

Wheaton, Illinois

Crusaders   **Orange and Blue**

Yr.	W	L	T	Coach
1951	4	3	1	Bob Baptista
1952	6	2	1	Bob Baptista
1953	6	2	1	Bob Baptista
1954	5	6	1	Bob Baptista
1955	6	1	2	Bob Baptista
1956	4	4	2	Bob Baptista
1957	3	2	4	Bob Baptista
1958	4	5	2	Cliff McCrath
1959	8	1	0	Bob Baptista
1960	5	5	0	Bob Baptista
1961	6	5	1	Bob Baptista
1962	9	3	2	Bob Baptista
1963	7	5	1	Bob Baptista
1964	10	4	1	Bob Baptista
1965	5	6	1	Bob Baptista
1966	11	0	3	Bob Baptista

The three key coaches in Wheaton soccer history were, in order of their appearance (right to left): Bob Baptista, Cliff McCrath and Joe Bean.

Yr.	W	L	T	Coach
1967	9	3	1	Bob Baptista
1968	10	1	2	Russ Enlow
1969	10	1	1	Joe Bean
1970	12	2	1	Joe Bean
1971	10	2	1	Joe Bean
1972	8	4	0	Joe Bean
1973	5	6	4	Joe Bean
1974	8	6	1	Joe Bean
1975	11	6	0	Joe Bean
1976	9	6	1	Joe Bean
1977	13	8	0	Joe Bean
1978	13	5	3	Joe Bean

WHEELING COLLEGE

Wheeling, West Virginia

Cardinals   **Red and Yellow**

Yr.	W	L	T	Coach
1976	1	7	1	Al Didriksen
1977	1	7	1	Keith Goudy
1978	1	9	1	Keith Goudy

WHITMAN COLLEGE

Walla Walla, Washington

Missionaries   **Blue and Gold**

Yr.	W	L	T	Coach
1969	3	3	0	Floyd Bunt
1970	8	1	0	Floyd Bunt

Yr.	W	L	T	Coach
1971	12	2	1	Floyd Bunt
1972	5	11	2	Floyd Bunt
1973	8	4	4	Floyd Bunt
1974	5	8	2	Floyd Bunt
1975	9	7	2	Floyd Bunt
1976	12	5	1	Floyd Bunt
1977	11	3	3	Floyd Bunt
1978	13	9	2	Floyd Bunt

WIDENER COLLEGE

Chester, Pennsylvania

Pioneers   **Blue and Gold**

Yr.	W	L	T	Coach
1961	3	1	1	Frank Robinson
1962	3	4	1	Frank Robinson
1963	3	6	0	Frank Robinson
1964	3	7	0	Frank Robinson
1965	2	9	0	Frank Robinson
1966	3	7	0	Daniel Horninger
1967	3	8	0	Daniel Horninger
1968	3	6	0	Daniel Horninger
1969	2	5	2	Daniel Horninger
1970	4	8	0	James Fallon
1971	1	12	0	Bruce Babcock
1972	3	9	0	Bruce Babcock
1973	3	8	2	Thomas Balent
1974	0	10	1	Thomas Balent
1975	2	10	0	Thomas Balent
1976	5	8	0	Thomas Balent
1977	2	11	0	Thomas Balent
1978	2	11	0	Richard Bonnette

The year is 1924, and this is how they looked at Williams College.

WILKES COLLEGE

Wilkes-Barre, Pennsylvania

Colonels				Blue and Gold
Yr.	W	L	T	Coach
1966	10	3	0	Jim Neddoff
1967	6	2	4	Jim Neddoff
1968	7	3	0	Jim Neddoff
1969	0	9	0	—
1970	6	4	2	Tom Rokita
1971	8	4	2	Tom Rokita
1972	5	7	1	Tom Rokita
1973	6	8	1	Tom Rokita
1974	2	6	2	Tom Rokita
1975	1	10	0	Charles Eaton
1976	6	6	0	Charles Eaton
1977	3	10	0	Charles Eaton
1978	4	9	0	Kurt Hagman

WILLIAM AND MARY UNIVERSITY

Williamsburg, Virginia

Indians				Green and Gold
Yr.	W	L	T	Coach
1965	0	6	0	McLaughlin
1966	0	8	0	McLaughlin
1967	3	6	0	Joe Agee
1968	5	4	0	Joe Agee
1969	5	6	2	Jim Carpenter

Yr.	W	L	T	Coach
1970	9	2	2	Jim Carpenter
1971	6	7	0	Al Albert
1972	5	7	0	Al Albert
1973	6	5	1	Al Albert
1974	5	5	2	Al Albert
1975	9	4	1	Al Albert
1976	10	4	1	Al Albert
1977	13	4	0	Al Albert
1978	10	6	3	Al Albert

WILLIAMS COLLEGE

Williamstown, Massachusetts

Ephs				Purple and White
Yr.	W	L	T	Coach
1922	0	5	0	William Taggart
1923	2	4	1	R. G. Leonard
1924	1	4	1	J. E. Bullock
1925	1	4	0	J. E. Bullock
1926	2	3	1	J. E. Bullock
1927	1	5	0	J. E. Bullock
1928	4	0	2	J. E. Bullock
1929	4	1	1	J. E. Bullock
1930	3	3	1	J. E. Bullock
1931	2	2	2	J. E. Bullock
1932	4	0	2	J. E. Bullock
1933	2	2	2	J. E. Bullock
1934	3	2	1	J. E. Bullock
1935	3	3	0	J. E. Bullock

Yr.	W	L	T	Coach
1936	3	2	1	J. E. Bullock
1937	4	2	1	J. E. Bullock
1938	5	2	0	J. E. Bullock
1939	4	2	1	J. E. Bullock
1940	3	3	1	J. E. Bullock
1941	0	4	2	J. E. Bullock
1942	2	3	0	—
1943	—	—	—	—
1944	3	1	0	J. E. Bullock
1945	2	3	0	J. E. Bullock
1946	6	1	0	J. E. Bullock
1947	4	3	0	J. E. Bullock
1948	2	4	0	J. E. Bullock
1949	2	5	0	Clarence Chaffee
1950	4	3	0	Clarence Chaffee
1951	0	6	1	Clarence Chaffee
1952	4	3	1	Clarence Chaffee
1953	3	5	0	Clarence Chaffee
1954	6	2	0	Clarence Chaffee
1955	4	4	0	Clarence Chaffee
1956	4	4	0	Clarence Chaffee
1957	2	4	2	Clarence Chaffee
1958	3	4	1	Clarence Chaffee
1959	6	1	2	Clarence Chaffee
1960	5	2	1	Clarence Chaffee
1961	7	1	0	Clarence Chaffee
1962	8	0	0	Clarence Chaffee
1963	6	1	1	Clarence Chaffee
1964	5	3	0	Clarence Chaffee
1965	2	6	0	Clarence Chaffee
1966	6	1	1	Clarence Chaffee
1967	4	4	0	Clarence Chaffee
1968	3	3	2	Clarence Chaffee
1969	3	4	1	Clarence Chaffee
1970	4	3	2	Jonathan Healy
1971	6	1	3	Jeffrey Vennell
1972	6	4	1	Jeffrey Vennell
1973	1	5	5	Jeffrey Vennell
1974	4	5	2	Jeffrey Vennell
1975	6	5	0	Jeffrey Vennell
1976	7	4	1	Jeffrey Vennell
1977	5	6	1	Jeffrey Vennell
1978	8	3	1	Jeffrey Vennell

WILMINGTON COLLEGE

Wilmington, Ohio

Quakers				Green and White
Yr.	W	L	T	Coach
1975	1	9	1	Bud Lewis
1976	2	9	1	Bud Lewis
1977	12	3	0	Bud Lewis
1978	9	5	1	Bud Lewis

WINTHROP COLLEGE

Rock Hill, South Carolina

Eagles				Garnet and Gold
Yr.	W	L	T	Coach
1975	3	7	0	Jim Casada
1976	4	11	2	Jim Casada
1977	11	9	1	Jim Casada
1978	15	11	0	Jim Casada

WISCONSIN, UNIVERSITY OF

Madison, Wisconsin

Badgers				Cardinal and White
Yr.	W	L	T	Coach
1968	7	1	1	Bill Reddan
1969	5	3	0	Bill Reddan
1970	3	2	3	Bill Reddan
1971	7	1	0	Bill Reddan
1972	9	1	0	Bill Reddan
1973	6	4	1	Bill Reddan
1974	10	4	4	Bill Reddan
1975	7	7	1	Bill Reddan
1976	6	6	3	Bill Reddan
1977	8	6	1	Bill Reddan
1978	9	7	3	Bill Reddan

WISCONSIN, UNIVERSITY OF (GREEN BAY)

Green Bay, Wisconsin

Phoenix				Red, Green, and White
Yr.	W	L	T	Coach
1969	12	2	1	Lou LeCalsey
1970	11	2	3	Lou LeCalsey
1971	8	5	3	Tom Griffith
1972	9	3	0	Tom Griffith
1973	9	3	0	Tom Griffith
1974	3	6	2	Hank Eichin
1975	15	5	0	Hank Eichin
1976	13	3	0	Hank Eichin
1977	14	4	2	Hank Eichin
1978	9	7	2	Aldo Santaga

WISCONSIN, UNIVERSITY OF (MILWAUKEE)

Milwaukee, Wisconsin

Panthers				Black and Gold
Yr.	W	L	T	Coach
1973	6	6	0	Dan Harris
1974	8	2	3	Dan Harris
1975	11	4	0	Dan Harris
1976	4	9	2	Dan Harris
1977	14	4	0	Dan Harris
1978	12	8	0	Dan Harris

WISCONSIN, UNIVERSITY OF (WHITEWATER)

Whitewater, Wisconsin

Warhawks				Purple and White
Yr.	W	L	T	Coach
1978	6	6	2	Gene Cardinal

WITTENBERG UNIVERSITY

Springfield, Ohio

Tigers				Red and White
Yr.	W	L	T	Coach
1967	2	6	0	Steve Farrar
1968	2	8	0	Bob Hamilton
1969	5	4	1	Bob Hamilton
1970	3	3	1	Bob Van Poppel

Yr.	W	L	T	Coach
1971	3	7	1	Bob Van Poppel
1972	6	6	0	Bob Van Poppel
1973	3	9	0	Larry Hunter
1974	3	7	0	Larry Hunter
1975	5	4	1	Larry Hunter
1976	3	7	1	Steve Moore
1977	6	4	1	Steve Moore
1978	9	2	2	Steve Moore

WOFFORD COLLEGE

Spartanburg, South Carolina

Terriers				Gold and Black
Yr.	W	L	T	Coach
1976	8	8	0	Charles McGinty
1977	7	7	2	Charles McGinty
1978	9	5	1	Charles McGinty

WOOSTER, THE COLLEGE OF

Wooster, Ohio

Scots				Black and Gold
Yr.	W	L	T	Coach
1914	1	0	0	R. R. Pike
1915	0	2	0	—
1933	3	0	1	Munson, Bainbridge
1934	3	1	1	Al Jones
1935	0	1	1	—
1960	3	3	1	Pete Parry
1961	1	5	0	Tom Bing
1962	2	6	0	Gary Barrette
1963	2	6	2	Jack Lammert
1964	5	3	1	Bob Nye
1965	5	3	2	Bob Nye
1966	6	3	2	Bob Nye
1967	9	4	1	Bob Nye
1968	9	3	1	Bob Nye
1969	7	5	1	Bob Nye
1970	11	2	1	Bob Nye
1971	5	7	0	Bob Nye
1972	8	3	1	Bob Nye
1973	5	4	4	Bob Nye
1974	9	4	1	Bob Nye
1975	7	6	0	Bob Nye
1976	8	5	2	Bob Nye
1977	14	5	0	Bob Nye
1978	9	6	1	Bob Nye

WORCESTER POLYTECHNIC INSTITUTE

Worcester, Massachusetts

Engineers				Maroon and Gray
Yr.	W	L	T	Coach
1921	4	2	1	Fordyce T. Blake
1922	4	2	0	W. L. Jenkins
1923	3	2	1	W. L. Jenkins
1924	3	3	1	—
1925	7	1	0	J. S. Miller
1926	5	2	0	W. L. Jenkins
1927	0	7	0	W. L. Jenkins
1928	2	5	0	Edwin Higginbottom
1929	2	4	1	Edwin Higginbottom

Wooster became a Division III power under the tutelage of coach Bob Nye.

Yr.	W	L	T	Coach
1930	3	2	2	Edwin Higginbottom
1931	3	4	0	Edwin Higginbottom
1932	3	4	0	Edwin Higginbottom
1933	2	3	1	Edwin Higginbottom
1934	3	2	1	Edwin Higginbottom
1935	4	2	0	Edwin Higginbottom
1936	3	2	0	Edwin Higginbottom
1937	4	2	0	Edwin Higginbottom
1938	6	0	0	Edwin Higginbottom
1939	5	1	0	Edwin Higginbottom
1940	2	4	0	Edwin Higginbottom
1941	2	2	2	Edwin Higginbottom
1942	5	3	0	Edwin Higginbottom
1943	4	3	0	Edwin Higginbottom
1944	5	1	1	Edwin Higginbottom
1945	3	2	0	Edwin Higginbottom
1946	1	2	2	Edwin Higginbottom
1947	0	7	0	Edwin Higginbottom
1948	1	5	0	Edwin Higginbottom
1949	2	5	0	Edwin Higginbottom
1950	2	3	1	Edwin Higginbottom
1951	2	2	2	James Geddes
1952	1	6	0	James Geddes
1953	1	6	0	James Geddes
1954	2	4	1	James Geddes
1955	2	5	1	James Geddes
1956	1	3	4	James Geddes
1957	3	5	0	Alan King
1958	3	3	2	Alan King
1959	3	5	0	Alan King
1960	7	2	1	Alan King
1961	4	4	1	Alan King
1962	5	6	0	Alan King
1963	3	8	1	Alan King
1964	7	2	1	Alan King
1965	11	1	1	Alan King
1966	9	2	0	Alan King

Yr.	W	L	T	Coach
1967	8	2	3	Alan King
1968	6	5	1	Alan King
1969	8	2	1	Alan King
1970	9	2	1	Alan King
1971	5	5	1	Alan King
1972	3	6	2	Alan King
1973	6	4	2	Alan King
1974	11	3	1	Alan King
1975	9	3	1	Alan King
1976	11	3	1	Alan King
1977	7	5	1	Alan King
1978	4	7	1	Alan King

WORCESTER STATE COLLEGE

Worcester, Massachusetts

Lancers   **Blue and Gold**

Yr.	W	L	T	Coach
1968	0	5	0	Jack Regele
1969	2	8	0	Bob Perry
1970	3	7	0	Bob Perry
1971	0	11	0	Ham Perkins
1972	2	10	2	Ham Perkins
1973	2	9	3	Ham Perkins
1974	1	11	2	Ham Perkins
1975	0	11	0	Ham Perkins
1976	2	9	1	Earl Bonett
1977	1	11	0	Earl Bonett
1978	0	13	0	Earl Bonett

YALE UNIVERSITY

New Haven, Connecticut

Eli, Bulldogs   **Blue and White**

Yr.	W	L	T	Coach
1912	5	0	0	Alexander B. Timm
1913	3	2	0	Henry J. Green, Dr. Cecil A. Herbert
1914	2	3	2	—
1915	4	5	2	—
1916	2	6	0	—
1917	1	3	0	—
1918	—	—	—	—
1919	0	4	1	—
1920	0	1	1	—
1921	2	6	0	Horace Wilson
1922	1	3	2	F. M. Touchton
1923	4	1	1	F. M. Touchton
1924	5	5	1	F. M. Touchton
1925	2	6	3	F. M. Touchton
1926	3	3	3	—
1927	6	2	0	Walter Leeman
1928	7	0	2	Walter Leeman
1929	7	1	1	Walter Leeman
1930	8	1	0	Walter Leeman
1931	3	3	2	Walter Leeman
1932	4	1	2	Walter Leeman
1933	5	3	2	Walter Leeman
1934	6	2	2	Walter Leeman

Yr.	W	L	T	Coach
1935	12	0	0	Walter Leeman
1936	6	5	1	Walter Leeman
1937	5	5	2	Walter Leeman
1938	9	5	0	Walter Leeman
1939	7	2	1	Walter Leeman
1940	6	0	4	Walter Leeman
1941	7	1	2	Walter Leeman
1942	4	1	2	Walter Leeman
1943	5	2	0	Walter Leeman
1944	7	3	0	Walter Leeman
1945	8	0	2	Walter Leeman
1946	3	3	3	Walter Leeman
1947	6	4	1	Walter Leeman
1948	5	5	0	Walter Leeman
1949	3	6	2	Walter Leeman
1950	9	2	1	Jack Marshall
1951	8	2	1	Jack Marshall
1952	9	1	2	Jack Marshall
1953	4	6	1	Jack Marshall
1954	8	1	2	Jack Marshall
1955	9	2	1	Jack Marshall
1956	9	2	1	Jack Marshall
1957	5	6	0	Jack Marshall
1958	5	4	2	Jack Marshall
1959	6	4	1	Jack Marshall
1960	7	3	2	Jack Marshall
1961	5	6	2	Jack Marshall
1962	4	7	0	Jack Marshall
1963	3	7	1	Jack Marshall
1964	4	5	2	Jack Marshall
1965	8	3	0	Jack Marshall
1966	5	4	2	Hubert Vogelsinger
1967	5	4	1	Hubert Vogelsinger
1968	6	3	3	Hubert Vogelsinger
1969	4	5	3	Hubert Vogelsinger
1970	4	10	0	Hubert Vogelsinger
1971	3	7	2	Hubert Vogelsinger
1972	4	8	1	Hubert Vogelsinger
1973	7	4	4	Hubert Vogelsinger
1974	2	6	6	Bill Killen
1975	3	8	2	Bill Killen
1976	4	8	2	Bill Killen
1977	8	7	0	Bill Killen
1978	6	8	1	Steve Griggs

YORK COLLEGE

York, Pennsylvania

Spartans   **Green and White**

Yr.	W	L	T	Coach
1968	4	6	0	Bob Cummings
1969	6	3	1	Bob Cummings
1970	5	4	1	Bob Cummings
1971	10	3	0	Bob Cummings
1972	5	4	0	Bob Cummings
1973	7	3	0	Jack Klingaman
1974	7	4	1	Jack Klingaman
1975	4	7	0	Jack Klingaman
1976	6	4	1	Jack Klingaman
1977	1	11	0	Keith Peterman
1978	2	10	1	Keith Peterman

THE PROFESSIONALS

Billy Gonsalves (right), the "Babe Ruth of Soccer," regarded as the United States' greatest player in the 1930s, finished his career with the ASL's Brooklyn Hispano.

7

The American Soccer League

The most important contribution of the American Soccer League to the development of the sport in the United States was its sponsorship of outstanding foreign teams here from 1946 into the 1960s. The ASL's own league games at the time were played in dusty ovals. They were underpublicized and poorly attended. Its franchises struggled to survive; its players were paid poorly. Yet each spring and summer, the inadequacies of America's oldest and then only professional soccer league were forgotten.

The teams from England, Scotland, Israel, Germany, Italy, Brazil, and other fabled soccer lands arrived. They played against each other. They played against selected ASL all-star teams. They drew crowds of between twenty thousand and forty-five thousand at New York's Yankee Stadium, the Polo Grounds, Ebbets Field, and Downing Stadium. These exhibitions kept the ASL afloat, since portions of the gate receipts were divided among ASL clubs. They also exposed the American public to some of the finest players in the world, gained worldwide fame for the ASL, and kept soccer alive in the U.S.

It often seemed that the ASL existed merely to welcome visitors like Liverpool, Manchester United, Glasgow Celtic, Tottenham Hotspurs, Hapoel, Inter-Milan, and Santos. But by staging its various "dream games," the ASL laid the groundwork for what eventually was termed the American soccer boom.

A secondary benefit was that the ASL helped keep the United States Soccer Football Association, now called the USSF, solvent. The ASL claims to have raised over three hundred thousand dollars for the governing body of American soccer, which took five percent of the gate from each tour game. "We got ten thousand dollars from the Liverpool tour [in 1946]," Joseph J. Barriskill, former USSF president, recalled, "and we've never looked back since."

Then president of the USSF, Walt Rechsteiner said in 1958 that the ASL's international presentations "encouraged others to follow in your footsteps," and helped soccer gain "prestige in the American press which is otherwise difficult to obtain."

There have been other ASL contributions to the growth of soccer in the U.S.:

• It pioneered indoor soccer at Madison Square Garden as early as 1939, the ASL's sixth year.

• It supplied four of the eleven starters on the 1950 U.S. World Cup team that produced a 1-0 victory over England in what is considered one of the greatest upsets in soccer history.

• It was the first pro league in the U.S. to have games televised, in October 1952, on WPIX, from Yankee Stadium.

• It brought Pelé to the U.S. for the first time on August 21, 1965, when his Santos team beat Benfica of Portugal with Eusebio, 4-0, at Downing Stadium before more than twenty-five thousand.

• It was a spawning ground for hundreds of coaches, referees, administrators, and boosters who remained in the game at the local, and in some cases, national level.

The success of the North American Soccer League since 1968 threatened the ASL with extinction in 1971 and kept it mired in an almost semipro status until 1975. But then the ASL formed its own marketing operation, expanded to the West Coast for the first time, attracted several responsible ownership groups, and tried to raise its standard of play.

Most ASL players in 1979 still worked full-time jobs outside of soccer—as always. So they were still viewed by fans as semipros. They still played in small stadiums, got little media coverage and part-time soccer salaries. The ASL's average attendance for the 1978 season was reported as 2,630, an increase of 4 percent over 1977, but still about 20 percent of the NASL's average.

The ASL expanded to eleven franchises in 1979, with newcomers in Pennsylvania, Las Vegas, and Columbus, Ohio. Its league officials talked hopefully of a "Soccer Bowl" showdown against the NASL champion within a decade. NASL officials sneered at the suggestion.

That is par for the course. The legacy of the American Soccer League consists mainly of breakthroughs that never came, dreams that died unfulfilled, hopes crushed by harsh reality. And yet somehow, the league has survived.

THE BEGINNING, 1933–41

The ASL was born in 1933 when the United States Football Association (later the USSFA and USSF) granted it exclusive rights to pro soccer on the Atlantic seaboard. Information is sketchy, and memories have clouded, but several old-timers interviewed in 1978 recalled a "soccer war of 1931" and an "old American Soccer League" in the 1920s. It seems that in 1931 several groups representing pro interests met in New York to form their own ASL, independent of all state associations. These interests refused to enter the National Open Cup competition and were suspended by the USFA. Two years later, the USFA

Hakoah, an all-Jewish team from Vienna, came to New York's Polo Grounds for an historic meeting with an ASL all-star team. The 1926 exhibition drew 46,000 fans and was won by the ASL, 3–0.

apparently relented and granted the ASL limited autonomy.

The highlight of the "old ASL" was a May 1, 1926, exhibition game between Hakoah of Vienna and an all-star team of ASL players which drew forty-six thousand—many with free tickets—to the Polo Grounds. Erno Schwarcz played for Hakoah and later returned to the United States as an ASL player, coach, league official, and promoter.

Pete Renzulli was the ASL goalie that day. He remembered that Hakoah "had the ball for eighty-seven minutes," but that the ASL scored three times on counter attacks and won, 3-0. Renzulli played for a team called the New York Nationals that year. He later became a clinician and youth soccer advocate.

Without question, the best player in the U.S. in the 1920s was Archie Stark, born in Scotland in 1897. Stark was the center forward for the famous Bethlehem (Pennsylvania) Steel Company team which during a 1919 tour compiled a 7-2-5 record against some of the best teams in Scandinavia. Stark scored sixty-seven goals in forty-four games for Bethlehem in 1924–25. The team drew as many as twenty thousand to road games, but often a mere two hundred at home. Stark concluded his playing career with the Kearny Irish, which won the first official ASL title in 1934.

"By then I was finished, really," Stark recalled. "Kearny was a social club. They were always after me to play for them. They finally got me out of retirement and we won the championship. But it was a social club, not a soccer club."

The pattern of ethnic clubs fielding ASL teams was to be repeated over the years among the Irish, Scots, Hispanics, Italians, Germans, Poles, and Ukrainians. "Every time there was a migration [from Europe]," said Walt Bahr, one of the best halfbacks in ASL history, "the most recent group fielded the best team and had the largest following. Then they gradually fell into the same mold."

The scourge of the prewar period was the Kearny (New Jersey) Scots, who won five straight ASL championships from 1937 to 1941. That streak never has been equalled. Phil Fox, a referee during the period, said there was a distinct difference in the ethnic composition of ASL teams before the war and after. "Before," he said, "it

was mainly English, Scotch, and American boys. After, the various nationalities came in."

The greatest player of the 1930s wasn't playing in the ASL. He was playing in various semipro leagues. Billy Gonsalves, born August 10, 1908, in Fall River, Massachusetts, took seven different teams to nine straight final appearances and six titles in the U.S. National Open Cup from 1930–39. The unanimously proclaimed "Babe Ruth" of American soccer finished his career with Brooklyn Hispano in the ASL, helping it win a league title in 1943 and national cups in 1943 and 1944. Gonsalves, a massive force at 6'2", 210 pounds, also was a member of the U.S. World Cup teams in 1930 and 1934.

"Pelé could hit a ball," said Jack Hynes, who was one of the ASL's greatest goal scorers himself, "but he was nothing compared to Billy Gonsalves. Billy could hit a ball and make it fly. He was the greatest."

In the early days the ASL established a reputation as a no-nonsense, professional circuit that would not tolerate violence. The ASL even tried to dictate a style of play, suggesting in 1938 that teams "see to it the ball is kept low and not kicked high like a ten-cent balloon. . . . The essence of good football is keeping the ball on the ground as much as possible, . . . kicking [it] into the air on the first time is an indication of hurry and fluster and unsoundness of technique."

But referee Fox remembers a lot of high balls being played in games he officiated and said that he suffered some narrow escapes—like the time he ejected a Philadelphia Germans' player late in a 1938 game in Philadelphia. The New York Americans won, Fox said, "and for a while there I didn't think I was ever going to blow another whistle. . . . The local gendarmes took me away in a squad car."

An October 9, 1938, issue of *American Soccer League News* states that Jose Aja of Brooklyn Hispano was suspended three months and fined twenty-five dollars after he allegedly began kicking a Scots' player, precipitating a free-for-all involving spectators at Celtic Park in Brooklyn. A month of the sentence was commuted after Aja wrote a letter of apology to the league saying "I'm cured."

According to Erwin Single, a longtime soccer broadcaster and writer, the ASL generally con-

The Manhattan Brewery team was one of many that featured the legendary Billy Gonsalves (rear, fifth from left).

sisted of ten teams in the 1930s and 1940s, "two from the Bronx, two from Brooklyn, two from Philadelphia, two from New Jersey, and two from Baltimore."

The teams usually represented social clubs. "The ASL always was composed of people who had soccer in their hearts and backgrounds, but to whom business was secondary," Single said. "They weren't sports promoters. It was never really a professional league. It was a semiprofessional league."

Julius G. Alonso, secretary of the Brooklyn Hispano club from 1936 to 1956 and an ASL official for two decades, kept vouchers from 1938 that show a net profit of eleven dollars for an exhibition game and a range of players' salaries of from four dollars to seventeen dollars a game. Fox remembered getting eight dollars a game to referee before World War II, though he did get twenty dollars plus twelve dollars expenses to handle a May 1939 game between ASL all-stars and the Scottish national team at the Polo Grounds.

As always, there were inequities in the ASL

and in U.S. soccer in general. Amateurs received under-the-table payments and jobs from some teams, and the USSFA sometimes overlooked them in return for the players' services in the Pan American and Olympic Games. Others who wished to remain amateurs often were professionalized by the USSF against their will and denied Olympic participation.

Three of those were among the best players the ASL ever produced: Walt Bahr, Jack Hynes, and Bennie McLaughlin. Hynes started his career at fifteen in 1936 with St. Mary's Celtic. That year he flew to Chicago to play in the National Cup final. "Imagine," Hynes said. "I was fifteen!" He said the USSFA professionalized him in 1941. Bahr and McLaughlin were professionalized in 1948. So they missed the Olympics. But they all were selected to virtually every other U.S. all-star team between 1947 and 1958. All three have been named to the USSF Hall of Fame.

Before and even after World War II, weather conditions determined how many league matches ASL teams would play. Games were always on

St. Mary's Celtic, one of the first soccer teams to take to the air, flew from New York to Chicago for the 1936 National Cup final.

Sundays, between September and April (until 1969). Alonso remembered the early players generally as "mechanics, restaurant workers, salesmen . . . even a couple of doctors." Alonso himself was a construction representative for Consolidated Edison.

Players and officials came from all walks of life. The only thing that bound them was devotion to the sport. "It was a hodgepodge, a mixture," Hynes said. "Certainly nothing big. . . . But it was the lifeblood—what kept the game going here. It was *the* league in the U.S. Truly the pioneers."

By 1939, the ASL had grown to twelve teams, was staging indoor matches at Madison Square Garden, and was considering applications from seven New England teams. The ASL has been criticized for lack of attention to junior soccer and poor promotion. But in the 1940–41 season it admitted ladies free to league games, held an amateur clinic at Rutgers, and even paid expenses for two Baltimore junior teams to travel to New York for a national junior cup final.

The next season, the ASL first ran a high school game as a preliminary to a league game. And it sold at its parks a magazine devoted to juniors called *Soccer*. So it appears that there was at least some effort to cultivate the youth. The trouble was, the ASL got relatively little space in the newspapers.

The ASL was proud of its caliber of play, generally believed to be the best in the U.S. in the prewar era. Its all-star teams tied Charlton AC of England, 1-1; held the Scottish nationals to a 180-minute draw before losing, 4-2, in overtime; tied Atlante of Mexico, 2-2, and beat South American champion Botafogo of Brazil, 3-1.

"Just imagine," the *ASL News* speculated on April 6, 1941, "if conditions in this country would permit 100 percent professional teams. What great teams we would have here."

But along came World War II.

THE WAR YEARS, 1941–45

Even the *ASL News* acknowledged a decline in the caliber of play during the war years. "[It] did not, except in spots, even approach that of prewar days," the publication noted in 1945. "Yet the league did an excellent job . . . games are being started on time more nearly than ever before.

Official Program

PRICE **10** CENTS

AMERICAN LEAGUE SOCCER

FOOTBALL

New York Americans

vs.

Baltimore Americans

ERNO SCHWARCZ
Player-Manager, N. Y. Americans

TRIBORO STADIUM

—

RANDALLS ISLAND

●

Sunday, November 2, 1941

A month before Pearl Harbor, they were playing soccer at New York's Randalls Island.

Player discipline . . . has been made severe. . . . leg-breaking play . . . has been practically eliminated."

The ASL had four different champions from 1942–46. The balance of power often shifted as various stars left their teams for the armed forces or defense plants. There was a nationalistic movement in late 1941 to Americanize the ASL by dispensing with ethnic affiliations in team nicknames. But the social clubs that sponsored the teams were too strong, too proud, and wanted the recognition. Ethnically named teams would continue into the 1970s.

The roster limit of wartime ASL teams was extended from eighteen players to twenty-one to provide extra players to replace those called into service. Still, there were occasions when teams claimed they were so depleted by defections that they were forced to miss games.

Jack Hynes remembers missing a couple of Sunday games with the New York Americans because of his job as a precision grinder of tools with Sperry Gyroscope Company. "But they kept the league going," he said, "and that was good."

Soccer fans listened to Terry Long's WBNX program, the only fifteen-minute broadcast in the United States devoted exclusively to soccer, on Saturday evenings at eight o'clock in New York. The membership of the ASL underwent few changes during the war. And, Erno Schwarcz and Jimmy McGuire, who would later be the guiding force of the tour programs, became intimately involved with the ASL.

McGuire had the distinction of being plucked away from the ASL's Brooklyn Wanderers in 1931 by the touring Glasgow Celtic team. He wound up playing six years for Northampton Town in the English League as a center halfback before cartilage trouble sidelined him. He returned to the St. Mary's Celtic in 1938, eventually became ASL president, and in the 1950s became its goodwill ambassador.

Julius Alonso noted that McGuire once signed a player for the St. Mary's Celtic who "wasn't very good, but was a fantastic accordion player. McGuire kept him all season—not as a player, but as a musician—to entertain on the way to road games."

There was a general feeling during the war that since U.S. troops had been stationed in far-flung lands where the sport had progressed more notably than in the U.S., they would come back more acquainted with the game than ever. There would be a fertile ground for the seeds of international games. In 1944, anticipating the war's end, the ASL formed a profit corporation within itself to promote foreign tours.

Among the best wartime players were: Stanley Chesney, the New York Americans' goalie who wore baseball pants and eventually made everybody's ASL all-time team; Laszlo Sternberg, Americans' fullback; Charlie Ernst of Baltimore, the first native-born American to score five goals in an ASL game; Gonsalves and Hynes; Bill Stark of the Brooklyn Wanderers, who was the son of Archie Stark; Fabri Salcedo of the Brooklyn Hispano; Duke Nanoski, Bob Gormley, and George Nemchik of Philadelphia; Rudy Kuntner of Brookhattan; and Fred Kropfelder of the Baltimore Americans.

Hynes finished first among soccer players in a 1944 war bond sports popularity contest in New York. He got more votes than baseball's Dizzy Dean and tennis' Bill Tilden. The same year, Ernst performed the Ruthian feat of scoring eleven goals in three games while on leave from the service.

By September 24, 1944, more than 140 ASL players had been inducted into the armed forces, but the league still reported an average of fourteen professionals signed with each of its clubs. For the first time, the ASL adopted a legal contract between player and club. Walt Bahr remembers getting five dollars a game during the war as a teenage amateur in the league, but, he explains, "In 1943, five dollars was nice spending money for a kid."

Any look at the war years would be incomplete without mentioning that when Archie Ballantyne of the Kearny Celtics landed in France, he parachuted onto a soccer field. Ballantyne eventually was awarded a Silver Star for heroism. The ASL should have awarded itself a medal for staying alive.

THE GLORY YEARS, 1946–68

The ASL went at staging international exhibition games in a big way. Eventually, teams from nineteen countries appeared under ASL auspices. Liverpool began the series in 1946 and made three more appearances. Manchester United came three times. For months in advance of their appearances, the *ASL News* whetted fans' appetites with player profiles, team historical data, and team itineraries.

There was no doubt that American fans would turn out for good soccer. The promoters proved that time after time. In 1947, the ASL presented Hapoel of Israel, cosponsored by the Jewish National Workers Alliance. The game, which the Israelis won, 2–0, reportedly had an advance sale of 53,000. A crowd of 43,177 showed up in the rain at Yankee Stadium May 4. The visitors first were greeted by Mayor William O'Dwyer and given a motorcade.

In 1948, a group calling itself Hakoah bought the Brooklyn Wanderers, long considered the ASL's physically toughest team, and decided to try to field an all-Jewish team. After a losing season (3–10), the management decided on open enrolment. At this time, Philadelphia took over dominance of the ASL. The Philadelphia Americans and Nationals won seven ASL titles between them from 1947–53 and sent Bahr and McLaughlin to the U.S. World Cup team.

The best soccer game of the period in the U.S. is believed by many to have been the Liverpool-Djurgarden of Sweden match at Brooklyn's Ebbets Field before twenty thousand in 1948. Liverpool won, 3–2. Soon after, Djurgarden beat an ASL all-star team, 3–1. ASL teams continued to turn in respectable results against foreign teams, leading ASL players and officials to conclude that the ASL was playing the finest soccer in the U.S.

The New York Americans tied two matches and lost one in Cuba in 1949. The U.S. team beat Cuba, 5–2, in Mexico City, to qualify for the sixteen-team World Cup finals in Rio de Janeiro. The 1–0 U.S. upset of England there focused attention on American soccer as never before. Many foreign newspapers refused to print the score until they had checked with Brazilian officials. Haitian Joe Gaetjens of Brookhattan scored the goal. He was one of the only three foreign-born starters on the U.S. team. The others were Joe Maca of Belgium and Ed McIlveney of Scot-

land. Four starters were ASL players: Maca, Gaetjens, Bahr, and McIlveney.

"It made me a hero in Belgium," Maca said. "But here, it never meant nothing. In Belgium, I had played for the national team. For seventy-five years my country had never been able to beat England. You have no idea what it was like. It was like playing against Joe DiMaggio and Babe Ruth, and beating 'em." Bahr grabbed the ball after the game and it was enshrined by the USSF under a glass cover.

There were those who thought the victory heralded a new era in American soccer. But it soon became clear that it was not to be. The game was an isolated instance and really had no lasting impact on the ASL or on soccer here. The 1950–51 ASL season was a peaceful one. The ASL went ahead bringing over European clubs and ran its league seasons almost anonymously.

There was a momentary triumph in October 1952, when WPIX televised ASL doubleheaders at Yankee Stadium. "Magazines, newspapers and columnists who formerly ignored us suddenly took notice," said Jack Flamhaft, newly elected ASL president. But poor attendance killed the series and it never was revived.

Even though the Philadelphia Nationals won three titles in four years, they folded after the 1953 season. So did the Americans, whose franchise was bought by Tony Uhrik and renamed the Uhrik Truckers. The Truckers won ASL titles in 1955 and 1956.

As displaced persons arrived from Europe, they formed soccer clubs and some sought admission to the ASL. The Polish Falcons, for instance. They'd existed in the United States since 1908 as part of a national order. In 1953, with displaced persons the inspiration, soccer was added to the club calendar. Before that, "only a few of the five hundred–odd members were acquainted with the rules of the game," the *ASL News* noted. But the team, playing in Elizabeth, New Jersey, was not successful and withdrew in a few years.

Between 1955 and 1965, the ASL tried several cooperative efforts to form a "super league" with the semipro German-American League in New York and New Jersey. These efforts collapsed due to jealousy, different philosophies, and other internal politics.

Jack Hynes (left) leads Brookhattan against the Philadelphia A's in 1954.

The ASL in 1955 invited the GAL to participate in its Lewis Cup competition (annual ASL play-offs) as a possible prelude to a jointly operated league. The two sent a combined select team to play Wacker SC of Vienna before sixty-four hundred at Zerega Oval in the Bronx on February 20, 1955. The Vienna team won, 4–1.

But in 1955, the USSFA suspended the GAL for refusing to stop playing interstate games. The USSFA said the ASL had the exclusive rights for such games. So the ASL-GAL rivalry was stoked. On February 12, 1956, the ASL all-stars lost, 7–1, to Austria FC before 4,312 at Gaelic Park on a muddy field. The GAL scheduled its best league match on the same day to attract fans away from the ASL game. It wasn't the last time the leagues refused to work together.

Despite the lack of cooperation, by 1956 the ASL tour matches were world-famous and still drawing well. On the same day that Maccabi of Israel played the ASL all-stars before 42,455 at

Yankee Stadium, baseball's Dodgers drew 22,609 at Ebbets Field and the Giants 18,689 for a Polo Grounds doubleheader.

There is some question as to just how profitable these dream matches with foreign teams were for the ASL. Eric Charleson wrote in the *ASL News* in 1957 that under-the-table payments to municipalities took "thousands of dollars" away from tour profits. Charleson said that when soccer people, in turn, asked for some publicity from city fathers to hype their gates, they "were hooted down."

In 1958, one of the most famous matches ever held in the United States pitted Hearts of Scotland against Manchester City. Hearts won, 6–5, in the rain and mud at Ebbets Field. The next year, the ASL brought Legia of Poland, the first team from an Iron Curtain country since World War II to visit the U.S. And when Napoli came to play the ASL all-stars June 21, 1959, at Ebbets Field, invitations were sent to Perry Como, Sophia

Ebbets Field was the site of this exhibition between Sunderland, one of the many foreign squads that toured the U.S., and a team of ASL all-stars in 1956.

Loren, Rocky Marciano, the Italian Ambassador in Washington, DC, and the Italian consul general in New York.

The 1960s saw the arrival and demise of William B. Cox's International Soccer League, which staged international games in the U.S. among foreign teams and also had a New York franchise. In 1960, Manchester United made its third visit; Red Star of Yugoslavia came over and the ASL and GAL continued feuding. The GAL refused to allow its American Czech team to play a preliminary to the Red Star–ASL All-Stars match at Gaelic Park.

Eventually, the GAL and ASL merged, though remaining independent in the 1961–62 season. And in 1964–65, the two leagues got USSFA permission to form a twelve-team Eastern Soccer Conference, which disbanded before the season was over. The lineup was:

New York Hungaria	New York Inter
Boston	Hota
Giuliana	Ukrainian Nationals
BW Gotschee	New York Americans
Newark Ukrainians	Minerva-Pfaelzer
German Hungarians	New York Ukrainian

"It was a wedding where neither the bride nor the groom had much enthusiasm," said Erwin Single, the former radio commentator, soccer writer, and GAL president. "Nobody had any money. There were few colorful foreign players left. The GAL didn't draw well in the ASL cities and vice versa. There was too much traveling. . . ." The same old story.

"Nobody could tell at that point," said Kurt Lamm, "if soccer ever was going to go big or how long it would take." Lamm was an ASL manager with Hakoah and became president of the league (1963–68).

"The ASL was supposed to be a professional league," said Walt Chyzowych, one of the most talented goal scorers of the 1960s. "But I considered it amateur. It was a higher standard of play, sure. But nobody was making any money. It was a joke. There was no money to be had. I got three dollars for expenses [with the Ukrainian Nationals] to practices and six dollars on Sundays.

"Every two or three years, players would leave because of management problems, coaching problems. You coached yourself, really. Somebody just made out the lineup. The weather was always a problem. Scheduling never was very stable. A lot of teams came in with a lot of enthusiasm and found they couldn't exist financially—Polish Falcons, Ludlow (Massachusetts), Brookhattan. . . .

"The teams went day to day, year to year. They didn't have the ability to project long-term planning. The people running the clubs had full-time professions and soccer to them was an avocation." Chyzowych eventually became coach of the U.S. National Team.

In the mid and late 1960s, Enzo Magnozzi picked up Erno Schwarcz's mantle and promoted matches of international stature: Santos of Brazil (without Pelé) vs. Milan, Napoli vs. Independiente of Argentina, and Santos vs. Inter-Milan.

Magnozzi says that he opened the first office in the United States devoted strictly to the buying and selling of soccer players and the staging of tours by foreign teams. He was long associated as owner and later honorary president of the New York Inter franchise, which has had a team in both the GAL and ASL. Magnozzi's presentations set the stage for the arrival of the better-financed NASL. He is one of many who feel the ASL almost killed itself.

The American Soccer League's decline began at a special meeting of the USSFA in Chicago on November 19, 1966. The USSFA stripped the ASL of its exclusive rights to professional soccer in the East and granted additional pro rights to the fledgling United Soccer Association. The next year, interests in Chicago, Milwaukee, Detroit, and Minnesota were refused permission by the USSFA to join the ASL. The stage was set for the merger of the USA and the National Professional Soccer League that produced the NASL in 1968.

"If that happened in 1978," Magnozzi said, "everybody would sue one another. We were hoping the new guys would come through the ASL. They didn't. . . . That's when I dropped out of the ASL. I wasn't gonna lose any more money." The handwriting was on the wall.

"It's like anything else," Walt Chyzowych said. "If you own a grocery store and across the street they start building a big shopping center, it's over for you. That's what happened to the ASL."

"It was like watching an old friend deteriorate," Walt Bahr noted.

Lamm finished his fifth year as ASL president in 1968 and left to join the USSFA, where he is now secretary. Two years earlier, Lamm had formed a committee to aid the organizers of what became the NASL, saying, "It is our sincere hope and wish that [the eventual NASL] be a flourishing organization." By adopting such a stance, the ASL was dooming itself to obscurity.

"How could the ASL compete with the NASL?" Magnozzi said. "Its [ASL] clubs operated strictly on the eastern seaboard. At Inter, my budget was thirty thousand to fifty thousand dollars a year. The NASL teams came in spending two hundred thousand to three hundred thousand dollars. But the ASL—dammit—shouldn't have been all for the NASL hogging the spotlight without indemnifying anybody. . . . I left the league because it was standing still."

A summary of the ASL's 1967 foreign tour program shows that the ASL lost $4,986.12, though it paid over $34,000 in gate receipts to Chelsea of England and Dundee of Scotland. The mismanagement was apparent. By 1967–68, the ASL had organized itself into a twelve-team, two-division league. It looked like this:

Rochester Lancers	New York Inter
Washington Britannica	Hartford SC
Newark Ukrainian	New Brunswick Hungarians
Boston Tigers	Roma (N.J.) SC
Ukrainian Nationals	Newark Portuguese
Baltimore St. Gerard's	Astros (Mass.)

The only noticeable changes from the early days were the admission of the Rochester and Washington clubs. The ASL teams still operated on small budgets, had ethnic followings, played in dusty ovals, had part-time players and small crowds. The ASL lived in the past and wasn't equipped to handle the future.

Edner Breton, picked up from Haiti by the NASL's Detroit Cougars, played a couple of exhibition games for Rochester's ASL team in 1968. "It was like a bunch of kids playing in a park with no organization whatsoever," he said.

FACING EXTINCTION, 1969–75

By 1970, the ASL had only eight teams, with just two of them left in the New York metropolitan area—Newark Sitch and New York Inter. The other members were: Washington Darts, Philadelphia Spartans, Philadelphia Ukes, Syracuse Scorpions, Rochester Lancers, and Boston Astros. The Washington and Rochester teams then defected to the NASL. Inter was suspended. The Philadelphia Ukrainians moved to the GAL. The Syracuse franchise folded. Newark Sitch withdrew.

For a time, there were only two teams lining up for the 1971 season: the Boston Astros and the Philadelphia Spartans. If not for the efforts of Eugene Chyzowych, Walt's brother, the oldest pro soccer league in the United States might have folded that year.

"I took the league over as president," Eugene Chyzowych said. "I called my friends around the U.S. and asked them if they'd possibly want to be owners in the ASL. I was very successful. I found coaches for them and I helped to organize each team."

He got a new group in New York to take over the vacant Inter franchise—calling itself the New York Greeks. That club won the 1971 title with a 7–1–2 record. There were four other clubs that year: Boston Astros, Philadelphia Spartans, Syracuse Suns, and the short-lived Virginians.

By 1972, with USSFA approval, Chyzowych had formed a twelve-team league with three conferences, and the patient had been revived; the set-up was:

MIDWEST	NORTHEAST
Cincinnati	New York
Cleveland	Boston
Detroit	Northeast
Pittsburgh	New Jersey

MID-ATLANTIC
Philadelphia
Delaware
Baltimore
Washington

It didn't much matter that within five years the ASL again would contract to nine teams, four of them on the West Coast. The important thing was that Chyzowych kept the league alive. And in doing so, he changed its emphasis from foreign tour promotion to the advocacy of American players.

"St. Louis used all American boys," Chyzowych said. "Delaware, too. I said we cannot continue playing with Ukrainians, Italians, and Portuguese; we have to open doors for Americans. I said the league should exist for the American kids. And we slowed down on the foreign tour business."

The franchise shifts and player turbulence continued for the ASL through the 1970s. Salaries hadn't improved much in twenty years. Breton remembers being one of the then New York Apollo's highest-paid players at fifty dollars a game in 1973. "Others were getting twenty-five dollars a game," he said. "But each year it got better."

There are those who will say privately that having Bob Cousy become ASL commissioner in December 1974 was farcical. What could a man who spent over two decades of his life playing and coaching basketball possibly know about, or do for, soccer? Cousy is a realist. He knew virtually nothing about the game when he was hired. He admitted that. But he felt he could contribute something: his image.

"Oh, hell," Cousy said in a 1976 interview. "That's what life's about. Whatever function we fulfill, someone uses our services. This [soccer] is what I sell. . . . The ASL needs exposure and it came to me as a national sports figure whose name is somewhat known and who hopefully can bring creditability to the league. People want a candid,

An American sports hero from another game, basketball's Bob Cousy became the ASL commissioner after the 1974 season.

Cleveland's Miguel Perrichon kicks over Pittsburgh's Mike Angeliotti in 1975.

tell-it-like-it-is approach rather than bull. The important thing is that if Bob Cousy says it, that's the way it is."

There is no doubt that the ASL started making a comeback by 1976 that boded well for the league's future. Franchises in Cincinnati, Boston, Pittsburgh, and New Jersey were dropped before the 1976 season, but the league still was able to field eleven teams, including one in Chicago for the first time and five in the West: Los Angeles, Tacoma, Utah, Oakland, and Sacramento. The ASL was trying to step out of its stereotype as a strictly eastern league and to "go national."

"The ASL has been around since 1933," Cousy said. "It has the tradition. The other league has no tradition, but it has the loot. . . . The West Coast teams are well funded and in for the long haul. . . . Pelé has helped us more than them [NASL] because he's given exposure to both leagues. I'm happy they're the ones who paid the tab."

The ASL has continued Gene Chyzowych's idea that it should deemphasize foreign tours and emphasize its own commitment to Americanizing pro soccer. The ASL has no limit on the amount of starters who can be foreign born, but it does prevent teams from importing any more than six foreign players a season.

"We have conducted tours," deputy ASL commissioner Otto Radich said, "but on a much more modest scale. With the advent of the NASL and because of the extension of league schedules, international tour games don't seem to be that profitable. Times have changed in Europe, too. Whereas ten years ago a First Division German team might come over for eight, ten games, that's impossible now because they play more games out of season over there. And there is the cost factor. Ten years ago I could get a top team for three thousand dollars a game and expenses. Now, they wouldn't come over for under ten thousand dollars a game."

The ASL finished the 1978 season with ten teams in two divisions that looked like this:

EASTERN	WESTERN
New York Apollo	California Sunshine
New Jersey Americans	Sacramento Spirits
Connecticut Yankees	Los Angeles Skyhawks
Cleveland Cobras	Los Angeles Lazers
New York Eagles	
Indy Daredevils	

The league completed its tenth summer season playing a twenty-four–match schedule from April to September that ended with New York Apollo taking its fourth championship since joining the ASL as "the Greeks" in 1971. It defeated the Skyhawks, 1–0, in the title game, for the Coors Cup, awarded to ASL champs by a beer company. If that is commercialism, the ASL welcomes it.

None of the ASL teams made any money in 1978, Radich said. Indeed, Apollo general manager Fred Bachman reported that his team lost one hundred and fifty thousand dollars, for a three-year total of five hundred thousand dollars since the Apollo moved from Westchester to Long Island's Hofstra University. The league seeks to equalize costs by having all teams share equally in travel expenses. Radich said that the ASL teams' average budgets in 1978 were three hundred thousand to three hundred and fifty thousand dollars, roughly ten times the average a decade ago, but still far behind the NASL's payrolls. The Indy club led the league with a total attendance of 46,512 at twelve home games; the Apollo drew a reported 38,032 at home, including 7,247 May 29 on opening night.

The signing of a major foreign star by the ASL might do for the ASL what Joe Namath's signing did for the American Football League—gain it publicity and possibly a merger with the other league.

The only name players the ASL signed in 1978 were aging internationals near the end of their careers who did little for their teams at the gate. Former Pelé teammates from Brazil, Ramon Mifflin and Rildo, signed with the New York Eagles and Los Angeles Lazers, respectively. Portuguese 1966 World Cup veterans Eusebio and Antonio Simoes signed with New Jersey Americans and managed just two goals and six assists between them in a dozen games. Eusebio reportedly scored the one thousandth goal of his career to enable him to join Pelé as the only players in history over that plateau. But he showed little of the brilliance of past decades.

The kind of players the ASL needs, it can't keep. Ringo Cantillo played four years with the now-defunct Cincinnati Comets, then was the league Most Valuable Player at age twenty-one in 1977 with the New Jersey Americans. Cantillo jumped to the North American Soccer League. Keith Van Eron, a college All-American at Hart-

New York Apollo Dave Power is closest to the ball in the 1978 Eastern Division championship game against the New Jersey Americans. The Apollo eliminated the defending ASL champions and went on to win the league title.

wick and the ASL's all-star keeper in 1977, deserted the low-paying Apollo for the NASL's Houston Hurricane.

The ASL has remained a "semipro" league played by part-time players. The salaries for some have crept near the ten thousand dollars-a-year range, but the players still can't make a living at that level. A look at the 1978 Apollo told the story. Goalie Jamil Canal, 29, was a building superintendent in Manhattan. Midfielder David Power handled baggage complaints at Kennedy Airport

for KLM. Left wing Edner Breton was a ticket agent there. Right back Chris Tyson, 26, drove a school bus.

Still, some who had been around the ASL awhile saw improvements. The Apollo played—and won—all twelve home games on a brand new four-hundred-thousand-dollar SuperTurf artificial surface at night at Hofstra. They attracted more media coverage on Long Island than ever before. They played exciting soccer. They attracted some commercial sponsors.

Trevor Dawkins, captain of Sacramento Gold, and coach Bill Williams celebrate their 1979 ASL championship. Dawkins is wearing the Columbus Magic jersey of Keith Peacock.

Early in the 1979 season, the New Jersey Americans pulled a major coup on behalf of the league by signing former New York Cosmos coach Eddie Firmani to a three-year contract for an estimated one hundred thousand dollars a year.

"It [the ASL] is definitely recovering," Breton said. "The ASL definitely needs the NASL, and everybody owes the NASL a debt of gratitude. But I think the ASL's going to make it, too."

He isn't the first to express that sentiment.

ASL Champions

1934 Kearny Irish
1935 Philadelphia Germans
1936 New York Americans
1937 Kearny Scots
1938 Kearny Scots
1939 Kearny Scots
1940 Kearny Scots
1941 Kearny Scots
1942 Philadelphia Americans
1943 Brooklyn Hispanos
1944 Philadelphia Americans
1945 New York Brookhattan

1946 Baltimore Americans
1947 Philadelphia Americans
1948 Philadelphia Americans
1949 Philadelphia Nationals
1950 Philadelphia Nationals
1951 Philadelphia Nationals
1952 Philadelphia Americans
1953 Philadelphia Nationals
1954 New York Americans
1955 Uhrik Truckers
1956 Uhrik Truckers
1957 New York Hakoah
1958 New York Hakoah
1959 New York Hakoah
1960 Colombo
1961 Ukrainian Nationals
1962 Ukrainian Nationals
1963 Ukrainian Nationals
1964 Urkanian Nationals
1965 Hartford SC
1966 Roma SC
1967 Baltimore St. Gerard's
1968 Ukrainian Nationals
1968 Washington Darts (interval season)
1969 Washington Darts
1970 Philadelphia Ukrainians
1971 New York Greeks
1972 Cincinnati Comets
1973 New York Apollo
1974 Rhode Island Oceaneers
1975 Boston Astros–New York Apollo
1976 Los Angeles Skyhawks
1977 New Jersey Americans
1978 New York Apollo
1979 Sacramento Gold

Most Valuable Player

1945 **Steve Rozbora**, New York Brookhattan
1946 **Ray McFaul**, Baltimore Americans
1947 **Joe "Lefty" Mervine**, Philadelphia Americans
1948 **John O'Connell**, Brooklyn Wanderers
1949 **John O'Connell**, New York Americans
1950 **Joe Maca**, Brooklyn Hispano
1951 **John Donald**, Kearny Scots
1952 Not available
1953 Not available
1954 **Cyril Hannaby**, Baltimore Rockets
1955 **Jack Ferris**, Uhrik Truckers
1956 **Jack Hynes**, New York Hakoah
1957 **John Oliver**, Uhrik Truckers
1958 **Walter Kudenko**, Ukrainian Nationals
1959 **Juri Kulishenko**, Ukrainian Nationals
1960 **Andy Racz**, Ukrainian Nationals
1961 **Mike Noha**, Ukrainian Nationals
1962 **Pete Millar**, Inter SC
1963 **Pete Millar**, Inter SC

1964 **Avner Wollanow**, New York Americans
1965 **Alberto Falak**, Roma
1966 **Walter Chyzowych**, Ukrainian Sitch
1967 **M. Worobec**, Newark Sitch
1968 **R. Waugh**, Inter SC
1969 **Robert Waugh**, New York Inter
1970 Not available
1971 **Bob Hatzos**, New York Greeks
1972 **Ringo Cantillo**, Cincinnati Comets
1973 **Helio "Boom-Boom" Barbosa**, Boston Astros
1974 **Ringo Cantillo**, Cincinnati Comets
1975 **Jose Neto**, Rhode Island Oceaneers
1976 **Jimmy Hinch**, Los Angeles Skyhawks
1977 **Ringo Cantillo**, New Jersey Americans
1978 **Jim Rolland**, Los Angeles Skyhawks
1979 **Poli Garcia**, California Sunshine

Coach of the Year

1956 **John Grabowski**, Falcons
1957 **Kurt Lamm**, Hakoah
1958 **Wassyl Borak**, Ukrainian Nationals
1959 **Charley McGill**, Fall River SC
1960 **Walter Medusha**, Ukrainian Nationals
1961 **Enzo Magnozzi**, Inter SC
1962 **Kurt Lamm**, Hakoah
1963 **Charley McGill**, Fall River SC
1964 **Enzo Magnozzi**, Inter SC
1965 **Paul Pantano**, Hartford SC
1966 **Louis Pietrocola**, Roma S.
1967 **Eugene Chyzowych**, Newark Sitch
1968 **Norman Sutherland**, Washington Darts
1969 **Norman Sutherland**, Washington Darts
1970 Not available
1971 **John Bertos**, Boston Astros
1972 **Nick Cappuro**, Cincinnati Comets
1973 **John Bertos**, Boston Astros
1974 **Manfred Schellscheidt**, Rhode Island Oceaneers
1975 **Herbie Haller**, Cleveland Cobras
1976 **Ron Newman**, Los Angeles Skyhawks
1977 **Bob Ridley**, Sacramento Spirits
1978 **Derek Lawther**, California Sunshine
1979 **Willie Ehrlich**, Pennsylvania Stoners

Rookie of the Year

1973 **Doug McMillan**, Cleveland Stars
1974 Not available
1975 **Roberto Taylor**, Connecticut Wildcats
1976 **John Roeslein**, New Jersey Americans
    Steve Ralbovsky, Los Angeles Skyhawks
1977 **Mal Roche**, Sacramento Spirits
1978 **Emilio John**, Sacramento Gold
1979 **John McDermott**, Las Vegas Seagulls

Pelé came and Pelé conquered; he turned the hearts of Americans toward soccer.

8

The North American Soccer League

The leisure and calm of the United States Soccer Football Association (USSFA) was shattered in the spring and summer of 1966. A small office with a two-person staff was suddenly besieged with applications from businessmen wanting to start professional soccer leagues.

Pro soccer in the true sense of the term had been only a dream in the United States for more than thirty years. The American Soccer League briefly had flourished before World War II, drawing a few respectable crowds in five figures in a few East Coast cities. But the ASL long since had settled back into semipro status, and few dreamers had mentioned pro soccer in decades.

But American sport was lunging out in all directions in the mid-1960s, like a hyperthyroid baby. The success of the American Football League and of baseball's West Coast expansion had changed the thinking of businessmen with extra dollars looking for investment. In particular, stadium owners with long-range debts to pay were casting about in search of new teams to rent their fields.

Slowly, word had filtered across the oceans about the successes of the great soccer teams of Europe—Manchester United, Benfica, Real Madrid, Inter Milan, Borussia Munchengladbach, Red Star Belgrade, and others. The word was out that soccer was a cheap sport, both in equipment and in salaries. Weren't there stadia of two hundred thousand and one hundred fifty thousand capacity brimmed to the top with wildly enthusiastic fans? Reports filtered across of the excite-

ment in England over the upcoming World Cup, about the huge crowds which would attend.

Suddenly there was a fever. The USSFA was shocked and unprepared when not one, not two, but three groups of wealthy would-be owners applied for sanction to operate a professional league in the U.S. beginning the following spring, 1967.

While the wheels were put in motion to choose among the three, NBC-TV threw a few coals on the fire. It televised, on a slight tape delay from the London suburb of Wembley, the World Cup final. England defeated West Germany, 4–2 in overtime, in an emotional if not classic match. The final alone amounted to a gate of $573,454. The entire tournament drew 1.5 million spectators paying $7 million—and that on the limited British economy, before television revenues were even figured.

Even the American media seemed to notice. The morning after the final, the Dallas *Morning News* ran a picture on the front of its sports section of Germany's dramatic tying goal in the last thirty seconds of regulation time. The caption read in part, "If you tuned in Channel 5 Saturday afternoon and wondered what the Cowboys and Rams were doing out there scrimmaging in short pants, you just didn't understand the name of the game. It was soccer, old chap."

Soon, the chaps with the big money arrived at decision time. In return for its sanction, which included the machinery with which to recruit players from other countries in the approved fashion, USSFA wanted 4 percent of the gate receipts, 10 percent of the television money and a twenty-five thousand dollar franchise fee from each club.

Two of the three groups said, "Hogwash." The third, which included probably the most money and surely the biggest names, agreed. This was the group headed by Lamar Hunt, Jack Kent Cooke, John Weston Adams, John Allyn, Gabe Paul, Vernon Stauffer, William Clay Ford, Judge Roy Hofheinz, and Earl Foreman. Initially it called itself the North American Soccer League. That was soon changed, to avoid conflict with another group's name, to the United Soccer Association (USA).

The other two groups merged and founded the National Professional Soccer League (NPSL). This league numbered among its owners Robert Hermann of St. Louis and Bill Bartholomay of Atlanta. Without USSFA sanction, the NPSL was branded an "outlaw" league, meaning that the players it recruited were subject to penalty from the international governing body, FIFA, for having signed with the league. But the NPSL didn't care. It had outfoxed the USA and signed what it publicized as a "ten-year contract" with CBS for a national TV Game of the Week.

Actually, the contract paid only a pittance for the TV rights, and it was renewable annually—at CBS' option. But it did give the NPSL, and the whole soccer experiment, some credibility.

Immediately the owners rented the biggest and most expensive stadia they could find. Coaches were hired virtually blindly—some good, some mediocre.

The USA believed it would not be able to put together its own teams from scratch in nine months, so it decided to import entire foreign teams to represent its franchises. It would construct its own teams for the 1968 season. Twelve cities were organized for the beginning in June 1967.

Of course, the NPSL had its own ideas. It would start two months earlier, with ten teams, all pieceworked together in a few months by signing itinerant players from virtually every country on the globe. Unproven amateurs, faded stars, and journeymen alike signed contracts for comfortable if not fat salaries.

The race was on.

1967

It was suspected by some that Ernie Kovacs wrote the script for pro soccer's initial season. There were clowns, jugglers, pratfalls, everything except the Nairobi Trio, and maybe even that.

It started April 16 in Baltimore, with the NPSL Baltimore Bays meeting the Atlanta Chiefs. The attendance was 8,434, not exactly the throng which had been anticipated. CBS' cameras saw a bitter defensive struggle which the Bays won, 1–0. The NPSL had adopted the scoring system of six points for a win and a point for each goal, so Baltimore chalked up seven points in the standings, the Chiefs zero.

Manning the microphones were the cool professional play-by-play man, Jack Whitaker, and former Irish soccer star Danny Blanchflower. Arguments still are heard over Blanchflower's commentary. The man was brutally frank, and such was the quality of play that he spent most of the summer telling the viewers how lacking was the soccer they were seeing. The league kept wishing he would be stranded permanently in the Lincoln Tunnel, as crowds and TV ratings dwindled.

St. Louis drew 20,985 fans for its season opener, but the spoiled and discriminating fans in that city, long America's soccer capital, soon turned their backs on the Stars. By the warmth of summer the NPSL was on its way to a league-wide average gate of 4,879. St. Louis would be its top draw, with a 7,613 average, while Chicago set a pattern of its soccer interest which has held true, averaging 2,588 per game. Chicago drew crowds of 870, 811, and 897.

The standard of play was erratic in the NPSL, but the league included some talented and smart players, such as Phil Woosnam, Ron Newman, Ken Bracewell, Cesar Luis Menotti (who in 1978 would coach Argentina to the World Cup championship), Gordon Bradley, John Best, Vic Crowe, Art Welch, Gabbo Gavric, Mirko Stojanovic, Ilija Mitic, and Warren Archibald, all of whom played in the NPSL in 1967.

But the NPSL teams were United Nations experiments—only eight Americans were in the league. It suffered also because of its television contract. On May 15, barely a month after the first game, referee Peter Rhodes admitted that eleven of the twenty-one fouls he called in the tele-

Ilija Mitic (10) was an NPSL pioneer with the Oakland Clippers. Shown here as a Dallas Tornado in 1975 against the Denver Dynamos, Mitic would finish his nine-year American career with the NASL San Jose Earthquakes in 1978, scoring 101 goals and 239 points, both league records.

vised Toronto–Pittsburgh game were phonies to allow CBS to work in commercials. On one occasion, Rhodes had to push one player down who was trying to get up and resume the game because the commercial hadn't finished.

In this atmosphere of snickers and rolled eyeballs, the USA began play on May 28. Its owners were confident of success, since it had brought in what it would tell the public were twelve of the best teams in the world. In fact, they were a mixed breed.

Wolverhampton of England, representing Los Angeles as the Los Angeles Wolves, proved to be the elite of the league, along with the Washington Whips (Aberdeen of Scotland) and the Cleveland Stokers (Stoke City of England). Other cities had the misfortune to be represented by a country's lesser light, such as Dundee United of Scotland (Dallas), Cerro of Uruguay (New York), and Bangu of Brazil (Houston). Two of the teams were actually amateur: Glentoran of Belfast (Detroit) and ADO of Holland (San Francisco). The others were Sunderland of England (Vancouver), Cagliari of Italy (Chicago), and Hibernian of Scotland (Toronto).

With a shorter season, a series of exhibition games which whetted appetites, and more lead time, the USA got off to a better start. Among the opening crowds were 34,965 in the Astrodome, 21,871 in Yankee Stadium, and 16,431 in Dallas' Cotton Bowl. No opener drew less than 7,400.

Crowds didn't keep pace, of course, and the league average finished at 7,890. Houston was the pacesetter with its 19,802 average, and Boston was lowest at 4,171. The low crowd was 648 in a rainstorm at Detroit.

Competition was heated in USA games. Detroit player-coach John Colrain was suspended for punching a linesman. A Detroit–Houston game was abandoned because of a brawl. Italian fans at a Chicago–New York game chased referee Leo Goldstein off the field, ending that game early. Two days later, the Chicago (Cagliari) team left the field in protest of a referee's decision, Italian Day fans invaded the field, and that game was also abandoned. USA Commissioner Dick Walsh had to suspend three Cagliari players and withhold the team's match fee. Eventually, both leagues came down to high-quality finishes.

The USA went into its play-offs first, the second week of July. The Los Angeles Wolves, by the flip of a coin, won the right to play host to the championship game against Eastern Division champion Washington. The game drew 17,824 to Memorial Coliseum, and they saw one of the most exciting games in U.S. soccer history.

After thirty-six minutes of overtime, Los Angeles won the championship, 6–5, when Washington defender Ally Shewan accidentally nudged a long Wolves pass into his own net. Four goals were scored within three and a half minutes midway through the second half, and each team scored during the thirty-minute overtime.

The entire Wolverhampton team received the handsome bonus of three thousand dollars for its championship. Later, Oakland Clippers players would receive one thousand five hundred dollars apiece for winning the NPSL title.

The Clippers prevailed over Baltimore in a two-game, total-goals series in September. Dennis Viollet's goal gave the Bays a 1–0 win for a home crowd of 16,619. But in the second leg at Oakland

Coliseum, Dragan Djukic scored the hat trick as coach Aleksander Obradovic's Clippers took a 4–1 triumph before 9,037 fans.

Yanko Daucik of Toronto led the NPSL in scoring with twenty goals and eight assists, and Philadelphia defender Ruben "The Hatchet" Navarro was MVP. Willie Roy scored seventeen goals and was Rookie of the Year. Chicago (Cagliari)'s Roberto Boninsegna was USA top scorer with ten goals, one assist, in only nine games.

1967 FINAL SEASON STANDINGS AND STATISTICS

UNITED SOCCER ASSOCIATION

Eastern Division	W	L	T	GF	GA	TP*
Washington	5	2	5	19	11	15
Cleveland	5	3	4	19	13	14
Toronto	4	3	5	23	17	13
Detroit	3	3	6	11	18	12
New York	2	4	6	15	17	10
Boston	2	7	3	12	26	7

Western Division						
Los Angeles	5	2	5	21	14	15
San Francisco	5	4	3	25	19	13
Chicago	3	2	7	20	14	13
Houston	4	4	4	19	18	12
Vancouver	3	4	5	20	28	11
Dallas	3	6	3	14	23	9

*USA TP-2 pts. win, 1 pt. tie, 0 pts. loss

PLAYOFF RESULTS

Championship Game
July 14 at Los Angeles—Los Angeles 6, Washington 5 (OT)

NATIONAL PROFESSIONAL SOCCER LEAGUE

Eastern Division						
Baltimore	14	9	9	53	47	162†
Philadelphia	14	9	9	53	43	157
New York	11	13	8	60	58	143
Atlanta	10	12	9	51	46	135
Pittsburgh	10	14	7	59	74	132

Western Division						
Oakland	19	8	5	64	34	185
St. Louis	14	11	7	54	57	156
Chicago	10	11	11	50	55	142
Toronto	10	17	5	59	70	127
Los Angeles	7	15	10	42	61	114

†NPSL TP-6 pts. win, 3 pts. tie, 1 pt. for each goal up to maximum of 3 per team, 0 pts. loss

PLAYOFF RESULTS

Championship Games
Sept. 3 at Baltimore—Baltimore 1, Oakland 0
Sept. 9 at Oakland—Oakland 4, Baltimore 1
Oakland wins on 4-2 goal difference

1967 UNITED SOCCER ASSOCIATION

Leading Scorers

	GP	G	A	TP
Roberto Boninsegna, Chicago	9	10	1	21
Henk Houwaart, San Francisco	12	9	2	20
Paulo Borges, Houston	8	6	3	15
Peter Dobing, Cleveland	8	7	0	14
Rene Pas, San Francisco	9	6	2	14
Peter Cormack, Toronto	11	6	1	13
Benedicto Ribeiro, New York	12	5	2	12
Colin Stein, Toronto	8	5	1	11
Jim Storrie, Washington	12	5	1	11

Leading Goalkeepers

	GP	Min.	SV	GA	SH	GAA
John Farmer, Cleveland	3	250	6	1	2	0.36
Paul Shardlow, Cleveland	4	254	18	2	0	0.71
Robert Clark, Washington	12	1080	71	11	5	0.92
Phil Parkes, Los Angeles	7	630	30	7	1	1.000
Pietro Pianta, Chicago	7	627	57	7	1	1.004
John Kennedy, Detroit	12	1017	105	14	4	1.24
Osmar Miguelucci, New York	7	582	27	9	1	1.39
Fred Davies, Los Angeles	5	450	37	7	1	1.40
Adriano Reginato, Chicago	5	442	29	7	1	1.425
Allan Thomson, Toronto	12	1072	60	17	1	1.427

1967 NATIONAL PROFESSIONAL SOCCER LEAGUE

Leading Scorers

	GP	G	A	TP
Yanko Daucik, Toronto	17	20	8	48
Willie Roy, Chicago	27	17	5	39
Eli Durate, Los Angeles	23	15	5	35
Rudi Kolbl, St. Louis	19	13	8	34
Manfred Rummel, Pittsburgh	19	14	4	32
Bora Kostic, St. Louis	23	13	5	31
Oscar Lopez, Toronto	19	13	5	31
George Kirby, New York	12	14	2	30
Ilija Mitic, Oakland	19	13	3	29
Norb Pogrzeba, St. Louis	24	11	6	28
Ernie Winchester, Chicago	13	13	2	28

Leading Goalkeepers

	GP	SV	GA	SH	GAA
Mirko Stojanovic, Oakland	29	287	29	10	1.00
Klaus Griletz, Chicago	3	20	3	1	1.00
Ernesto Lopera, Philadelphia	8	84	8	4	1.07
Terry Adlington, Baltimore	25	206	32	7	1.27
Sven Lindberg, Atlanta	16	134	22	3	1.37
Gernot Fraydl, Philadelphia	25	280	35	7	1.43
Nigel Sims, Toronto	2	27	3	0	1.50
Paul Freitag, New York	15	136	24	3	1.66

GP—Games Played
W—Won
L—Lost
T—Tie
G—Goals
GF—Goals For
GA—Goals Against

GAA—Goals Against Average
A—Assists
TP—Total Points
SV—Saves
SH—Shutouts
Min.—Minutes

1968

Seeing financial disaster ahead, the two leagues merged in December 1967 and formed the North American Soccer League—with two commissioners, one from each of the original circuits.

Seventeen of the original twenty-two teams were retained, and all played the entire 1968 sea-son. The merger was precipitated in part by an $18 million antitrust suit which the NPSL filed against virtually everybody, including the USA, USSFA, FIFA, and even the poor Canadian FA (Football Association). FIFA's blacklisting of NPSL players was one example cited. The suit never went to court.

CBS came back for another year, minus the volatile Blanchflower, who was replaced by the more mellow Mario Machado. A few North American citizens, thirty in all, were sprinkled among the seventeen teams, but there were still only ten native-born Americans.

New talent was recruited from overseas, including the little Pole, John Kowalik, the league MVP who scored thirty goals and nine assists to set records which stood for ten years. The great Ferenc Puskas was brought in to coach the Vancouver Royals, and Gordon Jago took over the Baltimore Bays. The Washington Whips fielded the only one-armed player in NASL history, Victorio Casa of Argentina.

The caliber of play reached new heights—in fact, a level of quality which was not matched again until 1977. Touring teams learned it the hard way. Both the Cleveland Stokers and the New York Generals defeated Pelé and his Santos of Brazil team. Malcolm Allison brought his proud Manchester City team over from England and promptly lost to the Atlanta Chiefs, coached by Phil Woosnam and numbering among its players Ron Newman, Peter McParland, Vic Crowe, Vic Rouse, Kaiser "Boy Boy" Motaung, and Emment Kapengwe. After the defeat, Allison churlishly told the press the Chiefs were a mediocre team.

Atlanta challenged Allison to a rematch, and he accepted. After going to the West Coast, where City lost to the Oakland Clippers, Allison took his team back through Atlanta. He lost again.

Of course the league had its casualties, the Dallas Tornado being No. 1. Owners Lamar Hunt and Bill McNutt hired a sly Yugoslav, Bob Kap, as coach. Kap recruited a team of untried teenagers, amateurs all, and took them on a winter world tour to season and meld them. They proved to be hopelessly outclassed, suffering beatings of 6–0 and 8–2 almost routinely, and failed to win in their first twenty-one games. After firing Kap, coaching the team themselves for a game, going through a second coach, Hunt and McNutt hired Ron Newman, who had never coached before. The team managed to finish with a 2-26-4 record, setting a standard of failure which has never since been approached.

Eventually, Atlanta won the Atlantic Division, Cleveland the Lakes Division, Kansas City the Gulf Division, and San Diego the Pacific Division, by one point over Oakland (the two had identical 18-8-6 records).

In best-of-three semifinals, Atlanta ousted Cleveland in two games, and San Diego did the same to Kansas City. The championship round was a two-game, total-goals series. Atlanta and San Diego drew 0-0 at San Diego, as league-leading Toros goalie Ataulfo Sanchez (0.93 average) starred. In the second leg at Atlanta, the Chiefs surged to a 3-0 triumph. Woosnam was Coach of the Year and Motaung was Rookie of the Year.

There were no real winners, though. Within two months, virtually every team in the league folded. As far as the general public and many of the owners were concerned, the NASL ceased to exist by Christmas. The St. Louis Stars admitted to having lost $1.5 million in two years. Losses from the first season alone had run to $6 million for the two leagues, and every club saw at least $200,000 go down the drain. In 1968, continued rental of big stadia and large salaries ended most of the owners' interest in soccer for good.

1968 FINAL SEASON STANDINGS AND STATISTICS

EASTERN CONFERENCE

Atlantic Division	W	L	T	GF	GA	BP	TP
Atlanta	18	7	6	50	32	48	174
Washington	15	10	7	63	53	56	167
New York	12	8	12	62	54	36	164
Baltimore	13	16	3	42	43	41	128
Boston	9	17	6	51	69	49	121

Lakes Division	W	L	T	GF	GA	BP	TP
Cleveland	14	7	11	62	44	58	175
Chicago	13	10	9	68	68	59	164
Toronto	13	13	6	55	69	48	144
Detroit	6	21	4	48	65	40	88

WESTERN CONFERENCE

Gulf Division	W	L	T	GF	GA	BP	TP
Kansas City	16	11	5	61	43	47	158
Houston	14	12	6	58	41	48	150
St. Louis	12	14	6	47	59	40	130
Dallas	2	26	4	28	109	28	52

Pacific Division	W	L	T	GF	GA	BP	TP
San Diego	18	8	6	65	38	60	186
Oakland	18	8	6	71	38	59	185
Los Angeles	11	13	8	55	52	49	139
Vancouver	12	15	5	51	60	49	136

PLAYOFF RESULTS

Eastern Conference
Sept. 11 at Cleveland—Atlanta 1, Cleveland 1.
Sept. 14 at Atlanta—Atlanta 2, Cleveland 1 in sudden-death overtime.

Western Conference
Sept. 11 at Kansas City—San Diego 1, Kansas City 1
Sept. 16 at San Diego—San Diego 1, Kansas City 0 in overtime.

League Championship
Sept. 21 at San Diego—Atlanta 0, San Diego 0.
Sept. 28 at Atlanta—Atlanta 3, San Diego 0.

Leading Scorers	GP	G	A	TP
John Kowalik, Chicago	28	30	9	69
Cirilo Fernandez, San Diego	29	30	7	67
Ilija Mitic, Oakland	28	18	12	48
Henry Klein, Vancouver	26	20	4	44
Iris DeBrito, Toronto	22	21	2	44

Leading Goalkeepers	GP	Min.	SV	GA	GAA
Ataulfo Sanchez, San Diego	22	1849	130	19	0.93
Vic Rouse, Atlanta	26	2340	106	25	0.96
Mirko Stojanovic, Oakland	30	2571	178	32	1.12
Lief Neilsen, Houston	30	2683	144	37	1.24
Bert Hoogerman, Kansas City	30	2676	189	38	1.28

1969

Credit must go to Lamar Hunt and Phil Woosnam for soccer even surviving its first two U.S. pro seasons. Most of the owners dropped out after 1968, and others argued over which way to go: the big-budget route which didn't work, or the low-budget approach.

A meeting was held in Atlanta on January 7, 1969, at which Atlanta Chiefs coach Woosnam was persuaded to try to convince ten owners to stay with the league. Five agreed. Woosnam was encouraged to move up, from player in 1967 and coach in 1968, to become the NASL's executive director, and he accepted.

Woosnam's first act was to impose a ceiling of two hundred fifty thousand dollars on each club's budget. He set up an "office" in a locker room in the bowels of Atlanta Stadium and arm-twisted

It was a championship season for the Kansas City Spurs.

Manfred Seissler (left), from Germany, and Eric Barber, from Ireland, were among the four Kansas City Spurs who earned spots on the all-star team in 1969.

Clive Toye, formerly general manager of the Baltimore Bays, to join him as director of administration and information.

So with Atlanta, Dallas, Kansas City, Baltimore, and St. Louis fielding teams, the NASL played a sixteen-game schedule. It was preceded by a bravura reprise of the 1967 USA, an International Cup in which again five teams (all British) were imported to represent the league cities. West Ham United of England, which included World Cup heroes Geoff Hurst, Bobby Moore, and Martin Peters, played Dundee United of Scotland at Dallas' Cobb Stadium before a rousing crowd of 714.

After that double round robin, the league bridged the old to the new by having the guest club play the home club in each city; for example, Wolverhampton vs Kansas City Spurs. Then the sixteen-game league schedule was run off, sans playoffs—another Woosnam economy measure.

The season climaxed with a controversial finish, aptly demonstrating the effects of the NASL scoring system. Atlanta had the best won-loss-tie record, 11–2–3. But Kansas City's 10–2–4 mark was accompanied by fifty-three goals scored, compared to Atlanta's forty-six. With four bonus points offsetting Atlanta's extra victory, Kansas City won the league championship by a single point, 110–109.

"Boy Boy" Motaung, the clever South African, was scoring champion with sixteen goals, four assists, and Atlanta teammate Manfred Kammerer led the goalies with a 1.07 average. Individual honors went to Kansas City's Cirilio Fernandez, MVP, and the Baltimore Bays' Siegfried Stritzl, Rookie of the Year.

Americanization finally was ventured in the NASL, as St. Louis had fourteen Yanks on its eighteen-man roster. It was the beginning of a three-year period during which the team bravely waved its American flags and got trounced for its efforts. Its record in 1969 was 3–11–2.

Crowds had fallen to around thirty-four hundred per game in 1968, and they dwindled almost out of sight in 1969. It's safe to say the league average was well below three thousand. But with low budgets and short schedule, the league survived the year and would never sink so low again.

1969 FINAL SEASON STANDINGS AND STATISTICS

No Play-offs were held this year

	W	L	T	GF	GA	BP	TP
Kansas City	10	2	4	53	28	38	110
Atlanta	11	2	3	46	20	34	109
Dallas	8	6	2	32	31	28	82
St. Louis	3	11	2	24	47	23	47
Baltimore	2	13	1	27	56	27	42

Leading Scorers	G	A	TP
Kaiser Motaung, Atlanta	16	4	36
George Benitez, Kansas City	15	5	35
Ilija Mitic, Dallas	11	4	26
Fons Stoffels, Kansas City	8	7	23
Manfred Seissler, Kansas City	8	6	22
Emment Kapengwe, Atlanta	7	6	20
Ademar Saccone, Kansas City	9	1	19
Peter Millar, Baltimore	8	2	18
Cirilo Fernandez, Kansas City	6	6	18
Everald Cummings, Atlanta	6	6	18
Freddie Mwila, Atlanta	7	1	15
Tom Ferguson, St. Louis	7	1	15
Peter Short, Dallas	6	2	14

Leading Goalkeepers	GP	SV	GA	GAA
Manfred Kammerer, Atlanta	14	56	15	1.07
Humberto Arrieta, Dallas	14	49	22	1.57
Leonel Conde, Kansas City	16	83	28	1.75
Dave Jokerst, St. Louis	14	111	39	2.78
Orrie Banach, Baltimore	13	99	42	3.23

1970

Midway through the 1969 season, at a meeting in Dallas, the Baltimore Bays had informed the league that they would not continue in 1970. Woosnam faced the prospect of another backward step, and a four-team league would have been intolerable. But with his usual perseverance, Woosnam kept Baltimore's plans quiet. He went out and persuaded the Rochester Lancers and the Washington Darts to transfer from the ASL and enter the NASL in 1970.

The plan worked. With two new teams, the league grew to six. The budgets were kept low, but the schedule was expanded to twenty-four games, and play-offs were reinstated.

Another International Cup was put on the schedule, but with a difference. This time it was the native league teams versus touring foreign clubs—and the games counted in the NASL standings. The Washington Darts, on their way to the league's best record, won the International Cup with a 2–2–0 record and twenty points, defeating Varzim of Portugal and Hapoel Petah

Ken Cooper started a 10-year career in goal for the Dallas Tornado in 1970. He sported a baseball cap when he faced Monterrey of Mexico in an International Cup match.

Tikvah of Israel. (Hapoel didn't make the complete league circuit. It didn't play in Dallas, because Lamar Hunt figured a match with Israelis wouldn't be good for his Arab oil business. Monterrey of Mexico was a substitute.)

During June, Phil Woosnam met Neshui Ertegun at a cocktail party and struck up a friendship. Ertegun was executive vice-president of Atlantic Records, a subsidiary of Warner Communications, and a soccer fanatic. Within a year the league would add a team called the New York Cosmos, backed by Warner Communications.

Defense dominated the league in 1970, personified by the Washington Darts. They were "led" by player-coach and goalkeeper Lincoln Phillips, if leading can be exemplified by shouting and scolding his teammates for ninety minutes. With Willie Evans and Chris Dunleavy on the back line and Warren Archibald leading the offense, the Darts pitched twelve shutouts, still a league record, including four in a row.

Phillips recorded a 0.95 goals-against average, and the entire team allowed only twenty-nine goals in twenty-four games. With a 14–6–4 record, the Darts were the favorites in the playoffs as Southern Division champs. But Rochester, only 9–9–6 in the regular season, upset them for the crown. The Lancers won at home, 3–0, before 9,321 fans, and though they lost the second leg, 3–1, in Washington before 5,543, they took the championship on total goals, 4–3. They were led by Carlos "Little Mouse" Metidieri, a 5'4" forward who was MVP and tied for the league scoring title with fourteen goals, seven assists. Kirk Apostolidis of Dallas also had thirty-five points, with sixteen goals and three assists. Rookie of the Year was Jim Leeker of the St. Louis Stars.

The NASL All-Stars capped the season by

drawing 13,222 to Soldier Field in Chicago to see Pelé and Santos beat them, 4–3, on a rebound of a Pelé shot. Pat McBride, Dragan Popovic, Art Welch, and Warren Archibald were among the All-Stars.

Crowds were up, to perhaps thirty-six hundred per game.

1970 FINAL SEASON STANDINGS AND STATISTICS

Northern Division	GP	W	L	T	GF	GA	BP	TP
Rochester	24	9	9	6	41	45	39	111
Kansas City	24	8	10	6	42	44	34	100
St. Louis	24	5	17	2	26	71	24	60
Southern Division								
Washington	24	14	6	4	52	29	41	137
Atlanta	24	11	8	5	53	33	42	123
Dallas	24	8	12	4	39	39	32	92

PLAYOFF RESULTS

Rochester 3, Washington 0
Washington 3, Rochester 1
Rochester won 4-3 on aggregate.

Leading Scorers	GP	G	A	TP
Kirk Apostolidis, Dallas	19	16	3	35
Carlos Metidieri, Rochester	22	14	7	35
Leroy DeLeon, Washington	21	16	1	33
Art Welch, Atlanta	21	12	8	32
Manfred Seissler, Kansas City	23	11	7	29
Nick Papadakis, Atlanta	22	11	2	24
Warren Archibald, Washington	20	8	7	23
Dave Metchick, Atlanta	20	8	6	22
Eli Durante, Kansas City	22	8	4	20
Bobby Moffat, Dallas	24	8	3	19
Raul Herrera, Rochester	18	8	3	19
Pat McBride, St. Louis	24	9	1	19
Joseph "Nana" Gyau, Washington	19	5	8	18
Henry Largie, Atlanta	21	8	2	18
Mike Renshaw, Dallas	23	6	5	17

Leading Goalkeepers	GP	SV	GA	SH	GAA
Lincoln Phillips, Washington	22	96	21	12	0.95
Vic Rouse, Atlanta	13	52	14	4	1.07
Kenny Cooper, Dallas	20	66	29	6	1.45
Manfred Kammerer, Atlanta	12	65	19	4	1.58
Leonel Conde, Kansas City	23	134	38	7	1.65
Dick Howard, Rochester	15	81	27	2	1.80
Claude Campos, Rochester	9	61	18	2	2.00
Miguel DeLima, St. Louis	12	74	29	0	2.41
Joe Right, St. Louis	13	85	34	2	2.61

1971

Solid, respectable growth came this season. Nobody dropped out, and three franchises were added. Each paid the league's new franchise fee, twenty-five thousand dollars. Coming in were the Montreal Olympics (or Les Olympiques de Montreal, to be exact), Toronto Metros and New York Cosmos.

The Cosmos signed a few American players, plus a forbidding 6'4'' Bermudian named Randy Horton, who would be the league's Rookie of the Year and second to Rochester's Carlos Metidieri in the scoring race with sixteen goals, five assists. Their games at Yankee Stadium were sparsely attended, though, and the Yankees retained the right to postpone any game if there were a threat of rain (and thus, of damage to the turf).

The focus of the league race was elsewhere. Rochester compiled the best record, 13-5-6 for 141 points, taking good advantage of its home-field supremacy at then-named Aquinas Stadium. The Lancers won the International Cup with a 2-0-2 record, against Hearts of Scotland, Lanerossi Vicenza of Italy, Apollon of Greece, and Bangu of Brazil.

After the twenty-four–game schedule, Rochester was champion of the Northern Division, and Atlanta was king of the South. For the first time, however, second-place teams were allowed into the playoffs, each round of which was best of three.

This led to the zaniest and most intriguing playoffs in the league's early years. Atlanta got past New York, 1-0 in overtime and 2-0. Meanwhile, Dallas was meeting Rochester. The opener, in Rochester, became the longest game in NASL history. It went 176 minutes, into its sixth sudden-death overtime, before Metidieri won it with a low shot, at 11:55 P.M.

Rochester figured that would take the wind out of Dallas, but with Mirko Stojanovic in goal, John Best and Gabbo Gavric in defense, Tony McLaughlin at forward, and Ron Newman coaching, the Tornado roared back to win 3-1 at home. The third game, at Rochester, went 148 minutes before Bobby Moffat scored and sent Dallas into the final series—against Atlanta.

Again Dallas lost the opener of the three-game set on the road, 2-1, on an overtime goal after 123 minutes by Mick Ash, who had just walked into the game as a substitute. Again at home, the Tornado waltzed to a 4-1 victory. That set up a championship game, at Atlanta Stadium, and with barely three thousand watching, Mike Renshaw

The New York Cosmos came into the league and had the top rookie in Randy Horton (left), who scored 16 goals. His teammate is Kyriakos Fitilis.

Tony McLaughlin (10) of Dallas tangled with Atlanta goalie Manfred Kammerer in the 1971 final. McLaughlin's four goals and two assists were a major factor in the three-game series won by the Tornado.

and Moffat scored first-half goals to give Dallas the title, 2-0.

McLaughlin, a young English forward who taped his knuckles before the game, was the leading playoff scorer with four goals, two assists, and he was never seen in the NASL again. Metidieri was league MVP and led the scorers with nineteen goals, eight assists. Stojanovic set a league record with a 0.79 goals-against average.

League attendance crept up to about 3,850 per game.

1971 FINAL SEASON STANDINGS AND STATISTICS

Northern Division	GP	W	L	T	GF	GA	BP	TP
Rochester	24	13	5	6	48	31	45	141
New York	24	9	10	5	51	55	48	117
Toronto	24	5	10	9	32	47	32	89
Montreal	24	4	15	5	29	59	26	65
Southern Division								
Atlanta	24	12	7	5	35	29	33	120
Dallas	24	10	6	8	38	24	35	119
Washington	24	8	6	10	36	34	33	111
St. Louis	24	6	13	5	37	47	35	86

PLAYOFF RESULTS

Semifinals
Sept. 1 at Rochester—Rochester 2, Dallas 1 (OT)
Sept. 4 at Dallas—Dallas 3, Rochester 1
Sept. 8 at Rochester—Dallas 2, Rochester 1 (OT)
Dallas won best of three series (2-1)
Sept. 2 at Atlanta—Atlanta 1, New York 0 (OT)
Sept. 5 at New York—Atlanta 2, New York 0
Atlanta won best of three series (2-0)

Championship Games
Sept. 12 at Atlanta—Atlanta 2, Dallas 1 (OT)
Sept. 15 at Dallas—Dallas 4, Atlanta 1
Sept. 19 at Atlanta—Dallas 2, Atlanta 0
Dallas won best of three series (2-1)

Leading Scorers	GP	G	A	TP
Carlos Metidieri, Rochester	24	19	8	46
Randy Horton, New York	22	16	5	37
Casey Frankiewicz, St. Louis	24	14	5	33
Jorge Siega, New York	24	9	9	27
Manfred Seissler, Rochester	22	10	7	27
Leroy DeLeon, Washington	24	8	7	23
Ken Wallace, Montreal	22	8	5	21
Ian McHattie, Toronto	22	8	5	21
Tommy Youlden, Dallas	18	8	4	20
Iris DeBrito, Rochester	17	6	8	20

Leading Goalkeepers*	Min.	SV	GA	SH	GAA
Mirko Stojanovic, Dallas	1359	91	11	8	0.79
Claude Campos, Rochester	1054	97	13	3	1.11
Manfred Kammerer, Atlanta	1820	142	23	8	1.14
Orest Banach, St. Louis	1170	115	17	2	1.31
Leonel Conde, Washington	2145	208	33	4	1.38
Conrad Kornek, New York	1215	100	29	1	2.15
Kieron Baker, Montreal	1593	145	46	1	2.60

*Need 1050 minutes to qualify.

1972

The league hardly changed at all from 1971. The Washington Darts moved to Miami, and in search of the worst nickname they could find became the Miami Gatos. They hired Sal DeRosa, former Rochester mentor, as coach. The New York Cosmos scaled down their games to twelve thousand-capacity Hofstra Stadium on Long Island. Montreal hired Graham Adams as coach, Rochester tried player Adolfo Gori as head coach, and St. Louis put Casey (né Kasi) Frankiewicz in charge, at the same time recruiting a couple of Englishmen named Wilf Tranter and John Sewell.

Suddenly, St. Louis and New York took off. The league played its shortest schedule ever, only fourteen games, and when it was over, the Cosmos had won the North with a 7-4-3 mark, and St. Louis received its reward for Americanization as southern champs with a 7-3-4 record.

In quick, one-game semifinals, New York ousted Dallas, 1-0, on Johnny Kerr's goal at Hofstra, and St. Louis polished off Rochester, 2-0, as Sewell and Gene Geimer scored. The championship game was played in the rain before 6,102 at Hofstra. Goals by Randy Horton and player-coach Frankiewicz sent the game level at 1-1 into its waning minutes, and at 86:00 the Cosmos' Josef Jelinek converted a penalty kick to give New York the championship.

Horton was Most Valuable Player, Frankiewicz made Coach of the Year, and Mike Winter of St. Louis was Rookie of the Year.

Dallas had the consolation of a 24,742 crowd at its new home, Texas Stadium, for an exhibition game against Moscow Dynamo, making its first appearance in North America. Goalie Ken Cooper was magnificent against the Russians in a 0-0 tie. Dynamo went on to Hofstra to beat the Cosmos, 2-1, before 13,205, a standing-room-only crowd. League attendance made a significant rise, up 39 percent to 5,340 per game. Toronto led the league in attendance with 7,274 fans per game.

A milestone was erected as the league changed its offside rule midway through the schedule, on June 26, to put an offside line across the field, thirty-five yards from the goal line. Thereafter, no player could be offside unless he had crossed the thirty-five yard line; in the rest of the world, off-

The Cosmos' Randy Horton (left), captain Barry Mahy (with trophy) and Stan Startzell (14) celebrate after 2–1 championship triumph over the St. Louis Stars.

St. Louis goalie Mike Winter was named Rookie of the Year at 19 for posting a 1.00 average and leading his team to the final.

side applies to the entire attacking half of the field. Players were slow to adjust to the new rule, and on its first weekend, scores were 1-0, 0-0, and 2-0. Gradually, the thirty-five–yard line began to open up attacking possibilities.

The Dallas Tornado showed a large measure of foresight by drafting a local boy who played college soccer at the University of the South. His name was Kyle Rote, Jr. The boy was such a raw talent that he was kept on the reserve team for an entire season, but Lamar Hunt and Ron Newman insisted they didn't draft him for the publicity value of his surname. His father had been a famous football player.

1972 FINAL SEASON STANDINGS AND STATISTICS

Northern Division	GP	W	L	T	GF	GA	BP	TP
New York	14	7	3	4	28	16	23	77
Rochester	14	6	5	3	20	22	19	64
Montreal	14	4	5	5	19	20	18	57
Toronto	14	4	6	4	18	22	17	53
Southern Division								
St. Louis	14	7	4	3	20	14	18	69
Dallas	14	6	5	3	15	12	15	60
Atlanta	14	5	6	3	19	18	17	56
Miami	14	3	8	3	17	32	17	44

PLAYOFF RESULTS

Semifinals
Aug. 15 at St. Louis—St. Louis 2, Rochester 0
Aug. 19 at New York—New York 1, Dallas 0

Championship Game
Aug. 26 at New York—New York 2, St. Louis 1

Leading Scorers	GP	G	A	TP
Randy Horton, New York	13	9	4	22
Michael Dillon, Montreal	10	8	2	18
Paul Child, Atlanta	12	8	1	17
Warren Archibald, Miami	14	6	5	17
Willie Roy, St. Louis	11	7	2	16
Everald Cummings, New York	13	5	3	13
Casey Frankiewicz, St. Louis	12	5	3	13
Mike Renshaw, Dallas	13	5	3	13
Leroy DeLeon, Miami	14	5	3	13
Art Welch, Atlanta	13	4	4	12
Carlos Metidieri, Rochester	12	5	1	11
Willie Mfum, New York	10	5	1	11
John Sewell, St. Louis	14	3	4	10
Carlo Dell'Omodarme, Rochester	14	1	8	10
Johnny Kerr, New York	14	3	4	10

Leading Goalkeepers*	Min.	SV	GA	SH	GAA
Ken Cooper, Dallas	1260	107	12	6	0.86
Mike Winter, St. Louis	1260	122	14	3	1.00
Manfred Kammerer, Atlanta	945	76	12	4	1.14
Richard Blackmore, New York	1260	129	16	3	1.14
Dick Howard, Toronto	1170	73	17	2	1.31
Claude Campos, Rochester	1133	64	18	4	1.43
Sam Nusum, Montreal	1260	113	20	4	1.43
Paulo Dias, Miami	1033	124	22	3	1.92

*Need 940 minutes to qualify.

1973

According to Tom McCluskey, his infatuation with soccer began when Lamar Hunt found eight Super Bowl tickets for him and said, "How would you like to have a soccer franchise in Philadelphia?" McCluskey, at that time doing beautifully in the construction business, agreed. The result was a franchise which was like a shot of Vitamin B-12 to the NASL: the Philadelphia Atoms.

McCluskey and general manager Bob Ehlinger and coach Al Miller put the Atoms together out of thin air in the late winter and early spring of 1973, and within eight months they were champions of the league. They were the first team to win a major league championship in their first year of existence in decades, and Miller was the NASL's first American-born Coach of the Year.

The league came into 1973 in modest shape. The addition of the Atoms increased the roster from eight to nine teams. Joe Robbie and his family bought the Miami franchise, mercifully burying its old nickname and calling the team the Toros. Atlanta found new owners and a new nickname, the Apollos.

New coaches were hired in Miami (John Young), Atlanta (Ken Bracewell), and Toronto (Arthur Rodrigues), and Rochester accepted the wayward Sal DeRosa back in the fold after his brief stop at Miami.

As soon as the season began, there was cautious hope for the future. Miami drew 12,766, Philadelphia had a surprising 21,000 for its opener, and Dallas 19,342 for its. By the end of the season, the Atoms would set a league record by averaging 11,382 per game, Dallas was up 86 percent to 7,465, and Miami brought in better than 6,000 per game. League attendance overall was up 18 percent, to 6,290 per contest.

Dallas' Tornado came up with the best regular-season record, 11-4-4, sparked by the playmaking of Ritchie Reynolds and Nick Jennings and the scoring of Ilija Mitic (twelve goals) and the Rookie of the Year, Kyle Rote, Jr. Rote ended up with ten goals, ten assists and thirty points, edging Miami winger Warren Archibald for the league scoring title by one point.

Rote remains the only American-born player ever to win the NASL scoring championship. Archibald had the consolation of receiving the Most Valuable Player award.

◄ *Philadelphia's Bill Straub (left) and Dallas' Ray Bloomfield battle for the ball in championship game. Straub scored a goal in the 2–0 victory.*

Dallas' Kyle Rote Jr., (far right) heading the ball for the only goal in a game against the Cosmos, won the scoring crown and was Rookie of the Year. No. 24, closest to the ball, is Cosmos player-coach Gordon Bradley.

Bob Rigby set an NASL goals-against-average record of 0.62 for the championship Atoms.

But the season was a chapter of The Philadelphia Story. It had all the elements: American coach, a rookie in the professional game; American goalie, Bob Rigby, blond and hip, setting an NASL record with an 0.62 goals-against average; burly seasoned Britons going unbeaten for thirteen consecutive games. They were Derek Trevis, Jim Fryatt, Andy Provan, George O'Neill, Chris Dunleavy. Provan scored eleven goals himself.

The Atoms lost only two games all season and allowed only fourteen goals in nineteen matches. They flattened the Toronto Metros, 3-0, in the play-off semifinals, with 18,766 fans at Veterans Stadium; they had drawn 18,824 for their last regular-season game.

The Tornado managed to beat the New York Cosmos, the wild-card team, 1-0, on another header goal by Rote, with a crowd of 9,009 at Texas Stadium. Dallas had the pleasure of playing host for the final.

Relationships with the English League being what they were at that stage, each team lost crucial players between the semifinals and the final. Dallas' three loan players from Portsmouth—Reynolds, Jennings, and fullback John Collins—departed, as did the Atoms' scoring tandem of Provan and Fryatt.

Philadelphia proved it was the readier team as it disappointed most of the 18,824 Dallas fans with a 2-0 victory for the championship. The game was scoreless for sixty minutes until Tornado center back John Best accidentally kicked a dangerous Philadelphia pass into the Dallas goal. Bill Straub netted a header in the last five minutes.

Rigby was on the cover of *Sports Illustrated* after the final. It was a great moment for the

Atoms, who would cease to exist two years later. The ill-fated Atlanta Apollos, however, had won only three games and quickly folded. Montreal did likewise, unable to make a dent in ice hockey country.

1973 FINAL SEASON STANDINGS AND STATISTICS

Eastern Division	GP	W	L	T	GF	GA	BP	TP
Philadelphia	19	9	2	8	29	14	26	104
New York	19	7	5	7	31	23	28	91
Miami	19	8	5	6	26	21	22	88
Northern Division								
Toronto	19	6	4	9	32	18	26	89
Montreal	19	5	10	4	25	32	22	64
Rochester	19	4	9	6	17	27	17	59
Southern Division								
Dallas	19	11	4	4	36	25	33	111
St. Louis	19	7	7	5	27	27	25	82
Atlanta	19	3	9	7	23	40	23	62

PLAYOFF RESULTS

Semifinals
Aug. 15 at Dallas—Dallas 1, New York 0
Aug. 18 at Philadelphia—Philadelphia 3, Toronto 0

Championship Game
Aug. 25 at Dallas—Philadelphia 2, Dallas 0

Leading Scorers	GP	G	A	TP
Kyle Rote, Jr., Dallas	18	10	10	30
Warren Archibald, Miami	17	12	5	29
Andy Provan, Philadelphia	19	11	6	28
Gene Geimer, St. Louis	19	10	5	25
Ilija Mitic, Dallas	18	12	1	25
Randy Horton, New York	14	9	5	23
Joe Fink, New York	14	11	0	22
Richard Reynolds, Dallas	12	8	6	22
Miguel Perrichon, Toronto	17	9	4	22
Willie Roy, St. Louis	19	7	4	18
Tom Ord, Montreal	17	6	6	18

Leading Goalkeepers**	Min.	SV	GA	SH	GAA
Bob Rigby, Philadelphia	1157	78	8	6	0.62
Dick Howard, Toronto	1530	91	17	6	1.00
Ruben Montoya, Miami	1695	151	21	7	1.11
Ken Cooper, Dallas	1620	156	21	5	1.17
Jerry Sularz, New York	1620	136	22	5	1.22
Mike Winter, St. Louis	1710	138	27	4	1.42
Claude Campos, Rochester	1157	89	19	3	1.63
Sam Nusum, Montreal	1710	156	32	4	1.68
John Forrest, Atlanta	1452	130	30	3	1.86

**Need 1100 minutes to qualify.

1974

Despite the loss of Atlanta and Montreal, the NASL made a giant stride in 1974, expanding to the West Coast. It made the league truly national for the first time since the debacle of 1968.

The league tripled the franchise fee to seventy-five thousand dollars, and eight clubs paid it. They quickly signed up owners in Los Angeles, Seattle, and Vancouver. Each required, however, another West Coast team. Under pressure of a deadline, Woosnam convinced the owners to look outside urban San Francisco and accept the application of a group in the growing city of San Jose. Denver, Baltimore, and Washington also came in.

The westward migration proved to be ingenius. In their first season, both Seattle and San Jose broke the Kansas City Spurs' 1968 season attendance record of 129,236. The Earthquakes averaged 16,576 fans in Spartan Stadium. Seattle's Sounders had the league's first regular-season sellout, 13,876 at little Memorial Stadium, and followed it with six more. With Philadelphia doing 11,784 and Vancouver 10,098, the league averaged 7,825 per game, up 24 percent from 1973.

Dallas' young forward, Kyle Rote, Jr., added some attention to the league by winning ABC-TV's "Superstars" competition, which he said "proved that soccer players are not second-class athletes."

The league divided again, into four divisions. The New York Cosmos moved into Downing Stadium, which gave new meaning to the word "crumbling." St. Louis' Stars became so tired of their almost All-American lineup bucking imported players, that before one game the starters presented each Dallas player with a tiny American flag.

What changed the play substantially was the NASL's elimination of ties. If a game were tied after ninety minutes, it was decided by a series of penalty kicks. The new venture was worked into the scoring table by the invention of the "tie-win," which went to the team that won the tie-breaker and was worth three points. The loser of the tie-breaker, even though it played the other team even for ninety minutes, received no points (except, of course, for goals).

Coaches as usual moved around the league. Ken Bracewell joined the new Denver Dynamos' franchise. Bill Hughes took over at Rochester, and John Sewell at St. Louis. Former Dallas captain John Best became coach at Seattle, while the new franchises picked Gabbo Gavric, San Jose; Doug Millward, Baltimore Bays; Dennis Viollet, Wash-

Paul Child joined the expansion San Jose Earthquakes from the defunct Atlanta Apollos and captured the league scoring title.

ington Diplomats; Hubert Vogelsinger, Boston Minutemen, and Alex Perolli, Los Angeles Aztecs.

Mastery of the tie-breaker, as well as the attacks of Warren Archibald and a youngster named Steve David, helped Miami win the East, by two points over Baltimore. The Toros were 6-0 in the penalty-kick sessions. Boston ran off with the North, Dallas took the Central, and Los Angeles' new club won the West, though few

showed up at East Los Angeles College to bear witness.

San Jose and Baltimore earned the wild-card spots and were quickly eliminated by Dallas and Boston, respectively. In the semis, Miami ran away from Dallas, 3-1, at Tamiami Stadium, and Los Angeles shut out Boston, 2-0.

CBS-TV carried the championship game live from the Orange Bowl, and though it received only a 3.8 rating, it was a dramatic game. Doug

McMillan tied it for the Aztecs in the last two minutes, 3-3, and Los Angeles won the game in the tie-breaker, 4-3—a great irony since Miami had been the king of the penalty kicks during the regular season. The game drew 15,507 fans.

Paul Child, the opportunistic San Jose forward, led the league in scoring with fifteen goals, six assists. Barry Watling of Seattle, who put good-luck dolls in his net, was the leading goalie with an 0.80 average. Los Angeles set a league record with eight consecutive victories. Dallas went fourteen games without a defeat during regulation time, but lost three tie-breakers along the way.

Individual laurels for the season were accorded Miami's John Young, Coach of the Year; Baltimore's Peter Silvester, Most Valuable Player; and Los Angeles' Doug McMillan, Rookie of the Year.

Washington made a negative impact by firing public relations director Debbie Goldstein for refusing to verify a padded crowd count.

1974 FINAL SEASON STANDINGS AND STATISTICS

Northern Division	GP	W	L	T	GF	GA	BP	TP
Boston	20	10	9	1	36	23	31	94
Toronto	20	9	10	1	30	31	30	87
Rochester	20	8	10	2	23	30	23	77
New York	20	4	14	2	28	40	28	58
Eastern Division								
Miami	20	9	5	6	38	24	35	107
Baltimore	20	10	8	2	42	46	39	105
Philadelphia	20	8	11	1	25	25	23	74
Washington	20	7	12	1	29	36	25	70
Central Division								
Dallas	20	9	8	3	39	27	37	100
St. Louis	20	4	15	1	27	42	27	54
Denver	20	5	15	0	21	42	19	49
Western Division								
Los Angeles	20	11	7	2	41	36	38	110
San Jose	20	9	8	3	43	38	40	103
Seattle	20	10	7	3	37	17	32	101
Vancouver	20	5	11	4	29	30	28	70

PLAYOFF RESULTS

Quarterfinals
Aug. 14 at Dallas—Dallas 3, San Jose 0
Aug. 15 at Boston—Boston 1, Baltimore 0

Semifinals
Aug. 17 at Los Angeles—Los Angeles 2, Boston 0
Aug. 17 at Miami—Miami 3, Dallas 1

Championship Game
Aug. 25 at Miami—Los Angeles 4, Miami 3 (TB)

Leading Scorers	GP	G	A	TP
Paul Child, San Jose	20	15	6	36
Peter Silvester, Baltimore	17	14	3	31
Douglas McMillan, Los Angeles	20	10	10	30
John Rowlands, Seattle	20	10	8	28
Steven David, Miami	19	13	0	26
Randy Horton, New York	16	9	4	22
David Butler, Seattle	15	10	1	21
Andy Provan, Philadelphia	20	9	3	21
Ilija Mitic, Dallas	20	10	1	21
John Coyne, Dallas-Boston	20	7	7	21
Archie Roboostoff, San Jose	19	6	8	20
Jim Fryatt, Philadelphia	20	8	4	20
Alvin Henderson, Baltimore	18	7	6	20
Frank Large, Baltimore	17	9	2	20
Gary Darrell, Washington	20	9	2	20

Leading Goalkeepers*	Min.	SV	GA	SH	GAA
Barry Watling, Seattle	1800	132	16	8	0.80
Ian McKechnie, Boston	1280	75	13	5	0.94
Bob Rigby, Philadelphia	1800	151	22	5	1.10
Ken Cooper, Dallas	1800	117	22	9	1.10
Claude Campos, Rochester	1579	111	20	8	1.14

*Need 1170 minutes to qualify.

1975

Pelé came to the NASL in 1975, and it was obvious that what went before was only a warmup. The league, or at least the New York Cosmos' part of it, was through fooling around and was ready to go into big-time sport.

Cosmos general manager Clive Toye completed five years of efforts by announcing Pelé's agreement to a Cosmos contract on June 3. He would play three years for $4.7 million, and, counting income taxes, it was a $7 million deal. A week later, Pelé signed his contract in a media mob scene at the 21 Club in the heart of Manhattan. When the Cosmos played in Philadelphia, the game drew 20,124 even though Pelé was in civvies and the crowd knew he wouldn't play.

On June 15, with national television cameras focused on him and 21,278 fans squirming at old Downing Stadium, Pelé made his Cosmos debut in a 2-2 tie with the Dallas Tornado. He assisted on one goal and scored another. It took him a few weeks to get in shape, but the Cosmos began breaking records. At Washington, they drew 35,620, then a league record, and they set records in Boston, Los Angeles, Seattle, Vancouver, wherever they stopped. Even so, NASL attendance was up only 2 percent over 1974, at 7,930 per game.

But Pelé's presence focused national attention on what had become a twenty-team league. All fifteen of the 1974 teams stayed around, and the

Accompanied by his wife, and backed up by Clive Toye (left) and Warner Communications chairman Steve Ross, Pelé signed the multi-million dollar contract that changed the face of American soccer.

Pelé made his Cosmos debut against the Dallas Tornado before a capacity crowd at creaky Downing Stadium and a national television audience of millions.

additions were in Tampa Bay, Chicago, Hartford, San Antonio, and Portland. Toronto's Metros merged with a local club, Croatia, to become the Metros-Croatia.

John Young moved to Denver to coach the Dynamos, Greg Myers took over at Miami, Toronto picked Aldo Principe, Rochester chose Ted Dumitru, Alex Perolli left Los Angeles for San Antonio, while the Aztecs chose twenty-three-year-old Terry Fisher out of UCLA. The new teams' coaches were Bill Foulkes at Chicago, Manfred Schellsheidt at Hartford, Ivan Toplak returning briefly to San Jose, Vic Crowe at Portland, and Eddie Firmani at Tampa Bay.

The tie-win was eliminated, overtimes were added, and the tie-breaker victories scored the same as regulation victories.

While Pelé was the center of media and fan attention, he wasn't able to make a mark on the league with his play, not coming in at mid-season with a lackluster team around him. The eye-catching moves were coming from Miami's Steve David, who had the first five-goal game in league history, against Washington, led the league with

The upstart Tampa Boy Rowdies vaulted to the NASL title in the first Soccer Bowl. Goalie Paul Hammond, battling the Portland Timbers' Peter Withe (9), shut out the opposition in three playoff games.

Tampa Bay's championship moment was celebrated by team captain John Boyle (left) and goaltender Paul Hammond.

Chris Bahr, who played for his father Walter at Penn State, was Rookie of the Year with the Philadelphia Atoms.

Flamboyant Shep Messing, New York-born, Harvard-educated, finished with a 0.93 average for the Boston Minutemen to lead league goaltenders.

twenty-three goals, six assists, and wound up as Most Valuable Player.

It was coming also from the Portland Timbers, with a virtually all-British team sparked by big Peter Withe, Jimmy Kelly, Willy Anderson, and Graham Day. And from Firmani's Tampa Bay Rowdies' forward line of Derek Smethurst, Clyde Best, and Stewart Scullion.

Boston again won the North, Tampa Bay climbed over Miami for the East title, St. Louis surged back into the limelight by winning the Central, and newcomer Portland enjoyed a season of soccer fever in the Pacific Northwest by winning the West.

Portland drew 31,523 fans, a league play-off record, for a 2-1 overtime win over Seattle in the first round, and 33,503 for a 1-0 squeaker over St. Louis in the semifinals. Tampa Bay downed Toronto, 1-0; Miami edged past Boston 2-1 in overtime; and St. Louis conquered Los Angeles, 2-1, in a tie-breaker to complete the quarterfinals. Tampa Bay overpowered Miami, 3-0, in the other semifinal.

That brought the play-offs to the NASL's first-ever Soccer Bowl, a fixed-site championship game copied from football's Super Bowl. Ironically, this game in Portland would have sold 35,000 tickets, but it was held in San Jose's little Spartan Stadium, and 17,009 plus TV cameras were shoe-horned in. Portland was the favorite, but Tampa Bay won, 2-0, on second-half goals by sub fullback Arsene Auguste and big Clyde Best. Paul Hammond didn't allow a goal in the Rowdies' three play-off games.

John Sewell was rewarded for St. Louis' finest season ever by receiving the Coach of the Year award. Chris Bahr of Philadelphia, later a pro football place-kicker, was the Rookie of the Year and never returned to soccer. Shep Messing demanded attention in Boston by leading the league in goalkeeping with an average of 0.93.

The NASL also experimented in 1975 with indoor soccer, the first time it was done on a league basis. Four regional tournaments were played, followed by the four-team finals in San Francisco's Cow Palace, where San Jose won the championship, beating Tampa Bay, 8-5. It was one of the few setbacks the Rowdies had in 1975.

1975 FINAL SEASON STANDINGS AND STATISTICS

Northern Division	GP	W	L	GF	GA	BP	TP
Boston	22	13	9	41	29	38	116
Toronto	22	13	9	39	28	36	114
New York	22	10	12	39	38	31	91
Rochester	22	6	16	29	49	28	64
Hartford	22	6	16	27	51	25	61
Eastern Division							
Tampa Bay	22	16	6	46	27	39	135
Miami	22	14	8	47	30	39	123
Washington	22	12	10	42	47	40	112
Philadelphia	22	10	12	33	42	30	90
Baltimore	22	9	13	34	52	33	87
Central Division							
St. Louis	22	13	9	38	34	37	115
Chicago	22	12	10	39	33	34	106
Denver	22	9	13	37	42	31	85
Dallas	22	9	13	33	38	29	83
San Antonio	22	6	16	24	46	23	59
Western Division							
Portland	22	16	6	43	27	42	138
Seattle	22	15	7	42	28	39	129
Los Angeles	22	12	10	42	33	35	107
Vancouver	22	11	11	38	28	33	99
San Jose	22	8	14	37	48	35	83

PLAYOFF RESULTS

Quarterfinals
Aug. 12 at Portland—Portland 2, Seattle 1 (OT)
Aug. 13 at St. Louis—St. Louis 2, Los Angeles 1 (TB 5-4)
Aug. 13 at Boston—Miami 2, Boston 1 (OT)
Aug. 13 at Tampa Bay—Tampa Bay 1, Toronto 0

Semifinals
Aug. 16 at Tampa Bay—Tampa Bay 3, Miami 0
Aug. 17 at Portland—Portland 1, St. Louis 0

Soccer Bowl-75
Aug. 24 at San Jose—Tampa Bay 2, Portland 0

Leading Scorers	GP	G	A	TP
Steven David, Miami	21	23	6	52
Gordon Hill, Chicago	21	16	7	39
Derek Smethurst, Tampa Bay	22	18	3	39
Peter Withe, Portland	22	16	6	38
Uri Banhoffer, Los Angeles	20	14	9	37
Tommy Ord, Rochester-New York	21	16	3	35
Ilija Mitic, San Jose	19	15	3	33
Ade Coker, Boston	15	10	6	26
Patrick Ntsoelengoe, Denver	21	10	5	25
John Rowlands, Seattle	21	10	5	25
John Coyne, Toronto	22	7	11	25
Chris Bahr, Philadelphia	22	11	2	24
Mike Flater, Denver	15	10	4	24
John Hawley, St. Louis	20	11	2	24
Keith Aqui, Baltimore	20	10	3	23
Glenn Johnson, Vancouver	21	8	7	23

Leading Goalkeepers*	Min.	SV	GA	SH	GAA
Shep Messing, Boston	1639	140	17	6	0.93
Barry Watling, Seattle	2032	140	26	6	1.15
Graham Brown, Portland	1948	144	26	5	1.20
Zeljko Bilecki, Toronto	1949	123	27	8	1.25
Greg Weber, Vancouver	1273	95	19	5	1.34

*Need 1260 minutes to qualify.

1976

It was Pelé's first full season in the U.S. The Denver Dynamos moved to Minnesota and became an instant success as the Kicks. The Cosmos began to build a super team around their superstar, adding Giorgio Chinaglia, Ramon Mifflin, Terry Garbett, and Dave Clements.

At the same time, the Kingdome was completed in Seattle, and its first sports event was a preseason game between the Sounders and the Cosmos. All previous NASL records were shattered as 58,128 fans attended.

By the end of the campaign, attendance had jumped by 38 percent, to 10,980 per game. The Cosmos averaged 18,226 fans at Yankee Stadium, Seattle did 23,828, and Minnesota came charging upward at the end to average 23,117, with a 42,065 crowd for the final regular-season game at home.

The influx of big-name players, sparked by Pelé, was obvious by a glance at the all-star team, which included Pelé, Chinaglia, Tony Simoes, George Best, Mifflin, Keith Eddy, Mike England, and Bobby Moore.

Coloring the picture the other way was the transition in Philadelphia, where a group of Mexican club owners took control—they would stay just one year—and dismal attendance in Miami, Chicago, San Antonio, Hartford and Boston. The Minutemen ran out of money in mid-season, and owner John Sterge gave the league two choices: either let him sell his players for enough cash to finish the season or he would fold then and there. The league let Sterge sell.

Boston coach Hubert Vogelsinger had assembled an awesome roster: Messing, Eusebio, Simoes, Wolfgang Suhnholz, Geoff Davies, and Ade Coker, among others. Toronto's opportunistic pickup of Eusebio and Suhnholz would send the Metros-Croatia on to the league championship.

Baltimore moved to San Diego in the league's other transfer of 1976. New York brought in Ken

The Pelé-enriched Cosmos got richer by signing high-▶ scoring striker Giorgio Chinaglia from Lazio of Rome.

Wolfgang Suhnholz, followed by Benny Alon of the Chicago Sting in the quarterfinals, helped take the Toronto Metros-Croatia to Soccer Bowl-76.

Eusebio (left) and Wolfgang Suhnholz celebrate Toronto's 3–0 victory over the first-year Minnesota Kicks in the Soccer Bowl.

Furphy as head coach, demoting Gordon Bradley. By mid-season, Furphy quit and was replaced by Bradley. Toronto started with Ivan Markovic, but halfway through the campaign Domagoj Kapetonovic took over. New coaches were Don Batie at San Antonio, Jesus Ponce at Philadelphia, Derek Trevis at San Diego, Gabbo Gavric returning to the reins at San Jose, and Eckhard Krautzun at Vancouver.

The New York Cosmos were prolific, with sixty-five goals, nineteen of them by Chinaglia, who led the league with forty-nine points. The Cosmos finished strong, 8-2 after Bradley replaced Furphy. Pelé set a league record with eighteen assists, a funny statistic for the sport's greatest goal scorer.

Tampa Bay seemed destined again, roaring to an 18-6 record. When Boston fell apart, the Minutemen suffered twelve straight losses, finishing the season with a lineup of amateurs and kids.

In the play-offs, Toronto nipped Rochester, 2-1; Dallas ousted Los Angeles, 2-0; Seattle edged Vancouver, 1-0; and the Cosmos topped Washington, 2-0. Minnesota, as West Division champ, beat Seattle, 3-0; South champ San Jose beat Dallas, 2-0; Toronto upset North champ Chicago away,

Steve Pecher dropped out of Florissant Valley Junior College in St. Louis to become Rookie of the Year with Dallas.

3-2; and East champ Tampa Bay downed the Cosmos, 3-1.

By this time, it was obvious that Toronto was for real, and the M-Cs proved it by upsetting Tampa Bay in Tampa, 2-0. The ethnics were in Soccer Bowl! They were joined by Minnesota, which drew 49,572 as it beat San Jose, 2-1, at the Met.

Soccer Bowl was held in style this time, at the Kingdome, and 25,765 showed up for what was expected to be a Minnesota triumph. But Freddie Goodwin's artistic and confident Kicks were overwhelmed by Toronto, 3-0. Though TV commentator Jon Miller was forbidden by league officials to mention the name Metros-Croatia on the air, it was an all-Toronto show. Eusebio's banana free kick proved to be the winning goal, followed by tallies from Ivan Lukacevic and Ivair Ferreira. Suhnholz was the Soccer Bowl MVP.

Unfortunately, that Toronto team was unraveled by salary and logistical problems and never played together again as a complete unit.

Tony Chursky of Seattle led the league's goalies with an 0.91 average. Pelé was the MVP, and Dallas center back Steve Pecher took the Rookie of the Year award. Chinaglia entered the record book with a hat trick inside 8:19—and four goals in only 16:15.

Tampa Bay won the league indoor championship, at home, with a 6-4 win over Rochester to cap a sixteen-game indoor schedule.

1976 FINAL SEASON STANDINGS AND STATISTICS

ATLANTIC CONFERENCE

Northern Division	GP	W	L	GF	GA	BP	TP
Chicago	24	15	9	52	32	42	132
Toronto	24	15	9	38	30	33	123
Rochester	24	13	11	36	32	36	114
Hartford	24	12	12	37	56	35	107
Boston	24	7	17	35	64	32	72

Eastern Division							
Tampa Bay	24	18	6	58	30	46	154
New York	24	16	8	65	34	52	148
Washington	24	14	10	46	38	42	126
Philadelphia	24	8	16	32	49	32	80
Miami	24	6	18	29	58	27	63

PACIFIC CONFERENCE

Western Division							
Minnesota	24	15	9	54	33	48	138
Seattle	24	14	10	40	31	39	123
Vancouver	24	14	10	38	30	36	120

Western Division	GP	W	L	GF	GA	BP	TP
Portland	24	8	16	23	40	23	71
St. Louis	24	5	19	28	57	28	58

Southern Division							
San Jose	24	14	10	47	30	39	123
Dallas	24	13	11	44	45	39	117
Los Angeles	24	12	12	43	44	36	108
San Antonio	24	12	12	38	32	35	107
San Diego	24	9	15	29	47	28	82

PLAYOFF RESULTS

First Round
Aug. 17 at New York—New York 2, Washington 0
Aug. 18 at Toronto—Toronto 2, Rochester 1
Aug. 18 at Dallas—Dallas 2, Los Angeles 0
Aug. 18 at Seattle—Seattle 1, Vancouver 0

Division Championships
Aug. 20 at San Jose—San Jose 2, Dallas 0
Aug. 20 at Chicago—Toronto 3, Chicago 2
Aug. 20 at Tampa Bay—Tampa Bay 3, New York 1
Aug. 21 at Minnesota—Minnesota 3, Seattle 0

Conference Championships
Aug. 24 at Tampa Bay—Toronto 2, Tampa Bay 0
Aug. 25 at Minnesota—Minnesota 3, San Jose 1

Soccer Bowl–76
Aug. 28 at Seattle—Toronto 3, Minnesota 0

Leading Scorers	GP	G	A	TP
Giorgio Chinaglia, New York	19	19	11	49
Derek Smethurst, Tampa Bay	24	20	5	45
Pelé, New York	22	13	18	44
Mike Stojanovic, Rochester	24	17	7	41
Alan Willey, Minnesota	23	16	7	39
George Best, Los Angeles	23	15	7	37
Ilija Mitic, San Jose	24	14	9	37
Eusebio, Toronto	21	16	4	36
Ron Futcher, Minnesota	20	14	6	34
Paul Child, San Jose	23	13	8	34
Jeff Bourne, Dallas	22	15	3	33
Rodney Marsh, Tampa Bay	21	11	9	31
Stewart Scullion, Tampa Bay	24	10	10	30
Mark Liveric, San Jose	20	10	9	29

Leading Goalkeepers*	Min.	SV	GA	SH	GAA
Tony Chursky, Seattle	1981	135	20	9	0.91
Mike Hewitt, San Jose	1657	150	17	6	0.92
Paolo Cimpiel, Toronto	2058	157	22	9	0.96
Arnold Mausser, Tampa Bay	2162	201	28	6	1.17
Mervyn Cawston, Chicago	2173	165	29	6	1.20
Phil Parkes, Vancouver	1836	111	25	6	1.23
Shep Messing, New York	1728	166	24	6	1.25

*Need 1365 minutes to qualify.

1977

The NASL had to retrench a bit in 1977, down to eighteen teams as Boston and Philadelphia entered receivership. But Pelé climaxed his three NASL seasons by helping the Cosmos win a championship. Attendance went up again, by 33 percent, Franz Beckenbauer entered the league, and the shootout was used to replace the penalty kick tie-breaker.

Franz Beckenbauer joined the Cosmos in midseason from Bayern Munich. The two-time European Footballer of the Year and captain of West Germany's 1974 World Cup champion reportedly signed for $2.8 million.

Steve David, league scoring champion with Miami in 1975, won another scoring title, this time playing for the Los Angeles Aztecs.

Added to that was the Cinderella season of the Fort Lauderdale Strikers, who were a much more attractive version of the old Miami Toros. Steve David, now at Los Angeles, added great flair with a league-leading twenty-six goals, including a record-setting stretch in which he scored in ten consecutive games.

When the Cosmos drew 77,691 fans for a play-off game at Giants Stadium against Fort Lauderdale, (which they won, 8-3), it was obvious what Pelé had contributed to the NASL. In fact, six of the league's seven best crowds were attracted in this one season, including a regular-season throng of 62,394 to see the Cosmos play Tampa Bay at Giants Stadium, the first home park worthy of Pelé, Chinaglia, and Beckenbauer.

The Cosmos (they dropped New York from their name when they moved their games to the Meadowlands complex in New Jersey) were the story of 1977. They drew 443,847 fans at home, an average of 34,142, dwarfing all previous efforts.

The Cosmos were in controversy—they kicked Gordon Bradley upstairs again—and named Ed-die Firmani head coach. Firmani had quit a winning team at Tampa, after a dinner with Chinaglia, and the Rowdies went downhill without him.

Meanwhile franchises were shifting: San Diego to Las Vegas, San Antonio to Hawaii, and Hartford to New Haven, Connecticut. Ivan Sangulin moved in at Toronto, Jimmy Gabriel at Seattle, and Brian Tiler at Portland. Derek Trevis (Las Vegas), Hubert Vogelsinger (Team Hawaii), Bobby Thomson (Connecticut), Bill Foulkes (Chicago), Dennis Viollet (Washington), and Eckhard Krautzun (Vancouver) failed to last the season.

Ron Newman did the most notable coaching job, taking Fort Lauderdale from a cellar team to a 19-7 record. His hiring of goalie Gordon Banks, in retirement since losing an eye in a car accident, was masterful, as Banks made the all-star team.

Dallas' Ken Cooper led the league goalies with an 0.90 average, and the Tornado had its best record ever, 18-8.

Seven league games were telecast on the TVS syndicated network, the most since 1968. The league also beefed up its corps of referees, hiring three internationals in Abraham Klein of Israel, Tom Reynolds of Wales, and Bob Matthewson of England.

The largest beefing up, though, was done by Warner Communications, which added Beckenbauer and Brazilian sweeper Carlos Alberto to the Cosmos. Alberto solidified a perennially weak defense, while Beckenbauer commanded the entire team from his midfield spot and was named the league's Most Valuable Player.

Nearly everybody made the play-offs, as the league saw the losses to be recouped by the large postseason crowds. Indeed, the play-off games averaged 29,251 fans.

Rochester, Los Angeles, Seattle, and the Cosmos came through the first round, Seattle winning at Vancouver, while the Cosmos pounded demoralized Tampa Bay, 3-0.

In the second round, the Cosmos enjoyed their shocking 8-3 pounding of Fort Lauderdale, and they won the second leg, 3-2, in a shootout. Los Angeles trimmed Dallas twice, Seattle eliminated Minnesota with a pair of wins, and Rochester shut Toronto out, 1-0 twice.

The semifinals were no less decisive. The Cosmos swatted Rochester aside, 2-1 and 4-1. Seattle won in Los Angeles, 3-1, and at home, 1-0. The Sounders had come from a 2-6 start to a place in the Soccer Bowl.

Portland's Civic Stadium sold out for Soccer Bowl, and 35,548 crammed in to see the Cosmos beat Seattle, 2-1, for the title. Steve Hunt stole the ball from Sounders goalie Tony Chursky to score early. Tommy Ord tied it, but Chinaglia's header from a Hunt cross was the winner, and all the Cosmos said they won the title as a going-away present to Pelé.

Pelé presented his shirt to Rookie of the Year

Goalie Gordon Banks of the Fort Lauderdale Strikers, who led England to the World Cup in 1966, came out of retirement and made the all-star team.

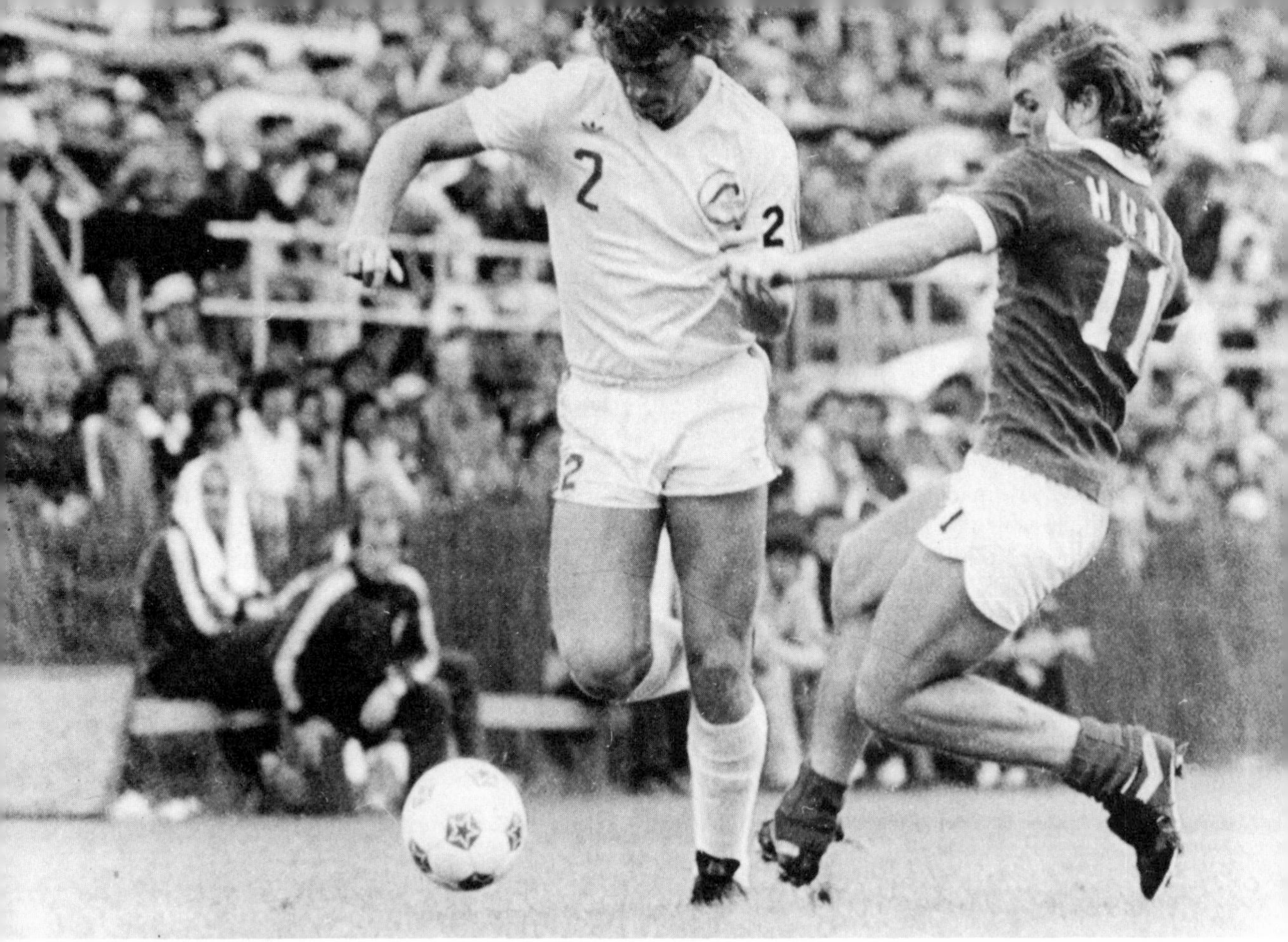
2
HUN
BECKENBAUER
6
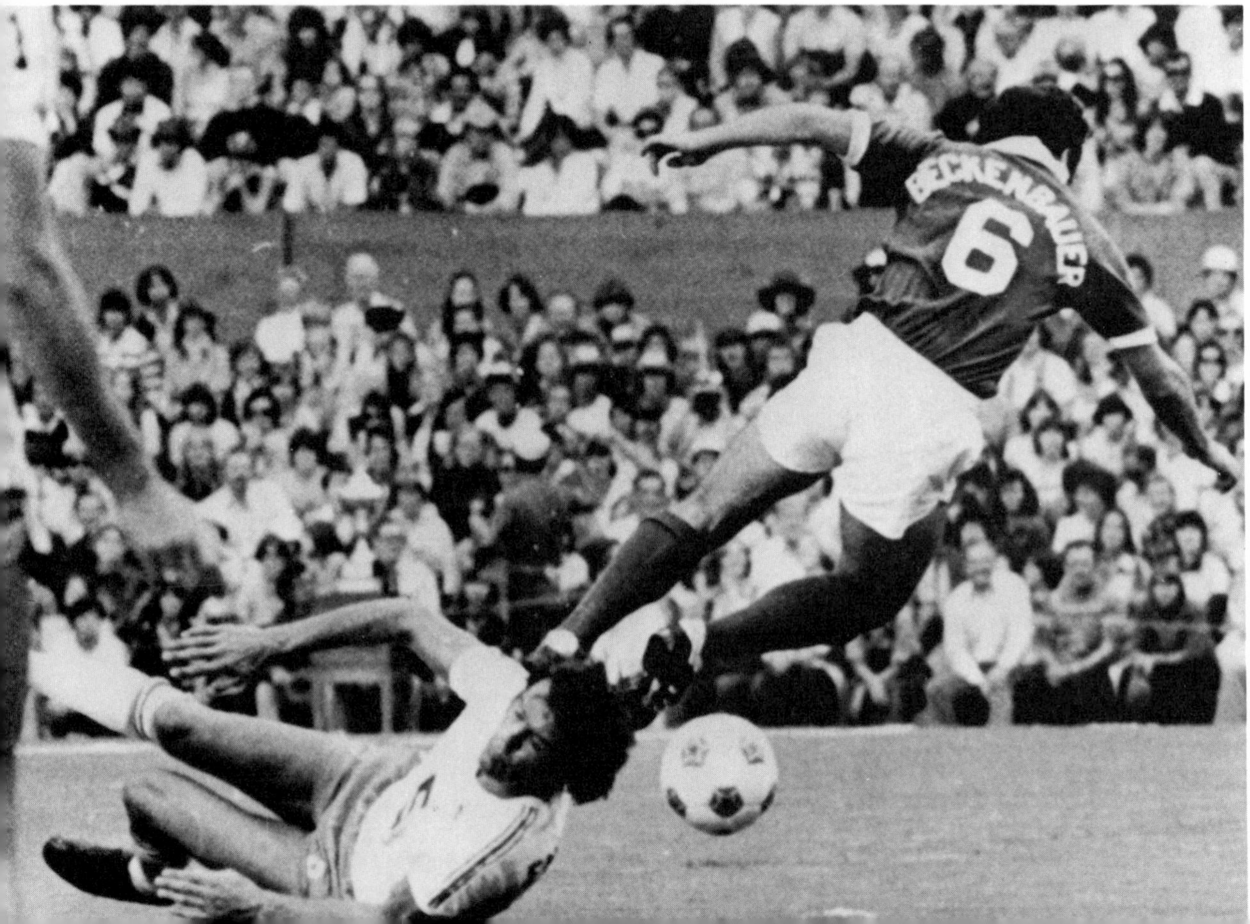

◀ *Steve Hunt (11), a flashy and speedy English forward, inspired the Cosmos' playoff drive toward Soccer Bowl-77. He's battling Don Droege of the Rochester Lancers during the semifinals.*

(Bottom left) League MVP Franz Beckenbauer (6) tangles with the Seattle Sounders' all-star defender, Mike England, in the Soccer Bowl won by the Cosmos.

Pelé spoke of love at his farewell game against his former club, Santos of Brazil, as more than 77,000 people came to Giants Stadium to pay their respects to the King, including Jimmy Carter's son, Chip (far left); Sonny Werblin; master of ceremonies Frank Gifford; Cosmos teammates Franz Beckenbauer and Carlos Alberto, and heavyweight champion Muhammad Ali.

Jim McAlister, the Seattle fullback, and went back to Giants Stadium for one more sellout, his farewell game in October against his original club, Santos of Brazil.

1977 FINAL SEASON STANDINGS AND STATISTICS

ATLANTIC CONFERENCE

Northern Division	GP	W	L	GF	GA	BP	TP
Toronto	26	13	13	42	38	37	115
St. Louis	26	12	14	33	35	32	104
Rochester	26	11	15	34	41	33	99
Chicago	26	10	16	31	43	28	88
Connecticut	26	7	19	34	65	30	72

Eastern Division							
Ft. Lauderdale	26	19	7	49	29	47	161
New York	26	15	11	60	39	50	140
Tampa Bay	26	14	12	55	45	47	131
Washington	26	10	16	32	49	32	92

PACIFIC CONFERENCE

Western Division	GP	W	L	GF	GA	BP	TP
Minnesota	26	16	10	44	36	41	137
Vancouver	26	14	12	43	46	40	124
Seattle	26	14	12	43	34	39	123
Portland	26	10	16	39	42	38	98

Southern Division							
Dallas	26	18	8	56	37	53	161
Los Angeles	26	15	11	65	54	57	147
San Jose	26	14	12	37	44	35	119
Hawaii	26	11	15	45	59	40	106
Las Vegas	26	11	15	38	44	37	103

PLAYOFF RESULTS

First Round
Aug. 10 at Los Angeles—Los Angeles 2, San Jose 1
Aug. 10 at Vancouver—Seattle 2, Vancouver 0
Aug. 10 at New York—New York 3, Tampa Bay 0
Aug. 10 at St. Louis—Rochester 1, St. Louis 0 (SO)

Division Championships
1st Round
Aug. 13 at Rochester—Rochester 1, Toronto 0 (SO)
Aug. 14 at Minnesota—Seattle 2, Minnesota 1 (OT)
Aug. 14 at Los Angeles—Los Angeles 3, Dallas 1
Aug. 14 at New York—New York 8, Ft. Lauderdale 3

2nd Round
Aug. 16 at Toronto—Rochester 1, Toronto 0
Aug. 17 at Dallas—Los Angeles 5, Dallas 1
Aug. 17 at Ft. Lauderdale—New York 3, Ft. Lauderdale 2 (SO)
Aug. 17 at Seattle—Seattle 1, Minnesota 0

Conference Championships
1st Round
Aug. 21 at Los Angeles—Seattle 3, Los Angeles 1
Aug. 21 at Rochester—New York 2, Rochester 1

2nd Round
Aug. 24 at New York—New York 4, Rochester 1
Aug. 25 at Seattle—Seattle 1, Los Angeles 0

Soccer Bowl-77
Aug. 28 at Portland—New York 2, Seattle 1

Leading Scorers	GP	G	A	TP
Steve David, Los Angeles	24	26	6	58
Derek Smethurst, Tampa Bay	21	19	4	42
George Best, Los Angeles	20	11	18	40
Giorgio Chinaglia, New York	24	15	8	38
Mike Stojanovic, Rochester	24	14	5	33
Micky Cave, Seattle	22	12	6	30
Alan Willey, Minnesota	20	14	1	29
Pele, New York	25	13	3	29
Paul Child, San Jose	26	13	3	29
Kyle Rote, Jr., Dallas	24	11	6	28
Derek Possee, Vancouver	16	11	5	27
Rodney Marsh, Tampa Bay	24	8	11	27
Drago Vabec, Toronto	15	11	4	26
Ron Futcher, Minnesota	20	11	4	26
Buzz Parsons, Vancouver	25	10	6	26
Steve Hunt, New York	23	8	10	26

Leading Goalkeepers*	Min.	SV	GA	SH	GAA
Ken Cooper, Dallas	2100	120	21	8	0.90
Gordon Banks, Ft. Lauderdale	2329	147	29	9	1.12
John Jackson, St. Louis	1526	103	20	7	1.18
Zeljko Bilecki, Toronto	2239	185	30	10	1.21
Geoff Barnett, Minnesota	2165	117	30	8	1.25
Tony Chursky, Seattle	2200	143	31	7	1.27
Alan Mayer, Las Vegas	1997	152	31	7	1.40
Mick Poole, Portland	1932	132	30	3	1.40
Mike Hewitt, San Jose	2225	135	35	8	1.42
Shep Messing, New York	1735	155	28	4	1.45
Jack Brand, Rochester	2373	167	39	6	1.48
Mervyn Cawston, Chicago	2370	179	40	3	1.52

*Need 1170 minutes to qualify

1978

Boldly, the NASL struck out in new directions. Despite a franchise fee of one million dollars, potential owners swarmed around commissioner Phil Woosnam, and he said yes to six of them.

At the same time that four franchises were moved—Connecticut to Oakland, St. Louis to Anaheim, California, Team Hawaii to Tulsa, and Las Vegas to San Diego (again)—six brand new ones were added, increasing the total to a record twenty-four. The newcomers were Colorado, Detroit, Houston, Memphis, New England, and Philadelphia, the last two buying the old Boston and Philadelphia franchises out of receivership.

Detroit and New England produced two of the best teams in the league, and Memphis was a mildly successful club at the gate despite an 0-9

Unheralded Mike Flanagan came from England to the ▶ first-year New England Tea Men and became the league's MVP.

Trevor Francis (20), on loan from England's Nottingham Forest, led the expansion Detroit Express to first place in the American Conference's Central Division.

start on the field. But few of the twenty-four teams could keep pace with the Cosmos, who surged to their second straight championship—the first time that had been done.

The Cosmos were 24-6 during the season, breaking league records for games won, points (212), goals (88), average attendance (47,856 at home), winning percentage (.800), and home victories (14, plus a two-year streak of 23 in a row).

Vancouver's Whitecaps, revamped by coaches Tony Waiters and Alan Hinton, kept pace with the Cosmos until the semifinals, also hanging up a 24-6 record including a league record thirteen straight wins. The Whitecaps also broke their home attendance record twice.

At the other end of the scale, San Jose crum-

bled to an 8-22 record, losing thirteen games in a row, also a league record. Los Angeles' Aztecs lost their first seven home games, fired coach Terry Fisher, and sold their five best players, including 1977 scoring champion Steve David and George Best.

Never was the league more of a coaching merry-go-round. Among those dislocated during the season were San Jose's Gabbo Gavric, Chicago's Malcolm Musgrove, Toronto's Domegoj Kapetonovic, Memphis' Malcolm Allison (fired during preseason after one month's tenure!), Colorado's Dave Clements, Philadelphia's Richard Dinnis; and Rochester coach Dragan Popovic was suspended for eight home games for abusing officials.

There was even a forfeited game, as Tulsa was

More high-quality Americans started to come into the league as exemplified by back-to-back Rookies of the Year Jim McAlister of the Seattle Sounders (left) in 1977 and Gary Etherington of the Cosmos in 1978.

Alan Willey of the Minnesota Kicks scored five goals in a quarterfinal match against the Cosmos.

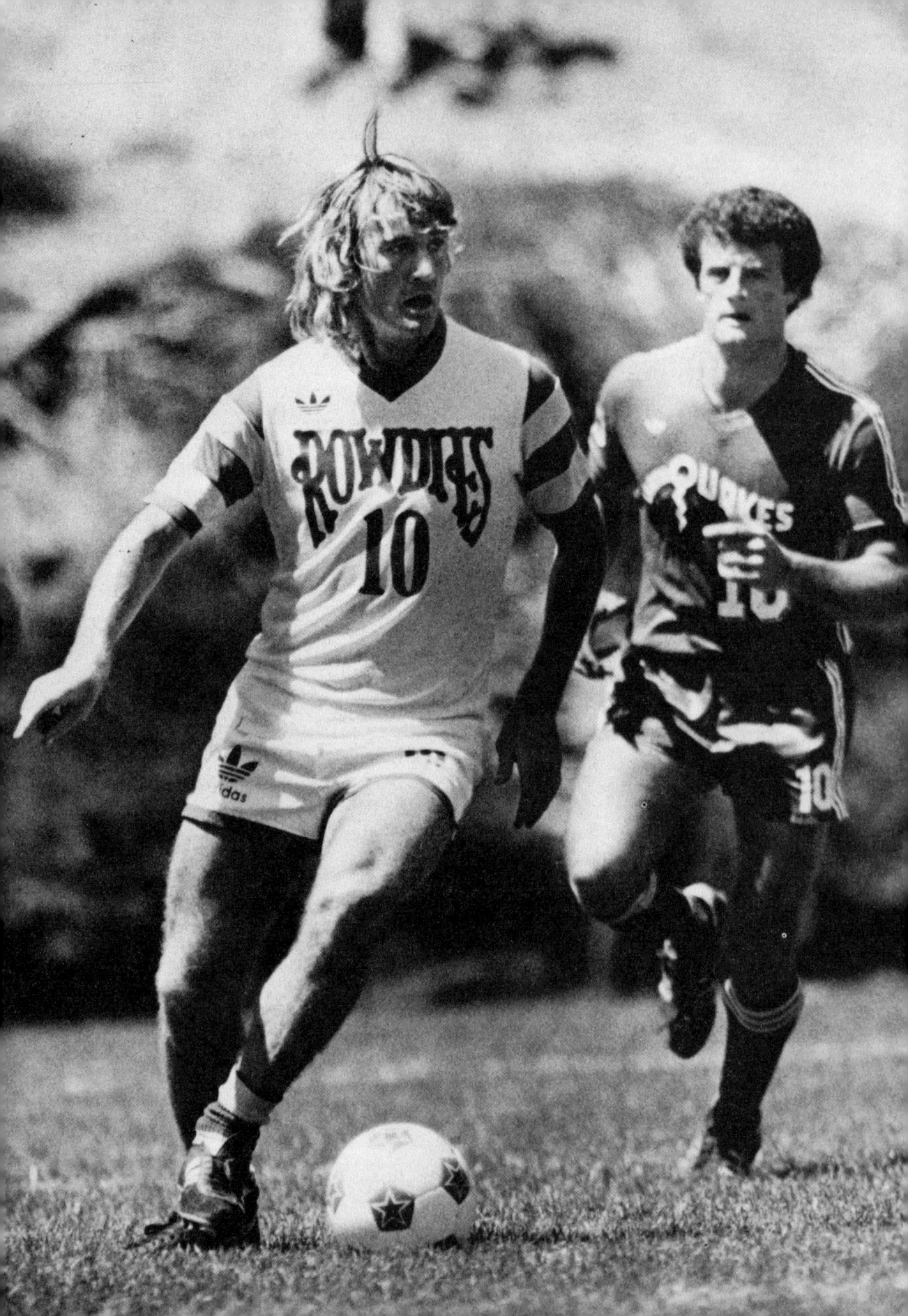

◀ Rodney Marsh led the Tampa Bay Rowdies into the Soccer Bowl, but a spike wound kept him out of the title game.

ruled to have used an ineligible player, Peter Nikezic, and its 3-2 win over Rochester was overturned.

League attendance was slightly down, at 12,997 per game, but the twenty-one playoff games drew 27,904 per game.

With the twenty-four teams, the league copied the National Football League's alignment, going to six divisions in two conferences. Sixteen of the twenty-four made the playoffs, leaving the remainder with very red faces.

The Cosmos won their division by sixty-seven points, and there was only one tight race, when New England and Tampa Bay tied for the American Conference East title with 165 points apiece.

New England's Tea Men were designated champs on the basis of one more win. Minnesota won the National Central, Vancouver the National West, Detroit the American Central, and San Diego the American West.

The play-offs bore out the cliché that they are "a new season." Despite its 19-11 record, New England was immediately ousted by Fort Lauderdale in the first round, 3-1. Detroit, with twenty-one-goal Trevor Francis, fell to those same Strikers in the second round, in the two-game-series, deciding mini-game. Vancouver fell in the second round, beaten twice by Portland.

So all the new blood was gone by the semifinals. The Cosmos had suffered a tremendous shock in the second round when they were crushed at Minnesota, 9-2, as Alan Willey scored five goals. The embarrassment reawakened the millionaires' team, easily the league's most talented, and it scrambled past Minnesota in the tie-breaker shoot-out. In the semis, the New York–New Jer-

Dennis Tueart scores the first of his two goals in the Cosmos' 3-1 victory over the Tampa Bay Rowdies in Soccer Bowl-78.

The Cosmos' Giorgio Chinaglia bicycle kicks in an exhibition game against a team of world all-stars after the season.

sey club swept Portland aside, 1-0 and 5-0, for a return berth in Soccer Bowl.

In the American Conference, Tampa Bay squeaked past Fort Lauderdale by one shoot-out kick, neatly scored by Rodney Marsh. The two teams each won at home, and goalies Winston DuBose (Tampa) and Ian Turner performed brilliantly in the shoot-out.

Tampa Bay's hopes of upsetting the Cosmos on their home field—the Soccer Bowl was awarded a year in advance to Giants Stadium—evaporated when Marsh's right shin became infected from a cleat wound. With Marsh out, and a sellout throng of 74,901 roaring, the Cosmos won Soccer Bowl handily, 3-1. English winger Dennis Tueart capped a fabulous postseason splurge with his fifth and sixth goals, and he set up the other.

The Cosmos' Giorgio Chinaglia broke a flock of scoring records with thirty-four goals and seventy-nine points, and his was judged the league's Goal of the Year, a floating header into the top corner during a regular-season win over Tampa Bay. With the addition of Tueart, fullbacks Pino Wilson and Robert Iarusci, and goalie Jack Brand, the Cosmos fielded the most powerful team in league history.

Vancouver's Bob Lenarduzzi was voted NASL North American Player of the Year.

Former Secretary of State Henry Kissinger is congratulated by Commissioner Phil Woosnam after becoming Chairman of the Board of the NASL following the 1978 season.

New England's Irish-born striker Mike Flanagan pumped in thirty goals, winning the MVP and Offensive Player of the Year awards, as well as Top Forward. Cosmos sweeper Carlos Alberto took the Defensive Player of the Year honor. Franz Beckenbauer of course was named Top Midfielder—an irony, he noted, after fourteen years as a sweeper in Germany. Cosmos winger Gary Etherington was selected Rookie of the Year. Phil Parkes of Vancouver led the league's goalies with an 0.95 average, though Kevin Keelan of the New England Tea Men was named Best Goalkeeper. Vancouver's Tony Waiters took the Coach of the Year honor. Bobby Lenarduzzi, Vancouver midfielder, was named North American Player of the Year by the Professional Soccer Reporters' Association, and the players voted San Diego goalie Alan Mayer the American Player of the Year.

The league continued to languish on television, forced to settle for a nine-game package with lightweight TVS, which placed games in some markets at 11:30 P.M. Mondays, a thirty-one hour delay. Ratings were low to medium.

The standard of play, however, was at an all-time high, and clubs such as Dallas, San Jose, and Seattle, which didn't improve, were left in the dust.

1978 FINAL SEASON STANDINGS AND STATISTICS

NATIONAL CONFERENCE

Eastern Division	GP	W	L	GF	GA	BP	TP
New York	30	24	6	88	39	68	212
Washington	30	16	14	55	47	49	145
Toronto	30	16	14	58	47	48	144
Rochester	30	14	16	47	52	47	131

Central Division							
Minnesota	30	17	13	58	43	54	156
Tulsa	30	15	15	49	46	42	132
Dallas	30	14	16	51	53	47	131
Colorado	30	8	22	34	66	33	81

Western Division							
Vancouver	30	24	6	68	29	55	199
Portland	30	20	10	50	36	47	167
Seattle	30	15	15	50	45	48	138
Los Angeles	30	9	21	36	69	34	88

AMERICAN CONFERENCE

Eastern Division	GP	W	L	GF	GA	BP	TP
New England	30	19	11	62	39	51	165
Tampa Bay	30	18	12	63	48	57	165
Ft. Lauderdale	30	16	14	50	59	47	143
Philadelphia	30	12	18	40	58	39	111

Central Division	GP	W	L	GF	GA	BP	TP
Detroit	30	20	10	68	36	56	176
Chicago	30	12	18	57	64	51	123
Memphis	30	10	20	43	58	41	101
Houston	30	10	20	37	61	36	96

Western Division							
San Diego	30	18	12	63	56	56	164
California	30	13	17	43	49	37	115
Oakland	30	12	18	34	59	31	103
San Jose	30	8	22	36	81	35	83

PLAYOFF RESULTS

First Round
Aug. 8 at San Diego—San Diego 2, California 1
Aug. 8 at Tampa Bay—Tampa Bay 3, Chicago 1
Aug. 8 at Detroit—Detroit 1, Philadelphia 0
Aug. 9 at Vancouver—Vancouver 4, Toronto 0
Aug. 9 at New York—New York 5, Seattle 2
Aug. 9 at Portland—Portland 2, Washington 1 (OT)
Aug. 9 at New England—Ft. Lauderdale 3, New England 1
Aug. 10 at Minnesota—Minnesota 3, Tulsa 1

Conference Semifinals
Aug. 12 at Portland—Portland 1, Vancouver 0
Aug. 16 at Vancouver—Portland 2, Vancouver 1
Aug. 13 at Ft. Lauderdale—Ft. Lauderdale 4, Detroit 3 (SO)
Aug. 16 at Detroit—Detroit 1, Ft. Lauderdale 0
   Ft. Lauderdale 1, Detroit 0 (OT)
Aug. 14 at San Diego—Tampa 1, San Diego 0
Aug. 16 at Tampa—San Diego 2, Tampa 1
   Tampa 1, San Diego 0 (OT)
Aug. 14 at Minnesota—Minnesota 9, New York 2
Aug. 16 at New York—New York 4, Minnesota 0
   New York 1, Minnesota 0 (SO)

Conference Championships
American Conference
Aug. 20 at Ft. Lauderdale—Ft. Lauderdale 3, Tampa 2
Aug. 23 at Tampa—Tampa 3, Ft. Lauderdale 1
   Tampa Bay 1, Ft. Lauderdale 0 (SO)

National Conference
Aug. 18 at Portland—New York 1, Portland 0
Aug. 23 at New York—New York 5, Portland 0

Soccer Bowl-78
Aug. 27 at East Rutherford, N.J.—New York 3, Tampa Bay 1

Leading Scorers	GP	G	A	TP
Giorgio Chinaglia, New York	30	34	11	79
Mike Flanagan, New England	28	30	8	68
Trevor Francis, Detroit	20	22	10	54
Kevin Hector, Vancouver	28	21	10	52
Rodney Marsh, Tampa Bay	26	18	16	52
Jeff Bourne, Dallas	30	21	8	50
Karl-Heinz Granitza, Chicago	22	19	9	47
Alan Willey, Minnesota	30	21	3	45
Ivan Lukacevic, Toronto	17	16	5	37
David Irving, Ft. Lauderdale	28	16	5	37
Bob Lenarduzzi, Vancouver	29	10	17	37
Vladislav Bogicevic, New York	30	10	17	37

Leading Goalkeepers*	G	Min.	SV	GA	SH	GAA
Phil Parkes, Vancouver	29	2650	133	28	10	0.95
Erol Yasin, New York	22	1916	129	24	6	1.13
Mick Poole, Portland	30	2783	173	36	9	1.16
Steve Hardwick, Detroit	30	2734	179	36	9	1.19
Kevin Keelan, New England	29	2609	158	36	7	1.24
Winston Dubose, Tampa Bay	15	1352	68	19	4	1.26
Zeljko Bilecki, Toronto	17	1550	122	23	6	1.34
Dave Jokerst, California	17	1574	79	24	6	1.37
Colin Boulton, Tulsa	29	2531	160	39	10	1.39
Tony Chursky, Seattle	28	2617	175	41	9	1.41
Bill Irwin, Washington	27	2362	178	39	5	1.49
Keith Van Eron, Houston	19	1737	114	31	6	1.60

*Need 1350 minutes to qualify.

1979

At last, the NASL found an alternative to the Cosmos.

The New York–New Jersey club's bid for a hat trick of league titles died in the semifinals at Giants Stadium, and the circuit hailed a new champion, the Vancouver Whitecaps.

Officially, the Whitecaps ascended the throne in Soccer Bowl IV as they defeated the Tampa Bay Rowdies, 2-1, making the Rowdies losing finalists two years running.

Yet the supreme moment seemed to be one week earlier, when the Whitecaps outfought the Cosmos in the second leg of the semifinals (for the National Conference title), over some three and a half hours of soccer. Having won the first leg at home, 2-0, Vancouver rallied to tie the second game, 2-2, only to lose in a shootout. The mini-game ended scoreless, despite a controversial near-goal by Vancouver wing Carl Valentine on a shot off the crossbar. But goalie Phil Parkes and his Vancouver teammates won the mini-game shootout, 3-2, as Cosmos defender Nelsi Morais exceeded the five-second time limit on his final shootout attempt.

With the Cosmos eliminated, only 50,699 of the 66,843 paid ticket-holders showed up for the Soccer Bowl, a game which will come to be known as the Trevor Whymark Final. Sparked by the bustling and playmaking of Alan Ball, Whymark collected two of Ball's passes and put them past Rowdies goalie Zeljko Bilecki to decide the game. Midfielder Jan Van Der Veen scored Tampa's goal in the first half, but Vancouver's league-leading defense smothered retiring Rodney Marsh and NASL scoring champion Oscar Fabbiani.

The final capped a zany season which saw:

• Dutch superstar Johan Cruyff come out of retirement to sign with the Los Angeles Aztecs for a reported $700,000 per year and win the NASL Most Valuable Player award;

• Rochester goalie Shep Messing charge that New England goalie Kevin Keelan suggested the two teams give each other an extra goal in a late-season game so both would make the playoffs;

• ABC-TV telecast live nine NASL games, including the final, though ratings were so low they were almost invisible;

• Timo Liekoski coached the no-star Houston Hurricane to the second best record in the league, 22–8, thus winning the Coach of the Year award, only to stumble in the first round of the playoffs and lose to lowly Philadelphia (10–20);

• The Cosmos dominate the all-star team to an extent unprecedented in league history, with Carlos Alberto, Wim Rijsbergen, Franz Beckenbauer, Johan Neeskens and Giorgio Chinaglia all on the first team, by vote of the players themselves. And Ricky Davis, a 20-year-old midfielder, was named North American Player of the Year.

Chinaglia topped everyone in goals with twenty-six, though the Argentine Fabbiani nosed him out for the scoring title by one point, fifty-eight to fifty-seven. Teammate Vladislav Bogicevic was the top assist maker with twenty-three. Yet despite adding Neeskens, Rijsbergen, Francisco Marinho and goalie Hubert Birkenmeier, the Cosmos were a fragmented, argumentative team.

Chinaglia went into the stands during practice and fought with maintenance workers. Four players were ejected when the Cosmos and the Whitecaps engaged in an eight-minute mid-season brawl. Sweeper Alberto was suspended for rest of the playoffs when he allegedly spat on an official after the playoff loss at Vancouver, and the Cosmos threatened to sue their own league for "anti-Cosmos feeling."

More successful stories were being told in Tampa Bay, where Gordon Jago's exciting team increased attendance by 57 percent over 1978 and lost only twice at home; and in Vancouver, where all of British Columbia seemed to fall hopelessly in love with the gritty, never-stop Whitecaps. Crowds at Empire Stadium were up 42 percent,

Despite the presence of NASL scoring champ Oscar Fabbiani (20), Tampa Bay lost to Vancouver in Soccer Bowl-79.

The Cosmos' 20-year-old Rick Davis was voted the top ▶
North American player by the writers.

sparking demand for a new, larger stadium. Fort Lauderdale was exhilarated by the world-class pairing of Gerd Mueller and Teofilo Cubillas.

Many of the smaller cities came up with surprisingly healthy attendance gains: San Diego 111 percent, Toronto 89 percent, Chicago 78 percent, Tulsa 46 percent, and fifteen of the twenty-four teams averaged 10,000 fans per game or better. The league as a whole was up by 7.5 percent, to 14,003 per contest.

While the Cosmos ran away with the National East, setting a league record with 216 points, Minnesota again won the National Central easily, and Vancouver held off the Aztecs to win the National West. Tampa Bay and Houston commanded their ASC divisions, and San Diego and California tied for the ASC West title with 140 points apiece.

Houston, Fort Lauderdale, Detroit, California, Dallas, Washington, Minnesota and Toronto fell by the wayside in the first round of the playoffs. In the conference semifinals, Tampa Bay nudged Philadelphia, San Diego blanked Chicago, and Vancouver and the Cosmos had to go to mini-games to beat L.A. and Tulsa, respectively.

Again in the conference finals, Vancouver and Tampa Bay both needed mini-games to scramble past San Diego and the Cosmos, making the '79 playoffs the closest in recent years.

In the end, the 34-year-old Ball was voted the MVP of the playoffs, and he and the Whitecaps flew home to a tumultuous heroes' welcome in the streets of Vancouver.

1979 FINAL SEASON STANDINGS AND STATISTICS

NATIONAL CONFERENCE

Eastern Division	GP	W	L	GF	GA	BP	TP
New York	30	24	6	84	52	72	216
Washington	30	19	11	68	50	59	172
Toronto	30	14	16	52	65	49	133
Rochester	30	15	15	43	57	42	132

Central Division							
Minnesota	30	21	9	67	48	58	184
Dallas	30	17	13	53	51	50	152
Tulsa	30	14	16	61	56	55	139
Atlanta	30	12	18	59	61	49	121

Western Division							
Vancouver	30	20	10	54	34	52	172
Los Angeles	30	18	12	62	47	54	162
Seattle	30	13	17	58	52	47	125
Portland	30	11	19	50	75	46	112

AMERICAN CONFERENCE

Eastern Division	GP	W	L	GF	GA	BP	TP
Tampa Bay	30	19	11	67	46	55	169
Ft. Lauderdale	30	17	13	75	65	63	165
Philadelphia	30	10	20	5	60	51	111
New England	30	12	18	41	56	38	110

Central Division							
Houston	30	22	8	61	46	5	187
Chicago	30	16	14	70	62	63	159
Detroit	30	14	16	61	56	49	133
Memphis	30	6	24	38	74	37	73

Western Division							
San Diego	30	15	15	59	55	50	140
California	30	15	15	53	56	50	140
Edmonton	30	8	22	43	78	40	88
San Jose	30	8	22	41	74	38	86

PLAYOFF RESULTS

Conference Quarterfinals
Aug. 14 at Philadelphia—Philadelphia 2, Houston 1
Aug. 20 at Houston—Philadelphia 2, Houston 1
Aug. 15 at Detroit—Tampa Bay 1, Detroit 0
Aug. 19 at Tampa Bay—Tampa Bay 3, Detroit 1
Aug. 15 at Chicago—Chicago 2, Ft. Lauderdale 0
Aug. 18 at Ft. Lauderdale—Chicago 1, Ft. Lauderdale 0
Aug. 16 at California—San Diego 4, California 2
Aug. 18 at San Diego—San Diego 7, California 2
Aug. 15 at Tulsa—Tulsa 2, Minnesota 1 (OT)
Aug. 19 at Minnesota—Tulsa 2, Minnesota 1 (OT)
Aug. 15 at Dallas—Vancouver 3, Dallas 2
Aug. 18 at Vancouver—Vancouver 2, Dallas 1
Aug. 15 at Los Angeles—Los Angeles 2, Washington 1
Aug. 19 at Washington—Los Angeles 4, Washington 3 (OT)
Aug. 16 at Toronto—Nw York 3, Toronto 1
Aug. 19 at New York—New York 2, Toronto 0

Conference Semifinals
Aug. 22 at San Diego—San Diego 2, Chicago 0
Aug. 25 at Chicago—San Diego 1, Chicago 0
Aug. 23 at Philadelphia—Tampa Bay 3, Philadelphia 2 (SO)
Aug. 25 at Tampa Bay—Tampa Bay 1, Philadelphia 0
Aug. 22 at Los Angeles—Los Angeles 3, Vancouver 2 (SO)
Aug. 25 at Vancouver—Vancouver 1, Los Angeles 0
   Mini-Game—Vancouver 1, Los Angeles 0
Aug. 23 at Tulsa—Tulsa 3, New York 0
Aug. 26 at New York—New York 3, Tulsa 0
   Mini-Game—New York 3, Tulsa 1

Conference Championships
American Conference
Aug. 30 at San Diego—San Diego 2, Tampa Bay 1
Sept. 2 at Tampa Bay—Tampa Bay 3, San Diego 2 (SO)
   Mini-Game—Tampa Bay 1, San Diego 0

National Conference
Aug. 29 at Vancouver—Vancouver 2, New York 0
Sept. 1 at New York—New York 3, Vancouver 2 (SO)
   Mini-Game—Vancouver 1, New York 0 (SO)

Soccer Bowl-79
 Sept. 8 at East Rutherford, N.J.—Vancouver 2, Tampa Bay 1

Leading Scorers	GP	G	A	TP
Oscar Fabbiani, Tampa Bay	26	25	8	58
Giorgio Chinaglia, New York	27	26	5	57
Gerd Mueller, Ft. Lauderdale	25	19	17	55
Jeff Bourne, Atlanta	29	18	15	51
David Robb, Philadelphia	30	16	20	52
Karl-Heinz Granitza, Chicago	30	20	10	50
Teofilo Cubillas, Ft. Lauderdale	30	16	18	50
Alan Willey, Minnesota	29	21	7	49
Dennis Tueart, New York	27	16	16	48
Laurie Abrahams, Cal/Tulsa	25	18	9	45

Leading Goalkeepers*	GP	Min.	SV	GA	SH	GAA
Phil Parkes, Vancouver	29	2704	100	29	7	0.96
Victor Nogueira, Atlanta	17	1432	79	20	5	1.26
Zeljko Bilecki, Tampa Bay	17	1549	93	22	5	1.28
Mike Ivanow, Seattle	28	2517	149	39	2	1.39
Bill Irwin, Washington	28	2603	134	42	4	1.45
Paul Hammond, Houston	29	2705	215	44	6	1.46
Volkmar Gross, SD/ Minnesota	24	2132	137	38	6	1.604
Kevin Keelan, New England	25	2242	133	40	6	1.605
Colin Boulton, LA/Tulsa	30	2746	109	49	7	1.606
Tino Lettieri, Minnesota	16	1378	95	25	2	1.63

*Goalkeepers need 1350 minutes to qualify.

Holland's Johan Cruyff conquered America in his first campaign, winning league Most Valuable Player honors as a Los Angeles Aztec.

Cosmo captain Werner Roth and the Soccer Bowl trophy say it all in 1978 after the Cosmos defeated Tampa Bay, 3–1.

9

All-Time NASL Records

NASL Honor Roll

Champions
1967—Oakland Clippers (NPSL)
1967—Los Angeles Wolves (USA)
1968—Atlanta Chiefs
1969—Kansas City Spurs
1970—Rochester Lancers
1971—Dallas Tornado
1972—New York Cosmos
1973—Philadelphia Atoms
1974—Los Angeles Aztecs
1975—Tampa Bay Rowdies
1976—Toronto Metros
1977—New York Cosmos
1978—New York Cosmos
1979—Vancouver Whitecaps

Runners-Up
1967—Baltimore Bays
1967—Washington Whips
1968—San Diego Toros
1969—Atlanta Chiefs
1970—Washington Darts
1971—Atlanta Chiefs
1972—St. Louis Stars
1973—Dallas Tornado
1974—Miami Toros
1975—Portland Timbers
1976—Minnesota Kicks
1977—Seattle Sounders
1978—Tampa Bay Rowdies
1979—Tampa Bay Rowdies

Most Valuable Player
1967—Ruben Navarro, Phila. Spartans
1968—John Kowalik, Chicago Mustangs
1969—Cirilio Fernandez, KC Spurs
1970—Carlos Metidieri, Rochester Lancers
1971—Carlos Metidieri, Rochester Lancers
1972—Randy Horton, NY Cosmos
1973—Warren Archibald, Miami Toros
1974—Peter Silvester, Baltimore Comets
1975—Steven David, Miami Toros
1976—Pelé, NY Cosmos
1977—Franz Beckenbauer, NY Cosmos
1978—Mike Flanagan, New England Tea Men
1979—Johan Cruyff, Los Angeles Aztecs

Coach of the Year
1968—Phil Woosnam, Atlanta Chiefs
1969—No selection made
1970—No selection made
1971—No selection made
1972—Casey Frankiewicz, St. Louis Stars
1973—Al Miller, Philadelphia Atoms
1974—John Young, Miami Toros
1975—John Sewell, St. Louis Stars
1976—Eddie Firmani, Tampa Bay Rowdies
1977—Ron Newman, Fort Lauderdale Strikers
1978—Tony Waiters, Vancouver Whitecaps
1979—Timo Liekoski, Houston Hurricane

Rookie of the Year
1967—Willie Roy, Chicago Spurs
1968—Kaizer Motaung, Atlanta Chiefs
1969—Siegfried Stritzl, Baltimore Bays
1970—Jim Leeker, St. Louis Stars
1971—Randy Horton, NY Cosmos
1972—Mike Winter, St. Louis Stars
1973—Kyle Rote, Jr., Dallas Tornado
1974—Douglas McMillan, LA Aztecs
1975—Chris Bahr, Philadelphia Atoms
1976—Steve Pecher, Dallas Tornado
1977—Jim McAlister, Seattle Sounders
1978—Gary Etherington, NY Cosmos
1979—Larry Hulcer, Los Angeles Aztecs

Leading Scorer

Year	Player, Team	GP	G	A	TP
1967	Yanko Daucik, Toronto Falcons	17	20	8	48
1968	John Kowalik, Chicago Mustangs	28	30	9	69
1969	Kaizer Motaung, Atlanta Chiefs	15	16	4	36
1970	Kirk Apostolidis, Dallas Tornado	19	16	3	35
	Carlos Metidieri, Rochester Lancers	22	14	7	35
1971	Carlos Metidieri, Rochester Lancers	24	19	8	46
1972	Randy Horton, New York Cosmos	13	9	4	22
1973	Kyle Rote, Jr., Dallas Tornado	18	10	10	30
1974	Paul Child, San Jose Earthquakes	20	15	6	36
1975	Steven David, Miami Toros	21	23	6	52
1976	Giorgio Chinaglia, New York Cosmos	19	19	11	49
1977	Steven David, Los Angeles Aztecs	24	26	6	58
1978	Giorgio Chinaglia, New York Cosmos	30	34	11	79
1979	Oscar Fabbiani, Tampa Bay	26	25	8	58

GP—Games Played
G—Games
A—Assists
TP—Total Points

Leading Goalkeeper

Year	Player, Team	GP	SV	G	SH	GAA
1967	Mirko Stojanovic, Oakland Clippers	29	NA	29	10	1.00
1968	Ataulfo Sanchez, San Diego Toros	22	130	19	NA	0.93
1969	Manfred Kammerer, Atlanta Chiefs	14	56	15	4	1.07
1970	Lincoln Phillips, Washington Darts	22	96	21	12	0.95
		Min.				
1971	Mirko Stojanovic, Dallas Tornado	1359	91	11	8	0.79
1972	Ken Cooper, Dallas Tornado	1260	107	12	6	0.86
1973	Bob Rigby, Philadelphia Atoms	1157	78	8	6	0.62
1974	Barry Watling, Seattle Sounders	1800	132	16	8	0.80
1975	Shep Messing, Boston Minutemen	1639	140	17	6	0.93
1976	Tony Chursky, Seattle Sounders	1981	135	20	9	0.91
1977	Ken Cooper, Dallas Tornado	2100	120	21	8	0.90
1978	Phil Parkes, Vancouver Whitecaps	2650	133	28	10	0.95
1979	Phil Parkes, Vancouver Whitecaps	2704	100	29	7	0.96

All-Time Scorers

*Player	Seasons	GP	G	A	TP
Ilija Mitic, San Jose	9	166	101	37	239
Giorgio Chinaglia, New York	4	100	94	35	223
Paul Child, San Jose	8	179	77	36	190
Steve David, California	6	131	81	25	187
Alan Willey, Minnesota	4	102	72	18	162
Derek Smethurst, Seattle	5	110	72	17	161
Warren Archibald, Rochester	9	162	58	39	155
Carlos Metidieri, Rochester	7	129	61	28	150
Leroy Deleon, San Jose	11	153	56	35	147
Rodney Marsh, Tampa Bay	4	94	54	50	146
Jeff Bourne, Atlanta	3	81	54	26	134
Randy Horton, Connecticut	6	89	51	23	125
Kyle Rote, Houston	7	142	43	38	124
Tommy Ord, Seattle	7	133	49	21	119
Kaiser Motaung, Atlanta	6	105	50	18	118
Clyde Best, Portland	5	122	43	31	117
Ron Futcher, Minnesota	4	80	46	24	116
Manfred Seissler, Rochester	7	108	43	28	114
Willy Roy, Chicago	5	99	42	29	113
Ace Ntsoelengoe, Minnesota	6	131	39	35	113
Art Welch, Washington	11	171	38	34	110
Casey Frankiewicz, St. Louis	7	110	44	20	108
Mike Stojanovic, Rochester	4	90	40	28	108
Pepe Fernandez, Seattle	5	75	42	18	102
Al Trost, Seattle	7	147	39	24	102
David Robb, Philadelphia	3	72	37	27	101

*Team as of 1979

NASL All-Star Teams 1967–1978

Selected by vote of players and coaches in conjunction with *The Sporting News*

1967—United Soccer Association

First Team
G—Bobby Clark, Washington
D—Mario Tito, Houston
D—Jose Fidelis, Houston
D—Pat Stanton, Toronto
M—Jim Baxter, Vancouver
M—Tommy McMillan, Washington
M—Ary Clemente, Houston
F—Paulo Borges, Houston

F—Peter Dobing, Cleveland
F—George Eastham, Cleveland
F—Roy Vernon, Cleveland
Second Team
G—Gordon Banks, Cleveland
D—Eric Skeels, Cleveland
D—Jan Villerius, San Francisco
D—Joe Davis, Toronto
M—John Moore, Cleveland
M—Miguel Angelo Longo, Chicago
M—Doug Smith, Dallas
F—Henk Houwaart, San Francisco
F—Roberto Boninsegna, Chicago
F—Benedicto Ribeiro, New York
F—Peter Cormack, Toronto

1967 National Professional Soccer League

First Team
G—Mirko Stojanovic, Oakland
D—Mel Scott, Oakland
D—Badu Da Cruz, Baltimore
M—Juan Santisteban, Baltimore
M—Ilija Mitic, Oakland
M—Ruben Navarro, Baltimore
F—Willie Roy, Chicago
F—Co Prins, Pittsburgh
F—Mario Baesso, Oakland
F—Art Welch, Baltimore
F—Emment Kapengwe, Atlanta

1968 NASL (Merger of USA and NPSL)

First Team
G—Mirko Stojanovic, Oakland
D—Mel Scott, Oakland
D—Momcilio Gavric, Oakland
M—David Davidovic, Oakland
M—Ron Crisp, San Diego
M—Ruben Navarro, Cleveland
F—John Kowalik, Chicago
F—Cirilo Fernandez, San Diego
F—Jorgen Kristensen, Detroit
F—Casey Frankiewicz, St. Louis
F—Ilija Mitic, Oakland
Second Team
G—Vic Rouse, Atlanta
D—John Worbye, Washington
D—John Cocking, Atlanta
M—Dennis Viollet, Baltimore
M—Milan Cop, Oakland
M—Tony Knapp, Los Angeles
F—Victorio Casa, Washington
F—Mario Baesso, Oakland
F—Eric Barber, Kansas City
F—Vava (Edvaldo Neto), San Diego
F—Enrique Mateos, Cleveland

1969

First Team
G—Leonel Conde, Kansas City
D—John Borodiak, Baltimore
D—Kirk Apostolidis, Dallas
M—William Quiros, Kansas City
M—John Best, Dallas
M—Joe Puis, St. Louis
F—Pepe Fernandez, Kansas City

F—Kaiser Motaung, Atlanta
F—Manfred Seissler, Kansas City
F—Ilija Mitic, Dallas
F—Emment Kapengwe, Atlanta
F—Art Welch, Baltimore

1970

First Team
G—Lincoln Phillips, Washington
D—Charlie Mitchell, Rochester
D—Uriel daVeiga, Atlanta
M—Willie Evans, Washington
M—John Best, Dallas
M—Willie Fraser, Washington
F—Carlos Metidieri, Rochester
F—Dave Metchik, Atlanta
F—Art Welch, Atlanta
F—Leroy DeLeon, Washington
F—Manfred Seissler, Kansas City
Second Team
G—Leonel Conde, Kansas City
D—John Cocking, Atlanta
D—Delroy Scott, Atlanta
M—Ray Bloomfield, Atlanta
M—Roy Turner, Dallas
M—Bob DeLuca, Rochester
F—Warren Archibald, Washington
F—Clarival Oliveira, Kansas City
F—Kirk Apostolidis, Dallas
F—Mike Renshaw, Dallas
F—Pat McBride, St. Louis

1971

First Team
G—Mirko Stojanovic, Dallas
D—Dick Hall, Dallas
D—Willie Evans, Washington
D—Peter Short, Rochester
D—John Best, Dallas
M—Dragan Popovic, St. Louis
M—Siggy Stritzl, New York
F—Carlos Metidieri, Rochester
F—Randy Horton, New York
F—Kaiser Motaung, Atlanta
F—Manfred Seissler, Rochester
Second Team
G—Leonel Conde, Washington
D—Clive Charles, Montreal
D—Uriel, Atlanta
D—John Cocking, Atlanta
D—Charles Mitchell, Rochester
M—Francisco Escos, Rochester
M—Felix Correia, Toronto
F—Warren Archibald, Washington
F—Casey Frankiewicz, St. Louis
F—Franco Gallina, Montreal
F—Jorge Siega, New York

1972

First Team
G—Ken Cooper, Dallas
D—John Best, Dallas
D—John Sewell, Saint Louis
D—Peter Short, Rochester
D—Willie Evans, Miami
M—John Kerr, New York
M—Graeme Souness, Montreal

M—Pat McBride, St. Louis
F—Randy Horton, New York
F—Paul Child, Atlanta
F—Michael Dillon, Montreal
Second Team
G—Dick Howard, Toronto
D—Dick Hall, Dallas
D—Clive Charles, Montreal
D—Wilf Tranter, Saint Louis
D—Brian Rowan, Toronto
M—Francisco Escos, Rochester
M—Dave Metchick, Miami
M—Siggy Stritzl, New York
F—Carlos Metidieri, Rochester
F—Art Welch, Atlanta
F—Jorge Siega, New York

1973

First Team
G—Ken Cooper, Dallas
D—John Best, Dallas
D—Chris Dunleavy, Philadelphia
D—David Sadler, Miami
D—Brian Rowan, Toronto
M—Ilija Mitic, Dallas
M—Fernando Pinto, Toronto
M—Ian McPhee, Toronto
F—Andy Provan, Philadelphia
F—Jim Fryatt, Philadelphia
F—Warren Archibald, Miami
Second Team
G—Bob Rigby, Philadelphia
D—Bob Smith, Philadelphia
D—Derek Trevis, Philadelphia
D—Dick Hall, Dallas
D—Roy Evans, Philadelphia
M—Pat McBride, St. Louis
M—Francisco Escos, Rochester
M—Roberto Aguirre, Miami
F—Joe Fink, New York
F—Rick Reynolds, Dallas
F—Randy Horton, New York

1974

First Team
G—Barry Watling, Seattle
D—Dick Hall, Dallas
D—Albert Jackson, Dallas
D—Christ Dunleavy, Philadelphia
D—Geoff Butler, Baltimore
M—Ronnie Sharp, Miami
M—Ilija Mitic, Dallas
M—Roberto Aguirre, Miami
F—Paul Child, San Jose
F—John Rowlands, Seattle
F—Peter Silvester, Baltimore
Second Team
G—Bob Rigby, Philadelphia
D—Ralph Wright, Miami
D—Derek Trevis, Philadelphia
D—Jim Gabriel, Seattle
D—Brian Rowan, Toronto
M—Hank Liotart, Seattle
M—Luis Marotte, Los Angeles
M—Fernando Pinto, Toronto
F—Ade Coker, Boston
F—Doug McMillan, Los Angeles
F—Warren Archibald, Miami

1975

First Team
G—Peter Bonetti, St. Louis
D—Bob Smith, Philadelphia
D—Mike England, Seattle
D—Werner Roth, New York
D—Farrukh Quraishi, Tampa
M—Arfon Griffiths, Seattle
M—Ronnie Sharp, Miami
M—Antonio Simoes, Boston
F—Steven David, Miami
F—Pele, New York
F—Gordon Hill, Chicago
Second Team
G—Ken Cooper, Dallas
D—Tony Want, Philadelphia
D—Stewart Jump, Tampa
D—Ralph Wright, Miami
D—Charlie Mitchell, Rochester
M—Barry Powell, Portland
M—John Boyle, Tampa
M—Bob Hope, Philadelphia
F—Peter Withe, Portland
F—Tommy Ord, Rochester/New York
F—Stewart Scullion, Tampa

1976

First Team
G—Arnold Mausser, Tampa Bay
D—Bobby Moore, San Antonio
D—Mike England, Seattle
D—Tommy Smith, Tampa Bay
D—Keith Eddy, New York
M—Ramon Mifflin, New York
M—Antonio Simoes, Boston/San Jose
M—Rodney Marsh, Tampa Bay
F—George Best, Los Angeles
F—Pele, New York
F—Giorgio Chinaglia, New York
Second Team
G—Eric Martin, Washington
D—Stewart Jump, Tampa Bay
D—George Ley, Dallas
D—Ron Webster, Minnesota
D—Bobby Smith, New York
M—Alan West, Minnesota
M—Bob Hope, Dallas
M—Al Trost, St. Louis
F—Derek Smethurst, Tampa Bay
F—Stewart Scullion, Tampa Bay
F—Jeff Bourne, Dallas

1977

First Team
G—Gordon Banks, Fort Lauderdale
D—Franz Beckenbauer, New York
D—Mike England, Seattle
D—Bruce Wilson, Vancouver
D—Mel Machin, Seattle
M—George Best, Los Angeles
M—Wolfgang Suhnholz, Las Vegas
M—Alan West, Minnesota
F—Steve David, Los Angeles
F—Pele, New York
F—Derek Smethurst, Tampa Bay
Second Team
G—Alan Mayer, Las Vegas

D—Ray Evens, St. Louis
D—Steve Pecher, Dallas
D—Humberto, Las Vegas
D—*George Ley, Dallas
D—*Arsene Auguste, Tampa Bay
M—Charlie Cooke, Los Angeles
M—Vito Dimitrijevic, New York
M—Rodney Marsh, Tampa Bay
F—Mike Stojanovic, Rochester
F—Steve Wegerle, Tampa Bay
F—Buzz Parsons, Vancouver
*Tied for 4th Defender

1978

First Team
G—Kevin Keelan, New England
D—Carlos Alberto, New York
D—Mike England, Seattle
D—Ray Evans, California
D—Chris Turner, New England
M—Franz Beckenbauer, New York
M—Gerry Daly, New England
M—Rodney Marsh, Tampa Bay
F—Mike Flanagan, New England
F—Trevor Francis, Detroit
F—Giorgio Chinaglia, New York
Second Team
G—Alan Mayer, San Diego
D—Bruce Wilson, Chicago
D—Arsene Auguste, Tampa Bay
D—John Craven, Vancouver
D—Alan Merrick, Minnesota
M—Vladislav Bogicevic, New York
M—Alan Ball, Philadelphia
M—Ray Hudson, Fort Lauderdale
F—Steve Hunt, New York
F—Steve Wegerle, Tampa Bay
F—Kevin Hector, Vancouver

1979

First Team
G—Phil Parkes, Vancouver
D—Carlos Alberto, New York
D—Bruce Wilson, Chicago
D—Mike Connell, Tampa Bay
D—Wim Rijsbergen, New York
M—Franz Beckenbauer, New York
M—Johan Neeskens, New York
M—Ace Ntsoelengoe, Minnesota
F—Johan Cruyff, Los Angeles
F—Trevor Francis, Detroit
F—Georgio Chinaglia, New York
Second Team
G—Paul Hammond, Houston
D—Marinho, New York
D—John Gorman, Tampa Bay
D—Mihalj Keri, Los Angeles
D—Bob Lenarduzzi, Vancouver
M—Vladislav Bogicevic, New York
M—Teofilo Cubillas, Fort Lauderdale
M—Alan Ball, Vancouver
F—Oscar Fabbiani, Tampa Bay
F—Karl-Heinz Granitza, Chicago
F—Gerd Mueller, Fort Lauderdale

REGULAR SEASON RECORDS

INDIVIDUAL

Most total points, season—79, Giorgio Chinaglia, New York 1978—34 goals, 11 assists in 30 games

Most total points, game—12, Giorgio Chinaglia, New York (vs. Miami) 8/10/76—5 goals, 2 assists

Most total points, one half—8, Andy Provan, Philadelphia (at Washington) 5/4/74—4 goals; Giorgio Chinaglia, New York (vs. Miami) 8/10/76—4 goals; Bob Rohrbach, Detroit (vs. Memphis) 4/14/79—4 goals

Most goals, season—34, Giorgio Chinaglia, New York 1978

Most goals, game—5, Steve David, Miami (vs. Washington) 6/20/75; Giorgio Chinaglia, New York (vs. Miami) 8/10/76; Ron Moore, Chicago (vs. Vancouver) 6/24/77; Mike Flanagan, New England (vs. California) 7/9/78; Trevor Francis, Detroit (vs. San Jose) 7/12/78; Oscar Fabbiani, Tampa Bay (vs. California) 7/11/79

Most goals, one half—4, Andy Provan, Philadelphia (at Washington) 5/4/74; Giorgio Chinaglia, New York (vs. Miami) 8/10/76; Bob Rohrbach, Detroit (vs. Memphis) 4/14/79

Most consecutive games scoring a goal—10, Steve David, Los Angeles 1977

Earliest goal—0:21, Willie Mfum, New York (vs. Rochester) 8/2/71

Latest goal, regulation time—90:00, Ilija Mitic, San Jose (vs. St. Louis) 5/2/75; Trevor Francis, Detroit (vs. San Jose) 7/12/78

Latest goal, overtime—104:59, Brian Tinnion, Colorado (at San Jose) 4/16/78

Shortest time to score two goals—0:41, Jeff Bourne, Dallas (vs. Houston) 7/29/78

Shortest time to score three goals—4:24, Jeff Bourne, Dallas (vs. New York) 8/4/78

Shortest time to score four goals—16:45, Giorgio Chinaglia, New York (vs. Miami) 8/10/76

Most goals on penalty kicks, season—8, Keith Eddy, New York 1976

Most penalty kicks missed, season—2, Carlos Metidieri, Rochester 1971; Charlie Mitchell, Rochester 1972; Tommy Ord, Seattle 1978; Stewart Scullion, Portland 1978; Gerry Ingram, California 1979; Keith Weller, New England 1979; Frank Worthington, Philadelphia 1979

Most goals on penalty kicks, game—3, Wayne Hughes, Tulsa (vs. Dallas) 4/21/79

Most assists, season—30, Alan Hinton, Vancouver 1978

Most assists, game—4, Miguel Perrichon, Toronto (at Miami) 5/6/72; Roberto Aguirre, Miami (vs. New York) 6/14/74; Pelé, New York (vs. Miami) 8/10/76; Vito Dimitrijevic, New York (vs. Toronto) 6/5/77; Vladislav Bogicevic, New York (vs. Fort Lauderdale) 4/2/78; Bob Bolitho, Vancouver (vs. Dallas) 7/12/78;Roberto DeOliveira, Detroit (vs. Memphis) 4/14/79; Vladislav Bogicevic, New York (vs. Rochester) 7/1/79

Most assists, one half—4, Roberto DeOliveira, Detroit (vs. Memphis) 4/14/79

Most consecutive games with an assist—8, Vladislav Bogicevic, New York 1979

GOALKEEPER

Most goals allowed, season—70, Mick Poole, Portland 1979

Best goals-against average, season—0.62, Bob Rigby, Philadelphia 1973—8 goals-against in 1157 minutes played

Fewest goals allowed, season—8, Bob Rigby, Philadelphia 1973

Most shutouts, season—12, Lincoln Phillips, Washington 1970

Most consecutive shutouts—4, Claude Campos, Rochester 1972, 1974; Ken Cooper, Dallas 1974, Zeljko Bilecki, Toronto 1975; Mick Poole, Portland 1978

Most consecutive minutes without allowing a goal—476, Claude Campos, Rochester 1972

Most saves, game—22, Mike Winter, St. Louis (at Rochester) 5/27/73

Fewest saves, game—0, held by many; last done by: Alex Stepney, Dallas (vs. Portland) 7/14/79; Phil Parkes, Vancouver (vs. Seattle) 7/7/79; Bob Rigby, Los Angeles (vs. San Diego) 6/13/79; Blagoje Tamindzic, Toronto (at San Jose) 6/9/79; Bob Rigby, Los Angeles (vs. Rochester) 5/23/79; Zeljko Bilecki, Tampa Bay (at Atlanta) 5/5/79; Slobodan Ilijevski, Detroit (at Dallas) 3/24/79

Fewest saves, game, both teams—2, San Diego (1 by Alan Mayer) at Vancouver (1 by Phil Parkes) 5/2/79

Most saves, game without allowing a goal—21, Sam Nusum, Montreal (at Miami) 5/5/73

Most minutes played, one season—2798, Alan Mayer, San Diego 1978

TEAM GENERAL

Most games won, season—24, New York 1978, 1979; Vancouver 1978

Highest winning percentage—80%, New York 1978, 1979; Vancouver 1978

Fewest games won, season—2, Dallas 1968; Baltimore 1969

Lowest winning percentage—6%, Dallas 1968 (2 of 32 games)

Most consecutive games won—13, Vancouver 1978

Most consecutive home games won—23, New York 1977–1978

Most consecutive road games won—8, Vancouver 1978

Most wins by an expansion team, season—20, Detroit 1978

Most consecutive games lost—14, Edmonton 1979

Most consecutive games without a victory—22, Dallas 1968

Most tie games, season (regulation time)—12, New York 1968

Highest percentage of tie games, season (regulation time)—47%, Toronto 1973 (9 of 19)

Fewest tie games, season (regulation time)—1, Baltimore 1969

Lowest percentage of tie games, season (regulation time)—6%, Baltimore 1969 (1 of 16)

Most consecutive games going over regulation time—7, San Jose 1978 (5 shootouts, 2 overtimes)

TEAM OFFENSIVE

Most goals scored, season—88, New York 1978

Highest goals per game average, season—3.3, Kansas City 1969 (53 goals in 16 games)

Fewest goals scored, season—15, Dallas 1972

Lowest goals per game average, season—0.88, Dallas 1968 (28 goals in 32 games)

Most goals, game—10, Detroit (vs San Jose) 7/12/78

Most goals, game, both teams—12, Chicago (4) at Toronto (8), 8/27/68

Largest margin of victory—10, San Jose (0) at Detroit (10), 7/12/78

Most consecutive games scoring one or more goals—30, New York 1979

Most goals, two consecutive games—13, Detroit 1978

Most goals, three consecutive games—17, Detroit 1978

Most goals, four consecutive games—19, Detroit 1978

Most goals, five consecutive games—23, Detroit 1978

Most games scoring two or more goals, season—24, New York 1979

Most games scoring three or more goals, season—18, New York 1979

Most games scoring four or more goals, season—10, New York 1978

Most games scoring five or more goals, season—5, New York 1978

Most goals, tie game (regulation time)—8, Chicago at Atlanta 6/4/67; Toronto at St. Louis 8/22/67

Shortest time to score two goals, game—0:15, Fort Lauderdale (vs Dallas) 6/25/77—Colin Fowles @ 66:30; George Nanchoff @ 66:45

Shortest time to score three goals, game—2:00, Philadelphia (vs Rochester) 6/22/73—Jim Fryatt @ 65:00; Barry Barto @ 66:00; Andy Provan @ 67:00

Shortest time to score four goals, game—5:01, Tampa Bay (vs Toronto) 4/14/79—Jan Van Der Veen @ 7:55; Wes McLeod @ 10:24; Wes McLeod @ 11:29; Peter Baralic @ 12:56

Most games held scoreless, season—12, Philadelphia 1979

Most consecutive games held scoreless—5, Denver 1974; Miami 1976; New England 1979

Most consecutive minutes held scoreless—524, Philadelphia 1978

Most own goals, season—4, Dallas 1977

Most shots, game—45, Hawaii (vs. Los Angeles) 7/22/77

Most shots, game, both teams—66, San Jose (24) at Baltimore (42) 5/24/74

Fewest shots, game—1, Rochester (vs. Toronto) 7/6/75

Fewest shots, game, both teams—16, Rochester (5) vs. Hearts-Scotland (11) 6/9/71; Dallas (9) vs. Toronto (7) 5/3/73; Hartford (7) vs. Vancouver (9) 5/24/75; California (9) vs. New England (7) 5/12/79; Vancouver (11) vs. Tulsa (5) 7/25/79

Most penalty kicks, game—3, Tulsa (vs. Dallas) 4/21/79

Most penalty kicks, game, both teams—3, Atlanta (2) vs. Lanerossi Vicenza, Italy 6/15/71; New York (1) vs. Dallas (2) 8/11/73; Boston (2) vs. Rochester (1) 7/20/74; San Antonio (1) vs. Dallas (2) 4/18/75; Tulsa (3) vs. Dallas (0) 4/21/79

Most penalty kicks converted, season—10, New York 1976

Most penalty kicks missed, season—4, Vancouver 1979

TEAM DEFENSIVE

Most goals allowed, season—109, Dallas 1968, 32 games

Highest average goals per game allowed, season—3.40, Dallas 1968—109 goals in 32 games

Fewest goals allowed, season—14, Philadelphia 1973, 19 games

Lowest average goals per game allowed, season—0.74, Philadelphia 1973—14 goals in 19 games

Most goals allowed, game—10, San Jose (at Detroit) 7/12/78

Most games holding the opposition scoreless—12, Washington 1970

Most consecutive games holding the opposition scoreless—4, Rochester 1972; Rochester 1974; Dallas 1974; Toronto 1975; Portland 1978

Most games holding the opposition to one goal or none—25, Vancouver 1978

Most consecutive games holding the opposition to one goal or none—12, Vancouver 1978

Most games holding the opposition to two goals or fewer—28, Vancouver 1979

Most penalty kicks against, season—10, Philadelphia 1979

Most own goals allowed, season—4, Minnesota 1978

ATTENDANCE RECORDS

Largest attendance, regular season game—72,342, New York (vs. Fort Lauderdale) 4/22/79

Largest attendance, international game—75,641, New York (vs. Santos) 10/1/77

Largest attendance, pre-season game—58,128, Seattle (vs. New York) 4/9/76

Largest opening day attendance—72,342, New York (vs. Fort Lauderdale) 4/22/79

Largest total attendance, season, one club—717,856, New York 1978

Highest average attendance, season, one club—47,856, New York 1978 (15 games)

Most number of sellouts, season—8, San Jose 1977 (San Jose Stadium capacity: 17,579)

Largest league attendance, regular season—5,111,861, 1979 (360 games)

Highest average per game attendance, regular season—14,199, 1979 (360 games)

Largest single game attendance in North America—77,691, New York (vs. Fort Lauderdale) 8/14/77

PLAY-OFF RECORDS

INDIVIDUAL

Most total points, career—32, Giorgio Chinaglia (New York)

Most points, one season—20, Giorgio Chinaglia (New York) 1977

Most points, one game—10, Alan Willey (Minnesota) vs. New York 8/14/78 (5 goals)

Most points, one half—8, Alan Willey (Minnesota) vs. New York 8/14/78 (4 goals)

Most goals, career—14, Giorgio Chinaglia (New York)

Most goals, one season—9, Giorgio Chinaglia (New York) 1977

Most goals, one game—5, Alan Willey (Minnesota) vs. New York 8/14/78

Earliest goal—0:52, Charlie George (Minnesota) vs. New York 8/14/78

Latest goal—176:00, Carlos Metidieri (Rochester) vs. Dallas 9/1/71

Shortest time to score two goals—5:37, Alan Willey (Minnesota) vs. New York 8/14/78

Most assists, career—11, Steve Hunt (New York)

Most assists, one season—7, Steve Hunt (New York) 1977

Most assists, one game—3, Steve Hunt (New York) vs. Tampa Bay 8/10/77; Ian "Chico" Hamilton (Minnesota) vs. Tulsa 8/10/78; Ian "Chico" Hamilton (Minnesota) vs. New York 8/14/78; Willie Morgan (Minnesota) vs. New York 8/14/78; Vladislav Bogicevic (New York) vs. Minnesota 8/16/78

GOALKEEPER

Most goals allowed, career—18, Ken Cooper (Dallas)

Most goals allowed, one season—10, Gordon Banks (Fort Lauderdale) 1977; Ian Turner (Fort Lauderdale) 1978; Winston Dubose (Tampa Bay) 1978

Most goals allowed, one game—8, Gordon Banks (Ft. Lauderdale) vs. New York 8/14/77; Jack Brand (New York) vs. Minnesota 8/14/78

Best goals-against average, one season—0.00, Bob Rigby (Philadelphia) 1973 (2 games); Paul Hammond (Tampa Bay) 1975 (3 games)

Best goals-against average, career (need 270 minutes)—0.75, Paul Hammond (Tampa Bay) (3 goals, 360 minutes)

Most shutouts, career—5, Jack Brand (Rochester, New York)

Fewest goals allowed, one season—0, Bob Rigby (Philadelphia) 1973; Paul Hammond (Tampa Bay) 1975

Most saves, one game—17, Jerry Sularz (New York) vs. Dallas 8/15/73

Fewest saves, one game—1, Jack Brand (Rochester) vs. Toronto 8/13/77; Jack Brand (Rochester) vs. New York 8/22/77

Fewest saves, one game, both teams—4, Dallas and Los Angeles 8/18/76; San Jose and Los Angeles 8/10/77

TEAM GENERAL

Most play-off games won—14, New York (2 in 1972, 1 in 1976, 6 in 1977, 6 in 1977, 5 in 1978)

Best winning percentage—1.000, Philadelphia (2 wins in 2 games)

Lowest winning percentage—.250, San Jose (1 win in 4 games)

Most play-off games participated in—19, New York

TEAM OFFENSIVE

Most goals, career—48, New York

Highest average goals per game, career—2.50, New York

Most goals, one game—9, Minnesota (vs. New York) 8/14/78

Most goals, two teams—11, New York (8) vs. Fort Lauderdale (3) 8/14/77; Minnesota (9) vs. New York (2) 8/14/78

Most games scoring one or more goals—16, New York

Shortest time to score two goals—0:41, Maurice Whittle and David Irving (Fort Lauderdale) vs. Tampa Bay 8/20/78

Shortest time to score three goals—3:29, Miro Rys, Des Backos, Charlie Cooke (Los Angeles) vs. Dallas 8/17/77

Most penalty kick goals—1, Joe Jelinek (New York) vs. St. Louis 8/26/72; Jim Fryatt (Philadelphia) vs. Toronto 8/18/73; Tommy Ord (Seattle) vs. Minnesota 8/17/77; Rodney Marsh (Tampa Bay) vs. Chicago 8/8/78; Maurice Whittle (Fort Lauderdale) vs. Tampa Bay 8/20/78

Fewest shots, one game—6, San Jose (vs. Minnesota) 8/25/76; Toronto (vs. Vancouver) 8/9/78

Fewest shots, one game, both teams—21, Minnesota (15) vs. San Jose (6) 8/25/76

Most shots, two teams—55, New York (31) vs. Fort Lauderdale (24) 8/17/77; New York (29) vs. Seattle (26) 8/28/77

Most games held scoreless—5, Toronto

TEAM DEFENSIVE

Most goals allowed, career—28, New York

Most games held opposition scoreless—6, New York

Most games held opposition to one goal or less—13, New York

Most goals allowed, one season—12, New York 1978

Most goals allowed, one game—9, New York (vs. Minnesota) 8/14/78

ATTENDANCE

Largest single game attendance—77,691, New York (Giants Stadium) vs. Fort Lauderdale 8/14/77

Largest Soccer Bowl attendance—74,901, 1978 (Giants Stadium) New York vs. Tampa Bay 8/27/78

FRANCHISES YEAR BY YEAR

1967

United Soccer Association: Boston Rovers, Chicago Mustangs, Cleveland Stokers, Dallas Tornado, Detroit Cougars, Houston Stars, Los Angeles Wolves, New York Skyliners, San Francisco Golden Gate Gales, Toronto City, Vancouver Royal Canadians, Washington Whips

National Professional Soccer League: Atlanta Chiefs, Baltimore Bays, Chicago Spurs, Los Angeles Toros, New York Generals, Oakland Clippers, Philadelphia Spartans, Pittsburgh Phantoms, St. Louis Stars, Toronto Falcons (An eleventh franchise was awarded to the Boston Beacons. However, the owners decided to wait until 1968 to begin operations.)

1968

North American Soccer League (merger of USA and NPSL) Atlanta Chiefs, Baltimore Bays, Boston Beacons, Chicago Mustangs, Cleveland Stokers, Dallas Tornado, Detroit Cougars, Houston Stars, Kansas City Spurs (relocated from Chicago), Los Angeles Wolves, New York Generals, Oakland Clippers, St. Louis Stars, San Diego Toros (relocated from Los Angeles Toros), Toronto Falcons, Vancouver Royals (merger of San Francisco and Vancouver), Washington Whips

1969

Atlanta Chiefs, Baltimore Bays Dallas Tornado, Kansas City Spurs, St. Louis Stars

1970

Atlanta Chiefs, Dallas Tornado, Kansas City Spurs, Rochester Lancers (expansion team), St. Louis Stars, Washington Darts (expansion team)

1971

Atlanta Chiefs, Dallas Tornado, Montreal Olympics (expansion team), New York Cosmos (expansion team), Rochester Lancers, St. Louis Stars, Toronto Metros (expansion team), Washington Darts

1972

Atlanta Chiefs, Dallas Tornado, Miami Gatos (relocated from Washington), Montreal Olympics, New York Cosmos, Rochester Lancers, St. Louis Stars, Toronto Metros

1973

Atlanta Apollos (change of ownership), Dallas Tornado, Miami Toros (change of ownership), Olympique de Montreal (name change), New York Cosmos, Philadelphia Atoms (expansion team), Rochester Lancers, St. Louis Stars, Toronto Metros

1974

Baltimore Comets (expansion team), Boston Minutemen (expansion team), Dallas Tornado, Denver Dynamos (expansion team), Los Angeles Aztecs (expansion team), Miami Toros, New York Cosmos, Philadelphia Atoms, Rochester Lancers, St. Louis Stars, San Jose Earthquakes (expansion team), Seattle Sounders (expansion team), Toronto Metros, Vancouver Whitecaps (expansion team), Washington Diplomats (expansion team)

1975

Baltimore Comets, Boston Minutemen, Chicago Sting (expansion team), Dallas Tornado, Denver Dynamos, Hartford Bicentennials (expansion team), Los Angeles Aztecs, Miami Toros, New York Cosmos, Philadelphia Atoms, Portland Timbers (expansion team), Rochester Lancers, St. Louis Stars, San Antonio Thunder (expansion team), San Jose Earthquakes, Seattle Sounders, Tampa Bay Rowdies (expansion team), Toronto Metros-Croatia (merger), Vancouver Whitecaps, Washington Diplomats

1976

Boston Minutemen, Chicago Sting, Dallas Tornado, Hartford Bicentennials, Los Angeles Aztecs, Miami Toros, Minnesota Kicks (relocated from Denver), New York Cosmos, Philadelphia Atoms, Portland Timbers, Rochester Lancers, St. Louis Stars, San Antonio Thunder, San Diego Jaws (relocated from Baltimore), San Jose Earthquakes, Seattle Sounders, Tampa Bay Rowdies, Toronto Metros-Croatia, Vancouver Whitecaps, Washington Diplomats

1977

Chicago Sting, Connecticut Bicentennials (relocated from Hartford), Dallas Tornado, Fort Lauderdale Strikers (relocated from Miami), Team Hawaii (relocated from San Antonio), Las Vegas Quicksilvers (relocated from San Diego), Los Angeles Aztecs, Minnesota Kicks, New York Cosmos, Portland Timbers, Rochester Lancers, St. Louis Stars, San Jose Earthquakes, Seattle Sounders, Tampa Bay Rowdies, Toronto Metros-Croatia, Vancouver Whitecaps, Washington Diplomats

1978

California Surf (relocated from St. Louis), Chicago Sting, Caribous of Colorado (expansion team), Dallas Tornado, Detroit Express (expansion team), Fort Lauderdale Strikers, Houston Hurricane (expansion team), Los Angeles Aztecs, Memphis Rogues (expansion team), Minnesota Kicks, New England Tea Men (expansion team), New York Cosmos, Oakland Stompers (relocated from Connecticut), Philadelphia Fury (expansion team), Portland Timbers, Rochester Lancers, San Diego Sockers (relocated from Las Vegas), San Jose Earthquakes, Seattle Sounders, Tampa Bay Rowdies, Toronto Metros-Croatia, Tulsa Roughnecks (relocated from Hawaii), Vancouver Whitecaps, Washington Diplomats

1979

Atlanta Chiefs (relocated from Colorado), California Surf, Chicago Sting, Dallas Tornado, Detroit Express, Ft. Lauderdale Strikers, Houston Hurricane, Los Angeles Aztecs, Memphis Rogues, Minnesota Kicks, New England Tea Men, New York Cosmos, Oakland Stompers, Philadelphia Fury, Portland Timbers, Rochester Lancers, San Diego Sockers, San Jose Earthquakes, Seattle Sounders, Tampa Bay Rowdies, Toronto Metros, Tulsa Roughnecks, Vancouver Whitecaps, Washington Diplomats

NASL COLLEGE DRAFT

1972

Team	Rd.	Player	Pos.	College
Montreal	1	Shep Messing	G	Harvard
	2	Phil Kydes	F	Harvard
	3	Barry Barto	D	Philadelphia Textile
	4	Manny Hernandez	F	San Jose
St. Louis	1	John Carenza	F	Southern Illinois
	2	William Smyth	D	Davis & Elkins
	3	Jim Drande	F	St. Louis
	4	Edmundo Camacho (from Toronto)	D	Quincy
	5	Steve Partenheimer (from Miami)	D	McMurray
	6	Tom Beaver (from Toronto)	F	Blackburn
	7	Mirko Gragas (from Miami)	F	Ottowa
	8	John Deinowski	F	Southern Illinois
	9	Gerald Mitchell	D	Rensselaer Poly
	10	Ed Palacio (from Toronto)	G	Wheaton University
Toronto	1	Cal Kern	G	Buffalo State
	2	Jean Tassy	F	Buffalo State
Miami	1	Alain Maca (from Montreal)	D	Brockport
	2	Jim Kane	F	Jacksonville
	3	Chris Furlong	G	Villanova
New York	1	Chris Wilmott	D	Harvard
	2	Stan Startzell	F	Pennsylvania
	3	Ali Hubey	D	Newark Engineering
	4	Terry Brewer	D	East Stroudsburg
	5	Czeslaw Maskiewicz	M	Newark Engineering
Rochester	1	Gary Barone	D	Brockport
	2	Alex Roboostoff	F	San Francisco
	3	Bill Kazdoba	F	Montclair
	4	Casey Trappenburg	F	Rensselaer Poly
	5	Jim McMillan	F	Cleveland State
Atlanta	1	Steve Twellman	D	Michigan State
	2	Gary Woodward	F	Campbell
	3	Ron Lindsay	G	NC State
Dallas	1	Kyle Rote, Jr.	F	U. of the South
	2	Clay Small	G	Ohio Wesleyan
	3	Otey Cannon	F	Chico State

1973

Team	Rd.	Player	Pos.	College
Philadelphia	1	Bob Rigby	G	East Stroudsburg
	2	Shoa Agonafer	F	UCLA
	3	Bob Smith	F	Rider
	4	Dale Harmon	D	St. Louis
	5	Ed Blaney	D	St. Josepn
Miami	1	Mike Seerey	F	St. Louis
	2	Galvin Turner	M	South Florida
	3	Max Kernick	M	South Florida
	4	Greg McElroy	F	South Florida
	5	Pass		
Toronto	1	Joe Casucci	F	Niagara
	2	Simon Buisman	D	Buffalo State
	3	Alvin Henderson	F	Howard
	4	Jim Geiger	G	Colgate
	5	Dennis Almeida	F	West Virginia
Atlanta	1	Joe Hamm	D	St. Louis
	2	Kevin Howe	D	Southern Illinois
	3	Steve Buckley	D	Missouri (St. Louis)
	4	Rick Benben	G	Southern Illinois
	5	Pass		
Montreal	1	Bill Straub	D	Pennsylvania
	2	Eugene Durham	D	Philadelphia Textile
	3	Chris Papagianis	F	St. Louis
	4	Ken Chartier	D	New Hampshire
	5	Rodney Hoover	F	Evangel Colgate
Dallas	1	Keith Aqui	F	Howard
	2	Gary Allison	G	Westmont
	3	Andy Smiles	F	Ohio University
	4	Vince Fassi	D	Southern Illinois
	5	Bill Gonzalez	D	Texas
Rochester	1	Andy Rymarczek	F	Penn State
	2	Brendon Keenan	M	Hartwick
	3	Mario Camacho	F	Quincy
	4	Victor Huerta	F	Cornell
	5	William McLean	F	Brockport
St. Louis	1	Alan Harte	D	Quincy
	2	Bob O'Leary	M	St. Louis
	3	John Schneider	D	Quincy
	4	John Garland	M	Missouri (St. Louis)
	5	Pat Leahy	M	St. Louis
New York	1	Joe Fink	F	New York University
	2	Herb Austin	M	New York University
	3	Mike D'Alessio	D	East Stroudsburg
	4	Len Taylor	M	Long Island University
	5	Bruce Arena	G	Cornell

1974

Team	Rd.	Player	Pos.	College
Los Angeles	1	Jose Lopez	D	UCLA
	2	Colm Kennan	M	Hartwick
	3	Efren Herrera	F	UCLA
	4	Marion Stoj	M	Wesleyan
Washington	1	Kurt Kuykendall	G	American
	2	George Taratsides	G	Maryland
	3	Mori Dinae	F	Howard
	4	Bill Bendenbaugh	D	Frostburg

Team	Rd.	Player	Pos.	College
Seattle	1	Dave D'Errico	D	Hartwick
	2	Denny Hadican	F	St. Louis
	3	Pato Gutierrez	F	Duke
	4	Henry Abadi	F	Clemson
Baltimore	1	Alan Mayer	G	Madison
	2	John Gribben	D	Pennsylvania
	3	Eric Winders	F	Ohio University
	4	Brian Gabrielson	D	East Stroudsburg
Boston	1	Dan Counce	F	St. Louis
	2	Gordon Cholmondeley	D	Philadelphia Textile
	3	Ferdinand Treusacher	F	Brown
	4	Denny Werner	D	St. Louis
Denver	1	Jim Zylker	F	San Jose
	2	Chuck Zorumski	G	St. Louis
	3	Tony Suffle	M	San Jose
	4	Bill Renaud	D	SIU-Edwardsville
Vancouver	1	Steve Baumann	F	Pennsylvania
	2	Mark Mathis	M	Quincy
	3	Tekeda Alemu	F	UCLA
	4	Yaregal Gebreysus	M	UCLA
San Jose	1	Mark Demling	D	St. Louis
	2	Joe Giovacchini	M	San Jose
	3	Mike Flater	F	Colorado Mines
	4	Rod Garcia	F	Stanford
Rochester	1	Jim May	G	Brockport
	1	Frank Tusinski (from Toronto)	G	Missouri (St. Louis)
	2	Doug Wark	F	Hartwick
	2	Dave Dyminski (from Toronto)	D	Missouri (St. Louis)
	3	Dan Snyder	F	East Stroudsburg
	4	Tom Gentile	F	Brockport
St. Louis	1	to Miami		
	2	to Miami		
	3	Tom Twellman	F	SIU-Edwardsville
	4	Jim Bokern	F	St. Louis
Miami	1	Don Ries	D	Pennsylvania
	1	Kip Jordan (from St. Louis)	M	Cornell
	2	Larry Houston	M	Pennsylvania
	2	Bill Frost (from St. Louis)	M	Brown
	3	Tim Smith	F	Missouri (St. Louis)
	4	Bruce Allen	D	Penn State
Toronto	1	to Rochester		
	2	to Rochester		
	3	Bill Murray	D	Cornell
	4	Steve Purgavie	D	Westchester
New York	1	Rosario Camposto	D	Long Island University
	2	Ed Austin	F	Hartwick
	3	John Stavros	F	Long Island University
	4	Peter Goldschmidt	D	Stony Brook
Dallas	1	Bob Matteson	M	St. Louis
	2	Charles Gogaleski	G	SIU-Edwardsville
	3	Altamont McKenzie	M	Oneonta
	4	Richard Suit	F	Rockhurst

Team	Rd.	Player	Pos.	College
Philadelphia	1	Tom Galati	D	SIU-Edwardsville
	2	Joe Cozza	F	Montclair
	3	Bob Nelson	F	Indiana
	4	Joe Howarth	D	Oneonta

1975

Team	Rd.	Player	Pos.	College
Tampa Bay	1	Farrukh Quraishi	D	Oneonta
	2	Randy Garber	F	Penn State
	3	Bob Isaacson	F	Hartwick
	4	John Bleum	D	Hartwick
San Antonio	1	Sergio Velazquez	F	UCLA
	2	Chris Carenza	F	SIU-Edwardsville
	3	Mike Durr	D	North Texas State
	4	Mark Stahl	D	Chico State
Chicago	1	to Los Angeles		
	2	Mickey Rooney	M	Keene
	3	Tom Kazembe	F	Wooster
	4	Brad Steurer	G	Keene
Hartford	1	Kevin Welch	F	Bridgeport
	2	Kevin Missey	M	Missouri (St. Louis)
	3	Necdet Muldur	F	William Paterson
	4	Mike Barca	G	Fairleigh Dickinson
Denver	1	Solomon Ohriaki	F	Metro State
	2	Marty Friedman	D	Binghamton
	3	Frank Flesch	F	Missouri (St. Louis)
	4	Roland Lux	G	Metro State
St. Louis	1	Bruce Hudson	D	St. Louis
	2	to Seattle		
	3	Steve Elliott	D	SIU-Edwardsville
	4	John Roeslein	F	St. Louis
New York	1	Van Taylor	G	Erskine SC
	2	Mike Angelotti	D	Hartwick
	3	Tony Picciano	D	Long Island University
	4	Randy Nelson (from Miami)	F	Army
	4	Bob Stetler	G	East Stroudsburg
Washington	1	to Miami		
	2	Bill Williams	F	Washington
	3	Conn Davie	G	Davis and Elkins
	4	Chris Schmitt	M	Rollins
Philadelphia	1	Chris Bahr	M	Penn State
	2	Frank Brady	G	Drew
	3	Manny Matos	M	West Virginia
	4	Phil Santiago	F	Fairleigh Dickinson
Rochester	1	Nelson Cupello	M	Brockport
	1	Len Salvemini (from Boston)	M	Air Force
	2	James Young	F	Buffalo
	3	Keith Korte	M	Benedictine
	4	Elio Stamegna	D	Newark Engineering
Boston	1	to Rochester		
	2	Jon Ross	G	Cornell
	3	Dave Pizarro	F	Springfield
	4	Mark Woodbrey	F	Amherst

Team	Rd.	Player	Pos.	College
Dallas	1	Bob Kesson	D	SIU–Edwardsville
	1	Gary St. Clair	G	San Jose
		(from San Jose)		
	2	Frantz Innocent	F	Connecticut
	2	Bill Fann	F	Quincy
		(from San Jose)		
	3	Matt Weiss	G	Quincy
	4	Fabio Hurtado	F	Newark
Seattle	1	Monroe Matos	D	Adelphi
	2	Tim Logush	F	St. Louis
		(from St. Louis)		
	2	Dean Wurzberger	D	San Diego State
	3	Paul Gizzi	G	Biola
	4	Ed Pitney	D	San Jose
San Jose	1	to St. Louis		
	2	to Dallas		
	3	David Duffy	D	Colgate
	4	Chuck Carey	D	Chico State
Baltimore	1	Jesse Cox	D	Loyola (Baltimore)
	1	Alberto Cael	D	Catholic
		(from Washington)		
	2	Joe Okhakhu	D	West Virginia
	3	George Heyn	M	Adelphi
	4	Paul Geerling	F	Quincy
Miami	1	Trakoon Jirasuradet	D	Florida International
	1	Tim Hunter	D	Connecticut
		(from Vancouver)		
	2	Thomas Coburn	F	Massachusetts
	3	to New York		
	4	Steve Lee	F	Florida International
Los Angeles	1	Michael Bain	M	Howard
		(from Chicago)		
	1	Firoz Fowzi	F	UCLA
	2	Moshe Hoftman	D	UCLA
	3	Ben Mshila	M	Westmont
	4	Fernando Walker	M	San Diego

1976

Team	Rd.	Player	Pos.	College
San Antonio	1	to Los Angeles		
	2	Peter Mannos	G	Northern Illinois
	3	D. J. Harding	F	Chico State
	4	Mike Shue	F	Davis and Elkins
Hartford	1	Hugh O'Neill	F	Bridgeport
	2	Eugene DuChateau	G	Adelphi
	3	to Tampa Bay		
	4	Robert Smith	F	Akron
Rochester	1	Jim Pollihan	F	Quincy
	1	Dale Rothe	D	Baltimore
		(from Boston)		
	2	Steve Cacciatore	F	Southern Illinois
	2	Terry Lippman	D	UCLA
		(from Boston)		
	3	David Sarachan	F	Cornell
	4	Lyn Briggs	D	Brockport
San Jose	1	Terry Weeks	G	Santa Clara
	2	to Dallas		
	3	Tom Fleischi	D	Santa Clara
	4	Mark Dillon	D	San Francisco

Team	Rd.	Player	Pos.	College
Dallas	1	John Stremlau	F	Southern Illinois
	2	Charles Meyers	F	Baltimore
		(from San Jose)		
	2	Barry Small	F	Colgate
	3	Edward Jarrett	G	Springfield
		(from St. Louis)		
	3	John Borozzi	M	Pennsylvania
	3	Mark Rosen	D	Houston
		(from Minnesota)		
	4	Steve Tatum	M	Southern Methodist
Minnesota	1	Sam Bick	D	Quincy
	2	Don Droege	D	St. Louis
	3	to Dallas		
	4	Mark Wehking	D	Green Bay
San Diego	1	to Miami		
	2	Victor Arbalaez	F	San Francisco
	3	Hans Henchen	D	Brigham Young
	4	Bob Poaster	D	Claremont
Philadelphia	1	Brooks Cryder	F	Philadelphia Textile
	2	Tom Ross	G	Glassboro
	2	Jeffery Anstat	F	Kutztown
		(from Washington)		
	3	Mike Piccio	M	Rider
	4	Scott Schaffer	D	Gettysburg
New York	1	Phillip La Spisa	M	St. Francis (NY)
	2	John Russo	M	Lehman
	3	Craig Jeffries	M	Union
	4	Don Davis	D	Lehman
Vancouver	1	Bill Village	M	Simon Fraser
	2	to Tampa Bay		
	3	to Tampa Bay		
	4	to Tampa Bay		
Chicago	1	Tom Redmond	D	Indiana
	1	Paul Wenson	M	Northern Illinois
		(from Los Angeles)		
	2	Bruce Bokor	F	Dartmouth
	2	Kim Perez	M	Western Illinois
		(from Los Angeles)		
	3	Jim Waldschmidt	D	Indiana
	4	Marilyn Lange	F	Hawaii
Los Angeles	1	Steve Ralbovsky	F	Brown
		(from San Antonio)		
	1	to Chicago		
	2	to Chicago		
	3	Miguel Lopez	D	Whittier
	4	Francisco Salcedo	M	UC–Riverside
Washington	1	John Disalvo	F	Temple
	2	to Philadelphia		
	3	Don Reiter	D	Yale
	4	Craig Sheftell	D	South Florida
Toronto did not participate				
St. Louis	1	Joe Clarke	D	St. Louis
	2	to Dallas		
	3	Mike Beck	F	Missouri (St. Louis)
	3	Ted O'Neil	F	Missouri (St. Louis)
		(from Seattle)		
	4	Mark Dorsey	F	Missouri (St. Louis)

Team	Rd.	Player	Pos.	College
Boston	1	to Rochester		
	2	to Rochester		
	3	Tom Walsh	M	Brown
	4	James Power	D	Babson
Miami	1	Roman Rosul	F	Cleveland State
		(from San Diego)		
	1	John Shields	D	Loyola (Baltimore)
	2	Denny Lee	F	Rockhurst
	3	Tom Nowicki	D	Cleveland State
	4	Raoul Luzarraga	D	Florida International
Seattle	1	Matt O'Sullivan	D	Chico State
	2	Ward Forrest	F	Washington
	3	to St. Louis		
	4	Tim Allen	F	Seattle
Portland	1	John Smillie	D	San Jose
	2	Kit Zell	F	Seattle-Pacific
	3	Chip Smallwood	D	Delaware
	4	Ron Lee	G	Oregon
Tampa Bay	1	Colin Fowles	M	Long Island University
	2	Bill Polak	D	Akron
		(from Vancouver)		
	2	Paul Korn	F	San Francisco
	3	Chris Whitworth	D	Washington
		(from Hartford)		
	3	Larry Byrne	M	South Florida
		(from Vancouver)		
	3	Conn Foley	D	South Florida
	4	Jose Casais	F	Jersey City
		(from Vancouver)		
	4	B. J. Woodward	F	North Carolina

1977

Team	Rd.	Player	Pos.	College
St. Louis	1	to Dallas		
	2	to Ft. Lauderdale		
	3	Don Doran	D	St. Louis
	4	Tom Henson	D	Southern Illinois
Ft. Lauderdale	1	Fred Pereira	F	Brown
	2	Franz Grueter	D	Babson
		(from St. Louis)		
	2	Curtis Leeper	F	Florida International
	2	George Nanchoff	F	Akron
		(from Boston)		
	3	Charlie Krupansky	D	Dartmouth
	4	Robbie Moore	F	Bowdoin
Portland	1	Dale Russel	F	Philadelphia Textile
	2	Neil Fredrickson	M	Quincy
	3	Tim Murphy	D	Davis & Elkins
	4	Jim Rippey	M	Davis & Elkins
Las Vegas	1	to Seattle		
	2	Dave Bragg	G	Temple
	3	Dave Stahl	D	Chico State
	4	Ray Sparks	F	Nevada (Las Vegas)
Connecticut	2	James Bolster	F	Denison
	3	Mal Roche	F	San Francisco
	4	John Taft	M	Yale

Team	Rd.	Player	Pos.	College
Hawaii	1	to Washington		
	1	to Tampa Bay		
	2	Alfonso Guzman	F	Westmont
	2	Howard Mattfield	D	Chico State
	3	to Tampa Bay		
	3	Bruce Gant	D	Simon Fraser
		(from Dallas)		
	3	Tom Tronstad	D	San Francisco
	4	Flavio Vozila	D	St. Francis
	4	Kenny Hall	G	Seattle-Pacific
Los Angeles	1	to New York		
	1	Steve Burks	F	Indiana
		(from San Jose)		
	1	Ken Whitehead	F	Simon Fraser
	2	to Dallas		
	3	Ron Thomas	D	Pomona Pitzer
	4	Dave Goldstein	F	Claremont
Rochester	1	Don Droege	M	St. Louis
	2	Dennis Bozesky	F	Missouri (St. Louis)
	3	Arn Armstrong	D	Brockport
	4	Richard Spray	M	Indiana
Dallas	1	Glenn Myernick	D	Hartwick
		(from St. Louis)		
	1	Keith Van Eron	G	Hartwick
	2	Lincoln Peddie	F	Howard
		(from Los Angeles)		
	2	Gino Pennachio	D	Baltimore
	3	to Hawaii		
	4	Dave Grimmaldi	M	Rutgers
Vancouver	1	to New York		
	2	to Tampa Bay		
	3	Pass		
	4	Pass		
Seattle	1	Bruce Rudroff	M	St. Louis
		(from Las Vegas)		
	1	Elson Seale	F	Philadelphia Textile
	2	Ian Reid	M	Loyola (Baltimore)
	3	Terry White	M	Seattle Pacific
	4	Paul Mendes	M	Washington
San Jose	1	to Los Angeles		
	2	Greg McKeown	F	San Francisco
	3	Frank Fudenna	D	Cal State (Hayward)
	4	Mike Benton	F	Santa Clara
Toronto	1	to New York		
	3	Pass		
	4	Pass		
Washington	1	Gene Mishalow	G	Southern Illinois
		(from San Antonio from Connecticut)		
	1	to Los Angeles		
	2	Mark Griffiths	F	Brown
	3	to Hawaii		
	4	Fergus Hopper	D	South Florida
Chicago	1	Dave Flashen	G	Brown
	2	Paul Pringle	F	Howard
	3	Charlie O'Donnell	F	Adelphi
	4	Tim Holstein	F	Southern Illinois

Team	Rd.	Player	Pos.	College
Minnesota	1	Mike Strahler	D	Northern Illinois
	2	Tim Twellman	F	Southern Illinois
	3	Mark Moran	M	Southern Illinois
	4	John Mayer	F	Chicago Circle
New York	1	Paul Hunter (from Vancouver)	D	Connecticut
	1	Bob Rohrbach	F	Dayton
	1	Greg Kourtesis	M	St. Francis
	1	Marcelo Curi (from Toronto)	F	Brockport
	2	Shane Kennedy	G	Babson
	3	Scott Strasburg	F	Bucknell
	4	Tom Lang	M	Adelphi
Tampa Bay	1	Paul Dueker (from Hawaii)	G	Akron
	1	Kevin Eagan	D	South Florida
	2	Mike Knott (from Vancouver)	F	South Florida
	2	Steve Klaasen	F	Brockport
	3	Ed Renaud	D	Quincy
	3	Frank Vinciguerri	M	Quincy
	4	Howie Charbonneau	D	Hartwick

1978

Team	Rd.	Player	Pos.	College
Colorado	1	Greg Makowski	D	Southern Illinois
	1	Matt Bahr (from Chicago)	D	Penn State
	2	Tad Delorm	G	Keene State
	3	to Vancouver, to Tampa Bay		
	4	Adam Abronski	M	Miami Palmetto High School
Detroit	1	David Shelton	M	Indiana
	1	Daniel Vaughn (from California)	F	Washington
	2	David Hoffmeyer	M	Akron
	3	to California		
	4	to Tulsa		
New England	1	to Tulsa		
	2	Kirk Pearson	G	Alderson-Broaddus
	3	to Tampa Bay		
	4	Mike Reitz	D	Davis & Elkins
Philadelphia	1	Rich Reice	F	Penn State
	2	Ray Schnettgoecke	D	Brown
	3	Kevin Murphy	D	Pennington Prep
	4	Bill Sautter	F	Temple
Houston	1	Art Napolitano (from New York, from Washington)	F	Hartwick
	1	to Minnesota		
	2	John Pablos	F	Worcester Poly
	2	to Tampa Bay, to Vancouver		
	3	Chris Turner	G	North Secondary Surrey, BC
	4	Pat Fidelia (from New York)	F	Mercer County College
	4	to New York		
Memphis	1	John Houska	G	Loyola (Baltimore)
	2	Fran Lemons	M	South Florida
	3	to Houston		
	4	Ray Knowland	M	Chico State

Team	Rd.	Player	Pos.	College
Oakland	1	Andy Atuegbu (from New York, from Toronto)	F	San Francisco
	1	to Ft. Lauderdale		
	3	to New York		
	4	Eric Price	M	Saratoga High School
Chicago	1	to Colorado		
	2	Dan McCrudden	M	Rhode Island
	3	Bill Drozd	M	Schurz High School
	4	Tom Nevers	F	Connecticut
Washington	1	to New York, to Houston		
	2	Joe Gantenhammer	G	Long Island University
	3	Sid Nolan	M	Cornell
	4	Pete Caringi	F	Baltimore
Portland	1	Paul Toomey	D	Pennsylvania
	2	Joe Marrello	F	Simon Fraser
	3	Waining Lee	D	Simon Fraser
	4	Tim Gibbons	D	Missouri (St. Louis)
Rochester	1	Jim Roth	F	Missouri (St. Louis)
	2	George Perry	D	Indiana
	3	Chris Cacciatore	F	SIU–Edwardsville
	4	Bob Cupello	M	Brockport
San Diego	1	to Minnesota		
	1	John Nusum (from Dallas)	D	Philadelphia Textile
	1	Paul Milone (from Dallas, from Boston)	F	Princeton
	2	to San Jose		
	3	Joe Hight	G	Southern Methodist
	4	Emilio John	F	Quincy
California	1	to Detroit		
	2	to Ft. Lauderdale		
	3	Jim Tietjens	G	Oakville High School
	3	John Hayes	F	Aquinas High School
	4	Kevin Dunne	F	Westmont College
Tulsa	1	Bill Gazonas (from New England)	M	Hartwick
	1	Jim McKeown	D	Rider
	2	Darryl Wallace	G	Simon Fraser
	2	Dave Ferrell (from Tampa Bay, from Los Angeles)	D	Delaware
	3	to Tampa Bay		
	4	Duncan MacDonald (from Detroit)	D	Hartwick
	4	Jim Boyle	D	San Francisco
Toronto	1	to New York, to Oakland		
	1	to Oakland, to New York		
	2	John Treschuk	G	Philadelphia Textile
	3	Ken Ivanchukov	D	Hartwick
	4	Denny Kinnevy	M	Bridgeport
San Jose	1	to Los Angeles		
	2	to Tulsa		
	2	Jerry Bevans (from San Diego)	D	San Jose State

Team	Rd.	Player	Pos.	College
	2	Mike Vanneman	G	UCLA
	3	John Anton	F	San Francisco
	4	Rich Jungling	G	Chico State
Seattle	1	Pete Collico	M	St. Louis
	2	Jose Reyes	F	Seattle Pacific
	3	Cliff Brown	G	Washington
	4	Todd Schilperoort	M	Seattle Pacific
Vancouver	1	Jack Attaidia (from Tampa Bay)	F	Simon Fraser
	2	Andy Salt	G	Simon Fraser
	3	Steve Neshin (from Tampa Bay)	F	Lord Byng High School, Vancouver
	3	Gerry Gray (from Houston)	M	Westwood Secondary, Ontario
	4	Gino Nonni	M	Simon Fraser
Tampa Bay	1	to Vancouver		
	2	Dave Andrzejewski	D	Maryland-Baltimore County
	2	Dan Flynn	D	St. Louis
	3	Perry Van Der Beck (from Vancouver, from Colorado)	M	Aquinas High School
	3	Sandje Ivanchukov (from New England)	D	Howell Township High School
	3	Tommy Mauer (from Tulsa)	F	Pennsbury
	3	Hyon Lee	F	St. Petersburg High School
	4	to Los Angeles		
Minnesota	1	Alex Rosul (from Houston)	D	Cleveland State
	1	Gary Vogel (from San Diego)	D	Hartwick
	1	Emilio Romero	F	Metro State
	2	Roman Stanko	M	Philadelphia Textile
	3	Dave Dolphas	G	SIU (Edwardsville)
	4	Gary LaGrand	G	Missouri (St. Louis)
New York	1	Ron Atanasio (from Oakland, from Toronto)	F	Adelphi
	1	Cleveland Lewis (from Ft. Lauderdale)	F	Brandeis
	1	Pete Mannino	M	Pennsylvania
	2	Bob Isleib	F	Southern Connecticut
	3	Jim Millinder (from Oakland)	M	El Camino Jr. College
	3	Joe Filian	F	Gordon High School
	4	David Dickey (from Houston)	D	New Trier High School
	4	to Houston		
Los Angeles	1	Alan Kelly (from San Jose)	M	San Diego State
	1	Leif Redal	D	UCLA
	2	to Tampa Bay, to Tulsa		
	3	Jim Popov	F	Golden West College
	4	Mark Frederickson (from Tampa Bay)	M	DuBorg High School
	4	Nimrod Dreyfus	D	Adelphi

Team	Rd.	Player	Pos.	College
Dallas	1	to San Diego		
	1	to San Diego		
	2	Chris Collins	M	Oneonta State
	3	Joe Smith	D	Southern Methodist
	4	Uwe von Schaman	G	Oklahoma
Ft. Lauderdale	1	to New York		
	1	Mike Ortiz-Velez (from Oakland)	M	Erskine
	2	Les Peterson (from California)	D	Florida International
	3	Ken Hammond	F	NJIT
	4	Jan Kapstad	F	North Adams State

1979

Team	Rd.	Player	Pos.	College
Atlanta	1	Adrian Brooks	M	Philadelphia Textile
	1	Mark MacKain	D	Winter Park High School
	2	Bob Robson	G	SIU (Edwardsville)
	2	Rod O'Savio	D	Davis and Elkins
	3	Gavin Timoney	F	SUNY (Brockport)
	4	Frank Schuler	D	St. Louis
San Jose	1	Mike Simon (from Rochester)	M	Chico State
	1	Steve Ryan	M	San Jose State
	2	Richard Rappolt	M	San Francisco State
	3	"Doc" Lawson	D	Southern Connecticut
	4	"Easy" Perez	F	San Jose State
Los Angeles	1	Larry Hulcer	M	St. Louis
	1	Angelo DiBernardo	F	Indiana
	3	Dave Morrison	G	California
Houston	2	Bill McKeon (from New York)	D	Desmet High School
	2	Joe James	D	O'Dea High School
	4	Sam Zighelboim	F	North Beach High School
Memphis	2	Chris Nwokocha	F	Clemson
	3	Ben Popoola	M	Clemson
Edmonton	2	to Tulsa		
	2	Peter Arnautoff	G	San Francisco
	2	Derek Evans	D	San Jose State
	2	Steve Swadley	F	San Jose State
	4	Dan Payne	M	Chico State
	4	Carlos Zavaleta	D	UCLA
Philadelphia	1	Matt Kennedy	G	Belmont Abbey
	3	Tom Weiboldt	F	Rider
	4	Scott Steward	D	Lawrence High School
California	2	Bjorn Dahl (from New York)	F	San Francisco
	3	Frank Campis	F	West Torrance High School
	4	Peter Young	F	Newbury Park High School
Chicago	1	Paul Coffee	G	San Jose State
	1	Peter Notaro	F	Loyola (Baltimore)
	2	Tasso Koutsoukis	F	Indiana
	3	Charlie Fajkus	F	Indiana
	4	Steve Long	F	Wheaton

St. Louis University's Larry Hulcer was a 1979 first-round draft choice of the Los Angeles Aztecs.

Team	Rd.	Player	Pos.	College
Dallas	1	Njego Pesa	F	Ulster Community
	1	Dave Taylor	M	Simon Fraser
	2	Mike Kelly	D	Southern Illinois
	3	to Tulsa		
	3	Bill Watson	D	William and Mary
	4	Doug Moyer	F	Fleetwood High School
Tulsa	1	Ty Keough	M	St. Louis
	2	Greg Ryan (from Edmonton)	D	Southern Methodist
	2	Ken McDonald	D	Penn State
	3	Larry Nees (from Dallas)	D	Chico State
	3	Don Huber (from Tampa Bay)	F	St. Louis
	4	Dom Pagano	D	St. Peter's
Rochester	1	to San Jose		
	1	Tom Maresca	F	Hartwick
	2	Tony Crescitelli	F	North Adams State
	3	Andy Leeker	D	Rollins
	4	Earl Joffman	M	SUNY (Binghamton)
Seattle	2	Mike Hoag	M	Ft. Steilacoom
	3	George Gorleku	D	Eastern Illinois
	4	Jamey Deming	D	Seattle Pacific
Ft. Lauderdale	1	Steve Zerhusen	G	Maryland
	2	John Jones, Jr.	D	Campbell
	3	Al Njie	F	Florida International
	4	George Lesyw	F	Temple
Toronto	3	Louis Nagy	F	Cardinal Newman High School
	3	Gord Miller (from Tampa Bay)	F	Georgetown District High School
	4	Peter Van Beek (from Tampa Bay)	F	Brown
	4	Graeme Coulton (from Memphis)	F	Dorval High School
	4	Damian Ogunsuyi	M	Clemson
	4	Paul Stevenson (from Tampa Bay)	F	Brown
	4	Medric Innocent (from New York)	M	Connecticut
	4	Chris Baudowin	G	California
Washington	1	Dan Salvemini	D	California
	1	Dragan Radovich	G	St. Francis
	3	Kip Germain	D	William and Mary
	3	Alex Mihailovic	M	Jacksonville
	4	Carlos Curling	M	Adelphi
Minnesota	1	Joe Olwig	F	Aquinas High School
	1	Mike McLenaghan	F	Simon Fraser
	2	Mike Fisher	D	Wisconsin
	3	Tom Groark	D	Desmet High School
	4	to Oakland		
San Diego	3	Jan Norby	M	San Diego State
	4	Ward Macauley	D	San Diego State
New England	1	John Lignos	D	Ulster Community
	2	Fran Pantuosco	M	Babson
	3	Trevor Franklin	D	Keene State
	4	Dale Peterson	F	Southeastern Mass.
Portland	1	Bruce Gant	D	Simon Fraser
	2	Bret Hall	M	Wheaton

Team	Rd.	Player	Pos.	College
	3	Frank Vizcarra	M	Ohio State
	4	Kenny Moreen	D	Golden West Community
Detroit	2	Neils Guldbjerg	F	Ulster Community
	2	Steve McLean	F	Kearny High School
	3	Boris Ilicic	G	Hackensack High School
	3	Mike Hince	F	Alderson Broaddus
	4	Hal Partenheimer	M	James Madison
Vancouver	1	Brent Barling	F	John Oliver High School
	1	Daryl Buckham	M	Richmond High School
	2	Alan Fabbro	M	South Burnaby High School
	3	Gord Creamer	D	Simon Fraser
	4	Pat Rohla	M	Simon Fraser
Tampa Bay	1	Dave MacWilliams	F	Philadelphia Textile
	2	Dan Gallagher	G	Penn State
	3	to Toronto		
	3	to Tulsa		
	4	to Toronto		
	4	to Toronto		
New York	1	Jeff Durgen	D	Stadium High School
	1	to San Jose		
	2	to Houston		
	2	to California		
	4	to Toronto		
	4	to Toronto		

ALL-TIME CLUB RECORDS

Yr.	Coach	W	L	T
Atlanta Apollos				
1973	Ken Bracewell	3	9	7
Atlanta Chiefs				
1967	Phil Woosnam	10	12	9
1968	Phil Woosnam	18	7	6
1969	Vic Crowe	11	2	3
1970	Vic Rouse	11	8	5
1971	Vic Rouse	12	7	5
1972	Vic Rouse	5	6	3
	Totals	67	42	31
Atlanta Chiefs*				
1978	Dave Clements (6-14) Dan Wood (2-8)	8	22	0
1979	Dan Wood	12	18	0
	Totals	20	40	0

Known as the Colorado Caribous, 1978

Yr.	Coach	W	L	T
Baltimore Bays				
1967	Doug Millward	14	9	9
1968	Gordon Jago	13	16	3
1969	Gordon Jago	2	13	1
	Totals	29	38	13

Yr.	Coach	W	L	T
	Baltimore Comets			
	See *San Diego Sockers*			
	Boston Beacons			
1968	Jack Mansell	9	17	6
	Boston Minutemen			
1974	Hubert Vogelsinger	10	9	1
1975	Hubert Vogelsinger	13	9	0
1976	Hubert Vogelsinger (5–4)			
	John Bertos (6–11)	11	15	0
	Totals	34	33	1
	Boston Rovers			
1967	Liam Tuohy	2	7	3
	California Surf*			
1967	Rudi Gutendorf	14	11	7
1968	Rudi Gutendorf	12	14	6
1969	Robert Kehoe	3	11	2
1970	Robert Kehoe			
	Don Range	5	17	2
1971	George Meyer			
	Casey Frankiewicz	6	5	13
1972	Casey Frankiewicz	7	4	3
1973	Casey Frankiewicz	7	7	5
1974	John Sewell	4	15	1
1975	John Sewell	13	9	0
1976	John Sewell	5	19	0
1977	John Sewell	12	14	0
1978	John Sewell	13	17	0
1979	John Sewell (4–4)			
	Peter Wall (11–11)	15	15	0
	Totals	116	158	39

Known as the St. Louis Stars, 1967–1977

Yr.	Coach	W	L	T
	Chicago Mustangs			
1967	(USA) Manlio Scopigno	3	2	7
1968	George Meyer	13	10	9
	Totals	16	12	16
	Chicago Spurs			
	See *Kansas City Spurs*			
	Chicago Sting			
1975	Bill Foulkes	12	10	0
1976	Bill Foulkes	15	9	0
1977	Bill Foulkes (4–10)			
	Willy Roy (6–6)	10	16	0
1978	Malcolm Musgrove (2–14)			
	Willy Roy (10–4)	12	18	0
1979	Willy Roy	16	14	0
	Totals	65	67	0
	Cleveland Stokers			
1967	Tony Waddington	5	3	4
1968	Norman Low	14	7	11
	Totals	19	10	15

Colorado Caribous
See *Atlanta Chiefs, 1979*

Connecticut Bicentennials
See *Edmonton Drillers*

Yr.	Coach	W	L	T
	Dallas Tornado			
1967	Jerry Kerr	3	6	3
1968	Bob Kap			
	Keith Spurgeon	2	26	4
1969	Ron Newman	8	6	2
1970	Ron Newman	8	12	4
1971	Ron Newman	10	6	8
1972	Ron Newman	6	5	3
1973	Ron Newman	11	4	4
1974	Ron Newman	12	8	0
1975	Ron Newman	9	13	0
1976	Al Miller	13	11	0
1977	Al Miller	18	8	0
1978	Al Miller	14	16	0
1979	Al Miller	17	13	0
	Totals	131	144	28

Denver Dynamos
See *Minnesota Kicks*

Yr.	Coach	W	L	T
	Detroit Cougars			
1967	John Colrain	3	3	6
1968	Len Julians			
	Andre Nagy	6	21	4
	Totals	9	24	10
	Detroit Express			
1978	Ken Furphy	20	10	0
1979	Ken Furphy	14	16	0
	Totals	34	26	0
	Edmonton Drillers*			
1975	Manfred Schellscheidt	6	16	0
1976	Manfred Schellscheidt	12	12	0
1977	Bobby Thomson (1-12)			
	Malcolm Musgrove (6-7)	7	19	0
1978	Mirko Stojanovic (4-4)			
	Ken Bracewell (7-13)			
	Shep Messing, Dick Berg,			
	Charlie Mrosko (1-1)	12	18	0
1979	Hans Kraay, Sr. (6-19)			
	Joe Petrone (2-3)	8	22	0
	Totals	45	87	0

Known as the Hartford Bicentennials, 1975–1976; Connecticut Bicentennials, 1977; Oakland Stompers, 1978

Yr.	Coach	W	L	T
	Fort Lauderdale Strikers*			
1970	Lincoln Phillips	14	6	4
1971	Alan Rogers	8	6	10
1972	Sal DeRosa			
	Norm Sutherland	3	8	3
1973	John Young	8	5	6
1974	John Young	9	5	6
1975	Greg Meyers	14	8	0
1976	Greg Meyers	6	18	0
1977	Ron Newman	19	7	0
1978	Ron Newman	16	14	0
1979	Ron Newman	17	13	0
	Totals	114	90	29

Known as the Washington Darts, 1970–1971; Miami Gatos, 1972; Miami Toros, 1973–1976

Yr.	Coach	W	L	T
	Hartford Bicentennials			
	See *Edmonton Drillers*			
	Houston Hurricane			
1978	Timo Liekoski	10	20	0
1979	Timo Liekoski	22	8	0
	Totals	32	28	0
	Houston Stars			
1967	Martim Francisco	4	4	4
1968	Geza Henni	14	12	6
	Totals	18	16	10
	Kansas City Spurs*			
1967	(NPSL) Alan Rogers	10	11	11
1968	Janos Bedl	16	11	5
1969	Janos Bedl	10	2	4
1970	Alan Rogers	8	10	6
	Totals	44	34	26

*Known as the Chicago Spurs, 1967

Yr.	Coach	W	L	T
	Las Vegas Quicksilvers			
	See *San Diego Sockers*			
	Los Angeles Aztecs			
1974	Alex Perolli	11	7	2
1975	Terry Fisher	12	10	0
1976	Terry Fisher	12	12	0
1977	Terry Fisher	15	11	0
1978	Terry Fisher (5-8)			
	Tommy Smith (3-13)			
	Peter Short (1-0)	9	21	0
1979	Rinus Michels	18	12	0
	Totals	77	73	2
	Los Angeles Toros			
	See *San Diego Toros*			
	Los Angeles Wolves			
1967	(USA) Ronnie Allen	5	2	5
1968	Ray Wood	11	13	8
	Totals	16	15	13
	Memphis Rogues			
1978	Eddie McCreadie	10	20	0
1979	Eddie McCreadie (2-6)			
	Charlie Cooke (4-18)	6	24	0
	Totals	16	44	0
	Miami Gatos			
	See *Fort Lauderdale Strikers*			
	Miami Toros			
	See *Fort Lauderdale Strikers*			
	Minnesota Kicks*			
1974	Ken Bracewell	5	15	0
1975	John Young	9	13	0
1976	Freddie Goodwin	15	19	0
1977	Freddie Goodwin	16	10	0
1978	Freddie Goodwin	17	13	0
1979	Roy McCrohan	21	9	0
	Totals	83	69	0

*Known as the Denver Dynamos, 1974–1975

Yr.	Coach	W	L	T
	Montreal Olympics			
1971	Renato Tofani	4	15	5
1972	Graham Adams	4	5	5
1973	Graham Adams	5	10	4
	Totals	13	30	14
	New England Tea Men			
1978	Noel Cantwell	19	11	0
1979	Noel Cantwell	12	18	0
	Totals	31	29	0
	New York Cosmos			
1971	Gordon Bradley	9	10	5
1972	Gordon Bradley	7	3	4
1973	Gordon Bradley	7	5	7
1974	Gordon Bradley	6	14	2
1975	Gordon Bradley	10	12	0
1976	Gordon Bradley (8-2)			
	Ken Furphy (8-6)	16	8	0
1977	Gordon Bradley (12-8)			
	Eddie Firmani (3-3)	15	11	0
1978	Eddie Firmani	24	6	0
1979	Eddie Firmani (9-2)			
	Ray Klivecka (15-4)	24	6	0
	Totals	118	75	18
	New York Generals			
1967	(NPSL) Freddie Goodwin	11	13	8
1968	Freddie Goodwin	12	8	12
	Totals	23	21	20
	New York Skyliners			
1967	(USA) Ondino Vierra	2	4	6
	Oakland Clippers			
1967	Ivan Toplak	19	8	5
1968	Ivan Toplak	18	8	6
	Totals	37	16	11
	Oakland Stompers			
	See *Edmonton Drillers*			
	Philadelphia Atoms			
1973	Al Miller	9	2	8
1974	Al Miller	8	11	1
1975	Al Miller	10	12	0
1976	Jesus Ponce	8	16	0
	Totals	35	41	9
	Philadelphia Fury			
1978	Richard Dinnis (6-10)			
	Alan Ball (6-8)	12	18	0
1979	Marko Valok	10	20	0
	Totals	22	38	0
	Philadelphia Spartans			
1967	John Szep	14	9	9
	Pittsburgh Phantoms			
1967	Co Prins	10	14	7

Yr.	Coach	W	L	T
	Portland Timbers			
1975	Vic Crowe	16	6	0
1976	Vic Crowe	8	16	0
1977	Brian Tiler	10	16	0
1978	Don Megson	20	10	0
1979	Don Megson	11	19	0
	Totals	65	67	0
	Rochester Lancers			
1970	Alex Perolli			
	Charles Schiano			
	Sal DeRosa	9	9	6
1971	Sal DeRosa	13	5	6
1972	Adolfo Gori	6	5	3
1973	Sal DeRosa	4	9	6
1974	Bill Hughes			
	John Petrossi			
	Ted Dumitru	8	10	2
1975	Ted Dumitru	6	16	0
1976	Don Popovic	13	11	0
1977	Don Popovic	11	15	0
1978	Don Popovic	14	16	0
1979	Don Popovic	15	15	0
	Totals	99	111	23

St. Louis Stars
See *California Surf*

San Antonio Thunder
See *Tulsa Roughnecks*

San Diego Jaws
See *San Diego Sockers*

Yr.	Coach	W	L	T
	San Diego Sockers*			
1974	Doug Millward	10	8	2
1975	Doug Millward	9	13	0
1976	Derek Trevis	9	15	0
1977	Derek Trevis (10-10)			
	Jim Fryatt (1-5)	11	15	0
1978	Hubert Vogelsinger	18	12	0
1979	Hubert Vogelsinger	15	15	0
	Totals	72	78	2

Known as the Baltimore Comets, 1974–1975; San Diego Jaws, 1976; Las Vegas Quicksilvers, 1977

Yr.	Coach	W	L	T
	San Diego Toros*			
1967	Max Wozniak	7	15	10
1968	George Curtis			
	Angel Papadopolus	18	8	6
	Totals	25	23	16

Known as the Los Angeles Toros, 1967

Yr.	Coach	W	L	T
	San Francisco Golden Gate Gales			
1967	Ernst Happel	5	4	3

Yr.	Coach	W	L	T
	San Jose Earthquakes			
1974	Gabbo Gavric (7-7-0)			
	Ivan Toplak (2-1-3)	9	8	3
1975	Gabbo Gavric (3-1)			
	Ivan Toplak (5-13)	8	14	0
1976	Gabbo Gavric	14	10	0
1977	Gabbo Gavric	14	12	0
1978	Gabbo Gavric (5-11)			
	Terry Fisher (3-11)	8	22	0
1979	Terry Fisher (0-8)			
	Peter Stubbe (8-14)	8	22	0
	Totals	61	88	3

Yr.	Coach	W	L	T
	Seattle Sounders			
1974	John Best	10	7	3
1975	John Best	15	7	0
1976	John Best	14	10	0
1977	Jim Gabriel	14	12	0
1978	Jim Gabriel	15	15	0
1979	Jim Gabriel	13	17	0
	Totals	81	68	3

Yr.	Coach	W	L	T
	Tampa Bay Rowdies			
1975	Eddie Firmani	16	6	0
1976	Eddie Firmani	18	6	0
1977	Eddie Firmani (7-3)			
	John Boyle (7-9)	14	12	0
1978	Gordon Jago	18	12	0
1979	Gordon Jago	19	11	0
	Totals	85	47	0

Team Hawaii
See *Tulsa Roughnecks*

Yr.	Coach	W	L	T
	Toronto City			
1967	(USA) Bob Shankly	4	3	5

Yr.	Coach	W	L	T
	Toronto Falcons			
1967	(NPSL) Hector Mariano	10	17	5
1968	Laddie Kubala	13	13	6
	Totals	23	30	11

Yr.	Coach	W	L	T
	Toronto Blizzard*			
1971	Graham Leggat	5	10	9
1972	Graham Leggat	4	6	4
1973	Arthur Rodrigues	6	4	9
1974	Arthur Rodrigues	9	10	1
1975	Ivan Markovic	13	9	0
1976	Ivan Markovic (10-6)			
	Domagoj Kapetanovic (5-3)	15	9	0
1977	Ivan Sangullian	13	13	0
1978	Domagoj Kapetanovic	16	14	0
1979	Keith Eddy	14	16	0
	Totals	95	91	23

Known as the Toronto Metros, 1971–1974; Toronto Metros-Croatia, 1974–1978

Toronto Metros
See *Toronto Blizzard*

Toronto Metros-Croatia
See *Toronto Blizzard*

Yr.	Coach	W	L	T
	Tulsa Roughnecks*			
1975	Alex Perolli (1-8)			
	Don Batie (5-8)	6	16	0
1976	Don Batie	12	12	0
1977	Hubert Vogelsinger (8-9)			
	Charlie Mitchell (3-6)	11	15	0
1978	Bill Foulkes (8-9)			
	Alex Skotarek (7-6)	15	15	0
1979	Alan Hinton	14	16	0
	Totals	58	74	0

Known as the San Antonio Thunder, 1975–1976; Team Hawaii, 1977

Yr.	Coach	W	L	T
	Vancouver Royals			
1967	(USA) Ian McCall	3	4	5
1968	Ferenc Puskas	12	15	5
	Totals	15	19	10
	Vancouver Whitecaps			
1974	Jim Easton	5	11	4
1975	Jim Easton	11	11	0
1976	Eckhard Krautzun	14	10	0
1977	Eckhard Krautzun (3-3)			
	Holger Osieck (0-3)			
	Tony Waiters (11-6)	14	12	0
1978	Tony Waiters	24	6	0
1979	Tony Waiters	20	10	0
	Totals	88	60	4

Washington Darts
See *Fort Lauderdale Strikers*

Yr.	Coach	W	L	T
	Washington Diplomats			
1974	Dennis Viollet	7	12	1
1975	Dennis Viollet	12	10	0
1976	Dennis Viollet	14	10	0
1977	Dennis Viollet (6-9)			
	Alan Spavin (4-7)	10	16	0
1978	Gordon Bradley	16	14	0
1979	Gordon Bradley	19	11	0
	Totals	78	73	1
	Washington Whips			
1967	Eddie Turnbull	5	2	5
1968	Andre Nagy			
	Hicabi "Turk" Emekli	15	10	7
	Totals	20	12	12

10

ALL-TIME NASL PLAYER REGISTER

The NASL All-Time Register contains the season statistics for every player who has appeared in the North American Soccer League. Also included are player statistics from the predecessors to the NASL, the United Soccer Association and the National Professional Soccer League. Chicago, Los Angeles, New York, and Toronto were represented in both leagues, and players for any of those teams are marked appropriately (USA) or (NPSL).

Where it was available, each player's record lists season, team, games played (GP), assists (A), and total points (Pts.). Dashes indicate information was not available.

The goalkeepers are listed by name only in this section but are covered in detail in a separate listing following this one.

The player's date and place of birth, height, weight, position, and country of citizenship are given when available.

Season	Club	GP	G	A	Pts.
AARTS, KEES *Forward*					
Ht. 5–9 Wt. 152					
1967	San Francisco	9	2	4	8
ABAUNZA, MANUEL *Forward*					
B. Costa Rica					
Ht. 5–7 Wt. 145					
Citizen—Costa Rica					
1967	L.A.(NPSL)	18	0	3	3
ABBONDANZA, ALESSANDRO *Midfielder*					
B. Napoli, Italy					
Ht. 5–9 Wt. 165					
Citizen—Italy					
1979	Toronto	3	0	1	1
ABBOTT, PETER *Forward*					
B. Rotherham, England					
Ht. 6–1 Wt. 175					
Citizen—England					
1976	Hartford	10	1	2	4

Season	Club	GP	G	A	Pts.
ABRAHAMS, LAURIE *Forward*					
B. Mar. 4, 1953 Mile End, London, England					
Ht. 5–10 Wt. 161					
Citizen—England					
1978	New England	17	7	10	24
1979	Tul.–Calif.	25	18	9	45
	Totals	42	25	19	69
ACQUAH, SAM *Defender*					
B. Ghana					
Ht. 5–9 Wt. 150					
Citizen—Ghana					
1968	Detroit	6	2	0	4
ADALMIR, NERI					
See *Goalkeeper*					
ADAMS, GRAHAM *Forward*					
1972	Montreal	2	0	0	0
1973	Montreal	2	0	0	0
	Totals	4	0	0	0

Season	Club	GP	G	A	Pts.

ADLINGTON, TERRENCE
See *Goalkeeper*

ADVOCAAT, DICK   *Midfielder*
B. Sept. 27, 1947   Hague, Holland
Ht. 5-7   Wt. 145
Citizen—Holland

Season	Club	GP	G	A	Pts.
1967	San Francisco	7	1	0	2
1978	Chicago	24	2	4	8
1979	Chicago	28	3	8	14
	Totals	59	6	12	24

AGOLIATI, CHRIS   *Midfielder*
B. Nov. 3, 1951   Staten Island, N.Y.
Ht. 5-9   Wt. 158
Citizen—U.S.

1975	Boston	6	1	0	2
1976	New York	1	0	0	0
	Totals	7	1	0	2

AGOSTINIS, RENO   *Defender*
Ht. 6-0   Wt. 165
Citizen—Canada

1979	Seattle	1	0	0	0

AGUIRRE, ROBERTO   *Midfielder*
B. Feb. 10, 1946   Buenos Aires, Argentina
Ht. 5-9   Wt. 160
Citizen—Argentina

1972	Miami	13	3	2	8
1973	Miami	17	1	4	6
1974	Miami	18	4	7	15
1975	Miami	21	0	3	3
1976	Miami	21	1	0	2
1977	Ft. L	13	1	1	3
1978	Ft. L	11	0	0	0
	Totals	114	10	17	37

AIRD, KENNY   *Forward*
B. Apr. 13, 1947   Glasgow, Scotland
Ht. 5-5   Wt. 142
Citizen—Scotland

1977	Toronto	9	0	1	1

AITKEN, CHARLIE   *Defender*
B. May 1, 1942   Edinburgh, Scotland
Ht. 5-10   Wt. 155
Citizen—Scotland

1976	New York	16	0	3	3
1977	New York	8	0	1	1
	Totals	24	0	4	4

ALAS, JULIO   *Defender*
B. July 19, 1943   Argentina
Ht. 5-5   Wt. 140
Citizen—Argentina

1967	N.Y. (NPSL)	14	7	3	17
1968	New York	21	5	0	10
1973	Dallas	1	0	0	0
	Totals	36	12	3	27

ALAS, ROBERTO   *Defender*

1973	Rochester	1	0	0	0

ALBERTO, CARLOS (Carlos Alberto Torres)   *Defender*
B. July 17, 1944   Rio de Janeiro, Brazil
Ht. 6-0   Wt. 170
Citizen—Brazil

1977	New York	4	0	2	2
1978	New York	25	2	2	6
1979	New York	28	2	6	10
	Totals	57	4	10	18

ALBERTO, LUIS   *Forward*
B. Oct. 6, 1953   Argentina
Ht. 5-5   Wt. 145
Citizen—Argentina

1979	Rochester	22	1	2	4

ALBERTS, ROBERT   *Midfielder*
B. Nov. 14, 1954   Amsterdam, Holland
Citizen—Holland

1975	Vancouver	9	2	1	5
1976	Vancouver	9	1	2	4
	Totals	18	3	3	9

ALBRECHT, DIETRICH   *Forward*
B. Feb. 4, 1940   Germany
Ht. 6-3   Wt. 165
Citizen—U.S.

1967	Philadelphia	17	5	1	11
1968	Cleveland	31	6	0	12
1969	Baltimore	—	—	—	—
	Totals	48	11	1	23

ALCOCK, TERRY   *Defender*
B. Dec. 9, 1946   Stoke, England
Ht. 6-1   Wt. 175
Citizen—England

1977	Portland	7	2	0	4

ALDERSON, BRIAN   *Midfielder*
B. May 5, 1950   Dundee, Scotland
Ht. 5-7   Wt. 155
Citizen—Scotland

1978	New England	21	1	1	3
1979	New England	27	6	7	19
	Totals	48	7	8	22

Season	Club	GP	G	A	Pts.

ALHINHO *Defender*
B. Dec. 9, 1953 Cape Verde Islands
Ht. 5–11 Wt. 178
Citizen—Portugal

| 1979 | New England | 16 | 1 | 1 | 3 |

ALLAN, THOMSON
See *Goalkeeper*

ALLEN, CRAIG *Forward*
B. Oct. 2, 1959 Guernsey Channel Islands
Ht. 5–11 Wt. 158
Citizen—Channel Islands

| 1979 | California | 14 | 4 | 2 | 10 |

ALLEN, RUSSELL *Forward*
B. Jan. 19, 1954 England
Ht. 5–9 Wt. 160
Citizen—England

| 1975 | Chicago | 16 | 4 | 2 | 10 |

ALLISON, GARY
See *Goalkeeper*

ALON, BENNY *Forward*
B. Sept. 13, 1950 Haifa, Israel
Ht. 5–11 Wt. 170
Citizen—Israel

1975	Chicago	8	1	1	3
1976	Chicago	22	4	2	10
1977	Chicago	18	2	1	5
	Totals	48	7	4	18

ALONSO, RICARDO *Forward*
B. Mar. 21, 1957 Tansil, Argentina
Ht. 6–3 Wt. 192
Citizen—Argentina

| 1979 | Minnesota | 12 | 2 | 2 | 6 |

ALSTON, ADRIAN *Forward*
B. Feb. 6, 1949 Preston, England
Ht. 6–0 Wt. 170
Citizen—Australia

1977	Tampa Bay	17	7	3	17
1978	Tampa Bay	2	1	1	3
	Totals	19	8	4	20

ALZEVEDO, FERNANDO *Forward*
B. Glasgow, Scotland
Ht. 6–1 Wt. 160
Citizen—Scotland

| 1967 | Baltimore | 13 | 8 | 4 | 20 |

ANASTASIO, ANGELO *Defender*
B. Sept. 24, 1951
Ht. 5–7 Wt. 145
Citizen—U.S.

1974	New York	4	0	0	0
1975	New York	1	0	0	0
	Totals	5	0	0	0

ANDERSON, IAN *Midfielder*
B. Sept. 11, 1954 Edinburgh, Scotland
Ht. 6–0 Wt. 166
Citizen—Scotland

1977	Tampa Bay	11	2	0	4
1978	Houston	25	3	3	9
1979	Houston	30	5	5	15
	Totals	66	10	8	28

ANDERSON, PETER *Forward*
B. May 31, 1949 London, England
Ht. 5–10 Wt. 155
Citizen—England

| 1978 | S.D.-T.B. | 27 | 9 | 7 | 25 |

ANDERSON, TERRY *Midfielder*
B. Nov. 30, 1944 England
Ht. 5–9 Wt. 170
Citizen—England

1974	Baltimore	17	0	4	4
1975	Baltimore	19	0	1	1
	Totals	36	0	5	5

ANDERSON, WILLIE *Forward*
B. Jan. 26, 1947 Wrexham, Wales
Ht. 5–11 Wt. 175
Citizen—Wales

1975	Portland	17	3	9	15
1977	Portland	19	1	6	8
1978	Portland	26	3	11	17
1979	Portland	25	0	11	11
	Totals	87	7	37	51

ANDRUSS, EUGENE *Forward*
B. Sept. 3, 1945 Austria
Ht. 5–10 Wt. 160
Citizen—U.S.

| 1975 | Chicago | 1 | 0 | 0 | 0 |

ANDRUSZEWSKI, MANNY *Defender*
B. Nov. 4, 1955 Southampton, England
Ht. 5–11 Wt. 155
Citizen—England

| 1979 | Tampa Bay | 16 | 1 | 1 | 3 |

Season	Club	GP	G	A	Pts.

ANTOINE, EDDIE   *Midfielder*
B. Aug. 27, 1949   Haiti
Ht. 5-9   Wt. 160
Citizen—Haiti

| 1978 | Chicago | 6 | 1 | 0 | 2 |

ANTON, JOHN   *Midfielder*
B. Apr. 4, 1955   San Francisco, Calif.
Ht. 5-8   Wt. 160
Citizen—U.S.

| 1979 | Edmonton | 22 | 3 | 3 | 9 |

APOSTOLIDIS, KIRK   *Forward*
B. Mar. 3, 1946   Greece
Ht. 5-10   Wt. 165
Citizen—Greece

1968	Vancouver	7	0	0	0
1969	Dallas	15	2	2	6
1970	Dallas	19	16	3	35
1971	Dallas	15	11	1	23
	Totals	56	29	6	64

AQUI, KEITH   *Forward*
B. Aug. 5, 1945   Trinidad
Ht. 5-11   Wt. 160
Citizen—Trinidad

1974	Baltimore	19	5	7	17
1975	Baltimore	20	10	3	23
1976	San Diego	14	1	3	5
	Totals	53	16	13	45

ARANGUIZ, ESTEBAN   *Midfielder*
B. Chile
Ht. 5-9   Wt. 165

1974	Miami	16	0	3	3
1975	Miami	18	1	1	3
	Totals	34	1	4	6

ARBALEZ, VICTOR   *Forward*
B. Aug. 14, 1953   Colombia
Ht. 5-3   Wt. 140
Citizen—U.S.

1976	San Diego	3	0	0	0
1977	Las Vegas	13	1	1	3
1978	San Diego	5	0	0	0
	Totals	21	1	1	3

ARCHIBALD, WARREN   *Midfielder*
B. Nov. 15, 1946   Point Fortin, Trinidad
Ht. 5-7   Wt. 154
Citizen—Trinidad

1967	N.Y. (NPSL)	16	7	3	17
1968	New York	23	9	3	21
1970	Washington	20	8	7	23
1971	Miami	14	6	5	17
1972	Miami	14	6	5	17
1973	Miami	17	12	5	29
1974	Miami	19	5	3	13

Season	Club	GP	G	A	Pts.
1975	Miami	21	4	7	15
1976	Mia.-Roch.	17	1	1	3
	Totals	161	58	39	155

ARDESCH, HENNY
See *Goalkeeper*

ARGUELLES, RAFAEL   *Forward*
Ht. 5-10   Wt. 150

1972	Miami	11	0	1	1
1973	Miami	11	0	0	0
1974	Miami	19	0	1	1
1975	Miami	9	0	0	0
	Totals	50	0	2	2

ARMSTRONG, TOM   *Forward*
B. Apr. 4, 1954   Belfast, N. Ireland
Ht. 6-0   Wt. 160
Citizen—N. Ireland

| 1979 | S.D.-S.J. | 27 | 6 | 6 | 18 |

ARNAUTOFF, PETER
See *Goalkeeper*

ARRANZ, JOSE   *Forward*
B. Spain
Ht. 5-9   Wt. 168
Citizen—Spain

| 1968 | Vancouver | 4 | 0 | 0 | 0 |

ARSLANOVIC, IBRAHIM   *Midfielder*
Ht. 5-8   Wt. 160

| 1975 | Toronto | 3 | 0 | 0 | 0 |

ARTUR (ARTUR MANUEL SOARES CORREIA)   *Defender*
B. Apr. 18, 1950   Lisbon, Portugal
Ht. 5-8   Wt. 140
Citizen—Portugal

| 1979 | New England | 23 | 0 | 2 | 2 |

ASH, MICHAEL   *Midfielder*
B. Sept. 4, 1943   Yorkshire, England
Ht. 5-5   Wt. 150
Citizen—England

1967	N.Y. (NPSL)	16	4	4	12
1968	New York	10	6	0	12
1969	Atlanta	—	—	—	—
1970	Atlanta	—	—	—	—
1971	Atlanta	9	0	0	0
	Totals	35	10	4	24

ASKEW, JOHN "SONNY"   *Forward*
B. Apr. 17, 1957   Baltimore, Md.
Ht. 6-0   Wt. 175
Citizen—U.S.

1977	Washington	11	0	1	1
1979	Washington	29	8	6	22
	Totals	40	8	7	23

Season	Club	GP	G	A	Pts.

ASTIGARRAGA, RUBEN *Forward*
B. Aug. 3, 1950 Buenos Aires, Argentina
Ht. 6-0 Wt. 170
Citizen—Argentina

| 1979 | Mem.-Tul. | 22 | 2 | 6 | 10 |

ATACK, LEE *Defender*
B. Jan. 10, 1953 Leeds, England
Ht. 6-0 Wt. 170
Citizen—U.S.

1975	Los Angeles	9	0	0	0
1976	Los Angeles	3	0	0	0
1978	Oakland	24	0	0	0
1979	Edmonton	24	2	1	5
	Totals	60	2	1	5

ATAIDE, BENE *Midfielder*
Ht. 5-8 Wt. 170

| 1971 | Toronto | 3 | 0 | 0 | 0 |

ATANASIO, RON *Forward*
B. Sept. 10, 1956 Oceanside, N.Y.
Ht. 5-7 Wt. 165
Citizen—U.S.

1978	New York	6	1	0	2
1979	New York	2	0	0	0
	Totals	8	1	0	2

ATTAIH, MOHAMMED *Midfielder*
Ht. 5-5 Wt. 140

| 1973 | Dallas | 3 | 1 | 0 | 2 |

ATUEGBU, ANDY *Midfielder*
B. Feb. 4, 1949 Nigeria
Ht. 5-8 Wt. 170
Citizen—Nigeria

1978	Oakland	26	0	1	1
1979	Edmonton	29	3	6	12
	Totals	55	3	7	13

AUGUSTE, ARSENE *Defender*
B. Feb. 3, 1951 Port-au-Prince, Haiti
Ht. 6-2 Wt. 185
Citizen—Haiti

1975	Tampa Bay	6	0	0	0
1976	Tampa Bay	17	0	0	0
1977	Tampa Bay	14	2	0	4
1978	Tampa Bay	24	1	0	2
1979	Tampa Bay	13	0	0	0
	Totals	74	3	0	0

AUSTIN, EDDIE *Forward*
B. Mar. 14, 1952 Glasgow, Scotland
Ht. 5-10 Wt. 170
Citizen—U.S.

1975	Tampa Bay	13	0	1	1
1976	Tampa Bay	4	0	0	0
	Totals	17	0	1	1

Season	Club	GP	G	A	Pts.

AVERELL, BOBBIE *Defender*
B. N. Ireland
Ht. 6-0 Wt. 155

1972	Toronto	9	0	2	2
1973	Toronto	16	2	0	4
	Totals	25	2	2	6

AYRE, GARY *Defender*
B. Oct. 12, 1953 Vancouver, Canada
Ht. 5-11 Wt. 175
Citizen—Canada

1977	Vancouver	23	1	2	4
1978	Van.-N.Y.	19	0	0	0
1979	N.Y.-Port.	19	0	1	1
	Totals	61	1	3	5

BACHMAIER, ADOLF *Midfielder*
B. Rumania
Ht. 5-5 Wt. 140
Citizen—U.S.

| 1968 | Chicago | 15 | 3 | 0 | 6 |

BACHNER, IGOR *Midfielder*
B. Sept. 16, 1946 Czechoslovakia
Ht. 5-10 Wt. 158
Citizen—Canada

1973	Montreal	19	5	4	14
1974	Boston	12	0	1	1
1975	Boston	2	0	0	0
1978	San Diego	21	0	8	8
1979	S.D.-Roch.	9	0	1	1
	Totals	63	5	14	24

BACHOFNER, CHRISTIAN "BAU-BAU" *Forward*
B. Nov. 23, 1947 Amsterdam, Holland
Ht. 5-10 Wt. 160
Citizen—Holland

| 1968 | Dallas | 30 | 1 | 3 | 5 |

BACKOS, DES *Forward*
B. Nov. 13, 1950 Johannesburg, S. Africa
Ht. 5-7 Wt. 160
Citizen—S. Africa

| 1977 | Los Angeles | 20 | 4 | 5 | 13 |

BAESSLER, CARL *Forward*
B. Germany
Ht. 5-7 Wt. 150
Citizen—Germany

| 1968 | Chicago | 2 | 0 | 0 | 0 |

BAESSO, MARIO *Forward*
B. Sept. 5, 1945 Sao Paulo, Brazil
Ht. 5-5 Wt. 156
Citizen—Brazil

1967	Oakland	17	11	4	26
1968	Oakland	20	1	0	2
	Totals	37	12	4	28

Season	Club	GP	G	A	Pts.
BAEZA, ALBERTO *Forward*					
B. Mexico					
Ht. 5-7 Wt. 140					
Citizen—Mexico					
1968	San Diego	25	4	0	8
BAHR, CASEY *Defender*					
Ht. 6-1 Wt. 170					
1973	Philadelphia	17	1	0	2
BAHR, CHRIS *Midfielder*					
Ht. 5-10 Wt. 160					
Citizen—U.S.					
1975	Philadelphia	22	11	2	24
BAHR, MATT *Defender*					
B. July 6, 1956 Philadelphia, Pa.					
Ht. 5-10 Wt. 157					
Citizen—U.S.					
1978	Col.-Tul.	26	0	3	3
BAIGER, CONRAD *Midfielder*					
B. 1945 Katowice, Poland					
Ht. 5-10 Wt. 165					
Citizen—Poland					
1977	Chicago	1	0	0	0
BAILEY, MIKE *Midfielder*					
B. Feb. 27, 1942 Wisbech, England					
Ht. 5-8 Wt. 155					
Citizen—England					
1977	Minnesota	14	0	2	2
1978	Minnesota	4	0	0	0
	Totals	18	0	2	2
BAIN, IAN *Midfielder*					
Ht. 6-0 Wt. 160					
1975	Washington	13	3	1	7
BAIN, JOHN *Midfielder*					
B. June 23, 1957 Glasgow, Scotland					
Ht. 5-7 Wt. 150					
Citizen—England					
1978	Portland	26	6	3	15
1979	Portland	29	8	11	27
	Totals	55	14	14	42
BAKER, KIERON					
See *Goalkeeper*					
BAKIC, MIKE *Forward*					
B. Dec. 30, 1952 Yugoslavia					
Ht. 6-0 Wt. 175					
Citizen—Canada					
1977	Rochester	23	2	4	8
1978	Washington	17	6	3	15
1979	Washington	3	0	3	3
	Totals	43	8	10	26

Season	Club	GP	G	A	Pts.
BALDIN, PAOLO					
See *Goalkeeper*					
BALDWIN, TOMMY *Forward*					
B. June 10, 1945 Gateshead, England					
Ht. 5-9 Wt. 160					
Citizen—England					
1975	Seattle	15	5	0	10
BALEVSKI, VANCO *Midfielder*					
B. July 3, 1947 Skopje, Yugoslavia					
Ht. 5-9 Wt. 160					
Citizen—Yugoslavia					
1978	Toronto	14	7	3	17
BALL, ALAN *Midfielder*					
B. Mar. 12, 1945 Farnsworth, England					
Ht. 5-6 Wt. 140					
Citizen—England					
1978	Philadelphia	25	5	10	20
1979	Phil.-Van.	23	8	13	29
	Totals	48	13	23	49
BALSON, MIKE *Defender*					
B. Sept. 9, 1947 England					
Ht. 6-0 Wt. 175					
Citizen—England					
1979	Atlanta	15	0	1	1
BAN, BOZIDAR *Forward*					
B. Zagreb, Yugoslavia					
Ht. 5-11 Wt. 170					
Citizen—Yugoslavia					
1978	Oakland	25	3	2	8
1979	Edmonton	3	0	0	0
	Totals	28	3	2	8
BANACH, OREST					
See *Goalkeeper*					
BANDLE, ALEX *Midfielder*					
B. Vienna, Austria					
Ht. 6-1 Wt. 165					
Citizen—Austria					
1967	N.Y. (NPSL)	4	0	1	1
1968	Dallas	10	0	1	1
	Totals	14	0	2	2
BANDOV, BORIS *Forward*					
B. Nov. 23, 1953 Bosnia, Yugoslavia					
Ht. 5-10 Wt. 175					
Citizen—U.S.					
1974	San Jose	17	3	1	7
1975	San Jose	21	5	2	12
1976	Seattle	4	2	1	5
1977	Sea.-T.B.	10	0	0	0
1978	Tampa Bay	3	0	0	0
1979	New York	10	1	0	2
	Totals	65	11	4	26

Season	Club	GP	G	A	Pts.

BANHOFFER, URI *Forward*
B. Jan. 14, 1948
Ht. 5–11 Wt. 152
Citizen—Uruguay

1974	Los Angeles	18	7	4	18
1975	Los Angeles	20	14	9	37
	Totals	38	21	13	55

BANKS, GORDON
See *Goalkeeper*

BANSCHEWITZ, HEINZ *Defender*
B. Gunnigfeld, Germany
Ht. 5–10 Wt. 174
Citizen—Germany

1967	Chi. (NPSL)	16	0	1	1
1968	Kansas City	31	1	0	2
	Totals	47	1	1	3

BARALIC, PETER *Midfielder*
B. Oct. 3, 1951 Govhja, Kravarica
Ht. 5–10 Wt. 150
Citizen—Yugoslavia

1979	Tampa Bay	28	9	8	26

BARASIC, RADOSLAV *Defender*
B. Mar. 4, 1953 Belgrade, Yugoslavia
Ht. 6–2 Wt. 200
Citizen—Yugoslavia

1978	Tulsa	12	0	0	0

BARBER, ERIC *Forward*
B. Ireland
Ht. 5–10 Wt. 170
Citizen—Ireland

1967	Chi. (NPSL)	12	8	2	18
1968	Kansas City	32	16	0	32
	Totals	44	24	2	50

BARBOZA, ANTONIO *Defender*

1971	Montreal	2	0	0	0

BARCA, MIGUEL
See *Goalkeeper*

BARCLAY, KELVIN
See *Goalkeeper*

BARENO, RUBEN *Forward*
Ht. 5–8 Wt. 159

1967	N.Y.(USA)	10	2	2	6

BARISON, PAOLO *Forward*

1972	Toronto	8	3	1	7

BARKER, ALAN *Defender*
B. Feb. 23, 1956 Bishop Auchland, England
Ht. 6–0 Wt. 168
Citizen—England

1978	Tulsa	4	0	0	0

BARKER, ED *Midfielder*
B. England
Ht. 6–0 Wt. 190
Citizen—England

1968	Toronto	24	0	0	0

BARLOW, FRANK *Defender*
Ht. 5–9 Wt. 158

1974	Boston	20	0	2	2

BARNETT, GEOFF
See *Goalkeeper*

BARONE, GARY *Defender*
Ht. 6–1 Wt. 170

1972	Rochester	7	0	0	0
1974	Rochester	7	0	0	0
	Totals	14	0	0	0

BARONE, MARIO *Forward*
B. Italy
Ht. 6–0 Wt. 170
Citizen—Italy

1968	Toronto	9	1	0	2

BARRETT, LES *Forward*
B. Oct. 22, 1947 London, England
Ht. 5–8 Wt. 145
Citizen—England

1978	California	20	3	3	9
1979	California	24	1	1	3
	Totals	44	4	4	12

BARRON, JIM
See *Goalkeeper*

BARRY, MIKE *Midfielder*
Ht. 5–9 Wt. 150

1975	Washington	22	6	9	21

BARTHELEMY, CLAUDE *Forward*
B. Haiti
Ht. 5–7 Wt. 150
Citizen—Haiti

1968	Detroit	2	0	0	0

BARTO, BARRY *Midfielder*
B. Philadelphia, Pa.
Ht. 5–8 Wt. 155
Citizen—U.S.

1972	Montreal	9	1	0	2
1973	Philadelphia	17	1	0	2

Season	Club	GP	G	A	Pts.
1974	Philadelphia	20	0	3	3
1975	Philadelphia	13	0	1	1
1976	Philadelphia	7	0	0	0
1977	Ft. Lauderdale	1	0	0	0
	Totals	67	2	4	8

BARTON, FRANK   *Midfielder*
B. Oct. 22, 1947   Barton-Upon-Humber, England
Ht. 5–8   Wt. 160
Citizen—England

Season	Club	GP	G	A	Pts.
1979	Seattle	26	6	4	16

BASON, BRIAN   *Midfielder*
B. Sept. 3, 1955   England
Ht. 5–10   Wt. 165
Citizen—England

Season	Club	GP	G	A	Pts.
1977	Vancouver	19	3	3	9

BATTISTA, JOHN   *Midfielder*
B. Argentina
Ht. 5–7   Wt. 161
Citizen—Argentina

Season	Club	GP	G	A	Pts.
1968	Chicago	5	0	0	0

BAUM, JOE
See *Goalkeeper*

BAUMAN, STEVE   *Midfielder*
B. Sept. 16, 1952   Middletown, Ohio
Ht. 5–11   Wt. 165
Citizen—U.S.

Season	Club	GP	G	A	Pts.
1974	Miami	14	1	7	9
1975	Miami	9	1	1	3
1976	Miami	20	2	2	6
	Totals	43	4	10	18

BAXTER, JIM   *Midfielder*
Ht. 5–11   Wt. 168

Season	Club	GP	G	A	Pts.
1967	Vancouver	12	2	3	7

BAYLIS, ROBERT   *Midfielder*

Season	Club	GP	G	A	Pts.
1973	Montreal	1	0	0	0

BAYLON, JULIO   *Forward*
B. Oct. 12, 1947   Lima, Peru
Ht. 5–10   Wt. 170
Citizen—Peru

Season	Club	GP	G	A	Pts.
1978	Rochester	8	5	3	13
1979	Rochester	12	1	2	4
	Totals	20	6	5	17

BEAL, PHIL   *Defender*
B. Jan. 8, 1945   Goston, England
Ht. 5–10   Wt. 160
Citizen—England

Season	Club	GP	G	A	Pts.
1977	Los Angeles	23	3	0	6
1978	Memphis	22	0	1	1
	Totals	45	3	1	7

BEAN, RALPH   *Forward*
Ht. 6–1   Wt. 165
Citizen—Bermuda

Season	Club	GP	G	A	Pts.
1975	Philadelphia	16	0	2	2

BEANY, BILL   *Defender*

Season	Club	GP	G	A	Pts.
1975	Washington	14	0	0	0

BECKENBAUER, FRANZ "KAIZER"   *Midfielder*
B. Sept. 11, 1945   Munich, W. Germany
Ht. 5–11   Wt. 165
Citizen—W. Germany

Season	Club	GP	G	A	Pts.
1977	New York	15	4	5	13
1978	New York	27	8	16	32
1979	New York	12	1	6	8
	Totals	54	13	27	53

BEDFORD, BRIAN

Season	Club	GP	G	A	Pts.
1967	Atlanta	4	3	2	8

BELFIORE, IVAN   *Defender*
B. Sept. 4, 1960
Ht. 5–11   Wt. 172
Citizen—Canada

Season	Club	GP	G	A	Pts.
1979	Detroit	3	0	0	0

BELL, BOBBY   *Defender*
B. Sept. 26, 1950   Cambridge, England
Ht. 6–0   Wt. 165
Citizen—England

Season	Club	GP	G	A	Pts.
1977	Ft. Lauderdale	15	0	0	0

BELL, GRAHAM   *Midfielder*
Ht. 5–10   Wt. 155

Season	Club	GP	G	A	Pts.
1974	Denver	17	0	2	2

BELLINGER, TONY   *Midfielder*
B. Dec. 8, 1957   Willingboro, N.J.
Ht. 5–11   Wt. 165
Citizen—U.S.

Season	Club	GP	G	A	Pts.
1977	Dallas	19	2	0	4
1978	Dallas	22	2	2	6
1979	Dallas	26	1	1	3
	Totals	67	5	3	13

BENA, STEVE   *Defender*
B. Aug. 23, 1935   Yugoslavia
Ht. 5–11   Wt. 170
Citizen—Yugoslavia

Season	Club	GP	G	A	Pts.
1968	Oakland	21	0	0	0

BENEDEK, JIM   *Forward*
B. June 9, 1941   Budapest, Hungary
Ht. 5–8   Wt. 154
Citizen—U.S.

Season	Club	GP	G	A	Pts.
1968	Houston	19	3	3	9
1969	Kansas City	—	—	—	—

Season	Club	GP	G	A	Pts.
1970	Dallas	19	0	0	0
1971	Dallas	9	0	1	1
1972	Dallas	9	0	0	0
1973	Dallas	8	0	1	1
	Totals	64	3	5	11

BENEGAS, JUAN
See *Goalkeeper*

BENITEZ, JORGE   *Forward*
B. Peru
Ht. 5–9   Wt. 182
Citizen—Peru

Season	Club	GP	G	A	Pts.
1968	Los Angeles	11	6	0	12

BENNETT, CHRIS   *Forward*
B. Jan. 15, 1952   London, England
Ht. 5–9   Wt. 165
Citizen—Canada

Season	Club	GP	G	A	Pts.
1974	Vancouver	8	2	1	5
1976	Seattle	14	0	1	1
1977	Seattle	3	0	0	0
1978	Memphis	5	0	1	1
	Totals	30	2	3	7

BENNETT, PETER   *Midfielder*
B. June 24, 1946   Ruislip, England
Ht. 5–11   Wt. 172
Citizen—England

Season	Club	GP	G	A	Pts.
1977	St. Louis	19	2	2	6

BEN-TOVIM, EHUD   *Forward*

Season	Club	GP	G	A	Pts.
1978	Oakland	1	0	0	0

BENTUGNA, JORGE   *Forward*
B. Buenos Aires, Argentina
Ht. 5–8   Wt. 165
Citizen—Argentina

Season	Club	GP	G	A	Pts.
1967	Tor. (NPSL)	6	5	1	11

BERG, MOGENS   *Forward*
Ht. 6–4   Wt. 160

Season	Club	GP	G	A	Pts.
1967	Dallas	10	2	2	6

BERICO, JOSE   *Defender*
B. Nov. 29, 1947   Sao Paolo, Brazil
Ht. 5–7   Wt. 170
Citizen—Brazil

Season	Club	GP	G	A	Pts.
1975	San Antonio	20	5	0	10
1976	San Antonio	15	3	1	7
	Totals	35	8	1	17

BERNARD, MIKE   *Midfielder*
Ht. 5–9   Wt. 149

Season	Club	GP	G	A	Pts.
1967	Cleveland	5	1	0	2

BERRIO, JORGE   *Defender*
Ht. 6–1   Wt. 180
Citizen—Argentina

Season	Club	GP	G	A	Pts.
1979	Memphis	12	0	1	1

BERTL, HORST   *Midfielder*
B. Mar. 24, 1947   Bremerhaven, W. Germany
Ht. 5–10   Wt. 164
Citizen—W. Germany

Season	Club	GP	G	A	Pts.
1979	Houston	13	0	7	7

BERTOCCO, J.   *Forward*

Season	Club	GP	G	A	Pts.
1971	Montreal	1	0	0	0

BEST, CLYDE   *Forward*
B. Feb. 24, 1957   Somerset, Bermuda
Ht. 6–2   Wt. 195
Citizen—Bermuda

Season	Club	GP	G	A	Pts.
1975	Tampa Bay	19	6	5	17
1976	Tampa Bay	19	9	6	24
1977	Portland	25	7	4	18
1978	Portland	30	12	9	33
1979	Portland	29	8	8	24
	Totals	122	42	32	116

BEST, GEORGE   *Forward*
B. May 22, 1946   Belfast, N. Ireland
Ht. 5–8   Wt. 160
Citizen—N. Ireland

Season	Club	GP	G	A	Pts.
1976	Los Angeles	23	15	7	37
1977	Los Angeles	20	11	18	40
1978	L.A.-Ft. L.	21	4	1	9
1979	Ft. Lauderdale	19	2	7	11
	Totals	83	32	33	97

BEST, JOHN   *Defender*
B. July 11, 1940   Liverpool, England
Ht. 5–10   Wt. 170
Citizen—England

Season	Club	GP	G	A	Pts.
1967	Philadelphia	12	1	0	2
1968	Cleveland	28	—	—	—
1971	Dallas	23	0	0	0
1972	Dallas	14	0	0	0
1973	Dallas	17	0	0	0
	Totals	94	1	0	2

BETTS, TONY   *Forward*
B. Oct. 31, 1957   Derby Devonshire, England
Ht. 5–11   Wt. 165
Citizen—England

Season	Club	GP	G	A	Pts.
1975	Portland	18	7	1	15
1976	Portland	24	5	0	10
1977	Portland	24	1	4	6
	Totals	66	13	5	31

Season	Club	GP	G	A	Pts.

BEVANS, JERRY   *Defender*
B. May 6, 1954
Ht. 5-8   Wt. 160
Citizen—U.S.

1978	San Jose	3	0	0	0

BICK, SAM   *Midfielder*
B. Jan. 30, 1955   St. Louis, Mo.
Ht. 5-11   Wt. 180
Citizen—U.S.

1976	Minnesota	9	0	3	3
1977	Minnesota	14	0	1	1
1978	Minnesota	6	0	0	0
1979	San Jose	29	1	1	3
	Totals	58	1	5	7

BIDIAK, TERRY   *Midfielder*

1971	Toronto	4	0	0	0

BILECKI, ZELJKO
See *Goalkeeper*

BINNEY, FRED   *Forward*
B. Aug. 12, 1946   Saltdean, England
Ht. 5-10   Wt. 170
Citizen—England

1977	St. Louis	18	9	2	20

BIRCHENALL, ALAN   *Midfielder*
B. 1948   England
Ht. 6-0   Wt. 180
Citizen—England

1977	San Jose	17	3	0	6
1978	Memphis	24	2	2	6
	Totals	41	5	2	12

BIRKENMEIER, HUBERT
See *Goalkeeper*

BJERRE, KRESTEN   *Midfielder*
B. Feb. 22, 1946   Copenhagen, Denmark
Ht. 5-9   Wt. 160
Citizen—Denmark

1968	Houston	31	6	1	13

BLACK, OSCAR
B. Feb. 26, 1943   Kingston, Jamaica

1968	St. Louis	4	0	0	0

BLACKMORE, RICHARD
See *Goalkeeper*

BLAIR, CORCEL   *Midfielder*
Ht. 5-11   Wt. 170

1975	Toronto	8	0	0	0

BLAIR, RONNIE   *Midfielder*
B. Coleraine, N. Ireland
Ht. 5-10   Wt. 161

1978	Colorado	18	1	1	3

BLANCO, ROBERTO
See *Goalkeeper*

BLANCO, SERGIO
See *Goalkeeper*

BLANKENBURG, HORST   *Defender*
B. July 10, 1947   Heidenheim, Germany
Ht. 6-0   Wt. 170
Citizen—W. Germany

1978	Chicago	9	0	1	1
1979	Chicago	21	0	0	0
	Totals	30	0	1	1

BLASCKE, HERMAN   *Forward*
B. Sept. 31, 1948   S. Africa
Ht. 5-10   Wt. 150

1973	Miami	10	1	2	4

BLASKOVIC, FILIP   *Defender*
B. July 5, 1945   Yugoslavia
Ht. 6-0   Wt. 175
Citizen—Yugoslavia

1976	Toronto	14	0	0	0
1977	Toronto	12	0	0	0
1978	Toronto	27	0	0	0
	Totals	53	0	0	0

BLOOMFIELD, RAY   *Forward*
B. Oct. 15, 1944   London, England
Ht. 5-10   Wt. 160
Citizen—England

1967	Atlanta	10	3	4	10
1968	Atlanta	28	2	0	4
1969	Atlanta	—	—	—	—
1970	Atlanta	—	—	—	—
1971	Dallas	15	1	0	2
1972	Dallas	6	0	0	0
1973	Dallas	8	0	0	0
	Totals	67	6	4	16

BLOOR, ALAN   *Midfielder*
Ht. 6-0   Wt. 182

1967	Cleveland	11	1	1	3

BLUEM, JOHN   *Defender*
B. Apr. 17, 1953   Wheeling, W. Va.
Ht. 5-10   Wt. 165
Citizen—U.S.

1975	Tampa Bay	2	0	0	0
1976	Tampa Bay	13	0	0	0
	Totals	15	0	0	0

Season	Club	GP	G	A	Pts.

BODONCZY, NICO   *Forward*
B. Feb. 26, 1955   Santiago, Chile
Ht. 6-0   Wt. 170
Citizen—U.S.

Season	Club	GP	G	A	Pts.
1976	Miami	19	4	2	10
1977	Ft. Lauderdale	2	0	1	1
1978	Ft. Lauderdale	2	1	1	3
1979	Ft. Lauderdale	8	1	1	3
	Totals	31	6	5	17

BOEL, HENNING   *Midfielder*
B. Aug. 15, 1945   Ikast, Denmark
Ht. 5-11   Wt. 170

Season	Club	GP	G	A	Pts.
1968	Bost.-Wash.	9	0	0	0
1974	Boston	10	1	0	2
1975	Boston	17	0	1	1
	Totals	36	1	1	3

BOGICEVIC, VLADISLAV   *Midfielder*
B. Nov. 7, 1950   Belgrade, Yugoslavia
Ht. 6-1   Wt. 180
Citizen—Yugoslavia

Season	Club	GP	G	A	Pts.
1978	New York	30	10	17	37
1979	New York	25	1	23	25
	Totals	55	11	40	62

BOKERN, JIM   *Forward*
B. Apr. 16, 1952   St. Louis, Mo.
Ht. 5-9   Wt. 155
Citizen—U.S.

Season	Club	GP	G	A	Pts.
1974	St. Louis	18	4	6	14
1975	St. Louis	17	1	1	3
1976	St. Louis	14	1	1	3
	Totals	49	6	8	20

BOKERN, TOM   *Forward*
B. St. Louis, Mo.
Ht. 5-6   Wt. 145
Citizen—U.S.

Season	Club	GP	G	A	Pts.
1971	St. Louis	9	0	2	2

BOLANOS, JORGE   *Midfielder*
Ht. 5-8   Wt. 140

Season	Club	GP	G	A	Pts.
1973	Miami	2	0	0	0

BOLITHO, BOB   *Midfielder*
B. July 20, 1952   Victoria, Canada
Ht. 5-9   Wt. 173
Citizen—Canada

Season	Club	GP	G	A	Pts.
1977	Vancouver	19	4	2	10
1978	Vancouver	29	0	7	7
1979	Vancouver	27	0	9	9
	Totals	75	4	18	26

BOLOTA, FRANCISCO   *Forward*
B. Apr. 20, 1946   Portugal
Ht. 6-1   Wt. 180
Citizen—Portugal

Season	Club	GP	G	A	Pts.
1978	Rochester	28	12	3	27

BOND, LEN
See *Goalkeeper*

BONE, JIM   *Forward*
B. Sept. 22, 1949   Bridge-of-Allen, Scotland
Ht. 5-10   Wt. 175
Citizen—Scotland

Season	Club	GP	G	A	Pts.
1979	Toronto	25	3	16	22

BONETTI, PETER
See *Goalkeeper*

BONINSEGNA, ROBERTO   *Forward*
Ht. 5-9   Wt. 165

Season	Club	GP	G	A	Pts.
1967	Chi. (USA)	9	0	1	1

BOOK, JAN   *Forward*
B. Aug. 22, 1947   Jonkoping, Sweden
Ht. 6-0   Wt. 160
Citizen—Sweden

Season	Club	GP	G	A	Pts.
1968	Dallas	3	0	0	0

BORGES, PAULO   *Forward*
Ht. 5-9   Wt. 145

Season	Club	GP	G	A	Pts.
1967	Houston	8	6	3	15

BORGHOUS, GERRIT   *Midfielder*
B. Holland
Ht. 6-1   Wt. 181
Citizen—Holland

Season	Club	GP	G	A	Pts.
1968	Kansas City	29	0	0	0

BORODIAK, JOHN   *Defender*
B. Buenos Aires, Argentina
Ht. 5-8   Wt. 155
Citizen—Argentina

Season	Club	GP	G	A	Pts.
1968	Cleveland	23	0	0	0
1969	Baltimore	—	—	—	—
	Totals	23	0	0	0

BOROZZI, JOHN   *Midfielder*
Ht. 5-9   Wt. 160
Citizen—U.S.

Season	Club	GP	G	A	Pts.
1976	Philadelphia	8	0	0	0

BOSCAY, IMRE
B. July 9, 1947   Budapest, Hungary

Season	Club	GP	G	A	Pts.
1973	Miami	1	0	0	0

Season	Club	GP	G	A	Pts.

BOULTON, COLIN
See *Goalkeeper*

BOURAZANIS, YANNIS   *Midfielder*

Season	Club	GP	G	A	Pts.
1978	Tulsa	1	0	1	1

BOURNE, JEFF   *Forward*
B. June 19, 1948   Linton, England
Ht. 5–10   Wt. 170
Citizen—England

Season	Club	GP	G	A	Pts.
1977	Dallas	22	15	3	33
1978	Dallas	30	21	8	50
1979	Atlanta	29	18	15	51
	Totals	81	54	26	134

BOWERY, BERT   *Forward*
B. Oct. 29, 1954   St. Kitts, West Indies
Ht. 6–1   Wt. 195
Citizen—England

Season	Club	GP	G	A	Pts.
1976	Boston	24	8	8	24
1977	Hawaii	10	1	1	3
	Totals	34	9	9	27

BOYLE, JOHN   *Midfielder*
B. Dec. 25, 1946   Motherwell, Scotland
Ht. 5–9   Wt. 161
Citizen—England

Season	Club	GP	G	A	Pts.
1975	Tampa Bay	21	3	4	10

BRACEWELL, KEN   *Defender*
B. England
Ht. 5–11   Wt. 165
Citizen—England

Season	Club	GP	G	A	Pts.
1967	Tor. (NPSL)	—	—	—	—
1968	Toronto	27	1	0	2
1969	Atlanta	—	—	—	—
1970	Atlanta	—	—	—	—
1971	Atlanta	23	1	0	2
1972	Atlanta	13	0	1	1
1973	Atlanta	12	0	0	0
1974	Atlanta	3	0	0	0
	Totals	78	2	1	5

BRADFORD, DAVID   *Midfielder*
B. Feb. 22, 1953   Manchester, England
Ht. 5–5   Wt. 138
Citizen—England

Season	Club	GP	G	A	Pts.
1978	Detroit	30	9	11	29
1979	Detroit	28	2	11	15
	Totals	58	11	22	44

BRADLEY, GORDON   *Defender*
B. Nov. 23, 1938   Sunderland, England
Ht. 5–10   Wt. 170
Citizen—U.S.

Season	Club	GP	G	A	Pts.
1968	New York	20	0	0	0
1969	Baltimore	—	—	—	—
1971	New York	18	0	0	0
1972	New York	12	0	1	1
1973	New York	9	0	0	0
1974	New York	8	0	0	0
1975	New York	1	0	0	0
	Totals	68	0	1	1

BRADVIC, MARJIAN   *Midfielder*
B. July 12, 1949   Zagreb, Yugoslavia
Ht. 5–7   Wt. 155
Citizen—Yugoslavia

Season	Club	GP	G	A	Pts.
1975	Toronto	9	3	2	8
1977	Toronto	14	2	2	6
	Totals	23	5	4	14

BRADY, DAVID   *Midfielder*
Ht. 5–6   Wt. 155

Season	Club	GP	G	A	Pts.
1975	Denver	5	0	0	0

BRAGG, DAVID
See *Goalkeeper*

BRAND, JACK
See *Goalkeeper*

BRAUN, THEO
See *Goalkeeper*

BRAVENBOER, FREDDY
See *Goalkeeper*

BRAZIL, ALAN   *Forward*
B. June 15, 1959   Glasgow, Scotland
Ht. 5–10   Wt. 157
Citizen—England

Season	Club	GP	G	A	Pts.
1978	Detroit	21	9	7	25

BRIC, DAVID
See *Goalkeeper*

BREEVOORT, RENE   *Midfielder*
B. Aug. 14, 1950   Amsterdam, Holland
Ht. 5–11   Wt. 170
Citizen—Holland

Season	Club	GP	G	A	Pts.
1979	Washington	19	2	3	7

BRETON, EDNER   *Forward*
B. Haiti
Ht. 5–9   Wt. 160
Citizen—Haiti

Season	Club	GP	G	A	Pts.
1968	Detroit	2	0	0	0
1971	Rochester	19	2	3	7
1972	Rochester	8	1	0	2
	Totals	29	3	3	9

Season	Club	GP	G	A	Pts.

BREWSTER, BEN   *Defender*
B. September 26, 1948   Newton, Mass.
Ht. 5–10   Wt. 160
Citizen—U.S.

Season	Club	GP	G	A	Pts.
1974	Boston	11	0	0	0
1975	Boston	9	0	0	0
1978	New England	11	0	1	1
	Totals	31	0	1	1

BRIDGE, IAN   *Defender*
B. Sept. 18, 1959   Victoria, Canada
Ht. 6–1   Wt. 170
Citizen—Canada

Season	Club	GP	G	A	Pts.
1979	Seattle	14	1	3	5

BRIGGS, JIM

Season	Club	GP	G	A	Pts.
1967	Dallas	5	0	0	0

BRIGIDA, MIGUEL   *Forward*

Season	Club	GP	G	A	Pts.
1974	Los Angeles	4	0	1	1
1975	Los Angeles	4	0	0	0
	Totals	8	0	1	1

BRINE, PETER   *Midfielder*
B. July 18, 1953   London, England
Ht. 5–10   Wt. 160
Citizen—England

Season	Club	GP	G	A	Pts.
1976	Minnesota	22	1	5	7

BRISCOE, JOHN   *Forward*
B. England
Ht. 5–10   Wt. 155
Citizen—England

Season	Club	GP	G	A	Pts.
1968	Los Angeles	6	0	0	0

BRISTOWE, ALAN   *Forward*
B. Montreal
Ht. 5–8   Wt. 153
Citizen—Canada

Season	Club	GP	G	A	Pts.
1971	Montreal	10	0	1	1
1972	Montreal	5	0	0	0
	Totals	15	0	1	1

BROGDEN, LEE   *Forward*
Ht. 5–7   Wt. 150

Season	Club	GP	G	A	Pts.
1974	Denver	18	2	1	5

BROOKES, JOHN   *Forward*
B. England
Ht. 5–10   Wt. 160

Season	Club	GP	G	A	Pts.
1968	Cleveland	19	1	0	2

BROOKS, ADRIAN   *Midfielder*
B. Oct. 2, 1957   England
Ht. 6–2   Wt. 185
Citizen—England

Season	Club	GP	G	A	Pts.
1979	Atlanta	28	4	4	12

BROOKS, DOUG   *Forward*
B. Sept. 14, 1953   St. Louis, Mo.
Ht. 5–10   Wt. 165
Citizen—U.S.

Season	Club	GP	G	A	Pts.
1976	Minnesota	1	0	0	0

BROWN, BARRY   *Forward*
B. N. Ireland
Ht. 5–10   Wt. 160
Citizen—N. Ireland

Season	Club	GP	G	A	Pts.
1968	Detroit	8	0	0	0

BROWN, BILL
See *Goalkeeper*

BROWN, BRUCE
See *Goalkeeper*

BROWN, CLIFF
See *Goalkeeper*

BROWN, GRAHAM
See *Goalkeeper*

BROWN, LESBURN   *Defender*
B. Jan. 28, 1948   Jamaica
Ht. 5–7   Wt. 135
Citizen—Jamaica

Season	Club	GP	G	A	Pts.
1968	Boston	2	0	0	0

BROWNE, GERRY   *Forward*
B. Dec. 9, 1944   Trinidad
Ht. 5–9   Wt. 150

Season	Club	GP	G	A	Pts.
1971	Washington	15	2	1	5

BRUCE, WALTER   *Midfielder*
B. N. Ireland
Ht. 5–7   Wt. 148
Citizen—N. Ireland

Season	Club	GP	G	A	Pts.
1968	Detroit	11	3	0	6

BUCHAN, MARTIN   *Forward*
Ht. 5–10   Wt. 150

Season	Club	GP	G	A	Pts.
1967	Washington	8	1	1	3

BUCKLEY, PADDY   *Forward*
Ht. 5–6   Wt. 160

Season	Club	GP	G	A	Pts.
1967	L.A. (USA)	5	2	0	4

Season	Club	GP	G	A	Pts.
BUCKLEY, STEVE *Defender*					
B. May 12, 1950 St. Louis, Mo.					
Ht. 6–0 Wt. 180					
Citizen—U.S.					
1977	St. Louis	18	1	0	2
BUDD, BRIAN *Forward*					
B. April 8, 1952 Toronto, Canada					
Ht. 6–1 Wt. 180					
Citizen—Canada					
1974	Vancouver	10	2	1	5
1975	Vancouver	15	4	2	10
1976	Vancouver	17	1	3	5
1977	Vancouver	9	0	1	1
1978	Col.-Tor.	13	5	3	13
1979	Toronto	5	1	0	2
	Totals	69	13	10	36
BULGARELLI, GIACOMO *Midfielder*					
1975	Hartford	2	0	0	0
BUNDSCHOKS, MANFRED					
B. Jan. 3, 1937 Cologne, Germany					
1968	St. Louis	2	0	0	0
BURGIN, ANDY *Defender*					
B. England					
Ht. 5–8 Wt. 137					
Citizen—England					
1968	Detroit	16	1	0	2
BUSBY, DREW *Midfielder*					
B. Dec. 8, 1947 Glasgow, Scotland					
Ht. 5–9 Wt. 175					
Citizen—Scotland					
1979	Toronto	23	2	1	5
BURNETT, DENNIS *Midfielder*					
B. Sept. 27, 1944 London, England					
Ht. 5–11 Wt. 170					
Citizen—England					
1975	St. Louis	21	4	4	12
1977	St. Louis	22	0	1	1
	Totals	43	4	5	13
BURNS, TIM *Midfielder*					
B. England					
Ht. 5–10 Wt. 150					
Citizen—Canada					
1972	Toronto	3	0	1	1
1973	Toronto	12	0	0	0
1974	Toronto	17	2	1	5
1975	Toronto	2	0	0	0
	Totals	34	2	2	6
BURNS, TONY					
See *Goalkeeper*					

Season	Club	GP	G	A	Pts.
BURNSIDE, DAVE *Midfielder*					
Ht. 5–9 Wt. 153					
1967	L.A. (USA)	12	1	0	2
BURROWS, HARRY *Forward*					
Ht. 5–7 Wt. 155					
1967	Cleveland	9	3	1	7
BUTLER, DAVE *Forward*					
B. Mar. 30, 1953 W. Bromwich, England					
Ht. 5–8 Wt. 152					
Citizen—England					
1974	Seattle	15	10	1	21
1975	Seattle	19	5	3	13
1976	Seattle	20	8	2	18
1977	Seattle	20	5	4	14
1978	Seattle	23	6	1	13
1979	Portland	20	6	6	18
	Totals	117	40	17	97
BUTLER, GEOFF *Defender*					
B. Sept. 26, 1947 England					
Ht. 5–9 Wt. 160					
Citizen—England					
1974	Baltimore	19	1	9	11
1975	Baltimore	22	1	5	7
	Totals	41	2	14	18
BUTTLE, STEVE *Midfielder*					
B. Jan. 1, 1953 Norwich, England					
Ht. 5–7 Wt. 138					
Citizen—England					
1977	Seattle	25	4	5	13
1978	Seattle	25	0	4	4
1979	Seattle	26	6	6	18
	Totals	76	10	15	35
BYRNE, EDDIE *Midfielder*					
B. Oct. 31, 1951 Dublin, Ireland					
Ht. 5–4 Wt. 150					
Citizen—Ireland					
1978	Philadelphia	18	1	0	2
BYRNE, PAT *Forward*					
B. May 15, 1956 Dublin, Ireland					
Ht. 5–8 Wt. 140					
Citizen—Ireland					
1978	Philadelphia	19	3	7	13
CABRALZINHO, CARLOS *Forward*					
Ht. 5–7 Wt. 152					
1967	Houston	7	2	0	4
CACCIATORE, STEVE *Forward*					
B. May 1, 1954 St. Louis, Mo.					
Ht. 5–7 Wt. 130					
Citizen—U.S.					
1977	St. Louis	1	0	0	0

Season	Club	GP	G	A	Pts.

CAETANO, OMAR   *Defender*
B. Nov. 8, 1941
Ht. 5–6   Wt. 150
Citizen—Uruguay

| 1975 | New York | 6 | 0 | 0 | 0 |

CAHILL, LIAM   *Forward*

| 1971 | Toronto | 1 | 0 | 0 | 0 |

CAHILL, PAUL   *Defender*
B. Sept. 29, 1955   Liverpool, England
Ht. 5–9   Wt. 160
Citizen—England

| 1979 | California | 26 | 0 | 1 | 1 |

CALADO, JORGE   *Defender*
B. June 7, 1943   Mozambique
Ht. 6–3   Wt. 190
Citizen—Portugal

1975	Boston	15	0	0	0
1976	Rochester	4	0	3	3
	Totals	19	0	3	3

CALDERON, CARLOS   *Forward*
Ht. 5–10   Wt. 155
Citizen—Mexico

| 1976 | Philadelphia | 5 | 1 | 0 | 2 |

CALDWELL, LARRY   *Midfielder*
B. Braintree, Mass.
Ht. 5–9   Wt. 155
Citizen—U.S.

| 1975 | Hartford | 7 | 0 | 0 | 0 |

CALIFANO, DANIEL   *Defender*
B. Argentina
Ht. 5–10   Wt. 180

| 1975 | San Antonio | 8 | 0 | 0 | 0 |

CALLAGHAN, IAN   *Midfielder*
B. Apr. 10, 1942   Liverpool, England
Ht. 5–7   Wt. 155
Citizen—England

| 1978 | Ft. Lauderdale | 19 | 0 | 4 | 4 |

CALLOWAY, LAURIE   *Defender*
B. June 17, 1945   Birmingham, England
Ht. 5–10   Wt. 170
Citizen—England

1974	San Jose	19	0	1	1
1975	San Jose	9	1	1	3
1976	San Jose	17	0	1	1
1977	San Jose	25	2	4	8
1979	San Jose	4	0	0	0
	Totals	74	3	7	13

Season	Club	GP	G	A	Pts.

CALVERT, CLIFF   *Midfielder*
B. Apr. 24, 1954   York, England
Ht. 5–10   Wt. 168
Citizen—England

| 1979 | Toronto | 29 | 8 | 6 | 22 |

CALVO, JOSE LUIS
See *Goalkeeper*

CAMACHO, EMILIO   *Forward*
Ht. 6–0   Wt. 158
Citizen—Mexico

| 1976 | Philadelphia | 7 | 0 | 1 | 1 |

CAMACHO, HENRY   *Forward*

| 1973 | Rochester | 4 | 0 | 0 | 0 |

CAMACHO, MANUEL
See *Goalkeeper*

CAMERON, JIM   *Defender*
Ht. 5–9   Wt. 154

| 1967 | Dallas | 10 | 1 | 0 | 2 |

CAMPBELL, BOB   *Forward*
B. Sept. 13, 1956   Belfast, N. Ireland
Ht. 6–1   Wt. 190
Citizen—England

| 1978 | Vancouver | 13 | 9 | 6 | 24 |

CAMPBELL, DANNY   *Midfielder*
B. England
Ht. 6–1   Wt. 150
Citizen—England

| 1968 | Los Angeles | 21 | 1 | 0 | 2 |

CAMPO, MICHEL   *Defender*
Ht. 5–7   Wt. 160

| 1971 | Montreal | 2 | 0 | 0 | 0 |

CAMPOS, CLAUDE
See *Goalkeeper*

CAMPOS, ROLANDO   *Midfielder*
B. Lima, Peru
Ht. 5–9   Wt. 140
Citizen—Peru

| 1967 | Chi. (NPSL) | 6 | 1 | 0 | 2 |

CANNELL, PAUL   *Forward*
B. Sept. 2, 1953   Newcastle, England
Ht. 5–11   Wt. 165
Citizen—England

1976	Washington	21	13	2	28
1978	Washington	24	14	7	35
1979	Washington	24	10	6	26
	Totals	69	37	15	89

Season	Club	GP	G	A	Pts.

CANNON, OTEY "BOOM-BOOM"   *Forward*
Ht. 5–10   Wt. 165
Citizen—U.S.

Season	Club	GP	G	A	Pts.
1972	Dallas	7	0	0	0
1973	Dallas	2	0	0	0
1974	Dal.-Sea.	10	1	1	3
1975	Seattle	2	0	0	0
	Totals	21	1	1	3

CANO, JUAN   *Midfielder*
B. July 12, 1956   Medellin, Colombia
Ht. 5–10   Wt. 155
Citizen—U.S.

Season	Club	GP	G	A	Pts.
1979	New England	10	0	0	0

CANO, MARINE
See *Goalkeeper*

CANTELLO, LEN   *Midfielder*
B. Sept. 11, 1951   Manchester, England
Ht. 5–9   Wt. 168
Citizen—England

Season	Club	GP	G	A	Pts.
1978	Dallas	19	1	2	4

CANTILLO, RINGO   *Midfielder*
B. May 21, 1956   Cartago, Costa Rica
Ht. 5–10   Wt. 175
Citizen—U.S.

Season	Club	GP	G	A	Pts.
1976	Tampa Bay	21	0	3	3
1978	New England	24	0	7	7
1979	New England	29	2	5	9
	Totals	74	2	15	19

CARBOGNIANI, ANTONIO   *Midfielder*
B. Nov. 5, 1953   Buenos Aires, Argentina
Ht. 6–1   Wt. 176
Citizen—Argentina

Season	Club	GP	G	A	Pts.
1979	New York	12	1	2	4

CARENZA, CHRIS J.   *Defender*
B. Mar. 3, 1952   St. Louis, Mo.
Ht. 6–2   Wt. 185
Citizen—U.S.

Season	Club	GP	G	A	Pts.
1975	San Antonio	18	0	1	1
1976	San Antonio	19	0	0	0
1977	Hawaii	13	0	0	0
	Totals	50	0	1	1

CARENZA, JOHN   *Defender*
B. Jan. 3, 1956   St. Louis, Mo.
Ht. 6–4   Wt. 190
Citizen—U.S.

Season	Club	GP	G	A	Pts.
1973	St. Louis	13	0	0	0
1974	St. Louis	8	1	1	3
1975	St. Louis	17	3	6	12
1976	St. Louis	14	1	0	2
	Totals	52	5	7	17

CAREY, CHUCK   *Defender*
B. Aug. 12, 1953   Bethesda, Md.
Ht. 5–10   Wt. 165
Citizen—U.S.

Season	Club	GP	G	A	Pts.
1975	San Antonio	8	0	0	0
1976	S.A.-Port.	4	0	0	0
	Totals	12	0	0	0

CARLOS, JOAO   *Defender*
B. 1948   Portugal
Ht. 6–0   Wt. 175
Citizen—Portugal

Season	Club	GP	G	A	Pts.
1977	Connecticut	21	1	1	3

CARLTON, DAVID   *Midfielder*
B. Nov. 21, 1952   London, England
Ht. 5–11   Wt. 156

Season	Club	GP	G	A	Pts.
1972	Dallas	9	1	0	2

CARLYLE, HILARY   *Forward*
B. Aug. 20, 1954   Derby City, Ireland
Ht. 6–1   Wt. 180
Citizen—Ireland

Season	Club	GP	G	A	Pts.
1976	San Diego	11	5	2	12
1977	L.V.-Haw.	24	5	1	11
	Totals	35	10	3	23

CARR, PETER   *Defender*
B. Aug. 25, 1951   Durham, England
Ht. 5–9   Wt. 155
Citizen—England

Season	Club	GP	G	A	Pts.
1978	New England	30	0	5	5
1979	New England	29	0	0	0
	Totals	59	0	5	5

CARRETTE, EMMANUEL   *Forward*
B. May 24, 1948   Brazil

Season	Club	GP	G	A	Pts.
1971	New York	1	0	0	0

CARTER, MANLEY "SONNY"   *Defender*
B. Aug. 15, 1947   Macon, Ga.
Ht. 6–0   Wt. 165
Citizen—U.S.

Season	Club	GP	G	A	Pts.
1970	Atlanta	—	—	—	—
1971	Atlanta	8	0	0	0
1972	Atlanta	1	0	0	0
	Totals	9	0	0	0

CARVALHO, NICANOR   *Forward*

Season	Club	GP	G	A	Pts.
1974	Miami	2	0	0	0

CASA, VICTORIO   *Forward*
B. Argentina
Ht. 5–7   Wt. 145
Citizen—Argentina

Season	Club	GP	G	A	Pts.
1968	Washington	27	5	0	10

Season	Club	GP	G	A	Pts.

CASIC, MIRKO
B. Yugoslavia
Citizen—Yugoslavia

| 1968 | Vancouver | 2 | 0 | 0 | 0 |

CASKEY, BILLY *Forward*
B. Dec. 10, 1954   Belfast, N. Ireland
Ht. 5–11 Wt. 170
Citizen—N. Ireland

| 1978 | Tulsa | 27 | 11 | 8 | 30 |

CASSARETO, ENRIQUE *Forward*
B. Apr. 29, 1945   Chiclayo, Peru
Ht. 6–2 Wt. 160
Citizen—Peru

| 1976 | Miami | 6 | 0 | 0 | 0 |

CASSIDY, BILL *Forward*
B. Scotland
Ht. 5–9 Wt. 168
Citizen—Scotland

| 1968 | Detroit | 4 | 1 | 0 | 2 |

CASSIDY, NIGEL *Forward*
Ht. 5–11 Wt. 175

| 1975 | Denver | 20 | 1 | 1 | 3 |

CATTANEO, CHRIS *Midfielder*
B. Nov. 6, 1957   Brooklyn, N.Y.
Ht. 5–7 Wt. 150
Citizen—U.S.

| 1979 | Atlanta | 1 | 0 | 0 | 0 |

CAVALLERO, TRINI
See *Goalkeeper*

CAVANAGH, TONY *Forward*
Ht. 5–10 Wt. 150
Citizen—N. Ireland

| 1975 | Philadelphia | 18 | 0 | 2 | 2 |

CAVE, MICKY *Midfielder*
B. Jan. 28, 1949   Weymouth, England
Ht. 5–8 Wt. 155
Citizen—England

1977	Seattle	22	12	6	30
1978	Seattle	30	13	6	32
1979	Seattle	22	6	7	19
	Totals	74	31	19	81

CAWSTON, MERVYN "THE MAGICIAN"
See *Goalkeeper*

CEBALLOS, SERGIO *Forward*
B. Feb. 15, 1951   Mexico
Ht. 5–11 Wt. 170
Citizen—Mexico

| 1977 | Ft. Lauderdale | 5 | 1 | 1 | 3 |

CECIC, TOM *Defender*
B. Aug. 18, 1941   Yugoslavia
Ht. 5–10 Wt. 170
Citizen—U.S.

1968	Chicago	4	1	0	2
1973	Miami	2	0	0	0
	Totals	6	1	0	2

CECIL, IRWIN *Defender*
Ht. 6–1 Wt. 180

| 1967 | Vancouver | 12 | 0 | 2 | 2 |

CEHAIC, MIRSAD *Defender*
Ht. 6–0 Wt. 170

| 1975 | Toronto | 9 | 0 | 0 | 0 |

CERESIA, DONALD
B. Jan. 4, 1944   St. Louis, Mo.
Citizen—U.S.

1967	St. Louis	—	—	—	—
1968	St. Louis	7	0	0	0
	Totals	7	0	0	0

CERIC, EMIR *Forward*
B. 1950   Yugoslavia
Ht. 5–10 Wt. 174
Citizen—Yugoslavia

| 1977 | Las Vegas | 10 | 2 | 1 | 5 |

CHADWICK, DAVID *Forward*
B. Aug. 19, 1943   Ootacamund, India
Ht. 5–8 Wt. 140
Citizen—England

1974	Dallas	15	3	6	12
1975	Dallas	20	2	6	10
1977	Ft. Lauderdale	22	2	6	10
1978	Ft. Lauderdale	1	0	0	0
	Totals	58	7	18	32

CHAILLET, JEAN PIERRE *Forward*
B. France
Ht. 5–5 Wt. 152
Citizen—France

| 1968 | Vancouver | 2 | 0 | 0 | 0 |

CHANDLER, PETER *Defender*
B. Mar. 19, 1953   Duxbury, Mass.
Ht. 6–0 Wt. 160
Citizen—U.S.

1976	Hartford	17	0	0	0
1977	Connecticut	9	0	0	0
1978	Tampa Bay	4	0	0	0
	Totals	30	0	0	0

CHAPLA, GEORGE *Defender*
Ht. 5–10 Wt. 160

| 1975 | Hartford | 5 | 0 | 0 | 0 |

Season	Club	GP	G	A	Pts.
CHAPMAN, LES *Midfielder*					
B. England					
Ht. 6-0 Wt. 175					
1978	San Jose	20	2	0	4
CHAPMAN, SAMMY *Defender*					
B. Aug. 14, 1946 Walsall, England					
Ht. 6-1 Wt. 180					
Citizen—England					
1979	Tulsa	30	7	1	15
CHARBONNEAU, HOWIE *Defender*					
B. June 12, 1955 Troy, N.Y.					
Ht. 5-10 Wt. 165					
Citizen—U.S.					
1978	Houston	7	0	0	0
1979	Houston	27	1	1	3
	Totals	34	1	1	3
CHARDIN, DELICES *Forward*					
1971	New York	1	0	1	1
CHARLES, CLIVE *Defender*					
B. Oct. 3, 1951 London, England					
Ht. 5-9 Wt. 155					
Citizen—England					
1971	Montreal	21	0	1	1
1972	Montreal	7	0	0	0
1978	Portland	25	0	2	2
1979	Portland	29	0	5	5
	Totals	82	0	8	8
CHEETHAM, ROY *Defender*					
B. England					
Ht. 5-11 Wt. 163					
Citizen—England					
1968	Detroit	13	7	0	14
CHI-DOY, CHEUNG *Forward*					
B. July 30, 1941 Hong Kong					
Ht. 5-8 Wt. 157					
Citizen—England					
1968	Van.-St. L	19	2	0	4
CHILD, PAUL *Forward*					
B. Dec. 8, 1952 Birmingham, England					
Ht. 5-10 Wt. 155					
Citizen—England					
1972	Atlanta	12	8	1	17
1973	Atlanta	19	8	1	17
1974	San Jose	20	15	6	36
1975	San Jose	21	4	7	15
1976	San Jose	23	13	8	34
1977	San Jose	26	13	3	29
1978	San Jose	29	8	4	20
1979	San Jose	29	8	6	22
	Totals	179	77	36	190

Season	Club	GP	G	A	Pts.
CHILINQUE, HIPOLITO *Forward*					
B. Rio de Janeiro, Brazil					
Ht. 5-9 Wt. 164					
Citizen—Brazil					
1967	Baltimore	7	4	0	8
1968	St. Louis	6	1	0	2
	Totals	13	5	0	10
CHINAGLIA, GIORGIO *Forward*					
B. Jan. 24, 1947 Carrara, Italy					
Ht. 6-1 Wt. 190					
Citizen—U.S.					
1976	New York	19	19	11	49
1977	New York	24	15	8	38
1978	New York	30	34	11	79
1979	New York	27	26	5	57
	Totals	100	94	35	223
CHI-WAI, CHEUNG *Forward*					
B. Hong Kong					
Ht. 5-7 Wt. 153					
Citizen—England					
1968	Vancouver	28	2	0	4
CHODAKOWSKI, MIROSLAW *Defender*					
B. Poland					
Ht. 5-11 Wt. 165					
1975	Hartford	21	0	0	0
CHRISTENSEN, CARL *Defender*					
B. July 5, 1956 Jackson, Mich.					
Ht. 5-11 Wt. 175					
Citizen—U.S.					
1978	Dal.-S.J.	8	0	0	0
1979	San Jose	6	0	0	0
	Totals	14	0	0	0
CHRISTIE, GORDON *Forward*					
Ht. 5-11 Wt. 148					
1973	Montreal	5	0	0	0
CHURLIN, ANDY *Forward*					
B. Oct. 26, 1959					
Ht. 5-10 Wt. 160					
Citizen—U.S.					
1979	Seattle	1	0	0	0
CHURSKY, TONY					
See *Goalkeeper*					
CHYZOWYCH, WALTER *Forward*					
B. Apr. 20, 1937					
Ht. 5-10 Wt. 175					
Citizen—U.S.					
1967	Philadelphia	15	3	3	9

Season	Club	GP	G	A	Pts.
CID, AMANCIO *Forward*					
B. Argentina					
Ht. 6-0 Wt. 180					
Citizen—Argentina					
1968	Cleveland	19	12	0	24
CIOCCA, RAFFAELLO *Forward*					
Ht. 5-7 Wt. 158					
1967	Chi. (USA)	2	1	0	2
CILA, RENATO *Defender*					
B. Nov. 23, 1951 Brazil					
Ht. 5-7 Wt. 154					
Citizen—Brazil					
1979	Rochester	26	0	5	5
CLARK, BOBBY					
See *Goalkeeper*					
CLARK, CLIVE *Forward*					
Ht. 5-9 Wt. 150					
Citizen—England					
1974	Washington	8	0	0	0
CLARK, RICHARD *Forward*					
B. Guatemala					
Ht. 6-0 Wt. 170					
Citizen—Guatemala					
1968	Toronto	7	1	0	2
CLARK, ROBERT					
See *Goalkeeper*					
CLARKE, COLIN *Defender*					
B. Apr. 4, 1946 Glasgow, Scotland					
Ht. 6-1 Wt. 180					
Citizen—England					
1978	Los Angeles	17	0	1	1
CLARKE, DANVILLE					
See *Goalkeeper*					
CLARKE, JOEY *Defender*					
B. Nov. 27, 1953 St. Louis, Mo.					
Ht. 5-9 Wt. 160					
Citizen—U.S.					
1976	St. Louis	20	0	1	1
1977	St. Louis	10	0	1	1
1978	California	26	0	0	0
1979	California	18	0	0	0
	Totals	74	0	2	2
CLEAR, EDWARD *Midfielder*					
B. May 15, 1944 St. Louis, Mo.					
Ht. 5-11 Wt. 165					
Citizen—U.S.					
1967	St. Louis	—	—	—	—
1968	St. Louis	11	0	0	0
	Totals	11	0	0	0

Season	Club	GP	G	A	Pts.
CLEMENTS, DAVE *Midfielder*					
B. Sept. 16, 1945 Millbrook, N. Ireland					
Ht. 5-10 Wt. 155					
Citizen—N. Ireland					
1976	New York	18	2	3	7
1978	Colorado	15	1	3	5
	Totals	33	3	6	12
CLIFF, EDDIE *Defender*					
B. Sept. 30, 1951 Liverpool, England					
Ht. 5-10 Wt. 165					
Citizen—England					
1975	Chicago	1	0	0	0
1976	Chicago	15	0	0	0
	Totals	16	0	0	0
COAKLEY, TOMMY *Forward*					
B. Scotland					
Ht. 5-6 Wt. 148					
Citizen—Scotland					
1968	Detroit	10	0	0	0
COCKING, JOHN *Defender*					
B. May 13, 1944 Sunderland, England					
Ht. 5-10 Wt. 160					
Citizen—England					
1968	Atlanta	27	0	0	0
1969	Atlanta	—	—	—	—
1970	Atlanta	—	—	—	—
1971	Atlanta	22	0	0	0
1972	Atlanta	13	1	1	3
1973	Atlanta	15	2	0	4
	Totals	77	3	1	7
COCKS, RONALD *Forward*					
B. Jan. 8, 1943 Gzira, Malta					
Ht. 5-6 Wt. 155					
1967	Pittsburgh	17	10	2	22
COFFEE, PAUL					
See *Goalkeeper*					
COHEN, MARTIN *Midfielder*					
B. Feb. 3, 1952 Johannesburg, S. Africa					
Ht. 5-10 Wt. 170					
Citizen—S. Africa					
1977	Los Angeles	21	0	3	3
1979	California	23	0	3	3
	Totals	44	0	6	6
COHEN, NEIL *Defender*					
B. Sept. 12, 1955 Dallas, Texas					
Ht. 6-1 Wt. 175					
Citizen—U.S.					
1974	Dallas	1	0	0	0
1975	Dallas	7	0	0	0
1976	Dallas	21	0	2	2
1977	Dallas	20	0	2	2

Season	Club	GP	G	A	Pts.
1978	Dallas	21	0	2	2
1979	S.J.-Tul.	9	1	0	2
	Totals	79	1	6	8

COHEN, SHIMON   *Forward*
B. Tel Aiv, Israel
Ht. 5–8   Wt. 150
Citizen—Israel

Season	Club	GP	G	A	Pts.
1967	Baltimore	11	4	2	10

COKER, ADE   *Forward*
B. May 19, 1954   Lagos, Nigeria
Ht. 5–8   Wt. 148
Citizen—England

Season	Club	GP	G	A	Pts.
1974	Boston	18	8	2	18
1975	Boston	15	10	6	26
1976	Bost.-Minn.	16	8	5	21
1977	Minnesota	24	7	3	17
1978	Minn.-S.D.	8	4	1	9
1979	San Diego	8	3	1	7
	Totals	89	40	18	98

COLE, ALLAN   *Forward*
B. Oct. 14, 1950   Kingston, Jamaica
Ht. 6–0   Wt. 155
Citizen—Jamaica

Season	Club	GP	G	A	Pts.
1968	Atlanta	1	0	0	0

COLE, PHIL   *Forward*
B. Sept. 19, 1956   Sacramento, Calif.
Ht. 5–7   Wt. 150
Citizen—U.S.

Season	Club	GP	G	A	Pts.
1976	San Diego	7	0	0	0

COLEMAN, KEITH   *Defender*
B. May 24, 1951   Newcastle-Upon-Tyne, England
Ht. 5–9   Wt. 155
Citizen—England

Season	Club	GP	G	A	Pts.
1977	Hawaii	17	0	5	5

COLHACO, SILVIO   *Midfielder*

Season	Club	GP	G	A	Pts.
1974	Rochester	4	0	2	2

COLLAR, ANTONIO   *Midfielder*
B. Spain
Ht. 5–11   Wt. 168
Citizen—Spain

Season	Club	GP	G	A	Pts.
1968	Vancouver	14	0	0	0

COLLINS, CHRIS   *Midfielder*
B. Mar. 8, 1956   Ontario, N.Y.
Ht. 5–9   Wt. 150
Citizen—U.S.

Season	Club	GP	G	A	Pts.
1978	Dallas	2	0	1	1
1979	Dallas	7	0	1	1
	Totals	9	0	2	2

COLLINS, DOUG   *Midfielder*
B. Aug. 28, 1946   Newton, England
Ht. 5–10   Wt. 160
Citizen—England

Season	Club	GP	G	A	Pts.
1978	Tulsa	5	0	1	1

COLLINS, JOHN   *Defender*
B. Jan. 21, 1949   Wales
Ht. 5–8   Wt. 155

Season	Club	GP	G	A	Pts.
1973	Dallas	19	0	0	0

COLQUHOUN, EDDIE   *Defender*
B. Mar. 29, 1945   Edinburgh, Scotland
Ht. 6–0   Wt. 170
Citizen—England

Season	Club	GP	G	A	Pts.
1978	Detroit	24	2	0	4
1979	Detroit	28	1	1	3
	Totals	52	3	1	7

COLRAIN, JOHN   *Forward*
Ht. 6–0   Wt. 180

Season	Club	GP	G	A	Pts.
1967	Detroit	3	1	0	2

CONNAGHAN, DENNIS
See *Goalkeeper*

CONNELL, MIKE   *Defender*
B. Nov. 1, 1956   Johannesburg, S. Africa
Ht. 6–0   Wt. 150
Citizen—S. Africa

Season	Club	GP	G	A	Pts.
1975	Tampa Bay	20	1	1	3
1977	Tampa Bay	26	0	1	1
1978	Tampa Bay	27	0	0	0
1979	Tampa Bay	30	1	2	4
	Totals	103	2	4	8

CONSTANCIA, JOSE   *Forward*
B. Mar. 19, 1945   Willenstad, Curacao
Ht. 5–11   Wt. 185
Citizen—Curacao

Season	Club	GP	G	A	Pts.
1968	Oakland	3	0	0	0

CONTERERAS, RAFAEL   *Defender*
B. Mexico
Ht. 5–9   Wt. 156
Citizen—Mexico

Season	Club	GP	G	A	Pts.
1976	Philadelphia	17	0	1	1

CONWAY, JIMMY   *Midfielder*
B. Oct. 8, 1946   Dublin, Ireland
Ht. 5–8   Wt. 160
Citizen—England

Season	Club	GP	G	A	Pts.
1978	Portland	25	1	5	7
1979	Portland	25	4	9	17
	Totals	50	5	14	24

Season	Club	GP	G	A	Pts.
COOKE, CHARLIE *Midfielder*					
B. Oct. 14, 1942 St. Monace, Scotland					
Ht. 5–9 Wt. 160					
Citizen—Scotland					
1976	Los Angeles	12	2	6	10
1977	Los Angeles	20	2	15	19
1978	L.A.-Mem.	23	2	5	9
1979	Memphis	22	2	4	8
	Totals	77	8	30	46
COOP, MICK *Defender*					
B. July 10, 1948 England					
Ht. 5–11 Wt. 177					
Citizen—England					
1979	Detroit	13	0	1	1
COOPER, KEN					
See *Goalkeeper*					
COP, MILAN *Midfielder*					
B. Oct. 5, 1938 Slawonski, Yugoslavia					
Ht. 5–10 Wt. 166					
Citizen—Yugoslavia					
1967	Oakland	12	3	1	7
1968	Oakland	23	3	0	6
	Totals	35	6	1	13
CORISH, BOB *Defender*					
B. Sept. 13, 1958 Liverpool, England					
Ht. 5–10 Wt. 158					
Citizen—England					
1979	Ft. Lauderdale	14	0	0	0
CORMACK, PETER *Forward*					
Ht. 5–8 Wt. 146					
1967	Tor. (USA)	11	6	1	13
CORREA, JULIO *Midfielder*					
B. July 9, 1948					
Ht. 5–4 Wt. 144					
Citizen—Uruguay					
1975	New York	21	4.	8	16
CORREIA, CARLOS *Forward*					
1971	Montreal	8	2	1	5
CORREORA, FELIX *Forward*					
1971	Toronto	16	6	3	15
CORSI, JAMES *Forward*					
Ht. 5–10 Wt. 167					
1971	Montreal	1	0	0	0
1973	Montreal	4	1	1	3
	Totals	5	1	1	3

Season	Club	GP	G	A	Pts.
CORTEZ, JULIO *Defender*					
B. Mar. 29, 1943					
Ht. 5–9 Wt. 160					
Citizen—Uruguay					
1974	Los Angeles	19	1	1	3
COSKUN, DAVIT *Forward*					
B. Turkey					
Ht. 5–8 Wt. 150					
Citizen—Turkey					
1967	L.A. (NPSL)	20	6	2	14
COSKUNIAN, DAVE *Midfielder*					
1974	San Jose	4	0	0	0
COSTA, DIAMANTINO *Midfielder*					
B. May 29, 1948 Portimao, Portugal					
Ht. 5–8 Wt. 155					
Citizen—Portugal					
1977	Haw.-L.V.	16	1	1	3
COSTA, JOSE *Forward*					
B. Oct. 31, 1953 Portugal					
Ht. 5–10 Wt. 165					
Citizen—Portugal					
1977	Rochester	8	1	2	4
COSTA, RAUL *Midfielder*					
1975	San Antonio	14	2	0	4
COSTA, RENATO *Midfielder*					
B. Feb. 12, 1948					
Ht. 5–10 Wt. 163					
Citizen—Brazil					
1974	Los Angeles	16	3	4	10
COUNCE, DAN *Forward*					
B. Oct. 22, 1951 St. Louis, Mo.					
Ht. 5–11 Wt. 178					
Citizen—U.S.					
1974	Boston	8	1	0	2
1975	San Antonio	10	2	0	4
1976	San Antonio	20	6	1	13
1977	Hawaii	22	2	1	5
1978	California	23	4	3	11
1979	Toronto	8	0	1	1
	Totals	91	15	6	36
COURAGE, NICK *Forward*					
1974	Toronto	11	1	2	4
COX, ERNIE *Midfielder*					
B. Baltimore, Md.					
Ht. 5–9 Wt. 160					
Citizen—U.S.					
1975	Baltimore	9	0	0	0

Season	Club	GP	G	A	Pts.

COYNE, JOHN *Forward*
B. July 18, 1951   Liverpool, England
Ht. 5–10   Wt. 165
Citizen—England

1974	Boston	16	7	7	21
1975	Toronto	22	7	11	25
1976	Hartford	24	8	1	17
	Totals	62	22	19	63

COYNE, LAURENCE *Midfielder*
B. Nov. 13, 1956   Luton, England
Ht. 5–10   Wt. 155
Citizen—England

1976	Hartford	21	1	1	3
1977	Connecticut	20	0	1	1
	Totals	41	1	2	4

COYNE, PETER *Forward*
B. Ashton, England
Ht. 5–9   Wt. 150

1978	Los Angeles	11	1	1	3

CRAIG, DEREK *Defender*

1975	San Jose	18	2	0	4

CRAM, BOBBY *Defender*
B. Nov. 19, 1939   England
Ht. 5–11   Wt. 172
Citizen—England

1968	Vancouver	26	2	0	4
1974	Seattle	5	0	2	2
	Totals	31	2	2	6

CRAVEN, JOHN *Defender*
B. July 20, 1952   St. Annes, England
Ht. 6–0   Wt. 190
Citizen—England

1978	Vancouver	28	8	0	16
1979	Vancouver	12	1	0	2
	Totals	40	9	0	18

CREAMER, PETER *Defender*

1975	Dallas	12	1	1	3

CRESCITELLI, TONY *Forward*
B. Jan. 11, 1957   Avellino, Italy
Ht. 5–11   Wt. 175
Citizen—U.S.

1979	Washington	7	0	2	2

CRISP, RONALD *Defender*
B. London, England
Ht. 6–0   Wt. 172
Citizen—England

1967	L.A. (NPSL)	17	1	0	2
1968	San Diego	24	5	0	10
	Totals	41	6	0	12

CRISPIN, ROLAND *Defender*
B. Mar. 22, 1939
Ht. 5–8   Wt. 145

1971	Washington	24	0	1	1

CROSBIE, WILLIAM "FLUSH" *Defender*
B. Feb. 19, 1948   Liverpool, England
Ht. 5–9   Wt. 160
Citizen—England

1968	Dallas	7	0	0	0

CROSS, ROGER *Forward*
B. Oct. 24, 1948   London, England
Ht. 6–0   Wt. 175
Citizen—England

1977	Seattle	8	2	3	7

CROSSLEY, PAUL *Forward*
B. July 14, 1948   Rochdale, England
Ht. 5–7   Wt. 150
Citizen—England

1975	Seattle	20	4	12	20
1977	Seattle	16	4	6	14
1978	Seattle	25	5	7	17
1979	Seattle	16	3	1	7
	Totals	77	16	26	58

CROWE, VIC *Midfielder*
B. Jan. 30, 1934   Abercynon, Wales
Ht. 5–11   Wt. 160
Citizen—Wales

1968	Atlanta	13	1	0	2
1969	Atlanta	—	—	—	—
	Totals	13	1	0	2

CRUDGINGTON, GEOFF
See *Goalkeeper*

CRUDO, TONY *Defender*
B. Mar. 25, 1959   Seattle, Wash.
Ht. 6–0   Wt. 160
Citizen—U. S.

1978	Tampa Bay	11	0	0	0
1979	T.B.-Calif.	14	0	1	1
	Totals	25	0	1	1

CRUYFF, JOHAN *Forward*
B. April 25, 1947   Amsterdam, Holland
Ht. 5–8   Wt. 150
Citizen—Holland

1979	Los Angeles	23	13	16	42

CRYDER, BROOKS *Defender*
B. Jan. 13, 1955   Philadelphia, Pa.
Ht. 5–10   Wt. 170
Citizen—U.S.

1978	Philadelphia	14	0	0	0
1979	Philadelphia	26	0	0	0
	Totals	40	0	0	0

Season	Club	GP	G	A	Pts.

CRYNS, WILLI *Defender*
B. Aug. 29, 1952 Cologne, W. Germany
Ht. 6-0 Wt. 185
Citizen—W. Germany

| 1979 | San Jose | 28 | 0 | 0 | 0 |

CUBILLA, PETER *Midfielder*
B. Uruguay
Ht. 5-9 Wt. 172
Citizen—Uruguay

| 1968 | Toronto | 16 | 1 | 0 | 2 |

CUBILLAS, TEOFILO *Midfielder*
B. Mar. 8, 1949 Lima, Peru
Ht. 5-9 Wt. 158
Citizen—Peru

| 1979 | Ft. Lauderdale | 30 | 16 | 18 | 50 |

CUELLAR, LEONARDO *Midfielder*
B. Jan. 14, 1952 Mexico City, Mexico
Ht. 5-8 Wt. 160
Citizen—Mexico

| 1979 | San Diego | 24 | 3 | 9 | 15 |

CUENCA, MANUEL *Forward*
B. Sept. 11, 1948 Madrid, Spain
Ht. 5-6 Wt. 140
Citizen—Spain

| 1978 | California | 16 | 3 | 3 | 9 |

CUKON, MLADEN *Defender*
B. Mar. 21, 1946 Pula, Yugoslavia
Ht. 5-10 Wt. 165
Citizen—Yugoslavia

1976	Toronto	21	0	0	0
1977	Toronto	26	0	0	0
	Totals	47	0	0	0

CUMBERBATCH, AUSTIN
Ht. 5-10 Wt. 165

| 1973 | Montreal | 4 | 0 | 1 | 1 |

CUMBES, JIM
See *Goalkeeper*

CUMMINGS, EVERALD *Forward*
B. Aug. 28, 1948 Port au Spain, Trinidad
Ht. 5-8 Wt. 140
Citizen—Trinidad

1967	Atlanta	5	1	0	2
1968	Atlanta	2	0	0	0
1969	Atlanta	—	6	6	18
1970	Atlanta	—	—	—	—
1972	New York	13	5	3	13
1973	New York	9	1	0	2
	Totals	29	13	9	35

Season	Club	GP	G	A	Pts.

CUMMINGS, JOHN

| 1975 | Philadelphia | 7 | 0 | 0 | 0 |

CUMMINS, STAN *Forward*
B. June 12, 1958 Ferryhill, England
Ht. 5-3 Wt. 140
Citizen—England

| 1977 | Minnesota | 19 | 2 | 1 | 5 |

CUNHA-CINESINHO, SIDNEY *Defender*
B. Jan. 1, 1935 Brazil

| 1972 | New York | 1 | 0 | 0 | 0 |

CUPELLO, NELSON *Defender*
B. Aug. 28, 1951 Brazil
Ht. 6-0 Wt. 160
Citizen—U.S.

1975	Rochester	12	1	0	2
1976	Rochester	7	0	0	0
1977	Rochester	7	0	0	0
1978	Rochester	8	0	0	0
1979	Rochester	4	0	0	0
	Totals	38	1	0	2

da COSTA, JOAO *Defender*

| 1971 | Toronto | 19 | 0 | 1 | 1 |

da COSTA, VIRGINIO *Forward*

| 1971 | Toronto | 1 | 0 | 0 | 0 |

DaCRUZ, BADU *Defender*
B. July 20, 1946 Niteroi, Brazil
Ht. 5-11 Wt. 175
Citizen—Brazil

| 1967 | Baltimore | 11 | 4 | 2 | 10 |

DAGDEVIRON, VOLKAN

| 1968 | Dallas | 1 | 0 | 0 | 0 |

D'AGOSTINO, PAUL *Defender*
B. July 13, 1956 Canada
Ht. 5-11 Wt. 165
Citizen—Canada

| 1978 | Memphis | 19 | 0 | 1 | 1 |

D'ALESSIO, DOMENICO
See *Goalkeeper*

D'ALFONSO, ALDO *Forward*
B. June 28, 1956 Pescara, Italy
Ht. 5-9 Wt. 165
Citizen—Canada

| 1979 | Toronto | 1 | 0 | 0 | 0 |

DALMAO, JULIO *Midfielder*
Ht. 6-1 Wt. 196

| 1967 | N.Y. (U.S.A.) | 11 | 0 | 1 | 1 |

Season	Club	GP	G	A	Pts.

DALY, GERRY   *Midfielder*
B. Apr. 30, 1954   Dublin, Ireland
Ht. 5–9   Wt. 140
Citizen—Ireland

Season	Club	GP	G	A	Pts.
1978	New England	18	7	5	19
1979	New England	23	9	5	23
	Totals	41	16	10	42

DALY, TERRY   *Forward*
B. July 9, 1953   Dublin, Ireland
Ht. 5–9   Wt. 155
Citizen—Ireland

Season	Club	GP	G	A	Pts.
1977	St. Louis	19	2	1	5

DANAIFARD, IRAJ   *Midfielder*
B. Mar. 19, 1951   Teheran, Iran
Ht. 5–6   Wt. 163
Citizen—Iran

Season	Club	GP	G	A	Pts.
1979	Tulsa	19	1	3	5

DANGERFIELD, CHRIS   *Forward*
B. Aug. 9, 1955   Birmingham, England
Ht. 5–11   Wt. 160
Citizen—England

Season	Club	GP	G	A	Pts.
1975	Portland	14	4	2	10
1976	Portland	22	1	3	5
1977	L.V.-Haw.	22	2	0	4
1978	Tul.-Calif.	24	0	2	2
1979	Los Angeles	22	9	4	22
	Totals	104	16	11	43

DANIEL, PETER   *Defender*
B. Dec. 22, 1946   Derby, England
Ht. 5–10   Wt. 160
Citizen—England

Season	Club	GP	G	A	Pts.
1978	Vancouver	20	1	0	2
1979	Vancouver	27	1	0	2
	Totals	47	2	0	4

DARGLE, BENNY   *Defender*
B. Jan. 2, 1957   Liverpool, England
Ht. 5–11   Wt. 160
Citizen—U.S.

Season	Club	GP	G	A	Pts.
1979	Detroit	6	0	0	0

DARRACOTT, TERRY   *Defender*
B. Dec. 6, 1950   Liverpool, England
Ht. 5–8   Wt. 180
Citizen—England

Season	Club	GP	G	A	Pts.
1979	Tulsa	29	1	5	7

DARRELL, GARY   *Midfielder*
B. Jan. 10, 1947   Hamilton, Bermuda
Ht. 5–8   Wt. 150
Citizen—Bermuda

Season	Club	GP	G	A	Pts.
1972	Montreal	4	1	0	2
1973	Montreal	19	3	5	11

Season	Club	GP	G	A	Pts.
1974	Washington	19	6	2	14
1975	Washington	22	9	1	19
1976	Washington	15	0	2	2
1977	Washington	20	3	0	6
1978	Washington	19	2	0	4
1979	Washington	1	0	0	0
	Totals	119	24	10	58

DaSILVA, DIEGO   *Forward*
Ht. 5–11   Wt. 165

Season	Club	GP	G	A	Pts.
1972	Miami	10	0	0	0

DAUCIK, YANKO

Season	Club	GP	G	A	Pts.
1967	Tor. (NPSL)	17	20	8	48

DAVEY, CON   *Defender*

Season	Club	GP	G	A	Pts.
1974	Toronto	11	0	1	1

DAVID, STEVE   *Forward*
B. Nov. 3, 1950   Point Fortin, Trinidad
Ht. 6–0   Wt. 165
Citizen—Trinidad

Season	Club	GP	G	A	Pts.
1974	Miami	19	13	0	26
1975	Miami	21	23	6	52
1976	Miami	13	1	0	2
1977	Los Angeles	24	26	6	58
1978	L.A.-Det.-Calif.	25	7	8	22
1979	California	29	11	5	27
	Totals	131	81	25	187

DAVIDOVIC, DAVID   *Defender*
B. May 21, 1944   Aleksandrovac, Yugoslavia
Ht. 5–11   Wt. 165
Citizen—Yugoslavia

Season	Club	GP	G	A	Pts.
1967	Oakland	3	1	1	3
1968	Oakland	25	7	0	14
1978	San Jose	27	1	0	2
	Totals	55	9	1	19

DAVIE, SANDY
See *Goalkeeper*

DAVIES, BRIAN
B. Aug. 21, 1947   Stainford, England

Season	Club	GP	G	A	Pts.
1968	Balt.-Bost.	8	2	0	4

DAVIES, FRED
See *Goalkeeper*

DAVIES, GEOFF   *Forward*
B. July 1, 1947   Ellesmere Port, England
Ht. 6–0   Wt. 175
Citizen—England

Season	Club	GP	G	A	Pts.
1975	Boston	17	6	8	20
1976	Bost.-Chi.	17	8	6	22
1977	San Jose	24	4	2	10
	Totals	58	18	16	52

Season	Club	GP	G	A	Pts.
DAVIES, IAN *Defender*					
B. Mar. 29, 1957 Bristol, England					
Ht. 5–10 Wt. 146					
Citizen—England					
1978	Detroit	30	3	4	10
DAVIES, ROGER *Forward*					
B. Oct. 25, 1950 Wolverhampton, England					
Ht. 6–2 Wt. 180					
Citizen—England					
1979	Tulsa	22	8	7	23
DAVIES, RON *Forward*					
B. May 25, 1942 Holywell, England					
Ht. 6–0 Wt. 186					
Citizen—England					
1976	Los Angeles	24	6	3	15
1977	Los Angeles	25	6	3	15
1978	L.A.-Tul.	24	3	6	12
1979	Seattle	22	1	1	3
	Totals	95	16	13	45
DAVIS, JOE *Defender*					
Ht. 5–9 Wt. 156					
1967	Tor. (USA)	12	3	1	7
DAVIS, PHIL *Defender*					
B. Sheffield, England					
Ht. 6–1 Wt. 180					
Citizen—England					
1971	Toronto	15	1	0	2
1973	Montreal	19	1	0	2
1974	Rochester	5	0	0	0
1975	Hartford	3	0	0	0
	Totals	42	2	0	4
DAVIS, RICK *Midfielder*					
B. Nov. 24, 1958 Denver, Col.					
Ht. 5–8 Wt. 155					
Citizen—U.S.					
1978	New York	11	0	1	1
1979	New York	29	6	13	25
	Totals	40	6	14	26
DAWES, MALCOLM *Defender*					
B. Mar. 3, 1944					
Ht. 6–0 Wt. 180					
Citizen—England					
1973	New York	19	0	2	2
1974	New York	16	2	1	5
1975	Denver	19	2	3	7
	Totals	54	4	6	14
DAY, GRAHAM *Defender*					
B. Nov. 22, 1953 Bristol, England					
Ht. 6–1 Wt. 170					
Citizen—England					
1975	Portland	20	2	4	8
1977	Portland	20	3	1	7

Season	Club	GP	G	A	Pts.
1978	Portland	24	0	0	0
1979	Portland	29	4	2	10
	Totals	93	9	7	25
DE *Defender*					
1975	New York	3	0	0	0
DEAK, ANDRAS "ANDY" *Defender*					
B. Jan. 22, 1941 Budapest, Hungary					
Ht. 5–9 Wt. 160					
Citizen—U.S.					
1968	Houston	2	0	0	0
DeBONO, ALFREDO					
See *Goalkeeper*					
DeBRITO, IRIS *Forward*					
B. Rio de Janeiro, Brazil					
Ht. 5–9 Wt. 172					
Citizen—Brazil					
1967	Chi. (NPSL)	1	1	0	2
1968	K.C.-Tor.	22	21	2	44
1971	Rochester	17	6	8	20
1972	Rochester	11	1	0	2
1974	Denver	16	1	5	7
	Totals	67	30	15	75
DeCARIA, RAUL *Defender*					
Ht. 5–10 Wt. 165					
1971	Montreal	21	0	0	0
1972	Montreal	10	0	2	2
	Totals	31	0	2	2
DeCARVALHO, CLAUDIO *Forward*					
Ht. 6–0 Wt. 162					
1967	Chi. (USA)	10	1	2	4
DeGROOT, PIETER *Defender*					
B. June 26, 1940 Schiedam, Holland					
Ht. 5–8 Wt. 165					
Citizen—Holland					
1967	Pittsburgh	11	2	5	9
de la FUENTE, LUIS *Defender*					
B. Feb. 7, 1948					
Ht. 5–10 Wt. 170					
Citizen—Spain					
1975	New York	12	1	1	3
DELEON, LEROY *Forward*					
B. Feb. 7, 1948 Port au Spain, Trinidad					
Ht. 5–9 Wt. 165					
Citizen—Trinidad					
1967	N.Y. (NPSL)	7	3	0	6
1968	New York	7	0	0	0
1970	Washington	20	16	1	33
1971	Washington	23	8	7	23

Season	Club	GP	G	A	Pts.
1972	Miami	14	5	3	13
1974	Washington	18	7	2	16
1975	Washington	13	4	4	12
1976	Washington	16	7	5	19
1977	Wash.-S.J.	23	6	10	22
1978	San Jose	11	0	3	3
1979	Seattle	1	0	0	0
	Totals	153	56	35	147

DELGADO, JAIME *Forward*

Season	Club	GP	G	A	Pts.
1971	Washington	6	0	0	0
1972	Miami	1	0	0	0
	Totals	7	0	0	0

DeLIMA, MIGUEL
See *Goalkeeper*

DEL LLANO, WINDSOR *Midfielder*
Ht. 5-7 Wt. 130

Season	Club	GP	G	A	Pts.
1974	Washington	20	2	3	7

DELL'OMODARME, CARLO *Forward*

Season	Club	GP	G	A	Pts.
1972	Rochester	14	1	8	10

DELONG, CHARLES *Defender*
B. Feb. 18, 1948 Carrol, Iowa
Ht. 5-6 Wt. 158
Citizen—U.S.

Season	Club	GP	G	A	Pts.
1975	Dallas	3	0	0	0

DELORM, THOMAS "TAD"
See *Goalkeeper*

DEMAINE, DAVID *Forward*
B. Cleveleys, England
Ht. 5-7 Wt. 161
Citizen—England

Season	Club	GP	G	A	Pts.
1967	Tor. (NPSL)	9	3	0	6

DEMLING ARTHUR "BUZZ" *Defender*
B. Sept. 21, 1948 St. Louis, Mo.
Ht. 5-10 Wt. 170
Citizen—U.S.

Season	Club	GP	G	A	Pts.
1974	San Jose	20	0	0	0
1975	San Jose	19	0	2	2
1976	San Jose	16	1	1	3
1977	San Jose	25	0	2	2
1978	San Jose	18	0	0	0
	Totals	98	1	5	7

DEMLING, MARK *Defender*
B. Oct. 4, 1951 St. Louis, Mo.
Ht. 6-0 Wt. 175
Citizen—U.S.

Season	Club	GP	G	A	Pts.
1975	San Jose	13	1	1	3
1976	San Jose	18	0	1	1

Season	Club	GP	G	A	Pts.
1977	San Jose	8	0	0	0
1978	S.J.-S.D.	10	0	0	0
1979	San Diego	1	0	0	0
	Totals	50	1	2	4

DEMPSEY, JOHN *Defender*
B. Mar. 15, 1946 London, England
Ht. 6-0 Wt. 165
Citizen—England

Season	Club	GP	G	A	Pts.
1978	Philadelphia	26	1	0	2
1979	Philadelphia	29	0	1	1
	Totals	55	1	1	3

DeOLIVEIRA, JOEL *Forward*

Season	Club	GP	G	A	Pts.
1971	Montreal	6	2	0	4

DeOLIVEIRA, ROBERTO *Forward*
B. Sept. 11, 1955 Brooklyn, N.Y.
Ht. 5-9 Wt. 165
Citizen—U.S.

Season	Club	GP	G	A	Pts.
1977	New York	1	0	0	0
1978	Detroit	3	0	1	1
1979	Detroit	13	1	4	6
	Totals	17	1	5	7

DeRIENZO, RICARDO *Defender*
B. Aug. 20, 1948
Ht. 5-10 Wt. 168
Citizen—Argentina

Season	Club	GP	G	A	Pts.
1974	Los Angeles	19	2	0	4

DeROBERTIS, GENO *Midfielder*
B. Palermo, Italy
Ht. 5-5 Wt. 146
Citizen—Italy

Season	Club	GP	G	A	Pts.
1967	Chi. (NPSL)	12	0	3	3
1968	Kansas City	18	2	0	4
	Totals	30	2	3	7

D'ERRICO, DAVE *Defender*
B. June 3, 1952 Newark, New Jersey
Ht. 5-11 Wt. 165
Citizen—U.S.

Season	Club	GP	G	A	Pts.
1974	Seattle	6	0	1	1
1975	Seattle	15	1	0	2
1976	Seattle	15	0	0	0
1977	Minnesota	21	0	3	3
1978	New England	24	0	4	4
1979	Rochester	23	1	2	4
	Totals	104	2	10	14

DE SALES, SEVERO *Midfielder*
B. Mexico
Ht. 5-6 Wt. 160
Citizen—Mexico

Season	Club	GP	G	A	Pts.
1968	San Diego	20	0	0	0

Season	Club	GP	G	A	Pts.

DESIR, JOHN   *Midfielder*
B. Haiti
Ht. 5–8   Wt. 138
Citizen—Haiti

Season	Club	GP	G	A	Pts.
1968	Detroit	4	1	0	2

de SOUSA, NEY MARQUES   *Midfielder*
B. Brazil
Ht. 5–5   Wt. 138
Citizen—Brazil

Season	Club	GP	G	A	Pts.
1968	Washington	10	0	0	0

DEVITO, ROBERTO
See *Goalkeeper*

DeVRIES, ROBERT   *Forward*
B. Apr. 5, 1943   Amsterdam, Holland
Ht. 5–9   Wt. 175
Citizen—Holland

Season	Club	GP	G	A	Pts.
1967	Pittsburgh	11	1	2	4

DeWOLF, CARNELIS "CEES"   *Forward*
Ht. 6–0   Wt. 165
Citizen—Holland

Season	Club	GP	G	A	Pts.
1968	Dallas	9	3	0	6

DEWSNIP, GEORGE   *Forward*
B. May 6, 1956   England
Ht. 5–7   Wt. 140
Citizen—England

Season	Club	GP	G	A	Pts.
1977	Ft. Lauderdale	12	0	6	6
1978	Ft. Lauderdale	28	6	5	17
1979	L.A.-Atl.	18	0	10	10
	Totals	58	6	21	33

DeZOETE, PIET   *Midfielder*
Ht. 5–7   Wt. 145

Season	Club	GP	G	A	Pts.
1967	San Francisco	10	1	0	2

DIANE, MORRIE   *Forward*
B. Nigeria
Ht. 5–9   Wt. 140

Season	Club	GP	G	A	Pts.
1974	Washington	19	3	2	8
1975	San Antonio	17	2	3	7
	Totals	36	5	5	15

DIAS, PAULO
See *Goalkeeper*

DiBERNARDO, ANGELO   *Forward*
B. May 16, 1956   Buenos Aires, Argentina
Ht. 5–9   Wt. 154
Citizen—U.S.

Season	Club	GP	G	A	Pts.
1979	Los Angeles	15	1	3	5

DILL, CARLTON "PEPE"   *Forward*
B. June 1, 1943   Hamilton, Bermuda
Ht. 5–6   Wt. 150
Citizen—Bermuda

Season	Club	GP	G	A	Pts.
1968	Houston	13	7	2	16
1969	Dallas	14	2	1	5
1970	Dallas	14	1	1	3
	Totals	41	10	4	24

DILLON, MIKE   *Defender*
B. Sept. 29, 1952   London, England
Ht. 5–11   Wt. 175
Citizen—England

Season	Club	GP	G	A	Pts.
1972	Montreal	10	8	2	18
1975	New York	12	1	0	2
1976	New York	16	1	1	3
1977	New York	13	1	0	2
1978	Washington	23	0	2	2
1979	Washington	25	1	1	3
	Totals	99	12	6	30

DiLUCA, BOB   *Midfielder*

Season	Club	GP	G	A	Pts.
1971	Toronto	6	0	0	0

DIMITRIJEVIC, VITOMIR   *Midfielder*
B. Dec. 11, 1948   Surdulica, Yugoslavia
Ht. 5–10   Wt. 170
Citizen—Yugoslavia

Season	Club	GP	G	A	Pts.
1977	New York	21	4	6	14
1978	New York	18	1	2	4
1979	Los Angeles	20	0	1	1
	Totals	59	5	9	19

DINSDALE, PETER   *Defender*
B. England
Ht. 5–11   Wt. 178
Citizen—England

Season	Club	GP	G	A	Pts.
1968	Vancouver	24	0	0	0

DiPALMA, ROSSANO   *Forward*
Ht. 6–0   Wt. 180

Season	Club	GP	G	A	Pts.
1972	Montreal	2	0	0	0

DIXON, BILLY   *Forward*
Ht. 5–8   Wt. 154

Season	Club	GP	G	A	Pts.
1967	Boston	11	2	0	4

DJORDJEVIC, MIRO   *Midfielder*
Ht. 5–10   Wt. 166
Citizen—Yugoslavia

Season	Club	GP	G	A	Pts.
1978	Oakland	12	6	2	14
1979	Philadelphia	25	6	4	16
	Totals	37	12	6	30

Season	Club	GP	G	A	Pts.

DJUKIC, DRAGAN   *Midfielder*
B. Mar. 29, 1939   Belgrade, Yugoslavia
Ht. 6-1   Wt. 160
Citizen—Yugoslavia

Season	Club	GP	G	A	Pts.
1967	Oakland	12	2	1	5
1968	Oakland	9	0	0	0
	Totals	21	2	1	5

DOBING, PETER   *Forward*
Ht. 5-9   Wt. 163

1967	Cleveland	8	7	0	14

DOGANCIC, BOB   *Defender*
B. Sept. 17, 1949   Lujblana, Yugoslavia
Ht. 6-0   Wt. 175
Citizen—Yugoslavia

1978	San Diego	9	1	0	2
1979	San Diego	25	1	1	3
	Totals	34	2	1	5

DOHERTY, JAMES   *Midfielder*
B. Scotland
Ht. 5-8   Wt. 160

1975	San Antonio	22	2	1	5

D'OLOVIERA, ANTONIO   *Forward*
B. Brazil
Ht. 5-5   Wt. 148
Citizen—Brazil

1968	Washington	12	7	0	14

DOMINGUES, TINO   *Defender*
B. Nov. 2, 1951   Coimbra, Portugal
Ht. 5-0   Wt. 160
Citizen—U.S.

1976	Hartford	5	1	1	3

DONLAVEY, FRANK   *Defender*
B. Feb. 22, 1945   Scotland
Ht. 5-11   Wt. 170
Citizen—England

1971	New York	24	0	0	0
1972	New York	11	0	0	0
1974	New York	14	0	0	0
	Totals	49	0	0	0

DONLIC, TONY   *Forward*
B. Mar. 24, 1956   Vincrouci, Yugoslavia
Ht. 6-2   Wt. 195
Citizen—Yugoslavia

1976	New York	1	0	0	0
1978	New York	1	0	0	0
1979	San Diego	2	0	0	0
	Totals	4	0	0	0

DONNELLY, MARTIN   *Defender*
B. Jan. 4, 1951   Belfast, N. Ireland
Ht. 5-10   Wt. 155
Citizen—N. Ireland

1979	San Diego	23	1	3	5

DOSSING, FINN   *Forward*
Ht. 6-0   Wt. 165

1967	Dallas	10	3	0	6

DOUGAN, DEREK   *Forward*
Ht. 6-3   Wt. 175

1967	L.A.(USA)	11	3	3	9

DOUGLAS, JIM   *Forward*
Ht. 6-0   Wt. 155

1974	Toronto	11	0	2	2

DOUGLAS, TONY   *Midfielder*
B. Aug. 16, 1952
Ht. 5-9   Wt. 138
Citizen—Trinidad

1974	Los Angeles	20	5	6	16
1975	Los Angeles	16	5	2	12
	Totals	36	10	8	28

DOVEDAN, MILAN   *Defender*
B. Yugoslavia

1978	Tulsa	1	0	0	0

DOWIE, JOHN   *Midfielder*
B. Dec. 12, 1955   Hamilton, Scotland
Ht. 6-1   Wt. 162
Citizen—Scotland

1978	Houston	21	1	6	8

DOWLING, AL   *Forward*

1974	Washington	5	0	1	1

DOWNS, GREG   *Forward*
B. 1960   England
Ht. 5-1   Wt. 150
Citizen—England

1977	Connecticut	16	1	2	4

DRANDE, JIM   *Midfielder*
B. 1949   St. Louis, Mo.
Ht. 5-8   Wt. 143
Citizen—U.S.

1972	St. Louis	6	0	0	0

DROBNIAK, BRAD   *Forward*
Ht. 5-9   Wt. 160
Citizen—Yugoslavia

1975	Toronto	8	3	0	6

Season	Club	GP	G	A	Pts.

DROEGE, DON   *Defender*
B. Jan. 21, 1955   St. Louis, Mo.
Ht. 6-0   Wt. 180
Citizen—U.S.

1977	Rochester	20	1	1	3
1978	Rochester	24	0	1	1
1979	Washington	22	2	1	5
	Totals	66	3	3	9

DROEGMOELLER, MENO
See *Goalkeeper*

DROZD, BILL   *Defender*
B. Nov. 24, 1959   Lesna, Poland
Ht. 6-0   Wt. 170
Citizen—U.S.

1978	Chicago	4	0	0	0

DuBOSE, WINSTON
See *Goalkeeper*

DUCCILLI, CHARLES   *Forward*
B. Feb. 14, 1940   Philadelphia, Pa.
Ht. 5-7   Wt. 195
Citizen—U.S.

1973	Philadelphia	4	1	0	2

DuCHATEAU, GENE
See *Goalkeeper*

DUCIK, BRANISLAO   *Forward*
B. Oct. 1, 1949   Spain
Ht. 6-2   Wt. 190
Citizen—Spain

1968	Toronto	5	0	0	0

DUDA, RICHIE   *Midfielder*
B. Aug. 11, 1945   Poland
Ht. 6-0   Wt. 165
Citizen—Poland

1978	Chicago	1	0	0	0

DUERDEN, PETER   *Defender*
B. England
Ht. 5-1   Wt. 175
Citizen—Canada

1971	Toronto	6	0	0	0
1972	Montreal	3	0	0	0
1973	Montreal	6	0	1	1
	Totals	15	0	1	1

DUNLEAVY, CHRIS   *Defender*
B. Liverpool, England
Ht. 5-10   Wt. 165
Citizen—England

1973	Philadelphia	18	0	1	1
1974	Philadelphia	19	0	0	0
	Totals	37	0	1	1

DUNNE, PAT
See *Goalkeeper*

DUNNE, TONY   *Defender*
B. July 24, 1941   Dublin, Ireland
Ht. 5-7   Wt. 140
Citizen—Ireland

1979	Detroit	12	0	2	2

DURANTE, ELI   *Forward*
B. Sao Paulo, Brazil
Ht. 5-6   Wt. 151
Citizen—Brazil

1967	L.A. (NPSL)	23	15	5	35
1968	San Diego	6	1	0	2
1971	Rochester	20	0	4	4
1972	Rochester	13	0	1	1
1973	Rochester	19	0	3	3
1974	Rochester	19	2	2	6
1975	Rochester	21	3	5	11
	Totals	121	21	20	62

DYREBORG, ERIK   *Forward*
B. Jan. 20, 1940   Copenhagen, Denmark
Ht. 5-8   Wt. 145
Citizen—Denmark

1968	Boston	20	13	0	26

EAGAN, KEVIN   *Defender*
B. Dec. 30, 1954   Florissant, Mo.
Ht. 6-3   Wt. 175
Citizen—U.S.

1977	Tampa Bay	21	0	0	0
1978	Tampa Bay	7	0	0	0
1979	New York	3	0	0	0
	Totals	31	0	0	0

EARLE, STEVE   *Forward*
B. Nov. 1, 1945   Felthim, England
Ht. 5-9   Wt. 153
Citizen—England

1978	Det.-Tul.	22	2	5	9
1979	Tulsa	21	3	4	10
	Totals	43	5	9	19

EARLE, WINSTON   *Defender*
B. Mar. 31, 1948   Kingston, Jamaica
Ht. 6-0   Wt. 180
Citizen—Jamaica

1968	Baltimore	9	0	0	0
1971	Rochester	5	0	0	0
1974	Baltimore	7	0	3	3
1975	Baltimore	8	0	1	1
	Totals	29	0	4	4

Season	Club	GP	G	A	Pts.

EASTHAM, GEORGE   *Forward*
Ht. 5–7   Wt. 151

| 1967 | Cleveland | 11 | 1 | 1 | 3 |

EASTON, JAMES   *Defender*
B. Sept. 3, 1940   Glasgow, Scotland
Ht. 5–1   Wt. 170

| 1973 | Miami | 19 | 0 | 0 | 0 |

EDDY, KEITH   *Defender*
B. Oct. 23, 1944   Barrow-In-Furness, England
Ht. 5–11   Wt. 155
Citizen—England

1976	New York	24	8	2	18
1977	New York	6	1	0	2
	Totals	30	9	2	20

EDMUNDS, ERROL
See *Goalkeeper*

EICKERLING, MANFRED   *Defender*
Ht. 6–1   Wt. 170

| 1974 | Boston | 18 | 6 | 1 | 13 |

ELISEU, deGODY   *Forward*
B. Oct. 17, 1945   Brazil
Ht. 6–0   Wt. 165
Citizen—Brazil

| 1968 | New York | 8 | 5 | 0 | 10 |

ELLAM, ROY   *Defender*
Ht. 6–1   Wt. 180
Citizen—England

| 1975 | Philadelphia | 16 | 1 | 0 | 2 |

ELLETT, NEIL   *Defender*
B. 1945
Ht. 6–0   Wt. 170
Citizen—Canada

1974	Vancouver	5	1	0	2
1975	Vancouver	19	0	5	5
	Totals	24	1	5	7

EL MOSTAFA, ABBADIA   *Forward*
Ht. 5–11   Wt. 170

| 1972 | Montreal | 5 | 1 | 2 | 4 |

ENDEMAN, JAN
See *Goalkeeper*

ENDERS, PETER   *Midfielder*
Ht. 5–9   Wt. 170
Citizen—W. Germany

| 1978 | Oakland | 18 | 3 | 0 | 6 |

ENGER, HANS
See *Goalkeeper*

Season	Club	GP	G	A	Pts.

ENGERTH, EDDIE
Ht. 5–11   Wt. 165

| 1976 | Philadelphia | 7 | 0 | 1 | 1 |

ENGLAND, MIKE   *Defender*
B. Dec. 2, 1941   Greenfields, Wales
Ht. 6–2   Wt. 184
Citizen—Wales

1975	Seattle	19	2	6	10
1976	Seattle	17	2	0	4
1977	Seattle	25	0	1	1
1978	Seattle	27	2	2	6
1979	Seattle	18	0	3	3
	Totals	106	6	12	24

ERCOLI, PAT   *Forward*
B. Sept. 30, 1957   Toronto, Canada
Ht. 5–10   Wt. 160
Citizen—Canada

1978	Rochester	29	6	10	22
1979	Rochester	23	2	4	8
	Totals	52	8	14	30

ESCOS, FRANCISCO   *Midfielder*
B. July 10, 1942   Argentina
Ht. 5–6   Wt. 145
Citizen—Argentina

1971	Rochester	18	4	3	11
1972	Rochester	12	1	2	4
1973	Rochester	18	1	1	3
1974	Rochester	18	1	2	4
1975	Rochester	15	1	1	3
1976	Rochester	21	2	1	5
1977	Rochester	18	0	2	2
1978	Rochester	4	0	0	0
	Totals	124	10	12	32

ESGALHA, VALDEMAR   *Forward*
B. Nov. 24, 1944   Brazil
Ht. 5–11   Wt. 165

| 1972 | Miami | 4 | 2 | 1 | 5 |

ESKANDARIAN (ANDRANIK ESKANDARIAN)   *Defender*
B. Dec. 31, 1951   Teheran, Iran
Ht. 5–7   Wt. 155
Citizen—Iran

| 1979 | New York | 14 | 0 | 3 | 3 |

ESPOSITO, TONY   *Defender*

| 1973 | Rochester | 11 | 3 | 2 | 8 |

ETHERINGTON, GARY   *Forward*
B. Apr. 22, 1958   London, England
Ht. 5–8   Wt. 140
Citizen—U.S.

1977	New York	4	0	0	0
1978	New York	21	3	11	17
1979	New York	11	1	0	2
	Totals	36	4	11	19

Season	Club	GP	G	A	Pts.

ETTERICH, GUNTER   *Midfielder*
B. Aug. 16, 1951   Bochum, W. Germany
Ht. 5–10   Wt. 165
Citizen—W. Germany

Season	Club	GP	G	A	Pts.
1979	San Jose	27	4	8	16

EUSEBIO (EUSEBIO FERREIRA)   *Forward*
B. Jan. 25, 1942   Laurenco Marques, Mozambique
Ht. 6–0   Wt. 175
Citizen—Portugal

1975	Boston	7	2	2	6
1976	Toronto	21	16	4	36
1977	Las Vegas	17	2	5	9
	Totals	45	20	11	51

EVANS, DEREK   *Defender*
B. Jan. 15, 1959   Guyana, Central America
Ht. 5–10   Wt. 175
Citizen—U.S.

1979	Edmonton	10	0	0	0

EVANS, DOUG   *Midfielder*
B. 1959   Wales
Ht. 5–10   Wt. 160
Citizen—Wales

1977	Connecticut	17	0	0	0

EVANS, RAY   *Defender*
B. Sept. 20, 1949   Enfield, England
Ht. 5–11   Wt. 175
Citizen—Engalnd

1977	St. Louis	18	0	4	4
1978	California	24	1	3	5
	Totals	42	1	7	9

EVANS, WILLIAM   *Defender*
B. Nov. 21, 1939   Ghana
Ht. 6–2   Wt. 190

1971	Washington	24	0	1	1
1972	Miami	9	0	0	0
1973	Miami	12	1	0	2
	Totals	45	1	1	3

EVANSON, JOHN   *Midfielder*
B. May 10, 1947   Newcastle, England
Ht. 5–10   Wt. 160
Citizen—England

1976	Miami	16	1	1	3

FABBIANI, OSCAR   *Forward*
B. Dec. 17, 1950   Buenos Aires, Argentina
Ht. 5–10   Wt. 165
Citizen—Argentina

1979	Tampa Bay	26	25	8	58

FAGAN, BERNIE   *Defender*
B. Jan. 29, 1949   Sunderland, England
Ht. 5–9   Wt. 156
Citizen—England

1974	Seattle	11	0	1	1
1975	Los Angeles	13	0	1	2
1976	Los Angeles	21	1	3	5
1977	Los Angeles	12	0	1	1
	Totals	57	2	5	9

FAGAN, CHRIS   *Midfielder*

1974	Philadelphia	4	0	0	0

FAGRI, ANDERS "NOBBY"   *Midfielder*
B. Aug. 18, 1948   Oslo, Norway
Ht. 5–9   Wt. 155
Citizen—Norway

1968	Dallas	9	0	0	0

FAHY, JOHN   *Forward*
Ht. 6–2   Wt. 175

1972	Toronto	10	3	1	7

FAJKUS, CHARLIE   *Forward*
B. Mar. 4, 1957   Chicago, Ill.
Ht. 5–10   Wt. 155
Citizen—U.S.

1979	Chicago	19	2	5	9

FARMER, JOHN
See *Goalkeeper*

FASS, VOLKER   *Defender*
B. May 21, 1944
Ht. 6–2   Wt. 180
Citizen—W. Germany

1978	Oak.–S.J.	26	1	2	4

FAULKNER, JOHN   *Defender*
B. Mar. 10, 1948   Orpington, England
Ht. 6–0   Wt. 175
Citizen—England

1978	Memphis	29	2	3	7
1979	Memphis	27	1	2	4
	Totals	56	3	5	11

FAZLIC, MIRALEM   *Defender*
B. June 10, 1947   Tuzla, Yugoslavia
Ht. 6–1   Wt. 180
Citizen—Yugoslavia

1975	Toronto	22	0	3	3
1976	Tor.–Roch.	21	0	0	0
1977	Rochester	23	0	1	1
1978	Rochester	27	1	1	3
1979	Rochester	18	1	1	3
	Totals	111	2	6	10

Season	Club	GP	G	A	Pts.
FEAR, KEITH *Forward*					
B. May 8, 1952 Bristol, England					
Ht. 5-9 Wt. 160					
Citizen—England					
1976	St. Louis	20	3	6	12
FEARNLEY, GORDON *Forward*					
B. Jan. 25, 1950 Yorkshire, England					
Ht. 5-10 Wt. 165					
Citizen—England					
1976	Tor.-Mia.	21	3	9	15
1977	Ft. Lauderdale	18	2	0	4
1978	Ft. Lauderdale	4	0	1	1
	Totals	43	5	10	20
FELLOWS, GREGORY *Forward*					
B. Oct. 10, 1953 Dudley, England					
1973	Atlanta	7	1	2	4
FERGUSON, DAMIEN *Forward*					
B. Oct. 9, 1951 Dublin, Ireland					
Citizen—Ireland					
1972	Dallas	8	1	0	2
FERGUSON, DREW *Midfielder*					
B. Sept. 11, 1957 Powell River, Canada					
Ht. 5-11 Wt. 160					
Citizen—Canada					
1978	Vancouver	1	0	0	0
1979	Edmonton	11	0	2	2
	Totals	12	0	2	2
FERGUSON, MIKE *Midfielder*					
Ht. 5-10 Wt. 165					
1975	Los Angeles	21	2	2	6
FERNANDEZ, CIRILO "PEPE" *Forward*					
B. July 14, 1943 Montevideo, Uruguay					
Ht. 5-6 Wt. 164					
Citizen—Uruguay					
1967	L.A. (NPSL)	15	4	1	9
1968	San Diego	29	30	7	67
1969	Kansas City	16	6	6	18
1974	Seattle	3	1	2	4
1975	Seattle	12	1	2	4
	Totals	75	42	18	102
FERREIRA, IVAIR *Midfielder*					
B. Jan. 27, 1945 Sao Paulo, Brazil					
Ht. 5-9 Wt. 150					
Citizen—Brazil					
1975	Toronto	14	5	2	12
1976	Toronto	22	6	10	22
1977	Toronto	24	7	7	21
1978	Toronto	24	3	4	10
1979	Toronto	20	1	3	5
	Totals	104	22	26	70

Season	Club	GP	G	A	Pts.
FERREIRA, PAULO *Midfielder*					
1971	Rochester	7	0	0	0
FERRY, GORDON *Midfielder*					
B. Dec. 22, 1943 Sunderland, England					
Ht. 5-10 Wt. 165					
Citizen—England					
1968	Atlanta	18	0	0	0
FIDELIA, PAT *Forward*					
B. Apr. 16, 1959 Port-au-Prince, Haiti					
Ht. 5-10 Wt. 165					
Citizen—U.S.					
1978	Philadelphia	25	8	1	17
1979	Philadelphia	17	9	1	19
	Totals	42	17	2	36
FIELD, TONY *Forward*					
B. June 7, 1946 Halifax, England					
Ht. 5-7 Wt. 154					
Citizen—England					
1976	New York	23	7	9	23
1977	New York	21	6	9	21
1978	Memphis	29	7	11	25
1979	Memphis	28	5	9	19
	Totals	101	25	38	88
FIGARO, SELRIS *Defender*					
B. Trinidad					
Ht. 6-2 Wt. 190					
1973	Miami	13	1	1	3
1974	Miami	20	1	1	3
1975	Miami	14	0	1	1
	Totals	47	2	3	7
FILBY, IAN *Forward*					
Ht. 5-11 Wt. 154					
1973	Montreal	19	3	8	14
FILOTIS, PAYNOF *Forward*					
B. Greece					
Ht. 5-5 Wt. 145					
1974	Los Angeles	17	3	3	9
1975	San Antonio	7	1	1	3
	Totals	24	4	4	12
FINK, JOE *Forward*					
B. July 31, 1951 Ridgewood, N.Y.					
Ht. 6-0 Wt. 160					
Citizen—U.S.					
1973	New York	14	11	0	22
1974	New York	12	3	4	10
1975	New York	16	6	2	14
1976	Tampa Bay	12	1	1	3
1977	Tampa Bay	13	0	0	0
1978	Tampa Bay	9	4	1	9
	Totals	76	25	8	58

Season	Club	GP	G	A	Pts.
FINKEN, HERB *Midfielder*					
B. Dec. 31, 1939 Cologne, Germany					
Ht. 5–10 Wt. 180					
Citizen—Germany					
1967	Pitt.–N.Y. (NPSL)	26	1	5	7
1968	New York	21	2	0	4
	Totals	47	3	5	11

Season	Club	GP	G	A	Pts.
FIRMAN, EDWIN "GOLDEN TURKEY" *Forward*					
B. Aug. 7, 1933 Capetown, S. Africa					
Ht. 5–10 Wt. 170					
Citizen—Italy					
1975	Tampa Bay	1	0	0	0

FISHER, HUGH *Midfielder*
Ht. 5–7 Wt. 155

1975	Denver	22	0	4	4

FISSHA *Midfielder*
Ht. 6–0 Wt. 180

1975	Los Angeles	12	3	2	8

FITILIS, KYRIAKOS *Midfielder*
B. June 21, 1942 Greece
Ht. 6–0 Wt. 185

1971	New York	6	0	1	1

FLANAGAN, MIKE *Forward*
B. Sept. 11, 1952 Ilford, Essex, England
Ht. 5–9 Wt. 164
Citizen—England

1978	New England	28	30	8	68

FLASCHEN, DAVE
See *Goalkeeper*

FLATER, MIKE *Forward*
B. Jan. 22, 1950 Chicago, Ill.
Ht. 5–11 Wt. 160
Citizen—U.S.

1975	Denver	15	10	4	24
1976	Minnesota	16	4	7	15
1977	Minnesota	12	1	0	2
1978	Oak–Port.	26	7	3	17
	Totals	69	22	14	58

FLEETING, JIM *Defender*
B. Apr. 8, 1955 Glasgow, Scotland
Ht. 6–1 Wt. 159
Citizen—England

1978	Tampa Bay	28	2	1	5

FLINDT, OVIE *Midfielder*
B. July 21, 1948 Aalborg, Denmark
Ht. 5–10 Wt. 160
Citizen—Denmark

1979	San Jose	23	2	5	9

FOGARTY, KEN *Defender*
B. Jan. 25, 1955 Manchester, England
Ht. 5–8 Wt. 157
Citizen—England

1979	Ft. Lauderdale	10	0	0	0

FOGGON, ALAN *Forward*
B. Feb. 23, 1950 Durham, England
Ht. 5–10 Wt. 170
Citizen—England

1976	Hartford	19	4	5	13

FONSECH, JULIO *Forward*
B. Honduras
Ht. 5–3 Wt. 155
Citizen—Honduras

1968	Toronto	11	0	0	0

FONTURA, LUIS *Forward*
Ht. 5–8 Wt. 159

1967	N.Y. (USA)	10	0	1	1

FORD, CLIVE *Forward*
B. England
Ht. 5–8 Wt. 170
Citizen—England

1968	Los Angeles	4	2	0	4

FORMOSO, SANTIAGO *Forward*
B. July 4, 1953 Vigo, Spain
Ht. 5–10 Wt. 150
Citizen—U.S.

1976	Hartford	24	0	0	0
1977	Connecticut	25	1	0	2
1978	New York	26	2	7	11
1979	New York	17	0	2	2
	Totals	92	3	9	15

FORREST, JIM *Forward*
Ht. 5–10 Wt. 155

1975	San Antonio	4	0	0	0

FORREST, JOHN
See *Goalkeeper*

FORREST, WARD *Forward*
B. Jan. 25, 1954 Seattle, Wash.
Ht. 5–9 Wt. 155
Citizen—U.S.

1977	Seattle	3	0	0	0
1978	Seattle	1	0	0	0
	Totals	4	0	0	0

FORSTER, DEREK
See *Goalkeeper*

Season	Club	GP	G	A	Pts.

FORTEIS, RAUL *Defender*
Ht. 5-8   Wt. 160
Citizen— Argentina

Season	Club	GP	G	A	Pts.
1975	San Antonio	5	0	0	0

FOSTER, RON *Midfielder*
B. England
Ht. 5-10   Wt. 155
Citizen—England

1968	Dallas	11	4	0	8

FOTIADIS, TOM *Defender*
B. Greece
Ht. 5-9   Wt. 155
Citizen—Greece

1968	Chicago	14	0	0	0

FOWLES, COLIN *Midfielder*
B. Aug. 6, 1953   Kingston, Jamaica
Ht. 5-10   Wt. 170
Citizen—U.S.

1977	Ft. Lauderdale	23	5	4	14
1978	Ft. Lauderdale	27	1	2	4
1979	Ft. Lauderdale	7	0	0	0
	Totals	57	6	6	18

FOX, PETER
See *Goalkeeper*

FRANCIS, TREVOR *Forward*
B. Apr. 19, 1954   Plymouth, England
Ht. 5-10   Wt. 161
Citizen—England

1978	Detroit	19	22	10	54
1979	Detroit	14	14	8	36
	Totals	33	36	18	90

FRANK, STEVE *Defender*
B. 1948   St. Louis, Mo.
Ht. 5-11   Wt. 185
Citizen—U.S.

1971	St. Louis	24	0	0	0
1972	St. Louis	14	0	0	0
1973	St. Louis	16	0	0	0
1974	St. Louis	20	0	2	2
1975	St. Louis	22	0	0	0
	Totals	96	0	2	2

FRANKS, COLIN *Midfielder*
B. Apr. 16, 1951   Wembley, England
Ht. 5-11   Wt. 170
Citizen—England

1979	Toronto	28	4	4	12

FRANKIEWICZ, KAZIMIR "CASEY" *Forward*
B. Jan. 8, 1939   Pultusk, Poland
Ht. 6-0   Wt. 165
Citizen—Poland

1967	St. Louis	17	3	1	7
1968	St. Louis	31	14	9	37

Season	Club	GP	G	A	Pts.
1969	St. Louis	6	4	0	8
1971	St. Louis	24	14	5	33
1972	St. Louis	12	5	3	13
1973	St. Louis	18	4	2	10
1974	Boston	2	0	0	0
	Totals	110	44	20	108

FRASER, WILLIAM *Forward*
B. Aug. 12, 1945   Scotland
Ht. 5-8   Wt. 165

1967	Washington	—	—	—	—
1968	Boston	15	3	0	6
1971	Washington	23	3	4	10
1972	Miami	14	1	0	2
	Totals	52	7	4	18

FRAYDL, GERNOT
See *Goalkeeper*

FREEMAN, RAY *Midfielder*
B. England
Ht. 6-0   Wt. 168
Citizen—England

1968	San Diego	13	0	0	0

FREITAG, PAUL
See *Goalkeeper*

FREITAS, JAIME *Midfielder*
Ht. 5-6   Wt. 132

1967	Houston	10	1	1	3

FRENCH, GRAHAM *Midfielder*

1974	Boston	3	0	0	0

FRYATT, JIM *Forward*
B. Southampton, England
Ht. 5-11   Wt. 170

1973	Philadelphia	17	7	3	17
1974	Philadelphia	20	8	4	20
1975	Philadelphia	11	1	1	3
	Totals	48	16	8	40

FUHRMANN, JOE *Defender*
B. Oct. 10, 1940   Cologne, Germany
Ht. 5-7   Wt. 155
Citizen—Germany

1968	St. Louis	29	0	0	0

FUNNELL, TONY *Forward*
B. Aug. 27, 1957   England
Ht. 5-7   Wt. 160
Citizen—England

1977	Vancouver	10	2	0	4

Season	Club	GP	G	A	Pts.

FURPHY, KEITH   *Forward*
B. July 30, 1958   Stockton, England
Ht. 6-2   Wt. 168
Citizen—England

Season	Club	GP	G	A	Pts.
1978	Detroit	30	11	12	34
1979	Detroit	30	14	8	36
	Totals	60	25	20	70

FUTCHER, RON   *Forward*
B. Sept. 26, 1956   Chester, England
Ht. 5-11   Wt. 170
Citizen—England

Season	Club	GP	G	A	Pts.
1976	Minnesota	20	14	6	34
1977	Minnesota	20	11	4	26
1978	Minnesota	16	7	7	21
1979	Minnesota	24	14	7	35
	Totals	80	46	24	116

GABRIEL, JIM   *Midfielder*
B. Oct. 10, 1940   Dundee, Scotland
Ht. 5-11   Wt. 170
Citizen—England

Season	Club	GP	G	A	Pts.
1974	Seattle	19	4	1	9
1975	Seattle	21	2	2	6
1976	Seattle	9	1	1	3
1977	Seattle	2	0	1	1
	Totals	51	7	5	19

GADEA, ROBERTO   *Midfielder*
B. Feb. 2, 1953   Uruguay
Ht. 6-1   Wt. 175
Citizen—Uruguay

Season	Club	GP	G	A	Pts.
1978	Chicago	4	0	0	0

GADOCHA, ROBERT   *Forward*
B. Jan. 10. 1946   Poland
Ht. 5-10   Wt. 154
Citizen—Poland

Season	Club	GP	G	A	Pts.
1978	Chicago	12	1	2	4

GADOKA, ROBERT   *Forward*
B. Apr. 6, 1953   Umtali, Rhodesia
Ht. 5-8   Wt. 150
Citizen—Rhodesia

Season	Club	GP	G	A	Pts.
1979	Toronto	1	1	0	2

GALASSIN, FLORIANO   *Defender*
Ht. 5-8   Wt. 155

Season	Club	GP	G	A	Pts.
1973	Rochester	15	3	1	7

GALATI, TOM   *Defender*
Ht. 5-8   Wt. 185
Citizen—U.S.

Season	Club	GP	G	A	Pts.
1974	Philadelphia	20	0	0	0
1975	Philadelphia	10	1	0	2
1976	Philadelphia	20	0	0	0
1977	Las Vegas	11	0	0	0
	Totals	61	1	0	2

GALICE, HECTOR   *Midfielder*
Ht. 5-8   Wt. 150

Season	Club	GP	G	A	Pts.
1974	Miami	3	0	0	0

GALINDO, SANCHEZ   *Defender*
B. Nov. 26, 1947   Mexico City, Mexico
Ht. 5-9   Wt. 160
Citizen—Mexico

Season	Club	GP	G	A	Pts.
1979	Los Angeles	10	0	2	2

GALLAGHER, BRIAN   *Defender*
B. England
Ht. 5-9   Wt. 168
Citizen—England

Season	Club	GP	G	A	Pts.
1968	Los Angeles	14	0	0	0

GALLINA, FRANCO   *Forward*
B. Italy
Ht. 5-6   Wt. 140

Season	Club	GP	G	A	Pts.
1971	Montreal	21	10	2	22

GALLUZZO, NORBERTO   *Forward*
B. Jan. 13, 1950   Buenos Aires, Argentina
Ht. 6-0   Wt. 160
Citizen—Argentina

Season	Club	GP	G	A	Pts.
1978	Toronto	1	0	0	0

GAMALDO, VICTOR   *Defender*
B. Jan 22, 1944   Trinidad
Ht. 6-0   Wt. 175

Season	Club	GP	G	A	Pts.
1971	Washington	24	0	0	0
1974	Baltimore	18	0	0	0
	Totals	42	0	0	0

GANNON, KEVIN   *Forward*
Ht. 5-8   Wt. 150
Citizen—U.S.

Season	Club	GP	G	A	Pts.
1975	Rochester	10	0	1	1
1976	Rochester	8	0	0	0
	Totals	18	0	1	1

GANO, PEDRO   *Defender*
B. Sept. 1, 1953   General Rodriguez, Argentina
Ht. 5-11   Wt. 160
Citizen—Argentina

Season	Club	GP	G	A	Pts.
1979	Dallas	28	0	2	2

GANSLER, BOB   *Defender*
Ht. 6-0   Wt. 175
Citizen—U.S.

Season	Club	GP	G	A	Pts.
1968	Chicago	17	0	0	0

GANT, BRIAN   *Midfielder*
B. Apr. 23, 1952   Vancouver, Canada
Ht. 6-0   Wt. 155
Citizen—Canada

Season	Club	GP	G	A	Pts.
1974	Vancouver	20	6	1	13
1975	Vancouver	18	1	7	9

Season	Club	GP	G	A	Pts.
1976	Vancouver	5	1	0	2
1977	Portland	20	2	1	5
1978	Portland	24	3	0	6
1979	Portland	21	6	4	16
	Totals	108	19	13	51

GANT, BRUCE   *Defender*
B. Sept. 26, 1956   Burnaby, Canada
Ht. 6-0   Wt. 155
Citizen—Canada

1979	Portland	20	0	2	2

GARBER, RANDY   *Midfielder*
B. Aug. 19, 1952   Abington, Pa.
Ht. 5-9   Wt. 165
Citizen—U.S.

1975	Tampa Bay	13	1	1	3
1976	T.B.-L.A.	11	0	2	2
1977	Washington	7	0	2	2
1978	Washington	13	0	0	0
	Totals	44	1	5	7

GARBETT, TERRY   *Midfielder*
B. Sept. 9. 1945   Durham, England
Ht. 5-9   Wt. 166
Citizen—England

1976	New York	22	1	8	10
1977	New York	15	0	0	0
1978	New York	15	2	1	5
1979	New York	14	0	2	2
	Totals	66	3	11	17

GARCETE, RUBEN   *Forward*
B. Mar. 30, 1941   Asuncion, Paraguay
Ht. 5-8   Wt. 145
Citizen—Paraguay

1967	Baltimore	5	1	2	4

GARCIA, EDUARDO
See *Goalkeeper*

GARCIA, FREDDIE   *Forward*
B. July 7, 1952   Guanajuato, Mexico
Ht. 5-8   Wt. 150
Citizen—U.S.

1974	Dallas	7	3	1	7
1975	Dallas	13	0	0	0
1976	Dallas	7	0	0	0
1977	Dallas	6	0	1	1
1978	Dallas	3	0	0	0
1979	Dallas	1	0	0	0
	Totals	37	3	2	8

GARCIA, JORGE   *Forward*
B. Mercedes, Uruguay
Ht. 5-5   Wt. 155
Citizen—Uruguay

1967	Philadelphia	14	4	4	12

Season	Club	GP	G	A	Pts.

GARCIA, ROBERT   *Midfielder*
B. Oct. 5, 1953   Bogota, Colombia
Ht. 5-7   Wt. 155
Citizen—U.S.

1975	Hartford	9	0	0	0
1976	Boston	10	1	1	3
	Totals	19	0	3	3

GARDENER, DON   *Forward*
B. 1957   Jamaica
Ht. 5-11   Wt. 160
Citizen—England

1975	Portland	13	0	2	2
1977	Connecticut	3	0	1	1
	Totals	16	0	3	3

GARLAND, JOHN   *Defender*
B. St. Louis, Mo.
Citizen—U.S.

1974	St. Louis	1	0	0	0

GAROV, PAVLE   *Defender*
B. Aug. 25, 1939   Belgrade, Yugoslavia
Ht. 5-9   Wt. 165
Citizen—Yugoslavia

1968	Houston	29	1	1	3

GARRO, ORLANDO   *Forward*
B. Buenos Aires, Argentina
Ht. 5-9   Wt. 165
Citizen—Argentina

1967	Philadelphia	20	12	2	26

GAUDEN, ALAN   *Forward*
Ht. 5-8   Wt. 155

1967	Vancouver	8	2	2	6

GAZONAS, BILLY   *Midfielder*
B. June 8, 1956   Trenton, N.J.
Ht. 5-5   Wt. 135
Citizen—U.S.

1978	Tulsa	14	2	1	5
1979	Tulsa	17	2	2	6
	Totals	31	4	3	11

GEIMER, GENE   *Forward*
B. Jan. 31, 1949   St. Louis, Mo.
Ht. 5-10   Wt. 170
Citizen—U.S.

1971	St. Louis	8	1	2	4
1972	St. Louis	14	1	6	8
1973	St. Louis	12	2	0	4
1974	St. Louis	12	2	0	4
1975	St. Louis	13	3	2	8
1976	Bost.-Chi.	16	4	2	10
1977	Chicago	16	4	0	8
	Totals	91	17	12	46

Season	Club	GP	G	A	Pts.
GEMERI, TIBOR *Midfielder*					
B. Apr. 29, 1951 Subotica, Yugoslavia					
Ht. 5–8 Wt. 160					
Citizen—Canada					
1978	Ft. Lauderdale	10	0	0	0
1979	Ft. Lauderdale	13	0	2	2
	Totals	23	0	2	2
GENTILE, CARL *Forward*					
B. Feb. 23, 1944 St. Louis, Mo.					
Ht. 5–8 Wt. 175					
Citizen—U.S.					
1967	St. Louis	10	1	0	2
1968	St. Louis	26	2	0	4
1971	St. Louis	4	0	0	0
	Totals	40	3	0	6
GERSDORFF, BERNIE *Midfielder*					
B. Nov. 18, 1945 West Berlin, West Germany					
Ht. 6–0 Wt. 185					
Citizen—W. Germany					
1979	San Jose	30	10	5	25
GEORGE, CHARLIE *Forward*					
B. Oct. 10, 1950 London, England					
Ht. 5–11 Wt. 165					
Citizen—England					
1978	Minnesota	18	9	8	26
GETZINGER, RUDY *Forward*					
B. Sept. 4. 1944 Yugoslavia					
Ht. 6–0 Wt. 175					
Citizen—U.S.					
1975	Chicago	16	1	1	3
1976	Chicago	3	0	0	0
	Totals	19	1	1	3
GIANI, ENZO *Midfielder*					
Ht. 5–10 Wt. 170					
1971	Toronto	10	0	0	0
GIBBINS, ROGER *Forward*					
B. June 9. 1955 Middlesex, England					
Ht. 5–11 Wt. 170					
Citizen—England					
1978	New England	22	5	4	14
1979	New England	27	3	4	10
	Totals	49	8	8	24
GIBBS, GEORGE *Midfielder*					
B. Dec. 23, 1953 London, England					
Ht. 5–11 Wt. 170					
Citizen—England					
1974	Rochester	13	1	1	3
1975	Rochester	17	4	2	10
1979	Toronto	30	6	8	20
	Totals	60	11	11	33

Season	Club	GP	G	A	Pts.
GIBSON, JIM *Midfielder*					
B. N. Ireland					
Ht. 6–0 Wt. 169					
Citizen—N. Ireland					
1968	Chicago	17	0	0	0
GILBERT, BOBBY *Forward*					
Ht. 5–11 Wt. 191					
1967	Boston	6	1	1	3
GILCHRIST, LEROY *Forward*					
1975	Rochester	1	0	0	0
GILES, JOHNNY *Midfielder*					
B. Nov. 6, 1940 Dublin, Ireland					
Ht. 5–7 Wt. 150					
Citizen—Ireland					
1978	Philadelphia	20	0	3	3
GILLESPE, DENNIS *Forward*					
Ht. 5–9 Wt. 160					
1967	Dallas	10	1	2	4
GILLETT, DAVE *Defender*					
B. Apr. 2, 1951 Edinburgh, Scotland					
Ht. 6–1 Wt. 175					
Citizen—England					
1974	Seattle	20	1	1	3
1975	Seattle	22	1	2	4
1976	Seattle	23	0	0	0
1977	Seattle	23	1	1	3
1978	Seattle	1	1	0	2
	Totals	89	4	4	12
GILLIVER, ALAN *Forward*					
B. Aug. 3, 1944 England					
Ht. 6–2 Wt. 190					
Citizen—England					
1975	Baltimore	5	0	0	0
GIZZI, PAUL					
See *Goalkeeper*					
GLANZ, WERNER *Defender*					
B. Germany					
Ht. 5–10 Wt. 180					
Citizen—Holland					
1968	Chicago	15	2	0	4

Season	Club	GP	G	A	Pts.

GLAVIN, TONY   *Midfielder*
B. Apr. 29, 1958   Glasgow, Scotland
Ht. 5-6   Wt. 142
Citizen—Scotland

Season	Club	GP	G	A	Pts.
1978	Philadelphia	25	5	4	14
1979	Philadelphia	10	1	1	3
	Totals	35	6	5	17

GLOCK, WOLFGANG   *Forward*
B. Germany
Ht. 5-5   Wt. 142
Citizen—Germany

Season	Club	GP	G	A	Pts.
1967	Chi. (NPSL)	17	3	3	9
1968	Kansas City	26	7	0	14
	Totals	43	10	3	23

GLOVER, LEN   *Midfielder*
B. Jan. 31, 1944   London, England
Ht. 5-10   Wt. 168
Citizen—England

Season	Club	GP	G	A	Pts.
1976	Tampa Bay	14	1	5	7
1977	Tampa Bay	19	0	3	3
	Totals	33	1	8	10

GOBEL, UWE   *Defender*
B. Germany
Ht. 5-7   Wt. 150
Citizen—Germany

Season	Club	GP	G	A	Pts.
1967	Pittsburgh	—	—	—	—
1968	Kansas City	2	0	0	0
	Totals	2	0	0	0

GODFREY, BRIAN   *Midfielder*
Ht. 5-10   Wt. 160
Citizen—England

Season	Club	GP	G	A	Pts.
1975	Portland	20	3	2	8

GOL, GEDIZ   *Forward*
B. Turkey
Ht. 5-8   Wt. 133
Citizen—Turkey

Season	Club	GP	G	A	Pts.
1968	Dallas	16	3	1	7

GOLDINGAY, ROGER   *Forward*
B. July 29, 1950   Leicester, England
Ht. 5-11   Wt. 175
Citizen—U.S.

Season	Club	GP	G	A	Pts.
1974	Seattle	4	0	0	0
1975	Portland	4	0	0	0
1976	Portland	11	0	0	0
	Totals	19	0	0	0

GOMEZ, JORGE   *Defender*
B. Mexico
Ht. 5-9   Wt. 163
Citizen—Mexico

Season	Club	GP	G	A	Pts.
1976	Philadelphia	24	0	0	0

GOMEZ, OMAR   *Midfielder*
B. Oct. 3, 1955   Quilmes, Argentina
Ht. 5-10   Wt. 175
Citizen—Argentina

Season	Club	GP	G	A	Pts.
1979	Dallas	12	4	3	11

GONZALES, JOSE   *Forward*
B. Nov. 15, 1947   El Llano, Mexico

Season	Club	GP	G	A	Pts.
1971	St. Louis	2	1	0	2

GONZALES, MIGUEL   *Forward*
Ht. 5-10   Wt. 160
Citizen—Argentina

Season	Club	GP	G	A	Pts.
1979	Memphis	6	1	0	2

GOODWIN, DAVID
B. Nov. 14, 1943   England

Season	Club	GP	G	A	Pts.
1973	Miami	8	1	1	3

GOODWIN, FREDDIE   *Defender*
B. June 28, 1933   Heywood, Lancashire, England
Ht. 6-2   Wt. 205
Citizen—England

Season	Club	GP	G	A	Pts.
1967	New York (NPSL)	1	0	0	0

GOOSENS, JAN   *Forward*
B. Dec. 18, 1958   Velp, Holland
Ht. 6-0   Wt. 160
Citizen—Holland

Season	Club	GP	G	A	Pts.
1979	Edmonton	23	6	4	16

GORE, TOMMY   *Midfielder*
B. England
Ht. 5-7   Wt. 158

Season	Club	GP	G	A	Pts.
1974	Dallas	20	3	3	9
1975	Dallas	15	0	2	2
	Totals	35	3	5	11

GORI, ADOLPHO   *Midfielder*
B. Italy
Ht. 5-8   Wt. 155

Season	Club	GP	G	A	Pts.
1971	Rochester	24	0	1	1
1972	Rochester	14	2	1	5
	Totals	38	2	2	6

GORMAN, JOHN   *Defender*
B. Aug. 16, 1949   Wichburon, Scotland
Ht. 5-8   Wt. 153
Citizen—Scotland

Season	Club	GP	G	A	Pts.
1979	Tampa Bay	29	0	3	3

GORSEK, JIM
See *Goalkeeper*

Season	Club	GP	G	A	Pts.

GRAHAM, GEORGE   *Midfielder*
B. Nov. 30, 1944   Bargeddie, Scotland
Ht. 5-11   Wt. 169
Citizen—Scotland

| 1978 | California | 17 | 0 | 3 | 3 |

GRAHAM, JACKIE   *Forward*
Ht. 5-7   Wt. 155

| 1967 | Dallas | 11 | 4 | 2 | 10 |

GRAHAM, TONY   *Forward*
Ht. 5-6   Wt. 140
Citizen—U.S.

| 1978 | Oakland | 13 | 0 | 0 | 0 |

GRANITZA, KARL-HEINZ   *Forward*
B. Nov. 1, 1951   Lunen, Germany
Ht. 6-0   Wt. 165
Citizen—Germany

1978	Chicago	22	19	9	47
1979	Chicago	30	20	10	50
	Totals	52	39	19	97

GRANT, COLIN   *Midfielder*
Ht. 5-9   Wt. 156

| 1967 | Tor.(USA) | 6 | 4 | 1 | 9 |

GRASSER, JOHN
See *Goalkeeper*

GRASSINI, CARLOS   *Midfielder*
B. Argentina
Ht. 6-1   Wt. 170
Citizen—Argentina

| 1968 | Dallas | 16 | 0 | 0 | 0 |

GRAVINA, NICOLA   *Forward*
B. Dec. 6, 1935   Rio de Janeiro, Argentina
Ht. 5-4   Wt. 143
Citizen—Brazil

| 1968 | Houston | 1 | 0 | 0 | 0 |

GRAYDON, RAY   *Forward*
B. July 21, 1949   Bristol, England
Ht. 5-10   Wt. 160
Citizen—England

| 1978 | Washington | 26 | 4 | 17 | 25 |

GRBIC, MILOS   *Midfielder*
B. Nice, Yugoslavia
Ht. 6-2   Wt. 189
Citizen—Yugoslavia

1967	Chi.(NPSL)	8	1	0	2
1968	Kansas City	9	0	0	0
	Totals	17	1	0	2

GRECO, PETER
See *Goalkeeper*

GREEN, ALAN   *Forward*
B. Jan. 1, 1954   Worcester, England
Ht. 5-10   Wt. 165
Citizen—England

1977	Washington	16	9	5	23
1979	Washington	23	16	9	41
	Totals	39	25	14	64

GREEN, JOHNNY   *Forward*
B. England
Ht. 5-9   Wt. 150
Citizen—England

| 1968 | Vancouver | 23 | 4 | 0 | 8 |

GREEN, RICHARD   *Midfielder*
B. Aug. 13, 1949   Lima, Peru
Ht. 5-11   Wt. 165
Citizen U.S.

1975	Chicago	12	1	5	7
1976	Chicago	1	0	0	0
	Totals	13	1	5	7

GREENWOOD, PADDY   *Defender*
B. Oct. 19, 1946   Hull, England
Ht. 6-0   Wt. 170
Citizen—England

1974	Boston	19	4	0	8
1976	Boston	5	0	0	0
	Totals	24	4	0	8

GRELITZ, KLAUS
See *Goalkeeper*

GRELL, ROBERT   *Forward*
Ht. 6-0   Wt. 180

1971	Washington	16	1	1	3
1974	Washington	20	0	1	1
1975	Washington	18	0	1	1
	Totals	54	1	3	5

GRGUREV, FRED   *Forward*
B. Sept. 14, 1951   Yugoslavia
Ht. 6-1   Wt. 166
Citizen—U.S.

1978	New York	13	0	2	2
1979	Rochester	24	3	3	9
	Totals	37	3	5	11

GRIBBEN, JOHN   *Defender*
Ht. 5-9   Wt. 160

| 1974 | Baltimore | 5 | 0 | 0 | 0 |

Season	Club	GP	G	A	Pts.

GRIFFITHS, ARFON   *Midfielder*
B. Aug. 23, 1941   Wrexam, Wales
Ht. 5-6   Wt. 155
Citizen—Wales

Season	Club	GP	G	A	Pts.
1975	Seattle	15	1	4	6

GRIFFITHS, CLIVE   *Defender*
B. Jan. 22, 1955   Ponttridd, Wales
Ht. 5-10   Wt. 160
Citizen—Wales

Season	Club	GP	G	A	Pts.
1975	Chicago	22	1	1	3
1976	Chicago	22	1	1	3
1977	Chicago	25	0	1	1
1978	Chicago	29	0	2	2
1979	Chicago	28	0	0	0
	Totals	126	2	5	9

GRIMMALDI, DAVID   *Defender*
B. Dec. 19, 1954
Ht. 5-11   Wt. 165
Citizen—U.S.

Season	Club	GP	G	A	Pts.
1978	Memphis	6	0	0	0
1979	Memphis	1	0	0	0
	Totals	7	0	0	0

GRNJA, JOHN   *Forward*
B. Apr. 26, 1949   Darda, Yugoslavia
Ht. 5-4   Wt. 141
Citizen—Yugoslavia

Season	Club	GP	G	A	Pts.
1976	Toronto	5	1	1	3
1979	Tampa Bay	10	0	3	3
	Totals	15	1	4	6

GROBBELAAR, BRUCE
See *Goalkeeper*

GROSS, VOLKMAR
See *Goalkeeper*

GRUMMETT, JIM   *Defender*
B. Maltby, England
Ht. 5-11   Wt. 173

Season	Club	GP	G	A	Pts.
1974	Denver	20	0	1	1

GULDBJERG, NIELS   *Forward*
B. Feb. 10, 1958   Aalestrup, Denmark
Ht. 5-8   Wt. 150
Citizen—Denmark

Season	Club	GP	G	A	Pts.
1979	Detroit	3	1	0	2

GULIN, TONY   *Forward*
B. Yugoslavia
Ht. 5-10   Wt. 160
Citizen—Yugoslavia

Season	Club	GP	G	A	Pts.
1968	Boston	7	2	—	4

GUTENDORF, RUDI   *B. Germany*

Season	Club	GP	G	A	Pts.
1968	St. Louis	1	1	0	2

GUZMAN, GULLIERMO   *Defender*
B. Mexico
Ht. 5-10   Wt. 162
Citizen—Mexico

Season	Club	GP	G	A	Pts.
1968	San Diego	2	0	0	0

GUZMAN, OLINDO   *Defender*

Season	Club	GP	G	A	Pts.
1975	Miami	20	2	0	4

GYAU, JOSEPH "NANA"   *Midfielder*
B. Ghana
Ht. 5-9   Wt. 150
Citizen—Ghana

Season	Club	GP	G	A	Pts.
1968	Washington	12	4	0	8
1974	Washington	7	1	0	2
	Totals	19	5	0	10

HAASKIVI, KAI   *Midfielder*
B. Dec. 28, 1955   Lahti, Finland
Ht. 5-10   Wt. 175
Citizen—Finland

Season	Club	GP	G	A	Pts.
1978	Dallas	20	1	2	4
1979	Houston	28	12	6	30
	Totals	48	13	8	34

HADICAN, DENNY   *Forward*
B. St. Louis, Mo.
Citizen—U.S.

Season	Club	GP	G	A	Pts.
1974	St. Louis	3	0	0	0

HAFIZOVIC, KEMAL   *Forward*
B. May 12, 1950   Zencia, Yugoslavia
Ht. 5-10   Wt. 160
Citizen—Yugoslavia

Season	Club	GP	G	A	Pts.
1978	Toronto	12	0	1	1

HAHN, ERIC   *Forward*
B. Munich, Germany
Ht. 5-8   Wt. 135
Citizen—Germany

Season	Club	GP	G	A	Pts.
1967	St. Louis	5	2	0	4

HAINEY, BILLY   *Forward*
Ht. 5-8   Wt. 164

Season	Club	GP	G	A	Pts.
1967	Dallas	11	2	0	4

HALL, BRETT   *Midfielder*
B. Nov. 16, 1956
Ht. 5-7   Wt. 148
Citizen—U.S.

Season	Club	GP	G	A	Pts.
1979	Chicago	6	0	0	0

Season	Club	GP	G	A	Pts.

HALL, EDWARD *Defender*
B. Sept. 8, 1946 Liverpool, England
Ht. 6–0 Wt. 175
Citizen—England

1968	Dallas	28	0	0	0

HALL, RICHARD *Defender*
B. July 3, 1945 Portland, England
Ht. 5–8 Wt. 165
Citizen—U.S.

1970	Dallas	24	0	0	0
1971	Dallas	24	0	1	1
1972	Dallas	14	0	0	0
1973	Dallas	19	0	0	0
1974	Dallas	20	0	0	0
1975	Dallas	8	0	0	0
1976	Dallas	24	0	1	1
	Totals	133	0	2	2

HAMILTON, IAN "CHICO" *Forward*
B. Oct. 31, 1950 London, England
Ht. 5–9 Wt. 155
Citizen—England

1978	Minnesota	24	2	13	17
1979	Minnesota	18	5	5	15
	Totals	42	7	18	32

HAMLYN, ALAN *Defender*
B. Jan. 5, 1947 London, England
Ht. 5–11 Wt. 160
Citizen—U.S.

1972	Atlanta	14	1	1	3
1973	Atlanta	11	0	0	0
1974	Miami	8	0	0	0
1975	Miami	12	0	0	0
1976	Miami	21	0	0	0
1977	Ft. Lauderdale	11	0	0	0
1978	Ft. Lauderdale	2	0	0	0
	Totals	79	1	1	3

HAMMOND, GEOFF *Defender*
B. 1952 England
Ht. 5–11 Wt. 175
Citizen—England

1977	Connecticut	16	2	0	4

HAMMOND, PAUL
See *Goalkeeper*

HANDLAN, KEVIN *Midfielder*
B. July 10, 1956 St. Louis, Mo.
Ht. 5–9 Wt. 155
Citizen—U.S.

1978	Tul.-S.J.	4	0	0	0

HANEK, JANOS *Forward*
B. Hungary
Ht. 5–8 Wt. 165
Citizen—Hungary

1968	Van.-K.C.	15	3	0	6

HANNIGAN, ERNIE *Forward*

1971	New York	1	0	0	0

HANSEN, HAROLD *Forward*
B. May 24, 1946 Vancouver, Canada
Ht. 5–7 Wt. 135
Citizen—Canada

1968	Atlanta	1	0	0	0

HANSEN, KAJ *Defender*
B. Denmark
Ht. 5–11 Wt. 166
Citizen—Denmark

1968	Washington	20	6	0	12

HARBA, DZELMALUDIN *Defender*
B. June 14, 1948 Sarajevo, Yugoslavia
Ht. 6–0 Wt. 170

1975	Hartford	9	0	0	0

HARDWICK, STEVE
See *Goalkeeper*

HARGREAVES, GARRY *Forward*
B. July 27, 1955 Preston, England
Ht. 5–11 Wt. 150
Citizen—England

1975	Chicago	1	0	0	0

HARKIN, TERRY *Forward*

1973	Toronto	11	5	5	15

HARRISON, STEVE *Defender*
B. Dec. 26, 1952 Blackpool, England
Ht. 5–8 Wt. 155
Citizen—England

1978	Vancouver	24	0	3	3

HARSANYI, LASZLO *Defender*
B. Mar. 13, 1951 Budapest, Hungary
Ht. 6–3 Wt. 185
Citizen—Hungary

1978	San Diego	29	0	4	4
1979	San Diego	28	2	3	7
	Totals	57	2	7	11

HARTLE, ROY

1967	N.Y.(NPSL)	3	0	0	0

Season	Club	GP	G	A	Pts.

HARTZE, BERNARD   *Midfielder*
B. Mar. 3, 1950   Pretoria, S. Africa
Citizen—S. Africa

1975	Tampa Bay	6	1	1	3

HARVEY, ALLAN   *Defender*
B. England
Ht. 5-9   Wt. 160
Citizen—Canada

1968	Toronto	28	3	3	9

HARVEY, BRIAN   *Forward*
B. Jan. 21, 1947   Liverpool, England
Ht. 5-7   Wt. 150
Citizen—England

1968	Dallas	32	1	0	2

HASANBEGOVIC, JOHN   *Forward*
B. Jan. 8, 1948   Sarajevo, Yugoslavia
Ht. 6-0   Wt. 175
Citizen—Yugoslavia

1975	San Antonio	11	0	2	2
1977	Connecticut	10	4	2	10
1978	Chicago	24	4	9	17
1979	Memphis	8	2	0	4
	Totals	53	10	13	33

HASEKIDIS, THEODORE "LOLOS"   *Midfielder*
B. Aug. 23, 1940   Greece
Ht. 5-9   Wt. 150

1971	New York	18	0	0	0

HASON, FRANK
See *Goalkeeper*

HATLEY, TONY   *Forward*
Ht. 6-1   Wt. 180

1974	Boston	3	0	0	0

HAUSMAN, LARRY   *Defender*
B. Aug. 11, 1941   St. Louis, Mo.
Ht. 5-9   Wt. 152
Citizen—U.S.

1968	Chicago	22	1	7	9
1969	St. Louis	12	3	2	8
1970	St. Louis	24	2	3	7
1971	St. Louis	21	5	4	14
1972	St. Louis	11	1	1	3
1973	St. Louis	7	0	1	1
1974	St. Louis	19	0	0	0
1975	St. Louis	13	0	0	0
1976	St. Louis	5	0	0	0
	Totals	134	12	18	42

HAVERTY, JOE   *Forward*
B. Dublin, Ireland
Ht. 5-5   Wt. 145
Citizen—Ireland

1967	Chi. (NPSL)	16	0	3	3
1968	Kansas City	22	1	0	2
	Totals	38	1	3	5

HAWLEY, JOHN   *Forward*
B. May 8, 1954   Hull, England
Ht. 6-1   Wt. 170
Citizen—England

1975	St. Louis	20	11	2	24

HAYES, AUSTIN   *Forward*
B. Southhampton, England
Ht. 5-6   Wt. 135

1978	Los Angeles	22	4	2	10

HEANEY, GERRY   *Defender*
B. 1945   Scotland
Ht. 5-11   Wt. 170
Citizen—Canada

1974	Vancouver	4	0	0	0
1975	Vancouver	19	0	1	1
	Totals	23	0	1	1

HECK, HAROLD   *Defender*
B. July 1, 1954   W. Germany
Ht. 6-1   Wt. 175
Citizen—Germany

1979	San Diego	13	0	1	1

HECTOR, KEVIN   *Forward*
B. Nov. 2, 1944   Leeds, England
Ht. 5-8   Wt. 150
Citizen—England

1978	Vancouver	28	21	10	52
1979	Vancouver	25	15	6	36
	Totals	53	36	16	88

HEDEAGER, VAGN   *Midfielder*
B. Denmark
Ht. 5-8   Wt. 152
Citizen—Denmark

1968	Wash.-Det.	9	2	0	4

HEINEMANN, LARS   *Forward*
B. Sweden
Ht. 6-1   Wt. 160
Citizen—Sweden

1968	Wash.-Det.	17	4	0	28

Season	Club	GP	G	A	Pts.

HENDERSON, ALVIN   *Forward*
B. Sept. 24, 1950   Trinidad
Ht. 5-9   Wt. 155
Citizen—Trinidad

Season	Club	GP	G	A	Pts.
1974	Baltimore	18	7	6	20
1975	Baltimore	19	9	1	19
	Totals	37	16	7	39

HENDERSON, DAVID
See *Goalkeeper*

HENDERSON, MARTIN   *Forward*
B. May 3, 1956   Kirkcaldy, Scotland
Ht. 6-2   Wt. 178
Citizen—Scotland

Season	Club	GP	G	A	Pts.
1978	Philadelphia	17	3	3	9

HENDERSON, WILLIAM   *Forward*
B. Jan. 24, 1944   Bailleston, Scotland
Ht. 5-6   Wt. 145

Season	Club	GP	G	A	Pts.
1973	Miami	7	0	1	1

HENDRIE, PAUL   *Midfielder*
B. March 27, 1954   Lennoktown, Scotland
Ht. 5-6   Wt. 142
Citizen—Scotland

Season	Club	GP	G	A	Pts.
1976	Portland	20	0	2	2
1977	Portland	17	1	4	6
	Totals	37	1	6	8

HENRY, JIM   *Midfielder*
B. Feb. 4, 1949   Dundee, Scotland
Ht. 6-1   Wt. 165
Citizen—Scotland

Season	Club	GP	G	A	Pts.
1976	San Antonio	18	0	3	3
1977	Hawaii	24	5	5	15
	Totals	42	5	8	18

HERD, GEORGE   *Forward*
Ht. 5-8   Wt. 154

Season	Club	GP	G	A	Pts.
1967	Vancouver	6	3	2	8

HERNANDEZ, MANI   *Forward*
B. Aug. 2, 1948   Madrid, Spain
Ht. 5-3   Wt. 165
Citizen—U.S.

Season	Club	GP	G	A	Pts.
1974	San Jose	18	4	2	10
1975	San Jose	22	0	0	0
1976	San Jose	11	0	1	1
	Totals	51	4	3	11

HERRADA, PEDRO   *Midfielder*
Ht. 5-8   Wt. 147
Citizen—Mexico

Season	Club	GP	G	A	Pts.
1976	Philadelphia	22	5	8	18

HERRERA, HELENIO   *Forward*
B. Jan. 27, 1952   Madrid, Spain
Ht. 5-10   Wt. 170

Season	Club	GP	G	A	Pts.
1972	New York	1	0	0	0

HERRERA, RAUL   *Midfielder*
Ht. 5-8   Wt. 155

Season	Club	GP	G	A	Pts.
1973	Rochester	2	0	0	0

HESLOP, BRIAN   *Midfielder*
Ht. 5-10   Wt. 162

Season	Club	GP	G	A	Pts.
1967	Vancouver	8	1	0	2

HETZKE, STEPHEN   *Defender*
B. June 3, 1955   Marlborough, England
Ht. 6-3   Wt. 190
Citizen—England

Season	Club	GP	G	A	Pts.
1976	Vancouver	18	0	1	1

HEWITT, MIKE
See *Goalkeeper*

HEYNEN, HARRY   *Forward*
Ht. 5-7   Wt. 150

Season	Club	GP	G	A	Pts.
1967	San Francisco	9	2	4	8

HICKTON, JOHN   *Forward*
B. Sept. 24, 1944   Chesterfield, England
Ht. 6-0   Wt. 168
Citizen—England

Season	Club	GP	G	A	Pts.
1978	Ft. Lauderdale	3	1	0	2

HIDDINK, CUS   *Midfielder*
B. Dec. 9, 1946   Holland
Ht. 6-0   Wt. 175
Citizen—Holland

Season	Club	GP	G	A	Pts.
1978	Washington	13	4	5	13

HILKES, LORENZ   *Forward*
B. Aug. 31, 1950   Grubbenoors, Holland
Ht. 5-10   Wt. 155
Citizen—Germany

Season	Club	GP	G	A	Pts.
1979	Edmonton	21	13	3	29

HILL, GORDON   *Forward*
B. Apr. 1, 1954   Staines, England
Ht. 5-8   Wt. 155
Citizen—England

Season	Club	GP	G	A	Pts.
1975	Chicago	21	16	7	39

HILL, HENRY   *Defender*
B. England
Ht. 5-9   Wt. 160
Citizen—England

Season	Club	GP	G	A	Pts.
1968	Van.-S.D.	14	3	0	6

Season	Club	GP	G	A	Pts.

HILL, KEN   *Defender*
B. July 3, 1953 Canterbury, England
Ht. 6-0 Wt. 165
Citizen—England

Season	Club	GP	G	A	Pts.
1974	Baltimore	19	0	2	2
1977	Washington	25	0	0	0
	Totals	44	0	2	2

HINDSON, GORDON   *Forward*
B. Jan. 8, 1950 Newcastle-Upon-Tyne, England
Ht. 5-10 Wt. 165
Citizen—England

Season	Club	GP	G	A	Pts.
1976	Hartford	15	3	0	6

HINTON, ALAN   *Forward*
B. Oct. 6, 1942 Wednesday, England
Ht. 5-11 Wt. 190
Citizen—England

Season	Club	GP	G	A	Pts.
1977	Dallas	24	4	9	17
1978	Vancouver	29	1	30	32
	Totals	53	5	39	49

HITCHENS, JERRY

Season	Club	GP	G	A	Pts.
1967	Chi. (USA)	2	1	0	2

HOBAN, MIKE   *Defender*
B. Apr. 6, 1952 Tipton, England
Ht. 5-10 Wt. 165
Citizen—England

Season	Club	GP	G	A	Pts.
1971	Atlanta	21	0	0	0
1972	Atlanta	14	0	1	1
1973	Atlanta	19	3	3	9
1974	Denver	17	3	0	6
1975	Portland	16	0	0	0
1976	Portland	24	0	0	0
1977	Portland	23	0	3	3
1978	Portland	1	0	0	0
	Totals	135	6	7	19

HOCKEY, TREVOR   *Midfielder*
B. Jan. 5, 1943 Keighley, England
Ht. 5-7 Wt. 150
Citizen—England

Season	Club	GP	G	A	Pts.
1976	San Diego	22	0	1	1
1977	L.V.-S.J.	20	0	0	0
	Totals	42	0	1	1

HOFFMEYER, DAVE   *Midfielder*
B. May 31, 1955 St. Louis, Mo.
Ht. 5-9 Wt. 160
Citizen—U.S.

Season	Club	GP	G	A	Pts.
1978	Detroit	1	0	0	0

HOFTVEDT, TROWD   *Midfielder*
B. May 30, 1941 Oslo, Norway
Ht. 5-10 Wt. 166
Citizen—Norway

Season	Club	GP	G	A	Pts.
1967	Oakland	12	0	2	2
1968	Oakland	25	2	0	4
	Totals	37	2	2	6

HOLDER, PHIL   *Midfielder*
B. Jan. 19, 1952 Kilburn, England
Ht. 5-4 Wt. 160
Citizen—England

Season	Club	GP	G	A	Pts.
1978	Memphis	24	1	2	4

HOLLAND, PAT   *Midfielder*
B. Sept. 13, 1950 Essex, England
Ht. 5-8 Wt. 160
Citizen—England

Season	Club	GP	G	A	Pts.
1977	Hawaii	16	4	2	10

HOLTON, JIM   *Defender*
B. Apr. 11, 1952 Lesmanagow, Scotland
Ht. 6-2 Wt. 190
Citizen—Scotland

Season	Club	GP	G	A	Pts.
1976	Miami	16	1	0	2

HOOD, HARRY   *Forward*
B. Oct. 3, 1944 Glasgow, Scotland
Ht. 5-9 Wt. 160
Citizen—Scotland

Season	Club	GP	G	A	Pts.
1976	San Antonio	20	9	7	25

HOOGERMAN, BERTUS
See *Goalkeeper*

HOPE, BOB   *Midfielder*
B. Sept. 28, 1943 Bridge-of-Allan, Scotland
Ht. 5-8 Wt. 155
Citizen—Scotland

Season	Club	GP	G	A	Pts.
1975	Philadelphia	20	4	6	14
1976	Dallas	22	3	7	13
1977	Dallas	18	0	8	8
1978	Dallas	18	0	7	7
	Totals	78	7	28	42

HORN, GRAHAM
See *Goalkeeper*

HORNE, STAN   *Midfielder*
B. Clanfield, England
Ht. 5-10 Wt. 174

Season	Club	GP	G	A	Pts.
1974	Denver	20	0	0	0

HORROCKS, CHRIS   *Defender*
B. 1954 Vancouver, Canada
Ht. 5-9 Wt. 170
Citizen—Canada

Season	Club	GP	G	A	Pts.
1972	Montreal	1	0	0	0
1976	Toronto	1	0	0	0
1977	Las Vegas	18	1	0	2
	Totals	20	1	0	2

HORTON, RANDY   *Forward*
B. Jan. 22, 1945 Somerset, Bermuda
Ht. 6-2 Wt. 200
Citizen—Bermuda

Season	Club	GP	G	A	Pts.
1971	New York	22	16	5	37
1972	New York	13	9	4	22

Season	Club	GP	G	A	Pts.
1973	New York	14	9	5	23
1974	New York	19	9	4	22
1975	Washington	17	7	4	18
1976	Hartford	4	1	1	3
	Totals	89	51	23	125

HORVATH, JOE   *Midfielder*
B. May 21, 1949   Hungary
Ht. 6-1   Wt. 175
Citizen—Hungary

Season	Club	GP	G	A	Pts.
1978	Rochester	29	6	11	23
1979	Washington	26	7	18	32
	Totals	54	13	29	55

HOULISTON, JIM   *Defender*
B. England
Ht. 5-9   Wt. 155
Citizen—England

Season	Club	GP	G	A	Pts.
1968	Los Angeles	15	0	0	0

HOURNE, PATRICK   *Forward*
B. Mar. 2, 1953
Ht. 6-1   Wt. 192
Citizen—U.S.

Season	Club	GP	G	A	Pts.
1978	Memphis	3	0	0	0
1979	New England	1	0	0	0
	Totals	4	0	0	0

HOUSKA, JOHN
See *Goalkeeper*

HOUWAART, HENK   *Midfielder*
Ht. 5-9   Wt. 150

Season	Club	GP	G	A	Pts.
1967	San Francisco	12	9	2	20

HOWARD, DICK
See *Goalkeeper*

HOWARD, PAT   *Defender*
B. Oct. 7, 1948   Barnsley, England
Ht. 6-0   Wt. 175
Citizen—England

Season	Club	GP	G	A	Pts.
1978	Portland	24	1	2	4

HOWE, BOBBY   *Defender*
B. Dec. 22, 1945   Essex, England
Ht. 5-8   Wt. 160
Citizen—England

Season	Club	GP	G	A	Pts.
1977	Seattle	5	0	1	1
1978	Seattle	5	0	0	0
	Totals	10	0	1	1

HOWE, KEVIN   *Defender*
B. St. Louis, Mo.
Ht. 5-11   Wt. 170
Citizen—U.S.

Season	Club	GP	G	A	Pts.
1973	Atlanta	11	1	0	2
1974	Denver	5	0	0	0
1975	Denver	9	1	0	2
	Totals	25	2	0	4

HOWE, TOM   *Midfielder*
B. Oct. 5, 1949   St. Louis, Mo.
Ht. 5-9   Wt. 165
Citizen—U.S.

Season	Club	GP	G	A	Pts.
1973	St. Louis	7	0	1	1
1974	St. Louis	15	0	0	0
1975	Denver	1	0	0	0
1976	Minnesota	6	0	1	1
	Totals	29	0	2	2

HRESKO, DENNIS   *Forward*

Season	Club	GP	G	A	Pts.
1975	Baltimore	1	0	0	0

HUDSON, ALAN   *Midfielder*
B. June 21, 1951   London, England
Ht. 5-11   Wt. 160
Citizen—England

Season	Club	GP	G	A	Pts.
1979	Seattle	26	2	11	15

HUDSON, BRUCE   *Defender*
B. Oct. 31, 1950   St. Louis, Mo.
Ht. 6-0   Wt. 170
Citizen—U.S.

Season	Club	GP	G	A	Pts.
1976	St. Louis	22	0	0	0

HUDSON, RAY   *Midfielder*
B. Mar. 24, 1955   Hexham, England
Ht. 5-11   Wt. 157
Citizen—England

Season	Club	GP	G	A	Pts.
1977	Ft. Lauderdale	25	3	3	9
1978	Ft. Lauderdale	29	7	8	22
1979	Ft. Lauderdale	23	6	13	25
	Totals	77	16	24	56

HUGHES, BRIAN   *Defender*
B. Nov. 22, 1937   Skewen, Wales
Ht. 5-11   Wt. 170
Citizen—Wales

Season	Club	GP	G	A	Pts.
1968	Atlanta	29	1	0	2

HUGHES, WAYNE   *Midfielder*
B. Mar. 8, 1958   Port Talbert, South Wales
Ht. 6-0   Wt. 175
Citizen—Wales

Season	Club	GP	G	A	Pts.
1979	Tulsa	29	12	9	33

HUGHES, WILLIAM   *Midfielder*
Ht. 5-8   Wt. 147

Season	Club	GP	G	A	Pts.
1967	Vancouver	8	0	1	1

HUHSE, HARTMUT   *Midfielder*
B. Aug. 22, 1952   Germany
Ht. 5-11   Wt. 165
Citizen—Germany

Season	Club	GP	G	A	Pts.
1979	Rochester	11	2	1	5

Season	Club	GP	G	A	Pts.

HULCER, LARRY   *Midfielder*
B. Apr. 26, 1957   St. Louis, Mo.
Ht. 5–9   Wt. 160
Citizen—U.S.

1979	Los Angeles	22	0	4	4

HUMBERTO (HUMBERTO COELHO)   *Defender*
B. 1951   Portugal
Ht. 6–0   Wt. 170
Citizen—Portugal

1977	Las Vegas	22	3	1	7

HUMPHREYS, CARL   *Forward*
B. Athlone, Ireland
Ht. 5–7   Wt.`150
Citizen—Ireland

1976	St. Louis	11	3	1	7

HUMPHRIES, STEVE
See *Goalkeeper*

HUNT, ERNIE   *Forward*
Ht. 5–7   Wt. 168

1967	L.A.(USA)	10	4	2	10

HUNT, STEVE   *Forward*
B. July 8, 1956   England
Ht. 5–7   Wt. 150
Citizen—England

1977	New York	23	8	10	26
1978	New York	25	12	12	36
	Totals	48	20	22	62

HUNTER, PAUL   *Defender*
B. Jan. 18, 1956   Toronto, Canada
Ht. 5–11   Wt. 155
Citizen—Canada

1977	New York	3	0	0	0
1978	Detroit	30	0	0	0
1979	Detroit	24	0	0	0
	Totals	57	0	0	0

HUNTER, TIM   *Forward*
B. Mar. 3, 1954   Toronto, Canada
Ht. 5–9   Wt. 152
Citizen—U.S.

1976	Boston	1	0	0	0
1977	Connecticut	4	1	1	3
1978	New England	2	0	0	0
	Totals	7	1	1	3

HUNTER, WILLIE   *Forward*
B. Scotland
Ht. 5–7   Wt. 132
Citizen—Scotland

1968	Detroit	14	4	0	8

Season	Club	GP	G	A	Pts.

HURST, GEOFF   *Forward*
B. Dec. 8, 1941   Ashton-Under-Lyne, England
Ht. 5–11   Wt. 180
Citizen—England

1976	Seattle	23	8	4	20

HUSBAND, JIMMY   *Forward*
B. Oct. 15, 1947   Newcastle, England
Ht. 5–8   Wt. 160
Citizen—England

1978	Memphis	28	9	4	22
1979	Memphis	27	9	5	23
	Totals	55	18	9	45

HUSON, DAVE   *Forward*
B. May 1, 1951   Jersey Channel Islands
Ht. 5–9   Wt. 150
Citizen—Channel Islands

1979	California	18	0	5	5

HUTTEL, NIELS   *Midfielder*
B. Denmark
Ht. 5–11   Wt. 162
Citizen—Denmark

1968	Washington	18	2	0	4

HYKEMA, GERARD   *Forward*
B. Holland
Ht. 6–1   Wt. 175

1975	San Antonio	3	0	0	0

IARUSCI, ROBERT   *Defender*
B. Nov. 8, 1954   Toronto, Canada
Ht. 6–0   Wt. 170
Citizen—Canada

1976	Toronto	24	1	1	3
1977	Tor.-N.Y.	22	2	1	5
1978	New York	18	0	2	2
1979	Washington	28	0	4	4
	Totals	92	3	8	14

IGLESIAS, RUBEN

1968	Dallas	1	0	0	0

IGNACIO, LAURIBERTO   *Forward*
B. June 4, 1947   San Paulo, Brazil

1971	Dallas	1	0	0	0

IGUARAN, MIGUEL   *Midfielder*
B. Spain
Ht. 6–0   Wt. 165
Citizen—Spain

1968	Toronto	26	1	2	4

ILIJEVSKI, SLOBODAN
See *Goalkeeper*

Season	Club	GP	G	A	Pts.

IMPEY, JOHN   *Defender*
B. Aug. 11, 1954   Exeter, England
Ht. 6–1   Wt. 168
Citizen—England

| 1979 | Seattle | 22 | 1 | 1 | 3 |

INE, SONNY   *Forward*
B. June 18, 1947   Nigeria
Ht. 5–6   Wt. 145

| 1971 | Washington | 4 | 0 | 0 | 0 |

INGOLD, BARRY   *Forward*
B. England
Ht. 5–11   Wt. 175
Citizen—England

| 1968 | Los Angeles | 1 | 0 | 0 | 0 |

INGRAM, GERRY   *Forward*
B. Aug. 19, 1947   Hull, England
Ht. 5–10   Wt. 160
Citizen—England

1975	Washington	21	7	5	19
1976	Washington	20	8	5	21
1977	Las Vegas	25	7	4	18
1978	S.D.-Chi.-S.J.	25	4	4	12
1979	California	27	10	7	27
	Totals	118	36	25	97

INGRAM, GODFREY   *Forward*
B. Oct. 26, 1959   Luton, England
Ht. 5–7   Wt. 150
Citizen—England

| 1979 | New York | 1 | 0 | 0 | 0 |

IRVING, DAVID   *Forward*
B. Sept. 10, 1951   Cumbria, England
Ht. 5–9   Wt. 170
Citizen—England

1977	Ft. Lauderdale	13	3	1	7
1978	Ft. Lauderdale	28	16	5	37
1979	Ft. Lauderdale	24	8	9	25
	Totals	65	27	15	69

IRWIN, BILL
See *Goalkeeper*

IVANCHUKOV, SANDJE   *Defender*
B. June 23, 1960   Howell Township, N.J.
Ht. 5–10   Wt. 170
Citizen—U.S.A.

1978	Tampa Bay	2	0	0	0
1979	Tampa Bay	1	0	0	0
	Totals	3	0	0	0

IVANOW, MIKE
See *Goalkeeper*

IZIVKIC, STEVE
B. Feb. 21, 1949
Citizen—Yugoslavia

| 1977 | Toronto | 11 | 0 | 0 | 0 |

JACKSON, ALBERT   *Defender*
B. England
Ht. 6–0   Wt. 165

1974	Dallas	17	5	1	11
1975	Dallas	16	2	0	4
	Totals	33	7	1	15

JACKSON, JOHN
See *Goalkeeper*

JACOB, NAINUDEL   *Forward*
Ht. 6–2   Wt. 171

| 1973 | Montreal | 1 | 0 | 0 | 0 |

JACQUES, JOSEF   *Defender*

| 1975 | Boston | 2 | 0 | 0 | 0 |

JAIRO   *Forward*
B. Aug. 29, 1952   Maceio Alagoas, Brazil
Ht. 5–8   Wt. 155
Citizen—Brazil

| 1979 | Dallas | 4 | 1 | 1 | 3 |

JAMES, JOHN   *Forward*
B. Oct. 24, 1948   Stone Staffs, England
Ht. 6–0   Wt. 180
Citizen—England

| 1976 | Chicago | 9 | 4 | 1 | 9 |

JANDUDA, JOSEF   *Defender*
Ht. 6–I   Wt. 180
Citizen—Poland

1974	Rochester	20	0	2	2
1975	Rochester	22	0	0	0
	Totals	42	0	2	2

JANI, FERENC   *Defender*
B. Aug. 16, 1939   Budapest, Hungary
Ht. 5–8   Wt. 160
Citizen—U.S.

| 1968 | Houston | 2 | 0 | 0 | 0 |

JARMAN, HAROLD   *Forward*
B. Apr. 5, 1939   Bristol, England
Ht. 5–9
Citizen—England

| 1974 | New York | 18 | 4 | 3 | 11 |

JASIC, VLADAMIR   *Defender*
Ht. 6–1   Wt. 175
Citizen—Yugoslavia

| 1978 | Tulsa | 2 | 0 | 0 | 0 |

Season	Club	GP	G	A	Pts.

JEAN-JOSEPH, ERNST   *Defender*
B. June 11, 1948   Cap Haitien, Haiti
Ht. 6-2   Wt. 160
Citizen—Haiti

Season	Club	GP	G	A	Pts.
1978	Chicago	9	0	0	0

JEFFERSON, DEREK   *Defender*
B. Newcastle, England
Ht. 5-11   Wt. 170
Citizen—England

| 1976 | Bost.-Wash. | 21 | 0 | 0 | 0 |

JELINEK, JOSEF   *Forward*
B. Czechoslovakia
Ht. 5-9   Wt. 165

Season	Club	GP	G	A	Pts.
1972	New York	14	2	5	9
1973	New York	12	2	4	8
1974	Roch.-Bost.	19	1	7	9
1975	Boston	8	0	2	2
1976	Boston	4	0	1	1
	Totals	57	5	19	29

JENKINS, TOM   *Midfielder*
B. Dec. 2, 1947   London, England
Ht. 5-9   Wt. 148
Citizen—England

1976	Seattle	20	1	3	5
1977	Seattle	16	1	1	3
1978	Seattle	5	0	3	3
1979	Seattle	1	0	1	1
	Totals	42	2	8	12

JENNINGS, BILL   *Forward*
B. 1953   Hackney, England
Ht. 5-9   Wt. 155
Citizen—England

| 1977 | Chicago | 19 | 6 | 4 | 16 |

JENNINGS, NICHOLAS   *Forward*
B. Jan. 18, 1946   England
Ht. 5-7   Wt. 150

| 1973 | Dallas | 18 | 3 | 4 | 10 |

JENSEN, HENNING MUNK   *Defender*
B. Jan. 12, 1947   Tonder, Denmark
Ht. 6-3   Wt. 180
Citizen—Denmark

| 1979 | S.J.-Edm. | 23 | 0 | 1 | 1 |

JENSEN, LARS   *Forward*
B. Dec. 12, 1956   Grena, Denmark
Ht. 6-0   Wt. 180
Citizen—Denmark

| 1979 | San Jose | 2 | 0 | 0 | 0 |

JENSEN, VAGN   *Midfielder*
B. Denmark
Ht. 5-8   Wt. 152
Citizen—Denmark

Season	Club	GP	G	A	Pts.
1968	Detroit	3	0	0	0

JENTAS, WAYNE   *Midfielder*
B. Mar. 9, 1954   Toronto, Canada
Ht. 5-11   Wt. 160
Citizen—Canada

| 1978 | Vancouver | 4 | 0 | 0 | 0 |

JIJON, EDWARD   *Forward*
Ht. 5-8   Wt. 145
Citizen—Ecuador

| 1971 | Rochester | 22 | 2 | 5 | 9 |

JIMENEZ, GUS   *Midfielder*
B. Costa Rica
Ht. 5-9   Wt. 155
Citizen—Costa Rica

| 1968 | Toronto | 20 | 1 | 0 | 2 |

JIRASURADET, TRAKOON   *Defender*
B. Sept. 1, 1948   Bangkok, Thailand
Ht. 5-8   Wt.150

| 1975 | Miami | 7 | 0 | 0 | 0 |

JOCHEMS, JOOP   *Midfielder*
Ht. 5-6   Wt. 141

| 1967 | San Francisco | 11 | 0 | 1 | 1 |

JOERGE, JIMMY
See *Goalkeeper*

JOHNS, NICKY
See *Goalkeeper*

JOHNSON, GLEN   *Forward*
B. Apr. 22, 1951   Vancouver, Canada
Ht. 5-9   Wt. 160
Citizen—Canada

1974	Vancouver	12	2	2	6
1975	Vancouver	21	8	7	23
1976	Vancouver	20	4	4	12
1977	Vancouver	6	1	1	3
	Totals	59	15	14	44

JOHNSON, RODNEY   *Midfielder*
B. Jan. 8, 1945   Leeds, England
Ht. 5-8   Wt. 160
Citizen—England

| 1975 | Chicago | 19 | 0 | 3 | 3 |

Season	Club	GP	G	A	Pts.

JOHNSTON, WILLIE *Forward*
B. Dec. 19, 1946 Scotland
Ht. 5-7 Wt. 155
Citizen—Scotland

| 1979 | Vancouver | 27 | 1 | 12 | 14 |

JOHNSTONE, JIMMY *Forward*

| 1975 | San Jose | 10 | 0 | 4 | 4 |

JOKERST, DAVE
See *Goalkeeper*

JONES, ALLAN *Defender*
Ht. 6-0 Wt. 185

| 1975 | Los Angeles | 20 | 0 | 1 | 1 |

JONES, GARY *Forward*
B. Boulton, England
Ht. 5-11 Wt. 170

| 1978 | Los Angeles | 25 | 4 | 1 | 9 |

JONES, GARY *Forward*
B. Jan. 5, 1951 Liverpool, England
Ht. 5-9 Wt. 161
Citizen—England

1978	Ft. Lauderdale	12	1	1	3
1979	Ft. Lauderdale	6	1	2	4
	Totals	18	2	3	7

JONES, PHILLIP *Defender*
B. S. Africa
Ht. 5-10 Wt. 170

| 1978 | Colorado | 10 | 0 | 0 | 0 |

JORDAN, KIP *Defender*
Ht. 6-0 Wt. 190
Citizen—U.S.

1974	Miami	1	0	0	0
1975	Miami	12	1	0	2
1976	Rochester	10	0	0	0
	Totals	23	1	0	2

JORGE, ART *Forward*
B. Feb. 13, 1946 Portugal
Ht. 6-0 Wt. 165
Citizen—Portugal

| 1977 | Rochester | 7 | 2 | 1 | 5 |

JOSEPH, BOBBY
See *Goalkeeper*

Season	Club	GP	G	A	Pts.

JOY, BRIAN *Defender*
B. Feb. 26, 1951 Manchester, England
Ht. 5-9 Wt. 160
Citizen—England

1976	San Diego	24	3	5	11
1977	Las Vegas	23	2	1	5
1978	San Diego	5	0	0	0
	Totals	52	5	6	16

JUAREZ, HAROLD *Forward*
B. Guatemala
Ht. 5-10 Wt. 164
Citizen—Guatemala

| 1968 | Chicago | 7 | 2 | 0 | 4 |

JULIANS, LEN
B. England
Citizen—England

| 1968 | Detroit | 1 | 0 | 0 | 0 |

JUMP, STEWART *Defender*
B. Jan. 27, 1952 Crumpsall, England
Ht. 5-10 Wt. 160
Citizen—England

1975	Tampa Bay	21	0	1	1
1976	Tampa Bay	17	1	0	1
1977	Tampa Bay	21	0	0	0
1978	Houston	28	1	2	4
1979	Houston	26	2	0	4
	Totals	113	4	3	11

JURACY, LUIS *Forward*
B. May 3, 1939 Brazil
Ht. 5-8 Wt. 170
Citizen—Brazil

1968	Houston	31	9	2	20
1969	Dallas	13	3	2	8
1970	Dallas	13	2	2	6
1971	Dallas	11	1	0	2
1972	Dallas	14	3	1	7
1973	Dallas	10	0	1	1
1974	Dallas	3	0	0	0
	Totals	95	18	8	44

JURISEVIC, VICTOR *Forward*
B. Yugoslavia
Ht. 5-9 Wt. 165
Citizen—Yugoslavia

| 1968 | Toronto | 20 | 6 | 5 | 17 |

JUSIC, EMIR *Forward*
Ht. 6-2 Wt. 168
Citizen—Yugoslavia

| 1975 | Toronto | 13 | 1 | 2 | 4 |

Season	Club	GP	G	A	Pts.

JUTT, MARIO   *Forward*
B. Oct. 27, 1948   Yugoslavia
Ht. 6-1   Wt. 180
Citizen—Yugoslavia

Season	Club	GP	G	A	Pts.
1977	Toronto	4	0	0	0

KALICANIN, MILONJA   *Defender*
B. May 31, 1938   Belgrade, Yugoslavia
Ht. 5-10   Wt. 160
Citizen—Yugoslavia

Season	Club	GP	G	A	Pts.
1967	St. Louis	—	—	—	—
1968	St. Louis	30	0	0	0
1971	St. Louis	20	0	0	0
	Totals	50	0	0	0

KAMINKE, DICK   *Forward*
B. W. Germany
Ht. 5-11   Wt. 150
Citizen—W. Germany

Season	Club	GP	G	A	Pts.
1968	Detroit	5	2	0	4

KAMMERER, MANFRED
See *Goalkeeper*

KAN-KAM, YAO   *Midfielder*
B. 1945
Ht. 6-2   Wt. 145
Citizen—Ghana

Season	Club	GP	G	A	Pts.
1968	Baltimore	3	1	0	2
1970	Rochester	—	—	—	—
1972	St. Louis	3	0	0	0
1973	St. Louis	9	1	0	2
	Totals	15	2	0	4

KAPCINSKI, KAROL   *Defender*
B. Apr. 6, 1943   Poland
Ht. 5-10   Wt. 175

Season	Club	GP	G	A	Pts.
1971	New York	9	0	0	0
1972	New York	10	0	0	0
1973	New York	12	I	0	2
	Totals	31	1	0	2

KAPENGWE, EMMENT   *Forward*
B. Apr. 27, 1943   Broken Hill, Zambia
Ht. 5-8   Wt. 158
Citizen—Zambia

Season	Club	GP	G	A	Pts.
1967	Atlanta	11	5	4	14
1968	Atlanta	31	3	0	6
1969	Atlanta	—	7	6	20
1973	Atlanta	I3	0	2	2
	Totals	55	15	12	42

KASZAS, LASZLO   *Midfielder*
B. Hungary
Ht. 5-8   Wt. 160
Citizen—Hungary

Season	Club	GP	G	A	Pts.
1967	Philadelphia	14	4	2	10
1968	St. L.-N.Y.	15	0	0	0
	Totals	29	4	2	10

KASZUKSKI, WALDEMAR   *Defender*
B. Sczecin, Poland
Ht. 6-3   Wt. 183
Citizen—Poland

Season	Club	GP	G	A	Pts.
1967	Chi. (NPSL)	10	1	1	3
1968	K.C.-St. L.	13	0	0	0
	Totals	23	1	1	0

KAZARIAN, JERRY   *Forward*
B. Mar. 25, 1954
Ht. 5-10   Wt. 155

Season	Club	GP	G	A	Pts.
1974	Los Angeles	6	4	1	9
1975	L.A.-S.J.	5	0	0	0
	Totals	11	4	1	9

KAZDOBA, WALTER   *Midfielder*
B. Russia
Ht. 5-11   Wt. 185

Season	Club	GP	G	A	Pts.
1967	Philadelphia	8	1	0	2

KAZMIERSKI, HANK   *Forward*
B. Oct. 30, 1949   Baltimore, Md.
Ht. 6-0   Wt. 175
Citizen—U.S.

Season	Club	GP	G	A	Pts.
1974	Baltimore	16	4	1	9
1975	Baltimore	18	2	3	7
	Totals	34	6	4	16

KEELAN, KEVIN
See *Goalkeeper*

KEITA (SALIF KEITA)   *Forward*
B. Dec. 6, 1946   Bamako, Mali
Ht. 6-1   Wt. 175
Citizen—Portugal

Season	Club	GP	G	A	Pts.
1979	New England	21	6	6	18

KELLER, RUDY   *Midfielder*
B. Mar. 6, 1942   Menninger, Germany
Ht. 5-11   Wt. 185
Citizen—U.S.

Season	Club	GP	G	A	Pts.
1975	Chicago	1	0	0	0

KELLETT, RICHARD   *Forward*
B. Mar. 6, 1954   Benoni, S. Africa
Ht. 6-0   Wt. 170
Citizen—S. Africa

Season	Club	GP	G	A	Pts.
1978	Chicago	3	0	0	0

KELLY, ALAN   *Midfielder*
B. June 29, 1956   Glasgow, Scotland
Ht. 5-11   Wt. 165
Citizen—U.S.

Season	Club	GP	G	A	Pts.
1978	Los Angeles	9	1	0	2

KELLY, EDMUND   *Midfielder*

Season	Club	GP	G	A	Pts.
1975	Hartford	17	1	4	6

Season	Club	GP	G	A	Pts.

KELLY, JIM *Defender*
B. Glasgow, Scotland
Ht. 6-0 Wt. 172
Citizen—Scotland

| 1967 | Tor. (NPSL) | 7 | 0 | 2 | 2 |

KELLY, JIMMY *Forward*
B. Feb. 6, 1954 Crumlin, N. Ireland
Ht. 5-6 Wt. 134
Citizen—N. Ireland

1975	Portland	20	2	8	12
1976	Portland	20	1	2	4
	Totals	40	3	10	16

KELLY, JIMMY *Midfielder*
B. May 2, 1957 Carlisle, Scotland
Ht. 5-6 Wt. 145
Citizen—Scotland

1976	Chicago	21	5	2	12
1977	Chicago	26	2	7	11
1978	Chi.-L.A.	18	1	0	2
	Totals	65	8	9	25

KELLY, THOMAS *Defender*
B. Dublin, Ireland
Ht. 5-8 Wt. 164
Citizen—Ireland

| 1968 | Boston | 9 | 1 | 0 | 2 |

KEMBER, STEVE *Midfielder*
B. Dec. 8, 1948 Croydon, England
Ht. 5-8 Wt. 150
Citizen—England

| 1978 | Vancouver | 29 | 5 | 11 | 21 |

KEMP, DAVIE *Defender*
B. Aug. 5, 1950 Dundee, Scotland
Ht. 5-5 Wt. 150
Citizen—Scotland

1974	San Jose	8	0	0	0
1975	San Jose	21	0	0	0
1976	San Jose	23	0	4	4
1977	San Jose	23	0	0	0
1978	San Jose	28	0	1	1
	Totals	103	0	5	5

KEMPF, FLORIAN *Midfielder*
B. May 25, 1956 Philadelphia, Pa.
Ht. 5-9 Wt. 155
Citizen—U.S.

| 1978 | Philadelphia | 4 | 0 | 0 | 0 |

KENNEDY, JOHN
See *Goalkeeper*

KENYON, ROGER *Defender*
B. Jan. 4, 1949 Blackpool, England
Ht. 6-0 Wt. 180
Citizen—England

| 1979 | Vancouver | 10 | 0 | 1 | 1 |

KEOHANE, SEAN
See *Goalkeeper*

KEOUGH, TY *Midfielder*
B. Dec. 19, 1956 St. Louis, Mo.
Ht. 5-10 Wt. 165
Citizen—U.S.

| 1979 | San Diego | 19 | 0 | 0 | 0 |

KERI, MIHALJ *Defender*
B. Jan. 15, 1951 Kikinda, Yugoslavia
Ht. 6-1 Wt. 180
Citizen—Yugoslavia

| 1979 | Los Angeles | 30 | 1 | 3 | 5 |

KERR, JOHN *Midfielder*
B. Oct. 15, 1943 Glasgow, Scotland
Ht. 5-7 Wt. 150
Citizen—Canada

1968	Detroit	18	9	0	18
1971	Washington	24	6	6	18
1973	New York	12	3	4	10
1974	New York	9	0	0	0
1975	New York	17	2	1	5
1976	Washington	20	0	2	2
1977	Washington	13	0	1	1
	Totals	113	20	14	54

KESSON, BOBBY *Defender*
Ht. 5-7 Wt. 140

| 1975 | Dallas | 3 | 0 | 0 | 0 |

KETEMA, YELMER *Forward*
B. Ethiopia
Ht. 5-7 Wt. 140
Citizen—Ethiopia

| 1968 | Boston | 2 | 0 | 0 | 0 |

KETTLE, BRIAN *Defender*
B. Apr. 22, 1956 Prescot, England
Ht. 5-9 Wt. 170
Citizen—England

| 1978 | Dallas | 19 | 1 | 2 | 4 |

KEWLEY, KEVIN *Midfielder*
B. Feb. 3, 1955 Liverpool, England
Ht. 5-9 Wt. 166
Citizen—England

1976	Dallas	24	6	2	14
1977	Dallas	26	6	5	17
1978	Dallas	29	2	7	11
1979	Dallas	16	1	1	3
	Totals	95	15	15	45

KILLY, JIM

| 1968 | Dallas | 5 | 0 | 0 | 0 |

Season	Club	GP	G	A	Pts.

KINDRATIW, ROSTYSLAW "RUSTY"   *Forward*
B. Nov. 2, 1945   Vienna, Austria
Ht. 5-10   Wt. 170
Citizen—U.S.

Season	Club	GP	G	A	Pts.
1968	Baltimore	3	1	0	2
1969	Baltimore	—	—	—	—
	Totals	3	1	0	2

KINEALY, JACK   *Forward*
B. Mar. 17, 1945   St. Louis, Mo.
Ht. 6-1   Wt. 170
Citizen—U.S.

Season	Club	GP	G	A	Pts.
1968	St. Louis	12	1	0	1

KINNELL, GEORGE   *Midfielder*
Ht 6-0   Wt. 168

Season	Club	GP	G	A	Pts.
1967	Vancouver	12	2	0	4

KINSELLA, TOMMY   *Forward*
Ht. 5-7   Wt. 152

Season	Club	GP	G	A	Pts.
1967	Boston	4	0	2	2

KIRBY, GEORGE   *Forward*
B. Dec. 20, 1933   Liverpool, England
Ht. 6-1   Wt. 170
Citizen—England

Season	Club	GP	G	A	Pts.
1967	N.Y. (NPSL)	12	14	2	30
1968	New York	22	9		18
	Totals	34	23	2	48

KIRKBRIDE, ERIC   *Midfielder*

Season	Club	GP	G	A	Pts.
1973	Montreal	3	0	0	0

KITCHENER, BARRY   *Defender*
B. Dec. 11, 1947   Essex, England
Ht. 6-2   Wt. 192
Citizen—England

Season	Club	GP	G	A	Pts.
1979	Tampa Bay	20	0	1	1

KLABOCH, JIRI   *Midfielder*
Ht. 5-8   Wt. 158

Season	Club	GP	G	A	Pts.
1971	Montreal	4	0	0	0

KLARA, ARMIN   *Forward*
B. Dec. 22, 1955   Bayern, W. Germany
Ht. 5-10   Wt. 154
Citizen—W. Germany

Season	Club	GP	G	A	Pts.
1979	Houston	1	0	0	0

KLASSON, LEIF   *Forward*
B. Dec. 17, 1940   Lidkoping, Sweden
Ht. 6-0   Wt. 175
Citizen—Sweden

Season	Club	GP	G	A	Pts.
1967	Baltimore	3	4	1	9
1968	Bal.-Van.	14	4	0	8
	Totals	17	8	1	17

KLEIN, HENRY   *Forward*
B. Luxemburg, Belgium
Ht. 5-11   Wt. 175
Citizen—Belgium

Season	Club	GP	G	A	Pts.
1968	Vancouver	26	20	4	44

KLINKENBERG, RON   *Forward*
B. Aug. 18, 1955   Bussum, Holland
Ht. 5-9   Wt. 165
Citizen—Holland

Season	Club	GP	G	A	Pts.
1979	Edmonton	27	0	6	6

KOBL, RUDOLF   *Forward*
B. June 11, 1937   Munich, Germany
Ht. 5-8   Wt. 156
Citizen—Germany

Season	Club	GP	G	A	Pts.
1967	St. Louis	19	13	8	34
1968	St. Louis	14	4	0	8
	Totals	33	17	8	42

KOCIJANIC, IVAN   *Defender*
B. Feb. 24, 1947   Dol, Yugoslavia
Ht. 5-8   Wt. 165
Citizen—Yugoslavia

Season	Club	GP	G	A	Pts.
1978	Toronto	20	0	0	0

KODELJA, VICTOR   *Forward*
B. Nov. 26, 1951   Capua Casserta, Italy
Ht. 5-10   Wt. 165
Citizen—Canada

Season	Club	GP	G	A	Pts.
1974	Vancouver	15	2	4	8
1976	San Antonio	20	4	6	14
1977	Hawaii	23	4	3	11
1978	San Jose	15	3	1	7
	Totals	73	13	14	40

KOEPPEL, HORST   *Midfielder*
B. May 17, 1948   Stuttgart, W. Germany
Ht. 5-10   Wt. 150
Citizen—W. Germany

Season	Club	GP	G	A	Pts.
1976	Vancouver	12	1	4	6
1977	Vancouver	8	0	1	1
	Totals	20	1	5	7

KOFIE, EMANUEL
See *Goalkeeper*

KOLONIC, GEORGE   *Midfielder*
B. Apr. 20, 1954   Yugoslavia
Ht. 5-11   Wt. 165
Citizen—Yugoslavia

Season	Club	GP	G	A	Pts.
1977	Rochester	8	0	2	2

KONSTANTINOU, VASILIOS
See *Goalkeeper*

Season	Club	GP	G	A	Pts.

KOREMANS, RENE   *Midfielder*

1975	Boston	6	0	0	0

KORNEK, CONRAD
See *Goalkeeper*

KORTE, KEITH   *Defender*

1975	Rochester	3	0	0	0

KOSTIC, BORA   *Forward*
B. Scrna, Yugoslavia
Ht. 6-3   Wt. 190
Citizen—Yugoslavia

1967	St. Louis	23	13	5	31

KOTTAN, GEORGE   *Midfielder*
B. Oct. 6, 1950   Budapest, Hungary
Ht. 6-1   Wt. 185
Citizen—Hungary

1979	Los Angeles	8	1	2	4

KOVACIC, GORAN   *Midfielder*
B. Jan. 20, 1949   Yugoslavia
Ht. 5-9   Wt. 165
Citizen—Yugoslavia

1977	Toronto	14	1	0	2

KNAPP, TONY   *Midfielder*
B. England
Ht. 5-9   Wt. 162
Citizen—England

1968	Los Angeles	20	1	0	2

KNOWLES, PETER   *Forward*
Ht. 5-11   Wt. 160

1967	L.A. (USA)	12	3	2	8

KOWALIK, JOHN   *Forward*
B. Mar. 26, 1944   Krakow, Poland
Ht. 5-7   Wt. 145
Citizen—Poland

1968	Chicago	28	30	9	69
1976	Chicago	14	9	3	21
1977	Chicago	5	1	0	2
	Totals	47	40	12	92

KRAAY, JR., HANS   *Midfielder*
B. Dec. 22, 1959   Utrecht, Holland
Ht. 6-1   Wt. 165
Citizen—Holland

1979	Edmonton	30	4	2	10

KRALJEVIC, BRANKO   *Forward*
B. Nov. 10, 1939   Novi, Yugoslavia
Ht. 5-8   Wt. 156
Citizen—Yugoslavia

1968	Houston	31	4	9	17

KRAT, NICKOLAS   *Defender*
B. Feb. 24, 1943   Ukraine, USSR
Ht. 6-1   Wt. 175
Citizen—U.S.

1967	Chi. (NPSL)	—	—	—	—
1968	St. Louis	26	0	0	0
	Totals	26	0	0	0

KRAUTHAUSEN, FRANZ   *Forward*
B. Feb. 27, 1946   W. Germany
Ht. 5-9   Wt. 160
Citizen-W. Germany

1977	Las Vegas	23	1	5	7
1978	San Diego	5	1	0	2
1979	California	5	0	0	0
	Totals	33	2	5	9

KREMER, KAROLY   *Midfielder*
B. Feb. 8, 1947   Nagybaracska, Hungary
Ht. 5-8   Wt. 145
Citizen—Hungary

1979	Philadelphia	10	0	4	4

KRESIC, SERGIO   *Midfielder*
B. Yugoslavia
Ht. 6-1   Wt. 170
Citizen—Yugoslavia

1968	Cleveland	6	2	0	4

KREUGER, EDDIE   *Defender*
B. Sept. 10, 1959   Buffalo, N.Y.
Ht. 6-1   Wt. 170
Citizen—U.S.

1978	Seattle	7	0	1	1
1979	Seattle	5	0	0	0
	Totals	12	0	1	1

KRISTENSEN, JORGEN   *Forward*
B. Dec. 12, 1946   Denmark
Ht. 5-8   Wt. 160
Citizen—Denmark

1968	Detroit	20	8	0	16
1978	Chicago	19	5	15	25
1979	Chicago	30	4	22	30
	Totals	69	17	37	71

KRIVITZ, TOMAS   *Midfielder*
B. Hungary
Ht. 5-9   Wt. 170

1968	Vancouver	22	0	0	0

KUBALA, BRANCO   *Forward*
B. Sahey, Czechoslovakia
Ht. 5-10   Wt. 170

1967	Tor. (NPSL)	6	3	7	13
1968	Dal-Tor-St. L	17	4	1	9
	Totals	23	7	8	22

Season	Club	GP	G	A	Pts.

KUBALA, LADISLAV   *Forward*
B. Nov. 1927   Budapest, Hungary
Ht. 5-8

Season	Club	GP	G	A	Pts.
1967	Tor. (NPSL)	7	4	4	12

KUK, TONYL

| 1967 | Tor. (NPSL) | 3 | 0 | 1 | 1 |

KUNZLI, FRITZ   *Forward*
B. Jan. 8, 1946   Zurich, Switzerland
Ht. 5-10   Wt. 160
Citizen—Switzerland

| 1978 | S.D.-Hou. | 10 | 3 | 0 | 6 |

KUYKENDALL, KURT
See *Goalkeeper*

KUZMAN, JOE   *Forward*
B. Hungary
Ht. 5-10   Wt. 180
Citizen—Spain

| 1968 | Cleveland | 13 | 2 | 0 | 4 |

KYDD, SAMMY
See *Goalkeeper*

KYNDBOL, JOHN   *Midfielder*
B. Denmark
Ht. 5-11   Wt. 175
Citizen—Denmark

| 1968 | Bos.-Wash. | 11 | 0 | 0 | 0 |

LACERDA, OLIVIO

| 1967 | Pittsburgh | 1 | 0 | 1 | 1 |

LADOVIC, JOE   *Defender*
B. Sept. 9, 1938   Zagreb, Yugoslavia
Ht. 6-1   Wt. 180
Citizen—Yugoslavia

| 1968 | Houston | 16 | 0 | 0 | 0 |

LAGENDIJK, GERRIT   *Defender*
B. Holland
Ht. 5-8   Wt. 163
Citizen—Holland

| 1968 | Vancouver | 5 | 0 | 0 | 0 |

LAMAS, ALFREDO   *Midfielder*
B. May 2, 1947   Montevideo, Uruguay
Ht. 6-4   Wt. 170
Citizen—Uruguay

| 1975 | New York | 16 | 0 | 0 | 0 |

LAMBERT, MICKEY   *Forward*
B. May 20, 1950   Cambridge, England
Ht. 5-8   Wt. 155
Citizen—England

| 1978 | Vancouver | 3 | 0 | 0 | 0 |

LAMPTEY, GEORGE   *Defender*
B. Aug. 27, 1951   Accra, Ghana
Ht. 6-2   Wt. 180
Citizen—Ghana

Season	Club	GP	G	A	Pts.
1975	Rochester	6	0	0	0
1976	Chicago	3	0	0	0
1977	Chicago	12	0	1	1
1978	Colorado	6	0	0	0
	Totals	27	0	1	1

LANDRY, DAVE
See *Goalkeeper*

LANG, TOMMY   *Defender*
B. July 14, 1956   Dublin, Ireland
Ht. 5-9   Wt. 150
Citizen—U.S.

1978	Colorado	13	0	0	0
1979	Atlanta	8	0	0	0
	Totals	21	0	0	0

LARGE, FRANK   *Forward*
Ht. 6-0   Wt. 185

| 1974 | Baltimore | 17 | 9 | 2 | 20 |

LARGIE, HENRY   *Forward/Defender*
B. Dec. 31, 1940   Kingston, Jamaica
Ht. 6-2   Wt. 180
Citizen—Jamaica

1968	Bal.-Wash.	21	7	0	14
1969	Atlanta	—	—	—	—
1970	Atlanta	21	8	2	18
1971	Atlanta	20	3	1	7
1972	Atlanta	11	2	1	5
	Totals	73	20	4	44

LARSEN, PETER   *Forward*
B. Oct. 21, 1945   Tromso, Norway
Ht. 5-9   Wt. 160
Citizen—Norway

| 1968 | Dallas | 11 | 2 | 1 | 5 |

LASEROMS, THEO   *Midfielder*
B. Aug. 20, 1940   Roosendaal, Holland
Ht. 5-8   Wt. 175
Citizen—Holland

| 1967 | Pittsburgh | 13 | 2 | 1 | 5 |

LAVALLE, SERGIO   *Forward*
Ht. 6-1   Wt. 177

| 1973 | Montreal | 1 | 0 | 0 | 0 |

LAWLER, CHRIS   *Defender*
B. Oct. 20, 1943   Liverpool, England
Ht. 6-1   Wt. 180
Citizen—England

| 1976 | Miami | 21 | 1 | 0 | 2 |

Season	Club	GP	G	A	Pts.

LAWSON, DOC *Defender*
B. Feb. 11, 1958   Liberia
Ht. 6–0   Wt. 180
Citizen—U.S.

| 1979 | S.J.-S.D. | 18 | 2 | 2 | 6 |

LAZAREVIC, VOJIN *Forward*
Ht. 5–10   Wt. 175

| 1974 | Toronto | 6 | 4 | 2 | 10 |

LEACH, MICK *Midfielder*
B. Jan. 16, 1947   Manchester, England
Ht. 5–7   Wt. 168
Citizen—England

| 1978 | Detroit | 23 | 3 | 0 | 6 |

LECARO, VICENTE *Defender*
B. June 8, 1936   Ecuador
Ht. 6–0   Wt. 170

| 1972 | Miami | 6 | 0 | 0 | 0 |

LECCE, TONY *Defender*
B. Jan. 1, 1945   Rome, Italy
Ht. 5–9   Wt. 165
Citizen—Canada

1968	Toronto	28	1	1	3
1971	Toronto	10	0	1	1
1972	Toronto	14	0	0	0
1973	Toronto	15	0	0	0
	Totals	67	1	2	4

LECHERMANN, PETER *Defender*
B. Sept. 28, 1950   Mulheim, Germany
Ht. 5–10   Wt. 180
Citizen—Germany

1978	San Diego	20	1	1	3
1979	San Diego	19	0	1	1
	Totals	39	1	2	4

LEE, ALAN *Forward*
B. June 19, 1960
Ht. 6–0   Wt. 154
Citizen—Scotland

| 1978 | Philadelphia | 6 | 0 | 1 | 1 |

LEE, DENNY *Forward*
B. June 3, 1953   St. Louis, Mo.
Ht. 5–10   Wt. 155
Citizen—U.S.

| 1976 | Miami | 21 | 1 | 0 | 2 |

LEECH, MICHAEL *Forward*
Ht. 5–9   Wt. 148

| 1967 | Boston | 5 | 2 | 0 | 4 |

LEEKER, JIM *Forward*
B. 1947   St. Louis, Mo.
Ht. 6–2   Wt. 198
Citizen—U.S.

1971	St. Louis	13	2	4	8
1972	St. Louis	11	1	2	4
	Totals	24	3	6	12

LEEPER, CURTIS *Forward*
B. Dec. 28, 1955   Miami, Fla.
Ht. 5–11   Wt. 160
Citizen—U.S.

1977	Ft. Lauderdale	4	0	0	0
1978	Ft. Lauderdale	7	0	0	0
1979	Ft.L-Phil.	7	0	1	1
	Totals	18	0	1	1

LEES, TERRY *Defender*
Ht. 5–8   Wt. 155

| 1975 | San Jose | 17 | 1 | 2 | 4 |

LEFKOS, JIM *Forward*
B. Cyprus
Ht. 6–0   Wt. 180

| 1971 | Toronto | 6 | 0 | 0 | 0 |

LEGGAT, GRAHAM *Forward*
B. Aberdeen, Scotland
Ht. 5–9   Wt. 150

| 1971 | Toronto | 11 | 2 | 2 | 6 |

LEIFSSON, GUDGEIR *Midfielder*
B. Sept. 25, 1951   Reykjavik, Iceland
Ht. 6–0   Wt. 170
Citizen—Iceland

| 1979 | Edmonton | 24 | 3 | 4 | 10 |

LEMON, JIM *Midfielder*
B. Jan. 6, 1949   Belfast, N. Ireland
Ht. 5–11   Wt. 160
Citizen—N. Ireland

1975	Chicago	21	0	3	3
1977	Chicago	10	0	1	1
	Totals	31	0	4	4

LENARDUZZI, DAN *Defender*
B. Aug. 31, 1959   Vancouver, Canada
Ht. 6–1   Wt. 170
Citizen—Canada

1978	Vancouver	2	0	0	0
1979	Vancouver	6	0	0	0
	Totals	8	0	0	0

Season	Club	GP	G	A	Pts.

LENARDUZZI, ROBERT   *Defender*
B. May 1, 1955   Vancouver, Canada
Ht. 6–l   Wt. 185
Citizen—Canada

Season	Club	GP	G	A	Pts.
1974	Vancouver	19	2	0	4
1975	Vancouver	20	3	3	9
1976	Vancouver	21	3	2	8
1977	Vancouver	26	0	4	4
1978	Vancouver	29	10	17	37
1979	Vancouver	28	3	3	9
	Totals	143	21	29	71

LENARDUZZI, SILVANO "SAM"   *Defender*
B. Dec. 19, 1948   Italy
Ht. 5–10   Wt. 165
Citizen—Canada

Season	Club	GP	G	A	Pts.
1974	Vancouver	17	0	1	1
1975	Vancouver	16	0	1	1
1976	Vancouver	22	2	1	5
1977	Vancouver	22	0	0	0
1978	Vancouver	16	0	0	0
1979	Toronto	6	0	0	0
	Totals	99	2	3	7

LENNARD, DAVE   *Midfielder*
B. Manchester, England
Ht. 5–10   Wt. 165

Season	Club	GP	G	A	Pts.
1978	Los Angeles	14	0	0	0

LENNOX, BOBBY   *Forward*
B. Aug. 30, 1943   Glasgow, Scotland
Ht. 5–8   Wt. 160
Citizen—Scotland

Season	Club	GP	G	A	Pts.
1978	Houston	29	3	6	12

LESH, ALEX   *Midfielder*
Ht. 5–11   Wt. 155
Citizen—U.S.

Season	Club	GP	G	A	Pts.
1978	Oakland	14	0	1	1

LESTER, MIKE   *Forward*
B. Apr. 8, 1954   Manchester, England
Ht. 5–11   Wt. 160
Citizen—England

Season	Club	GP	G	A	Pts.
1977	Washington	24	1	3	5

LETTIERI, TINO
See *Goalkeeper*

LEWINGTON, RAY   *Midfielder*
B. Sept. 7, 1956   London, England
Ht. 5–6   Wt. 150
Citizen—England

Season	Club	GP	G	A	Pts.
1979	Vancouver	29	2	4	8

LEWIS, CLEVELAND   *Forward*
B. Jan. 11, 1955
Ht. 6–2   Wt.180
Citizen—U.S.

Season	Club	GP	G	A	Pts.
1978	Memphis	3	0	1	1

LEWIS, FREDDIE   *Forward*
Ht. 5–4   Wt. 140
Citizen—Bermuda

Season	Club	GP	G	A	Pts.
1975	Philadelphia	17	2	2	6

LEWIS, KEVIN   *Forward*
Ht. 5–11   Wt. 165

Season	Club	GP	G	A	Pts.
1974	Washington	7	0	2	2

LEY, GEORGE   *Defender*
B. Apr. 1, 1946   Exminster, England
Ht. 5–10   Wt. 168
Citizen—England

Season	Club	GP	G	A	Pts.
1974	Dallas	11	0	1	1
1975	Dallas	18	4	5	13
1976	Dallas	21	2	4	8
1977	Dallas	24	2	5	9
1978	Dallas	29	0	3	3
1979	Dallas	22	0	6	6
	Totals	125	8	24	40

LEZINGER, HERBERT   *Defender*
B. Vienna, Austria
Ht. 5–7   Wt. 145
Citizen—Austria

Season	Club	GP	G	A	Pts.
1967	L.A. (NPSL)	14	1	1	3

LICHABA, WEBSTER   *Defender*
B. Oct. 6, 1954   S. Africa
Ht. 5–7   Wt. 150
Citizen—S. Africa

Season	Club	GP	G	A	Pts.
1979	Atlanta	30	0	2	2

LIEVAND, GEORGE   *Forward*
B. San Salvador, El Salvador
Ht. 5–5   Wt. 144
Citizen—El Salvador

Season	Club	GP	G	A	Pts.
1967	Oakland	9	1	5	7

LIGHTOWLER, GERALD   *Midfielder*
B. England
Ht. 5–9   Wt. 165
Citizen—England

Season	Club	GP	G	A	Pts.
1968	Los Angeles	22	3	0	6

LIGNOS, JOHN   *Defender*
B. Feb. 2, 1958   Chios Island, Greece
Ht. 5–11   Wt. 160
Citizen—U.S.

Season	Club	GP	G	A	Pts.
1979	New England	7	0	0	0

Season	Club	GP	G	A	Pts.

LIMA, JOHN   *Forward*
B. Spain
Ht. 5–10   Wt. 150
Citizen—Spain

Season	Club	GP	G	A	Pts.
1968	Toronto	31	4	10	18

LINDBERG, ODD
See *Goalkeeper*

LINDBERG, SVEN
See *Goalkeeper*

LINDSAY, ALEC   *Defender*
B. Feb. 27, 1948   Liverpool, England
Ht. 6–1   Wt. 180
Citizen—England

Season	Club	GP	G	A	Pts.
1978	Oakland	28	1	0	2
1979	Toronto	4	0	0	0
	Totals	32	1	0	2

LINDSAY, MARK   *Midfielder*
B. Mar. 6, 1955   London, England
Ht. 5–8   Wt. 155
Citizen—England

Season	Club	GP	G	A	Pts.
1975	Tampa Bay	18	1	2	4
1976	Tampa Bay	21	4	4	12
1977	Tampa Bay	20	1	3	5
1978	Houston	10	4	4	12
1979	Hou.-Calif.	27	4	12	20
	Totals	96	14	25	53

LINTON, MALCOLM   *Defender*
B. Feb. 13, 1952   Southend, England
Ht. 6–1   Wt. 180
Citizen—England

Season	Club	GP	G	A	Pts.
1975	Tampa Bay	20	0	0	0
1976	Los Angeles	23	0	1	1
	Totals	43	0	1	1

LIOTART, HANK   *Midfielder*
B. Nov. 15, 1943   Baarn, Holland
Ht. 5–11   Wt. 176
Citizen—U.S.

Season	Club	GP	G	A	Pts.
1974	Seattle	19	0	7	7
1975	Seattle	18	2	3	7
1976	Sea.-Port.	17	1	0	2
1977	Portland	20	1	1	3
1979	San Diego	8	0	0	0
	Totals	82	4	11	19

LIPOSINOVIC, JOHN   *Forward*
B. Yugoslavia
Ht. 5–10   Wt. 150
Citizen—Yugoslavia

Season	Club	GP	G	A	Pts.
1968	Boston	10	4	0	8

LIPPENS, WILLIE   *Forward*
B. Nov. 10, 1945   Hau-Kleve, W. Germany
Ht. 5–9   Wt. 170
Citizen—Holland

Season	Club	GP	G	A	Pts.
1979	Dallas	25	15	7	37

LIPTAK, GYORGY   *Defender*
B. Hungary
Ht. 5–10   Wt. 185

Season	Club	GP	G	A	Pts.
1968	Vancouver	12	0	0	0

LITT, STEVE   *Defender*
B. May 21, 1954   Carlisle, England
Ht. 5–11   Wt. 185
Citizen—England

Season	Club	GP	G	A	Pts.
1976	Minnesota	22	4	2	10
1977	Minnesota	25	3	3	9
1978	Minnesota	26	0	2	2
1979	Minnesota	29	3	4	10
	Totals	102	10	11	31

LIVERIC, MARK   *Forward*
B. Aug. 16, 1953   Zadar, Yugoslavia
Ht. 5–11   Wt. 175
Citizen—U.S.

Season	Club	GP	G	A	Pts.
1974	New York	18	2	3	7
1975	New York	21	5	5	15
1976	San Jose	20	10	9	29
1977	S.J.-Wash.	16	2	1	5
1978	Oakland	11	0	1	1
1979	Edm.-N.Y.	27	10	9	29
	Totals	113	29	28	86

LLEWELLYN, SAMMY   *Forward*
B. Dec. 24, 1951   Port of Spain, Trinidad
Ht. 5–8   Wt. 130
Citizen—Trinidad

Season	Club	GP	G	A	Pts.
1979	Los Angeles	4	0	0	0

LLOYD, BARRY   *Midfielder*
B. Feb. 19, 1949   Hillingdon, England
Ht. 5–8   Wt. 155
Citizen—England

Season	Club	GP	G	A	Pts.
1978	Houston	10	0	3	3

LOCHHEAD, ANDY   *Forward*
B. Minngie, Scotland
Ht. 6–1   Wt. 165

Season	Club	GP	G	A	Pts.
1974	Denver	20	2	1	5

LODEWEGES, DWIGHT   *Defender*
B. Oct. 26, 1957   Turner Valley, Canada
Ht. 5–10   Wt. 175
Citizen—Canada

Season	Club	GP	G	A	Pts.
1979	Edmonton	30	1	4	6

Season	Club	GP	G	A	Pts.

LOEHR, WILLIAM   *Midfielder*
Ht. 5–9   Wt. 170

Season	Club	GP	G	A	Pts.
1974	Baltimore	1	0	0	0

LOGUSH, TIM   *Forward*
B. Sept. 16, 1952   St. Louis, Mo.
Ht. 5–11   Wt. 165
Citizen—U.S.

1975	Seattle	4	0	0	0

LOMAS, DAN   *Defender*
B. Mar. 24, 1954   Victoria, Canada
Ht. 5–8   Wt. 157
Citizen—Canada

1976	Portland	4	0	0	0

LONARDO, ROBERTO   *Defender*
Ht. 5–10   Wt. 176

1971	Rochester	23	0	0	0
1972	Rochester	12	0	0	0
1973	Rochester	19	0	0	0
1974	Rochester	14	0	0	0
	Totals	68	0	0	0

LONG, STEVE   *Forward*
B. Apr. 23, 1957   Babonga, Zaire
Ht. 5–7   Wt. 145
Citizen—U.S.

1979	Chicago	12	1	1	3

LONGONI, GIUSEPPI   *Defender*
Ht. 5–10   Wt. 156

1967	Chi. (USA)	8	2	0	4

LOPARIC, STJEPAN   *Defender*
B. July 24, 1951   Zagreb, Yugoslavia
Ht. 6–0   Wt. 175
Citizen—Yugoslavia

1978	Toronto	28	0	1	1

LOPERA, ERNESTO
See *Goalkeeper*

LOPEZ, ARCHANEL   *Forward*
B. Sept. 18, 1941   La Plata, Argentina
Ht. 5–9   Wt. 160
Citizen—Argentina

1968	Baltimore	10	7	0	14

LOPEZ, BELISARIO   *Forward*
Ht. 5–8   Wt. 145
Citizen—Mexico

1976	Philadelphia	24	6	5	17

LOPEZ, JOSE   *Defender*
B. Apr. 25, 1951   Mexicali, Mexico
Ht. 5–10   Wt. 150
Citizen—U.S.

1968	San Diego	12	1	0	2
1974	Los Angeles	9	0	0	0
1975	Los Angeles	16	2	1	5
1976	Los Angeles	10	0	0	0
	Totals	47	3	1	7

LOPEZ, MIGUEL   *Defender*
B. Oct. 1, 1953   El Salvador
Ht. 5–9   Wt. 145
Citizen—U.S.

1976	Los Angeles	15	0	0	0

LOPEZ, OSCAR   *Forward*
B. Buenos Aires, Argentina
Ht. 5–6   Wt. 160
Citizen—Argentina

1967	Tor. (NPSL)	19	13	5	31
1968	Toronto	28	10	7	27
	Totals	47	23	12	58

LORD, MALCOLM   *Midfielder*
B. Oct. 25, 1946   Driffield, England
Ht. 5–8   Wt. 164
Citizen—England

1978	California	22	3	4	10

LORIMER, PETER   *Forward*
B. Dec. 4, 1946   Dundee, Scotland
Ht. 5–10   Wt. 170
Citizen—Scotland

1979	Toronto	29	9	13	31

LOVELL, STEVE   *Defender*
Ht. 5–11   Wt. 160
Citizen—Wales

1979	Memphis	18	0	3	3

LOWENSTEIN, MARK   *Defender*
B. Paterson, New Jersey
Ht. 5–6   Wt. 145
Citizen—U.S.

1976	Washington	3	0	0	0

LOWEY, JOHN   *Forward*
B. Mar. 7, 1958   Manchester, England
Ht. 6–0   Wt. 170
Citizen—England

1976	Chicago	17	5	7	17
1977	Chicago	5	0	0	0
	Totals	22	5	7	17

Season	Club	GP	G	A	Pts.

LUCIANO, ALADIM   *Forward*
Ht. 5-7   Wt. 147

1967	Houston	12	4	2	10

LUDWIG, ROBERT   *Forward*

1974	Philadelphia	7	0	0	0

LUGG, RAY   *Defender*
B. July 18, 1948   Durham, England
Ht. 5-9   Wt. 150
Citizen—England

1977	Ft. Lauderdale	24	0	3	3

LUKACEVIC, IVAN   *Forward*
B. Oct. 7, 1946   Yugoslavia
Ht. 6-0   Wt. 175
Citizen—Yugoslavia

1975	Toronto	10	8	2	18
1976	Toronto	8	3	1	7
1978	Toronto	17	16	5	37
1979	Toronto	20	12	7	31
	Totals	55	39	15	93

LUKIC, DUSAN   *Midfielder*
B. Dec. 13, 1948   Belgrade, Yugoslavia
Ht. 5-10   Wt. 165
Citizen—Yugoslavia

1978	S.J.-Tul.	26	3	2	8
1979	Philadelphia	29	6	12	24
	Totals	55	9	14	32

LUKIC, ILIJA   *Forward*
B. Yugoslavia
Ht. 5-9   Wt. 150
Citizen—Yugoslavia

1967	Oakland	2	2	0	4
1968	Oakland	12	0	0	0
	Totals	14	2	0	4

LUND, FLEMMING   *Midfielder*
B. Oct. 6, 1952   Copenhagen, Denmark
Ht. 5-7   Wt. 150
Citizen—Denmark

1979	Dallas	21	0	5	5

LUXBACHER, JOE   *Forward*
Ht. 6-0   Wt. 180

1974	Philadelphia	5	0	0	0

LYNCH, BARRY   *Defender*
B. June 8, 1951   Birmingham, England
Ht. 5-11   Wt. 175
Citizen—England

1971	Atlanta	21	8	1	17
1975	Portland	22	1	3	5
1976	Portland	16	1	1	3
	Totals	59	10	5	25

MAASSEN, LAMBERT   *Forward*
Ht. 6-1   Wt. 172

1967	San Francisco	4	3	1	7

MACA, ALAIN   *Defender*
B. Feb. 10, 1950   Brussels, Belgium
Ht. 6-2   Wt. 170
Citizen—U.S.

1972	Miami	10	0	0	0
1974	Washington	16	1	0	2
1975	Washington	11	0	0	0
1976	Washington	4	0	0	0
	Totals	41	1	0	2

MacDOUGALL, TED   *Forward*
B. Jan. 8, 1947   Inverness, Scotland
Ht. 5-11   Wt. 168
Citizen—Scotland

1979	Detroit	19	9	11	29

MacHATTIE, IAN   *Forward*
B. Scotland
Ht. 6-0   Wt. 160

1971	Toronto	22	8	5	21
1972	Toronto	9	2	1	5
	Totals	31	10	6	26

MACHIN, MEL   *Defender*
B. Newcastle-Under-Lyne, England
Ht. 5-10   Wt. 168
Citizen—England

1977	Seattle	19	0	2	2

MACIAS, LUCIANO   *Defender*
Ht. 5-10   Wt. 170

1972	Miami	10	0	0	0

MacKAIN, MARK   *Defender*
B. Mar. 10, 1961   Orlando, Fla.
Ht. 5-10   Wt. 160
Citizen—U.S.

1979	Atlanta	1	0	0	0

Season	Club	GP	G	A	Pts.

MACKAY, DONALD
See *Goalkeeper*

MACKAY, IKE   *Forward*
B. Aug. 2, 1948   Gabriola Island, Canada
Ht. 6-0   Wt. 170
Citizen—Canada

Season	Club	GP	G	A	Pts.
1968	Vancouver	8	2	0	4
1976	Portland	10	3	0	6
1977	Portland	17	1	0	2
1978	Portland	24	0	2	2
	Totals	59	6	2	14

MacKAY, JOHN   *Defender*
B. Dec. 15, 1957   Falkirk, Scotland
Ht. 5-9   Wt. 160
Citizen—Scotland

Season	Club	GP	G	A	Pts.
1979	Toronto	3	0	0	0

MACKEN, TONY   *Midfielder*
B. Dublin, Ireland
Ht. 5-9   Wt. 165
Citizen—Ireland

Season	Club	GP	G	A	Pts.
1976	Washington	21	5	6	16
1977	Wash.-Dal.	19	2	0	4
	Totals	40	7	6	20

MACRAE, KEITH
See *Goalkeeper*

MacWILLIAMS, DAVE   *Forward*
B. May 20, 1957   Philadelphia, Pa.
Ht. 5-9   Wt. 158
Citizen—U.S.

Season	Club	GP	G	A	Pts.
1979	Tampa Bay	6	1	0	2

MAGANA, RAUL
See *Goalkeeper*

MAGYAR, TIBOR   *Midfielder*
B. Feb. 27, 1941   Budapest, Hungary
Ht. 5-10   Wt. 157
Citizen—Australia

Season	Club	GP	G	A	Pts.
1968	Houston	25	1	1	3

MAHONEY, JOHN   *Forward*
Ht. 5-8   Wt. 154

Season	Club	GP	G	A	Pts.
1967	Cleveland	12	0	1	1

MAHONEY, MIKE
See *Goalkeeper*

MAHY, BARRY   *Defender*
B. Jan. 21, 1943   England
Ht. 5-8   Wt. 150
Citizen—England

Season	Club	GP	G	A	Pts.
1967	New York	18	8	2	18
1968	New York	15	0	0	0
1971	New York	24	2	5	9
1972	New York	11	0	1	1
1973	New York	10	0	0	0
1974	New York	19	0	1	1
1975	New York	15	1	1	3
	Totals	112	11	10	32

MAJEWSKI, RAY   *Midfielder*
B. Uruguay
Ht. 6-0   Wt. 165
Citizen—Uruguay

Season	Club	GP	G	A	Pts.
1968	Chicago	4	0	0	0

MAJOR, ERNST   *Defender*
B. Zagreb, Yugoslavia
Citizen—Yugoslavia

Season	Club	GP	G	A	Pts.
1975	Toronto	7	0	0	0

MAKOWSKI, GREG   *Defender*
B. July 5, 1956   St. Louis, Mo.
Ht. 5-11   Wt. 185
Citizen—U.S.

Season	Club	GP	G	A	Pts.
1978	Colorado	30	2	5	9
1979	Atlanta	29	3	6	12
	Totals	59	5	11	21

MALISZEWSKI, MIGUEL "MIKE"
B. Sept. 30, 1948   San Lorenzo, Argentina
Ht. 5-8   Wt. 150
Citizen—U.S.

Season	Club	GP	G	A	Pts.
1968	Baltimore	4	4	0	8

MALLENDER, KEN   *Defender*
Ht. 5-11   Wt. 170

Season	Club	GP	G	A	Pts.
1974	Miami	17	0	0	0

MAMELEDZIJA, ENES   *Forward*
B. Aug. 16, 1949   Yugoslavia
Ht. 6-2   Wt. 185
Citizen—Yugoslavia

Season	Club	GP	G	A	Pts.
1978	Chicago	6	0	0	0

MANACA, CARLOS ALBERTO   *Defender*

Season	Club	GP	G	A	Pts.
1975	Boston	5	0	3	3

MANAFA, TONY   *Midfielder*
B. Oct. 7, 1947   Guinea
Ht. 5-9   Wt. 165
Citizen—Portugal

Season	Club	GP	G	A	Pts.
1977	Rochester	12	0	1	1

MANCINI, TERRY   *Defender*
B. Oct. 4, 1944   London, England
Ht. 6-0   Wt. 170
Citizen—England

Season	Club	GP	G	A	Pts.
1977	Los Angeles	25	3	0	6

Season	Club	GP	G	A	Pts.

MANFREDI, NESTOR *Forward*
Ht. 5–8 Wt. 150

1967	N.Y. (NPSL)	7	6	2	14

MANNINO, PETER *Midfielder*
B. Apr. 11, 1955 Italy
Ht. 5–9 Wt. 155
Citizen—U.S.

1978	Philadelphia	6	0	0	0
1979	Philadelphia	24	0	4	4
	Totals	30	0	4	4

MANNOS, PETER
See *Goalkeeper*

MANZINI, GORDON *Defender*
B. Jan. 28, 1953 Vernon, Canada
Ht. 6–1 Wt. 175
Citizen—Canada

1979	Edmonton	3	0	0	0

MANZO, MANUEL *Midfielder*
B. Feb. 10, 1952 Mexico City, Mexico
Ht. 6–0 Wt. 172
Citizen—Mexico

1979	Houston	10	2	1	5

MARASCO, EDUARDO *Forward*
B. Feb. 22, 1953 Mar del Plata, Argentina
Ht. 5–7 Wt. 153
Citizen—Argentina

1978	Houston	17	3	1	7
1979	Houston	23	12	3	27
	Totals	40	15	4	34

MARCANTONIO, CARMINE *Midfielder*
B. Nov. 21, 1954 Castel del Sangro, Italy
Ht. 5–8 Wt. 150
Citizen—Canada

1976	Toronto	23	0	1	1
1978	Washington	23	0	0	0
1979	Washington	13	1	0	2
	Totals	59	1	1	3

MARCIO, JOSE *Forward*

1975	San Antonio	13	5	3	13

MARCON, LUIGI *Forward*
Ht. 5–10 Wt. 160

1971	Montreal	4	0	0	0

MARDARESCA, GIL *Midfielder*
Ht. 6–0 Wt. 163
Citizen—Romania

1975	Rochester	7	0	0	0

MARIA, MANOEL *Forward*
B. Feb. 29, 1948
Ht. 5–10 Wt. 140
Citizen—Brazil

1975	New York	12	0	0	0

MARIC BOZIDAR "BOZE" *Defender*
B. Dec. 13, 1942 Zagreb, Yugoslavia
Ht. 6–1 Wt. 165
Citizen—Yugoslavia

1968	Houston	10	0	0	0

MARIN, EDGAR *Forward*
B. San Jose, Costa Rica
Ht. 5–5 Wt. 135
Citizen—Costa Rica

1967	Oakland	19	8	3	19
1968	Oakland	20	4	0	8
	Totals	39	12	3	27

MARINHO (FRANCISCO CHAGAS MARINHO) *Midfielder*
B. Feb. 8, 1952 Natal, Rio Grande do Norte, Brazil
Ht. 5–9 Wt. 160
Citizen—Brazil

1979	New York	24	8	8	24

MARKOVIC, MIKE
B. Yugoslavia

1968	St. Louis	1	0	0	0

MARKUS, DOV *Forward*
B. Jan. 31, 1946 Donbas, USSR
Ht. 5–8 Wt. 150
Citizen—U.S.

1968	New York	1	0	0	0

MAROTTE, LUIS *Midfielder*
B. Oct. 14, 1944 Montevideo, Uruguay
Ht. 5–6 Wt. 148
Citizen—Uruguay

1974	Los Angeles	19	4	4	12
1975	San Antonio	20	2	1	5
	Totals	39	6	5	17

MARQUEZ, RICARDO *Forward*
Ht. 5–8 Wt. 150
Citizen—Mexico

1976	Philadelphia	4	2	1	5

MARSH, JOHN *Defender*
B. May 31, 1948 Stoke, England
Ht. 5–1 Wt. 175
Citizen—England

1976	Los Angeles	15	1	2	4

Season	Club	GP	G	A	Pts.

MARSH, RODNEY *Forward*
B. Oct. 11, 1944 London, England
Ht. 6-1 Wt. 185
Citizen—England

Season	Club	GP	G	A	Pts.
1976	Tampa Bay	21	11	9	31
1977	Tampa Bay	24	8	11	27
1978	Tampa Bay	26	18	16	52
1979	Tampa Bay	23	11	14	36
	Totals	94	48	50	146

MARSHALL, CLIFF *Forward*
Ht. 5-10 Wt. 160
Citizen—England

Season	Club	GP	G	A	Pts.
1976	Miami	16	5	2	12

MARTIN, ERIC
See *Goalkeeper*

MARTIN, NEIL *Forward*
Ht. 6-0 Wt. 168

Season	Club	GP	G	A	Pts.
1967	Vancouver	11	1	1	3

MARTIN, RAY *Defender*
B. Jan. 23, 1945 Wolverhampton, England
Ht. 5-9 Wt. 155
Citizen—England

Season	Club	GP	G	A	Pts.
1975	Portland	16	0	0	0
1976	Portland	22	0	0	0
1977	Portland	24	0	2	2
	Totals	62	0	2	2

MARTINEZ, PEDRO *Midfielder*
B. Feb. 21, 1948 Mexico
Ht. 5-8 Wt. 163
Citizen—Mexico

Season	Club	GP	G	A	Pts.
1974	Los Angeles	15	0	0	0
1975	San Antonio	18	0	1	1
	Totals	33	0	1	1

MARTINI, LUIGI *Defender*
B. June 15, 1949 Capannori Lucca, Italy
Ht. 5-11 Wt. 175
Citizen—Italy

Season	Club	GP	G	A	Pts.
1979	Chicago	7	0	3	3

MARTINOVIC, RADI *Defender*
B. Apr. 21, 1949 Madenovac, Yugoslavia
Ht. 5-10 Wt. 162
Citizen—Yugoslavia

Season	Club	GP	G	A	Pts.
1979	Philadelphia	25	0	0	0

MARTIRINA, OSCAR *Forward*
Ht. 5-9 Wt. 158

Season	Club	GP	G	A	Pts.
1967	N.Y. (U.S.)	12	2	1	5

MAS, LUIS *Midfielder*
B. Sept. 18, 1944 San Martin, Argentina
Ht. 5-5 Wt. 140
Citizen—Argentina

Season	Club	GP	G	A	Pts.
1967	N.Y. (NPSL)	19	0	0	0
1968	New York	14	1	0	2
	Totals	33	1	0	2

MASCALITO, LUIGI *Defender*
Ht. 6-2 Wt. 181

Season	Club	GP	G	A	Pts.
1972	Montreal	8	1	0	2

MASEKO, ANDRIES *Forward*
B. Dec. 25, 1953 Transvaal, S. Africa
Ht. 5-9 Wt. 155
Citizen—S. Africa

Season	Club	GP	G	A	Pts.
1978	Washington	12	0	2	2
1979	Washington	9	1	1	3
	Totals	21	1	3	5

MASNIK, JUAN *Defender*
B. Mar. 2, 1943
Ht. 6-0 Wt. 157
Citizen—Uruguay

Season	Club	GP	G	A	Pts.
1975	New York	6	0	0	0

MASON, JOHN *Midfielder*
B. June 24, 1953 Scotland
Ht. 5-8 Wt. 150
Citizen—U.S.

Season	Club	GP	G	A	Pts.
1975	Los Angeles	8	0	2	2
1976	Los Angeles	19	6	2	14
1977	Los Angeles	12	2	0	4
	Totals	39	8	4	20

MATA, PAULO *Forward*
B. July 16, 1946 Bahia, Brazil
Ht. 5-10 Wt. 170
Citizen—Brazil

Season	Club	GP	G	A	Pts.
1979	Toronto	3	1	0	2

MATA, RONALD *Midfielder*
B. Costa Rica
Ht. 5-6 Wt. 155

Season	Club	GP	G	A	Pts.
1967	L.A. (NPSL)	11	0	1	1

MATAS, BORIS *Forward*
B. Sept. 1, 1957 Dakovo, Yugoslavia
Ht. 5-7 Wt. 150
Citizen—Yugoslavia

Season	Club	GP	G	A	Pts.
1978	Toronto	1	1	1	3

MATE, ANDREW *Forward*
B. Mar. 19, 1940 Budapest, Hungary
Ht. 5-11 Wt. 160

Season	Club	GP	G	A	Pts.
1971	New York	2	2	3	7

Season	Club	GP	G	A	Pts.

MATEOS, ENRIQUE *Forward*
B. Spain
Ht. 5-10 Wt. 150
Citizen—Spain

Season	Club	GP	G	A	Pts.
1968	Cleveland	31	16	0	32

MATEUS, MARIO SILVA *Forward*
B. Sept. 30, 1953 Lisbon, Portugal
Ht. 5-7 Wt. 150
Citizen—Portugal

Season	Club	GP	G	A	Pts.
1979	Toronto	3	0	0	0

MATOS, MANNY *Midfielder*
Ht. 5-11 Wt. 165
Citizen—Portugal

Season	Club	GP	G	A	Pts.
1975	Philadelphia	16	1	1	3
1976	Philadelphia	4	0	1	1
	Totals	20	1	2	4

MATOS, MANNY *Defender*
B. May 9, 1953 Mineola, New York
Ht. 5-9 Wt. 160
Citizen—U.S.

Season	Club	GP	G	A	Pts.
1975	Seattle	2	0	0	0
1976	Seattle	11	0	0	0
1977	Seattle	1	0	0	0
1978	Seattle	15	0	0	0
	Totals	29	0	0	0

MATTESON, BOB *Defender*
B. June 2, 1952 St. Louis, Missouri
Ht. 6-0 Wt. 170
Citizen—U.S.

Season	Club	GP	G	A	Pts.
1974	St. Louis	9	1	0	2
1975	St. Louis	20	0	2	2
1976	St. Louis	21	0	1	1
1977	St. Louis	19	1	1	3
	Totals	69	2	4	8

MAURO, ROBERTO *Forward*
B. Brazil
Ht. 5-8 Wt. 155
Citizen—Brazil

Season	Club	GP	G	A	Pts.
1968	Washington	9	4	0	8

MAUSSER, ARNOLD
See *Goalkeeper*

MAY, EDDIE *Defender*
B. May 19, 1945 London, England
Ht. 6-3 Wt. 175
Citizen—England

Season	Club	GP	G	A	Pts.
1975	Chicago	18	7	3	17

MAY, JIM
See *Goalkeeper*

MAY, LARRY *Defender*
B. Dec. 28, 1958 Birmingham, England
Ht. 6-1 Wt. 175
Citizen—England

Season	Club	GP	G	A	Pts.
1978	New England	4	0	0	0

MAYER, ALAN
See *Goalkeeper*

MAYER, JOHN *Forward*
B. June 29, 1955 Unz, Austria
Ht. 5-8 Wt. 155
Citizen—U.S.

Season	Club	GP	G	A	Pts.
1977	Minnesota	2	0	0	0

MAYER, RUDI *Midfielder*
B. Sept. 23, 1949 Linz, Austria
Ht. 5-10 Wt. 170
Citizen—U.S.

Season	Club	GP	G	A	Pts.
1976	Chicago	7	1	0	2

MAYORAL, LUIS *Midfielder*
B. Aug. 10, 1947 Madrid, Spain
Ht. 6-0 Wt. 155
Citizen—Spain

Season	Club	GP	G	A	Pts.
1967	Baltimore	5	1	0	2
1968	Boston	3	0	0	0
	Totals	8	1	0	2

McALINDEN, BOB *Forward*
B. May 22, 1946 Manchester, England
Ht. 5-7 Wt. 140
Citizen—England

Season	Club	GP	G	A	Pts.
1976	Los Angeles	23	3	5	11
1977	Los Angeles	25	2	6	10
1978	Los Angeles	29	4	5	13
1979	Memphis	14	1	2	4
	Totals	91	10	18	38

McALISTER, JIM *Defender*
B. Apr. 5, 1957 Seattle, Wash.
Ht. 5-8 Wt. 140
Citizen—U.S.

Season	Club	GP	G	A	Pts.
1976	Seattle	2	0	0	0
1977	Seattle	22	0	0	0
1978	Seattle	29	1	1	3
1979	Seattle	19	1	1	3
	Totals	72	2	2	6

McALLISTER, DON *Defender*
B. May 26, 1953 Manchester, England
Ht. 5-10 Wt. 160
Citizen—England

Season	Club	GP	G	A	Pts.
1977	Washington	25	0	1	1

Season	Club	GP	G	A	Pts.

McANDREW, TONY *Midfielder*
B. Apr. 11, 1956 Glasgow, Scotland
Ht. 5-10 Wt. 166
Citizen—Scotland

Season	Club	GP	G	A	Pts.
1976	Vancouver	21	6	1	13

McBRIDE, ANDY *Defender*
B. Mar. 15, 1954 Nakuru, Kenya
Ht. 6-2 Wt. 179
Citizen—England

Season	Club	GP	G	A	Pts.
1978	California	17	1	0	2
1979	California	22	1	1	3
	Totals	39	2	1	5

McBRIDE, PAT *Midfielder*
B. Nov. 13, 1943 St. Louis, Mo.
Ht. 5-9 Wt. 155
Citizen—U.S.

Season	Club	GP	G	A	Pts.
1967	St. Louis	20	1	4	6
1968	St. Louis	27	2	0	4
1969	St. Louis	10	2	2	6
1970	St. Louis	21	9	1	19
1971	St. Louis	22	7	4	18
1972	St. Louis	14	1	4	6
1973	St. Louis	19	2	3	7
1974	St. Louis	20	4	3	11
1975	St. Louis	15	1	3	5
1976	St. Louis	21	2	2	6
	Totals	189	31	26	88

McCALL, ALEX *Forward*
B. Scotland
Ht. 5-6 Wt. 140
Citizen—Scotland

Season	Club	GP	G	A	Pts.
1968	Kansas City	8	1	0	2

McCALL, WALKER *Forward*
B. Mar. 29, 1954 Irvin, Scotland
Ht. 6-3 Wt. 190
Citizen—Scotland

Season	Club	GP	G	A	Pts.
1978	San Diego	19	11	7	29
1979	San Diego	17	6	4	16
	Totals	36	17	11	45

McCALLIOG, JIM *Midfielder*
B. 1948 Glasgow, Scotland
Ht. 5-9 Wt. 155
Citizen—Scotland

Season	Club	GP	G	A	Pts.
1977	Chicago	19	0	6	6

McCONVILLE, TOM *Defender*
B. Dundalk, Ireland
Ht. 5-11 Wt. 170
Citizen—Ireland

Season	Club	GP	G	A	Pts.
1974	Washington	18	0	3	3
1975	Washington	18	0	0	0
1976	Washington	21	1	2	4
	Totals	57	1	5	7

McCRUDDEN, DAN *Forward*
B. Dec. 25, 1955 Queens, New York
Ht. 6-3 Wt. 180
Citizen—U.S.

Season	Club	GP	G	A	Pts.
1978	Chicago	13	0	0	0

McCRUDDEN, JOHN *Midfield*

Season	Club	GP	G	A	Pts.
1976	Boston	1	0	0	0

McCULLOCH, ANDY *Forward*
Ht. 6-2 Wt. 180
Citizen—England

Season	Club	GP	G	A	Pts.
1978	Oakland	18	3	1	7

McCULLY, CHARLIE *Defender*
B. Motherwell, Scotland
Ht. 6-0 Wt. 180
Citizen—U.S.

Season	Club	GP	G	A	Pts.
1968	Boston	5	0	0	0
1971	New York	24	6	3	15
1972	New York	7	0	1	1
1973	New York	3	0	0	0
1975	Hartford	20	4	2	10
	Totals	59	10	6	26

McCULLY, HENRY *Forward*
B. Apr, 30, 1948 Motherwell, Scotland
Ht. 6-0 Wt. 175
Citizen—U.S.

Season	Club	GP	G	A	Pts.
1973	New York	5	0	0	0
1975	Hartford	16	2	2	6
1976	Hartford	21	4	4	12
1977	Connecticut	17	0	1	1
1978	Memphis	26	8	3	19
1979	Memphis	23	1	1	3
	Totals	108	15	11	41

McCURDY, COLIN *Forward*
B. July 18, 1954 Belfast, N. Ireland
Ht. 6-0 Wt. 161
Citizen—N. Ireland

Season	Club	GP	G	A	Pts.
1978	Philadelphia	19	7	2	16

McDONALD, JIM *Defender*
B. May 3, 1954
Ht. 5-10 Wt. 180
Citizen—Canada

Season	Club	GP	G	A	Pts.
1973	Toronto	4	0	0	0

McDONALD, KEN *Defender*
B. Scotland
Ht. 5-9 Wt. 158
Citizen—Scotland

Season	Club	GP	G	A	Pts.
1968	Detroit	16	0	0	0

Season	Club	GP	G	A	Pts.

McDONALD, KEN   *Defender*
B. Sept. 26, 1957   Philadelphia, Pa.
Ht. 6-3   Wt. 190
Citizen—U.S.

1979	San Jose	1	0	0	0

McDONNELL, PETER
See *Goalkeeper*

McGILL, JIM   *Midfielder*
B. Nov. 27, 1946   Glasgow, Scotland
Ht. 5-8   Wt. 154
Citizen—Scotland

1976	San Diego	20	0	1	1

McGRANE, JOHN   *Forward*
B. Oct. 12, 1953   Glasgow, Scotland
Ht. 5-9   Wt. 160
Citizen—Canada

1977	Los Angeles	15	0	0	0
1978	Los Angeles	30	2	2	6
1979	Los Angeles	28	0	0	0
	Totals	73	2	2	6

McGRAW, ALAN   *Forward*
Ht. 5-10   Wt. 149

1967	Tor. (U.S.)	11	1	1	3

McGUIRE, MIKE   *Midfielder*
B. Sept. 4, 1952   Blackpool, England
Ht. 5-8   Wt. 140
Citizen—England

1978	Tampa Bay	25	2	0	4

McINTOSH, WILLIAM   *Forward*
B. July 30, 1939   Loanhead, Scotland
Ht. 5-8   Wt. 145
Citizen—Scotland

1968	Atlanta	22	3	0	6

McKECHNIE, IAN
See *Goalkeeper*

McKENZIE, ALTAMONT "ALTIE"   *Defender*
B. Mar. 5, 1951   Kingston, Jamaica
Ht. 5-7   Wt. 153

1975	Dallas	21	3	0	6

McKEOWN, GREG   *Forward*
B. 1957
Ht. 6-0   Wt. 165
Citizen—U.S.

1977	San Jose	2	0	0	0

McKEOWN, JEFF   *Forward*

1971	Washington	3	0	0	0

McKEOWN, JIM   *Defender*
B. Mar. 6, 1956   Trenton, New Jersey
Ht. 5-11   Wt. 160
Citizen—U.S.

1978	Tulsa	16	0	3	3
1979	Philadelphia	5	0	0	0
	Totals	21	0	3	3

McKERNAN, JOHN   *Defender*
B. Glasgow, Scotland
Ht. 5-8   Wt. 165

1975	San Antonio	20	0	1	1

McLAREN, THOMAS   *Midfielder*
Ht. 5-9   Wt. 156

1975	Portland	20	1	1	3

McLAUGHLIN, JOHN   *Midfielder*
B. Feb. 25, 1942   Liverpool, England
Ht. 5-9   Wt. 145
Citizen—England

1975	Philadelphia	22	7	4	18
1976	Dallas	5	0	0	0
	Totals	27	7	4	18

McLAUGHLIN, JOHN   *Defender*
B. Jan. 3, 1948   Stirling, Scotland
Ht. 5-6   Wt. 136
Citizen—England

1976	Seattle	19	0	0	0

McLEAN, GEORGE   *Forward*
B. 1944   Scotland
Ht. 6-0   Wt. 175
Citizen—England

1974	Vancouver	19	5	5	15

McLEAN, LLOYD   *Forward*
B. Aug. 24, 1947   Kingston, Jamaica
Ht. 5-6   Wt. 140

1968	Boston	4	0	0	0

McLENAGHEN, MIKE   *Defender*
B. June 10, 1954   Burnaby, Canada
Ht. 5-10   Wt. 155
Citizen—Canada

1979	Minnesota	20	0	4	4

McLEOD, WES   *Midfielder*
B. Oct. 24, 1957   Vancouver, Canada
Ht. 5-8   Wt. 149
Citizen—Canada

1977	Tampa Bay	20	1	5	7
1978	Tampa Bay	29	5	5	15
1979	Tampa Bay	30	5	9	19
	Totals	79	11	19	41

Season	Club	GP	G	A	Pts.

McLOCKLAN, COLIN *Forward*
B. Apr. 6, 1952
Ht. 6-0 Wt. 175
Citizen—England

Season	Club	GP	G	A	Pts.
1977	Connecticut	4	1	1	3
1978	Chicago	7	1	0	2
	Totals	11	2	1	5

McLOUGHLIN, ANTHONY *Forwqrd*
B. Sept. 24, 1946 Liverpool, England
Ht. 5-11 Wt. 173

1971	Dallas	15	6	2	14

McLOUGHLIN, JIM *Defender*
B. May 2, 1957 England
Ht. 6-1 Wt. 165
Citizen—Canada

1979	Rochester	12	0	0	0

McMAHON, PAT *Midfielder*
B. Sept. 19, 1945 Croy, Scotland
Ht. 5-11 Wt. 160
Citizen—Scotland

1976	Portland	18	1	2	4
1977	Portland	23	1	0	2
1978	Colorado	26	0	1	1
1979	Atlanta	22	0	1	1
	Totals	89	2	4	8

McMANUS, JACK *Defender*
Ht. 5-11 Wt. 178

1974	Boston	18	1	0	2

McMILLAN, DOUGLAS *Forward*
B. Oct. 14, 1944
Ht. 5-7 Wt. 140
Citizen—U.S.

1974	Los Angeles	20	10	10	30
1975	Los Angeles	14	1	1	3
	Totals	34	11	11	33

McNAB, ALLIE *Forward*
B. Montego Bay, Jamaica
Ht. 5-11 Wt. 147
Citizen—Jamaica

1967	St. Louis	5	1	2	4

McNAB, BOB *Defender*
B. July 20, 1944 London, England
Ht. 5-8 Wt. 155
Citizen—England

1976	San Antonio	11	1	1	3
1979	Vancouver	2	0	0	0
	Totals	13	1	1	3

McNEILL, BRIAN *Defender*
B. Apr. 1, 1956 Newcastle, England
Ht. 5-9 Wt. 165
Citizen—England

1978	Portland	27	1	1	3

McPARLAND, PETER *Forward*
B. Apr. 25, 1934 Newry, Ireland
Ht. 5-11 Wt. 174
Citizen—England

1967	Atlanta	11	5	8	18
1968	Atlanta	19	7	—	14
	Totals	30	12	8	32

McPHEE, IAN *Midfielder*
B. Scotland
Ht. 6-0 Wt. 160
Citizen—Canada

1973	Toronto	19	0	5	5
1974	Toronto	18	3	1	7
1975	Toronto	11	0	0	0
	Totals	48	3	6	12

McTAVISH, CRESWELL *Forward*

1975	San Antonio	11	2	0	4

McVIE, WILLIE *Defender*
B. Apr. 7, 1950 Lark Hall, Scotland
Ht. 6-1 Wt. 188
Citizen—Scotland

1979	Toronto	25	0	1	1

MEDEIROS, ANTONIO *Midfielder*
B. Portugal
Ht. 5-11 Wt. 170
Citizen—U.S.

1971	Toronto	9	1	0	2
1972	Toronto	13	1	1	3
1973	Toronto	5	0	0	0
	Totals	27	2	1	5

MEDINA, VICTOR *Midfielder*
Ht. 5-8 Wt. 148
Citizen—Mexico

1976	Philadelphia	21	0	0	0

MEEHL, LEW *Midfielder*
B. Philadelphia, Pa.
Ht. 5-8 Wt. 165
Citizen—U.S.

1973	Philadelphia	11	0	0	0
1974	Philadelphia	5	0	1	1
	Totals	16	0	1	1

Season	Club	GP	G	A	Pts.

MEGALOUDIS, NICKY *Defender*
B. Sept. 24, 1957 New York, N.Y.
Ht. 6-0 Wt. 170
Citizen—U.S.

Season	Club	GP	G	A	Pts.
1978	Houston	27	0	1	1
1979	Houston	12	0	3	3
	Totals	39	0	4	4

MEGRAW, ROBIN *Defender*
B. Aug. 9, 1950 Liverpool, England
Ht. 5-11 Wt. 155
Citizen—Canada

Season	Club	GP	G	A	Pts.
1977	Toronto	4	0	0	0
1979	Toronto	1	0	0	0
	Totals	5	0	0	0

MELLA, RON
See *Goalkeeper*

MELLEDEW, STEVEN *Midfielder*

Season	Club	GP	G	A	Pts.
1975	Boston	22	6	5	17

MELROSE, HARRY *Forward*
Ht. 5-7 Wt. 150

Season	Club	GP	G	A	Pts.
1967	Washington	5	0	1	1

MENDEZ, CALIXTO *Defender*
B. Dec. 10, 1938 Las Palmas, Spain
Ht. 5-10 Wt. 160
Citizen—Spain

Season	Club	GP	G	A	Pts.
1968	Baltimore	19	1	0	2

MENDOZA, MANUEL *Forward*
B. Portugal
Ht. 5-9 Wt. 165
Citizen—Portugal

Season	Club	GP	G	A	Pts.
1968	Cleveland	23	10	0	20

MENOTTI, LUIS *Forward*
B. Nov. 5, 1938 Rosario, Argentina
Ht. 6-1 Wt. 175
Citizen—Argentina

Season	Club	GP	G	A	Pts.
1967	N.Y.(NPSL)	12	4	3	11
1968	New York	11	5	0	10
	Totals	23	9	3	21

MERAYO, JACINTO *Forward*
B. Argentina
Ht. 5-6 Wt. 160
Citizen—Argentina

Season	Club	GP	G	A	Pts.
1968	Houston	15	4	4	12

MERRICK, ALAN *Defender*
B. June 20, 1950 Birmingham, England
Ht. 5-10 Wt. 160
Citizen—England

Season	Club	GP	G	A	Pts.
1976	Minnesota	24	1	1	3
1977	Minnesota	26	0	5	5
1978	Minnesota	26	0	4	4
1979	Minnesota	27	3	7	13
	Totals	103	4	17	25

MESKOVIC, GORAN *Forward*
B. Oct. 13, 1949 Yugoslavia
Ht. 6-0 Wt. 185
Citizen—Yugoslavia

Season	Club	GP	G	A	Pts.
1978	Chicago	8	1	2	4

MESSING, BERND *Forward*
B. Germany
Ht. 5-8 Wt. 160
Citizen—Germany

Season	Club	GP	G	A	Pts.
1968	Cleveland	8	0	0	0

MESSING, SHEP
See *Goalkeeper*

MESTRE, JULIO AMADOR *Forward*

Season	Club	GP	G	A	Pts.
1971	Toronto	10	1	1	3

MESZAROS, MIHALJ *Forward*
B. Tuzla, Yugoslavia
Ht. 5-9 Wt. 165
Citizen—Yugoslavia

Season	Club	GP	G	A	Pts.
1967	L.A.(NPSL)	16	3	4	10

METCHICK, DAVE *Midfielder*
B. Aug. 14, 1943 Derbyshire, England
Ht. 5-7 Wt. 140
Citizen—England

Season	Club	GP	G	A	Pts.
1970	Atlanta	20	8	6	22
1971	Atlanta	8	3	0	6
1972	Miami	9	0	1	1
1973	Atlanta	18	2	3	7
	Totals	55	13	10	36

METIDIERI, CARLOS "TOPOLINO" *Forward*
B. Dec. 18, 1942 Sorocaba, Brazil
Ht. 5-4 Wt. 150
Citizen—Brazil

Season	Club	GP	G	A	Pts.
1967	Boston	—	—	—	—
1968	Los Angeles	32	16	5	37
1970	Rochester	22	14	7	35
1971	Rochester	24	19	8	46
1972	Rochester	12	5	1	11
1973	Rochester	19	2	4	8
1974	Boston	20	5	3	13
	Totals	129	61	28	150

Season	Club	GP	G	A	Pts.

METIDIERI, GILSON   *Forward*
B. Brazil
Ht. 5–4   Wt. 140
Citizen—Brazil

Season	Club	GP	G	A	Pts.
1967	Boston	—	—	—	—
1968	Los Angeles	14	4	0	8
	Totals	14	4	0	8

MEYER, HORST   *Midfielder*
B. Sept. 28, 1937   Germany
Ht. 5–6   Wt. 150

1971	New York	10	0	0	0

MFUM, WILBERFORCE   *Forward*
B. Aug. 28, 1936   Ghana
Ht. 5–10   Wt. 170
Citizen—Ghana

1968	Baltimore	4	2	0	4
1971	New York	19	6	1	13
1972	New York	10	5	1	11
	Totals	33	13	2	28

MICHALLIK, KRYSTIAN   *Midfielder*
B. May 13, 1944   Chorzow, Poland
Ht. 6–1   Wt. 170
Citizen—Poland

1976	Hartford	9	0	0	0

MICHIA, JUAN CARLOS   *Forward*
B. Mar. 3, 1956   Sarandi, Argentina
Ht. 5–7   Wt. 150
Citizen—Argentina

1979	Houston	23	3	0	6

MICHNIEWSKI, JAN
See *Goalkeeper*

MICKELWRIGHT, JOHN   *Forward*

1975	San Antonio	1	0	0	0

MIELKE, HANS-PETER   *Midfielder*
B. Nov. 30, 1951   Golsen, Germany
Ht. 6–2   Wt. 180
Citizen—Germany

1978	San Deigo	9	0	1	1

MIFFLIN, RAMON   *Midfielder*
B. Apr. 5, 1947   Lima, Peru
Ht. 5–9   Wt. 160
Citizen—Peru

1976	New York	15	6	6	18
1977	New York	23	1	0	2
1978	Los Angeles	6	0	0	0
	Totals	44	7	6	20

MIGUEL, JORGE   *Defender*
B. Nov. 3, 1943   Votorantim, Brazil
Ht. 5–10   Wt. 145
Citizen—Brazil

1968	Boston	13	0	0	0

MIGUELUCCI, OSMAR
See *Goalkeeper*

MIHAILOVICH, ANE   *Midfielder*
B. Nov. 16, 1951   Yugoslavia
Ht. 5–9   Wt. 155
Citizen—U.S.

1977	Los Angeles	12	2	0	4
1978	L.A.-Wash.	20	0	1	1
1979	Washington	10	0	1	1
	Totals	42	2	2	6

MIJATOVIC, NIKOLA   *Defender*
B. May 17, 1947   Yugoslavia
Ht. 6–0   Wt. 180
Citizen—Yugoslavia

1976	Rochester	24	1	0	2
1977	Rochester	18	0	1	1
1978	Rochester	30	0	0	0
1979	Rochester	29	0	2	2
	Totals	101	1	3	5

MIKE-MAYER, MIKLOS   *Forward*
B. Italy
Ht. 5–8   Wt. 147
Citizen—Italy

1968	Washington	1	0	0	0

MILANOVIC, MIRO   *Defender*
B. Yugoslavia
Ht. 5–6   Wt. 155
Citizen—Yugoslavia

1968	L.A.(NPSL)	—	—	—	—
1968	San Deigo	20	1	0	2
	Totals	20	1	0	2

MILICEVIC, TOM   *Defender*
B. Yugoslavia
Ht. 5–10   Wt. 145
Citizen—Yugoslavia

1968	Chicago	14	0	0	0

MILLAR, TOMMY   *Defender*
Ht. 5–7   Wt. 155

1967	Dallas	10	0	0	0

Season	Club	GP	G	A	Pts.

MILLER, BRUCE   *Forward*
B. May 23, 1957   Vancouver, Canada
Ht. 5–9   Wt. 165
Citizen—Canada

Season	Club	GP	G	A	Pts.
1975	Seattle	1	0	0	0
1978	Seattle	6	1	0	2
1979	Seattle	13	1	0	2
	Totals	20	2	0	4

MILLER, JIM
See *Goalkeeper*

MILLINDER, JIM   *Midfielder*
B. Nov. 27, 1958   Salina, Kansas
Ht. 5–8   Wt. 150
Citizen—U.S.

Season	Club	GP	G	A	Pts.
1979	Los Angeles	4	0	1	1

MILLS, STEVE   *Defender*
B. Dec. 9, 1953   Portsmouth, England
Ht. 5–10   Wt. 156
Citizen—England

Season	Club	GP	G	A	Pts.
1976	Miami	12	0	0	0

MILNER, JOHN   *Defender*
B. May 14, 1942   Huddersfield, England
Ht. 5–9   Wt. 159
Citizen—England

Season	Club	GP	G	A	Pts.
1968	Boston	15	2	0	4
1974	Denver	1	0	0	0
	Totals	16	2	0	4

MILOSEVIC, SELIMIR   *Forward*
B. Sabac, Yugoslavia
Ht. 6–0   Wt. 167
Citizen—Yugoslavia

Season	Club	GP	G	A	Pts.
1967	Oakland	12	12	0	24
1968	Oakland	19	16	0	32
	Totals	31	28	0	56

MILTON   *Forward*
B. Aug. 1, 1957   Santos, Brazil
Ht. 6–1   Wt. 170
Citizen—Brazil

Season	Club	GP	G	A	Pts.
1979	Dallas	16	8	1	17

MINNOCK, JOHN   *Midfielder*
B. Nov. 12, 1949   Tullamore, Ireland
Ht. 5–9   Wt. 162
Citizen—Ireland

Season	Club	GP	G	A	Pts.
1976	San Diego	14	1	0	2

MINOR, KARL   *Forward*
B. Heilbron, W. Germany
Ht. 6–0   Wt. 175
Citizen—Australia

Season	Club	GP	G	A	Pts.
1973	Washington	16	4	4	12
1974	Washington	20	3	2	8
1975	Washington	19	2	1	5
	Totals	55	9	7	25

MINTON, ROGER   *Defender*
B. Staffordshire, England
Ht. 5–9   Wt. 160
Citizen—England

Season	Club	GP	G	A	Pts.
1975	Washington	12	0	0	0
1976	Washington	22	0	1	1
	Totals	34	0	1	1

MIRANDA, ANTONIO   *Defender*
B. Portugal
Ht. 5–8   Wt. 145

Season	Club	GP	G	A	Pts.
1971	Montreal	23	0	1	1
1972	Montreal	5	0	0	1
	Totals	28	0	1	1

MIRANDINHA (SEBASTIO MIRANDA DA SILVA FILHO)
Forward
B. Feb. 26, 1952   Sao Paulo, Brazil
Ht. 5–10   Wt. 160
Citizen—Brazil

Season	Club	GP	G	A	Pts.
1978	Tampa Bay	14	1	3	5
1979	T.B.-Mem.	18	7	5	19
	Totals	32	8	8	26

MISHALOW, BILL
See *Goalkeeper*

MISHALOW, GENE   *Defender*
B. Aug. 10, 1953   Chicago, Ill.
Ht. 5–8   Wt. 150
Citizen—U.S.

Season	Club	GP	G	A	Pts.
1977	Washington	4	0	0	0

MISSEY, KEVIN   *Midfielder*
Ht. 5–8   Wt. 175
Citizen—U.S.

Season	Club	GP	G	A	Pts.
1976	San Antonio	1	0	0	0

MITCHELL, BARRIE   *Midfielder*
B. 1947   Aberdeen, Scotland
Ht. 6–0   Wt. 160
Citizen—Scotland

Season	Club	GP	G	A	Pts.
1975	Vancouver	18	5	4	14
1976	Vancouver	8	0	1	1
	Totals	26	5	5	15

Season	Club	GP	G	A	Pts.

MITCHELL, CHARLIE *Defender*
B. May 18, 1948 Paisley, Scotland
Ht. 5–10 Wt. 160
Citizen—U.S.

Season	Club	GP	G	A	Pts.
1970	Rochester	24	2	0	0
1971	Rochester	23	1	2	4
1972	Rochester	14	2	0	4
1973	Rochester	18	0	3	3
1974	Rochester	20	0	4	4
1975	Rochester	22	0	1	1
1976	New York	7	0	1	1
1977	Hawaii	23	0	1	1
1978	Tulsa	25	0	5	5
1979	Toronto	30	0	2	2
	Totals	206	5	19	29

MITCHELL, DALE *Midfielder*
B. Apr. 21, 1958 Vancouver, Canada
Ht. 6–0 Wt. 160
Citizen—Canada

Season	Club	GP	G	A	Pts.
1977	Vancouver	1	0	0	0
1978	Vancouver	4	0	0	0
1979	Portland	12	5	2	12
	Totals	17	5	2	12

MITCHELL, KEN *Forward*
B. Sunderland, England
Ht. 6–0 Wt. 170
Citizen—England

Season	Club	GP	G	A	Pts.
1978	Tulsa	3	0	0	0

MITIC, ILIJA *Midfielder*
B. July 19, 1940 Belgrade, Yugoslavia
Ht. 5–10 Wt. 163
Citizen—Yugoslavia

Season	Club	GP	G	A	Pts.
1963	Oakland	19	13	3	29
1968	Oakland	28	18	12	48
1969	Dallas	12	11	4	26
197	Dallas	18	12	1	25
1974	Dallas	19	10	1	21
1975	Dal.-S.J.	19	15	3	33
1976	San Jose	24	14	9	37
1977	San Jose	11	3	1	7
1978	San Jose	16	5	3	13
	Totals	166	101	37	239

MITROVIC, RADI *Forward*
B. Nov. 2, 1940 Yugoslavia
Ht. 5–10 Wt. 170
Citizen—Yugoslavia

Season	Club	GP	G	A	Pts.
1971	New York	11	4	2	10

MOFFAT, ANGUS *Forward*
B. May 15, 1948 Carluke, Scotland
Ht. 5–7 Wt. 140
Citizen—Canada

Season	Club	GP	G	A	Pts.
1968	Detroit	12	2	0	4
1971	Toronto	24	1	6	8
1972	Toronto	14	1	2	4

Season	Club	GP	G	A	Pts.
1978	Detroit	27	1	6	8
1979	Detroit	28	0	8	8
	Totals	105	5	22	32

MOFFAT, ROBERT *Defender*
B. Oct. 7, 1945 Portsmouth, England
Ht. 5–11 Wt. 165
Citizen—England

Season	Club	GP	G	A	Pts.
1970	Dallas	24	8	3	19
1971	Dallas	12	1	2	4
1972	Dallas	14	0	2	2
1973	Dallas	13	0	1	1
1974	Dallas	20	1	1	3
1975	Dallas	22	1	0	2
1976	Dallas	17	0	0	0
1977	Dallas	21	2	4	8
	Totals	143	13	13	39

MOHRMANN, PETER *Midfielder*
B. June 29, 1955
Ht. 5–10 Wt. 154
Citizen—U.S.

Season	Club	GP	G	A	Pts.
1978	Memphis	6	0	0	0

MOIA, VITOR *Forward*
Ht. 6–1 Wt. 168
Citizen—Portugal

Season	Club	GP	G	A	Pts.
1976	Rochester	19	11	3	25
1977	Connecticut	14	2	0	4
	Totals	33	13	3	29

MOKJOGOA, KEN *Midfielder*
B. Sept. 9, 1954 Transvaal, S. Africa
Ht. 5–11 Wt. 165
Citizen—S. Africa

Season	Club	GP	G	A	Pts.
1978	Washington	26	10	6	26
1979	Washington	19	4	1	9
	Totals	45	14	7	35

MOLNAR, TIBOR *Midfielder*
B. June 6, 1952 Budapest, Hungary
Ht. 6–0 Wt. 180
Citizen—Hungary

Season	Club	GP	G	A	Pts.
1971	Dallas	2	0	0	0
1976	Roch.-S.J.	17	0	3	3
1977	San Jose	19	0	1	1
	Totals	38	0	4	4

MOLENDYK, DANNY *Midfielder*
B. Oct. 6, 1955 Schiedam, Holland
Ht. 5–11 Wt. 165
Citizen—Holland

Season	Club	GP	G	A	Pts.
1979	Washington	1	0	0	0

MONOKI, BELA *Midfielder*
B. Feb. 27, 1942 Budapest, Hungary

Season	Club	GP	G	A	Pts.
1974	New York	1	0	0	0

Season	Club	GP	G	A	Pts.

MONTGOMERY, JIMMY
See *Goalkeeper*

MONTOYA, RUBEN
See *Goalkeeper*

MOORCROFT, DAVID   *Midfielder*
B. Mar. 16, 1947 Liverpool, England
Ht. 5-11 Wt. 175
Citizen—England

1968	Dallas	25	1	1	3

MOORE, BOBBY   *Defender*
B. Apr. 12, 1941 Barking, England
Ht. 6-0 Wt. 185
Citizen—England

1976	San Antonio	24	1	0	1
1978	Seattle	7	0	1	1
	Totals	31	1	1	3

MOORE, IAN   *Forward*
B. Jan. 25, 1945
Ht. 5-11 Wt. 170

1975	Chicago	14	2	1	5

MOORE, JIM   *Defender*
Ht. 5-9 Wt. 165

1967	Dallas	10	0	0	0

MOORE, JOHN   *Forward*
B. Dec. 2, 1944 St. Louis, Mo.
Ht. 5-11 Wt. 175
Citizen—U.S.

1968	Dallas	1	0	0	0

MOORE, JOHNNY   *Midfielder*
B. Aug. 28, 1947 Glasgow, Scotland
Ht. 5-5 Wt. 142
Citizen—U.S.

1974	San Jose	11	2	4	8
1975	San Jose	19	2	3	7
1976	San Jose	19	4	6	14
1977	San Jose	13	0	0	0
1978	Oakland	7	1	0	2
	Totals	69	9	13	31

MOORE, MICKEY   *Forward*
Ht. 5-9 Wt. 153

1975	Dallas	20	5	2	12

MOORE, RON   *Forward*
Ht. 6-0 Wt. 176
Citizen—England

1977	Chicago	22	8	2	18

MORAIS, NELSI   *Midfielder*
B. Oct. 22, 1951 Santos, Brazil
Ht. 5-9 Wt. 155
Citizen—Brazil

1976	New York	12	0	2	2
1977	New York	22	1	3	5
1978	New York	15	0	1	1
1979	New York	12	0	3	3
	Totals	61	1	9	11

MORALES, RUBEN   *Forward*
B. Oct. 2, 1952 Montevideo, Uruguay
Ht. 5-7 Wt. 150
Citizen—Uruguay

1979	Houston	25	2	8	12

MORALDO, RAMON   *Defender*
B. July 18, 1951
Ht. 6-1 Wt. 165
Citizen—Trinidad

1974	Los Angeles	18	0	0	0
1975	Los Angeles	22	1	0	2
1976	Los Angeles	15	1	0	2
	Totals	55	2	0	4

MORAES, JOSE   *Forward*
Ht. 5-8 Wt. 160
Citizen—Brazil

1972	Toronto	12	3	2	8

MORAN, MARK   *Midfielder*
B. Sept. 26, 1954 St. Louis, Mo.
Ht. 5-11 Wt. 165
Citizen—U.S.

1977	Minnesota	12	0	3	3
1978	Minnesota	16	2	0	4
1979	Minnesota	12	0	1	1
	Totals	40	2	4	8

MOREIRA, ISMAEL

1977	Hawaii	6	0	0	0

MORELAND, VICTOR   *Defender*
B. June 15, 1957 Belfast, N. Ireland
Ht. 6-0 Wt. 165
Citizen—England

1978	Tulsa	28	0	6	6

MORGAN, WILLIE   *Forward*
B. Glasgow, Scotland
Ht. 5-9 Wt. 160
Citizen—Scotland

1977	Chicago	20	3	7	13
1978	Minnesota	16	2	7	11
1979	Minnesota	24	1	14	16
	Totals	60	6	28	40

Season	Club	GP	G	A	Pts.

MORIELLI, GERRY   *Forward*
B. Feb. 9, 1958   Montorio, Italy
Ht. 5–10   Wt. 165
Citizen—Canada

1978	Houston	9	1	1	3
1979	Houston	2	0	0	0
	Totals	11	1	1	3

MORIPE, LUCAS   *Midfielder*
Ht. 5–9   Wt. 160
Citizen—S. Africa

1979	Chicago	1	0	0	0

MORROW, TOM

1967	Detroit	8	1	1	3

MOSINA, TARCISIO "CZECHO"   *Defender*
B. Jan. 15, 1951   Yugoslavia
Ht. 5–6   Wt. 157
Citizen—U.S.

1975	Chicago	1	0	0	0

MOTAUNG, KAISER "BOY-BOY"   *Forward*
B. Oct. 10, 1944   Johannesburg, S. Africa
Ht. 5–11   Wt. 170
Citizen—S. Africa

1968	Atlanta	30	11	3	25
1969	Atlanta	16	16	4	36
1971	Atlanta	23	5	3	13
1974	Denver	16	7	1	15
1975	Denver	20	4	7	15
	Totals	105	43	18	104

MOTTA, UBIRAJARA
See *Goalkeeper*

MOYERS, STEVE   *Forward*
B. Sept. 23, 1956   St. Louis, Mo.
Ht. 5–10   Wt. 150
Citizen—U.S.

1977	St. Louis	3	1	1	3
1978	California	26	7	4	18
1979	California	17	4	3	11
	Totals	46	12	8	32

MRDULJAS, STANKO
See *Goalkeeper*

MROSKO, CHARLIE   *Midfielder*
Ht. 5–10   Wt. 165
Citizen—W. Germany

1978	Oakland	26	11	3	25

MUELLER, GERD   *Forward*
B. Nov. 3, 1945   Munich, W. Germany
Ht. 5–10   Wt. 170
Citizen—Germany

1979	Ft. Lauderdale	15	19	17	55

MUELLER, JERRY   *Forward*
B. Oct. 20, 1944   St. Louis, Mo.
Ht. 5–8   Wt. 155
Citizen—U.S.

1968	Houston	1	0	0	0

MUELLER, JOHN   *Forward*
Ht. 5–8   Wt. 150
Citizen—U.S.

1968	Cleveland	5	1	0	2

MUGOSA, GEORGE   *Midfielder*
B. Yugoslavia
Ht. 5–8   Wt. 165
Citizen—Yugoslavia

1968	Boston	5	0	0	0

MUIR, WALTER   *Forward*
B. Scotland
Ht. 5–7   Wt. 150
Citizen—Canada

1971	Toronto	20	5	2	12
1972	Toronto	10	1	0	2
1973	Toronto	1	1	0	2
	Totals	31	7	2	16

MULHALL, GEORGE   *Forward*
Ht. 5–9   Wt. 154

1967	Vancouver	10	3	0	6

MULLIGAN, PATRICK "PADDY"   *Midfielder*
B. Mar. 17, 1945   Dublin, Ireland
Ht. 5–8   Wt. 157
Citizen—Ireland

1967	Boston	6	1	0	2
1968	Boston	12	4	0	8
	Totals	18	5	0	10

MULROY, TOMMY   *Defender*
B. Sept. 28, 1956   New York, N.Y.
Ht. 6–0   Wt. 165
Citizen—U.S.

1976	Miami	13	1	1	3

MUNGUIA, RICHARDO   *Defender*
B. Mexico
Ht. 5–5   Wt. 155
Citizen—Mexico

1968	San Diego	14	0	0	0

Season	Club	GP	G	A	Pts.

MUNOZ, RUBEN   *Forward*
B. Mexico
Ht. 5-9   Wt. 145
Citizen—Mexico

Season	Club	GP	G	A	Pts.
1968	San Diego	5	0	0	0

MUNRO, FRANCIS   *Midfielder*
Ht. 6-0   Wt. 176

1967	Washington	11	2	1	5

MURPHY, ED   *Forward*
B. Scotland
Ht. 6-1   Wt. 185
Citizen—U.S.

1968	Chicago	9	1	0	2

MURPHY, KEVIN   *Defender*
B. July 6, 1960   Trenton, N.J.
Ht. 6-1   Wt. 165
Citizen—U.S.

1978	Philadelphia	3	0	0	0
1979	Philadelphia	3	0	0	0
	Totals	7	0	0	0

MURPHY, TIM   *Defender*
B. 1957   Trenton, N.J.
Ht. 5-9   Wt. 150
Citizen—U.S.

1977	Portland	1	0	0	0

MWIKUTA, HOWARD   *Defender*
B. June 20, 1943   Broken Hill, Zambia
Ht. 5-8   Wt. 155
Citizen—Zambia

1967	Atlanta	11	1	0	2

MWILA, FREDDIE   *Forward*
B. July 6, 1946   Kasama, Zambia
Ht. 5-8   Wt. 145
Citizen—Zambia

1967	Atlanta	10	3	0	6
1968	Atlanta	24	6	0	12
1969	Atlanta	—	7	1	15
1971	Atlanta	23	5	4	14
1973	Atlanta	19	3	1	7
	Totals	76	24	6	54

MYERNICK, GLENN   *Defender*
B. Dec. 29, 1954   Trenton, N.J.
Ht. 5-11   Wt. 180
Citizen—U.S.

1977	Dallas	21	0	2	2
1978	Dallas	27	1	2	4
1979	Dallas	17	1	2	4
	Totals	65	2	6	10

NANCHOFF, GEORGE   *Forward*
B. Apr. 17, 1954   Yugoslavia
Ht. 5-11   Wt. 160
Citizen—U.S.

Season	Club	GP	G	A	Pts.
1977	Ft. Lauderdale	21	8	6	22
1978	Ft. Lauderdale	10	0	1	1
1979	Atlanta	21	2	5	9
	Totals	52	10	12	32

NANCHOFF, LOUIE   *Forward*
B. May 13, 1956   Yugoslavia
Ht. 5-10   Wt. 149
Citizen—U.S.

1978	Colorado	23	4	3	11
1979	Atlanta	17	4	2	10
	Totals	40	8	5	21

NAPIER, JOHN   *Defender*
B. Sept. 23, 1946   Lurgan, N. Ireland
Ht. 6-2   Wt. 175
Citizen—N. Ireland

1975	Baltimore	22	1	1	3
1976	San Diego	21	1	1	3
	Totals	42	2	2	6

NAPOLITANO, ART   *Forward*
B. Jan. 7, 1956   Mobile, Ala.
Ht. 5-10   Wt. 150
Citizen—U.S.

1978	Houston	7	0	0	0

NAVARRO, RUBEN   *Midfielder*
B. Santiago Del Estero, Argentina
Ht. 5-7   Wt. 190
Citizen—Argentina

1967	Philadelphia	14	1	0	2
1968	Cleveland	32	0	0	0
	Totals	46	1	0	2

NAVARRO, SALVADOR   *Forward*
Ht. 5-9   Wt. 145
Citizen—Mexico

1976	Philadelphia	21	0	0	0

NEESKENS, JOHAN   *Midfielder*
B. Sept. 15, 1951   Haarlem, Holland
Ht. 5-9   Wt. 170
Citizen—Holland

1979	New York	13	4	7	15

NEIGHBOUR, JIMMY   *Midfielder*
B. Nov. 15, 1950   London, England
Ht. 5-8   Wt. 150
Citizen—England

1979	Seattle	21	1	8	10

Season	Club	GP	G	A	Pts.

NEILSON, TOMMY   *Midfielder*
Ht. 5-7   Wt. 165

1967	Dallas	11	0	0	0

NELSON, FERNANDO   *Forward*

1975	Boston	10	5	1	11

NELSON, PAUL   *Defender*
B. Nov. 12, 1958   Vancouver, Canada
Ht. 5-8   Wt. 160
Citizen—Canada

1978	Vancouver	2	0	0	0

NERSEPIAN, YEPREM   *Defender*
B. Dec. 4, 1946   Istanbul, Turkey
Ht. 5-9   Wt. 160

1974	Los Angeles	7	0	0	0
1975	San Antonio	9	0	0	0
	Totals	16	0	0	0

NESIN, STEVAN   *Forward*
B. Apr. 17, 1960   Canada
Ht. 5-9   Wt. 160
Citizen—Canada

1979	Vancouver	2	0	1	1

NETO, JOSE   *Forward*
B. June 5, 1955   Aracaju, Brazil
Ht. 6-1   Wt. 175
Citizen—Brazil

1979	San Diego	10	6	1	13

NEUBAUER, ROBERT   *Defender*
B. 1940
Ht. 5-8   Wt. 155
Citizen—W. Germany

1972	New York	4	0	0	0

NEUMANN, AXEL   *Midfielder*
B. Apr. 22, 1952   West Berlin, W. Germany
Ht. 6-1   Wt. 165
Citizen—W. Germany

1975	Boston	13	0	1	1
1977	Haw.-L.V.	19	3	2	8
1978	San Diego	26	3	0	6
1979	California	3	0	0	0
	Totals	61	6	3	15

NEUSEL, ED   *Defender*
B. St. Louis, Mo.
Ht. 5-8   Wt. 148
Citizen—U.S.

1971	St. Louis	19	0	1	1

NEVERS, TOM   *Forward*
B. June 8, 1956   Middletown, Conn.
Ht. 5-8   Wt. 160
Citizen—U.S.

1978	Chicago	3	0	0	0
1979	Memphis	18	0	0	0
	Totals	21	0	0	0

NEWMAN, GUY   *Defender*
B. Nov. 26, 1957   Portsmouth, England
Ht. 5-11   Wt. 165
Citizen—U.S.

1979	Ft. Lauderdale	5	0	0	0

NEWMAN, RON   *Forward*
B. Jan. 19, 1936   Fareham, England
Ht. 5-9   Wt. 160
Citizen—England

1967	Atlanta	10	2	3	7
1968	Atl.-Dal.	8	1	0	2
	Totals	18	3	3	9

NEWSTEAD, COLIN   *Forward*
B. Jan. 31, 1948   Rye, Sussex, England
Ht. 5-10   Wt. 155
Citizen—England

1978	Houston	1	0	0	0

NEWTON, GRAHAM   *Forward*
B. Dec. 22, 1942   Bilston, England
Ht. 5-11   Wt. 178
Citizen—England

1967	Atlanta	11	8	3	19
1968	Atlanta	20	10	0	20
1969	Atlanta	—	—	—	—
1970	Atlanta	—	—	—	—
	Totals	31	18	3	39

NGLOBO, CHAKA   *Forward*
B. May 10, 1950
Ht. 5-7   Wt. 150
Citizen—South Africa

1975	Denver	20	5	6	16
1976	Minnesota	3	0	0	0
	Totals	23	5	6	16

NIBLOCK, MICHAEL   *Forward*
B. Ireland

1973	New York	7	0	1	1

NICOLINI, HUGO   *Defender*
B. Nov. 15, 1949   Buenos Aires, Argentina
Ht. 6-0   Wt. 175
Citizen—Canada

1978	Rochester	24	1	2	4

Season	Club	GP	G	A	Pts.

NIEDZIOLKA, FELIKS   *Defender*
Ht. 6-0   Wt. 165
Citizen—Poland

1975	Rochester	18	0	0	0

NIELSEN, LEIF
See *Goalkeeper*

NIKEZIC, PETAR   *Midfielder*

1978	Tulsa	2	0	1	1

NIKOLIC, ALEXANDER
B. Aug. 17, 1939   Nis, Yugoslavia
Citizen—Yugoslavia

1968	Baltimore	3	1	0	2

NIKOLIC, STOJAN   *Defender*
B. Sept. 13, 1949   Nis, Yugoslavia
Ht. 6-0   Wt. 180
Citizen—Yugoslavia

1978	Tulsa	21	1	0	2
1979	Philadelphia	26	0	0	0
	Totals	47	1	0	2

NISH, DAVID   *Defender*
B. Sept. 26, 1947   Burton-On-Trent, England
Ht. 5-10   Wt. 172
Citizen—England

1979	Tulsa	28	6	8	20

NJIE, AL   *Forward*
B. Apr. 15, 1955   Atlanta, Ga.
Ht. 6-1   Wt. 160
Citizen—U.S.

1979	Ft. Lauderdale	6	0	1	1

NOGUEIRA, VICTOR
See *Goalkeeper*

NOLAN, RONNIE   *Midfielder*
Ht. 5-9   Wt. 168

1967	Boston	9	0	1	1

NORDQVIST, BJORN   *Defender*
B. Oct. 6, 1942   Hallsberg, Sweden
Ht. 5-10   Wt. 170
Citizen—Sweden

1979	Minnesota	30	1	3	5

NORMAN, KELVIN   *Defender*
B. Oct. 10, 1955   Cambridge, Mass.
Ht. 5-10   Wt. 168
Citizen—U.S.

1978	Portland	4	0	0	0

NOVER, PETER   *Defender*
B. Oct. 29, 1954   Holzheim, W. Germany
Ht. 6-5   Wt. 195
Citizen—W. Germany

1976	Boston	18	2	6	10
1977	Hawaii	26	7	0	14
1978	San Diego	30	4	6	14
1979	San Diego	29	8	2	18
	Totals	103	21	14	56

NTSOELENGOE, PATRICK "ACE"   *Forward*
B. Feb. 26, 1956   S. Africa
Ht. 5-8   Wt. 155
Citizen—S. Africa

1973	Miami	9	3	2	8
1975	Denver	21	10	5	25
1976	Minnesota	22	6	4	16
1977	Minnesota	21	3	5	11
1978	Minnesota	29	9	8	26
1979	Minnesota	29	8	11	27
	Totals	131	39	35	103

NUSUM, JOHN   *Defender*
B. July 6, 1954   Paget, Bermuda
Ht. 6-1   Wt. 175
Citizen—Bermuda

1978	San Diego	18	0	1	1

NUSUM, SAMUEL
See *Goalkeeper*

NUTTALL, BILL
See *Goalkeeper*

NWOKOCHA, CHRIS   *Forward*
Ht. 6-0   Wt. 180
Citizen—Nigeria

1979	Memphis	5	1	0	2

OAK, DARRELL   *Forward*
B. Aug. 30, 1954   Jameston, North Dakota
Ht. 6-0   Wt. 170
Citizen—U.S.

1976	Seattle	2	0	0	0
1977	Seattle	2	0	0	0
1978	Seattle	2	0	0	0
	Totals	6	0	0	0

OATES, GRAHAM   *Defender*
B. Mar. 14, 1949   Bradford, England
Ht. 6-2   Wt. 172
Citizen—England

1978	Detroit	27	2	3	7
1979	Detroit	29	5	12	22
	Totals	56	7	15	29

Season	Club	GP	G	A	Pts.

OBREBSKI, WALDEMAR *Forward*
B. May 23, 1944 Warsaw, Poland
Ht. 5-11 Wt. 170
Citizen—Poland

Season	Club	GP	G	A	Pts.
1975	Chicago	2	0	0	0

O'BRIEN, FRAN *Defender*
B. Apr. 7, 1955 Dublin, Ireland
Ht. 5-8 Wt. 140
Citizen—Ireland

Season	Club	GP	G	A	Pts.
1978	Philadelphia	24	1	2	4
1979	Philadelphia	27	4	10	18
	Totals	51	5	12	22

O'CONNELL, PAT *Forward*
B. England
Ht. 5-8 Wt. 159
Citizen—England

Season	Club	GP	G	A	Pts.
1968	Vancouver	19	6	0	12

O'CONNOR, PAT *Midfielder*
B. Scotland
Ht. 5-8 Wt. 156
Citizen—Scotland

Season	Club	GP	G	A	Pts.
1967	Chi.(NPSL)	4	1	0	2

O'DEA, TOM *Defender*
Ht. 6-0 Wt. 165

Season	Club	GP	G	A	Pts.
1975	Hartford	12	0	0	0

ODOI, FRANK *Midfielder*
B. Feb. 23, 1943 Ghana
Ht. 5-6 Wt. 155
Citizen—Ghana

Season	Club	GP	G	A	Pts.
1968	Washington	—	—	—	—
1970	Rochester	5	1	0	2
1971	Rochester	13	0	1	1
1972	Rochester	8	0	0	0
1973	Rochester	18	2	2	6
1974	Rochester	20	1	2	4
1975	Rochester	17	2	2	6
1976	Rochester	17	1	3	5
1977	Rochester	19	1	3	5
1978	Rochester	6	0	0	0
	Totals	123	8	13	29

OFORI, GLADSTONE *Forward*
B. Ghana
Ht. 5-7 Wt. 143

Season	Club	GP	G	A	Pts.
1971	Rochester	20	3	9	15
1972	Rochester	5	1	1	3
	Totals	25	4	10	18

OGNJANAC, JOSIP *Midfielder*
Ht. 6-1 Wt. 190

Season	Club	GP	G	A	Pts.
1971	Montreal	4	0	0	0

OGUNSUYI, DAMIAN *Forward*
B. May 3, 1954 Benin City, Nigeria
Ht. 5-11 Wt. 150
Citizen—Nigeria

Season	Club	GP	G	A	Pts.
1979	Toronto	2	0	0	0

O'HARA, TOMMY *Defender*
B. Aug. 17, 1952 Bellshill, Scotland
Ht. 5-9 Wt. 165
Citizen—Scotland

Season	Club	GP	G	A	Pts.
1978	Washington	28	0	2	2
1979	Washington	29	2	7	11
	Totals	57	2	9	13

O'HARE, JOHN *Forward*
B. Sept. 24, 1946 Renton, Scotland
Ht. 5-8 Wt. 180
Citizen—Scotland

Season	Club	GP	G	A	Pts.
1967	Vancouver	11	1	1	3
1977	Dallas	21	10	3	23
1978	Dallas	19	4	4	12
	Totals	51	15	8	38

OHMAN, JAN *Forward*
B. July 4, 1942 Stockholm, Sweden
Ht. 5-10 Wt. 155
Citizen—Sweden

Season	Club	GP	G	A	Pts.
1968	St. Louis	7	0	0	0

O'KANE, GERRY *Forward*
B. Jan. 20, 1955 Belfast, N. Ireland
Ht. 5-10 Wt. 160
Citizen—N. Ireland

Season	Club	GP	G	A	Pts.
1978	San Diego	3	0	0	0

OLAGUE, JUAN *Midfielder*
Ht. 5-10 Wt. 152
Citizen—Mexico

Season	Club	GP	G	A	Pts.
1976	Philadelphia	17	4	2	10

O'LEARY, BOB *Midfielder*
B. Jan. 3, 1952 St. Louis, Mo.
Ht. 5-10 Wt. 152
Citizen—U.S.

Season	Club	GP	G	A	Pts.
1974	St. Louis	12	0	0	0
1975	St. Louis	10	2	1	5
1976	St. Louis	22	0	4	4
1977	St. Louis	23	1	0	2
1978	California	19	0	1	1
1979	California	6	0	0	0
	Totals	92	3	6	12

O'LEARY, PIERCE *Defender*
B. Nov. 5, 1959 Dublin, Ireland
Ht. 6-0 Wt. 144
Citizen—Ireland

Season	Club	GP	G	A	Pts.
1978	Philadelphia	14	0	1	1

Season	Club	GP	G	A	Pts.

OLIVERIA, MIRANDA "FLASH"   *Forward*
Ht. 6–2   Wt. 190

1971	Washington	21	5	2	12
1972	Montreal	7	0	1	1
	Totals	28	5	3	13

OLSEN, JOHN   *Forward*
B. Jan. 4, 1943   Copenhagen, Denmark
Ht. 5–9   Wt. 158
Citizen—Denmark

| 1968 | Boston | 9 | 2 | 0 | 4 |

O'NEILL, ALAN   *Midfielder*
B. Newcastle, England

| 1971 | New York | 3 | 1 | 1 | 3 |

O'NEILL, FRANK   *Forward*
Ht. 5–9   Wt. 161

| 1967 | Boston | 12 | 3 | 4 | 10 |

O'NEILL, GEORGE   *Midfielder*
B. July 26, 1942   Port Glasgow, Scotland
Ht. 5–8   Wt. 155
Citizen—U.S.

1973	Philadelphia	17	1	9	11
1974	Philadelphia	19	0	2	2
1975	Philadelphia	5	1	1	3
1976	Philadelphia	11	2	1	5
	Totals	52	4	13	21

O'NEILL, HUGH   *Forward*
B. July 16, 1954   Kearny, N.J.
Ht. 5–10   Wt. 160
Citizen—U.S.

1976	Hartford	16	2	1	5
1977	Conn.–Dal.	5	1	0	2
1978	Memphis	12	2	0	4
	Totals	33	5	1	11

ORD, TOMMY   *Forward*
B. Oct. 15, 1952   London, England
Ht. 5–10   Wt. 165
Citizen—England

1973	Montreal	17	6	6	18
1974	Rochester	20	7	2	16
1975	Roch.–N.Y.	21	16	4	36
1976	N.Y.–Van.	17	5	1	11
1977	Van.–Sea.	20	7	7	23
1978	Seattle	26	7	1	15
1979	Seattle	12	1	1	3
	Totals	133	49	22	120

ORDONEZ, RICARDO
See *Goalkeeper*

ORECO (Waldemar Rodrigues Martins)   *Defender*
B. June 13, 1937   Brazil
Ht. 5–9   Wt. 170
Citizen—Brazil

1971	Dallas	16	0	0	0
1972	Dallas	5	0	0	0
	Totals	21	0	0	0

ORHAN, YILMAZ   *Forward*
B. Mar. 13, 1955   Cyprus
Ht. 5–9   Wt. 155
Citizen—Cyprus

1977	Hawaii	23	2	5	9
1978	Hou.–S.D.	25	3	6	12
1979	San Diego	21	3	9	15
	Totals	69	8	20	36

O'RIORDAN, DON   *Defender*
B. May 14, 1957   Dublin, Ireland
Ht. 6–1   Wt. 165
Citizen—Ireland

1978	Tulsa	30	2	1	5
1979	Tulsa	22	0	0	0
	Totals	52	2	1	5

ORTA, FELIPE   *Forward*
B. Mexico
Ht. 5–7   Wt. 163
Citizen—Mexico

| 1968 | San Diego | 8 | 2 | 0 | 4 |

ORTIZ-VELEZ, MIKE   *Midfielder*
B. May 13, 1957   Sumter, S.C.
Ht. 5–8   Wt. 150
Citizen—U.S.

1978	Ft. Lauderdale	1	0	0	0
1979	Ft. Lauderdale	1	0	0	0
	Totals	1	0	0	0

OSBORNE, ROGER   *Midfielder*
B. Mar. 9, 1950   Otley, England
Ht. 5–9   Wt. 151
Citizen—England

| 1979 | Detroit | 22 | 3 | 11 | 17 |

OSGOOD, PETER   *Forward*
B. Feb. 20, 1947   Windsor, England
Ht. 6–2   Wt. 180
Citizen—England

| 1978 | Philadelphia | 22 | 1 | 8 | 10 |

OSIECK, HOLGER   *Defender*
B. Aug. 31, 1948   W. Germany
Ht. 6–0   Wt. 180
Citizen—W. Germany

| 1977 | Vancouver | 21 | 3 | 1 | 7 |

Season	Club	GP	G	A	Pts.

OSTOJIC, STEVAN   *Midfielder*

Season	Club	GP	G	A	Pts.
1974	San Jose	2	0	0	0

O'SULLIVAN, MATT   *Defender*
B. July 1, 1955   San Francisco, Calif.
Ht. 6-0   Wt. 180
Citizen—U.S.

Season	Club	GP	G	A	Pts.
1978	Houston	22	0	1	1
1979	Houston	28	0	3	3
	Totals	50	0	4	4

OUWEHAND, ROB   *Defender*
B. Sept. 11, 1951   Gravenhage, Holland
Ht. 6-3   Wt. 180
Citizen—Holland

Season	Club	GP	G	A	Pts.
1979	Edmonton	17	1	2	4

OWCHARUCK, NICK
See *Goalkeeper*

OXFORD, NEVILLE   *Forward*
B. Nov. 18, 1948   Kingston, Jamaica
Ht. 5-10   Wt. 150
Citizen—Jamaica

Season	Club	GP	G	A	Pts.
1967	N.Y. (NPSL)	2	0	0	0
1968	New York	1	0	0	0
	Totals	3	0	0	0

PACHAME, CARLOS   *Midfielder*
B. Feb. 25, 1948   Argentina
Ht. 5-10   Wt. 153
Citizen—Argentina

Season	Club	GP	G	A	Pts.
1979	Rochester	3	0	0	0

PADDON, GRAHAM   *Midfielder*
B. Aug. 24, 1950   Manchester, England
Ht. 5-9   Wt. 161
Citizen—England

Season	Club	GP	G	A	Pts.
1978	Tampa Bay	25	5	3	13

PAEZ, OSCAR   *Midfielder*
B. Dec. 29, 1953   Buenos Aires, Argentina
Ht. 6-1   Wt. 165
Citizen—Argentina

Season	Club	GP	G	A	Pts.
1978	Toronto	1	0	0	0
1979	Houston	1	0	0	0
	Totals	2	0	0	0

PALETTA, JOHN   *Forward*
B. Argentina
Ht. 5-9   Wt. 175
Citizen—Argentina

Season	Club	GP	G	A	Pts.
1968	Washington	15	8	0	16
1974	Philadelphia	8	1	1	3
	Totals	23	9	1	19

PALMER, CHARLIE   *Defender*
B. 1949   Scotland
Ht. 5-11   Wt. 164
Citizen—England

Season	Club	GP	G	A	Pts.
1974	Vancouver	15	1	2	4
1975	Vancouver	7	1	1	3
	Totals	22	2	3	7

PALMIERI, HORATIO   *Midfielder*
B. Jan. 28, 1952   Buenos Aires, Argentina
Ht. 6-1   Wt. 170
Citizen—Argentina

Season	Club	GP	G	A	Pts.
1978	Rochester	27	0	4	4

PAPADAKIS, ALEC   *Midfielder*
B. Jan. 27, 1948   Athens, Greece
Ht. 5-9   Wt. 155

Season	Club	GP	G	A	Pts.
1971	Atlanta	13	0	1	1
1972	Atlanta	14	0	0	0
1973	Atlanta	12	0	0	0
1974	Boston	1	0	0	0
	Totals	40	0	1	1

PAPADAKIS, NICK   *Forward*
B. Mar. 6, 1943   Athens, Greece
Ht. 5-11   Wt. 155
Citizen—Canada

Season	Club	GP	G	A	Pts.
1968	Atlanta	2	0	0	0
1969	Atlanta	—	—	—	—
1970	Atlanta	22	11	2	24
1971	Atlanta	24	8	1	17
1972	Atlanta	9	1	0	2
1973	Atlanta	3	0	0	0
	Totals	60	20	3	43

PAPADOPOULOS, PAMPOS   *Forward*
B. May 29, 1948   Cyprus
Ht. 5-8   Wt. 160
Citizen—Cyprus

Season	Club	GP	G	A	Pts.
1978	Toronto	8	1	1	3

PAPAMAKARIOS, JOHN   *Forward*

Season	Club	GP	G	A	Pts.
1971	Montreal	7	1	0	2

PAPANDREA, LUIS   *Defender*
B. Aug. 8, 1952   Buenos Aires, Argentina
Ht. 5-8   Wt. 160
Citizen—Argentina

Season	Club	GP	G	A	Pts.
1978	Tampa Bay	15	0	1	1

PAREDES, AMERICO   *Forward*
B. Sept. 29, 1946
Ht. 5-8   Wt. 167
Citizen—Uruguay

Season	Club	GP	G	A	Pts.
1975	New York	15	3	1	7

Season	Club	GP	G	A	Pts.

PARK, TERRY *Midfielder*
B. Feb. 7, 1957 Liverpool, England
Ht. 5–11 Wt. 160
Citizen—England

| 1979 | Ft. Lauderdale | 27 | 5 | 7 | 17 |

PARKES, PHIL
See *Goalkeeper*

PARKIN, TIM *Defender*
B. May 29, 1953 England
Ht. 6–2 Wt. 175
Citizen—England

| 1977 | Ft. Lauderdale | 4 | 0 | 0 | 0 |

PARKIN, TOM *Midfielder*
Citizen—England

| 1977 | Connecticut | 17 | 2 | 1 | 5 |

PARODI, LES *Defender*
B. Apr. 1, 1954 Condon, England
Ht. 6–0 Wt. 160
Citizen—England

| 1978 | Seattle | 21 | 1 | 6 | 8 |

PARRIS, RAYMOND *Forward*
B. Sept. 25, 1946 Kingston, Jamaica
Ht. 5–10 Wt. 160

| 1973 | Philadelphia | 5 | 0 | 0 | 0 |

PARSONS LES "BUZZ" *Midfielder*
B. Dec. 16, 1950 Vancouver, Canada
Ht. 5–9 Wt. 160
Citizen—Canada

1976	Vancouver	9	4	1	9
1977	Vancouver	25	10	6	26
1978	Vancouver	16	1	1	3
1979	Vancouver	22	1	5	7
	Totals	72	16	13	45

PARVIZ (PARVIZ GHYLICHKHANI) *Defender*
B. Nov. 11, 1948
Citizen—Iran

| 1978 | San Jose | 16 | 0 | 1 | 1 |

PAS, RENE *Forward*
Ht. 5–8 Wt. 158

| 1967 | San Francisco | 9 | 6 | 2 | 14 |

PATON, DANNY *Midfielder*
B. Jan. 27, 1936 Scotland
Ht. 5–9 Wt. 160
Citizen—Scotland

1971	Atlanta	13	0	1	1
1972	Atlanta	13	2	1	5
1973	Atlanta	6	0	0	0
	Totals	32	2	2	6

PAUNOVICH, PAKI *Defender*
Ht. 5–11 Wt. 175
Citizen—Yugoslavia

| 1978 | Oakland | 23 | 0 | 0 | 0 |

PAVKOVIC, VLADIMIR *Forward*
B. Yugoslavia
Citizen—Yugoslavia

| 1968 | Houston | 6 | 0 | 0 | 0 |

PAVLOVIC, MIRO *Defender*
B. Oct. 15, 1942 Belgrade, Yugoslavia
Ht. 5–10 Wt. 165
Citizen—Yugoslavia

1976	San Jose	24	0	4	4
1977	San Jose	26	1	1	3
	Totals	50	1	5	7

PEARCE, RUDOLPH *Defender*
B. Dec. 18, 1945 Kingston, Jamaica
Ht. 5–9 Wt. 155
Citizen—Jamaica

| 1971 | New York | 19 | 0 | 0 | 0 |

PEARSON, KIRK
See *Goalkeeper*

PECHER, STEVE *Defender*
B. Feb. 13, 1956 St. Louis, Mo.
Ht. 6–0 Wt. 194
Citizen—U.S.

1976	Dallas	17	2	0	4
1977	Dallas	25	4	1	9
1978	Dallas	29	0	3	3
1979	Dallas	27	0	0	0
	Totals	98	6	4	16

PEDRO, JOHN *Forward*
B. 1952 Portugal
Ht. 5–9 Wt. 145
Citizen—Portugal

1976	Rochester	21	0	6	6
1977	Rochester	25	1	7	9
	Totals	46	1	13	15

PEIXNHO, CARLOS *Forward*
Ht. 5–6 Wt. 162

| 1967 | Houston | 6 | 1 | 1 | 3 |

PELÉ (EDSON ARANTES DO NASCIMENTO) *Forward*
B. Oct. 23, 1940 Tres Coracoes, Brazil
Ht. 5–9 Wt. 165
Citizen—Brazil

1975	New York	9	5	4	14
1976	New York	22	13	18	44
1977	New York	25	13	3	29
	Totals	56	31	25	87

Season	Club	GP	G	A	Pts.

PENMAN, WILLIE *Midfielder*
B. July 8, 1939 Wemyss Fite, England
Ht. 5-6 Wt. 155
Citizen—England

1974	Seattle	13	1	0	2

PEPLOW, STEVE *Forward*
B. Jan. 8, 1944 Liverpool, England
Ht. 5-9 Wt. 160
Citizen—England

1976	Chicago	20	4	9	17

PERANI, MARINO *Midfielder*
B. Oct. 27, 1939 Ponte Nossa, Italy
Ht. 5-8 Wt. 155
Citizen—Italy

1975	Toronto	8	1	2	4

PERAU, DIETER *Forward*
B. Feb. 2, 1938 Diepholz, Germany
Ht. 5-9 Wt. 185
Citizen—Germany

1967	Pittsburgh	21	8	6	22
1968	New York	32	13	7	33
	Totals	53	21	13	55

PEREIRA, FRED *Forward*
B. Feb. 17, 1954 Valanta, Portugal
Ht. 5-10 Wt. 165
Citizen—U.S.

1977	Ft. L-Conn.	22	6	3	15
1978	Colorado	12	2	2	6
1979	Atlanta	8	2	0	4
	Totals	42	10	5	25

PEREIRA, MIGUEL *Defender*
B. Sept. 20, 1949 Rio de Janeiro, Brazil
Ht. 5-9 Wt. 169
Citizen—Brazil

1978	Chicago	2	0	0	0

PEREZ, EASY *Forward*
B. Feb. 20, 1957
Ht. 5-8 Wt. 140
Citizen—U.S.

1979	San Jose	3	0	0	0

PEREZ, GONZALO
Ht. 5-10 Wt. 175

1974	San Jose	15	2	2	6

PEREZ, LUIS *Defender*
Ht. 6-0 Wt. 175
Citizen—Mexico

1976	Philadelphia	7	0	0	0

PEREZ, VICTOR *Forward*
Ht. 5-9 Wt. 143
Citizen—Mexico

1976	Philadelphia	21	7	0	14

PERIC, GORAN *Forward*
Ht. 5-8 Wt. 155
Citizen—Canada

1975	Toronto	10	1	0	2

PEROVIC, VUKAN *Forward*
B. Yugoslavia

1978	Tulsa	8	0	1	1

PERRI, ARDO
See *Goalkeeper*

PERRICHON, MIGUEL *Forward*
B. Argentina
Ht. 5-6 Wt. 170

1972	Toronto	13	0	9	9
1973	Toronto	17	9	4	22
	Totals	30	9	13	31

PESA, NJEGO *Forward*
B. May 30, 1958 Zadar, Yugoslavia
Ht. 5-10 Wt. 165
Citizen—U.S.

1979	Dallas	12	1	1	3

PESIC, TOMISLAV *Forward*
B. Sept. 8, 1949 Surdulica, Yugoslavia
Ht. 5-11 Wt. 154
Citizen—Yugoslavia

1978	Tulsa	2	0	1	1

PESUT, IVICA *Defender*
B. 1951
Ht. 6-1 Wt. 178
Citizen—Yugoslavia

1977	Las Vegas	16	0	1	1

PETERSON, DALE *Forward*
B. July 3, 1957 Brockton, Mass.
Ht. 5-8 Wt. 155
Citizen—U.S.

1979	New England	1	0	0	0

PETERSON, JENS *Midfielder*
Ht. 6-0 Wt. 156

1967	Washington	12	0	2	2

PETERSON, JOHN *Midfielder*
B. Apr. 4, 1943 Hridovre, Denmark
Ht. 6-0 Wt. 175
Citizen—Denmark

1968	Boston	5	0	—	0

Season	Club	GP	G	A	Pts.

PETERSON, LES   *Defender*
B. Dec. 29, 1954   Miami, Fla.
Ht. 5–10   Wt. 155
Citizen—U.S.

| 1978 | Ft. Lauderdale | 5 | 0 | 0 | 0 |

PHILLIPS, LINCOLN
See *Goalkeeper*

PIANTA, PIETRO
See *Goalkeeper*

PICCIANO, TONY   *Defender*
B. June 15, 1952
Ht. 6–0   Wt. 155
Citizen—U.S.

| 1975 | New York | 10 | 0 | 0 | 0 |

PIKE, GEOFF   *Forward*
B. Sept. 28, 1956   London, England
Ht. 5–8   Wt. 150
Citizen—England

1976	Hartford	19	4	6	14
1977	Connecticut	20	3	4	10
	Totals	39	7	10	24

PILAS, BRUNO   *Forward*
B. Nov. 21, 1950   Zagreb, Yugoslavia
Ht. 5–8   Wt. 165
Citizen—Canada

1973	Toronto	15	8	2	18
1974	Toronto	16	5	1	11
1975	Toronto	11	1	2	4
1976	Toronto	16	2	0	4
1977	Toronto	18	2	0	4
	Totals	76	18	5	41

PILLINGER, BRIAN   *Defender*
B. July 24, 1941   London, England
Ht. 6–0   Wt. 180

1974	Washington	14	0	1	1
1975	Washington	22	1	1	3
	Totals	36	1	2	4

PINTO, FERNANDO   *Midfielder*
B. Beugla, Portugal
Ht. 5–10   Wt. 172
Citizen—Portugal

1973	Toronto	17	2	3	7
1974	Toronto	18	3	3	9
	Totals	35	5	6	16

PINTOS, JUAN   *Forward*
Ht. 5–4   Wt. 159

| 1967 | N.Y. (USA) | 9 | 3 | 0 | 6 |

PIOTTI, JORGE   *Forward*
B. Argentina
Ht. 5–7   Wt. 155
Citizen—Argentina

| 1968 | Los Angeles | 13 | 3 | 0 | 6 |

PIPER, NORMAN   *Forward*
B. Jan. 8, 1948   England
Ht. 5–7   Wt. 145
Citizen—England

1977	Ft. Lauderdale	17	3	4	10
1978	Ft. Lauderdale	24	4	6	14
	Totals	41	7	10	24

PIRES, TELMO   *Defender*
B. Apr. 4, 1953   Cacia, Portugal
Ht. 6–1   Wt. 185
Citizen—U.S.

| 1976 | Hartford | 11 | 0 | 0 | 0 |

PISANI, JOHN   *Forward*
B. St. Louis, Mo.
Ht. 5–11   Wt. 167
Citizen—U.S.

1971	St. Louis	6	0	0	0
1972	St. Louis	4	0	0	0
1975	St. Louis	15	1	2	4
	Totals	25	1	2	4

PISANI, PAUL   *Midfielder*
B. June 9, 1938   St. Louis, Mo.
Ht. 5–9   Wt. 164
Citizen—U.S.

| 1971 | St. Louis | 6 | 0 | 0 | 0 |

PIZARRO, OSCAR   *Forward*
Ht. 5–8   Wt. 140

| 1971 | Montreal | 19 | 2 | 5 | 9 |

PLA, JOSE   *Forward*
B. Rosario, Argentina
Ht. 5–11   Wt. 163
Citizen—Argentina

| 1967 | N.Y. (NPSL) | 4 | 1 | 0 | 2 |

PLESSAS, JIMMY   *Midfielder*
B. Greece
Ht. 5–8   Wt. 156
Citizen—Greece

| 1968 | Kansas City | 32 | 2 | 0 | 4 |

PLETIKOSIC, ANTE "TONY"   *Defender*
B. Jan. 22, 1939   Supetar, Yugoslavia
Ht. 6–0   Wt. 180
Citizen—Yugoslavia

| 1968 | Houston | 16 | 0 | 0 | 0 |

Season	Club	GP	G	A	Pts.

POGRZEBA, NORBERT   *Forward*
B. June 23, 1939
Ht. 5-10   Wt. 175
Citizen—Poland

1967	St. Louis	24	11	6	28

POINTER, KEITH   *Midfielder*
B. Norwich, England
Ht. 5-11   Wt. 170

1971	Montreal	18	0	4	4
1972	Montreal	10	1	2	4
	Totals	28	1	6	8

POLAK, TED   *Defender*
B. Nov. 17, 1944   Vienna, Austria
Ht. 6-0   Wt. 175
Citizen—Canada

1974	Toronto	18	1	2	4
1975	Toronto	20	2	4	8
1976	Toronto	20	1	1	3
1977	Toronto	25	2	0	4
1978	Toronto	23	0	1	1
	Totals	106	6	8	20

POLJAK, IVAN   *Midfielder*
B. Nov. 23, 1951   Ogvoin, Yugoslavia
Ht. 5-11   Wt. 170
Citizen—Yugoslavia

1978	Toronto	16	2	3	7

POLLARD, DOUG   *Defender*
B. Aug. 28, 1957   Canada
Ht. 6-2   Wt. 165
Citizen—Canada

1979	Rochester	3	0	0	0

POLLIHAN, JIM   *Forward*
B. Feb. 13, 1954   St. Louis, Mo.
Ht. 6-1   Wt. 185
Citizen—U.S.

1976	Rochester	23	0	0	0
1977	Rochester	26	1	4	6
1978	Rochester	28	5	3	13
1979	Rochester	22	0	1	1
	Totals	99	6	8	20

POLYVIOU, PANOS   *Midfielder*

1971	Toronto	1	0	0	0

PONCE, JOE   *Defender*
B. Spain
Ht. 5-9   Wt. 165
Citizen—Spain

1968	Toronto	30	0	1	1

POOLE, MICK
See *Goalkeeper*

POOLE, ROBIN   *Defender*
B. Dec. 1, 1948   Liverpool, England
Ht. 5-10   Wt. 160

1972	Dallas	10	0	0	0

POPOOLA, BEN   *Forward*
Ht. 5-10   Wt. 160
Citizen—Nigeria

1979	Memphis	17	1	3	5

POPOVIC, DON   *Midfielder*
B. Jan. 1, 1941   Ivangrad, Yugoslavia

1967	St. Louis	5	1	0	2
1968	Kansas City	23	0	0	0
1969	St. Louis	—	—	—	—
1970	St. Louis	—	—	—	—
1971	St. Louis	23	1	7	9
	Totals	51	2	7	11

POPOVIC, MLADEN   *Midfielder*
B. Yugoslavia
Ht. 6-1   Wt. 170
Citizen—Yugoslavia

1968	Boston	3	0	0	0

POSSEE, DEREK   *Forward*
B. Feb. 14, 1946   England
Ht. 5-5   Wt. 135
Citizen—England

1977	Vancouver	16	11	5	27
1978	Vancouver	19	3	1	7
1979	Vancouver	18	3	2	8
	Totals	53	17	8	42

POWELL, BARRY   *Midfielder*
B. Kenilworth, England
Ht. 5-8   Wt. 144
Citizen—England

1975	Portland	18	4	2	10

POWELL, PADDY   *Forward*
B. July 7, 1948   Hendon, England
Ht. 5-10   Wt. 166
Citizen—England

1978	New England	20	2	2	6

POWELL, STEVE   *Midfielder*
B. Sept. 20, 1955   Derby County, England
Ht. 5-9   Wt. 160
Citizen—England

1979	Tulsa	19	1	0	2

PRATI, PIERO   *Forward*
B. Dec. 13, 1946   Italy
Ht. 5-11   Wt. 165
Citizen—Italy

1979	Rochester	6	3	0	6

Season	Club	GP	G	A	Pts.

PRATT, HUGH *Defender*
B. Oct. 11, 1943 Hexham, England
Ht. 5-9 Wt. 150
Citizen—England

| 1968 | San Diego | 9 | 0 | 0 | 0 |

PRENTICE, ROB *Midfielder*
B. Sept. 27, 1953 Lanark, Scotland
Ht. 5-9 Wt. 161
Citizen—Scotland

| 1979 | Toronto | 5 | 0 | 0 | 0 |

PRICE, PAUL *Defender*
B. Mar. 23, 1954 St. Albans, England
Ht. 5-11 Wt. 162
Citizen—England

1977	Minnesota	3	0	0	0
1978	Minnesota	21	2	4	8
	Totals	24	2	4	8

PRIMO, DAVID *Defender*
B. May 5, 1946 Tel Aviv, Israel
Ht. 5-10 Wt. 151
Citizen—Israel

1967	Baltimore	7	0	1	1
1968	Baltimore	16	0	0	0
1975	New York	11	0	0	0
	Totals	34	0	1	1

PRINGLE, ALEX *Defender*
B. Nov. 8, 1948 Edinburgh, Scotland
Ht. 5-9 Wt. 160
Citizen—Scotland

1975	Tampa Bay	14	1	0	2
1976	Tampa Bay	22	0	0	0
1977	T.B.-Wash.	17	0	0	0
1978	Washington	11	0	0	0
	Totals	64	1	0	2

PRINGLE, PAUL *Defender*
B. 1955 Kingston, Jamaica
Ht. 5-10 Wt. 155
Citizen—Jamaica

| 1977 | Chicago | 19 | 0 | 0 | 0 |

PRINS, JACOB "CO" *Forward*
B. May 6, 1938 Amsterdam, Holland
Ht. 5-7 Wt. 160
Citizen—Holland

1967	Pittsburgh	21	8	9	25
1968	New York	19	5	0	10
	Totals	40	13	9	35

PROCTOR, DAVID *Forward*
B. Dec. 26, 1951 Chiswick, England
Ht. 6-1 Wt. 175
Citizen—Canada

| 1974 | Den.-Roch. | 15 | 4 | 1 | 9 |
| 1975 | Miami | 15 | 9 | 3 | 21 |

Season	Club	GP	G	A	Pts.
1976	Miami	1	0	0	0
1977	Ft. Lauderdale	14	3	2	8
1978	Washington	3	1	0	2
	Totals	48	17	6	40

PROVAN, ANDY *Forward*
B. Greenock, Scotland
Ht. 5-5 Wt. 140

1973	Philadelphia	19	11	6	28
1974	Philadelphia	20	9	3	21
	Totals	39	20	9	49

PSAKER, BORIS *Forward*
Ht. 5-11 Wt. 161

| 1975 | Toronto | 12 | 2 | 0 | 4 |

PSIFIDIS, VASILLIS "BILLY" *Defender*
B. June 1, 1944 Thessaloniki, Greece
Ht. 5-8 Wt. 160
Citizen—Greece

1968	Houston	31	0	1	1
1972	Dallas	5	2	0	4
1974	Dallas	5	0	0	0
	Totals	41	2	1	5

PUGH, DAVID *Midfielder*
B. July 9, 1943 Ireland
Ht. 5-11 Wt. 175

1967	Boston	—	—	—	—
1968	Boston	14	2	0	4
	Totals	14	2	0	4

PUGLIA, FERNANDO *Forward*
Ht. 5-5 Wt. 141

| 1967 | Houston | 9 | 3 | 0 | 6 |

PULITA, JORGE *Forward*
Ht. 6-2 Wt. 185
Citizen—Mexico

| 1976 | Philadelphia | 1 | 0 | 0 | 0 |

PULS, JOACHIM *Midfielder*
B. Aug. 20, 1939 Sierakow, Poland
Ht. 6-2 Wt. 165
Citizen—Poland

1967	St. Louis	18	3	0	6
1968	St. Louis	7	1	0	2
1971	St. Louis	18	1	0	2
1972	St. Louis	14	1	0	2
1973	St. Louis	13	0	1	1
	Totals	70	6	1	13

PUSELJ, MLADEN *Midfielder*
B. Dec. 29, 1952 Zagreb, Yugoslavia
Ht. 5-7 Wt. 145
Citizen—Yugoslavia

| 1977 | Toronto | 7 | 1 | 0 | 2 |

Season	Club	GP	G	A	Pts.

PUSKAS, STANKO
See *Goalkeeper*

QUINN, PAT   *Forward*
Ht. 5–5   Wt. 140

| 1967 | Tor. (USA) | 11 | 0 | 2 | 2 |

QUIROS, WILLIAM   *Forward*
B. Oct. 10, 1941   Alajuela, Costa Rica
Ht. 5–5   Wt. 143
Citizen—Costa Rica

1967	Oakland	6	0	2	2
1968	Oakland	20	3	0	6
1975	San Jose	1	0	0	0
	Totals	27	3	2	8

QURAISHI, FARRUKH   *Defender*
B. Nov. 13, 1951   Masjid-I-Sulaiman, Iran
Ht. 5–9   Wt. 145
Citizen—England

1975	Tampa Bay	21	0	1	1
1976	Tampa Bay	15	0	0	0
1977	Tampa Bay	15	0	0	0
1979	Tampa Bay	18	0	0	0
	Totals	69	0	1	1

RADONJIC, MOJAS   *Forward*
B. Feb. 23, 1950   Njegusi
Ht. 6–3   Wt. 185
Citizen—Yugoslavia

| 1979 | Tampa Bay | 9 | 2 | 5 | 9 |

RADOVIC, BRANKO   *Midfielder*
B. Oct. 18, 1950   Yugoslavia
Ht. 5–9   Wt. 160
Citizen—Yugoslavia

1978	Colorado	29	0	1	1
1979	Atlanta	29	0	5	5
	Totals	58	0	6	6

RADUKA, JOE   *Defender*
B. Jan. 18, 1954   Bastaji, Yugoslavia
Ht. 5–10   Wt. 165
Citizen—Yugoslavia

1978	Oakland	6	0	1	1
1979	Edmonton	19	0	0	0
	Totals	25	0	1	1

RAINEY, JERRY
See *Goalkeeper*

RAJSKI, MIKE   *Forward*
B. Sept. 19, 1946   Sopot, Poland
Ht. 5–9   Wt. 155

| 1975 | Hartford | 7 | 4 | 0 | 8 |

Season	Club	GP	G	A	Pts.

RALBOVSKY, STEVE   *Midfielder*
B. Jan. 9, 1953   Backa, Yugoslavia
Ht. 5–9   Wt. 150
Citizen—U.S.

1977	Chicago	10	0	1	1
1978	Colorado	23	0	4	4
1979	Tul.-Ft. L	12	0	1	1
	Totals	45	0	6	6

RAMIREZ, WILLIAM FLEMING   *Defender*
B. Sept. 4, 1941   Peru
Ht. 5–11   Wt. 170

| 1972 | Miami | 10 | 0 | 0 | 0 |

RANOGALEC, BOZIDAR   *Forward*
B. Feb. 4, 1948   Zagreb, Yugoslavia
Ht. 5–8   Wt. 170
Citizen—Yugoslavia

| 1976 | Chicago | 1 | 0 | 1 | 1 |

RAUSCH, WOLFGANG   *Midfielder*
B. Apr. 30, 1947   Aachen, W. Germany
Ht. 5–9   Wt. 170
Citizen—W. Germany

| 1979 | Dallas | 21 | 5 | 7 | 17 |

RAUTMANN, WALTER   *Midfielder*

| 1975 | Dallas | 9 | 0 | 1 | 1 |

RAZAK, ABDUL   *Forward*
B. Apr. 18, 1956   Ghana
Ht. 5–8   Wt. 175
Citizen—Ghana

| 1979 | New York | 3 | 0 | 1 | 1 |

REDFERN, JIM   *Forward*
B. Jan. 8, 1952   Liverpool, England
Ht. 5–9   Wt. 150
Citizen—England

1977	Washington	21	4	3	11
1978	Tulsa	29	8	4	20
1979	Philadelphia	15	1	2	4
	Totals	65	13	9	35

REDKNAPP, HARRY   *Forward*
B. Mar. 2, 1947   Poplar, England
Ht. 5–10   Wt. 150
Citizen—England

1976	Seattle	15	0	6	6
1977	Seattle	5	0	2	2
1978	Seattle	3	0	1	1
1979	Seattle	1	0	0	0
	Totals	24	0	9	9

Season	Club	GP	G	A	Pts.

REDMOND, TOM *Defender*
B. Aug. 2, 1954 St. Louis, Mo.
Ht. 6–1 Wt. 170
Citizen—U.S.

Season	Club	GP	G	A	Pts.
1976	Chicago	6	0	0	0
1977	Chicago	3	0	0	0
	Totals	9	0	0	0

REEVES, EDWARD *Midfielder*
B. England
Ht. 5–9 Wt. 165
Citizen—England

Season	Club	GP	G	A	Pts.
1968	Los Angeles	20	3	0	6

REGINATO, ADRIANO
See *Goalkeeper*

REICE, RICH *Forward*
B. June 18, 1956 Levittown, Pa.
Ht. 5–6 Wt. 160
Citizen—U.S.

Season	Club	GP	G	A	Pts.
1978	Philadelphia	17	1	2	4
1979	Philadelphia	12	1	0	2
	Totals	29	2	2	6

REID, STEVE *Forward*
B. Apr. 6, 1955 Montreal, Canada
Ht. 5–10 Wt. 155
Citizen—U.S.

Season	Club	GP	G	A	Pts.
1979	New England	14	1	0	2

RENERY, LEN *Defender*
B. Nov. 9, 1949 London, England
Ht. 5–10 Wt. 175
Citizen—U.S.

Season	Club	GP	G	A	Pts.
1973	New York	16	1	2	4
1974	New York	15	0	0	0
1975	Baltimore	20	1	0	2
1976	San Diego	15	0	0	0
1978	California	22	0	0	0
1979	California	17	0	1	1
	Totals	105	2	3	7

RENKERT, PAUL *Forward*
B. Feb. 7, 1957 Seattle, Wash.
Ht. 5–6 Wt. 132
Citizen—U.S.

Season	Club	GP	G	A	Pts.
1977	Seattle	1	0	0	0

RENSHAW, MIKE *Forward*
B. Apr. 28, 1948 Manchester, England
Ht. 5–10 Wt. 140
Citizen—England

Season	Club	GP	G	A	Pts.
1968	Dallas	24	3	3	9
1969	Dallas	15	1	2	4
1970	Dallas	23	6	5	17

Season	Club	GP	G	A	Pts.
1971	Dallas	22	3	8	14
1972	Dallas	14	5	3	13
1973	Dallas	19	0	6	6
1974	Dallas	9	1	2	4
1975	Dallas	14	2	2	6
	Totals	140	21	31	73

RENSING, GARY *Defender*
B. Oct. 5, 1947 St. Louis, Mo.
Ht. 5–10 Wt. 150
Citizen—U.S.

Season	Club	GP	G	A	Pts.
1970	St. Louis	16	0	0	0
1971	St. Louis	22	0	0	0
1972	St. Louis	12	0	0	0
1973	St. Louis	19	0	1	1
1974	St. Louis	20	0	0	0
1975	St. Louis	22	0	0	0
1976	St. Louis	22	0	0	0
1977	St. Louis	15	0	0	0
1978	St. Louis	16	0	0	0
	Totals	164	0	1	1

RESSEL, PETER *Forward*
B. Dec. 4, 1945
Ht. 5–10 Wt. 160
Citizen—Holland

Season	Club	GP	G	A	Pts.
1978	San Jose	29	8	7	23
1979	Chicago	28	10	18	38
	Totals	57	18	25	61

RESZNECKI, TIBOR *Defender*
B. Hungary
Ht. 5–8 Wt. 165

Season	Club	GP	G	A	Pts.
1967	N.Y. (NPSL)	10	0	0	0

REY, JOAQUIN *Midfielder*
B. Spain
Ht. 5–10 Wt. 160
Citizen—Spain

Season	Club	GP	G	A	Pts.
1968	Vancouver	19	4	0	8

REYES, SALVADOR *Forward*
B. Guadalajara, Mexico
Ht. 5–10 Wt. 160
Citizen—Mexico

Season	Club	GP	G	A	Pts.
1967	L.A. (NPSL)	11	6	1	13

REYNOLDS, CRAIG *Defender*
B. Aug. 11, 1953 Webster, N.Y.
Ht. 5–10 Wt. 165
Citizen—U.S.

Season	Club	GP	G	A	Pts.
1976	Rochester	20	0	4	4
1977	Rochester	15	2	1	5
1978	Rochester	12	0	0	0
1979	Rochester	4	1	0	2
	Totals	51	3	5	11

Season	Club	GP	G	A	Pts.

REYNOLDS, RICHARD *Forward*
B. Feb. 15, 1948   Looe, England
Ht. 6-0   Wt. 180

Season	Club	GP	G	A	Pts.
1973	Dallas	13	8	6	22
1975	Dallas	18	3	6	12
	Totals	31	11	12	34

REYNOLDS, TOM
See *Goalkeeper*

RIBEIRO, BENEDICTO *Forward*
Ht. 5-5   Wt. 154

| 1967 | N.Y. (USA) | 12 | 5 | 2 | 12 |

RICHARDSON, JOHN *Forward*
Ht. 6-0   Wt. 164

| 1972 | Dallas | 9 | 1 | 1 | 3 |

RIDLEY, BOB *Midfielder*
Ht. 5-8   Wt. 155

1973	Dallas	17	1	0	2
1974	Dallas	13	0	4	4
1975	Denver	1	0	0	0
	Totals	31	1	4	6

RIDLEY, JOHN *Defender*
B. Apr. 27, 1952 Durham, England
Ht. 6-1   Wt. 166
Citizen—England

| 1978 | Ft. Lauderdale | 22 | 1 | 1 | 3 |

RIELY, HOWARD *Forward*
B. Leicester, England
Ht. 5-6   Wt. 152
Citizen—England

| 1967 | Atlanta | 5 | 2 | 1 | 5 |

RIES, DON *Defender*

| 1975 | Miami | 7 | 0 | 0 | 0 |

RIGAS, THEMIS
B. Patra, Greece
Citizen—Greece

| 1976 | Toronto | 10 | 0 | 1 | 1 |

RIGBY, BOB
See *Goalkeeper*

RIGHT, JOE
See *Goalkeeper*

RIJSBERGEN, WILHELMUS "WIM" *Midfielder*
B. Jan. 18, 1952   Leiden, Holland
Ht. 6-0   Wt. 155
Citizen—Holland

| 1979 | New York | 25 | 0 | 2 | 2 |

RIJZENBURG, ORLANDO
B. Mar. 23, 1948   Paramaribo, Surinam

| 1968 | Balt.-Bost. | 9 | 2 | 0 | 4 |

RILDO *Defender*
B. Jan. 23, 1942   Rio de Janeiro, Brazil
Ht. 5-9   Wt. 155
Citizen—Brazil

| 1977 | New York | 12 | 0 | 1 | 1 |

RIOCH, NEIL *Defender*
B. Apr. 13, 1951   London, England
Ht. 5-11   Wt. 180
Citizen—England

1971	Toronto	11	1	0	2
1976	Portland	23	3	1	7
	Totals	34	4	1	9

RIVERA, GERMY *Midfielder*
B. Mar. 6, 1946
Ht. 5-7   Wt. 145
Citizen—Ecuador

| 1974 | New York | 7 | 0 | 0 | 0 |

RIZZO, FRANCESCO *Forward*
Ht. 5-9   Wt. 154

| 1967 | Chi. (USA) | 10 | 4 | 1 | 9 |

ROA, MANUEL *Midfielder*
B. Sept. 6, 1952   Argentina
Ht. 5-10   Wt. 155
Citizen—Argentina

| 1978 | Washington | 1 | 0 | 0 | 0 |

ROACH, ROBERT *Midfielder*
B. Jan. 12, 1949   Liverpool, England
Ht. 5-9   Wt. 155
Citizen—England

| 1968 | Dallas | 23 | 2 | 0 | 4 |

ROBB, DAVID *Forward*
B. Dec. 15, 1947   Scotland
Ht. 5-11   Wt. 172
Citizen—Scotland

1977	Tampa Bay	15	8	1	17
1978	Tampa Bay	27	13	6	32
1979	Philadelphia	30	16	20	52
	Totals	72	37	27	101

ROBERTS, DALE *Defender*
B. Oct. 8, 1956   England
Ht. 5-10   Wt. 160
Citizen—England

| 1979 | Atlanta | 14 | 0 | 0 | 0 |

Season	Club	GP	G	A	Pts.
ROBERTS, DAVE *Defender*					
Ht. 5–11 Wt. 172					
1977	Chicago	13	0	0	0
ROBERTS, NEILL *Forward*					
B. Mar. 30, 1954 Durban, S. Africa					
Ht. 6–2 Wt. 175					
Citizen—S. Africa					
1979	Atlanta	19	14	3	31
ROBERTSON, JIMMY *Forward*					
B. Dec. 17, 1944 Glasgow, Scotland					
Ht. 5–8 Wt. 147					
Citizen—Scotland					
1976	Seattle	12	1	4	6
1977	Seattle	17	2	3	7
	Totals	29	3	7	13
ROBERTSON, LAMMIE *Midfielder*					
B. Sept. 27, 1947 Paisley, Scotland					
Ht. 5–11 Wt. 160					
Citizen—Scotland					
1976	Chicago	14	1	3	5
ROBINS, IAN *Forward*					
B. Bury, England					
Ht. 5–9 Wt. 158					
1974	Denver	20	4	4	12
ROBINSON, BRIAN *Midfielder*					
B. June 29, 1948 Victoria, Canada					
Ht. 5–8 Wt. 155					
Citizen—Canada					
1976	Vancouver	23	0	2	2
ROBOOSTOFF, ARCHIE *Forward*					
B. Oct. 9, 1951 Shanghai, China					
Ht. 5–0 Wt. 175					
Citizen—U.S.					
1974	San Jose	19	6	8	20
1975	San Jose	21	4	7	15
1976	San Diego	22	4	2	10
1977	Portland	20	4	1	9
1978	Port.-Oak.	20	2	1	5
	Totals	102	20	19	59
ROBSON, BOB					
See *Goalkeeper*					
RODERICK, SKIP *Midfielder*					
Ht. 5–11 Wt. 168					
1974	Philadelphia	5	0	1	1
RODRIGUES, JOSE					
See *Goalkeeper*					

Season	Club	GP	G	A	Pts.
ROE, PAUL *Forward*					
B. Nov. 21, 1959 Manchester, England					
Ht. 5–7 Wt. 145					
Citizen—Canada					
1978	Toronto	7	0	0	0
1979	Edmonton	1	0	0	0
	Totals	8	0	0	0
ROE, PETER *Forward*					
B. Sept. 23, 1955 Manchester, England					
Ht. 5–8 Wt. 150					
Citizen—Canada					
1973	Toronto	6	2	0	4
1974	Toronto	5	1	0	2
1975	Toronto	17	3	3	9
1977	Toronto	25	4	2	10
1978	Toronto	29	0	2	2
1979	Toronto	28	3	3	9
	Totals	110	13	10	36
ROGERS, JOHN *Forward*					
B. Sept. 16, 1950 Liverpool, England					
Ht. 6–0 Wt. 170					
Citizen—England					
1976	Portland	14	2	3	7
ROHRBACH, BOB *Forward*					
B. Apr. 2, 1955					
Ht. 6–2 Wt. 170					
Citizen—U.S.					
1978	Colorado	26	6	2	14
1979	Detroit	8	4	0	8
	Totals	34	10	2	22
ROLLAND, ANDY *Defender*					
B. Dundee, Scotland					
Ht. 5–9 Wt. 170					
Citizen—Scotland					
1978	Ft. L.-L.A.	27	1	1	3
RONDANINI, FRANCO *Forward*					
B. Milano, Italy					
Ht. 5–11 Wt. 166					
Citizen—Italy					
1967	Tor. (NPSL)	13	3	3	9
RONGEN, THOMAS *Midfielder*					
B. Oct. 31, 1956 Amsterdam, Holland					
Ht. 6–0 Wt. 175					
Citizen—Holland					
1979	Los Angeles	30	6	5	17
RONSON, BILL *Forward*					
B. Jan. 22, 1957 Fleetwood, England					
Ht. 5–4 Wt. 140					
Citizen—England					
1978	Ft. Lauderdale	17	1	2	4

Season	Club	GP	G	A	Pts.

ROSENTHAL, SAM   *Midfielder*
Ht., 5–11   Wt. 175
Citizen—Israel

Season	Club	GP	G	A	Pts.
1978	Oakland	18	0	2	2

ROSS, ERIC   *Forward*
Ht. 5–11   Wt. 140

Season	Club	GP	G	A	Pts.
1967	Detroit	7	0	1	1

ROSS, GEORGE   *Defender*
Ht. 6–0   Wt. 170

Season	Club	GP	G	A	Pts.
1974	Washington	17	1	0	2

ROSUL, ALEX   *Defender*
B. July 20, 1956   Cleveland, Ohio
Ht. 6–3   Wt. 185
Citizen—U.S.

Season	Club	GP	G	A	Pts.
1978	Minnesota	5	0	0	0
1979	Min.-Mem.	5	0	0	0
	Totals	10	0	0	0

ROSUL, ROMAN   *Forward*
B. May 10, 1953   Cleveland, Ohio
Ht. 6–0   Wt. 175
Citizen—U.S.

Season	Club	GP	G	A	Pts.
1976	Miami	14	4	3	11
1977	Ft. Lauderdale-Conn.	16	4	1	9
1978	Memphis	12	7	2	16
1979	Memphis	11	2	0	4
	Totals	53	17	6	40

ROTE, KYLE   *Forward*
B. Dec. 25, 1950   Dallas, Texas
Ht. 6–0   Wt. 180
Citizen—U.S.

Season	Club	GP	G	A	Pts.
1973	Dallas	18	10	10	30
1974	Dallas	18	7	2	16
1975	Dallas	21	5	6	16
1976	Dallas	19	3	3	9
1977	Dallas	24	11	6	28
1978	Dallas	21	6	7	19
1979	Houston	21	1	4	6
	Totals	142	43	38	124

ROTH, JIM   *Forward*
B. Nov. 8, 1955   St. Louis, Mo.
Ht. 5–8   Wt. 150
Citizen—U.S.

Season	Club	GP	G	A	Pts.
1978	Rochester	2	0	0	0

ROTH, WERNER   *Defender*
B. Apr. 4, 1948   Yugoslavia
Ht. 6–1   Wt. 185
Citizen—U.S.

Season	Club	GP	G	A	Pts.
1972	New York	11	0	2	2
1973	New York	16	0	0	0
1974	New York	16	0	0	0
1975	New York	22	0	0	0
1976	New York	12	0	1	1
1977	New York	23	1	1	3
1978	New York	25	1	2	4
1979	New York	1	0	0	0
	Totals	125	2	6	10

ROTNER, KAROL
B. Mar. 8, 1948   Rumania
Citizen—Israel

Season	Club	GP	G	A	Pts.
1973	New York	3	0	0	0

ROUSE, RAYMOND
See *Goalkeeper*

ROWAN, BARRY   *Forward*
B. Apr. 24, 1943   Newcastle, England
Ht. 5–9   Wt. 160
Citizen—England

Season	Club	GP	G	A	Pts.
1967	Oakland	12	1	5	7
1968	Detroit	10	2	0	4
1971	Dallas	15	0	1	1
1972	Toronto	13	1	0	2
	Totals	50	4	6	14

ROWAN, BRIAN   *Defender*
B. June 28, 1948   Glasgow, Scotland
Ht. 5–9   Wt. 142
Citizen—England

Season	Club	GP	G	A	Pts.
1971	Toronto	22	0	1	1
1972	Toronto	9	0	1	1
1973	Toronto	17	0	2	2
1974	Toronto	19	1	0	2
1975	Tor.-N.Y.	16	0	0	0
1976	New York	11	0	1	1
	Totals	94	1	5	7

ROWLANDS, JOHN   *Defender*
B. Feb. 7, 1947   Liverpool, England
Ht. 6–1   Wt. 175
Citizen—England

Season	Club	GP	G	A	Pts.
1974	Seattle	20	10	8	28
1975	Seattle	21	10	5	25
1976	San Jose	20	1	1	3
1977	San Jose	23	0	1	1
1978	S.J.-Oak.	20	1	3	5
1979	S.J.-Tul.	27	0	0	0
	Totals	131	22	18	62

ROY, WILLY   *Forward*
B. Feb. 8, 1943   Germany
Ht. 5–11   Wt. 172
Citizen—U.S.

Season	Club	GP	G	A	Pts.
1967	Chi. (NPSL)	27	17	5	39
1968	Kansas City	29	6	7	19
1971	St. Louis	13	5	11	21
1972	St. Louis	11	7	2	16
1973	St. Louis	19	7	4	18
	Totals	99	42	29	113

Season	Club	GP	G	A	Pts.

RUDROFF, BRUCE *Midfielder*
B. May 11, 1955 Jefferson City, Mo.
Ht. 6-0 Wt. 160
Citizen—U.S.

Season	Club	GP	G	A	Pts.
1977	Seattle	9	0	0	0
1978	Seattle	23	1	0	2
1979	Seattle	4	0	0	0
	Totals	36	1	0	2

RUMMEL, MANFRED *Forward*
B. Jan. 22, 1938 Essen, Germany
Ht. 5-6 Wt. 165
Citizen—Germany

Season	Club	GP	G	A	Pts.
1967	Pittsburgh	19	14	4	32
1968	Kansas City	28	11	0	22
	Totals	47	25	4	54

RUNAC, ANTUN *Forward*
B. Yugoslavia
Ht. 5-11 Wt. 150

Season	Club	GP	G	A	Pts.
1973	Rochester	9	3	0	6
1974	Rochester	9	2	0	4
	Totals	18	5	0	10

RUS, MILENKO *Defender*
B. June 14, 1941 Kikinos, Yugoslavia
Ht. 5-10 Wt. 165
Citizen—Yugoslavia

Season	Club	GP	G	A	Pts.
1968	St. Louis	23	0	0	0

RUSSEL, ALEX *Midfielder*
Ht. 5-8 Wt. 160

Season	Club	GP	G	A	Pts.
1975	Los Angeles	20	2	2	6

RUSSEL, DALE *Midfielder*
B. Jan. 19, 1955 Warwick Parrish, Bermuda
Ht. 5-10 Wt. 165
Citizen—Bermuda

Season	Club	GP	G	A	Pts.
1978	Houston	21	3	0	6
1979	Houston	28	6	6	18
	Totals	49	9	6	24

RUSSO, PHIL *Forward*

Season	Club	GP	G	A	Pts.
1973	Rochester	3	0	0	0

RUZIK, DARIO
See *Goalkeeper*

RYAN, GREG *Defender*
B. Jan. 21, 1957 Frankfurt, West Germany
Ht. 5-9 Wt. 160
Citizen—U.S.

Season	Club	GP	G	A	Pts.
1979	Tul.-N.Y.	18	0	2	2

RYAN, JIM *Forward*
B. May 12, 1945 Stirling, England
Ht. 5-9 Wt. 151
Citizen— England

Season	Club	GP	G	A	Pts.
1976	Dallas	23	9	7	25
1977	Dallas	26	4	2	10
1978	Dallas	27	8	12	28
1979	Dallas	21	0	6	6
	Totals	97	21	27	69

RYAN, STEVE *Midfielder*
B. Oct. 27, 1956
Ht. 5-10 Wt. 175
Citizen—U.S.

Season	Club	GP	G	A	Pts.
1979	San Jose	24	2	3	7

RYMARCZUK, ANDY *Forward*
Ht. 6-1 Wt. 186
Citizen—U.S.

Season	Club	GP	G	A	Pts.
1973	Rochester	15	1	1	3
1974	Rochester	16	1	2	4
1975	Rochester	21	1	2	4
	Totals	52	3	5	11

RYS, MIRO *Forward*
B. July 18, 1957 Kladno, Czechoslovakia
Ht. 6-1 Wt. 160
Citizen—U.S.

Season	Club	GP	G	A	Pts.
1976	Chicago	17	4	2	10
1977	Los Angeles	2	2	0	4
	Totals	19	6	2	14

SABANKAYA, MUSTAFA
See *Goalkeeper*

SACCONE, ADEMAR *Forward*
B. Montevideo, Uruguay
Ht. 5-10 Wt. 160
Citizen—Uruguay

Season	Club	GP	G	A	Pts.
1967	Oakland	12	5	3	13
1968	Oakland	13	10	0	20
	Totals	25	15	3	33

SADLER, DAVID *Defender*
B. Feb. 5, 1946 Yalding, Kent, England
Ht. 6-1 Wt. 175

Season	Club	GP	G	A	Pts.
1973	Miami	19	1	0	2

SAFIOTI, NORBERTO *Forward*
Ht. 5-10 Wt. 162

Season	Club	GP	G	A	Pts.
1967	Houston	3	1	1	3

SAGOSTUME, LUIS *Defender*

Season	Club	GP	G	A	Pts.
1975	San Antonio	9	0	0	0

ST. CLAIR, GARY
See *Goalkeeper*

Season	Club	GP	G	A	Pts.

ST. LOT, FRANTZ   *Defender*
B. Dec. 13, 1951   Haiti
Ht. 5–8   Wt. 150
Citizen—U.S.

Season	Club	GP	G	A	Pts.
1977	Tampa Bay	5	0	0	0
1978	Tampa Bay	22	0	1	1
1979	Memphis	12	0	3	3
	Totals	39	0	4	4

ST. VIL, GUY   *Forward*
B. Oct. 21, 1942   Port-au-Prince, Haiti
Ht. 5–8   Wt. 140
Citizen—Haiti

Season	Club	GP	G	A	Pts.
1967	Baltimore	13	8	2	18
1968	Baltimore	11	3	0	6
1975	Baltimore	6	0	0	0
	Totals	30	11	2	24

SALCEDO, IGNACIO   *Midfielder*
B. May 22, 1947   Madrid, Spain
Ht. 5–10   Wt. 165
Citizen—Spain

Season	Club	GP	G	A	Pts.
1978	Toronto	7	0	0	0

SALVAGE, BARRY   *Forward*
B. Dec. 21, 1947   Elbourne, England
Ht. 5–10   Wt. 156
Citizen—England

Season	Club	GP	G	A	Pts.
1977	St. Louis	25	1	4	6

SAMBU, JOSE

Season	Club	GP	G	A	Pts.
1971	Toronto	1	0	0	0

SAMMELS, JOHN   *Midfielder*
B. July 23, 1945   Ipswich, England
Ht. 5–10   Wt. 160
Citizen—England

Season	Club	GP	G	A	Pts.
1978	Vancouver	25	4	4	12
1979	Vancouver	29	3	7	13
	Totals	54	7	11	25

SAMSON, DARYL   *Midfielder*
B. Aug. 25, 1952   Vancouver, Canada
Ht. 5–10   Wt. 160
Citizen—Canada

Season	Club	GP	G	A	Pts.
1974	Vancouver	5	1	2	4
1975	Vancouver	6	0	0	0
1976	Vancouver	10	2	0	4
1977	Vancouver	1	0	0	0
	Totals	22	3	2	8

SAMUELSSON, KJELL   *Midfielder*
B. Aug. 22, 1951   Stockholm, Sweden
Ht. 5–10   Wt. 170
Citizen—Sweden

Season	Club	GP	G	A	Pts.
1976	San Diego	3	0	0	0

SANCHEZ, ATAULFO
See *Goalkeeper*

SANCHEZ, BLAS
See *Goalkeeper*

SANCHEZ, HUGO   *Forward*
B. July 11, 1958   Mexico City, Mexico
Ht. 5–7   Wt. 150
Citizen—Mexico

Season	Club	GP	G	A	Pts.
1979	San Diego	10	6	5	17

SANCHEZ, MIGUEL   *Defender*

Season	Club	GP	G	A	Pts.
1972	Miami	1	0	0	0

SANDOR, ATILLA   *Forward*
B. Germany
Ht. 5–7   Wt. 140
Citizen—U.S.

Season	Club	GP	G	A	Pts.
1968	Vancouver	1	0	0	0

SANTISTEBAN, JUAN   *Midfielder*
B. Dec. 8, 1937   Seville, Spain
Ht. 5–8   Wt. 155
Citizen—Spain

Season	Club	GP	G	A	Pts.
1967	Baltimore	14	2	7	11
1968	Baltimore	14	0	0	0
	Totals	28	2	7	11

SARACHAN, DAVID   *Forward*
B. June 7, 1954
Ht. 5–5   Wt. 135
Citizen—U.S.

Season	Club	GP	G	A	Pts.
1976	Rochester	2	0	0	0
1977	Rochester	1	0	0	0
	Totals	3	0	0	0

SASS, HENRY   *Forward*
B. Poland
Ht. 5–7   Wt. 141
Citizen—Poland

Season	Club	GP	G	A	Pts.
1968	Chicago	5	0	0	0

SAUTTER, BILL   *Forward*
B. Mar. 5, 1958   Abington, Pa.
Ht. 6–2   Wt. 180
Citizen—U.S.

Season	Club	GP	G	A	Pts.
1978	Tulsa	26	6	2	14
1979	Tulsa	14	0	3	3
	Totals	40	6	5	17

SCHAFER, HELMUT   *Defender*
B. W. Germany
Ht. 5–10   Wt. 150

Season	Club	GP	G	A	Pts.
1973	Toronto	15	0	2	2
1974	Toronto	19	0	2	2
	Totals	34	0	4	4

Season	Club	GP	G	A	Pts.

SCHARMANN, JOHANN *Midfielder*
B. Feb. 23, 1949   Austria
Ht. 5–9   Wt. 158
Citizen—Austria

1979	Det.-Calif.	23	1	5	7

SCHELLSCHEIDT, MANFRED *Midfielder*
B. Jan. 7, 1941   Germany
Ht. 5–10   Wt. 155
Citizen—U.S.

1973	Philadelphia	14	1	4	6
1975	Hartford	17	2	2	6
	Totals	31	3	6	12

SCHEPERS, JOHN
B. Tiel, Holland
Citizen—Canada

1971	Toronto	3	1	0	2

SCHIRALDI, JOE *Forward*
B. Sannicandro, Italy
Ht. 5–8   Wt. 155
Citizen—Canada

1973	Toronto	11	0	2	2
1974	Toronto	1	0	0	0
	Totals	12	0	2	2

SCHNETTGOECKE, RAY *Defender*
B. Mar. 2, 1956   St. Louis, Mo.
Ht. 6–1   Wt. 180
Citizen—U.S.

1978	Philadelphia	10	1	0	2

SCHOENMAKER, ALEX *Midfielder*
B. Aug. 23, 1947   Holland
Ht. 6–0   Wt. 185
Citizen—Holland

1979	Edmonton	22	6	8	20

SCHOENMAKER, LEY *Forward*
Ht. 6–1   Wt. 169

1967	San Francisco	9	1	1	3

SCHUBERTH, WALTER *Midfielder*
B. Apr. 1, 1950   Strassdorf, W. Germany
Ht. 5–8   Wt. 163
Citizen—W. Germany

1979	Houston	27	5	11	21

SCORSE, DOUG *Midfielder*
B. 1951   Vancouver
Ht. 5–10   Wt. 170
Citizen—Canada

1974	Vancouver	3	0	0	0

SCOTT, CARLOS *Midfielder*
B. Jan. 18, 1952   La Paz, Bolivia
Ht. 5–9   Wt. 160
Citizen—Bolivia

1975	New York	2	0	0	0

SCOTT, DELROY *Midfielder*
B. Jan. 22, 1947   Jamaica
Ht. 5–8   Wt. 150
Citizen—Jamaica

1968	Atlanta	9	1	0	2

SCOTT, IAN *Forward*
Ht. 6–0   Wt. 169

1967	Dallas	4	0	0	0

SCOTT, JIM *Forward*
Ht. 5–8   Wt. 147

1967	Tor. (USA)	12	2	3	7

SCOTT, JOCKY *Forward*
B. Jan. 1, 1948   Aberdeen, Scotland
Ht. 5–8   Wt. 160
Citizen—Scotland

1977	Seattle	17	6	3	15
1978	Seattle	22	3	8	14
	Totals	39	9	11	29

SCOTT, MELVYN *Midfielder*
B. Sept. 26, 1939   England
Ht. 5–11   Wt. 168
Citizen—England

1967	Chicago	11	1	0	2
1968	Oakland	21	0	0	0
	Totals	32	1	0	2

SCULLION, STEWART *Forward*
B. Apr. 18, 1947   Bo'Ness, Scotland
Ht. 5–7   Wt. 155
Citizen—Scotland

1975	Tampa Bay	18	7	7	21
1976	Tampa Bay	24	10	10	30
1977	Portland	24	11	3	25
1978	Portland	22	7	2	16
1979	Portland	17	2	3	7
	Totals	105	37	25	99

SCURTI, PAUL *Midfielder*
B. Feb. 10, 1951   Spoltore, Italy
Ht. 5–7   Wt. 147
Citizen—U.S.

1974	Baltimore	18	0	1	1
1975	Baltimore	19	0	2	2
1976	San Diego	15	1	1	3
1978	California	2	1	1	3
	Totals	54	2	5	9

Season	Club	GP	G	A	Pts.

SEALE, ELSON *Midfielder*
B. June 13, 1955   Bridgetown, Barbados
Ht. 5-7   Wt. 150
Citizen—Barbados

		GP	G	A	Pts.
1978	Portland	18	3	3	9
1979	Portland	17	2	1	5
	Totals	35	5	4	14

SEARGEANT, STEVE *Defender*
B. Jan. 2, 1951   Liverpool, England
Ht. 5-8   Wt. 154
Citizen—England

		GP	G	A	Pts.
1978	Detroit	30	0	3	3
1979	Detroit	28	0	5	5
	Totals	58	0	8	8

SECCHI, VINNY *Midfielder*
B. Feb. 2, 1958   Aracatuba, Brazil
Ht. 5-9   Wt. 140
Citizen—Brazil

		GP	G	A	Pts.
1979	Dallas	2	0	0	0

SEEMANN, FINN *Forward*
Ht. 6-0   Wt. 170

		GP	G	A	Pts.
1967	Dallas	5	1	1	3

SEERY, MIKE *Forward*
B. Oct. 23, 1950   St. Louis, Mo.
Ht. 6-0   Wt. 170
Citizen—U.S.

		GP	G	A	Pts.
1973	Miami	14	3	4	10
1974	St. Louis	20	1	0	2
1975	St. Louis	13	0	3	3
1976	St. Louis	9	0	0	0
	Totals	56	4	7	15

SEGOTA, BRANKO *Forward*
B. June 8, 1961   Yugoslavia
Ht. 5-9   Wt. 150
Citizen—Canada

		GP	G	A	Pts.
1979	Rochester	13	14	4	32

SEISSLER, MANFRED *Forward*
B. Aug. 8, 1939   Germany
Ht. 5-10   Wt. 175
Citizen—Germany

		GP	G	A	Pts.
1967	Pittsburgh	16	9	4	22
1968	Kansas City	24	8	6	22
1971	Rochester	22	10	7	27
1972	Rochester	11	4	1	9
1973	Roch.-Mont.	11	1	3	5
1974	Rochester	1	0	0	0
	Totals	85	32	21	85

SELMO, RENZO *Midfielder*
Ht. 5-8   Wt. 160

		GP	G	A	Pts.
1971	Montreal	20	1	5	7
1972	Montreal	14	2	3	7
	Totals	34	3	8	14

SEMEDO, QUINTO *Defender*
Ht. 5-10   Wt. 175

		GP	G	A	Pts.
1973	Toronto	14	1	0	2

SEMPLE, BILLY *Forward*
B. Nov. 2, 1947   Bells Hill, Scotland
Ht. 5-7   Wt. 150
Citizen—England

		GP	G	A	Pts.
1976	San Antonio	21	0	4	4

SENINHO (ARSENIO JARDIM) *Forward*
B. July 1, 1949   Sada Bandeira, Angola
Ht. 5-9   Wt. 154
Citizen—Angola

		GP	G	A	Pts.
1978	New York	5	0	0	0
1979	New York	19	3	8	14
	Totals	24	3	8	14

SERGE, LUIS
B. Feb. 5, 1940   Hungary

		GP	G	A	Pts.
1968	Dallas	3	0	0	0

SETTERS, MAURICE *Forward*
Ht. 5-8   Wt. 161

		GP	G	A	Pts.
1967	Cleveland	9	3	2	8

SETTIN, SERGIO *Midfielder*
Ht. 5-6   Wt. 145

		GP	G	A	Pts.
1971	Montreal	17	3	2	8

SEVASTOPOULOS, NICK

		GP	G	A	Pts.
1976	Toronto	3	0	0	0

SEWELL, JOHN *Defender*
B. July 7, 1936   London, England
Ht. 5-8   Wt. 163

		GP	G	A	Pts.
1972	St. Louis	14	3	4	10
1973	St. Louis	18	0	3	3
1974	St. Louis	19	1	1	3
1975	St. Louis	7	0	3	3
	Totals	58	4	11	19

SHARDLOW, PAUL
See *Goalkeeper*

Season	Club	GP	G	A	Pts.

SHARP, RONNIE   *Midfielder*
B. Jan. 30, 1948
Ht. 5–10   Wt. 175
Citizen—Scotland

Season	Club	GP	G	A	Pts.
1973	Miami	19	1	6	8
1974	Miami	11	2	1	5
1975	Miami	12	1	12	14
1976	Miami	21	1	2	4
1977	Miami	1	0	1	1
	Totals	64	5	22	32

SHEARER, CARL   *Defender*
B. Mar. 11, 1960   Canada
Ht. 6–3   Wt. 200
Citizen—Canada

Season	Club	GP	G	A	Pts.
1979	Vancouver	2	0	0	0

SHELTON, DAVE   *Midfielder*
B. Feb. 27, 1956   Chicago, Ill.
Ht. 5–9   Wt. 155
Citizen—U.S.

Season	Club	GP	G	A	Pts.
1978	Detroit	5	0	0	0
1979	Los Angeles	10	0	1	1
	Totals	15	0	1	1

SHERWOOD, STEVE
See *Goalkeeper*

SHEWAN, ALLY   *Defender*
Ht. 5–10   Wt. 170

Season	Club	GP	G	A	Pts.
1967	Washington	12	1	1	3

SHIELDS, JOHN   *Defender*
B. July 28, 1954   Baltimore, Md.
Ht. 6–1   Wt. 175
Citizen—U.S.

Season	Club	GP	G	A	Pts.
1976	Miami	4	0	0	0

SHORT, PETER   *Defender*
B. Oct. 27, 1944   Liverpool, England
Ht. 6–0   Wt. 170
Citizen—U.S.

Season	Club	GP	G	A	Pts.
1967	Philadelphia	12	4	1	9
1968	Cleveland	24	0	6	6
1969	Dallas	16	6	2	14
1970	Rochester	28	3	3	9
1971	Rochester	13	1	0	2
1972	Rochester	13	2	0	4
1973	Rochester	16	2	0	4
1974	Dallas	8	0	0	0
1975	Van.-Den.	20	3	1	7
1976	Minnesota	10	0	1	1
1977	Minnesota	10	0	0	0
	Totals	170	21	14	56

SHOULDER, JIM   *Defender*
Ht. 5–8   Wt. 157

Season	Club	GP	G	A	Pts.
1967	Vancouver	5	1	0	2

SHPIGLER, MORDECHAI   *Forward*

Season	Club	GP	G	A	Pts.
1975	New York	17	6	5	17

SIBBALD, BOBBY   *Defender*
B. Jan. 25, 1948   Newcastle, England
Ht. 5–6   Wt. 160
Citizen—England

Season	Club	GP	G	A	Pts.
1975	Los Angeles	22	3	3	9
1977	Los Angeles	25	1	4	6
1978	Los Angeles	29	0	4	4
1979	Los Angeles	30	1	5	7
	Totals	106	5	16	26

SICILIANO, BRUNO   *Forward*
B. Paola Calabria, Italy
Ht. 5–11   Wt. 161
Citizen—Italy

Season	Club	GP	G	A	Pts.
1967	N.Y. (NPSL)	8	0	3	3

SIDEBOTTOM, GEOFFREY
See *Goalkeeper*

SIDEROPOULOS, PAUL   *Forward*
B. Apr. 13, 1944   Greece
Ht. 5–8   Wt. 150
Citizen—Greece

Season	Club	GP	G	A	Pts.
1968	Boston	1	0	0	0

SIEGA, JORGE   *Forward*
B. Apr. 3, 1947   Cotipora, Brazil
Ht. 5–10   Wt. 165
Citizen—U.S.

Season	Club	GP	G	A	Pts.
1968	Washington	29	6	4	16
1971	New York	24	9	9	27
1972	New York	5	2	4	8
1973	New York	18	2	5	9
1974	New York	12	1	3	5
1975	New York	13	1	3	5
1976	New York	8	0	1	1
	Totals	109	21	29	71

SIKINGER, ROLAND
See *Goalkeeper*

SILVA, CARLOS   *Defender*
Ht. 6–2   Wt. 180
Citizen—Portugal

Season	Club	GP	G	A	Pts.
1976	Rochester	17	1	2	4

Season	Club	GP	G	A	Pts.

SILVA, IBRAIM   *Forward*
B. Nov. 29, 1953   Portugal
Ht. 6–0   Wt. 150
Citizen—Portugal

Season	Club	GP	G	A	Pts.
1976	Rochester	23	1	7	9
1977	Rochester	24	6	3	15
1978	Rochester	26	2	4	8
1979	Rochester	24	6	7	19
	Totals	97	15	21	51

SILVA, JAIR SANTON   *Midfielder*
Ht. 5–5   Wt. 132

1967	Houston	7	1	0	2

SILVA, MARIO   *Forward*
B. Sept. 30, 1943   Lisbon, Portugal
Ht. 5–7   Wt. 150
Citizen—Portugal

1979	Toronto	1	0	0	0

SILVA, SERGIO   *Forward*
Ht. 5–7   Wt. 159

1967	N.Y. (USA)	10	3	0	6

SILVEIRA, ADILSON

1967	N.Y. (NPSL)	3	1	0	2

SILVESTER, PETER   *Forward*
B. Feb. 19, 1948   Workingham, England
Ht. 6–0   Wt. 170
Citizen—England

1974	Baltimore	17	14	4	32
1975	Baltimore	19	5	7	17
1976	S.D.-Van.	17	5	1	11
1977	Washington	12	3	0	6
	Totals	65	27	12	66

SIMMONS, RICHARD   *Midfielder*
Ht. 5–8   Wt. 138

1972	Montreal	4	0	2	2
1973	Montreal	15	1	0	2
	Totals	19	1	2	4

SIMOES, ANTONIO   *Midfielder*
B. Dec. 14, 1943   Lisbon, Portugal
Ht. 5–8   Wt. 150
Citizen—Portugal

1975	Boston	17	3	9	15
1976	Bost.-S.J.	18	1	6	8
1977	San Jose	23	0	7	7
1979	Dallas	6	1	1	3
	Totals	64	5	23	33

SIMPSON, PETER   *Defender*
B. Jan. 13, 1945   Norfolk, England
Ht. 5–11   Wt. 163
Citizen—England

1978	New England	28	0	2	2
1979	New England	21	0	0	0
	Totals	49	0	2	2

SINCLAIR, BILLY   *Midfielder*
Ht. 5–7   Wt. 150

1967	Detroit	10	0	1	1

SINCLAIR, ROY   *Midfielder*
B. Dec. 10, 1944   Liverpool, England
Ht. 5–8   Wt. 147
Citizen—England

1974	Seattle	20	1	3	5
1975	Sea.-Den.	11	0	0	0
1978	Detroit	3	0	1	1
	Totals	34	1	4	6

SINGLETON, TONY   *Midfielder*
B. England
Ht. 6–0   Wt. 175
Citizen—England

1968	New York	12	0	0	0

SISSONS, JOHN   *Forward*
B. Sept. 30, 1945   Hayes, Middlesex, England
Ht. 5–7   Wt. 154
Citizen—England

1975	Tampa Bay	19	5	8	18

SJOBERG, THOMAS   *Forward*
B. July 6, 1952   Malmo, Sweden
Ht. 6–0   Wt.185
Citizen—Sweden

1979	Chicago	17	13	4	30

SKALA, LOTHAR   *Defender*
B. May 2, 1952   Gross-Greau, Germany
Ht. 6–1   Wt. 180
Citizen—W. Germany

1979	Chicago	9	0	0	0

SKEELS, ERIC   *Midfielder*
B. Nov. 27, 1939   Manchester, England
Citizen—England

1967	Cleveland	12	1	0	2
1976	Seattle	16	2	2	6
	Totals	28	3	2	8

Season	Club	GP	G	A	Pts.

SKOTAREK, ALEX *Defender*
B. Apr. 2, 1949 Sindelfingen, Germany
Ht. 6–1 Wt. 175
Citizen—U.S.

Season	Club	GP	G	A	Pts.
1975	Chicago	21	1	3	5
1976	Chicago	24	1	0	2
1977	Chicago	21	0	0	0
1978	Tulsa	18	0	1	1
1979	Tulsa	24	0	2	2
	Totals	108	2	6	10

SLATER, MAURICE *Defender*
Ht. 5–11 Wt. 160

Season	Club	GP	G	A	Pts.
1974	Washington	5	0	1	1

SMALLWOOD, CHIP *Defender*
B. June 14, 1954 Lancaster, Pa.
Ht. 6–2 Wt. 175
Citizen—U.S.

Season	Club	GP	G	A	Pts.
1976	Portland	9	0	0	0
1977	Portland	2	0	0	0
	Totals	11	0	0	0

SMEETS, HUBERT *Forward*
B. Sept. 20, 1953 Sittard, Holland
Ht. 6–5 Wt. 185
Citizen—Holland

Season	Club	GP	G	A	Pts.
1979	Los Angeles	24	8	3	19

SMETHURST, DEREK *Forward*
B. Oct. 24, 1947 Durban, S. Africa
Ht. 6–I Wt. 175
Citizen—S. Africa

Season	Club	GP	G	A	Pts.
1975	Tampa Bay	22	18	3	39
1976	Tampa Bay	24	20	5	45
1977	Tampa Bay	21	19	4	42
1978	T.B.-S.D.	21	2	3	7
1979	Seattle	22	13	2	28
	Totals	110	72	17	161

SMILLIE, JOHN *Forward*
B. Apr. 16, 1954 Glasgow, Scotland
Ht. 5–6 Wt. 145
Citizen—U.S.

Season	Club	GP	G	A	Pts.
1976	Portland	1	0	0	0
1977	San Jose	1	0	0	0
1978	San Jose	12	0	0	0
	Totals	14	0	0	0

SMILLIE, NEIL *Midfielder*
B. July 19, 1958
Ht. 5–7 Wt. 145
Citizen—England

Season	Club	GP	G	A	Pts.
1978	Memphis	28	2	4	8
1979	Memphis	20	5	7	17
	Totals	48	7	11	25

SMIT, CEES *Defender*
B. Haarlem, Holland
Ht. 6–0 Wt. 200
Citizen—Holland

Season	Club	GP	G	A	Pts.
1967	Pittsburgh	7	1	1	3

SMITH, BOB *Defender*
B. Sept. 23, 1951 Trenton, N.J.
Ht. 5–11 Wt. 165
Citizen—U.S.

Season	Club	GP	G	A	Pts.
1973	Philadelphia	19	0	0	0
1974	Philadelphia	20	1	4	6
1975	Philadelphia	22	2	1	5
1976	New York	22	0	2	2
1977	New York	10	1	0	2
1978	New York	9	0	0	0
1979	N.Y.-S.D.	20	0	1	1
	Totals	122	4	8	16

SMITH, BRIAN *Midfielder*
B. Sept. 12, 1955 Bolton, England
Ht. 5–8 Wt. 160
Citizen—England

Season	Club	GP	G	A	Pts.
1978	Tulsa	20	4	5	13

SMITH, DAVE *Defender*
B. Nov. 14, 1943 Aberdeen, Scotland
Citizen—England

Season	Club	GP	G	A	Pts.
1976	Los Angeles	15	0	0	0

SMITH, DEAN *Forward*
B. Nov. 28, 1958 Leicester, England
Ht. 5–10 Wt. 160
Citizen—England

Season	Club	GP	G	A	Pts.
1978	Houston	17	6	7	19

SMITH, FREDDIE *Defender*
Ht. 5–6 Wt. 140

Season	Club	GP	G	A	Pts.
1974	Dallas	15	0	0	0

SMITH, JIMMY *Forward*
Ht. 6–0 Wt. 154

Season	Club	GP	G	A	Pts.
1967	Washington	12	4	0	8

SMITH, MALCOLM *Forward*
B. Sept. 21, 1953 Ferryhill, England
Ht. 5–9 Wt. 155
Citizen—England

Season	Club	GP	G	A	Pts.
1976	Portland	19	3	3	9

SMITH, PETER *Defender*
B. Oct. 21, 1952 Liverpool, England
Ht. 5–11 Wt. 175
Citizen—England

Season	Club	GP	G	A	Pts.
1976	Los Angeles	10	0	0	0

Season	Club	GP	G	A	Pts.

SMITH, PETER

| 1975 | Philadelphia | 1 | 0 | 0 | 0 |

SMITH, STANFIELD *Defender*
B. Apr. 5, 1950   Bermuda
Ht. 6-0   Wt. 175
Citizen—Trinidad

1974	Baltimore	19	0	0	0
1975	Baltimore	19	0	0	0
	Totals	38	0	0	0

SMITH, TOMMY *Midfielder*
B. Apr. 5, 1945   Liverpool, England
Ht. 5-10   Wt. 175
Citizen—England

1976	Tampa Bay	17	0	0	0
1978	Los Angeles	12	0	1	1
	Totals	29	0	1	1

SMITH, WALTER *Midfielder*
Ht. 5-11   Wt. 168

| 1967 | Dallas | 3 | 0 | 0 | 0 |

SMOLCIC, VLADIMIR *Forward*
B. May 12, 1952   Split, Yugoslavia
St. 5-6   Wt. 150
Citizen—Yugoslavia

| 1978 | Toronto | 10 | 3 | 2 | 8 |

SMUDA, FRANZ *Defender*
B. June 22, 1949   Wodzislaw, Poland
Ht. 6-2   Wt. 175
Citizen—Poland

1975	Hartford	20	3	0	6
1978	Oak.-L.A.-S.J.	25	0	0	0
	Totals	45	3	0	6

SNEDDON, IAN *Defender*
Ht. 5-11   Wt. 160

| 1975 | Denver | 21 | 0 | 1 | 1 |

SNOWDON, BRYAN *Midfielder*
B. England
Ht. 6-0   Wt. 175
Citizen—England

| 1968 | Detroit | 15 | 0 | 0 | 0 |

SOLAK, ALEJA *Forward*
Ht. 5-8   Wt. 150
Citizen—Canada

| 1975 | Toronto | 6 | 1 | 0 | 2 |

Season	Club	GP	G	A	Pts.

SOLEM, JEFF *Defender*
B. Jan. 28, 1948   Fargo, North Dakota
Ht. 5-11   Wt. 170
Citizen—U.S.

1973	Atlanta	10	0	0	0
1974	Denver	18	0	0	0
1975	Denver	5	0	0	0
1976	Minnesota	1	0	0	0
	Totals	34	0	0	0

SONO, JOMO *Forward*
B. June 28, 1955   Johannesburg, S. Africa
Ht. 5-8   Wt. 165
Citizen—S. Africa

1977	New York	12	1	0	2
1978	Colorado	30	8	5	21
1979	Atlanta	29	5	12	22
	Totals	71	14	17	45

SORENSEN, FINN WILLY *Defender*
B. Denmark
Ht. 6-4   Wt. 189
Citizen—Denmark

| 1968 | Washington | 18 | 0 | 0 | 0 |

SORGIC, GEORGE *Forward*
B. Feb. 22, 1948   Ruma, Yugoslavia
Ht. 6-0   Wt. 165
Citizen—Yugoslavia

| 1976 | S.J.-L.A. | 23 | 8 | 2 | 18 |

SOROA, JOSE *Midfielder*
B. July 10, 1949   Montevideo, Uruguay
Ht. 6-0   Wt. 170
Citizen—Uruguay

1974	Boston	6	0	0	0
1975	Boston	11	0	1	1
1976	Boston	21	0	0	0
	Totals	38	0	1	1

SOSA, HECTOR RUBEN *Forward*
B. Nov. 14, 1936   Argentina
Ht. 6-0   Wt. 175
Citizen—Argentina

| 1968 | Boston | 8 | 5 | 0 | 10 |

SOTO, CHARLES *Forward*
B. Costa Rica
Ht. 5-7   Wt. 145
Citizen—Costa Rica

| 1968 | Toronto | 13 | 0 | 0 | 0 |

SOTTO MAIOR, JOSE *Midfielder*
Ht. 6-0   Wt. 180

| 1971 | Montreal | 17 | 0 | 1 | 1 |

Season	Club	GP	G	A	Pts.

SOUNESS, GRAHAM *Midfielder*
Ht. 6-0 Wt. 180

1972	Montreal	10	2	2	6

SPAJIC, BOZO *Forward*
B. Yugoslavia
Ht. 6-2 Wt. 180
Citizen—Yugoslavia

1968	Chicago	1	0	0	0

SPALDING, DEREK *Defender*
B. Dec. 20, 1954 Dundee, Scotland
Ht. 5-9 Wt. 170
Citizen—England

1978	Chicago	29	2	3	7
1979	Chicago	23	7	3	17
	Totals	52	9	6	24

SPANN, LEROY *Forward*
B. June 26, 1953
Ht. 5-11 Wt. 170
Citizen—Trinidad

1978	San Jose	17	1	2	4

SPARKS, RAY *Forward*
B. 1953 Henderson, New York
Ht. 5-10 Wt. 155
Citizen—U.S.

1977	Las Vegas	6	0	0	0

SPAVIN, ALAN *Midfielder*
B. Feb. 20, 1942 Lancaster, England
Ht. 5-8 Wt. 160
Citizen—England

1974	Washington	20	5	0	10
1975	Washington	20	0	6	6
1976	Washington	16	2	4	8
1977	Washington	12	0	0	0
	Totals	68	7	10	24

SPECA, JOE *Defender*
B. July 1, 1937 Baltimore, Md.
Ht. 5-9 Wt. 165
Citizen—U.S.

1967	Baltimore	9	1	1	3
1968	Baltimore	3	0	0	0
	Totals	12	1	1	3

SPEIWAK, WALTER *Forward*

1971	St. Louis	13	0	3	3

SPIRING, PETER *Forward*
B. Dec. 13, 1950 England
Ht. 5-11 Wt. 160

1971	Washington	4	0	1	1

Season	Club	GP	G	A	Pts.

SPRAGGON, FRANK *Defender*
B. Oct. 27, 1945 Marley Hill, England
Ht. 5-9 Wt. 170
Citizen—England

1976	Minnesota	24	0	4	4

SPRANGER, LOTHAR
See *Goalkeeper*

SPROATES, ALAN *Forward*

1973	Miami	10	0	1	1

STAHL, GERD *Forward*
B. 1954

1977	Dallas	2	0	0	0

STAHL, MARK *Defender*
B. Aug. 25, 1953 San Francisco, Calif.
Ht. 5-8 Wt. 160
Citizen—U.S.

1975	San Antonio	16	0	0	0
1976	San Antonio	20	0	0	0
1977	Hawaii	15	0	0	0
1978	Houston	14	0	0	0
1979	Houston	4	0	1	1
	Totals	69	0	1	1

STANLEY, GARY *Midfielder*
B. Mar. 4, 1954 Burton-on-Trent, England
Ht. 5-9 Wt. 170
Citizen—England

1979	Ft. Lauderdale	20	0	2	2

STANLEY, PETER *Defender*
B. Sept. 17, 1955 Vancouver, Canada
Ht. 5-9 Wt. 160
Citizen—Canada

1978	Portland	9	0	0	0
1979	Portland	10	0	1	1
	Totals	19	0	1	1

STANTON, PAT *Midfielder*
Ht. 5-9 Wt. 147

1967	Tor.(US)	11	0	1	1

STARTZELL, STAN *Midfielder*
B. Sept. 3, 1950 McClure, Pa.
Ht. 5-7 Wt. 150
Citizen—U.S.

1972	New York	3	0	0	0
1973	Philadelphia	13	1	0	2
1974	Philadelphia	6	0	0	0
	Totals	22	1	0	2

Season	Club	GP	G	A	Pts.
STASTNY, MILOSLAV					
B. Mar. 7, 1940 Bratislava, Czechoslovakia					
1968	Dallas	2	0	0	0
STEADMAN, JAN *Defender*					
B. Oct. 31, 1947 Trinidad					
Ht. 5-10 Wt. 170					
Citizen—Trinidad					
1967	N.Y.(NPSL)	7	0	1	1
1968	New York	7	0	0	0
1971	New York	5	0	0	0
	Totals	19	0	1	1
STEELE, JIM *Defender*					
B. Mar. 11, 1950 Scotland					
Ht. 6-1 Wt. 190					
Citizen—Scotland					
1977	Washington	14	0	2	2
1978	Washington	22	0	2	2
1979	Washington	17	1	3	5
	Totals	53	1	7	9
STEELE, KEITH *Defender*					
B. Oct. 9, 1958 Trinidad					
Ht. 5-8 Wt. 160					
Ciziten—Canada					
1977	Minnesota	3	0	0	0
STEFANOVICH, RADOMIR *Defender*					
B. Belgrade, Yugoslavia					
Ht. 5-10 Wt. 165					
Citizen—Yugoslavia					
1977	Tampa Bay	2	0	0	0
1978	Houston	27	1	0	2
	Totals	29	1	0	2
STEFFENHAGEN, ARNO *Forward*					
B. Sept. 24, 1949 Berlin, West Germany					
Ht. 5-9 Wt. 150					
Citizen—Germany					
1978	Chicago	12	13	3	29
1979	Chicago	1	0	0	0
	Totals	13	13	3	29
STEFONOVIC, MALDEN *Forward*					
B. Oct. 21, 1951					
Ht. 5-10 Wt. 175					
Citizen—Yugoslavia					
1977	Vancouver	2	0	0	0
STEIN, COLIN					
1967	Tor. (USA)	8	5	1	11
STEINROTTER, WILLIE *Defender*					
Ht. 5-11 Wt. 155					
1973	Rochester	11	0	0	0

Season	Club	GP	G	A	Pts.
STENSON, JOHN *Midfielder*					
1974	Denver	10	1	0	2
STEPHANS, ALAN *Defender*					
B. Oct. 13, 1952 Liverpool, England					
Ht. 5-9 Wt. 168					
Citizen—England					
1974	Seattle	18	0	2	2
1975	Seattle	22	0	2	2
1976	San Diego	24	1	1	3
	Totals	64	1	5	7
STEPHEN, MIKE *Midfielder*					
1974	Toronto	2	0	0	0
STEPNEY, ALEX					
See *Goalkeeper*					
STETLER, BOB					
See *Goalkeeper*					
STEURER, BRAD					
See *Goalkeeper*					
STEVENSON, BILLY *Midfielder*					
B. Scotland					
Ht. 5-11 Wt. 170					
Citizen—England					
1974	Vancouver	19	0	1	1
STEVENSON, ERIC *Forward*					
Ht. 5-7 Wt. 151					
1967	Tor.(USA)	11	1	1	3
STEWART, ARTHUR *Midfielder*					
Ht. 5-9 Wt. 154					
1967	Detroit	12	2	0	4
STEWART, JOHN *Defender*					
B. Feb. 18, 1948 Liverpool, England					
Ht. 5-11 Wt. 170					
Citizen—England					
1968	Dallas	9	0	0	0
STICKEL, HEINZ *Defender*					
B. May 9, 1949 Tubingen, Germany					
Ht. 6-0 Wt. 180					
Citizen—Germany					
1978	San Diego	7	1	0	2
STOFFELS, ALPHONSIUS *Forward*					
B. Feb. 3, 1945 Amsterdam, Holland					
Ht. 5-10 Wt. 177					
Citizen—Holland					
1968	K.C.-Dal.	18	2	2	6
1969	Kansas City	—	8	7	23
	Totals	18	10	9	29

Season	Club	GP	G	A	Pts.

STOJANOVIC, MIKE   *Forward*
B. Jan. 26, 1947   Yugoslavia
Ht. 6-0   Wt. 175
Citizen—Yugoslavia

Season	Club	GP	G	A	Pts.
1976	Rochester	24	17	7	41
1977	Rochester	25	14	5	33
1978	Rochester	11	5	3	13
1979	Rochester	30	4	13	21
	Totals	90	40	28	108

STOJANOVIC, MIRKO
See *Goalkeeper*

STOJOVIC, DAN   *Forward*
B. Yugoslavia
Ht. 6-1   Wt. 170
Citizen—Yugoslavia

1968	Chicago	14	9	0	18

STOKES, BOBBY   *Forward*
B. Jan. 30, 1951   Portsmouth, England
Ht. 5-9   Wt. 160
Citizen—England

1977	Washington	20	6	4	16
1978	Washington	26	3	6	12
1979	Washington	29	8	6	22
	Totals	75	17	16	50

STOLLWERK, PETER   *Midfielder*
B. June 5, 1949   W. Germany
Ht. 6-0   Wt. 160
Citizen—W. Germany

1977	Vancouver	16	0	0	0

STONE, IAN   *Forward*
B. May 18, 1950   Chicago, Ill.
Ht. 6-0   Wt. 165
Citizen—U.S.

1975	Chicago	1	0	0	0

STORRIE, JIM   *Forward*
Ht. 5-8   Wt. 156

1967	Washington	12	5	1	11

STRASBURG, SCOTT   *Midfielder*
B. July 12, 1955
Ht. 5-11   Wt. 175
Citizen—U.S.

1978	Colorado	13	0	1	1

STRATTON, REG
B. England

1968	Vancouver	4	0	0	0

STRAUB, BILL   *Defender*
Ht. 6-1   Wt. 165
Citizen—U.S.

1973	Mont.-Phil.	6	1	2	4
1974	Philadelphia	12	0	0	0

1975	Philadelphia	14	0	0	0
1976	Philadelphia	12	0	0	0
1978	Philadelphia	25	0	1	1
	Totals	69	1	3	5

STREMLAU, JOHN   *Midfielder*
B. Oct. 23, 1953   St. Louis, Mo.
Ht. 5-9   Wt. 150
Citizen—U.S.

1976	Dallas	8	1	0	2
1977	St. Louis	19	1	3	5
1978	Houston	22	0	0	0
1979	Houston	15	0	0	0
	Totals	64	2	3	7

STRENICER, GENE   *Midfielder*
B. Aug. 12, 1945   Budapest, Hungary
Ht. 5-6   Wt. 140
Citizen—Canada

1973	Toronto	17	2	3	7
1974	Toronto	20	1	2	4
1975	Toronto	22	0	3	3
1976	Toronto	19	0	1	1
1977	Toronto	17	0	1	1
1978	Chicago	19	2	0	4
1979	Chicago	20	2	3	7
	Totals	134	7	13	27

STRIDE, DAVID   *Defender*
B. Mar. 14, 1958   Lymington, England
Ht. 5-10   Wt. 160
Citizen—England

1978	Memphis	24	1	7	9

STRITZL, SIEGFRIED "SIGGY"   *Midfielder*
B. Apr. 12, 1944   Yugoslavia
Ht. 5-6   Wt. 150
Citizen—U.S.

1971	New York	20	3	9	15
1972	New York	11	1	2	4
1973	New York	6	1	2	4
	Totals	37	5	13	23

STRONG, CARL   *Midfielder*
B. Jan. 21, 1958   Washington, DC
Ht. 5-10   Wt. 162
Citizen—U.S.

1978	Colorado	7	0	1	1
1979	Atlanta	25	2	3	7
	Totals	32	2	4	8

STUCKEY, BRUCE   *Midfielder*
B. 1947   England
Ht. 5-10   Wt. 165
Citizen—England

1977	Connecticut	13	1	3	5

Season	Club	GP	G	A	Pts.

STULCKEN, DIRK   *Midfielder*
B. West Germany
Ht. 6-4   Wt. 150
Citizen—West Germany

| 1968 | Detroit | 13 | 0 | 0 | 0 |

SUFFLE, TONY   *Midfielder*
Ht. 5-9   Wt. 160
Citizen—U.S.

1974	Denver	3	0	0	0
1978	San Jose	1	0	0	0
	Totals	4	0	0	0

SUGGETT, COLIN   *Forward*
Ht. 5-9   Wt. 152

| 1967 | Vancouver | 12 | 3 | 0 | 6 |

SUHNHOLZ, WOLFGANG   *Midfielder*
B. Sept. 14, 1946   Berlin, West Germany
Ht. 5-10   Wt. 170
Citizen—West Germany

1975	Boston	20	6	6	18
1976	Toronto	22	1	4	6
1977	Las Vegas	19	4	1	9
1978	L.A.-Calif.	20	5	2	12
1979	California	26	2	10	14
	Totals	107	18	23	59

SULARZ, BRONISLAW "JERRY"
See *Goalkeeper*

SULINCEVSKI, PETER   *Forward*
B. Yugoslavia
Ht. 6-2   Wt. 170
Citizen—Yugoslavia

| 1968 | Chicago | 22 | 14 | 0 | 28 |

SUSIC, SEAD   *Forward*
B. Jan. 3, 1953   Zavidovici, Yugoslavia
Ht. 5-10   Wt. 180
Citizen—Yugoslavia

| 1978 | Col.-Tor. | 22 | 11 | 5 | 27 |

SUTEVSKI, DAMIR   *Defender*
B. Sept. 28, 1954   Zagreb, Yugoslavia
Ht. 5-9   Wt. 150
Citizen—Yugoslavia

1975	Toronto	9	0	0	0
1976	Toronto	24	1	1	3
1977	Toronto	25	1	2	4
1978	Toronto	24	1	0	2
1979	Rochester	25	1	1	3
	Totals	107	4	4	12

SUURBIER, WILLEM   *Defender*
B. Jan. 16, 1945   Eindhoven, Holland
Ht. 5-10   Wt. 155
Citizen—Holland

| 1979 | Los Angeles | 24 | 1 | 0 | 2 |

Season	Club	GP	G	A	Pts.

SVILAR, RATKO
See *Goalkeeper*

SWIERNIAK, JAN   *Forward*
Ht. 5-9   Wt. 160

| 1975 | Hartford | 15 | 0 | 0 | 0 |

SZALAY, TIBOR   *Forward*
B. Jan. 26, 1938   Kobolkut, Hungary
Ht. 5-7   Wt. 155
Citizen—Hungary

1967	Philadelphia	23	8	6	22
1968	Houston	21	8	1	17
1971	Washington	22	4	2	10
	Totals	66	20	9	49

SZCZEPANIAK, FRED   *Midfielder*
B. June 10, 1941   Gelsenkirchen, Germany
Ht. 5-7   Wt. 170
Citizen—Germany

| 1967 | Pittsburgh | 6 | 1 | 0 | 2 |

SZEFER, STEFAN   *Defender*
B. May 8, 1942   Poland
Ht. 6-0   Wt. 175
Citizen—U.S.

1975	Chicago	22	3	1	7
1977	Chicago	22	1	0	2
1978	Chicago	12	1	0	2
1979	Chicago	6	1	0	2
	Totals	62	6	1	13

SZYMANICK, HORST   *Forward*
B. Germany
Ht. 5-11   Wt. 174
Citizen—Germany

| 1967 | Chi.(NPSL) | 12 | 1 | 3 | 5 |

TAFT, JOHN   *Midfielder*
B. 1957
Ht. 5-9   Wt. 160
Citizen—U.S.

| 1977 | Connecticut | 3 | 0 | 0 | 0 |

TALBOT, BRIAN   *Midfielder*
B. Ipswich, England
Ht. 5-8   Wt. 160

1971	Toronto	10	2	1	5
1972	Toronto	10	2	2	6
	Totals	20	4	3	11

TAMINDZIC, BLAGOJE
See *Goalkeeper*

TARASIDES, GEORGE
See *Goalkeeper*

Season	Club	GP	G	A	Pts.

TARTILAN, JESUS *Midfielder*
B. Spain
Ht. 5–9 Wt. 160
Citizen—Spain

| 1968 | Cleveland | 26 | 0 | 0 | 0 |

TAYLOR, GORDON *Forward*
B. Dec. 18, 1944
Ht. 5–6 Wt. 160
Citizen—England

| 1977 | Vancouver | 16 | 1 | 9 | 11 |

TAYLOR, JOHN
See *Goalkeeper*

TAYLOR, ROBERTO *Midfielder*
B. Sept. 28, 1949 Guatemala
Ht. 6–3 Wt. 190
Citizen—Guatemala

| 1976 | Hartford | 9 | 1 | 0 | 2 |

TAYLOR, TOMMY *Defender*
B. Sept. 26, 1951 Essex, England
Ht. 6–1 Wt. 180
Citizen—England

| 1977 | Hawaii | 18 | 0 | 5 | 5 |

TAYLOR, VAN
See *Goalkeeper*

TEIXEIRA, NEVE *Forward*

| 1975 | Rochester | 2 | 0 | 0 | 0 |

TEJADA, CONSTANTINO *Midfielder*
B. Mar. 29, 1940 Buenos Aires, Argentina
Ht. 5–11 Wt. 167
Citizen—Argentina

| 1968 | Baltimore | 7 | 0 | 0 | 0 |

THIE, TON
See *Goalkeeper*

TAVERA, JORGE *Forward*
Ht. 5–8 Wt. 160

| 1972 | Miami | 7 | 0 | 0 | 0 |

THOMAS, PETER
See *Goalkeeper*

THOMPSON, ALAN *Defender*
B. Feb. 20, 1952 Liverpool, England
Ht. 5–1 Wt. 168
Citizen—England

| 1979 | Portland | 25 | 2 | 1 | 5 |

THOMPSON, GARY *Forward*
B. Sept. 28, 1945 Vancouver, Canada
Ht. 5–11 Wt. 160
Citizen—Canada

1974	Vancouver	3	0	1	1
1975	Vancouver	4	1	0	2
1976	Vancouver	12	1	1	3
1977	Vancouver	8	0	1	1
	Totals	27	2	3	7

THOMPSON, MAX *Defender*
B. Dec. 31, 1956 Liverpool, England
Ht. 6–3 Wt. 178
Citizen—England

1977	Dallas	21	2	4	8
1978	Dallas	22	2	2	6
	Totals	43	4	6	14

THOMPSON, TREVOR *Defender*
B. Newcastle, England
Ht. 5–9 Wt. 155
Citizen—England

1967	Detroit	4	3	0	6
1976	Washington	18	1	1	3
	Totals	22	4	1	9

THOMSON, BOBBY *Defender*
B. Dec. 5, 1953 Smethwick, England
Ht. 6–0 Wt. 175
Citizen—England

1967	L.A.(USA)	12	3	1	7
1976	Hartford	24	0	3	3
1977	Connecticut	25	0	2	2
1978	Memphis	22	0	4	4
1979	Memphis	29	1	0	2
	Totals	112	4	10	18

THOMSON, DAVE *Midfielder*
B. Scotland
Ht. 5–10 Wt. 155

1971	Toronto	12	0	1	1
1972	Toronto	5	0	0	0
	Totals	17	0	1	1

THOMSON, EDDIE *Midfielder*
B. Feb. 25, 1947 Midlothian, Scotland
Ht. 5–11 Wt. 165
Citizen—England

| 1976 | San Antonio | 19 | 3 | 1 | 7 |

TILER, BRIAN *Defender*
B. Mar. 15, 1943 Rotherham, England
Ht. 5–11 Wt. 170
Citizen—England

| 1976 | Portland | 6 | 0 | 1 | 1 |

Season	Club	GP	G	A	Pts.

TIMULA, MESSIAS *Defender*
Ht. 6-1   Wt. 180
Citizen—Portugal

Season	Club	GP	G	A	Pts.
1977	Rochester	15	0	1	1

TINNEY, PHILIP *Forward*
B. Jan. 15, 1945   Liverpool, England
Ht. 5-9   Wt. 171
Citizen—England

Season	Club	GP	G	A	Pts.
1967	Philadelphia	14	1	8	10
1970	Dallas	19	1	8	10
1971	Dallas	21	2	5	9
1972	Dallas	14	1	2	4
	Totals	68	5	23	33

TINNION, BRIAN *Forward*
B. June 11, 1948   Workington, England
Ht. 5-9   Wt. 155
Citizen—England

Season	Club	GP	G	A	Pts.
1976	New York	20	8	6	22
1977	Hawaii	26	7	9	23
1978	Col.-Det.	28	4	3	11
1979	Detroit	16	3	1	7
	Totals	90	22	19	63

TINSLEY, ALAN *Midfielder*
B. Jan. 1, 1951   Fleetwood, England
Ht. 5-11   Wt. 155
Citizen—England

Season	Club	GP	G	A	Pts.
1975	Miami	14	3	1	7
1976	Miami	8	0	0	0
	Totals	22	3	1	7

TIRADO, TONY
See *Goalkeeper*

TODD, COLIN *Midfielder*
Ht. 5-9   Wt. 154

Season	Club	GP	G	A	Pts.
1967	Vancouver	12	1	0	2

TODD, MICHAEL *Defender*

Season	Club	GP	G	A	Pts.
1975	Dallas	5	0	0	0

TOGACIC, ILIJA *Defender*
B. June 1, 1941   Gracac, Yugoslavia
Ht. 5-10   Wt. 160
Citizen—Yugoslavia

Season	Club	GP	G	A	Pts.
1967	St. Louis	15	1	2	4
1968	Houston	30	2	1	5
	Totals	45	3	3	9

TOMIC, NOVAK *Midfielder*
B. Yugoslavia
Ht. 6-0   Wt. 165
Citizen—Yugoslavia

Season	Club	GP	G	A	Pts.
1967	L.A.(NPSL)	—	—	—	—
1968	San Diego	23	3	0	6

TOMKINS, LEN *Forward*
Ht. 5-9   Wt. 160

Season	Club	GP	G	A	Pts.
1971	Toronto	9	3	0	6

TOMLJENOVIC, MILE *Midfielder*
B. June 10, 1937   Rijeka, Yugoslavia
Ht. 5-10   Wt. 170
Citizen—Yugoslavia

Season	Club	GP	G	A	Pts.
1968	Houston	17	0	1	1

TONI *Midfielder*
B. 1948
Ht. 6-2   Wt. 185
Citizen—Portugal

Season	Club	GP	G	A	Pts.
1977	Las Vegas	16	0	0	0

TONNING, CHRISTER *Forward*
B. Nov. 19, 1946   Halmstad, Sweden
Ht. 6-3   Wt. 150
Citizen—Sweden

Season	Club	GP	G	A	Pts.
1968	Dallas	29	2	1	5

TOOMEY, PAUL *Defender*
B. June 28, 1956   New London, Conn.
Ht. 6-0   Wt. 175
Citizen—U.S.

Season	Club	GP	G	A	Pts.
1979	Portland	8	0	0	0

TOPALOVIC, BRONCO
See *Goalkeeper*

TOPIC, JADRANKO *Forward*
B. Apr. 20, 1949   Mostar, Yugoslavia
Ht. 5-11   Wt. 163
Citizen—Yugoslavia

Season	Club	GP	G	A	Pts.
1977	New York	6	1	3	5

TORIANI, OSVALDO
See *Goalkeeper*

TRAINOR, DANNY *Forward*
Ht. 5-11   Wt. 154

Season	Club	GP	G	A	Pts.
1967	Detroit	8	2	2	6

TRANTER, WILFRED *Defender*
B. Mar. 5, 1945   Manchester, England
Ht. 5-10   Wt. 154
Citizen—England

Season	Club	GP	G	A	Pts.
1968	Baltimore	9	2	0	4
1972	St. Louis	14	0	1	1
	Totals	23	2	1	5

TRAVLJANIN, EMIR *Midfielder*
B. Yugoslavia
Ht. 5-9   Wt. 155

Season	Club	GP	G	A	Pts.
1975	Hartford	21	5	2	12

Season	Club	GP	G	A	Pts.

TREACY, RAY   *Forward*
B. June 18, 1946   Dublin, Ireland
Ht. 5-9   Wt. 158
Citizen—Ireland

1978	Toronto	23	5	3	13

TRENTOR, PHIL   *Midfielder*
B. June 26, 1953
Ht. 5-8   Wt. 165
Citizen—England

1974	Seattle	7	0	0	0

TREVIS, DEREK   *Defender*
B. Sept. 9, 1942   Birmingham, England
Ht. 6-2   Wt. 170
Citizen—England

1973	Philadelphia	19	0	0	0
1974	Philadelphia	20	0	0	0
1975	Philadelphia	22	0	1	1
1976	San Diego	16	1	0	2
1977	Las Vegas	6	0	0	0
1978	Philadelphia	4	1	0	2
	Totals	87	2	1	5

TRICKOVIC, STOJAN   *Forward*
B. Belgrade, Yugoslavia
Ht. 5-9   Wt. 150
Citizen—Yugoslavia

1976	Washington	9	3	2	8

TRIFUNOVIC, VLADIMIR   *Midfielder*
B. July 7, 1949   Yugoslavia
Ht. 5-9   Wt. 150
Citizen—Yugoslavia

1978	Rochester	19	3	3	9

TRINKLEIN, GERT   *Defender*
B. June 19, 1949   Frankfurt, West Germany
Ht. 6-3   Wt. 180
Citizen—West Germany

1979	Dallas	25	2	4	8

TRIPKOVIC, ZLATKO   *Midfielder*
Ht. 5-8   Wt. 170

1974	Baltimore	10	0	4	4

TROST, AL   *Midfielder*
B. Feb. 7, 1949   St. Louis, Mo.
Ht. 6-2   Wt. 166
Citizen—U.S.

1973	St. Louis	17	1	2	4
1974	St. Louis	19	6	4	16
1975	St. Louis	22	6	2	14
1976	St. Louis	24	12	3	27
1977	St. Louis	26	3	8	14
1978	California	28	10	3	23
1979	Seattle	11	1	2	4
	Totals	147	39	24	102

TRZSKOWSKI, ANTONIO   *Defender*
B. Apr. 6, 1941   Poland
Ht. 5-9   Wt. 170
Citizen—Poland

1973	Rochester	9	0	1	1
1974	Rochester	19	0	1	1
1975	Rochester	19	1	3	5
	Totals	47	1	5	7

TUEART, DENNIS "THE MENACE"   *Forward*
B. Nov. 27, 1949   Newcastle, England
Ht. 5-8   Wt. 156
Citizen—England

1978	New York	20	10	12	32
1979	New York	27	16	16	48
	Totals	47	26	28	80

TUKSA, VAL   *Midfielder*
B. Nov. 21, 1950   Zagreb, Yugoslavia
Ht. 5-9   Wt. 150
Citizen—Yugoslavia

1977	Toronto	15	4	1	9
1970	Rochester	12	0	1	1
	Totals	27	4	2	10

TUOHY, LIAM   *Forward*
Ht. 5-6   Wt. 140

1967	Boston	9	3	0	6

TURNER, CHRIS   *Defender*
B. Mar. 4, 1951   St. Neots, England
Ht. 6-1   Wt. 190
Citizen—England

1977	Connecticut	20	3	0	6
1978	New England	26	2	6	10
1979	New England	29	2	2	6
	Totals	75	7	8	22

TURNER, CHRIS
See *Goalkeeper*

TURNER, IAN
See *Goalkeeper*

TURNER, ROY   *Midfielder*
B. Oct. 30, 1943   Liverpool, England
Ht. 5-9   Wt. 172
Citizen—U.S.

1967	Phil.-Tor.(NPSL)	23	1	2	4
1968	Cleveland	28	4	0	8
1969	Dallas	13	0	0	0
1970	Dallas	24	0	0	0
1971	Dallas	24	2	1	5
1972	Dallas	14	1	0	2
1973	Dallas	19	0	0	0
1974	Dallas	20	1	0	2
1975	Dallas	14	1	1	3
1976	Dallas	23	0	1	1

Season	Club	GP	G	A	Pts.
1977	Dallas	8	0	0	0
1978	Dallas	1	0	0	0
	Totals	211	10	5	25

TURUDIJA, BOGDAN   *Forward*
B. June 30, 1948   Lornica, Yugoslavia
Ht. 5-10   Wt. 175
Citizen—Yugoslavia

Season	Club	GP	G	A	Pts.
1978	Oakland	11	1	2	4
1979	Edmonton	24	1	4	6
	Totals	35	2	6	10

TWAMLEY, BRUCE   *Defender*
B. May 23, 1952   Victoria, Canada
Ht. 5-9   Wt. 150
Citizen—Canada

Season	Club	GP	G	A	Pts.
1975	Vancouver	18	2	0	4
1977	N.Y.-Minn.	5	0	0	0
1978	Minn.-Oak.	16	0	0	0
1979	Edmonton	9	0	0	0
	Totals	48	2	0	4

TWELLMAN, STEVE   *Defender*
B. Dec. 14, 1949   St. Louis, Mo.
Ht. 5-11   Wt. 170
Citizen—U.S.

Season	Club	GP	G	A	Pts.
1972	Atlanta	6	0	0	0
1973	Atlanta	14	0	1	1
1974	Boston	10	0	0	0
	Totals	30	0	1	1

TWELLMAN, TIM   *Forward*
B. May 1, 1955   St. Louis, Mo.
Ht. 5-11   Wt. 175
Citizen—U.S.

Season	Club	GP	G	A	Pts.
1977	Minnesota	8	0	0	0
1978	Minnesota	25	1	3	5
1979	Minnesota	14	1	1	3
	Totals	47	2	4	8

TYER, IAN   *Defender*
B. Manchester, England
Ht. 5-9   Wt. 164

Season	Club	GP	G	A	Pts.
1971	Montreal	20	0	0	0
1972	Montreal	13	0	0	0
1973	Montreal	17	0	1	1
	Totals	50	0	1	1

TYNAN, BOBBY   *Forward*

Season	Club	GP	G	A	Pts.
1977	Chicago	15	2	0	4

TYNAN, TOMMY   *Forward*
B. Nov. 17, 1955   Liverpool, England
Ht. 5-10   Wt. 170
Citizen—England

Season	Club	GP	G	A	Pts.
1976	Dallas	17	2	3	7

UHLANDER, BERT
See *Goalkeeper*

ULLIVARI, FRANCISCO   *Midfielder*
B. Mexico
Ht. 5-11   Wt. 165

Season	Club	GP	G	A	Pts.
1971	Rochester	6	0	1	1
1972	Rochester	2	0	0	0
	Totals	8	0	1	1

URANIN, KOZIMIERZ   *Forward*

Season	Club	GP	G	A	Pts.
1972	St. Louis	1	0	0	0

URIEL (URIEL da VEIGA FONTOURA)   *Defender*
B. Aug. 28, 1940   Rio de Janeiro, Brazil
Ht. 5-10   Wt. 168
Citizen—Brazil

Season	Club	GP	G	A	Pts.
1967	Baltimore	7	2	2	6
1968	Baltimore	15	1	0	2
1970	Atlanta	—	—	—	—
1971	Atlanta	24	0	1	1
1972	Atlanta	13	0	0	0
1973	Atlanta	16	1	0	2
	Totals	75	4	3	11

VABEC, DRAGO   *Forward*
B. Oct. 26, 1950   Zagreb, Yugoslavia
Ht. 5-8   Wt. 145
Citizen—Yugoslavia

Season	Club	GP	G	A	Pts.
1977	Toronto	15	11	4	26

VALENTINE, CARL   *Forward*
B. July 4, 1958   Manchester, England
Ht. 5-9   Wt. 160
Citizen—England

Season	Club	GP	G	A	Pts.
1979	Vancouver	29	4	7	15

VAN DER BECK, PERRY   *Midfielder*
B. Nov. 5, 1959   Florissant, Mo.
Ht. 5-10   Wt. 150
Citizen—U.S.

Season	Club	GP	G	A	Pts.
1978	Tampa Bay	2	0	0	0
1979	Tampa Bay	16	0	3	3
	Totals	18	0	3	3

VAN DER BURK, THEO   *Defender*
Ht. 5-9   Wt. 152

Season	Club	GP	G	A	Pts.
1967	San Francisco	12	0	1	1

VAN DER LEE, FREEK   *Defender*
Ht. 5-10   Wt. 175

Season	Club	GP	G	A	Pts.
1967	San Francisco	9	0	1	1

Season	Club	GP	G	A	Pts.

VAN DER VEEN, JAN *Midfielder*
B. July 6, 1948 Meppel, Holland
Ht. 5–11 Wt. 165
Citizen—Holland

Season	Club	GP	G	A	Pts.
1978	San Diego	23	0	5	5
1979	Tampa Bay	29	4	12	20
	Totals	52	4	17	25

VAN DER VEN, HENNY *Midfielder*
B. May 22, 1954 Holland
Ht. 5–10 Wt. 160
Citizen—Holland

Season	Club	GP	G	A	Pts.
1978	Washington	4	0	0	0

VAN ERON, KEITH
See *Goalkeeper*

VAN HANEGEM, WIM *Midfielder*
B. Feb. 20, 1944 Breskens, Holland
Ht. 6–2 Wt. 180
Citizen—Holland

Season	Club	GP	G	A	Pts.
1979	Chicago	27	6	7	19

VANINGER, DENNIS *Forward*
B. Mar. 14, 1952 St. Louis, Mo.
Ht. 6–2 Wt. 185
Citizen—U.S.

Season	Club	GP	G	A	Pts.
1973	St. Louis	3	2	0	4
1974	St. Louis	17	6	6	18
1975	St. Louis	4	2	1	5
1976	St. Louis	23	5	7	17
1977	St. Louis	23	8	2	18
1978	Ft. Lauderdale	19	3	5	11
1979	Ft. Lauderdale	1	0	0	0
	Totals	90	26	21	73

VAN'T LAND, TJEERT *Forward*
B. Feb. 25, 1954 Voorthuizen, Holland
Ht. 6–2 Wt. 160
Citizen—Holland

Season	Club	GP	G	A	Pts.
1974	Seattle	17	5	2	12
1975	Seattle	19	6	2	14
	Totals	36	11	4	26

VAN VEEN, LEO *Forward*
B. June 6, 1946 Utrecht, Holland
Ht. 6–3 Wt. 175
Citizen—Holland

Season	Club	GP	G	A	Pts.
1979	Los Angeles	26	13	6	32

VARGAS, BERNARDO *Forward*
B. Mendoza, Argentina
Ht. 5–6 Wt. 156
Citizen—Argentina

Season	Club	GP	G	A	Pts.
1967	Tor.(NPSL)	9	4	1	9
1968	Toronto	26	0	4	4
	Totals	35	4	5	13

VAUGHN, DANNY *Forward*
B. Sept. 7, 1956 Tacoma, Wash.
Ht. 6–1 Wt. 180
Citizen—U.S.

Season	Club	GP	G	A	Pts.
1978	Detroit	9	2	0	4
1979	Detroit	15	2	3	7
	Totals	24	4	3	11

VAVA (EDVALDO NETO) *Forward*
B. Brazil
Ht. 5–2 Wt. 160
Citizen—Brazil

Season	Club	GP	G	A	Pts.
1968	San Diego	22	5	0	10

VEALL, RAY *Midfielder*
B. England
Ht. 5–8 Wt. 145
Citizen—England

Season	Club	GP	G	A	Pts.
1968	Los Angeles	23	4	0	8

VEEE, JULIE *Midfielder*
B. Feb. 22, 1950 Budapest, Hungary
Ht. 6–0 Wt. 180
Citizen—U.S.

Season	Club	GP	G	A	Pts.
1975	Los Angeles	20	6	5	17
1976	San Jose	11	0	6	6
1978	San Diego	27	7	13	17
1979	San Diego	27	10	8	28
	Totals	85	23	32	78

VEITCH, TOM *Midfielder*
Ht. 5–10 Wt. 170

Season	Club	GP	G	A	Pts.
1975	Denver	21	1	3	5

VELASQUEZ, MANUEL *Midfielder*
B. Jan. 14, 1943 Madrid, Spain
Ht. 5–9 Wt. 160
Citizen—Spain

Season	Club	GP	G	A	Pts.
1978	Toronto	16	1	3	5

VELAZQUEZ, SERGIO *Forward*
B. Feb. 25, 1952 Leon, Mexico
Ht. 5–7 Wt. 140
Citizen—U.S.

Season	Club	GP	G	A	Pts.
1975	Los Angeles	8	1	2	4
1976	Los Angeles	9	1	2	4
1977	Seattle	4	0	0	0
	Totals	21	2	4	8

VERDI, ROGER *Defender*
B. Feb. 4, 1953 Kenya, Africa
Ht. 5–7 Wt. 150
Citizen—England

Season	Club	GP	G	A	Pts.
1972	Montreal	6	0	0	0
1973	Montreal	19	1	0	2
1974	Miami	11	0	0	0
1975	St. Louis	21	0	0	0

Season	Club	GP	G	A	Pts.
1976	St. Louis	23	0	3	3
1977	St. Louis	15	0	0	0
1978	San Jose	9	0	0	0
	Totals	104	1	3	5

VERNON, ROY   *Forward*
Ht. 5-8   Wt. 153

Season	Club	GP	G	A	Pts.
1967	Cleveland	11	2	5	9

VERSEN, DIETER   *Defender*
B. June 22, 1945   Bochum, W. Germany
Ht. 5-9   Wt. 170
Citizen—W. Germany

Season	Club	GP	G	A	Pts.
1979	San Jose	29	1	2	4

VESCOVI, RAFFAELLO   *Midfielder*
Ht. 5-10   Wt. 165

Season	Club	GP	G	A	Pts.
1967	Chi.(USA)	10	0	2	2

VESELINOVIC, BOB   *Forward*
B. July 12, 1951
Ht. 6-0   Wt. 170
Citizen—Yugoslavia

Season	Club	GP	G	A	Pts.
1977	Rochester	2	0	0	0

VESTERGAARD, HENRIK   *Midfielder*
B. Soborg, Denmark
Ht. 6-0   Wt. 172
Citizen—Denmark

Season	Club	GP	G	A	Pts.
1967	N.Y.(NPSL)	10	1	1	3

VICEK, LAJOS   *Forward*
B. Yugoslavia
Ht. 5-7   Wt. 140
Citizen—Yugoslavia

Season	Club	GP	G	A	Pts.
1968	Vancouver	15	2	0	4

VICIOSO, ANSELMO   *Forward*
B. Oct. 28, 1952   Madrid, Spain
Ht. 5-11   Wt. 170
Citizen—Spain

Season	Club	GP	G	A	Pts.
1978	California	21	2	0	4

VIDAL, JOSE   *Forward*
B. Spain
Ht. 5-10   Wt. 155

Season	Club	GP	G	A	Pts.
1967	Philadelphia	8	5	2	12

VIDNIC, BLAGJOE
See *Goalkeeper*

VIEIRA, ADEMIR   *Forward*
Citizen—Brazil

Season	Club	GP	G	A	Pts.
1974	Toronto	11	3	4	10

VIERI, ROBERTO   *Midfielder*
B. Feb. 14, 1946   Prato, Italy
Ht. 5-10   Wt. 165
Citizen—Italy

Season	Club	GP	G	A	Pts.
1975	Toronto	9	3	2	8

VIGH, TIBOR   *Forward*
Ht. 6-0   Wt. 175

Season	Club	GP	G	A	Pts.
1968	Houston	28	13	3	29
1973	N.Y.-Mont.	15	0	6	6
	Totals	43	13	9	35

VILLA, GREG   *Forward*
B. Dec. 15, 1956   St. Louis, Mo.
Ht. 6-1   Wt. 190
Citizen—U.S.

Season	Club	GP	G	A	Pts.
1977	Minnesota	8	0	0	0
1978	Minnesota	13	1	0	2
1979	Min.-Tul.	10	3	1	7
	Totals	31	4	1	9

VILLARRUEL, OSCAR   *Midfielder*
B. Jan. 8, 1952   Buenos Aires, Argentina
Ht. 5-7   Wt. 160
Citizen—Argentina

Season	Club	GP	G	A	Pts.
1976	Miami	4	0	0	0

VINCENT, JOHN   *Midfielder*
B. 1948
Ht. 5-11   Wt. 170
Citizen—England

Season	Club	GP	G	A	Pts.
1977	Connecticut	10	4	0	8

VIOLLET, DENNIS   *Midfielder*
B. Sept. 20, 1933   Manchester, England
Ht. 5-9   Wt. 151
Citizen—U.S.

Season	Club	GP	G	A	Pts.
1967	Baltimore	9	3	1	7
1968	Baltimore	18	3	0	6
	Totals	27	6	1	13

VISENTIN, BRUNO   *Forward*
Ht. 5-10   Wt. 171

Season	Club	GP	G	A	Pts.
1967	Chi.(USA)	8	1	0	2

VITESKIC, SAKIB   *Midfielder*
B. Dec. 27, 1952   Yugoslavia
Ht. 5-11   Wt. 170
Citizen—Yugoslavia

Season	Club	GP	G	A	Pts.
1978	Washington	30	7	7	21
1979	Washington	17	1	6	8
	Totals	47	8	13	29

Season	Club	GP	G	A	Pts.

VIZCAINO, RENE
See *Goalkeeper*

VOGEL, GARY *Defender*
B. Mar. 3, 1956 Buffalo, N.Y.
Ht. 5–8 Wt. 155
Citizen—U.S.

Season	Club	GP	G	A	Pts.
1978	Minn.	7	0	0	0
1979	Minn.	10	0	0	0
	Totals	17	0	0	0

VOLPATI, SALVADOR

Season	Club	GP	G	A	Pts.
1971	Toronto	2	0	0	0

VOOYS, GERRIT
See *Goalkeeper*

VORBE, PHILIPE *Midfielder*
B. Sept. 14, 1947 Port-au-Prince, Haiti
Ht. 6–0 Wt. 163
Citizen—Haiti

Season	Club	GP	G	A	Pts.
1967	N.Y.(NPSL)	5	1	0	2
1968	New York	8	0	0	0
	Totals	13	1	0	2

VORST, SCOTT *Defender*
B. St. Louis, Mo.
Ht. 6–0 Wt. 175
Citizen—U.S.

Season	Club	GP	G	A	Pts.
1978	Los Angeles	9	0	0	0

VOWDEN, GEOFF *Midfielder*
B. Barnsley, England

Season	Club	GP	G	A	Pts.
1974	New York	15	2	4	8

VRANKOVIC, MLADEN *Midfielder*
B. Yugoslavia
Ht. 6–1 Wt. 180
Citizen—Yugoslavia

Season	Club	GP	G	A	Pts.
1968	Kansas City	32	1	0	2

VUJKOVIC, MARKO *Midfielder*
B. Jan. 26, 1950 Subotica, Yugoslavia
Ht. 5–8 Wt. 170
Citizen—Yugoslavia

Season	Club	GP	G	A	Pts.
1977	Van.-Minn.	19	3	1	7
1978	Minn.-Tor.	28	8	11	27
	Totals	47	11	12	34

WADDELL, BOB *Defender*
Ht. 5–11 Wt. 170

Season	Club	GP	G	A	Pts.
1974	Toronto	15	0	0	0

WADDINGTON, JOHN *Defender*
B. Feb. 26, 1952
Ht. 5–11 Wt. 160
Citizen—England

Season	Club	GP	G	A	Pts.
1977	Vancouver	6	0	0	0

WAGNER, WALTER *Forward*
B. July 26, 1949 Altenvars, Germany
Ht. 6–0 Wt. 170
Citizen—West Germany

Season	Club	GP	G	A	Pts.
1979	Los Angeles	21	8	1	17

WAGSTAFFE, DAVE *Forward*
Ht. 5–8 Wt. 148

Season	Club	GP	G	A	Pts.
1967	L.A.(USA)	10	0	1	1

WALDRON, ALAN *Midfielder*
B. Sept. 6, 1951 Royton, England
Ht. 5–9 Wt. 150
Citizen—England

Season	Club	GP	G	A	Pts.
1976	Chicago	20	3	7	13

WALDRON, COLIN *Defender*
B. June 22, 1948 Bristol, England
Ht. 6–2 Wt. 180
Citizen—England

Season	Club	GP	G	A	Pts.
1978	Tul-Phil.	27	2	0	4
1979	Atlanta	14	0	3	3
	Totals	41	2	3	7

WALDROP, MICHAEL *Midfielder*
B. Dec. 23, 1955 England
Ht. 5–9 Wt. 146
Citizen—England

Season	Club	GP	G	A	Pts.
1974	New York	13	0	2	2

WALKER, CLIVE *Forward*
B. July 1, 1958 Oxford, England
Ht. 5–7 Wt. 165
Citizen—England

Season	Club	GP	G	A	Pts.
1979	Ft. Lauderdale	22	9	7	25

WALKER, DENNIS *Defender*
Ht. 5–10 Wt. 170

Season	Club	GP	G	A	Pts.
1972	Montreal	10	0	0	0

WALKER, MICKEY *Midfielder*
B. Ireland
Ht. 5–8 Wt. 155
Citizen—Ireland

Season	Club	GP	G	A	Pts.
1968	Los Angeles	22	7	0	14

WALL, PETER *Defender*
B. Sept. 13, 1944 London, England
Ht. 5–11 Wt. 170
Citizen—England

Season	Club	GP	G	A	Pts.
1977	St. Louis	18	0	0	0
1978	California	30	0	2	2
1979	California	29	3	4	10
	Totals	77	3	6	12

Season	Club	GP	G	A	Pts.

WALLACE, DARRYL
See *Goalkeeper*

WALLACE, GORDON   *Midfielder*
B. May 20, 1943   Dundee, Scotland
Ht. 5–9   Wt. 155
Citizen—England

Season	Club	GP	G	A	Pts.
1976	Seattle	21	12	4	28
1978	Seattle	24	4	3	11
	Totals	45	16	7	39

WALLACE, KEN   *Forward*
B. Islington, England
Ht. 5–10   Wt. 170

Season	Club	GP	G	A	Pts.
1971	Montreal	21	8	5	21
1972	Montreal	9	2	2	6
	Totals	30	10	7	27

WALLEY, KEITH   *Midfielder*
B. Oct. 19, 1954   Weymouth, England
Ht. 6–0   Wt. 165
Citizen—England

Season	Club	GP	G	A	Pts.
1978	California	2	0	0	0

WALSH, TOM   *Defender*
B. Dec. 11, 1953   St. Louis, Mo.
Ht. 5–11   Wt. 175
Citizen—U.S.

Season	Club	GP	G	A	Pts.
1976	Boston	24	2	1	5

WANT, TONY   *Defender*
B. Dec. 13, 1948   London, England
Ht. 5–8   Wt. 160
Citizen—England

Season	Club	GP	G	A	Pts.
1975	Philadelphia	19	0	1	1
1978	Minnesota	26	0	0	0
1979	Minnesota	27	0	5	5
	Totals	72	0	6	6

WARDANJAN, LOTHAR   *Forward*
B. Oct. 20, 1951
Citizen—W. Germany

Season	Club	GP	G	A	Pts.
1973	Toronto	11	0	3	3

WARK, DOUG   *Forward*
B. Dec. 24, 1951   Glasgow, Scotland
Ht. 5–10   Wt. 160
Citizen—U.S.

Season	Club	GP	G	A	Pts.
1974	Rochester	6	1	2	4
1975	Tampa Bay	21	0	1	1
1976	T.B.-S.D.	11	4	1	9
1977	Las Vegas	17	2	3	7
1978	S.D.-Chic.-S.J.	12	0	1	1
	Totals	67	7	8	22

WATLING, BARRY
See *Goalkeeper*

WATSON, WILLIAM   *Midfielder*
B. Dec. 4, 1949   Motherwell, Scotland
Ht. 5–10   Wt. 180

Season	Club	GP	G	A	Pts.
1973	Miami	18	0	0	0

WATTS, DEREK   *Forward*
Ht. 5–11   Wt. 165

Season	Club	GP	G	A	Pts.
1974	Miami	17	3	2	8

WEATHERUP, JIM   *Forward*
Ht. 5–6   Wt. 147

Season	Club	GP	G	A	Pts.
1967	Detroit	9	2	1	5

WEBB, JOHN   *Defender*
B. Feb. 10, 1952   Liverpool, England
Ht. 5–10   Wt. 155
Citizen—England

Season	Club	GP	G	A	Pts.
1975	Chicago	21	0	0	0
1976	Chicago	24	1	9	11
1977	Chicago	9	0	1	1
	Totals	54	1	10	12

WEBER, GREG
See *Goalkeeper*

WEBERS, DETLEF   *Forward*
B. Sept. 12, 1949   W. Germany
Ht. 6–0   Wt. 170
Citizen—W. Germany

Season	Club	GP	G	A	Pts.
1979	San Jose	8	1	0	2

WEBSTER, ADRIAN   *Defender*
B. Nov. 6, 1951   Colchester, England
Ht. 5–9   Wt. 155
Citizen—England

Season	Club	GP	G	A	Pts.
1974	Seattle	16	0	0	0
1975	Seattle	21	0	0	0
1976	Seattle	24	1	0	2
1977	Seattle	25	1	1	3
1978	Seattle	13	1	0	2
1979	Seattle	12	0	0	0
	Totals	111	3	1	7

WEBSTER, RON   *Defender*
B. Apr. 21, 1943   Belper, England
Ht. 5–9   Wt. 163
Citizen—England

Season	Club	GP	G	A	Pts.
1976	Minnesota	20	1	2	4
1978	Minnesota	7	0	2	2
	Totals	27	1	4	6

Season	Club	GP	G	A	Pts.

WEEKES, TERRY
See *Goalkeeper*

WEGERLE, GEOFF   *Forward*
B. June 9, 1954   Pretoria, S. Africa
Ht. 5–11   Wt. 170
Citizen—S. Africa

1978	Oakland	26	1	6	8

WEGERLE, STEVE   *Forward*
B. May 15, 1953   Pretoria, S. Africa
Ht. 5–10   Wt. 145
Citizen—S. Africa

1977	Tampa Bay	25	5	11	21
1978	Tampa Bay	26	7	12	26
1979	Tampa Bay	29	3	21	27
	Totals	80	15	44	74

WEISS, MATT
See *Goalkeeper*

WELBOURNE, DONALD   *Defender*
Ht. 5–10   Wt. 154

1975	Boston	17	0	1	1

WELCH, ART   *Midfielder*
B. Apr. 16, 1944   Jamaica
Ht. 5–8   Wt. 160
Citizen—U.S.

1967	Baltimore	16	5	5	15
1968	Baltimore	26	6	0	12
1969	Baltimore	—	—	—	—
1970	Atlanta	21	12	8	32
1971	Atlanta	16	2	5	9
1972	Atlanta	13	4	4	12
1973	Atlanta	7	2	1	5
1974	San Jose	19	4	6	14
1975	San Jose	22	2	4	8
1976	Van.-S.D.	17	0	1	1
1977	Washington	14	1	0	2
	Totals	171	38	34	110

WELCH, ASHER   *Forward*
B. Apr. 16, 1944   Kingston, Jamaica
Ht. 5–7   Wt. 148
Citizen—Jamaica

1967	Baltimore	8	1	1	3
1968	Baltimore	21	3	0	6
1969	Baltimore	—	—	—	—
1970	Kansas City	—	—	—	—
	Totals	29	4	1	9

WELLER, KEITH   *Midfielder*
B. June 11, 1946   Islington, England
Ht. 5–10   Wt. 170
Citizen—England

1978	New England	24	5	7	17
1979	New England	30	9	10	28
	Totals	54	14	17	45

WELSH, KEVIN   *Forward*
B. Oct. 26, 1953   Trenton, N.J.
Ht. 5–10   Wt. 160
Citizen—U.S.

1975	Hartford	16	0	0	0
1976	Hartford	20	1	0	2
1978	New England	19	1	2	4
1979	New England	17	1	1	3
	Totals	72	3	3	9

WELSH, PETER   *Forward*
B. July 19, 1959   Coatsbridge, Scotland
Ht. 6–1   Wt. 185
Citizen—England

1978	Houston	15	4	1	9

WERNEID, LEIF-DAG   *Forward*
B. Norway
Ht. 5–10   Wt. 154
Citizen—Norway

1968	Los Angeles	17	4	0	8

WERSTEIN, CHRIS   *Defender*
B. St. Louis, Mo.
Ht. 6–0   Wt. 182
Citizen—U.S.

1971	St. Louis	4	0	0	0

WEST, ALAN   *Midfielder*
B. Dec. 18, 1951   Hyde, England
Ht. 5–10   Wt. 170
Citizen—England

1976	Minnesota	22	2	8	12
1977	Minnesota	23	0	11	11
1978	Minnesota	15	2	6	10
1979	Minnesota	19	3	10	16
	Totals	79	7	35	49

WHARTON, TERRY   *Forward*
Ht. 5–8   Wt. 160

1967	L.A.(USA)	10	3	1	7

WHEELER, CHRIS   *Forward*
Ht. 6–1   Wt. 177

1972	Montreal	2	0	0	0
1973	Montreal	1	0	0	0
	Totals	3	0	0	0

WHELAN, TONY   *Forward*
B. Nov. 20, 1952   Lancashire, England
Ht. 6–I   Wt. 170
Citizen—England

1977	Ft. Lauderdale	26	4	2	10
1978	Ft. Lauderdale	30	0	4	4
1979	Ft. Lauderdale	29	1	3	5
	Totals	85	5	9	19

Season	Club	GP	G	A	Pts.

WHITE, TERRY   *Defender*
B. Nov. 20, 1955   Tokyo, Japan
Ht. 5–10   Wt. 160
Citizen—U.S.

		GP	G	A	Pts.
1978	California	4	0	0	0

WHITEHEAD, KEN   *Forward*
B. Vancouver, Canada
Ht. 5–10   Wt. 170
Citizen—Canada

		GP	G	A	Pts.
1977	Los Angeles	1	0	0	0

WHITTLE, MAURICE   *Defender*
B. July 15, 1948   Wigan, England
Ht. 5–8   Wt. 150
Citizen—England

		GP	G	A	Pts.
1977	Ft. Lauderdale	21	5	0	10
1978	Ft. Lauderdale	29	4	6	14
1979	Ft. Lauderdale	30	6	5	17
	Totals	80	15	11	41

WHYMARK, TREVOR   *Forward*
B. May 5, 1950   Burston, England
Ht. 5–11   Wt. 160
Citizen—England

		GP	G	A	Pts.
1979	Vancouver	27	10	2	22

WHYTE, JIM   *Defender*
Ht. 5–11   Wt. 174

		GP	G	A	Pts.
1967	Washington	11	1	0	2

WIEBOLDT, TOM   *Forward*
B. Aug. 23, 1956   Point Pleasant Borough, N.J.
Ht. 5–11   Wt. 180
Citizen—U.S.

		GP	G	A	Pts.
1979	Philadelphia	1	0	0	0

WIECZORKOWSKI, GERT   *Midfielder*
B. July 24, 1948   Hamburg, Germany
Ht. 6–1   Wt. 175
Citizen—Germany

		GP	G	A	Pts.
1979	San Deigo	25	0	6	6

WIEDEMEIER, GERHARD   *Midfielder*
B. Feb. 8, 1938   Essen, Germany
Ht. 5–6   Wt. 160
Citizen—Germany

		GP	G	A	Pts.
1967	Pittsburgh	15	1	1	3
1968	Kansas City	31	0	0	0
	Totals	46	1	1	3

WIESTAL, KAY-ARNE
B. Oct. 16, 1940   Unea, Sweden
Ht. 5–10   Wt. 165
Citizen—Sweden

		GP	G	A	Pts.
1968	Oak.-St. L.	17	1	0	2

WIGGEMANSEN, ROY   *Defender*
B. Dec. 2, 1959   Pretoria, S. Africa
Ht. 6–2   Wt. 290
Citizen—S. Africa

		GP	G	A	Pts.
1979	Ft. Lauderdale	11	0	0	0

WILKINSON, WILLIAM   *Defender*
Ht. 5–8   Wt. 165

		GP	G	A	Pts.
1975	Boston	15	0	3	3

WILLEY, ALAN   *Forward*
B. Oct. 18, 1956   Houghton Le Spring, England
Ht. 5–11   Wt. 163
Citizen—England

		GP	G	A	Pts.
1976	Minnesota	23	16	7	39
1977	Minnesota	20	14	1	29
1978	Minnesota	21	21	3	45
1979	Minnesota	29	21	7	49
	Totals	93	72	18	162

WILLIAMS, CHARLES   *Midfielder*
B. 1944   Valletta, Malta
Ht. 5–7   Wt. 165
Citizen—Malta

		GP	G	A	Pts.
1967	Pittsburgh	9	0	1	1
1968	Dallas	3	0	0	0
	Totals	12	0	1	1

WILLINER, ROY   *Midfielder*
B. Oct. 22, 1949   Baltimore, Md.
Ht. 5–7   Wt. 145
Citizen—U.S.

		GP	G	A	Pts.
1974	Washington	14	0	0	0
1975	Washington	12	1	1	3
1976	Washington	11	0	1	1
1977	Washington	20	0	0	0
1978	Washington	12	0	0	0
	Totals	69	1	2	4

WILLRICH, JEAN   *Forward*
B. Apr. 27, 1953   Koblenz, Germany
Ht. 6–0   Wt. 185
Citizen—Germany

		GP	G	A	Pts.
1978	San Diego	30	9	13	31
1979	San Deigo	26	3	12	18
	Totals	56	12	25	49

WILSON, BRUCE   *Defender*
B. June 20, 1951   Vancouver, Canada
Ht. 5–10   Wt. 160
Citizen—Canada

		GP	G	A	Pts.
1974	Vancouver	20	1	1	3
1975	Vancouver	22	2	4	8
1976	Vancouver	24	1	4	6
1977	Vancouver	26	0	10	10
1978	Chicago	30	0	0	0
1979	Chicago	30	0	4	4
	Totals	152	4	23	31

Season	Club	GP	G	A	Pts.

WILSON, GIUSEPPE "PINO" *Defender*
B. Oct. 27, 1945 Darlington, England
Ht. 5-9 Wt. 170
Citizen—Italy

Season	Club	GP	G	A	Pts.
1978	New York	16	0	0	0

WILSON, JIMMY *Forward*
Ht. 5-1 Wt. 140

| 1967 | Washington | 12 | 2 | 2 | 6 |

WILSON, JIMMY *Forward*
B. Jan. 6, 1958 Dallas, Texas
Ht. 5-8 Wt. 160
Citizen—U.S.

| 1979 | Dallas | 1 | 0 | 0 | 0 |

WILSON, LES *Defender*
B. July 10, 1946 Manchester, England
Ht. 5-9 Wt. 162
Citizen—Canada

Season	Club	GP	G	A	Pts.
1974	Vancouver	18	0	0	0
1975	Vancouver	16	1	2	4
1976	Vancouver	3	0	3	3
1977	Vancouver	1	0	0	0
	Totals	38	1	5	7

WILSON, PAT *Forward*
Ht. 5-3 Wt. 150

| 1967 | Washington | 10 | 2 | 2 | 6 |

WINCHESTER, ERNIE *Forward*
B. Scotland
Ht. 6-2 Wt. 168
Citizen—Scotland

Season	Club	GP	G	A	Pts.
1967	Chi. (NPSL)	13	13	2	28
1969	Kansas City	27	9	0	18
	Totals	40	22	2	46

WINGERT, NORM
See *Goalkeeper*

WINTER, MIKE
See *Goalkeeper*

WIT, DENNIS *Midfielder*
B. July 25, 1951 Baltimore, Md.
Ht. 6-2 Wt. 165
Citizen—U.S.

Season	Club	GP	G	A	Pts.
1974	Baltimore	9	0	2	2
1975	Baltimore	19	2	1	5
1976	S.D./T.B.	14	0	0	0
1977	Tampa Bay	7	0	1	1
1978	New England	27	2	7	11
1979	New England	14	0	2	2
	Totals	90	4	13	21

WITHE, PETER *Forward*
Ht. 6-1 Wt. 175
Citizen—England

Season	Club	GP	G	A	Pts.
1975	Portland	22	16	6	38

WOLF, EDE *Midfielder*
B. Munich, W. Germany
Ht. 5-8 Wt. 170
Citizen—W. Germany

| 1979 | Dallas | 16 | 2 | 3 | 7 |

WOLF, EDUARDO *Midfielder*

| 1975 | San Antonio | 1 | 0 | 0 | 0 |

WOLF, KLAUS *Forward*
B. July 3, 1948 Dankelshausen, Germany
Ht. 6-1 Wt. 180
Citizen—Germany

| 1978 | San Diego | 9 | 4 | 1 | 9 |

WOOD, IAN *Defender*
B. Jan. 15, 1948
Ht. 5-9 Wt. 162
Citizen—England

Season	Club	GP	G	A	Pts.
1974	Denver	6	0	0	0
1978	San Jose	27	1	3	5
1979	San Jose	22	4	2	10
	Totals	55	5	5	15

WOODFIELD, DAVE *Midfielder*
Ht. 5-11 Wt. 170

| 1967 | L.A.(USA) | 6 | 1 | 0 | 2 |

WOODWARD, DENNIS *Defender*
Ht. 6-2 Wt. 170

Season	Club	GP	G	A	Pts.
1969	Baltimore	—	—	—	—
1974	Washington	3	0	0	0

WOOF, BILLY *Forward*
B. Aug. 16, 1952 Durham, England
Ht. 5-10 Wt. 162
Citizen—England

| 1976 | Vancouver | 21 | 5 | 4 | 14 |

WOOLER, ALAN *Defender*
B. Aug. 17, 1953 Poole, England
Ht. 6-1 Wt. 170
Citizen—England

Season	Club	GP	G	A	Pts.
1974	Boston	20	0	1	1
1975	Boston	22	2	5	9
1976	Boston	24	0	1	1
	Totals	66	2	7	11

Season	Club	GP	G	A	Pts.

WOOSNAM, PHIL *Forward*
B. Dec. 22, 1932   Caersws, Wales
Ht. 5–11   Wt. 178

Season	Club	GP	G	A	Pts.
1967	Atlanta	9	8	7	23
1968	Atlanta	7	1	0	2
	Totals	16	9	7	25

WORBYE, JOHN *Defender*
B. Denmark
Ht. 5–8   Wt. 144
Citizen—Denmark

Season	Club	GP	G	A	Pts.
1968	Washington	18	0	0	0

WORTHINGTON, DAVE *Defender*
Ht. 5–10   Wt. 155

Season	Club	GP	G	A	Pts.
1974	Denver	16	0	0	0

WORTHINGTON, FRANK *Forward*
B. Nov. 23, 1948   Yorkshire, England
Ht. 5–10   Wt. 168
Citizen—England

Season	Club	GP	G	A	Pts.
1979	Philadelphia	21	10	7	27

WOODWARD, ALAN *Forward*
B. Sept. 7, 1946   Sheffield, England
Ht. 5–10   Wt. 180
Citizen—England

Season	Club	GP	G	A	Pts.
1979	Tulsa	19	4	12	20

WOZNIAK, MAX
See *Goalkeeper*

WRENGER, WILHELM *Midfielder*
B. Apr. 5, 1938   Essen, Germany
Ht. 5–9   Wt. 163
Citizen—Germany

Season	Club	GP	G	A	Pts.
1968	St. Louis	20	4	0	8

WRIGHT, BARRIE *Defender*
B. Bradford, England
Ht. 5–9   Wt. 150
Citizen—England

Season	Club	GP	G	A	Pts.
1967	N.Y. (NPSL)	26	0	0	0
1968	New York	32	0	0	0
	Totals	58	0	0	0

WRIGHT, RALPH *Defender*
B. Aug. 3, 1947   Newcastle, England
Ht. 6–0   Wt. 180
Citizen—England

Season	Club	GP	G	A	Pts.
1974	Miami	20	3	0	6
1975	Miami	17	1	2	4
1976	Mia.-Dal.	20	1	0	2
	Totals	57	5	2	12

YASIN, EROL
See *Goalkeeper*

YAZAR, CEYHAN *Forward*
B. Feb. 1, 1944   Turkey
Ht. 5–8   Wt. 160
Citizen—Turkey

Season	Club	GP	G	A	Pts.
1971	New York	9	2	6	10

YBARRA, RUDY *Forward*
B. Apr. 3, 1958   Santa Barbara, Calif.
Ht. 5–6   Wt. 135
Citizen—U.S.

Season	Club	GP	G	A	Pts.
1978	Los Angeles	27	4	1	9
1979	Memphis	8	0	1	1
	Totals	35	4	2	10

YOULDEN, THOMAS *Defender*
B. Aug. 7, 1940   London, England
Ht. 6–1   Wt. 175

Season	Club	GP	G	A	Pts.
1971	Dallas	15	8	4	20

YOUNG, JOHN *Midfielder*
B. Nov. 3, 1935
Ht. 6–1   Wt. 175
Citizen—Scotland

Season	Club	GP	G	A	Pts.
1971	New York	19	0	0	0

YOUNG, ROBY *Forward*
B. Oct. 3, 1943   Israel
Ht. 5–9   Wt. 160
Citizen—Israel

Season	Club	GP	G	A	Pts.
1972	New York	7	1	2	4
1973	New York	11	1	1	3
	Totals	18	2	3	7

ZABARAC, VLADE *Forward*
B. 1948   Yugoslavia
Ht. 5–9   Wt. 165
Citizen—Yugoslavia

Season	Club	GP	G	A	Pts.
1977	San Jose	2	0	0	0

ZACZYNSKI, ZENON *Midfielder*
Ht. 5–8   Wt. 155

Season	Club	GP	G	A	Pts.
1975	San Jose	1	0	0	0

ZAIJA, WALTER *Defender*
Ht. 5–11   Wt. 165
Citizen—U.S.

Season	Club	GP	G	A	Pts.
1973	Atlanta	1	0	0	0
1974	Denver	5	0	0	0
	Totals	6	0	0	0

Season	Club	GP	G	A	Pts.

ZAJDEL, DIETER *Midfielder*
B. July 7, 1931 Poland
Ht. 5-8 Wt. 160

Season	Club	GP	G	A	Pts.
1972	New York	10	0	0	0
1973	New York	13	1	1	3
1974	San Jose	17	1	0	1
	Totals	40	2	1	5

ZANATTA, SERGIO *Forward*
B. Italy
Ht. 5-10 Wt. 170
Citizen—Canada

Season	Club	GP	G	A	Pts.
1975	Vancouver	16	6	4	16

ZANELLI, ANDREA *Defender*
Ht. 5-10 Wt. 155

Season	Club	GP	G	A	Pts.
1971	Montreal	6	0	0	0

ZANOTTI, MARIO *Defender*
B. Mar. 8, 1947
Ht. 5-8 Wt. 164
Citizen—Argentina

Season	Club	GP	G	A	Pts.
1974	Los Angeles	15	0	1	1

ZEC, NINOSLAV *Forward*
B. July 22, 1949 Belgrade, Yugoslavia
Ht. 5-10 Wt. 165
Citizen—Yugoslavia

Season	Club	GP	G	A	Pts.
1978	Tulsa	28	9	9	27
1979	Atl.-Hou.	23	6	5	17
	Totals	51	15	14	44

ZELL, KIT *Forward*
B. Aug. 19, 1954 Seattle, Wash.
Ht. 6-2 Wt. 170
Citizen—U.S.

Season	Club	GP	G	A	Pts.
1976	Portland	2	0	0	0

ZELTSER, ZEEV *Forward*
Ht. 5-11 Wt. 165

Season	Club	GP	G	A	Pts.
1967	L.A. (NPSL)	14	5	1	11

ZEMARIA (ZEMARIA dos SANTOS) *Defender*
B. May 27, 1939 Brazil
Ht. 6-I Wt. 188
Citizen—Brazil

Season	Club	GP	G	A	Pts.
1967	Baltimore	12	2	1	5
1968	Baltimore	5	0	0	0
	Totals	17	2	1	5

ZEQUINHA *Forward*
B. Nov. 7, 1949 Leopoldina, Brazil
Ht. 5-8 Wt. 154
Citizen—Brazil

Season	Club	GP	G	A	Pts.
1979	Dallas	27	8	14	30

ZERHUSEN, STEVE
See *Goalkeeper*

ZERILLO, HECTOR *Midfielder*
B. Argentina
Ht. 6-1 Wt. 180

Season	Club	GP	G	A	Pts.
1967	Philadelphia	5	2	1	5

ZIADIE, DENNIS *Forward*
B. Oct. 1, 1946 Montego Bay, Jamaica
Ht. 5-8 Wt. 140

Season	Club	GP	G	A	Pts.
1968	Boston	2	0	0	0

ZIEMANN, GERD *Forward*
B. Nov. 19, 1943 Gelsenkirchen, W. Germany
Ht. 5-9 Wt. 165
Citizen—W. Germany

Season	Club	GP	G	A	Pts.
1967	Chi. (NPSL)	11	0	1	1
1968	San Diego	3	0	0	0
	Totals	14	0	1	1

ZUTELIJA, DINKO *Forward*
B. Oct. 4, 1948 Belgrade, Yugoslavia
Ht. 5-8 Wt. 150
Citizen—Yugoslavia

Season	Club	GP	G	A	Pts.
1977	Toronto	17	3	6	12

ZYLKER, JIM *Defender*

Season	Club	GP	G	A	Pts.
1975	San Jose	16	1	2	4

GOALKEEPERS

Where it was available, the goalkeeper records list the player's date and place of birth, height, weight, and country of citizenship in addition to season, team, minutes played (Min.), saves, goals against (GA) shutouts (SO), and goals-against average (Avg.).

Season	Club	Min.	Saves	GA	SO	Avg.
ADALMIR, NERI						
Ht. 5-10 Wt. 147						
1967	Hou.	252	15	1	1	1.42
ADLINGTON, TERRENCE						
B. Nov. 21, 1935 Torquay Devon, England						
Ht. 6-0 Wt. 175						
Citizen—England						
1967	Balt.	2268	206	32	7	1.27
1968	Dal.	720	36	20	0	2.50
	Totals	2988	242	52	7	1.57
ALLAN, THOMSON						
Ht. 5-9 Wt. 140						
1967	Tor. (NPSL)	1072	60	17	1	1.43
ALLISON, GARY						
B. Oct. 14, 1952 W. Germany						
Ht. 6-0 Wt. 170						
Citizen—W. Germany						
1973	Dal.	90	9	4	0	4.00
1975	L.A.	810	87	16	2	1.77
1979	S. D.	90	6	2	0	2.00
	Totals	990	102	22	2	2.00
ARDESCH, HENNY						
Ht. 6-1 Wt. 165						
1967	S.F.	45	1	1	0	2.00
ARNAUTOFF, PETER						
B. Dec. 29, 1951 Oakland, Calif.						
Ht. 5-11 Wt. 165						
Citizen—U.S.						
1979	Edm.	90	8	9	0	9.00
BAKER, KIERON						
Ht. 6-0 Wt. 160						
1971	Mont.	1593	145	46	1	2.60
BALDIN, PAOLO						
1972	Tor.	90	6	5	0	5.00

Season	Club	Min.	Saves	GA	SO	Avg.
BANACH, OREST						
B. Mar. 31, 1948 Neu Ulm, Germany						
Ht. 6-1 Wt. 185						
Citizen—U.S.						
1968	Boston	—	—	—	—	—
1969	Balt.	1170	99	42	0	3.23
1971	St. L.	1170	115	17	2	1.31
	Totals	2340	214	59	2	2.27
BANKS, GORDON						
B. Dec. 30, 1939 Sheffield, England						
Ht. 5-11 Wt. 170						
Citizen—England						
1967	Cle.	576	27	10	1	1.56
1977	Ft. L.	2329	147	29	9	1.12
1978	Ft. L.	948	64	22	2	2.09
	Totals	3853	238	61	12	1.42
BARCA, MIGUEL						
1975	Hart.	14	1	0	0	0.00
BARCLAY, KELVIN						
B. Feb. 26, 1945 Trinidad						
Ht. 5-10 Wt. 175						
1974	Wash.	900	61	18	2	1.80
BARNETT, GEOFF						
B. Oct. 16, 1946 Northwich, England						
Ht. 6-0 Wt. 166						
Citizen—England						
1976	Minn.	1984	115	28	7	1.27
1977	Minn.	2165	117	30	8	1.25
1978	Minn.	1761	103	33	3	1.69
1979	Minn.	45	3	1	0	2.00
	Totals	5955	338	92	18	1.39
BARRON, JIM						
B. 1945 England						
Ht. 6-1 Wt. 175						
Citizen—England						
1977	Conn.	842	88	26	0	2.78

Season	Club	Min.	Saves	GA	SO	Avg.

BAUM, JOE
B. St. Louis, Mo.
Citizen—U.S.

Season	Club	Min.	Saves	GA	SO	Avg.
1971	St. L.	90	9	4	0	4.00

BENEGAS, JUAN
B. Spain
Ht. 5-9   Wt. 170
Citizen—Spain

Season	Club	Min.	Saves	GA	SO	Avg.
1967	Tor. (NPSL)	1170	117	29	1	2.23
1968	Tor.	1640	99	44	3	2.44
	Totals	2810	216	73	4	2.34

BILECKI, ZELJKO
B. Apr. 28, 1950   Yugoslavia
Ht. 6-1   Wt. 180
Citizen—Canada

Season	Club	Min.	Saves	GA	SO	Avg.
1975	Tor.	1950	129	27	8	1.25
1976	Tor.	180	11	6	0	3.00
1977	Tor.	2239	185	30	10	1.21
1978	Tor.	1550	122	23	6	1.34
1979	T.B.	1549	93	22	5	1.28
	Totals	7468	540	108	29	1.30

BIRKENMEIER, HUBERT
B. May 24, 1949   Hartaheim, West Germany
Ht. 5-9   Wt. 169
Citizen—West Germany

Season	Club	Min.	Saves	GA	SO	Avg.
1979	N.Y.	630	46	10	2	1.43

BLACKMORE, RICHARD
Ht. 6-0   Wt. 170

Season	Club	Min.	Saves	GA	SO	Avg.
1972	N.Y.	1260	129	16	3	1.14
1975	Den.	995	65	21	1	1.90
	Totals	2255	194	37	4	1.48

BLANCO, ROBERTO
B. Puebla, Mexico
Ht. 5-10   Wt. 165

Season	Club	Min.	Saves	GA	SO	Avg.
1975	S.A.	1204	122	24	2	1.79

BOND, LEN
B. Feb. 12, 1954   Bristol, England
Ht. 6-0   Wt. 170
Citizen—England

Season	Club	Min.	Saves	GA	SO	Avg.
1976	St. L.	1326	113	40	0	2.71

BONETTI, PETER

Season	Club	Min.	Saves	GA	SO	Avg.
1975	St. L.	1830	189	28	5	1.38

BOULTON, COLIN
B. Dec. 9. 1945   Cheltenham, England
Ht. 6-0   Wt. 165
Citizen—England

Season	Club	Min.	Saves	GA	SO	Avg.
1978	Tul.	2531	159	39	10	1.39
1979	Tul.-L.A.	2746	109	49	7	1.61
	Totals	5277	268	88	17	1.50

BRAGG, DAVID
B. Mar. 5, 1953   Baltimore, Md.
Ht. 6-0   Wt. 175
Citizen—U.S.

Season	Club	Min.	Saves	GA	SO	Avg.
1977	L.V.	67	5	3	0	4.03
1978	Phil.	380	27	8	0	1.89
	Totals	447	32	11	0	2.21

BRAND, JACK
B. Aug. 4, 1953   Germany
Ht. 6-1   Wt. 175
Citizen—Canada

Season	Club	Min.	Saves	GA	SO	Avg.
1974	Tor.	1260	107	20	3	1.43
1975	Tor.	61	10	0	0	0.00
1977	Roch.	2373	167	39	6	1.48
1978	N.Y.	763	49	12	1	1.42
1979	N.Y.-Tul.	902	66	18	0	1.80
	Totals	5359	399	89	10	1.49

BRAUN, THEO
Ht. 5-8   Wt. 160

Season	Club	Min.	Saves	GA	SO	Avg.
1973	Tor.	180	6	1	1	0.50

BRAVENBOER, FREDDY
B. May 22, 1943   Rotterdam, Holland
Ht. 6-2   Wt. 215
Citizen—Holland

Season	Club	Min.	Saves	GA	SO	Avg.
1967	Pitt.	103	6	4	0	3.50

BRCIC, DAVID
B. Jan. 21, 1957   St. Louis, Mo.
Ht. 6-2   Wt. 173
Citizen—U.S.

Season	Club	Min.	Saves	GA	SO	Avg.
1978	N.Y.	45	2	2	0	4.00
1979	N.Y.	599	50	10	1	1.50
	Totals	644	52	12	1	1.68

BROWN, BILL
B. London, England
Ht. 6-1   Wt. 158
Citizen—England

Season	Club	Min.	Saves	GA	SO	Avg.
1967	Tor. (NPSL)	1443	6	34	2	2.12

BROWN, BRUCE
Ht. 6-3   Wt. 190

Season	Club	Min.	Saves	GA	SO	Avg.
1974	Den.	180	29	5	0	2.50
1975	Den.	839	69	19	0	2.04
	Totals	1019	98	24	0	2.12

BROWN, CLIFF
B. May 23, 1956   Valdosta, Ga.
Ht. 5-11   Wt. 160
Citizen—U.S.

Season	Club	Min.	Saves	GA	SO	Avg.
1978	Sea.	180	22	2	1	1.00
1979	Sea.	244	18	11	0	4.06
	Totals	424	40	13	1	2.76

Season	Club	Min.	Saves	GA	SO	Avg.

BROWN, GRAHAM
B. Mar. 21, 1946   Matlock Derbyshire, England
Ht. 6-0   Wt. 175
Citizen—England

Season	Club	Min.	Saves	GA	SO	Avg.
1975	Port.	1949	144	26	5	1.20
1977	Port.	224	14	4	0	1.61
	Totals	2173	158	30	5	1.24

BURNS, TONY
B. Mar. 27, 1945   England
Ht. 6-0   Wt. 190
Citizen—England

Season	Club	Min.	Saves	GA	SO	Avg.
1978	Mem.	1061	63	22	1	1.87

CALVO, JOSE LUIS
B. Argentina
Ht. 5-1   Wt. 158

Season	Club	Min.	Saves	GA	SO	Avg.
1967	Chi. (NPSL)	90	10	3	0	3.00

CAMACHO, MANUEL
Ht. 5-10   Wt. 174
Citizen—Mexico

Season	Club	Min.	Saves	GA	SO	Avg.
1967	Chi. (NPSL)	2514	256	50	3	1.79

CAMPOS, CLAUDE
Ht. 5-10   Wt. 160

Season	Club	Min.	Saves	GA	SO	Avg.
1971	Roch.	1054	97	13	3	1.11
1972	Roch.	1133	64	18	4	1.43
1973	Roch.	1050	89	19	3	1.63
1974	Roch.	1571	111	20	8	1.14
	Totals	4808	361	70	18	1.31

CANO, MARINE
B. Sept. 13, 1954   Los Angeles, Calif.
Ht. 6-1   Wt. 175
Citizen—U.S.

Season	Club	Min.	Saves	GA	SO	Avg.
1978	Ft. L.	711	40	16	2	2.02

CAVALLERO, TRINI

Season	Club	Min.	Saves	GA	SO	Avg.
1975	S.A.	450	29	12	0	2.40

CAWSTON, MERVYN "THE MAGICIAN"
B. Feb. 4, 1952   Norwich, England
Ht. 6-2   Wt. 170
Citizen—England

Season	Club	Min.	Saves	GA	SO	Avg.
1975	Chi.	1586	96	23	4	1.35
1976	Chi.	2173	165	29	6	1.20
1977	Chi.	2370	179	40	3	1.52
1978	Chi.	2106	170	46	2	1.97
	Totals	8235	610	138	15	1.51

CHURSKY, TONY
B. June 13, 1953   Vancouver, Canada
Ht. 5-10   Wt. 165
Citizen—Canada

Season	Club	Min.	Saves	GA	SO	Avg.
1976	Sea.	1981	135	20	9	0.91
1977	Sea.	2200	143	31	7	1.27
1978	Sea.	2617	175	41	9	1.41
1979	Calif.-Chi.	1276	74	24	4	1.69
	Totals	8074	527	116	29	1.29

CLARK, BOBBY
B. Sept. 26, 1945   Glasgow, Scotland
Ht. 5-11   Wt. 175
Citizen—Scotland

Season	Club	Min.	Saves	GA	SO	Avg.
1976	S.A.	1775	97	25	4	1.27

CLARK, ROBERT
Ht. 6-1   Wt. 170

Season	Club	Min.	Saves	GA	SO	Avg.
1967	Wash.	1080	71	11	5	0.92

CLARKE, DANVILLE

Season	Club	Min.	Saves	GA	SO	Avg.
1971	Roch.	580	36	8	3	1.24
1973	Roch.	660	39	8	3	1.09
	Totals	1240	75	16	6	1.16

COFFEE, PAUL
B. Nov. 12, 1956   Santa Clara, Calif.
Ht. 6-1   Wt. 170
Citizen—U.S.

Season	Club	Min.	Saves	GA	SO	Avg.
1979	Chi.	1454	76	33	0	2.04

CONNAGHAN, DENNIS
B. Glasgow, Scotland
Ht. 6-2   Wt. 175
Citizen—Scotland

Season	Club	Min.	Saves	GA	SO	Avg.
1967	Balt.	584	65	12	3	1.85

COOPER, KEN
B. Feb. 2, 1946   Blackpool, England
Ht. 5-10   Wt. 187
Citizen—England

Season	Club	Min.	Saves	GA	SO	Avg.
1970	Dal.	1800	66	29	6	1.45
1971	Dal.	720	34	13	2	1.44
1972	Dal.	1260	109	12	6	0.86
1973	Dal.	1620	156	21	5	1.17
1974	Dal.	1800	105	22	9	1.10
1975	Dal.	1871	125	31	4	1.49
1976	Dal.	2179	116	45	5	1.73
1977	Dal.	2100	120	21	8	0.90
1978	Dal.	1905	90	35	3	1.65
1979	Dal.	180	7	2	1	1.00
	Totals	15,435	928	231	49	1.35

CRUDGINGTON, GEOFF
Ht. 5-11   Wt. 175

Season	Club	Min.	Saves	GA	SO	Avg.
1971	Tor.	494	41	12	0	2.19

CUMBES, JIM
B. May 4, 1944   Manchester, England
Ht. 6-3   Wt. 200
Citizen—England

Season	Club	Min.	Saves	GA	SO	Avg.
1976	Port.	2031	123	34	5	1.51

Season	Club	Min.	Saves	GA	SO	Avg.
D'ALESSIO, DOMENICO						
1971	Roch.	90	16	3	0	3.00
DAVIE, SANDY						
Ht. 6-0 Wt. 165						
1967	Dal.	500	34	9	2	1.62
DAVIES, FRED						
1967	L.A. (USA)	450	37	7	1	1.40
DeBONO, ALFREDO						
B. Jan. 20, 1944 Sliema, Malta						
Ht. 5-8 Wt. 165						
1967	Pitt.	1617	183	46	11	2.56
DeLIMA, MIGUEL						
B. Sept. 9, 1937 Brazil						
1967	St. L.	1397	172	27	3	1.74
DELORM, THOMAS "TAD"						
B. Dec. 7, 1955 Trier, West Germany						
Ht. 6-4 Wt. 195						
Citizen—U.S.A.						
1978	Col	180	19	3	0	1.50
1979	Atl.	1243	85	33	1	2.39
	Totals	1423	104	36	1	2.28
DEVITO, ROBERTO						
1967	Hou.	2	0	1	0	45.00
DIAS, PAULO						
B. Feb. 27, 1944 Brazil						
Ht. 6-1 Wt. 170						
1972	Mia.	1033	124	22	3	1.92
DROEGMOELLER, MENO						
Ht. 6-1 Wt. 180						
Citizen—U.S.						
1976	Roch.	8	2	0	0	0.00
DuBOSE, WINSTON						
B. July 28, 1955 Orlando, Fla.						
Ht. 6-2 Wt. 180						
Citizen—U.S.						
1977	T.B.	197	19	4	0	1.83
1978	T.B.	1352	68	19	4	1.26
1979	T.B.	1189	92	24	2	1.82
	Totals	2738	179	47	6	1.54
DuCHATEAU, GENE						
B. Jan. 23, 1954 Ridgewood, N.J.						
Ht. 6-2 Wt. 175						
Citizen—U.S.						
1976	Hart.	1172	92	25	1	0.92
1977	Conn.	1546	140	38	1	2.21

Season	Club	Min.	Saves	GA	SO	Avg.
1978	Oak.	460	32	9	1	1.76
1979	Mem.-Tul.	1012	59	23	0	2.04
	Totals	4190	323	95	3	2.04
DUNNE, PAT						
Ht. 6-0 Wt. 196						
1967	Bost.	1080	85	26	1	2.17
EDMUNDS, ERROL						
Ht. 6-0 Wt. 165						
1973	Mia.	15	0	0	0	0.00
ENDEMAN, JAN						
B. May 22, 1957 Eibergen, Holland						
Ht. 6-2 Wt. 180						
Citizen—Holland						
1979	Edm.	2657	174	67	3	2.27
ENGER, HANS						
B. Jan. 22, 1947 Oslo, Norway						
Ht. 5-9 Wt. 150						
Citizen—Norway						
1968	Dal.	191	12	18	0	8.48
FARMER, JOHN						
Ht. 6-1 Wt. 182						
1967	Cle.	250	6	1	2	0.36
FLASCHEN, DAVE						
B. Dec. 10, 1955 Conn.						
Ht. 6-1 Wt. 170						
Citizen—U.S.						
1977	Chi.	55	4	2	0	3.27
1978	Chi.	649	58	17	0	2.36
	Totals	704	62	19	0	2.43
FORREST, JOHN						
Ht. 5-10 Wt. 165						
1973	Atl.	1452	130	30	3	1.86
FORSTER, DEREK						
Ht. 5-9 Wt. 155						
1967	Van.	585	64	15	1	2.31
FOX, PETER						
B. July 5, 1957 Scunthorpe, England						
Ht. 5-11 Wt. 165						
Citizen—England						
1977	Haw.	2282	187	52	1	2.05
FRAYDL, GERNOT						
B. Austria						
Ht. 6-0 Wt. 180						
Citizen—Austria						
1967	Phil.	2203	280	35	7	1.43
1968	St. L.	—	—	—	—	—
	Totals	2203	280	35	7	1.43

Season	Club	Min.	Saves	GA	SO	Avg.
FREITAG, PAUL						
B. May 12, 1940 Vienna, Austria						
Ht. 5-10 Wt. 175						
Citizen—U.S.						
1967	N.Y. (NPSL)	1305	136	34	0	1.65
1968	N.Y.	—	—	—	—	—
	Totals	1305	136	24	—	1.65
GARCIA, EDUARDO						
Ht. 5-8 Wt. 165						
1967	N.Y. (USA)	495	30	8	0	1.45
GIZZI, PAUL						
B. Dec. 19, 1952 Keebo, Japan						
Ht. 6-1 Wt. 180						
Citizen—U.S.						
1976	Sea.	90	8	2	0	2.00
1978	S.J.	166	16	6	0	3.25
	Totals	256	24	8	0	2.81
GORSEK, JIM						
B. Oct. 12, 1955 Oregon City, Oregon						
Ht. 6-0 Wt. 160						
Citizen—U.S.						
1977	Port.	252	11	5	0	1.79
1979	Port.	90	2	2	0	2.00
	Totals	342	13	7	0	1.84
GRASSER, JOHN						
Ht. 6-3 Wt. 185						
Citizen—U.S.A.						
1974	Roch.	229	18	9	0	3.67
GRECO, PETER						
B. 1947 Italy						
Ht. 6-2 Wt. 185						
Citizen—Canada						
1975	Van.	720	66	9	2	1.13
GRELITZ, KLAUS						
B. Vienna, Austria						
Ht. 5-10 Wt. 170						
Citizen—Austria						
1967	Chi. (NPSL)	270	20	3	1	1.00
GROBELAAR, BRUCE						
B. Sept. 11, 1957 South Africa						
Ht. 6-1 Wt. 175						
Citizen—South Africa						
1979	Van.	90	6	2	0	2.00
GROSS, VOLKMAR						
B. Jan. 31, 1948 Berlin, West Germany						
Ht. 6-3 Wt. 215						
Citizen—West Germany						
1979	Minn.-S.D.	2042	137	38	6	1.60

Season	Club	Min.	Saves	GA	SO	Avg.
HAMMOND, PAUL						
B. July 26, 1953 Nottingham, England						
Ht. 6-1 Wt. 190						
Citizen—England						
1975	T.B.	1096	79	14	3	1.15
1977	T.B.	2184	174	41	4	1.69
1978	T.B.-Hou.	1369	88	35	1	2.73
1979	Hou.	2705	213	44	6	1.46
	Totals	7354	554	134	14	1.64
HARDWICK, STEVE						
B. Sept. 6, 1956 Mansfield, England						
Ht. 5-11 Wt. 174						
Citizen—England						
1978	Det.	2734	179	36	9	1.19
HASON, FRANK						
B. June 8, 1935 Bratislava, Czechoslovakia						
Ht. 5-10 Wt. 165						
1971	Dal.	15	0	0	0	0.00
HENDERSON, DAVID						
B. June 11, 1960 Dublin, Ireland						
Ht. 6-2 Wt. 180						
Citizen—Ireland						
1979	Tor.	540	21	17	0	2.83
HEWITT, MIKE						
B. July 14, 1944 Dundee, Scotland						
Ht. 5-11 Wt. 165						
Citizen—Scotland						
1975	T.B.	919	60	12	3	1.18
1976	S.J.	1657	150	17	6	0.92
1977	S.J.	2225	135	35	8	1.42
1978	S.J.	1976	159	48	6	2.19
1979	S.J.	1506	91	39	1	2.35
	Totals	8283	595	151	24	1.64
HOOGERMAN, BERTUS						
B. Holland						
Ht. 6-1 Wt. 183						
Citizen—Holland						
1967	Pitt.	990	135	21	2	1.91
1968	K.C.	2676	189	38	0	1.28
	Totals	3666	324	59	2	1.45
HORN, GRAHAM						
B. Aug. 23, 1954 London, England						
Ht. 6-2 Wt. 200						
Citizen—England						
1976	L.A.	1361	94	28	2	1.85

Season	Club	Min.	Saves	GA	SO	Avg.

HOUSKA, JOHN
B. May 13, 1956
Ht. 6-0   Wt. 190
Citizen—U.S.

Season	Club	Min.	Saves	GA	SO	Avg.
1978	Mem.	1725	88	35	4	1.83
1979	Mem.	2187	103	53	2	2.18
	Totals	3912	191	88	6	2.02

HOWARD, DICK
B. June 10, 1943   Cheshire, England
Ht. 6-2   Wt. 185
Citizen—England

Season	Club	Min.	Saves	GA	SO	Avg.
1968	Det.	497	42	10	0	1.80
1970	Roch.	1350	81	27	2	1.80
1971	Tor.	946	74	20	0	1.90
1972	Tor.	1170	73	17	2	1.31
1973	Tor.	1530	91	17	6	1.00
1974	Tor.	540	28	9	0	1.50
	Totals	6033	389	100	10	1.49

HUMPHRIES, STEVE
B. May 29, 1961   Leicester, England
Ht. 6-0   Wt. 175
Citizen—England

Season	Club	Min.	Saves	GA	SO	Avg.
1978	Van.	90	4	1	0	1.00

ILIJEVSKI, SLOBODAN
B. Oct. 24, 1949   Skopje, Yugoslavia
Ht. 5-11   Wt. 175
Citizen—Yugoslavia

Season	Club	Min.	Saves	GA	SO	Avg.
1978	Det.	16	0	0	0	0.00
1979	Det.	90	0	1	0	1.00
	Totals	106	0	1	0	0.85

IRWIN, BILL
B. July 23, 1951   Newtown Ards, N. Ireland
Ht. 6-3   Wt. 203
Citizen—N. Ireland

Season	Club	Min.	Saves	GA	SO	Avg.
1978	Wash.	2361	178	39	5	1.49
1979	Wash.	2603	134	42	4	1.45
	Totals	4964	312	81	9	1.47

IVANOW, MIKE
B. Jan. 9, 1948   Shanghai, China
Ht. 6-4   Wt. 200
Citizen—U.S.

Season	Club	Min.	Saves	GA	SO	Avg.
1974	S.J.	1349	96	20	4	1.33
1975	S.J.	1905	193	41	1	1.94
1976	S.J.-Sea.	694	57	17	2	2.20
1977	Sea.	195	13	1	1	0.46
1979	Sea.	2517	151	39	2	1.39
	Totals	6660	410	118	10	1.59

JACKSON, JOHN
B. Sept. 5, 1942   England
Ht. 6-0   Wt. 188
Citizen—England

Season	Club	Min.	Saves	GA	SO	Avg.
1977	St. L.	1526	103	20	7	1.18
1978	Calif.	1170	101	24	3	1.85
	Totals	2696	204	44	10	1.47

JOERGE, JIMMY
B. Mar. 25, 1954   Chur, Switzerland
Ht. 6-3   Wt. 185
Citizen—U.S.

Season	Club	Min.	Saves	GA	SO	Avg.
1977	Haw.	150	7	4	1	2.40

JOHNS, NICKY
B. June 8, 1957   Orpington, Kent, England
Ht. 6-2   Wt. 180
Citizen—England

Season	Club	Min.	Saves	GA	SO	Avg.
1978	T.B.	731	39	15	2	1.85

JOKERST, DAVE
B. Jan. 1, 1948   St. Louis, Mo.
Ht. 6-2   Wt. 170
Citizen—U.S.

Season	Club	Min.	Saves	GA	SO	Avg.
1969	St. L.	1260	111	39	0	2.78
1970	St. L.	194	17	9	0	4.17
1974	St. L.	90	20	2	0	2.00
1975	St. L.	270	33	4	1	1.33
1976	St. L.	855	57	17	1	1.79
1977	St. L.	905	86	13	3	1.29
1978	Calif.	1484	75	19	6	1.15
1979	Calif.	1958	127	38	2	1.75
	Totals	7016	526	141	13	1.81

JOSEPH, BOBBY

Season	Club	Min.	Saves	GA	SO	Avg.
1975	Wash.	445	30	15	0	3.03

KAMMERER, MANFRED
B. Sept. 28, 1944   Germany
Ht. 5-11   Wt. 163
Citizen—Germany

Season	Club	Min.	Saves	GA	SO	Avg.
1968	Det.	—	—	—	—	—
1969	Atl.	1260	56	15	0	1.07
1970	Atl.	1080	65	19	4	1.58
1971	Atl.	1819	142	23	8	1.14
1972	Atl.	945	76	12	4	1.14
1973	Atl.	258	32	10	0	3.49
	Totals	5362	371	79	16	1.33

KEELAN, KEVIN
B. Jan. 5, 1946   Calcutta, India
Ht. 5-11   Wt. 175
Citizen—England

Season	Club	Min.	Saves	GA	SO	Avg.
1978	N.E.	2621	158	36	7	1.24
1979	N.E.	2234	133	40	6	1.61
	Totals	4855	291	76	13	1.41

Season	Club	Min.	Saves	GA	SO	Avg.
KENNEDY, JOHN						
Ht. 5–11 Wt. 158						
1967	Det.	1017	105	14	4	1.24
KEOHANE, SEAN						
Ht. 5–11 Wt. 170						
Citizen—U.S.						
1978	S.J.	45	4	7	0	14.00
KOFIE, EMANUEL						
B. Feb. 10, 1947						
Ht. 5–6 Wt. 150						
1971	N.Y.	945	91	26	1	2.48
KONSTANTINOU, VASILIOS						
B. June 4, 1947 Athens, Greece						
Ht. 5–11 Wt. 180						
Citizen—Greece						
1978	Tor.	1180	87	23	3	1.75
KORNEK, CONRAD						
B. Feb. 12, 1937						
Ht. 5–11 Wt. 170						
Citizen—Poland						
1971	N.Y.	1215	100	29	1	2.15
KUYKENDALL, KURT						
B. Oct. 30, 1952 Chicago, Ill.						
Ht. 6–0 Wt. 165						
Citizen—U.S.						
1974	Wash.	810	65	16	1	1.78
1975	N.Y.	375	9	34	1	2.25
1976	N.Y.	104	12	6	0	5.19
1979	Roch.	90	3	5	0	5.00
	Totals	1379	89	61	2	3.98
KYDD, SAMMY						
Ht. 5–11 Wt. 175						
1967	Det.	45	3	4	0	8.00
LANDRY, DAVE						
B. July 21, 1951 Tisdale, Canada						
Ht. 6–3 Wt. 190						
Citizen—Canada						
1975	Port.	90	4	1	0	1.00
1976	Port.	180	9	5	0	2.50
	Totals	270	13	6	0	2.00
LETTIERI, TINO						
B. Sept. 27, 1957 Torito Bari, Italy						
Ht. 5–8 Wt. 165						
Citizen—Canada						
1977	Minn.	245	7	3	1	1.10
1978	Minn.	1003	55	7	7	0.63
1979	Minn.	1378	91	25	2	1.63
	Totals	2626	153	35	10	1.20

Season	Club	Min.	Saves	GA	SO	Avg.
LINDBERG, ODD						
B. Dec. 20, 1948 Oslo, Norway						
Ht. 5–11 Wt. 140						
Citizen—Norway						
1968	Dal.	907	56	37	0	3.67
LINDBERG, SVEN						
B. Jan. 30, 1934 Sunne, Sweden						
Ht. 6–0 Wt. 174						
Citizen—Sweden						
1967	Atl.	1445	134	22	3	1.37
1968	Atl.	—	—	—	—	—
	Totals	1445	134	22	3	1.37
LOPERA, ERNESTO						
Ht. 5–7 Wt. 160						
1967	Phil.	673	84	8	4	1.07
MACKAY, DONALD						
Ht. 5–11 Wt. 168						
1967	Dal.	580	22	14	0	2.17
MACRAE, KEITH						
B. Feb. 5, 1951						
Ht. 6–1 Wt. 170						
Citizen—England						
1978	Phil.	1958	167	42	2	1.93
MAGANA, RAUL						
B. El Salvador						
Ht. 5–10 Wt. 158						
Citizen—Guatemala						
1968	Tor.	1240	100	25	3	1.78
MAHONEY, MIKE						
B. Oct. 25, 1950 Bristol, England						
Ht. 6–2 Wt. 185						
Citizen—England						
1979	Chi.-Calif.	899	54	20	0	2.00
MANNOS, PETER						
B. July 20, 1954 Chicago, Ill.						
Ht. 5–11 Wt. 165						
Citizen—U.S.						
1976	S.A.	458	24	6	1	1.18
1977	Dal.	270	27	9	0	3.00
	Totals	728	51	15	1	1.85
MARTIN, ERIC						
B. Mar. 31, 1946 Perth, Scotland						
Ht. 6–0 Wt. 175						
Citizen—Scotland						
1976	Wash.	2193	148	37	5	1.51
1977	Wash.	2192	133	41	4	1.68
	Totals	4385	281	78	9	1.60

Season	Club	Min.	Saves	GA	SO	Avg.

MAUSSER, ARNOLD
B. Feb. 28, 1954   Brooklyn, N.Y.
Ht. 6–2   Wt. 185
Citizen—U.S.

Season	Club	Min.	Saves	GA	SO	Avg.
1975	Hart.	2011	223	50	2	2.24
1976	T.B.	2162	201	28	6	1.17
1977	Van.	2386	149	44	8	1.66
1978	Colo.	2585	198	61	3	2.12
1979	Ft.L.	2637	193	58	3	1.98
	Totals	11,781	964	241	22	1.84

MAY, JIM
B. Mar. 22, 1953   Kings Ferry, N.Y.
Ht. 6–1   Wt. 165
Citizen—U.S.

Season	Club	Min.	Saves	GA	SO	Avg.
1975	Roch.	379	28	11	2	2.61
1977	Roch.	24	1	1	0	3.75
1978	Roch.	921	53	20	2	1.95
	Totals	1324	82	32	4	2.18

MAYER, ALAN
B. July 3, 1952   Bayshore, N.Y.
Ht. 6–0   Wt. 185
Citizen—U.S.

Season	Club	Min.	Saves	GA	SO	Avg.
1974	Balt.	502	58	15	0	2.68
1975	Balt.	1646	149	38	4	2.11
1976	S.D.	2081	218	41	3	1.77
1977	L.V.	1997	152	31	7	1.40
1978	S.D.	2978	217	55	6	1.77
1979	S.D.	1880	120	37	4	1.77
	Totals	11,084	914	217	24	1.76

McDONNELL, PETER
B. June 11, 1953   Kendall, England
Ht. 6–1   Wt. 175
Citizen—England

Season	Club	Min.	Saves	GA	SO	Avg.
1978	Dal.	825	33	18	3	1.96

McKECHNIE, IAN
Ht. 6–0   Wt. 186

Season	Club	Min.	Saves	GA	SO	Avg.
1974	Bost.	1208	75	13	5	0.86

MELLA, RON
Ht. 6–1   Wt. 175

Season	Club	Min.	Saves	GA	SO	Avg.
1971	Roch.	450	47	17	0	3.40
1972	Roch.	117	12	4	0	3.07
	Totals	567	59	21	0	3.33

MESSING, SHEP
B. Oct. 9, 1949   Bronx, N.Y.
Ht. 6–0   Wt. 180
Citizen—U.S.

Season	Club	Min.	Saves	GA	SO	Avg.
1973	N.Y.	90	9	1	0	1.00
1974	N.Y.	719	59	15	0	1.88
1975	Bost.	1640	144	17	6	0.93
1976	Bost.-N.Y.	1728	166	24	6	1.25
1977	N.Y.	1737	155	28	4	1.45

Season	Club	Min.	Saves	GA	SO	Avg.
1978	Oak.	2332	185	48	5	1.85
1979	Roch.	2707	187	50	4	1.66
	Totals	10,953	905	183	25	1.50

MICHNIEWSKI, JAN
Ht. 6–2   Wt. 183
Citizen—Poland

Season	Club	Min.	Saves	GA	SO	Avg.
1974	Bost.	592	54	7	2	1.00
1975	Bost.	383	36	11	0	2.58
	Totals	975	90	18	2	1.66

MIGUELUCCI, OSMAR
Ht. 6–0   Wt. 172

Season	Club	Min.	Saves	GA	SO	Avg.
1967	N.Y. (USA)	582	27	9	1	1.39

MILLER, JIM
Ht. 6–0   Wt. 175
Citizen—U.S.

Season	Club	Min.	Saves	GA	SO	Avg.
1976	Phil.	187	15	4	0	1.93
1978	Phil.	418	29	8	0	1.72
1979	Phil.	76	8	2	0	2.37
	Totals	681	52	14	0	1.85

MISHALOW, BILL
B. Mar. 6, 1952   Chicago, Ill.
Ht. 5–11   Wt. 170
Citizen—U.S.

Season	Club	Min.	Saves	GA	SO	Avg.
1976	L.A.	854	65	11	2	1.16
1977	L.A.	705	58	8	3	1.02
1978	L.A.	463	37	11	0	2.14
1979	N.E.-Mem.	270	22	8	0	2.67
	Totals	2292	182	38	5	1.49

MONTGOMERY, JIMMY
Ht. 6–0   Wt. 168

Season	Club	Min.	Saves	GA	SO	Avg.
1967	Van.	495	33	13	0	2.36

MONTOYA, RUBEN
B. June 18, 1940
Ht. 6–2   Wt. 203

Season	Club	Min.	Saves	GA	SO	Avg.
1973	Mia.	1695	151	21	7	1.11

MOTTA, UBIRAJARA
Ht. 5–8   Wt. 154

Season	Club	Min.	Saves	GA	SO	Avg.
1967	Hou.	808	46	13	1	1.45

MRDULJAS, STANKO
B. Aug. 26, 1938   Split, Yugoslavia
Ht. 6–1   Wt. 185
Citizen—Yugoslavia

Season	Club	Min.	Saves	GA	SO	Avg.
1968	Hou.	197	9	4	0	1.82

Season	Club	Min.	Saves	GA	SO	Avg.

NIELSEN, LEIF
B. May 28, 1942   Copenhagen, Denmark
Ht. 6–0   Wt. 175
Citizen—Denmark

Season	Club	Min.	Saves	GA	SO	Avg.
1968	Hou.	2683	144	37	10	1.24

NOGUEIRA, VICTOR
B. July 17, 1959   Mozambique
Ht. 6–1   Wt. 180
Citizen—Mozambique

Season	Club	Min.	Saves	GA	SO	Avg.
1979	Atl.	1432	82	20	5	1.26

NUSUM, SAMUEL
B. Oct. 3, 1943
Ht. 5–10   Wt. 181
Citizen—Bermuda

Season	Club	Min.	Saves	GA	SO	Avg.
1972	N.Y.	1260	113	20	4	1.43
1973	N.Y.	1710	156	32	4	1.68
1974	N.Y.	1530	111	15	6	0.88
1975	N.Y.	1555	130	25	3	1.56
	Totals	6055	510	92	17	1.37

NUTTALL, BILL
B. Mar. 10, 1948   Norristown, Pa.
Ht. 6–3   Wt. 180
Citizen—U.S.

Season	Club	Min.	Saves	GA	SO	Avg.
1975	Mia.	765	64	10	2	1.18
1976	Mia.	769	74	24	0	2.80
	Totals	1534	138	34	2	1.99

ORDONEZ, RICARDO
B. Spain
Ht. 5–8   Wt. 155
Citizen—Spain

Season	Club	Min.	Saves	GA	SO	Avg.
1968	Dal.	270	23	9	0	3.00

OWCHARUCK, NICK
B. May 29, 1953   Chicago, Ill.
Ht. 6–1   Wt. 175
Citizen—U.S.

Season	Club	Min.	Saves	GA	SO	Avg.
1976	Minn.	114	10	1	1	0.86

PARKES, PHIL
B. July 14, 1947   West Bromwich, England
Ht. 6–4   Wt. 200
Citizen—England

Season	Club	Min.	Saves	GA	SO	Avg.
1967	L.A. (USA)	630	30	7	1	1.00
1976	Van.	1836	111	25	6	1.25
1978	Van.	2650	133	28	10	0.95
1979	Van.	2705	100	29	7	0.96
	Totals	7821	374	89	24	1.02

PEARSON, KIRK
B. Nov. 30, 1956   Reading, Pa.
Ht. 5–11   Wt. 170
Citizen—U.S.

Season	Club	Min.	Saves	GA	SO	Avg.
1978	N.E.	142	13	1	1	0.63
1979	N.E.	302	16	10	0	2.98
	Totals	444	29	11	1	2.23

PERRI, ARDO
Ht. 5–11   Wt. 180
Citizen—Canada

Season	Club	Min.	Saves	GA	SO	Avg.
1975	Roch.	1632	154	37	2	2.07

PHILLIPS, LINCOLN
B. Sept. 4, 1941
Ht. 6–1   Wt. 185
Citizen—Trinidad

Season	Club	Min.	Saves	GA	SO	Avg.
1968	Balt.	—	—	—	—	—
1974	Balt.	1326	137	33	1	2.24
1975	Balt.	378	38	14	1	3.33
	Totals	1794	175	47	2	2.48

PIANTA, PIETRO
Ht. 5–10   Wt. 169

Season	Club	Min.	Saves	GA	SO	Avg.
1967	Chi. (USA)	627	57	7	1	1.00

POOLE, MICK
B. Apr. 23, 1955   Yorkshire, England
Ht. 6–1   Wt. 185
Citizen—England

Season	Club	Min.	Saves	GA	SO	Avg.
1974	Den.	1440	174	36	2	2.23
1977	Port.	1932	132	30	3	1.40
1978	Port.	2783	180	36	9	1.16
1979	Port.	2736	178	70	2	2.30
	Totals	8891	664	172	23	1.74

PUSKAS, STANKO

Season	Club	Min.	Saves	GA	SO	Avg.
1971	Mont.	90	4	2	0	2.00

RAINEY, JERRY
Ht. 5–9   Wt. 164

Season	Club	Min.	Saves	GA	SO	Avg.
1971	Mont.	548	46	11	0	1.81

REGINATO, ADRIANO
Ht. 6–0   Wt. 165

Season	Club	Min.	Saves	GA	SO	Avg.
1967	Chi. (USA)	442	29	7	1	1.43

REYNOLDS, TOM
B. Sept. 6, 1955   Alameda, Calif.
Ht. 5–11   Wt. 180
Citizen—U.S.

Season	Club	Min.	Saves	GA	SO	Avg.
1977	Dal.	90	5	4	0	4.00

RIGBY, BOB
B. July 3, 1951   Ridley Park, Pa.
Ht. 6–0   Wt. 175
Citizen—U.S.

Season	Club	Min.	Saves	GA	SO	Avg.
1973	Phil.	1157	78	8	6	0.62
1974	Phil.	1800	151	22	3	1.10
1975	Phil.	1803	149	31	4	1.59
1976	N.Y.	1184	102	15	5	1.14
1977	L.A.	1680	137	46	1	2.46
1978	L.A.	2314	167	56	1	2.18
1979	L.A.-Phil.	2532	142	49	6	1.74
	Totals	12,470	926	227	26	1.64

Season	Club	Min.	Saves	GA	SO	Avg.

RIGHT, JOE
B. July 26, 1950   St. Louis, Mo.
Ht. 6–0   Wt. 183
Citizen—U.S.

1971	St. L.	397	47	9	1	2.04

ROBSON, BOB
B. June 11, 1957   St. Louis, Mo.
Ht. 6–0   Wt. 175
Citizen—U.S.

1979	Atl.	15	0	1	0	6.00

RODRIGUES, JOSE

1971	Tor.	720	49	15	1	1.88

ROUSE, RAYMOND "VIC"
B. Mar. 16, 1936   Swansea, Wales
Ht. 6–1   Wt. 174
Citizen—Wales

1967	Atl.	1263	122	24	2	1.71
1968	Atl.	2340	106	25	—	0.96
1971	Atl.	341	34	6	1	1.58
1972	Atl.	315	32	6	0	1.72
	Totals	4259	294	61	3	1.29

RUZIK, DARIO
B. Pula, Yugoslavia
Ht. 6–0   Wt. 178
Citizen—Yugoslavia

1978	Hou.	195	8	5	0	2.31

SABANKAYA, MUSTAFA
B. June 29, 1948   Ankara, Turkey
Ht. 5–9   Wt. 150
Citizen—Turkey

1968	Dal.	612	59	16	0	2.35

ST. CLAIR, GARY
B. Aug. 7, 1952   Glendale, Calif.
Ht. 6–3   Wt. 175
Citizen—U.S.

1975	S.J.	138	11	4	0	2.60
1976	S.D.	145	9	3	1	1.86
	Totals	283	20	7	1	2.23

SANCHEZ, ATAULFO
B. Argentina
Ht. 5–10   Wt. 167
Citizen—Argentina

1968	S.D.	1849	130	19	—	0.93

SANCHEZ, BLAS
B. Mexico City, Mexico
Ht. 5–10   Wt. 165

1974	L.A.	1530	120	30	4	1.76
1975	S.A.	388	20	8	0	1.86
	Totals	1918	140	38	4	1.78

Season	Club	Min.	Saves	GA	SO	Avg.

SHARDLOW, PAUL
B. England
Ht. 5–9   Wt. 172
Citizen—England

1967	Cle.	254	18	2	0	0.71
1968	Cle.	—	—	—	—	—
	Totals	254	18	2	0	0.71

SHERWOOD, STEVE
B. Shelby, England
Ht. 6–3   Wt. 190
Citizen—England

1976	Hart.	1090	97	29	1	2.39

SIDEBOTTOM, GEOFFREY
B. Maplewell, England
Ht. 5–10   Wt. 174
Citizen—England

1967	N.Y. (NPSL)	1577	179	34	0	1.94
1968	N.Y.	—	—	—	—	—
	Totals	1577	179	34	0	1.94

SIKINGER, ROLAND
B. Mar. 20, 1959   Milwaukee, Wis.
Ht. 6–2   Wt. 195
Citizen—U.S.

1978	Hou.	103	5	2	0	1.75
1979	Hou.	90	7	2	0	2.00
	Totals	193	12	4	0	1.86

SPRANGER, LOTHAR
B. Germany
Ht. 5–10   Wt. 185
Citizen—Germany

1967	L.A. (NPSL)	1137	137	23	3	1.82

STEPNEY, ALEX
B. Sept. 18, 1942   Surrey, England
Ht. 6–1   Wt. 180
Citizen—England

1979	Dal.	2597	134	48	6	1.66

STETLER, BOB
B. Oct. 10, 1952   East Stroudsburg, Pa.
Ht. 6–1   Wt. 170
Citizen—U.S.

1976	T.B.	43	3	1	0	4.19
1977	Wash.	202	21	8	0	3.56
1978	Wash.	401	21	6	0	1.34
1979	Wash.	195	14	4	0	1.85
	Totals	841	59	19	0	2.03

STEURER, BRAD
B. Jan. 11, 1953   Manchester, Conn.
Ht. 5–10   Wt. 180
Citizen—U.S.

1976	Chi.	90	10	2	0	2.00

Season	Club	Min.	Saves	GA	SO	Avg.
STOJANOVIC, MIRKO						
B. June 11, 1939 Zagreb, Yugoslavia						
Ht. 6-1 Wt. 194						
Citizen—Yugoslavia						
1967	Oak.	2610	287	29	10	1.00
1968	Oak.	2571	178	32	—	1.12
1971	Dal.	1425	91	11	8	0.69
1974	S.J.	450	45	15	0	3.00
	Totals	7056	601	87	18	1.11
SULARZ, BRONISLAW "JERRY"						
B. Jan. 27, 1942 Wieruszow, Poland						
Ht. 6-0 Wt. 180						
Citizen—Poland						
1973	N.Y.	1620	136	22	5	1.22
1974	N.Y.	1081	107	21	1	1.75
1975	N.Y.	90	8	3	0	3.00
1976	Bost.	620	54	16	2	2.32
	Totals	3411	305	62	8	1.64
SVILAR, RATKO						
B. May 8, 1942 Yugoslavia						
Ht. 6-1 Wt. 180						
Citizen—Yugoslavia						
1978	Roch.	1398	87	26	3	1.67
TAMINDZIC, BLAGOJE						
Ht. 6-0 Wt. 175						
Citizen—Yugoslavia						
1976	Roch.	2193	157	31	4	1.28
1979	Tor.	2151	140	40	4	1.67
	Totals	4344	297	71	8	1.47
TARASIDES, GEORGE						
Ht. 5-10 Wt. 160						
Citizen—Greece						
1974	Wash.	270	20	6	0	2.00
1975	Wash.	150	11	12	0	7.23
	Totals	420	31	18	0	3.86
TAYLOR, JOHN						
Ht. 6-1 Wt. 174						
1975	L.A.	1194	113	17	4	1.27
TAYLOR, VAN						
B. May 16, 1953 Portsmouth, Ohio						
Ht. 6-0 Wt. 160						
Citizen—U.S.						
1976	Mia.	1455	138	31	3	1.92
THIE, TON						
Ht. 6-2 Wt. 167						
1967	S.F.	1035	57	18	3	1.57

Season	Club	Min.	Saves	GA	SO	Avg.
THOMAS, PETER						
Ht. 5-9 Wt. 160						
Citizen—England						
1975	Wash.	514	45	6	3	1.05
1977	L.V.	288	17	5	1	1.56
	Totals	802	62	11	4	1.23
TIRADO, TONY						
Ht. 6-1 Wt. 170						
1972	Mia.	227	10	11	0	4.00
TOPALOVIC, BRONCO						
B. Cezrna, Yugoslavia						
Ht. 6-2 Wt. 180						
Citizen—Yugoslavia						
1967	St. L.	1450	167	29	1	1.80
TORIANI, OSVALDO						
Ht. 6-1 Wt. 170						
1974	Mia.	1800	184	24	6	1.20
1975	Mia.	1228	83	20	4	1.47
	Totals	3028	267	44	10	1.31
TURNER, CHRIS						
B. Feb. 1, 1960						
Ht. 6-1 Wt. 185						
Citizen—Canada						
1979	S.J.	1316	90	33	0	2.32
TURNER, IAN						
B. Jan. 17, 1953 Middlesborough, England						
Ht. 5-11 Wt. 182						
Citizen—England						
1978	Ft. L.	1095	68	21	4	1.73
UHLANDER, BERT						
1971	St. L.	450	47	17	0	3.40
VAN ERON, KEITH						
B. Nov. 17, 1955 Brooklyn, N.Y.						
Ht. 6-1 Wt. 180						
Citizen—U.S.						
1978	Hou.	1737	114	31	6	1.60
1979	Phil.	1831	125	36	4	1.77
	Totals	3568	239	67	10	1.69
VIDNIC, BLAGOJE						
B. June 11, l934 Skopje, Yugoslavia						
Ht. 6-5 Wt. 190						
Citizen—Yugoslavia						
1967	L.A. (NPSL)	1667	194	35	3	1.89
1968	St.L.-S.D.	—	—	—	—	—
	Totals	1667	194	35	3	1.89

Season	Club	Min.	Saves	GA	SO	Avg.

VIZCAINO, RENE
Ht. 5–8   Wt. 150
Citizen—Mexico

| 1976 | Phil. | 2069 | 202 | 41 | 4 | 1.78 |

VOOYS, GERRIT
B. Oct. 11, 1947
Citizen—Holland

| 1978 | S.J. | 645 | 50 | 15 | 0 | 2.09 |

WALLACE, DARRYL
B. Feb. 10, 1953   Abbettsford, Canada
Ht. 5–11   Wt. 165
Citizen—Canada

1978	Tul.	204	11	5	1	2.21
1979	Tul.	20	2	0	0	0.00
	Totals	224	13	5	1	2.00

WATLING, BARRY
B. July 16, 1944
Ht. 5–11   Wt. 170
Citizen—England

1974	Sea.	1800	132	16	8	0.80
1975	Sea.	2033	140	26	6	1.15
	Totals	3833	272	42	⌃14	0.99

WEBER, GREG
B. Apr. 15, 1950   Winnepeg, Canada
Ht. 6–1   Wt. 175
Citizen—Canada

1974	Van.	270	9	5	0	1.67
1975	Van.	1274	95	19	5	1.34
1976	Van.	383	17	5	1	1.17
	Totals	1927	121	29	6	1.35

WEEKES, TERRY
B. May 6, 1954   Hayward, Calif.
Ht. 6–0   Wt. 180
Citizen—U.S.

| 1976 | S.J. | 15 | 2 | 1 | 0 | 6.00 |

WEISS, MATT
B. Oct. 21, 1952   St. Louis, Mo.
Ht. 6–0   Wt. 188
Citizen—U.S.

| 1975 | Dal. | 180 | 14 | 6 | 0 | 3.00 |

WINGERT, NORM
Ht. 5–11   Wt. 160

1973	Phil.	553	38	6	1	0.98
1975	Phil.	397	29	9	0	2.04
	Totals	950	67	15	1	1.42

WINTER, MIKE
B. Sept. 2, 1952   Austria
Ht. 5–11   Wt. 161
Citizen—U.S.

1972	St. L.	1260	122	14	3	1.00
1973	St. L.	1710	138	27	4	1.41
1974	St. L.	1710	158	36	2	1.89
1975	Chi.	471	43	7	1	I.34
	Totals	5151	461	84	10	1.47

WOZNIAK, MAX
B. Germany

| 1967 | L.A. (NPSL) | 90 | 11 | 4 | 0 | 4.00 |

YASIN, EROL (YASIN EROL OZDENAK)
B. Oct. 11, 1948   Iskenderun, Turkey
Ht. 6–I   Wt. 170
Citizen—Turkey

1977	N.Y.	677	42	8	3	1.06
1978	N.Y.	1916	130	24	6	1.13
1979	N.Y.	1012	82	20	2	1.78
	Totals	3605	254	52	11	1.30

ZERHUSEN, STEVE
B. Aug. 20, 1957   Baltimore, Md.
Ht. 6–1   Wt. 180
Citizen—U.S.

| 1979 | Ft. L. | 18 | 1 | 2 | 0 | 10.00 |

The United States National Team shocked the world with a 1–0 first-round upset of England during 1950 World Cup play. Here is the U.S. squad, pictured before it took off for Rio de Janeiro. Front row (left to right): Jeff Coombs, Nick DiOrio, Adal Molanin, Gino Pariani, Robert Annis and Walter Bahr. Second row: Robert Craddock, Frank Borghi, Joe Maca, Gino Gardassanich, Ed McIlveney, Ed Souza and John Souza. Back row: Chubby Lyons, Frank Valecenti, Joe Gaetjens, Charles Colombo, Harry Keough and coach Bill Jeffrey.

11
World Cup

Immediately upon its formation in 1904, the Fédération Internationale de Football Association (FIFA) did a rather ridiculous thing: it announced, grandiosely, that it alone had the right to organize a world championship of soccer. To which the rest of the world, and particularly the all-important British nations, which had not joined FIFA, replied with a monster yawn. There was, at that date, not the slightest likelihood of, or even a demand for, a world championship.

Yet the FIFA founders, and in particular Frenchman Jules Rimet and Dutchman C. A. Hirschman, persisted. It took them twenty-five years, but their dream came true in 1930. By then certain key elements had fallen neatly into place. Alas, the British nations were still aloofly pooh-poohing the whole idea, but in their place the South Americans had suddenly burst upon the scene. In 1924 and 1928 the Olympic soccer title—the only worldwide competition then in existence—had been won in most convincing fashion by little Uruguay. In fact, the 1928 final had been an all-Latin affair, with Argentina on the losing end of a 2-1 score. Clearly, the level of South American soccer was now on a par with that in Europe. There was, too, the emergence of professionalism in Europe; this had led to improved standards and better organization—but the pro players (from Italy, Czechoslovakia, Austria, etc.) could not play in the amateur Olympics. Here was FIFA's moment. Messrs. Rimet, Hirschman, and their colleagues went to work.

And with their first important move, they nearly blew the whole project. They awarded the staging of the first competition not to one of the powerful European nations, not even to M. Rimet's native France—but to far-away Uruguay. The reason was simple enough: money was short, and the Uruguayans had come up with an irresistible offer. They would foot all the bills, build a brand new stadium, even pay the transportation costs of the European teams to South America.

The decision may have been easy on FIFA's coffers, but it did not go down well with the European countries. Some felt snubbed at not getting the tournament themselves, and all were decidedly reluctant to send their teams off on the long transatlantic trip. Jets and sonic booms were things of the distant future, and the boat trip plus tournament meant a two-month outing.

I—URUGUAY 1930

Eventually, thirteen nations agreed to participate. Only four of them were European—Belgium, Yugoslavia, Romania, and France—and none was exactly a major power. It had been an embarrassing experience for M. Rimet, who had to indulge in much arm-twisting to get France to participate; the Romanians had joined in only after the personal intervention of King Carol, who guaranteed the players' employers that he would make up any losses the firms incurred while the team was in South America.

The thirteen teams were divided into three

groups of three and one of four, with each team playing the others in its group once. The winners of the four groups would then advance to the semifinals. The system ensured, at least, that no team played less than two games. The big surprise was the United States, which, with victories over Belgium and Paraguay, marched into the semifinals—there to be crushed, 6–1, by the Argentines. In the other semifinal, Uruguay swept past Yugoslavia by the same 6–1 score, thus setting up a repeat of the 1928 Olympic final.

An argument over which make of ball should be used in the game was resolved by using an Argentine ball in the first half, a Uruguayan in the second. As it happened, the nationality of the ball did seem to have an effect; the Argentines led at halftime, 2–1, but the Uruguayans came back in the second half to win, 4–2. Jules Rimet handed over the trophy that bore his name to the Uruguayan captain as the ninety thousand-plus crowd that had jammed the barely completed stadium sang its national anthem.

Uruguay was the first official world champion of the world's sport. The tournament had suffered from assorted incidents, (in particular, there had been an alarming variation in the way that different referees had interpreted the rules), but it had survived. Nobody had made any money out of it, but then nobody had expected to. The vital thing was that the tournament was now a reality, and the organizers could now start thinking about where they would hold the next edition, four years away.

World Cup I, Uruguay, 1930

Group 1: France 4, Mexico 1; Argentina 1, France 0; Chile 3, Mexico 0; Chile 3, France 0; Argentina 6, Mexico 3; Argentina 3, Chile 1.
  Qualifier: Argentina

Group 2: Yugoslavia 2, Brazil 1; Yugoslavia 4, Bolivia 0; Brazil 4, Bolivia 0.
  Qualifier: Yugoslavia

Group 3: Romania 3, Peru 1; Uruguay 1, Peru 0; Uruguay 4, Romania 0.
  Qualifier: Uruguay

Group 4: United States 3, Belgium 0; United States 3, Paraguay 0; Paraguay 1, Belgium 0.
  Qualifier: United States

Semifinals: Argentina 6, United States 1; Uruguay 6, Yugoslavia 1.

Final: Uruguay 4, Argentina 2.

Champion: Uruguay

II—ITALY 1934

Politics entered the World Cup with a vengeance in 1934. Italy, under the grip of the flamboyant Mussolini and his Fascist regime, saw in the competition a fine opportunity to display its glories before the world. Mussolini himself is said to have told the organizing committee, in ominous tones, "Italy *will* win the World Cup, gentlemen."

The Italian lobbying of FIFA was successful, and in 1932 Italy was awarded the 1934 tournament. The first move was to appoint Vittorio Pozzo as coach. Although he had never been a player of any consequence, Pozzo was a shrewd tactician and a master psychologist, the ideal "strong man" to deal with Italy's talented but erratic players. He would also be helped by the Fascist dictum that any Italian born overseas of Italian parentage was, in fact, an Italian. In this way, he was able to add four experienced Argentines to his team: one of them, center half Luisito Monti, had actually played for Argentina in the 1930 final!

The growing attraction of the World Cup was obvious in the number of entries: thirty-two this time, so that preliminary regional rounds had to be played to reduce the number to a manageable sixteen. The British nations were still ignoring the whole thing, while another regrettable absentee was the holder of the trophy, Uruguay. Its decision not to compete was, at least in part, a return snub to those European teams (Italy among them) that had refused to travel to Uruguay four years earlier.

This time the competition would be a sudden-death affair—one loss, and the team could go home. This proved a disastrous state of affairs for Argentina, which ended up playing—and losing—just one game. The United States beat Mexico in a qualifying game, then was unlucky enough to be drawn against the victory-hungry Italians. Italy 7, U.S. 1 was the score: a result that surprised no one, for the Italians were, for soccer reasons alone, joint favorites to win. The other fancied team was Austria, the so-called *Wunderteam*, under the guidance of Hugo Meisl. Like Pozzo, Meisl had never been a player, but he had a burning passion for the sport and a profound knowledge of its intricacies. He had made Austria the masters of Europe, unbeaten in eighteen games. Its last loss had been in England—no disgrace that, for no continental team had ever won, or even tied, there—and the closeness of the score, 4–3, revealed that the English were no longer in a class of their own.

Having disposed so easily of the Americans, the Italians ran into trouble in the second round when they faced Spain. The inspiration of the Spaniards was their legendary goalkeeper Ricardo Zamora—fearless, acrobatic, seemingly unbeatable in his day. And against Italy, he played as only he could play; the Italians got a goal from Ferrari to match one from Regueiro, but that was all. Tied, 1–1, the game went into overtime; thirty minutes later it was still 1–1, and a replay would be necessary—twenty-four hours later! Both teams had suffered badly in the physically brutal game. Poor Spain had had to field seven reserves for the replay, and among those unable to play was the redoubtable Zamora. Even so, it was a close thing, the Italians advancing to the semifinals, 1–0, on a goal by Giuseppe Meazza, who was emerging as the star of their team.

At the same time the Austrians were struggling along, not looking too impressive but scoring narrow victories over France and Hungary, scoring enough to get them into the semifinals, where the luck of the draw brought them up against Italy.

Meisl, always pessimistic, said his team had no chance. Pozzo, always optimistic, predicted victory for the Italians, and so it worked out. Another 1–0 win for Italy, this time on a goal by the Argentine-born Guaita. The Austrians, without Horwarth, one of their key players, were further handicapped by the rain which produced a muddy surface totally unsuitable for their short-passing ground game.

In the other semifinal, Czechoslovakia had beaten Germany, 3–1. The final would pit the Italians (probably the fittest team in the tournament, with a rugged defense and devastatingly fast counterattacks) against the Czechs (whose game was closer to the artistry of the Austrians although it featured more than a touch of the hardness that the sport now seemed to require).

Mussolini and a large party of Fascist dignitaries came to the final in Rome ready to celebrate the victory of the forces of the new Italian empire. They were to be given an uncomfortable afternoon. Throughout a tense first half, it became clearer and clearer that the Czechs were taking

command of the game; the Italian defense was frequently at desperation point, the attack simply not clicking. They hung on, but with twenty minutes left in the game, the Czechs struck—left winger Puc smashed a shot past the Italian goalkeeper Combi. Minutes later it looked as though it was all over as Svoboda broke through the Italian team and beat Combi again, only to see his blistering shot bounce back off the goalpost.

As time ran out, as the crowd grew apprehensively quieter, as the stares of Mussolini and his cohorts grew blacker, the Italians grew more nervous, more inept. Their forwards were shooting from ridiculous angles, they were not coming close to scoring when, suddenly, they did score. From an unlikely shot. Left winger Orsi (yet another Argentine) tried a right-foot shot from way out on the wing; the ball floated, then dipped and twisted as Czech goalie Planicka went for it. It ended up in the net.

That incredible slice of luck was all the Italians needed. Tied at 1–1, the game went to overtime. Fittingly, for he had been Italy's most consistent player, it was Meazza who started the move that led to the winning goal, scored by Schiavio. Mussolini, still stern-faced, watched as Jules Rimet presented the trophy to Combi, the Italian captain, and for the second time in two tournaments the host country had come out on top.

World Cup II, Italy, 1934

First Round: Italy 7, United States 1; Czechoslovakia 2, Romania 1; Germany 5, Belgium 2; Austria 3, France 2; Sweden 3, Argentina 2; Switzerland 3, Netherlands 2; Hungary 4, Egypt 2.

Second Round: Germany 2, Sweden 1; Austria 2, Hungary 1; Italy 1, Spain 1; Italy 1, Spain 0 (replay); Czechoslovakia 3, Switzerland 2.

Semifinals: Czechoslovakia 3, Germany 1; Italy 1, Austria 0.

Third-place Game: Germany 3, Austria 2.

Final: Italy 2, Czechoslovakia 1 (OT).

Champion: Italy

III—FRANCE 1938

France was not exactly an obvious choice for the staging of the World Cup. Soccer had never been the No. 1 sport there, but it was the prestige and the persuasion of Jules Rimet that brought the competition to his homeland. More teams than ever—thirty-six this time—entered the preliminary rounds. The British teams still stood on the sidelines, though by now they were beginning to get the message that they were missing something. Austria, so recently the shining beacon of European soccer, would not compete; the country did not exist any more, swallowed up by the spreading menace of Nazi Germany. Spain, too, swept with civil war, would be absent.

The only major Latin American power to enter was Brazil (the Argentines were particularly annoyed at the way that Italy was filching so many of their best players), joined by Cuba. Another strange survivor into the finals was the Dutch Antilles, which got through without playing a game when Japan withdrew.

It was left to unfancied Switzerland to produce the first real upset in World Cup history. Drawn against the powerful Germans (who now included some of the Austrian players on their team), the Swiss played them to a 1–1 tie, then won the replay in surprisingly easy fashion by 4–2. This highly inglorious exit was not at all what the Nazi leaders had been expecting. Cuba, too, pulled off a surprise by beating Romania, while down in Marseilles the biggest surprise of all didn't quite happen. The holders, Italy, confidently took on the inexperienced Norwegians and very nearly paid the price for underestimating them. After the Italians had given the Fascist salute to the crowd, and had been roundly booed for their efforts, they scored an early goal and began to relax. The Norwegians took over the game, hit the goalposts three times, scored the equalizer, then scored again, only to have the goal disallowed. The Italians got the only goal in overtime, an opportunistic effort from their new star Silvio Piola, and, by the skin of their teeth, passed on to the next round.

There was plenty to talk about up at Strasbourg, too, where Brazil and Poland traded goals in abundance before Brazil took the game, 6–5, in overtime. The star of the game was a lithe, magically gifted black forward, Leonidas, who introduced European spectators to the beauties of the bicycle kick. He scored four goals, one with a bare foot, as, racing for a pass, he left his boot firmly wedged in the mud!

There was to be no goal-scoring spree for the Brazilians in the quarterfinals, however. Against the rugged Czechs, it was 1–1 after overtime in a game that was never far from being an out-and-out brawl. Two Brazilians and one Czech were ejected; for the replay, two days later, the Brazilians fielded what was virtually a reserve team—and still won by 2–1. Their confidence was now high, but the overtime games and the replay had cost them dearly. After only two days' rest, they had to meet Italy in the semifinal—and the Italians had had an easy 3–1 win over France, followed by four days to recuperate.

The game finished with the Italians as 2–1 winners, but it could so easily have gone the other way. And the unpalatable fact for the Brazilians was that they had only themselves to blame for the loss. Admittedly, they were without Leonidas, out with a knee injury, but they had played well enough to win, despite giving up the first goal to the ever-dangerous Piola. If only the Brazilians had kept their heads and had continued to play their skilful game; but it was not to be. When the goals would not come, they became nervous; and when Italy scored first, through Colaussi, the Brazilians simply fell apart. Four minutes later, in the Brazilian penalty area and yards away from the ball, Piola was blatantly kicked. The referee spotted the foul, gave the penalty kick, and Meazza scored to put Italy 2–0 up. The Brazilians scored later, but the Italians were well in command by then.

The Italians (the *azzurri*, after the blue color of their shirts) were certainly a better all-around team than the one that had won four years earlier, and they were hitting top form at precisely the right moment. In the final, they had little trouble sweeping aside the rather old-fashioned Hungarians by a score of 4–2. By the same score, Brazil beat Sweden in the game for third place and returned home convinced that it should have won the World Cup, but not at all certain about the reasons for its failure. It would take another twenty years, and two more ignominious failures, before Brazil could put things right.

The Italians had proved that they could win outside their country and were masters of the Rimet Trophy for another four years. Sadly, those four years stretched to twelve as World War II put a temporary end to the World Cup.

First Round: Switzerland 1, Germany 1; Switzerland 4, Germany 2 (replay); Cuba 3, Romania 3; Cuba 2, Romania 1 (replay); Hungary 6, Dutch East Indies 0; France 3, Belgium 1; Czechoslovakia 3, Netherlands 0; Brazil 6, Poland 5; Italy 2, Norway 1.

Second Round: Sweden 8, Cuba 0; Hungary 2, Switzerland 0; Italy 3, France 1; Brazil 1, Czechoslovakia 1; Brazil 2, Czechoslovakia 1 (replay).

Semifinals: Italy 2, Brazil 1; Hungary 5, Sweden 1.

Third-place Game: Brazil 4, Sweden 2.

Final: Italy 4, Hungary 2.

Champion: Italy

IV—BRAZIL 1950

The Brazilians got their opportunity to show their skills in 1950. As organizers, they had the undoubted advantage of playing before their own crowds, and they had a team that was considered to be by far the best they had ever had. In particular, it glittered with attacking players like Ademir, Jair, and Friaca, marvellously skilled ball-artists and prolific goal-scorers.

They were cofavorites, along with—England. Yes, at last, the British nations had joined FIFA and had agreed to put their formidable reputations on the line. Or nearly so. Scotland originally agreed to participate, played its qualifying games, qualified, then withdrew, miffed because it had failed to beat its old enemy England. Even more shocking was the defection of Argentina, which accused the Brazilian soccer federation of showing "disrespect" to them and bowed out in a huff.

There were, eventually, only thirteen qualifiers for the final rounds, among them the United States, which had been heavily beaten twice by Mexico, but had survived by dint of a tie and victory over Cuba. It was a feeble record, one that gave no indication of the sensation that the Americans were to cause in the first round. Drawn in the same group as England, they were obviously given no chance at all. Yet when the two teams met, the final score was U.S. 1, England 0, one that caused universal astonishment and set many an editor frantically trying to check its accuracy. True it was, and it was a genuine win. The English had not played well, the Americans had hung in

there until, at the final whistle, they had been carried off the field by jubilant Brazilian fans, ever eager to see a threat to their own team removed.

England then lost to Spain, while the U.S. lost to Chile, so that neither team moved into the next round. Spain advanced to the next round, there to join Uruguay, Sweden, and Brazil. The Swedes had done remarkably well, beating out Paraguay and Italy, though the Italians were still in a state of shock and rebuilding after the Superga air disaster in May 1949 when ten members of their national team had been killed. Uruguay had been the lucky ones—its qualifying "group" had included only Bolivia, hastily dispatched by an 8–0 score. Brazil had not quite lived up to its promise; good victories over Mexico and Yugoslavia were tarnished by a labored draw with Switzerland.

But in the final round, the Brazilian brilliance exploded. A new system was in operation; the four teams would play each other once, and the winner would be decided by the usual process of awarding two points for a win and one for a tie. Thus, there would be no "final game"—at least that was the way it was planned.

The Brazilians were irresistible, crushing Sweden, 7–1, then brushing aside Spain, 6–1. While they were scoring goals almost at will, the Uruguayans were toiling to a 2–2 tie with Spain and a narrow 3–2 win over Sweden. So the final game of the group turned out to be the deciding game after all—Brazil vs. Uruguay in the huge new Maracaná Stadium in Rio de Janeiro, the world's largest, capacity two hundred thousand. To win the World Cup, all Brazil had to do was to tie. Uruguay would win the trophy only if it beat the Brazilians. Hardly anyone thought that was possible; most people were busy guessing how many goals the Brazilians would score this time.

National glory awaited the Brazilian team, yet it was almost certainly this intense pressure, this linking of national pride to a soccer game, that made things go wrong. Before the game, an impassioned plea came from the Governor of Rio down on the field, "Fifty million Brazilians await your victory!"

All this hysteria made the Brazilians intense and nervous, while it seemed only to strengthen the resistance of the Uruguayans. Throughout the first half, the Brazilians just could not get their goal-scoring machine going. The Uruguayan defense was solid and surprisingly cool; when the Brazilians did break through, they were repelled by goalkeeper Maspoli, in unbeatable form.

The huge crowd had to wait until two minutes into the second half to roar for a goal; Friaca was the scorer, and surely Brazil was now on its way. But the expected avalanche of goals simply would not come. Instead, it was Uruguay that moved into top gear. Twenty minutes later its right winger Ghiggia raced away to put over a perfect cross which Schiaffino calmly controlled and blasted past the Brazilian goalie Barbosa from twenty yards out. Brazil was struggling now, the crowd ominously hesitant to cheer. They knew now that if more goals were scored, they would come from Uruguay—they were just praying that Brazil could hold on for a tie. For ten minutes it did, but then Ghiggia struck again, racing down the right wing just as on the first goal. But as the Brazilian defense waited for his cross, Ghiggia cut inside and unleashed a violent swerving shot that smashed into the net between Barbosa and the near post. Schiaffino was to say later, "That was when I knew we could win. I could feel the silence."

The silence deepened as time ran out, and when Jules Rimet presented the trophy to Obdulio Varela, the Uruguayan captain, the vast stadium was an echoing shell.

World Cup IV, Brazil, 1950

Group 1: Brazil 4, Mexico 0; Yugoslavia 3, Switzerland 0; Yugoslavia 4, Mexico 1; Brazil 2, Switzerland 2; Brazil 2, Yugoslavia 0; Switzerland 2, Mexico 1.
    Qualifier: Brazil

Group 2: Spain 3, United States 1; England 2, Chile 0; United States 1, England 0; Spain 2, Chile 0; Spain 1, England 0; Chile 5, United States 2.
    Qualifier: Spain

Group 3: Sweden 3, Italy 2; Sweden 2, Paraguay 2; Italy 2, Paraguay 0.
    Qualifier: Sweden

Group 4: Uruguay 8, Bolivia 0.
    Qualifier: Uruguay

Final Pool: Uruguay 2, Spain 2; Brazil 7, Sweden 1; Uruguay 3, Sweden 2; Brazil 6, Spain 1; Sweden 3, Spain 1; Uruguay 2, Brazil 1.

Champion: Uruguay

V—SWITZERLAND 1954

If Brazil had been the favorite in 1950, then Hungary was the superfavorite in 1954. Unbeaten in four years, a team of all-stars, the first continental team ever to beat England in England—Hungary looked irresistible.

Its stiffest opposition would come from the holders, Uruguay, and the Brazilians, who retained only two of the team members who had lost the 1950 final.

Throughout the tournament, the rains poured down, and an extravagant number of goals was scored: the average was 5.38 per game!

Lopsided scores abounded: Hungary thrashed Korea, 9–0, Austria beat Czechoslovakia, 5–0, and the Uruguayans welcomed Scotland to World Cup play by murdering them, 7–0. The Germans, coached by Sepp Herberger (he had been the coach in 1938, but had somehow survived the debacle) beat Turkey, 7–2, in a play-off game to qualify for the quarterfinals, where the promiscuous scoring continued. Switzerland scored five goals but went down to Austria, which scored seven. Uruguay beat England, 4–2, while Hungary beat Brazil by the same score, in a game which has since become notorious as The Battle of Bern. Two Brazilians and a Hungarian were ejected, and as the game ended, a general free-for-all broke out on the field. In the other quarterfinal, a rather dull game ended with West Germany beating Yugoslavia, 2–0.

From the disgraceful game against the Brazilians, the Hungarians moved on to a semifinal against Uruguay, a game between the two classic teams of the era. It is remembered still as one of the greatest, perhaps the greatest, of all World Cup games. The Hungarians, playing without their star forward Ferenc Puskas, scored first through Czibor, then added another, a marvelous diving header from Hidegkuti, at the beginning of the second half. The Uruguayans moved over to all-out offense, with Schiaffino and Hohberg as the spearheads. With fifteen minutes left, Schiaffino's perfect through pass was rammed home by Hohberg, and with only four minutes left, Hohberg scored again to tie it up. In extratime, two goals from Czibor gave the Hungarians victory and the Uruguayans their first-ever defeat in a World Cup game.

The other finalist would be Germany, 6–1 victors over Austria. Apparently an easy game for Hungary, for the Germans had little to offer but speed and power.

Hungarian coach Gustav Sebes decided to reinsert Puskas in the lineup, and that was the beginning of Hungary's woes. For Puskas was not really recovered, while the rest of the team had had to work awfully hard to beat Brazil and Uruguay.

But nobody was thinking about that after eight minutes of the final game. Hungary had scored twice, through Puskas and Czibor, and was surely coasting to its destiny, the World Championship. Far from it, the Hungarians had in fact shot their bolt. When the German power game began its relentless advance, the Magical Magyars had no answer. First Max Morlock scored for the Germans, and a few minutes later Helmut Rahn tied it up. It was Rahn again who got the winner in the second half. After four glorious years, the Hungarians tasted defeat, in the most important game of all.

The Germans had won on strength and speed—aided, claimed the Italian press, by some mysterious drug that a few days after the final brought on attacks of jaundice.

The 1954 finals were also notable for a technological advance: on June 16, the game between France and Yugoslavia became the first World Cup game to be televised, the thin end of a wedge that was soon to become a financial gold mine for FIFA.

World Cup V, Switzerland, 1954

Group 1: Yugoslavia 1, France 0; Brazil 5, Mexico 0; France 3, Mexico 2; Brazil 1, Yugoslavia 1.
   Qualifiers: Brazil and Yugoslavia

Group 2: Hungary 9, Korea 0; West Germany 4, Turkey 1; Hungary 8, West Germany 3; Turkey 7, Korea 0; West Germany 7, Turkey 2 (play-off).
   Qualifiers: Hungary and West Germany

Group 3: Austria 1, Scotland 0; Uruguay 2, Czechoslovakia 0; Austria 5, Czechoslovakia 0; Uruguay 7, Scotland 0.
   Qualifiers: Uruguay and Austria

Group 4: England 4, Belgium 4; England 2, Switzerland 0; Italy 4, Belgium 1; Switzerland 2, Italy 1; Switzerland 4, Italy 1 (play-off).
   Qualifiers: England and Switzerland

Quarterfinals: West Germany 2, Yugoslavia 0; Hungary 4, Brazil 2; Austria 7, Switzerland 5; Uruguay 4, England 2.

Semifinals: West Germany 6, Austria 1; Hungary 4, Uruguay 2.

Third-place Game: Austria 3, Uruguay 1.

Final: West Germany 3, Hungary 2.

Champion: West Germany

VI—SWEDEN 1958

This was the year when the Brazilians finally put all the dazzling facets of their talent together. After the lean years, they had indulged in much soul searching, and had produced official reports demanding much better organization and preparation for their teams. The 1958 team was the most thoroughly prepared ever, yet it owed its success to a whimsical decision by its coach and to the brilliance of two individual players who were not at first considered as starters.

The players were the irrepressible Garrincha, bowlegged, stooping, but a winger capable of beating any fullback in the world; and, of course, the seventeen-year-old Pelé. Neither played in Brazil's first two games, but after an uninspired tie with England, a deputation of players went to coach Vicente Feola to ask that Garrincha and Pelé start the next game against Russia. Feola agreed, and in one game Brazil suddenly realized all the brilliance that had been frustrated for so long.

Poor Russia, it was simply unable to cope with the corkscrew runs of Garrincha, the electrifying brilliance of Pelé, the scoring power of Vava, the midfield omniscience of Didi. The score was 2–0, but the Brazilians, with any luck, would have scored six. This was fast-moving, modern soccer, exciting and entertaining. Where the Hungarians in 1954 had introduced the withdrawn center forward, and replaced him with twin strikers, the Brazilians of 1958 unveiled the 4–2–4 formation.

One of the ironies of the 1958 finals was that Italy did not qualify while Argentina did. The Argentines were without a number of world-class players who had been lured to play in Italy and who had been included in the Italian national team! The host Swedes too had suffered at the hands of the Italians but had been able to recall most of their stars from their Italian clubs.

Italy was eliminated in the qualifying rounds by Northern Ireland, which meant that for the first and only time, all four British nations were in the finals. Of these, it was not England or Scotland, but Wales that did the best, battling Brazil almost to a standstill in a quarterfinal game, until Pelé calmly lifted the ball over a Welsh defender's head, ran around him, and volleyed the ball home for the only score of the game, a goal that Pelé would later rate as "the most important of my career."

The surprise of the tournament was the French, scoring goals freely, with inside forwards Raymond Kopa and Juste Fontaine in fine form. Their semifinal against Brazil produced much brilliant soccer, but Brazil was rampant now and won by a score of 5–2, three of its goals coming from Pelé.

In the final, Brazil would meet, of all teams, the hosts, Sweden. A real surprise this, for no one had given the Swedes any chance at all, despite their home-field advantage. They were considered slow and too old—even their coach, Englishman George Raynor, admitted it. But he said they would win the final, and he raised the old accusations about the Brazilian temperament: "If we score first, the Brazilians will fall apart."

It was a rotten prophesy. The Swedes did score first, after only four minutes, an event that merely unleashed all the Brazilian brilliance. By halftime they were 2–1 up, with Pelé and Garrincha dazzling and tormenting the Swedish defense at will. In the second half, Zagalo scored a third, and Pelé added two more of the breathtaking goals that were his trademark; Sweden scored again, but it never really had a chance in this game.

Brazil had not only won the World Championship, it had served up soccer so skillfully that the whole world marvelled. And it had done what no other team had ever done before and has never done since: it won the title playing outside its own continent.

World Cup VI, Sweden, 1958

Group 1: West Germany 3, Argentina 1;
Northern Ireland 1, Czechoslovakia 0;
West Germany 2, Czechoslovakia 2;
Argentina 3, Northern Ireland 1;
West Germany 2, Northern Ireland 2;
Czechoslovakia 6, Argentina 1;
Northern Ireland 2, Czechoslovakia 1 (play-off).
  Qualifiers: West Germany and Northern Ireland

Group 2: France 7, Paraguay 3; Yugoslavia 1, Scotland 1;
Yugoslavia 3, France 2; Paraguay 3, Scotland 2;
France 2, Scotland 1; Yugoslavia 3, Paraguay 3.
  Qualifiers: France and Yugoslavia

Group 3: Sweden 3, Mexico 0; Hungary 1, Wales 1; Mexico 1, Wales 1;
Sweden 2, Hungary 1; Sweden 9, Wales 0; Hungary 4, Mexico 0;
Wales 2, Hungary 1 (play-off).
  Qualifiers: Sweden and Wales

Group 4: England 2, USSR 2; Brazil 3, Austria 0; England 0, Brazil 0;
USSR 2, Austria 0; Brazil 2, USSR 0; England 2, Austria 2;
USSR 1, England 0 (play-off).
  Qualifiers: Brazil and USSR

Quarterfinals: France 4, Northern Ireland 0;
West Germany 1, Yugoslavia 0; Sweden 2, USSR 0;
Brazil 1, Wales 0.

Semifinals: Brazil 5, France 2; Sweden 3, West Germany 1.

Third-place Game: France 6, West Germany 3.

Final: Brazil 5, Sweden 2.

Champion: Brazil

VII—CHILE 1962

By 1962 soccer was becoming a truly international sport. It was not just *played* everywhere but, thanks to film and television, the top players and teams were now known the world over. By general consent, the greatest of this new generation of world superstars were Brazil's twenty-one-year-old Pelé and the thirty-six-year-old Argentine Alfredo di Stefano.

This would be di Stefano's first World Cup, and he would play for Spain, being now a citizen of that country. The promise was great, but it all fell through. Injuries prevented di Stefano from playing at all, while Pelé played only one and a half games, before a pulled muscle sidelined him for the rest of the tournament.

Lacking its two brightest jewels, the 1962 World Cup produced little in the way of memorable soccer. It did, alas, produce a very clear trend towards defensive tactics and rather cynical, rough play. And it featured yet another brawl, with the unhappy Italians as the victims.

Before the tournament started, an Italian journalist (not a soccer writer) had visited Chile and had written a highly critical account of the life there, calling it, in effect, an underdeveloped nation. Amidst a wave of anti-Italian feeling, the poor *azzuri* were called upon to face Chile before

In 1962 in Chile, the Brazilians rose above the loss of young Pelé, out for most of the tournament due to a pulled muscle. They turned back the challenge of upstart Czechoslovakia, 3–1, after which jubilant fans saluted winning goalkeeper Gilmar.

sixty-six thousand decidedly hostile fans in Santiago. In this game, soccer never had a chance. The kicking and fouling was almost constant, reaching a climax when Chile's Sanchez swung a prodigious punch at Italy's Maschio and broke his nose. English referee Ken Aston could do little; he sent two Italians off the field, but no Chileans. A highly tarnished 2–0 win sent Chile into the quarterfinals and the *azzurri* back to Italy.

In the quarterfinals the Chileans showed that they could play soccer when they beat the Russians 2–1, helped by an uncharacteristically poor performance from the great Russian goalkeeper Lev Yashin.

The Brazilians, without Pelé now, struggled against Spain, but two late goals from his deputy Amarildo saw them through. After an easy 3–1 win, with Garrincha in devastating form, against England, they had to face Chile in the semifinals. It was a game that produced much good soccer, mostly from Brazil, and much ugliness, mostly from Chile. Garrincha, kicked and fouled throughout the game, finally retaliated and was sent off. As he walked away, he was hit on the head by a bottle thrown from the crowd. He had scored two goals, enough to provide the margin of Brazil's 4–2 win.

In the other semifinal, Czechoslovakia beat Yugoslavia, 3–1, a surprise result, but the Czechs seemed to have a knack of winning games where they were outplayed, the reason usually being the superb displays of their goalkeeper Schroiff.

Brazil and Czechoslovakia met for the final then, a repeat of the first-round game in which Pelé had pulled his muscle and which had ended in a 0–0 tie.

The Czechs scored first, when midfielder Masopust ran through the middle unmarked to score. After that, it looked as though it was all going to depend on Schroiff again, for Brazil was unmistakably the better team. But Schroiff had an off-day; Amarildo caught him leaning the wrong way and rapped a shot past him inside the near post. Zito made it 2–1, then Schroiff goofed again, dropping a long, high ball from fullback Djalma Santos right on the feet of Vava, who banged the ball straight into the net for a 3–1 victory for Brazil.

This was not the Brazilian team of 1958. From 4–2–4 they had gone to 4–3–3, with Zagalo, primarily a winger in Sweden, now playing as a midfielder. This more defensive alignment was merely a reflection of a worldwide trend. The Italians were bringing the infamous *catenaccio* to its perverted perfection, and goal scoring was dropping. After the 5.38 per game glut in the 1954 World Cup, it had gone down to 3.6 per game in 1958, and now it slumped to 2.78 per game.

World Cup VII, Chile, 1962

Group 1: Uruguay 2, Colombia 1; USSR 2, Yugoslavia 0; Colombia 4, USSR 4; Yugoslavia 3, Uruguay 1; USSR 2, Uruguay 1; Yugoslavia 5, Colombia 0.
    Qualifiers: USSR and Yugoslavia

Group 2: Chile 3, Switzerland 1; West Germany 0, Italy 0; Chile 2, Italy 0; West Germany 2, Switzerland 1; West Germany 2, Chile 0; Italy 3, Switzerland 0.
    Qualifiers: West Germany and Chile

Group 3: Brazil 2, Mexico 0; Czechoslovakia 1, Spain 0; Brazil 0, Czechoslovakia 0; Spain 1, Mexico 0; Brazil 2, Spain 1; Mexico 3, Czechoslovakia 1.
    Qualifiers: Brazil and Czechoslovakia

Group 4: Argentina 1, Bulgaria 0; Hungary 2, England 1; England 3, Argentina 1; Hungary 6, Bulgaria 1; Argentina 0, Hungary 0; England 0, Bulgaria 0.
    Qualifiers: Hungary and England

Quarterfinals: Yugoslavia 1, West Germany 0; Brazil 3, England 1; Chile 2, USSR 1; Czechoslovakia 1, Hungary 0.

Semifinals: Brazil 4, Chile 2; Czechoslovakia 3, Yugoslavia 1.

Third-place Game: Chile 1, Yugoslavia 0.

Final: Brazil 3, Czechoslovakia 1.

Champion: Brazil

VIII—ENGLAND 1966

World Cup Willie appeared in 1966, a chubby little lion drawn all dressed up in the English flag, the official mascot of the tournament, and a sign of the growing commercialism of the sport. Willie's face would smile from a million flags and posters and mementos, collecting royalties all the while.

Ever since his appointment in 1963, English coach Alf Ramsey had been saying, "We shall win." Increasingly, it looked probable that England would win, for there were no really strong competitors. Brazil had grown old, they had Pelé, of course, still only twenty-five, but they desperately needed new, young blood. Argentina looked the better side from South America, as skilled as ever, with a clever and experienced coach in Juan Carlos Lorenzo. Of the Europeans, the Italians were much fancied, but they provided their usual sensation by being beaten, 1–0, by North Korea and failing to make the second round.

The North Koreans, playing with almost boyish abandon but incredible tactical naïveté, played Portugal in the quarterfinal and were 3–0 up in twenty minutes. A more experienced team would have protected that commanding lead; the Koreans squandered it, and Portugal scored five. Four of these goals came from the young Eusebio, now being hailed as "the new Pelé." The two had confronted each other earlier in a crucial game for Brazil. Eusebio had scored twice in Portugal's 3–1 victory, Pelé had been viciously and systematically fouled, and Brazil was eliminated. Pelé, who had already suffered grievously at the hands (or the feet) of the Bulgarians in Brazil's first game, swore he would not play again the World Cup.

England advanced to the quarterfinals in solid, if unspectacular fashion. In three games it scored only four goals, but its defense had given up none.

Against Argentina in the quarterfinals, it was

West Germany's Wolfgang Weber (left) unloaded a shot that eluded British defender Ray Wilson (center) and goalkeeper Gordon Banks (right) for the goal that tied the 1966 final with less than a minute to play. Alan Ball and Geoff Hurst scored in overtime to give the English the Cup, 4–2, in a tournament played on their home turf.

in real trouble until the Argentine captain Antonio Rattin started to get on the referee's nerves with his constant carping. Eventually Rattin was ordered off, refused to go, and the game was held up for twenty minutes while things were sorted out. Against ten men, England scraped home, 1–0. It did not look like a championship team, but in the semifinal England suddenly found its form, beating Portugal, 2–1, in a pulsating game, thanks to two splendid goals from Bobby Charlton. In the other semifinal, the West Germans had little trouble disposing of the unimaginative Russians.

The omens for the Germans were not good. In the past thirty years they had played England seven times, losing six and managing just one tie. They brought thousands of supporters to Wembley, waving their gold and black flags, and they started well. After thirteen minutes Haller scored, and England was a goal down for the first time in the competition. The equalizer came six minutes later, a sweetly-timed header from Geoff Hurst, with the German defenders seemingly rooted in the ground. As the second half wore on, England slowly gained a slight advantage, and with twelve minutes left, Martin Peters seized on a bad clearance and scored the go-ahead goal. Germany threw everyone forward and, as time ran out, it got its last chance—a free kick outside the English penalty area. The ball was lofted into the goal-mouth, misplayed by the English defense, and there was fullback Weber to push in a last-minute equalizer.

In extratime the English lasted a little better, thanks largely to the inexhaustible Alan Ball, but even so their first goal was tinged with doubt—a stinging shot from Geoff Hurst that hit the underneath of the crossbar, bounced down to the ground, and was headed away by Weber. Was the ball over the goal line as the English players insisted? Yes, said the Russian linesman. The Germans, sportingly, made no great fuss. They again attacked in waves, but this time England was ready, and it was Geoff Hurst yet again who got another goal in a counterattack exactly as the final whistle went.

Hurst was the first player ever to score a hat trick in the World Cup final, while coach Alf Ramsey was soon after knighted by Queen Elizabeth. England had deserved its victory, but it cannot be said that it was an exciting team to watch. It had played a 4–4–2 formation, with only two genuine forwards. The defensive trend of soccer seemed to be accelerating.

World Cup VIII, England, 1966

Group 1: England 0, Uruguay 0; France 1, Mexico 1; Uruguay 2, France 1; England 2, Mexico 0; Uruguay 0, Mexico 0;

England 2, France 0.
Qualifiers: Uruguay and England

Group 2: West Germany 5, Switzerland 0; Argentina 2, Spain 1; Spain 2, Switzerland 1; Argentina 0, West Germany 0; Argentina 2, Switzerland 0; West Germany 2, Spain 1.
Qualifiers: West Germany and Argentina

Group 3: Brazil 2, Bulgaria 0; Portugal 3, Hungary 1; Hungary 3, Brazil 1; Portugal 3, Bulgaria 0; Portugal 3, Brazil 1; Hungary 3, Bulgaria 1.
Qualifiers: Portugal and Hungary

Group 4: USSR 3, North Korea 0; Italy 2, Chile 0; USSR 1, Italy 0; Chile 1, North Korea 1; USSR 2, Chile 1; North Korea 1, Italy 0.
Qualifiers: USSR and North Korea

Quarterfinals: England 1, Argentina 0; West Germany 4, Uruguay 0; Portugal 5, North Korea 2; USSR 2, Hungary 1.

Semifinals: West Germany 2, USSR 1; England 2, Portugal 1.

Third-place Game: Portugal 2, USSR 1.

Final: England 4, West Germany 2 (OT)

Champion: England

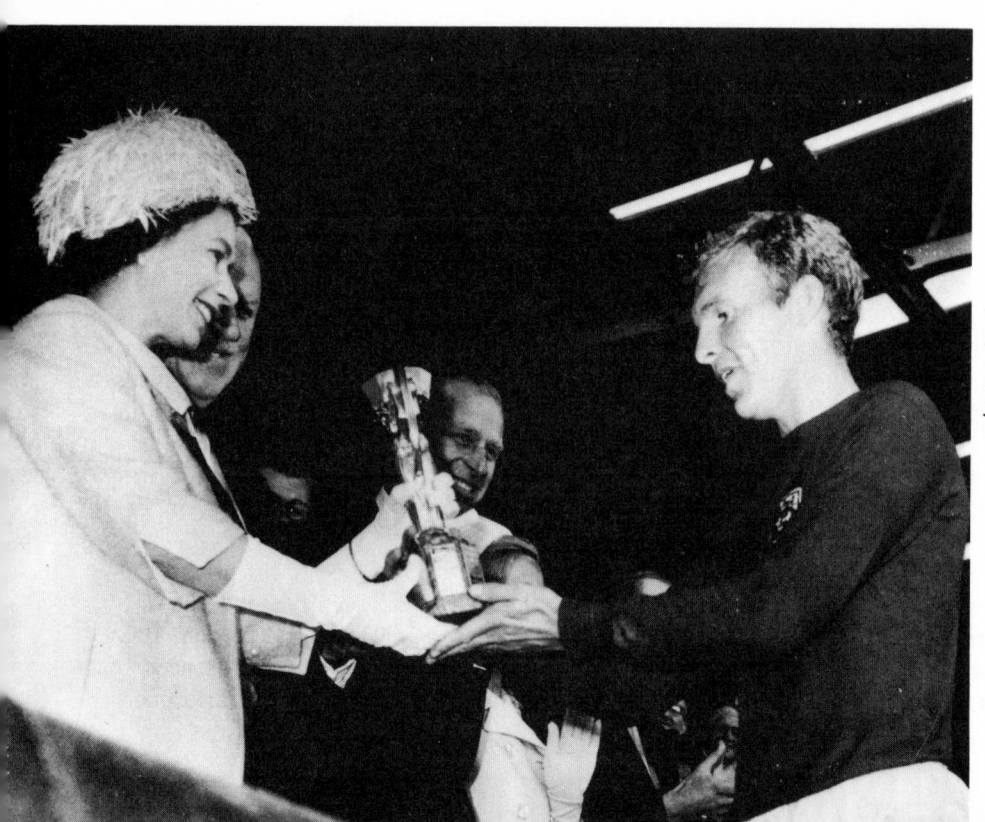

Queen Elizabeth made the presentation of the Jules Rimet Cup to English captain Bobby Moore following his team's World Cup triumph in 1966.

Pelé beat goalie Ivo Victor of Czechoslovakia during a 4–1 early-round conquest and went on to turn in his greatest World Cup performance in leading Brazil to the 1970 crown in Guadalajara, Mexico.

IX—MEXICO 1970

And so to Mexico, site of the 1968 Olympics and, of course, center of all sorts of disputes about the effects of altitude on athletic performance. It seems probable that the altitude factor was marginally important in the 1970 championships. It made teams play a little slower, a little more thoughtfully. In this sense it encouraged more attractive soccer. The result was a superb performance and a universally popular win for the Brazilians.

Pelé had decided to play after all, and how he played! Now aged thirty, the slight loss of speed more than offset by experience and wiliness, Pelé was the undisputed star of the tournament, no mean achievement for someone playing on a team that included players such as Jairzinho, Carlos Alberto, Tostao, and Gerson.

The Brazilian defense was considered weak, but it didn't really matter; they always seemed to have the inspiration to score when they wanted to. This was soccer with a smile, fluid, entertaining, immensely skilled, and acrobatic. England, Czechoslovakia, and Romania were all beaten in the first round; Peru went down, 4–2, in the quarterfinals, and Uruguay (always a problem for Brazil—remember 1950?) was beaten, 3–1, in the semifinal.

This was all in such contrast to the progress of the other finalist, Italy. In the first round, the Italians scored only *one* goal, beating Sweden, 1–0, then tying Uruguay and Israel, 0–0. This lone goal was enough to get them into the quarterfinals

England's Geoff Hurst (fallen) headed the ball away from Brazil's Everaldo, but the 1966 World Cup hero couldn't prevent his team from suffering a 1–0 defeat at the hands of the 1970 champions.

where they scored four against a weak Mexican team. The semifinal game against Germany promised to be the usual Italian defensive game, when Italy took an early one-goal lead and held it right up until the final minute when Schnellinger equalized. The goals came thick and fast in a wild overtime, with Italy eventually scrambling home by 4–3.

The Germans were to win the third-place game against Uruguay, rather luckily, but in sweeper Franz Beckenbauer and goal scorer Gerd Mueller they had two of the finest players of the tournament.

The final, then, pitted the carefree, attacking Brazilians against the *catenaccio* defensive game of the Italians. In retrospect, it appears a crucial game for the whole philosophy of the sport—so much the better, then, that it was the Brazilians

who triumphed so handsomely. First blood went to Brazil, and to Pelé, who turned an innocent-looking cross from Rivelino into a lethal header that the Italian goalkeeper Albertosi just couldn't reach. The sloppy Brazilian defense gave the Italians a goal later in the first half, which finished tied at 1–1.

In the second half, it was a stalemate until Gerson suddenly unleashed an unstoppable twenty-five-yard, left-footed shot to give Brazil the lead. There followed a goal from Jairzinho (assist from Pelé) and a final, breathtaking goal from fullback

A joyous Pelé holds the Jules Rimet Cup which Brazil ▶ retired after winning the World Cup for the third consecutive time.

Carlos Alberto (assist, again, Pelé), and the Italians had no answer to all that brilliance.

In the most emphatic way possible, the 1970 Brazilians had called a halt to the defensive negativism of the 1960s. This was Pelé's farewell to the World Cup, and it was only fitting that he should leave as the key player of one of the most brilliant teams of all time.

Mention should also be made of a genuine—and largely successful—attempt on the part of FIFA to enforce strong measures against rough play. The system of red and yellow cards was introduced in Mexico and worked well, as did the introduction of substitutes: for the first time, teams were allowed two substitutes per game. Another disciplinary measure, one that had been started in England in 1966, was continued, the random testing of player's urine samples as a means of banning the use of stimulants.

World Cup IX, Mexico, 1970

Group 1: Mexico 0, USSR 0; Belgium 3, El Salvador 0; USSR 4, Belgium 1; Mexico 4, El Salvador 0; USSR 2, El Salvador 0; Mexico 1, Belgium 0.
  Qualifiers: USSR and Mexico

Group 2: Uruguay 2, Israel 0; Italy 1, Sweden 0; Uruguay 0, Italy 0; Israel 1, Sweden 1; Sweden 1, Uruguay 0; Israel 0, Italy 0.
  Qualifiers: Italy and Uruguay

Group 3: England 1, Romania 0; Brazil 4, Czechoslovakia 1; Romania 2, Czechoslovakia 1; Brazil 1, England 0; Brazil 3, Romania 2; England 1, Czechoslovakia 0.
  Qualifiers: Brazil and England

Group 4: Peru 3, Bulgaria 2; West Germany 2, Morocco 1; Peru 3, Morocco 0; West Germany 5, Bulgaria 2; West Germany 3, Peru 1; Bulgaria 1, Morocco 1.
  Qualifiers: West Germany and Peru

Quarterfinals: Uruguay 1, USSR 0; Italy 4, Mexico 1; Brazil 4, Peru 2; West Germany 3, England 2 (OT).

Semifinals: Italy 4, West Germany 3 (OT); Brazil 3, Uruguay 1.

Third-place Game: West Germany 1, Uruguay 0.

Final: Brazil 4, Italy 1.

Champion: Brazil

X—WEST GERMANY 1974

Brazil's third World Cup triumph in 1970 had entitled it to take permanent possession of the venerable Jules Rimet Trophy. A new cup, officially named The FIFA World Cup, was now the prize—it was of eighteen-carat gold, worth some twenty thousand dollars.

Brazil, despite having spent over $4 million preparing its team, was not among the favorites, mainly because Pelé had at last stepped down. The favorites were the West Germans: they had won the European championship in 1972 and had the immense advantage of playing at home. The strongest challengers would be the Dutch, led by the brilliant Johan Cruyff, and the surprising Poles, who had eliminated England in the qualifying rounds.

The West Germans started poorly, struggling to a 1–0 win over Chile, booed by their own fans, and with clear signs of dissension among the players. They were pulled together by their captain, Franz Beckenbauer, a commanding figure both on and off the field. A win over a weak Australian team was followed by a loss to East Germany in the first-ever meeting of the two countries. The loss meant that West Germany finished second in its group; more significantly, it meant that in the second round it would play in Group B, thus avoiding the Dutch, who had won their group, and would be in Group A.

By now the Dutch, with their "Total Football," were the clear favorite. Three straight wins over Brazil, East Germany, and Argentina in the second round took them to the final with a record of fourteen goals scored, only one given up.

The West Germans did eventually top Group B, but it was a close thing between them and Poland. The deciding game between the teams was played on a field that was almost under water, with the ball constantly sticking in the mud. Poland had the better of the play, but West Germany, thanks to a lone goal from the invincible Gerd Mueller, was the winner.

Immediate sensation in the final. Within a minute, Cruyff had dribbled the ball into the West German penalty area and was brought crashing to the ground. From the resulting penalty kick, Neeskens scored, and the Dutch were off to a flying start. They did not press it home; their Total Football continued to delight, but it was the Germans who threatened. At twenty-five minutes they leveled the score when Paul Breitner scored from a penalty kick, and two minutes before half-

West Germany's Bertie Vogts (airborne) gives support to his team's pledge to stop Holland's Johan Cruyff (14) as West Germany defeated Holland, 2–1, for the 1974 World Cup.

◄ *West Germany's Franz Beckenbauer (left) led his team's second-half defense as the host nation took the trophy in Munich.*

time Gerd Mueller—who else?—gave them the lead. The second half was virtually all Holland, but, with Cruyff playing an oddly withdrawn role, they could not break down the German defense, in which Beckenbauer and goalkeeper Sepp Maier were in grand form.

And so once again it was the host nation that took the trophy, and once again the team that had scored the first goal had lost (that had happened in seven of the ten finals).

The 1974 tournament, despite all the talk of positive-attacking football, proved the worst yet in goal scoring. The average was only 2.55 a game. On a more positive note, the four goals scored by Gerd Mueller, added to the ten he had scored in Mexico in 1970, moved him into first place in the list of all-time World Cup goal scorers.

World Cup X, West Germany, 1974

Group 1: West Germany 1, Chile 0; East Germany 2, Australia 0; West Germany 3, Australia 0; East Germany 1, Chile 1; Australia 0, Chile 0; East Germany 1, West Germany 0.
  Qualifiers: East Germany and West Germany

Group 2: Brazil 0, Yugoslavia 0; Scotland 2, Zaire 0; Brazil 0, Scotland 0; Yugoslavia 9, Zaire 0; Scotland 1, Yugoslavia 1; Brazil 3, Zaire 0.
  Qualifiers: Brazil and Yugoslavia

Group 3: Netherlands 2, Uruguay 0; Sweden 0, Bulgaria 0; Sweden 0, Netherlands 0; Bulgaria 1, Uruguay 1; Netherlands 4, Bulgaria 1; Sweden 3, Uruguay 0.
  Qualifiers: Netherlands and Sweden

Group 4: Italy 3, Haiti 1; Poland 3, Argentina 2; Argentina 1, Italy 1; Poland 7, Haiti 0; Argentina 4, Haiti 1; Poland 2, Italy 1.
  Qualifiers: Poland and Argentina

Semifinal Group A: Brazil 1, East Germany 0; Brazil 2, Argentina 1; Netherlands 4, Argentina 0; Netherlands 2, East Germany 0; Netherlands 2, Brazil 0; Argentina 1, East Germany 1.
  Winner: Netherlands. Runner-up: Brazil.

Semifinal Group B: Poland 1, Sweden 0; West Germany 2, Yugoslavia 0; Poland 2, Yugoslavia 1; West Germany 4, Sweden 2; West Germany 1, Poland 0; Sweden 2, Yugoslavia 1.

Winner: West Germany. Runner-up: Poland.

Third-place Game: Poland 1, Brazil 0.

Final: West Germany 2, Netherlands 1.

Champion: West Germany

XI—ARGENTINA 1978

The selection of Argentina was controversial, to put it mildly. Many Europeans objected on the grounds of the unstable political situation, but the military government that took over in 1975 saw to it that preparations (including the building of three new stadiums) were completed on time.

Then again, this looked rather like Hamlet without the prince: Franz Beckenbauer, engaged by the New York Cosmos, would not play, nor would Johan Cruyff, who opted out for "personal reasons."

The beginning was not promising, either. Two of the brightest teams from the 1974 World Cup, Poland and West Germany, met in the opener and produced a game of stupefying boredom. The score was 0–0, the fourth consecutive time that the grand ceremonial opening game of the World Cup had ended without a goal.

The Italians delighted everyone in the first round, beating France, Hungary, and host Argentina with spirited attacking soccer, the inspiration coming from the wizardry of the twenty-one-year-old Paolo Rossi. Despite its loss to Italy, Argentina passed into the second round, another team that had impressed with its commitment to attacking soccer.

Elsewhere, reputations were taking all sorts of knocks. The Brazilians, looking nervous and uninspired, should have been beaten by Spain but survived, and, thanks to a 1–0 win over Austria, went into the second round. The West Germans too, although qualifying for the second round, were clearly lacking the inspiration of Beckenbauer. The Dutch had looked good in their first two games but then had lost to Scotland. The Scots, who arrived full of confidence, left in disgrace after a loss to Peru and a tie with lowly Iran and the scandal of having one of their players sent home for failing the dope test.

In the second round, the Italians seemed to lose their nerve, or perhaps they simply weren't fit enough. They played a ponderous 0–0 tie with the West Germans, a 1–0 win over Austria, and then their first loss, 2–1 to Holland, a loss that put Holland, not Italy, into the final. The sad thing for Italy was that both of Holland's goals had come on long-range shots that should surely have been saved by their veteran goalkeeper Dino Zoff.

Referee Antonio Garrido (left) sends Tibor Nyilast (8) off the field after the Hungarian player fouled Argentina's Alberto Tarantini (prone) during a 2–1 Argentina triumph in Buenos Aires.

Holland's Robert Rensenbrink made history of sorts in 1978 when he scored the 1,000th World Cup goal since the inaugural match in 1930. His goal came against Scotland.

Argentine captain Daniel Passarella rides high around River Plate stadium after his team captures the 1978 World Cup, 3–1, over Holland.

In Group B, both Argentina and Brazil beat Poland, then tied with each other, 0–0, in an ill-tempered game. It all boiled down to which of them could score more goals against the hapless Peruvians, another team, like the Italians, that was clearly running out of steam as the tournament went on. The Brazilians put three goals past the Peruvian goalkeeper; the Argentines, needing to score four times, racked up six goals and so went on to the final to meet Holland.

Even without Cruyff, the Dutch were a formidable team of physically strong, multitalented players. But somehow the glitter of Total Football was missing, while its physical aspects—in particular the heavy tackling of the Dutch defenders—were now more evident.

Urged on by eighty thousand supporters in River Plate Stadium (every one of them, it seemed, waving a blue and white flag), the Argentines had the better of a stirring first half and went ahead on a fine goal by Mario Kempes, who took the ball calmly past two Dutch defenders before sliding it under the advancing goalkeeper. The second half belonged to Holland, but they had to wait until nine minutes from the end before they equalized on a header from substitute Nanninga. The Dutch came agonizingly close—they hit the post in the final minute—but they could not get the winner. But it seemed not to matter, for surely they would win in overtime; they looked faster, stronger, and fitter than the Argentines.

All the more amazing then that it was Argentina, right from the whistle, which controlled the extra thirty minutes. Two more goals, another from the brilliant Kempes and one from Bertoni, gave them victory.

Their coach, Cesar Menotti, had had the courage to go with attacking players, had eschewed the caution of defensive formations, and had been rewarded. A victory, then, not for any particular formation or tactical ploy, but for the skill of individual players and for attacking soccer.

And should anyone be left in any doubt about the popularity of the World Cup, a look at the final financial figures for the 1978 tournament should alter those views: income: $42 million ($23 million from radio, television, and advertising rights); expenses: $14 million; profit: $28 million.

World Cup XI, Argentina, 1978

Group 1: Argentina 2, Hungary 1; Italy 2, France 1; Argentina 2, France 1; Italy 3, Hungary 1; Italy 1, Argentina 0; France 3, Hungary 1.
  Qualifiers: Italy and Argentina

Group 2: West Germany 0, Poland 0; Tunisia 3, Mexico 1; Poland 1, Tunisia 0; West Germany 6, Mexico 0; West Germany 0, Tunisia 0; Poland 3, Mexico 1.
  Qualifiers: Poland and West Germany

Group 3: Sweden 1, Brazil 1; Austria 2, Spain 1; Brazil 0, Spain 0; Austria 1, Sweden 0; Brazil 1, Austria 0; Spain 1, Sweden 0.
  Qualifiers: Austria and Brazil

Group 4: Netherlands 3, Iran 0; Peru 3, Scotland 1; Netherlands 0, Peru 0; Scotland 1, Iran 1; Scotland 3, Netherlands 2; Peru 4, Iran 1.
  Qualifiers: Peru and Netherlands

Semifinals Group A: West Germany 0, Italy 0; Italy 1, Austria 0; Netherlands 5, Austria 1; Netherlands 2, West Germany 2; Netherlands 2, Italy 1; Austria 3, West Germany 2.
  Winner: Netherlands. Runner-up: Italy.

Semifinals Group B: Argentina 2, Poland 0; Brazil 3, Peru 0; Poland 1, Peru 0; Argentina 0, Brazil 0; Brazil 3, Poland 1; Argentina 6, Peru 0.
  Winner: Argentina. Runner-up: Brazil.

Third-place Game: Brazil 2, Italy 1.

Final: Argentina 3, Netherlands 1 (OT).

Champion: Argentina

Intercontinental Cup Champions

1960—Real Madrid (Spain)
1961—Penarol (Uruguay)
1962—Santos (Brazil)
1963—Santos (Brazil)
1964—Internazionale (Italy)
1965—Internazionale (Italy)
1966—Penarol (Uruguay)
1967—Racing Club (Argentina)
1968—Estudiantes de la Plata (Argentina)
1969—Milan (Italy)
1970—Feyenoord (Netherlands)
1971—Nacional (Uruguay)
1972—Ajax (Netherlands)
1973—Independiente (Argentina)
1974—Atlético Madrid (Spain)
1975—Atlético Madrid (Spain)
1976—Bayern Munich (West Germany)
1977—Boca Juniors (Argentina)
1978—No competition

European Cup Winners' Cup Champions

1961—Fiorentina (Italy)
1962—Atlético Madrid (Spain)
1963—Tottenham Hotspur (England)
1964—Sporting Portugal (Portugal)
1965—West Ham United (England)
1966—Borussia Dortmund (West Germany)
1967—Bayern Munich (West Germany)
1968—Milan (Italy)
1969—Slovan Bratislava (Czechoslovakia)
1970—Manchester City (England)
1971—Chelsea (England)
1972—Rangers (Scotland)
1973—Milan (Italy)
1974—FC Magdeburg (East Germany)
1975—Dynamo Kiev (USSR)
1976—RSC Anderlecht (Belgium)
1977—Hamburg Sport Verein (West Germany)
1978—RSC Anderlecht (Belgium)
1979—Barcelona (Spain)

European Cup Champions

1956—Real Madrid (Spain)
1957—Real Madrid (Spain)
1958—Real Madrid (Spain)
1959—Real Madrid (Spain)
1960—Real Madrid (Spain)
1961—Benfica (Portugal)
1962—Benfica (Portugal)
1963—Milan (Italy)
1964—Internazionale (Italy)
1965—Internazionale (Italy)
1966—Real Madrid (Spain)
1967—Celtic (Scotland)
1968—Manchester United (England)
1969—Milan (Italy)
1970—Feyenoord (Netherlands)
1971—Ajax (Netherlands)
1972—Ajax (Netherlands)
1973—Ajax (Netherlands)
1974—Bayern Munich (West Germany)
1975—Bayern Munich (West Germany)
1976—Bayern Munich (West Germany)
1977—Liverpool (England)
1978—Liverpool (England)
1979—Nottingham Forest (England)

Union of European Football Associations (UEFA) Cup Champions

1958—Barcelona (Spain)
1959—No competition
1960—Barcelona (Spain)
1961—Roma (Italy)
1962—Valencia (Spain)
1963—Valencia (Spain)
1964—Real Zaragoza (Spain)
1965—Ferencvaros (Hungary)
1966—Barcelona (Spain)
1967—Dynamo Zagreb (Yugoslavia)
1968—Leeds United (England)
1969—Newcastle United (England)
1970—Arsenal (England)
1971—Leeds United (England)
1972—Tottenham Hotspur (England)
1973—Liverpool (England)
1974—Feyenoord (Netherlands)
1975—Borussia Mönchengladbach (West Germany)
1976—Liverpool (England)
1977—Juventus (Italy)
1978—PSV Eindhoven (Holland)
1979—Borussia Möenchengladbach (West Germany)

371

The ball is gone, but with their synchronization these opposing players from Chile and Portugal could have made anybody's chorus line. It happened during the 1928 Olympic Games in Amsterdam, Holland. Portugal won the game, but Uruguay won the gold medal.

12
The Olympic Games

Soccer officially became an Olympic sport in 1908, but a soccer tournament was held and a champion was crowned as early as the second modern Olympic Games in Paris in 1900. Great Britain won the 1900 event when a team from Upton Park defeated France. Canada prevailed in 1904 at St. Louis, and Denmark led the way in 1906 at Athens, where an Olympic festival was held even though it didn't have the normal four-year interval.

Great Britain took the gold medals at London in 1908 and in Stockholm in 1912, but it lost its momentum with the advent of World War I and the loss of talent to its professional teams. The 1920 Olympics at Antwerp, Belgium, brought victory to the host country in a competition highlighted by the final game against Czechoslovakia. The latter, protesting foul play by a Belgian player, walked off the field en masse.

In 1924 in Paris, the British withdrew from Olympic competition in protest of payments it claimed were being made to so-called amateur players. It was one of the early signs of the long-standing controversy over the definition of amateur status which many felt, and feel, has relegated Olympic soccer to secondary importance. It was in 1924 that the United States sent a team to the Olympics for the first time, beginning an unwelcome tradition of failing to make it past the preliminary rounds. Uruguay brought home the gold medal from Paris and made it two in a row in Amsterdam in 1928 when it took a replayed final

against Argentina. Uruguay went on to host and win the first World Cup two years later.

In 1936 in Berlin, Italy captured the Olympic title two years after its World Cup victory, and both triumphs were trumpeted by the Mussolini regime. Sweden enjoyed a brief ascendency to the winners' stand in London in 1948, but was then ruined by talent-raiding, checkbook-bearing Italian club teams.

The Hungarians became the first communist national team to challenge Western Europe by running away with the 1952 title at Helsinki, defeating Yugoslavia in the finals. The victory marked the beginning of a string of Eastern European domination that saw Hungary equal the English record of three titles (in 1952, 1964, 1968) and Russia (1956), Poland (1972), East Germany (1976), and Yugoslavia (1960) each emerge as a champion.

This Eastern European domination threatened the very nature of the Olympic tournament, since the event had become the exclusive property of the nations that claimed to have no professional players at all. The countries that continued to field truly amateur sides found that they could not keep pace.

In 1978, a decision was handed down by the Fédération Internationale de Football Association (FIFA) that prohibits the appearance of World Cup players in subsequent Olympic Games competition. The ruling allows nations to use the Olympics as a trial run for the World Cup but it

It's not how you do the Olympic salute, but how you play the game. This is the U.S. Olympic team prior to its match against Argentina in 1928. Argentina won, 11–2.

prevents nations from fielding key players in appearances in another Olympics.

The United States' participation in the Olympics has been undistinguished. In 1972, the United States won its way into the Olympic tournament for the first time since the system of qualifying rounds was introduced in 1960. In the early days of U.S. participation, the teams consisted largely of amateurs who were not collegians. Beginning with the 1946 team, the U.S. adopted the use of "select games" held across the nation to make the selection process more equitable.

In advance of the 1980 Olympics in Moscow, the implementation of an Olympic Registration Form gave new hope to the U.S. in its Olympic program. The innovation, worked out by the Uni-

ted States Soccer Federation in concert with the pro leagues, makes it possible for players to maintain their amateur standing while playing for a professional team. It is all in accordance with international rules. An immediate result was that most of the members of the 1980 U.S. Olympic team were from North American Soccer League teams.

Olympic Champions

1900—Great Britain
1904—Canada
1906—Denmark
1908—Great Britain
1912—Great Britain

1920—Belgium
1924—Uruguay
1928—Uruguay
1932—No soccer competition
1936—Italy
1948—Sweden
1952—Hungary
1956—Russia
1960—Yugoslavia
1964—Hungary
1968—Hungary
1972—Poland
1976—East Germany

United States Olympic Team Results

1924, Paris: United States 1, Estonia 0; Uruguay 3, United States 0.

1928, Amsterdam: Argentina 11, United States 2.

1932: No soccer tournament.

1936, Berlin: Italy 1, United States 0.

1940, 1944: Olympic games not held.

1948, London: Italy 9, United States 0.

1952, Helsinki: Italy 8, United States 0.

1956, Melbourne: Yugoslavia 9, United States 1.

1960, Qualifying Round: Mexico 2, United States 0; United States 1, Mexico 1. Team failed to qualify for final round in Rome.

1964, Qualifying Round: Surinam 1, United States 0; United States 4, Panama 2; Mexico 2, United States 1. Team failed to qualify for final round in Tokyo.

1968, Qualifying Round: United States 1, Bermuda 1; Bermuda 1, United States 0. Team failed to qualify for final round in Mexico City.

1972, Qualifying Round: United States 1, El Salvador 1; United States 3, Barbados 0; United States 1, El Salvador 1; United States 3, Barbados 1. Play-off: United States 1, El Salvador 1 (OT; game decided on penalty kicks). Second Preliminary Round: United States 1, Jamaica 1; United States 1, Mexico 1; Guatemala 3, United States 2; United States 2, Guatemala 1; United States 2, Mexico 2; United States 2, Jamaica 1. Team qualified for final round in Munich. Final Round: United States 0, Morocco 0; Malaysia 3, United States 0; West Germany 7, United States 0.

1976, Qualifying Round: Bermuda 3, United States 2; United States 2, Bermuda 0; Mexico 8, United States 0; Mexico 4, United States 2. Team failed to qualify for final round in Montreal.

A Czechoslovakian player marks his Hungarian opponent in the 1964 Olympic final in Tokyo. Hungary won the gold medal, 2–1, and repeated in Mexico City in 1968.

Goalkeeper Shep Messing stymied the Cincinnati Kids in the Major Indoor Soccer League's inaugural game in 1978 and then wrapped up the season with a playoff MVP-winning effort that brought a title to his New York Arrows.

13

The Indoor Game

Indoor soccer is a hybrid game which combines many traditional soccer skills with the more physical play and faster tempo of ice hockey. The game arrived in a major way on the American professional sports scene in 1978 with the birth of the six-team Major Indoor Soccer League (MISL), but it was played in a slightly different form for many years prior to that date. Indoor soccer originated as a training device for European soccer teams. The American Soccer League promoted an indoor match with a touring international team at Madison Square Garden as early as 1939.

The version of the game arrived at by Earl Foreman and Ed Tepper, the cofounders of the MISL, is contested on a field with the dimensions of a hockey rink (200 feet by 85 feet) which is covered with an artificial turf surface. Dasher boards, topped by plexiglass, surround the field as in hockey, and balls can be played on the rebound off the sideboards. The goal is 6½ feet high and 12 feet wide; there are six players on each team (including the goalkeeper); there is free substitution; and there are virtually no stops in play. Teams play four 15-minute periods, with a sudden-death overtime in case of a tie.

Although the net is actually smaller than in the outdoor version (8 by 24 feet), the indoor game features more scoring and the possibility of power plays (in the event of two-minute penalties for delay of game or ungentlemanly conduct). There was an average of a fraction under twelve goals scored per game in MISL's inaugural season.

The charter members of the Major Indoor Soccer League were the New York Arrows (winner of the league's first championship), the Cincinnati Kids, the Houston Summit, the Philadelphia Fever, the Cleveland Force, and the Pittsburgh Spirit. Baseball star Pete Rose, a coowner of the Cincinnati franchise, kicked out the first ball prior to the league's first game, won by the Arrows over the Kids at New York's Nassau Coliseum.

Although Houston compiled the league's best regular-season record, New York, led by goalkeeper Shep Messing, tabbed the Most Valuable Player in the play-offs, defeated Philadelphia in the finals to win its crown.

Most of the MISL teams filled their rosters with former local collegiate stars, in keeping with a league rule limiting the number of foreign imports on each roster to four.

In 1980, MISL became a 10-team, two-division circuit with Buffalo, Hartford, New York, Philadelphia, and Pittsburgh in the Atlantic Division; Cleveland, Detroit, Houston, St. Louis, and Wichita in the Central Division.

At the same time, the North American Soccer League, which had previously had indoor tournaments and exhibitions, launched NASL Indoor Soccer with 10 teams in two divisions: Atlanta, Detroit, Fort Lauderdale, New England, and Tampa Bay in the Eastern Division; California, Los Angeles, Memphis, Minnesota, and Tulsa in the Western Division.

14

United States Soccer Federation

The United States Soccer Federation (USSF), originally known as the United States Soccer Football Association (USSFA), was founded in 1913 as the governing body for the sport of soccer on all levels in the United States. Under the leadership of G. Randolph Manning, its first president, the Federation gained the exclusive recognition of soccer's world governing body, the Fédération Internationale (FIFA) in 1914.

Membership in the Federation is achieved through participation and membership in the various organizations that function autonomously but remain under the official auspices of the USSF. Federation members and associate members include fifty-three state associations in the United States Youth Soccer Association (California, Pennsylvania, New York, and Ohio each have two associations), the North American Soccer League, the American Soccer League and the Major Indoor Soccer League, the National Soccer Coaches Association, the Intercollegiate Soccer Football Association, the National Collegiate Athletic Association, the Federation of State High School Associations, the United States Olympic Committee, and the Amateur Athletic Union.

◀ *Heady play of young stars like Perry Van Der Beck enabled the U.S. National Team to earn a berth in the 1979 Pan American Games.*

The basic responsibility of the USSF is the supervision and promotion of the game on all levels—local, national and international.

Community youth teams serve as the foundation for USSF programs. The Federation acts as a clearing house for organizational problems, and it provides local organizers with materials relevant to field procurement, financing, publicity, rules of play, and the training of players, coaches, and referees.

On the national level, the Federation works to promote sponsorship and endorsement of programs with corporations. A percentage of these revenues is turned over by the Federation to the various state associations. Among the most important functions of the USSF is the choosing and preparing of U.S. National teams to compete in Pan American, Olympic, World Cup, and international youth competitions. The U.S. National coach, in charge of supervising the development of both the U.S. National Team and the U.S. Youth Team, is Walt Chyzowych.

The United States Soccer Federation supervises all international matches in this country and sees that the rules of the game are consistent with international rules. It sponsors clinics and coaching schools, invites speakers from foreign countries, and conducts a variety of national and state amateur competitions.

The James P. McGuire National Junior Cup competition, for amateur players under the age of 19, named in honor of a former president of the

USSF, is a tournament which attracts much attention. The USSF also oversees the Dewar's National Open Challenge Cup, the National Amateur Challenge Cup, and the D. J. Niotis Cup competitions.

In its role as promoter of the game in this country, the USSF distributes textbooks, films, charts, and rulebooks for use by players and coaches.

In 1979, the president of the USSF was Gene Edwards. The Executive Secretary is Kurt Lamm. Federation offices are located in the Empire State Building in New York.

◀ *The U.S. National Team's Angelo DiBernardo vies with France's Didier Six in a 1979 match won by the French, 6–0, at Giants Stadium, East Rutherford, N.J.*

Jack Hynes of the New York Americans (left) and Gene Olaff of the Brooklyn Hispano, opponents in 1948, are members of the National Soccer Hall of Fame.

15

National Soccer Hall of Fame

In January 1950, the Old Timers' Soccer Association of Philadelphia held an awards banquet honoring fifteen individuals for their contributions to the growth of soccer in America. Three years and thirty-eight inductees later, the United States Soccer Football Association granted official recognition to the Old Timers' Association, became its parent body, and renamed it the National Soccer Hall of Fame.

Through 1978, 137 players and administrators have been inducted into the Hall of Fame, including 19 recipients of the Meritorious Award and 40 players in this country's first professional league, the American Soccer League. Though still in search of an official home base, the Hall of Fame conducts annual induction ceremonies honoring America's soccer pioneers.

Selections are made from a list of candidates submitted by the various leagues, state associations, and a veterans committee, to the Hall of Fame Committee, a group of five former presidents of the United States Soccer Federation. Included in the ranks of the enshrined are: players with careers ranging from ownership of a brewery to working on the Manhattan project which produced the atomic bomb during World War II; newspapermen; an entire U.S. World Cup team; a father-son combination; a famous football coach; and a woman.

The fifteen charter members of the Hall of Fame included seven players, seven officials and one coach—Dr. John Brock, who captained and coached the first team at Springfield College in 1906 and who came out of retirement to lead the same school to national championship designations in 1946 and 1947.

One of the original fifteen was an inside forward from Fall River, Massachusetts, named Billy Gonsalves. Regarded by his peers as the best player of his time and characterized as "The Babe Ruth of Soccer," Gonsalves turned down lucrative offers to play other sports and chose to play soccer in Italy following his performance in 1934 World Cup play in Rome.

Gonsalves' physique—he was 6'1" and a muscular 185 pounds—and his powerful shot earned him a variety of nicknames, including "Big Bertha," "The Big Bomber," "Piano Legs," and "Mr. Soccer." The holder of a record eight National Challenge Cup championship medals and one of the few American players of his day with the talent to have played abroad, Gonsalves recalled with delight one particular goal which he scored while playing for the St. Louis Shamrocks:

"I kicked a hard shot about three–four feet high, but it had a hook on it. You know how a goalkeeper has his hands up to his chest as if to clutch the ball? Well, the ball just curved around him and into the net. The goalkeeper just stood there. He was dumbfounded. You should have seen his face."

One of Gonsalves' contemporaries and another charter member of the Hall of Fame was Archie Stark, who scored a record sixty-seven goals in forty-four games while playing for Bethlehem Steel during the 1924–1925 American Soccer

One of the 15 Hall of Fame charter members, Billy Gonsalves played for eight National Challenge Cup champions and was known as "Mr. Soccer."

League season. Stark was asked by Ed Sullivan, who was a sportswriter prior to his career as a nationally-syndicated columnist and television personality, to pose for an action photograph during an interview. When Stark asked how he was supposed to pose with his leg up in the air for an extended period of time, Sullivan produced a nail and hammered Stark's soccer shoe into the wall of the newspaper office. Then Stark wiggled his foot into the shoe and posed for the photographer.

Joseph Barriskill, a 1953 inductee, had a run-in with the late Vice President Nelson Rockefeller, who was playing left fullback at Dartmouth College at the time. Barriskill jumped to head a ball and became tangled with Rockefeller's foot. When Barriskill took exception to this, Rocky called him a "sissy." The next time the ball came Joe's way, he got underneath Rocky and straightened up, sending his opponent crashing to the turf. Picking Rocky up, Barriskill said, "This is not a parlor game." The two men became close friends.

The members of the 1950 U.S. World Cup team, which pulled off a landmark 1–0 upset of an English team that was reportedly insured for $3 million by Lloyd's of London, were all inducted into the Hall of Fame as a group in 1976.

Charles Colombo, a center halfback with a reputation for toughness whose trademark was wearing gloves in all kinds of weather, saved the Americans' victory over England when he cut down England's dangerous Stan Mortenson with a football tackle and saved an almost certain game-tying goal. The English team anticipated that Colombo would receive a stiff punishment and that it would be awarded a penalty kick. Instead, the referee, who, like Colombo, was Italian, blew his whistle, ran up to Colombo and yelled, "Bono, bono, bono."

Pete Renzulli was another popular Italian Hall of Famer. In the 1920s, when Tony Lazzeri was starring for baseball's New York Yankees in Yankee Stadium, Renzulli was the goalkeeper for the Nationals and the soccer Giants at the Polo Grounds. Both players were great favorites of New York's Italian fans, who traditionally urged slugging Tony to "poosh 'em up" and goalie Pete to "poosh 'em out."

One soccer Hall of Famer is best known for his achievements as an American football coach. Buff

Donelli, who scored a World Cup-record four goals against Mexico in 1934, went on to gain recognition as the head coach of two National Football League teams and college gridiron squads at Duquesne, Boston University, and Columbia.

Perhaps the most famous of the referees in the Hall is Jimmy Walder, affectionately termed the "Dean of Referees" after an officiating career that began in 1909 and spanned six decades before he refereed his last game at the age of seventy.

For several members of the Hall, soccer was a family affair. David Brown, a 1951 inductee, was one of six generations of professional players in his family, dating back to his grandfather on his mother's side, goalkeeper James Douglas. Walter Bahr, one of the stars of the 1950 World Cup team and a long-time Penn State coach, sired U.S. Olympians Casey and Chris as well as Matt, a professional player.

The only father-son combination in the Hall is Powys A. L. "PAL" Foulds and his son Sam. The elder Foulds was identified with the sport for almost sixty years as a player and an official, while Sam earned recognition as a historian for the USSF. Foulds continues to be active in the Hall's search for a home. He is joined in that effort by another Hall of Famer, Julius Alonso, the secretary of the Veterans' Committee. His involvement with soccer has included playing, managing, refereeing, and administrative work.

Several newspapermen who contributed to the growth of the sport during their journalistic careers also gained entrance to the select group of dignitaries. They include Frank McGrath of the Fall River (Massachusetts) *Herald News* and Jack Johnston, a soccer reporter for the Chicago *Tribune* who wrote under the pen name "Offside."

The lone female member of the Hall is Alfredda Inglehart of Maryland. She gained admittance in 1951 after a teaching career that spanned more than thirty years during which she instructed more than twelve hundred boys—many of whom later became professionals—in the fundamentals of soccer.

Thomas Sager, chairman of the National Hall of Fame Committee in 1979, summed up the common ground shared by the wide range of personalities whose contributions have been commemo-rated by their inclusion in the Hall: "All the members of the Hall of Fame, both living and dead, deserve a resounding 'thank you' from all of us and those in the future, for they have left something that money cannot buy—loyalty and the love of soccer."

SOCCER HALL OF FAME MEMBERS THROUGH 1978
(Year of induction in parentheses)

Alonso, Julius J. (1972)
Andersen, William (1956)
Armstrong, James (1952)
Bahr, Walter (1976)
Barriskill, Joseph J. (1953)
Beardsworth, Fred (1965)
Bernabei, Raymond (1978)
Booth, Joseph (1952)
Borghi, Frank (1976)
Boxer, Matthew (1961)
Brittan, Harold (1951)
Brock, John (1950)
Brown, Andrew M. (1950)
Brown, David (1951)
Cahill, Thomas W. (1950)
Carrafi, Ralph (1959)
Chesney, Stanley (1966)
Collins, George M. (1951)
Colombo, Charles (1976)
Commander, Colin (1967)
Craddock, Robert (1959)
Craggs, Edward (1969)
Cummings, Wilfred R. (1953)
Donaghy, Edward J. (1951)
Donelli, Aldo T. (1954)
Douglas, James E. (1954)
Dresmich, John W. (1968)
Dugan, Thomas (1955)
Epperleim, Rudy (1951)
Fairfield, Harry (1951)
Ferguson, John (1950)
Fernley, John A. (1951)
Ferro, Charles (1958)
Fishwick, George E. (1974)
Flamhaft, Jack (1964)
Fleming, Harry G. (1967)
Foulds, Powys A. L. (1953)
Foulds, Sam T. N. (1969)
Fowler, Daniel W. (1970)
Fryer, William J. (1951)
Gaetjens, Joseph (1976)
Garcia, Peter (1964)
Giesler, Walter (1962)
Glover, Charles E. (1965)
Gonsalves, William (1950)
Gould, David L. (1953)
Govier, Sheldon (1950)
Gryzik, Joseph (1973)
Healy, George (1951)
Hemmings, William (1961)
Hudson, Maurice (1966)
Hynes, John (1977)
Inglehart, Alfredda (1951)
Jaap, John (1953)

Jeffrey, William (1951)
Johnson, Jack (1952)
Kempton, George (1950)
Keough, Harry (1976)
Klein, Paul (1953)
Koszma, Oscar (1964)
Kraus, Harry A. (1963)
Kuntner, Rudy (1963)
Lang, Millard (1950)
Lewis, H. Edgar (1950)
Maca, Joseph (1976)
Mac Ewan, John J. (1953)
McGuire, James P. (1951)
McGuire, John (1951)
McIlveney, Edward (1976)
McLaughlin, Bernard (1977)
McSkimming, Den (1951)
Magnozzi, Enzo (1977)
Maher, Jack (1970)
Manning, Rudolph R. (1950)
Marre, John (1953)
Mieth, Werner (1974)
Millar, Robert (1950)
Mills, James (1954)
Morrison, Robert (1951)
Morrissette, William (1967)
Netto, Fred (1958)
Niotis, Dimitrios J. (1963)
Olaff, Gene (1971)
Oliver, Arnold (1968)
Palmer, William (1952)
Pariani, Gino (1976)
Patenaude, Bertrand A. (1971)
Peel, Peter J. (1951)
Peters, Wally (1967)
Pomeroy, Edgar (1955)
Ramsden, Arnold (1957)
Ratican, Harry (1950)
Reese, Vernon R. (1957)
Renzulli, Peter (1951)
Ryan, John (1958)
Sager, Thomas (1968)
Schillinger, Emil (1960)
Schroeder, Elmer (1951)
Schwarcz, Erno (1951)

Shields, Fred (1968)
Smith, Alfred (1951)
Souza, Ed (1976)
Souza, John C. (1976)
Spalding, Richard (1950)
Stark, Archie (1950)
Steur, August (1969)
Stewart, Douglas (1950)
Swords, Thomas (1951)
Tintle, George (1952)
Triner, Joseph (1951)
Wallace, Frank (1976)
Weir, Alex (1975)
Weston, Victor (1956)
Wilson, Peter (1950)
Woods, John W. (1952)
Young, John (1958)
Zampini, Daniel (1963)
Zerhusen, Al (1978)

MERITORIOUS AWARD

Abronzino, Umberto (1971)
Ardizzone, John (1971)
Briggs, Lawrence E. (1978)
Cordery, Ted (1975)
Delach, Joseph (1973)
Di Orio, Nick (1974)
Duff, Duncan (1972)
Dunn, James (1974)
McClay, Allan (1971)
McGrath, Frank (1978)
Merovich, Peter (1971)
Miller, Milton (1971)
Moore, James F. (1971)
Piscopo, Giorgio (1978)
Rottenberg, Jack J. (1971)
Steelink, Nicolas (1971)
Stone, Robert T. (1971)
Walder, James A. (1971)
Washauer, Adolph (1977)

APPENDIX A
Glossary

ADVANTAGE RULE: The referee does not have to stop play every time he detects a foul, but he will if the offending team gains an advantage. Sometimes it is penalizing the innocent team to stop play; for example, if a defender deliberately handles the ball to bring it under control but only succeeds in deflecting it to an opponent who is well placed for a shot at goal. To stop play at this moment would penalize the attacking team by allowing the defenders time to regroup. In such a case, the referee would allow play to go on.

AGGREGATE SCORE: The combined scores of two home-and-home games. Playing at home before the hometown fans is considered a big advantage in soccer, particularly in international club competitions. For this reason, most international games at the club level are played on a home-and-home basis, and the scores from the two games are added together. A team losing 1–2 away from home but winning 2–0 at home wins by an aggregate score of 3–2. In some competitions if aggregate scores are tied, goals scored away from home count double.

ASL: American Soccer League.

ASSOCIATION FOOTBALL: Soccer's official title. Back in the 1860s the word *football* was being used in England for two different sports. To distinguish the two the terms Rugby *football* (because rugby was first played in the town of Rugby) and *association football* (because the first soccer rules were drawn up by the London Football Association) were used. It is believed that the word soccer is a corruption of the abbreviation

assoc., just as *rugger* became the commonly used word for rugby.

BACKHEEL: To pass the ball backward with the back of the heel. It is a highly deceptive pass, particularly if performed at speed, as the ball travels in the opposite direction from the way the passer is moving and looking.

BALL: The spherical object the players use in a game. It must be made of leather or "other approved materials," which include various forms of plastic. It must have a circumference of twenty-seven to twenty-eight inches, weigh between fourteen and sixteen ounces, and be pumped up to a pressure of fifteen pounds per square inch. If the ball should burst during a game, play is restarted with the new ball at the point where the old one was last played. If a kick results in a goal and a burst ball, the goal does not count. It is assumed that the moment the ball was kicked it started to deflate and was therefore no longer a regulation ball.

BALL IN AND OUT OF PLAY: For the ball to pass out of play, *all* of it must be over *all* of the sideline or goal line (the lines are about five inches wide). Thus, a ball on the line is in play. Even a ball resting on the ground just outside the touchline is still in play if any part of it is projecting over the line. Similarly, a goal is not scored until all of the ball has passed over all of the goal line. A shot that hits the crossbar and bounces down onto the goal line and then out is not a goal.

BALLPLAYER: A player who is especially skilled at controlling and moving with the ball.

BALL WINNER: A rather euphemistic term used to describe hard-tackling players, usually midfielders and usually lacking in constructive skills.

BANANA SHOT: A hard shot at goal in which the ball is kicked off-center, giving it a spin that makes it curve in flight. It is usually used on free kicks near the goal to "bend" the ball around a defensive wall.

BAR: The crossbar of the goal.

BEND: To kick the ball so that it curves in flight. It is done by kicking the ball off-center, making it spin.

BICYCLE KICK: See Overhead Kick.

BLIND SIDE: The side of a player that is farthest from the ball. A defender watching an attack develop on his right must also be aware of movement on his left, his blind side, in case an attacker should sneak behind him to receive a pass.

BOOT: To kick the ball clumsily and aimlessly. Hence the term should not be used simply as an alternative for *kick*, and it should never be used in the form of *booters* to mean soccer players or the *booting game* to mean soccer.

BOX: The penalty area (the eighteen-yard box). Also, less frequently, the goal area (the six-yard box).

BREAKDOWN PERIOD: The period immediately following a change of ball possession. Soccer is a game in which, like hockey, possession is constantly and abruptly passing from one team to the other. The team gaining possession must immediately switch from defense to attack, the team losing possession from attack to defense.

CALLING: Shouting on the field by soccer players to let a teammate with the ball know that they are backing him up or running alongside him to receive a pass. In a rapidly moving game like soccer, the player with the ball does not usually have the time to look all around him to note exactly where his teammates are positioned. This is particularly true for those playing behind him.

CANNONBALL SHOT: Any very fast, powerful shot on goal. The hardest shooters in soccer can make the ball travel at more than 70 miles per hour.

CAP: To select a player to play for his country's national team. The phrase comes from the British custom, still observed, of awarding such players an elaborately decorated cap, complete with a large dangling tassel.

CARPET: The playing surface. A team that specializes in ground passes is "keeping it on the carpet."

CATENACCIO (kat-ten-AH-cho): A defensive system, perfected by Italian clubs in the 1960s. It employs a single, extradeep fullback who plays behind a line of three or four fullbacks. He is called the libero, or sweeper, or freeback. His main job is to provide cover for the defenders in front of him.

CAUTION: See Yellow Card.

CENTER: To pass the ball from near the touchlines into the opposing goalmouth. Also called crossing the ball.

CENTERBACK: See Tactics.

CENTER CIRCLE: A circle of ten yards radius marked out around the center spot of the field. It has only one official function—at the moment of a kickoff, players on the team not taking the kick must be ten yards from the ball; so they must stay out of the circle.

CENTER FORWARD: See Tactics.

CHALLENGE: To approach a player who has possession of the ball with the apparent intention of tackling him. In fact, a tackle may not come. The idea is to force the player in possession to commit himself, either to pass or to run with the ball.

CHARGE: Physical contact with an opponent in an attempt to force him off the ball. The charge must be a shoulder-to-shoulder contact. If the elbows, hands, or hips are used, or if the charge is made from behind or with unnecessary roughness, it is illegal. Although shoulder-charging the goalkeeper when he is holding the ball is permitted by the international rules, most countries do not allow it.

CHIP: A short, lofted pass made with only a small movement of the kicking foot and no follow-through. The foot is jammed underneath the ball, which is made to rise steeply in the air. The chip is used in passing to lift the ball over a nearby defender.

CLEAR: To kick or head the ball away from the goalmouth, thus killing an immediate threat to the goal.

CLOGGER: A player who tackles roughly, aiming more for his opponent's legs than for the ball.

COIN TOSS: Before each game a coin is tossed, and the winner has the choice either of ends or the kickoff. In soccer, possession at the kickoff means virtually nothing, so that the captain winning the coin toss will invariably select which end he wishes to defend.

CORNER KICK: What the attacking side is awarded when a defending player kicks the ball over his own goal line (other than into the goal). The ball is placed in the corner area and kicked, usually in the air, so that it will reach the opposing goalmouth, where attackers are hoping to head or kick it into the goal, the defenders to clear it.

COVER: To back up a teammate in defense.

CROSSBAR: The horizontal bar that forms the top of the goal.

CROSS-SHOT: A shot on goal made from the right side toward the left of the goal, or vice versa.

DANGEROUS PLAY: This is not defined in the rules, and it is up to the referee to decide what is and what is not dangerous. Two common examples are high kicking, particularly when an opponent is trying to head the ball, and kicking at the ball when it is held by the goalkeeper.

DEAD BALL: When play has been stopped by the referee and the ball is not moving. All free kicks have to be taken from a dead ball.

DECOY: An attacker who indulges in much running about without the ball, trying to make the opposing defense believe that he is about to receive a pass. Decoy running is also called off-the-ball running.

DEFENDER: Primarily a defensive player who assists the goalkeeper in protecting the goal. See Tactics.

DIAGONAL RUNNING: An attacking maneuver. Although the most direct way to goal for an attacker is straight down the field, it is not usually the most successful. Attackers do much of their running diagonally across the field, rapidly interchanging positions. This creates problems of marking for the defense and makes it easier for the forwards to control passes coming through from midfield.

DIPPER: A long, hard shot at goal that suddenly dips downward in its flight. It is top spin that makes the ball dip; hence dippers are usually shots taken on the volley when the kicker can get his foot well over the ball.

DIRECT FREE KICK: A kick awarded against a team that has committed one of the nine serious fouls. A goal can be scored directly from the kick. If the foul was committed within its own penalty area, the team has a penalty kick awarded against it. All opposing players must be at least ten yards from the ball when the kick is taken.

DRIBBLE: To run with the ball under control, tapping it ahead with the inside or the outside of the foot, and taking it past opponents by tricking them with feints, body swerves, and tricky footwork.

DROP BALL: Soccer's equivalent of basketball's jump ball. When the referee has stopped the game—for example, to allow treatment of an injured player—he will restart it by dropping the ball between two opposing players. They must let it touch the ground before they attempt to kick it.

ELEVEN: This is the number of players on a soccer team, and the word, or the roman numeral XI, is sometimes used to mean team.

EQUIPMENT: Players wear a shirt, shorts, stockings, and what the rules insist on calling boots. In fact the old soccer boots—heavy, ankle high, with hard, reinforced toes—went out of style years ago. Today's "boots" are low-cut, light-weight shoes of supple leather, allowing a much more delicate control of the ball. Some players wear shin guards, flexible shields that cover the front of the leg between the ankle and the knee; they are tucked down inside the socks.

EUROPEAN CUP: Started in 1956, this is the most successful of the international competitions for clubs. It is held yearly and involves the champion clubs from over thirty European countries. In 1960, a similar competition was started in South America, thus opening the way for championship games between the European and South American winners. This is the International Cup, and the winner can truly claim to be the champion club of the world.

FIELD: Under international rules the playing area in soccer can vary greatly in size, but the length (100 to 130 yards) must always be greater than the width (50 to 100 yards).

FIFA: The Fédération Internationale de Football Association, the international organization that governs world soccer. Formed in 1904, it now has a membership of over 140 countries. Its functions include ruling on differences among member nations over interpretation of the rules, and organizing the World Cup.

50-50 BALL: A loose ball that both teams have an equal chance of controlling.

FINISHING: The final touch to an attacking move. It includes any type shot on goal. Good finishing means accurate shooting.

FIRST-TIME: To play a ball—to pass or to shoot—immediately after it arrives without attempting to bring it under control.

FLANK(S): The side areas of the playing field.

FLAT POSITIONS: Players alongside each other, forming a line across the field, are in flat, or square, positions.

FLICK PASS: A short pass, made on the run with the outside of the foot.

FOOTBALL: Soccer is a game played with the feet and with a ball. Its natural name is football. And this is the word that is used in one form or another in most of the world to describe the sport. In the British Isles it's football, in France it's *le football*, in Spain and most of South America *el futbol*, in Brazil *o futebol*, in Germany it's *fussball*. In fact, most of the world finds it rather hard to understand how Americans can use the word *football* for a game in which the foot is much less important than the hand.

FORWARD: Primarily an attacking player whose responsibility is to create and score goals. See Tactics.

FOUL(S): There are two types of fouls in soccer: serious and not serious. The more serious are: dangerous charging, charging from behind, holding, striking, pushing, tripping, or kicking an opponent, jumping at an opponent, and handling the ball. These offenses will result in a direct free kick given against the guilty team, or a penalty kick if the foul occurred in its penalty area. The less serious fouls include obstruction, ungentlemanly conduct, and the taking of more than four steps by a goalkeeper while holding the ball. For these, an indirect free kick is given.

FOUL THROW: See Throw-in.

FREEBACK: See Sweeper.

FULLBACK: See Tactics.

FUNNELING: A defensive tactic. When a team that is attacking loses possession of the ball, its players immediately retreat toward their own goal and concentrate in the center of the field toward their penalty area.

GOAL: What is at each end of the field, consisting of two goalposts (or uprights) and a crossbar, backed with a cage of netting. The goals are eight feet high and eight yards wide. They are also what counts in soccer; the method of deciding who wins. Each time the ball, all of it, goes over the goal line, between the posts and beneath the crossbar, a goal has been scored.

GOAL AREA: A rectangular area, marked by a line, in front of each goal. It is twenty yards wide and six yards deep. Inside this area the goalkeeper cannot be charged unless he has possession of the ball—although the modern trend is to bar all charges on the goalkeeper.

GOAL AVERAGE: A figure obtained by dividing the number of goals a team scores by the number scored against it. A team scoring one hundred goals and giving up fifty has a goal average of 2.00, while a team that scores only fifty but gives up one hundred has a goal average of 0.50. In some countries the goal average is used to determine league placings among teams that have the same number of points. Another method is by goal difference, in which goals against are subtracted from goals for. Thus, a team that scores one hundred goals and allows fifty has a goal difference of 50. See also Standings.

GOALKEEPER or GOALIE: The player who defends the goal. It is a little difficult to think of him as a soccer player because his functions are so different from those of the other ten members of the team. His main weapons are his hands, not his feet. He may handle the ball anywhere within his own penalty area. Should he venture beyond this, he becomes just another player, and if he then handles the ball, a foul will be called against him. When he has possession of the ball, he can take only four steps before he must get rid of it. The goalie is required to wear different colors from the rest of the team.

GOAL KICK: When the attacking team plays the ball over the opponent's goal line (other than into the goal), play is restarted by the defending team taking a goal kick. The ball is placed at the edge of the goal area and kicked upfield by the goalkeeper or a defender.

GROUNDER: A shot on goal in which the ball is kept low, in contact with the ground.

HACKING: Kicking at an opponent's legs. It is, of course, banned, but when the first soccer rules were published in 1863, many clubs protested vigorously that it was an important and legitimate part of the game.

HALFTIME: The interval between the halves. Under international rules it should not exceed five minutes, but this is a rule that is rarely observed. Ten minutes is the average.

HALF-VOLLEY: To kick the ball immediately after it has bounced, when it is only a fraction of an inch off the ground. The dropkick, sometimes used by goalies to clear the ball, is a form of half-volley.

HALFWAY LINE: The line marked across the width of the field, dividing it into two halves. Players must be in their own half of the field at kickoffs, and they cannot be offside in their own half. See also Offside.

HANDS: The only soccer player allowed to use his hands is the goalkeeper, and then only inside his own penalty area. Any other player who handles the ball will be penalized by a direct free kick against his team, or—if he is within his own penalty area—a penalty kick. But the handling must be intentional. If the referee judges it to be accidental, he will let play go on. In soccer, *hand* means any part of the arm below the armpit.

HAT TRICK: Three goals by one player in one game. The term is borrowed from cricket where it used to be the custom for the club to present a new hat to any bowler (the equivalent of a pitcher) who dismissed three batsmen with three successive balls.

HEADING: Playing the ball with the head, a very important basic soccer skill. The ball is met with the middle of the forehead; the skull is at its hardest and thickest at this point, and great power can be put into head shots.

HOLDING: Grabbing hold of an opponent or his uniform. It's illegal.

HOSPITAL BALL: A badly directed pass that is a little nearer to an opponent than the teammate it was intended for. Both players will run for the ball

and the unfortunate teammate, who will arrive second, stands a fair chance of being injured.

INDIRECT FREE KICK: A kick awarded against a team that has committed one of the less serious offenses. A goal cannot be scored directly from the kick; the ball must first be played by a player other than the kicker. All opposing players must be at least ten yards from the ball. See also Fouls.

INJURY TIME: Time added on by the referee (who is the official timekeeper) at the end of each half to make up for any time lost when play was stopped for treatment to an injured player.

INSTEP: The hard, bony part of the top of the foot. It is the surface that makes contact with the ball in the normal soccer kick.

INSWINGER: A type of corner kick or center that curls in the air toward the goal.

INTERCONTINENTAL CUP: This annual tournament matches the winners of the European Cup and the Copa Libertadores, which is the South American equivalent of the European Cup. It is also known as the world club championship.

JOCKEYING: When a player in possession of the ball faces a defender, each will be trying to jockey the other into an unfavorable position. A defender who feels that he is stronger on his left side (that is, off his right foot) may allow an attacker more room on that side, almost inviting him to run that way.

KEEP BALL: Soccer's version of freezing the ball, involving a succession of short, safe, ground passes to teammates. There is no attempt to advance the ball, which often travels backward and ends up being passed back to the goalkeeper.

KICK AND RUN: A crude type of soccer, without any plan or system and with very little skill. The ball is kicked in the air, as hard as possible, toward the opponent's goal, and the forwards run downfield after it, hoping for the best.

KICKER: A rough player, one who is always fouling opponents. It's another word like *booter*, that is sometimes used incorrectly to denote a soccer player.

KICKOFF: The start of the game. The ball is placed on the center spot and is kicked forward. It is not in play, and the game has not started, until it has rolled the distance of its circumference, about twenty-seven inches. The kickoff is also used to restart play after a goal has been scored, the team that gave up the goal taking the kick.

LINESMAN: A subordinate official who assists the referee. There is one on each side of the field. His job is to run up and down the touchline and to signal with his flag when the ball goes out of play, indicating which team is to get the throw-in. When he spots players offside, or other infringements, he also raises his flag. This is only a signal to the referee; if the referee disagrees with the linesman's judgment, he will simply ignore the signal.

LINKMAN: See Tactics.

LOOSE BALL: A ball that is not controlled by either team and is up for grabs.

MARK: In man-to-man coverage the defender is said to mark the attacker. The closer he plays to him, the tighter the marking; the further away, the looser the marking.

MIDFIELD: An ill-defined area, but corresponding roughly to the middle third of the field. It is the area in which attacking moves are built up but from which there is no direct threat to the goal. Goals are rarely scored from the midfield area, and unless penetrating attacking moves can be started, control of midfield is valuable only as a defensive measure.

LOB: A high, soft kick taken on the volley, lifting the ball over the head of an opponent.

MIDFIELDER: See Tactics.

MINI-GAME: Under 1979 NASL playoff procedures, each series consisted of two home-and-home games. A team had to win both games to proceed to the next round; if the series ended with one victory apiece, this called for a 30-minute mini-game. If the teams were deadlocked after 30 minutes, a shootout was held. See Shootout.

MISKICK: The player's nightmare. There are as many ways of miskicking a soccer ball as there are ways of mishitting a golf ball. It can be sliced, pulled, topped, ballooned, or—horror of horrors—missed altogether.

NARROWING THE ANGLE: This is what the goalie and, to a lesser extent, the other defensive players seek to do. It means reducing the area of the goal that an attacker can shoot at, and it is a matter of simple geometry. With the goalie standing in the middle of his goal line, a forward twelve yards out should be able to score easily with any fairly hard shot wide of the goalie's reach—which gives him quite a large area of the goal to aim at. If the goalie advances six yards, however, the ball will have to be kicked at a much sharper angle, and much more accurately, to get it past him and into the goal. The angles available for scoring shots have been considerably reduced. Flying leaps and diving saves have their place, but a goalie who is forever flinging himself spectacularly all over the place is usually one whose positional play is at fault.

NASL: The North American Soccer League.

NATIONAL TEAM: An all-star team composed of the eleven best players in the nation. FIFA has issued regulations outlining who may play for which country. Generally, it is determined by where a player was born rather than where he plays. Naturalized citizens may play for their adopted country, provided they have not already played on another national team. Competitions for national teams include the Olympics (for amateurs) and the World Cup (for professionals).

NISOA: National Intercollegiate Soccer Officials Association.

NSCAA: National Soccer Coaches Association of America.

NUMBERING: It has always been the custom in soccer to number positions rather than players. The traditional numbering was 1—goalkeeper, 2—right fullback, 3—left fullback, 4—right halfback, 5—center halfback, 6—left halfback, 7—outside right, 8—inside right, 9—center forward, 10—inside left, and 11—outside left. So, for example, whoever played center forward wore number 9. If, in his next game, the same player were switched to outside right, he changed his number to 7. The above system was based on the so-called pyramid formation, but the coming of modern tactical formations has outdated this system, and the numbers no longer have much positional meaning. In the NASL, the American—and more sensible—system of assigning a different number to each player, which they wear whatever position they play, has been adopted. See also Tactics.

OBSTRUCTION: When a player who is not attempting to play the ball uses his body to prevent an opponent from getting to it. The referee will give an indirect free kick against the guilty team.

OFFSIDE: The offside rule requires that an attacker must have at least two opponents between him and the opposing goal line when the ball is passed to him. Under normal circumstances one of these two players will be the goalkeeper. A player cannot be offside in his own half of the field; he cannot be offside if he receives the ball directly from a corner kick, a goal kick, or a throw-in or if he receives it from an opponent; and he cannot be offside if he is behind the ball—that is, if he is running toward the opposing goal and the ball is in front of him. It is not the player's position when he receives the ball that matters. It is where he was when the pass to him was made that counts. The NASL, with permission from FIFA, has modified this rule by limiting its application to a thirty-five-yard zone at each end of the field.

OLYMPICS: Soccer has been an official Olympic sport since 1908.

ONE-FOOTED: Something no soccer player can afford to be. He must be able to kick and control the ball equally well with either foot.

OUTSIDE LEFT: See Tactics.

OUTSIDE RIGHT: See Tactics.

OUTSWINGER: A type of corner kick or center that curls in the air, swinging away from the goal.

OVERHEAD KICK: A spectacular kick useful when a player finds himself facing the wrong way with no time to turn around, or as a surprise move. The player literally upends himself, throwing his feet up and his torso downward. When contact is made with the ball the body is parallel to the ground and some three or four feet above it. The pumping action of the legs just before the ball is kicked resembles the motion of pedaling a bicycle. Also called a somersault or bicycle kick.

OVERLAP: An attacking move in which a defender—usually a fullback—comes forward to join in the attack, taking position on the wing.

OVER THE TOP: A dangerous play in which a player tackling another for possession of the ball comes in with his foot high so that he goes over the top of the ball, making life very unpleasant for the legs and feet of the man in possession. It is, of course, illegal.

OWN GOAL: If a player miskicks or misheads, and the ball goes into his own goal, it counts—for the other team. The player's name will appear among the list of his opponent's scorers with the letters o.g. (for own goal) after it.

PENALTY: A penalty kick. The term should not be applied indiscriminately to any offense.

PENALTY KICK: When the defending team commits one of the nine serious offenses (see Fouls) inside its own penalty area, the attacking team is awarded a penalty kick. The ball is placed on the penalty spot, twelve yards from the goal, and the player taking the kick has only the goalkeeper to beat. All the other players of both teams must be outside the penalty area. The goalie must stand on his goal line and is not allowed to move his feet until the ball is kicked. The chances of the goalkeeper saving the shot are not high—most penalty kicks result in goals.

PITCH: A British term for the playing field.

PLACE-KICK: Any free kick, direct or indirect.

PLAYERS' POSITIONS: See Tactics.

POSTS: The two eight-foot-high uprights that support the crossbar and together with it make up the goal.

READING THE GAME: To size up accurately and quickly the opposing team's strengths and weaknesses; being quick to anticipate its moves.

RED CARD: When the referee ejects a player from the game, he will call the player to him, enter his name in his notebook, then wave a red card in the air, indicating to everyone that the player is being sent off the field. The player's name is sent on to the appropriate disciplinary authorities. See also Yellow Card.

REFEREE: The man in charge. His word on the field is law, and his decisions are final. He starts the game, and because he is also the official timekeeper, he alone says when it is over. No player can enter or leave the field without his consent. He calls the fouls and has the power to caution or eject players. He is also responsible for seeing that the ball and the players' equipment conform to the rules. Under American college and high school rules, two referees are used, and timekeeping is performed by an official timekeeper.

SAVE: The goalkeeper makes a save when he stops an attempted goal by catching or deflecting the ball away from the goal.

SCHEMER: The brains of the team, the player who schemes out attacking moves, usually from a midfield or link position.

SCREENING: The way in which a player in possession uses his body to shield the ball from an opponent. By putting himself between the opponent and the ball, he can make tackling extremely difficult. This is not the same thing as obstruction, in which a player not in possession of the ball attempts to block an opponent.

SHOOT: To make a scoring attempt on the goal, especially by kicking the ball hard. Head shots are also referred to as headers.

SHOOTOUT: The tie-breaking procedure used in North American Soccer League games when teams are tied after playing two sudden-death overtime periods. The shootout involves players on each team challenging the opposing goalkeeper in a one-on-one situation. The visiting team kicks first and each team has five chances in alternate order. The attacker starts with the ball on the 35-yard line and he must shoot within five seconds. The procedure ends when one team has achieved an insurmountable margin. If the teams are tied after the prescribed five attempts, they continue to take alternate kicks until one has scored more than the other after an equal number of attempts.

SIDELINE: See Touchline.

SLIDE TACKLE: An effective method of taking the ball away from an opponent but one that is usually used only as a last resort. It is employed by a defender who has been beaten; running alongside or slightly behind the man who has beaten him, he gains the extra yard by lunging at full stretch with one leg to poke the ball away. In performing the slide tackle, the tackler ends up on his back and thus puts himself out of the game for a brief moment.

SOMERSAULT KICK: See Overhead Kick.

SPOT-KICK: A penalty kick, so called because the ball is placed on the penalty spot, a round mark twelve yards in front of the goal.

STANDINGS: The method most commonly used in soccer to determine places in league standings is a point system allowing two for a win, one for a tie, and none for a loss. The NASL uses a system awarding six points for a win, three for a tie, and none for a loss, plus bonus points for each goal scored (by both winning and losing team) up to a maximum of three. In a game ending 4–2, for example, the winning team would get six points for the win plus the maximum number of bonus points, three, a total of nine points. The losing team would get two points for its two goals. In giving score lines, it is the worldwide soccer custom to give the home team first: Cosmos 1, Celtics 2 means that the Cosmos were beaten, 2–1, on their own ground. U.S. style, however, is to give the winner's score first.

STOPPER: Originally applied to the center half of the old pyramid system when he was moved back to become a third fullback with the role of tightly marking the opposing center forward. It is still used to denote a defender who has the job of tightly marking a striker. See also Tactics.

STRIKER: Any of the central attacking players in the 4–2–4, 4–3–3, and 4–4–2 formations. See also Tactics.

SUBSTITUTION: The use of substitutes—even to replace an injured player—was for years forbidden by the soccer authorities. In the 1960s the international rules were at last relaxed to allow a maximum of two substitutes for each team. There is no free substitution; once a player has been taken out of a game, he cannot reenter it. In America, the NASL permits three substitutes per team per game; the colleges allow five, with resubstitution permitted; and the high schools allow free substitution.

SUDDEN-DEATH OVERTIME: If a regular-season NASL game is tied at the end of regulation play, it is extended by fifteen minutes of sudden-death overtime (two 7½-minute periods). The first team to score a goal wins the game. If the teams are still tied after the sudden-death periods, a shootout is held. See Shootout.

SWEEPER: A fullback who plays an ultradefensive role in the *catenaccio* formation. Also called a libero, or freeback. See also Tactics.

TACKLE: An attempt to take the ball away from an opponent. It is the feet that do the tackling, though the shoulder may also be used to charge a player off the ball.

TACTICS: For over fifty years, until 1925, soccer was dominated by the pyramid formation:

```
                         Goalkeeper
                             x

             Right fullback        Left fullback
                   x                     x

        Right halfback      Center halfback      Left halfback
              x                   x                   x

Outside          Inside          Center         Inside          Outside
right            right           forward        left            left
  x                x               x              x                x
```

a goalkeeper, two fullbacks, three halfbacks, and five forwards—also referred to as a 2-3-5 formation. Tactics were straightforward: the goalkeeper and the fullbacks played defense, the forwards played offense, while the halfbacks played both. Despite the heavy emphasis on attack, it was felt that defenders were favored by the old offside rule, which required an attacker to have *three* opponents in front of him. In 1925 the rule was changed and the number reduced to two. The result was a great jump in the number of goals scored, and defensive play had to be reorganized to cope with the new situation. The center half, who up until then had primarily been an attacking player, was withdrawn into an entirely defensive role, playing as a third fullback between the other two. He became known as the stopper. This gave a 3-2-5 formation, which, it was soon realized, was

weak in midfield. The answer was to withdraw first one, later both, of the inside forwards to midfield giving a 3-4-3 formation, also known as the W-M. This was the common formation throughout the 1930s and 1940s. In the 1950s the accent in soccer became heavily defensive, and the 4-3-3 was developed, with a line of four fullbacks. The Italians perfected an even more defensive system, the *catenaccio*, with a single fullback playing behind the other four, a 1-4-2-3. A less defensive modern system is the 4-2-4, developed by the Brazilians.

The coming of new systems has meant that the old player position names, based on the pyramid, have become outdated. New names are now used and are shown below as applied to the 4-2-4 formation:

It should be remembered, however, that soccer

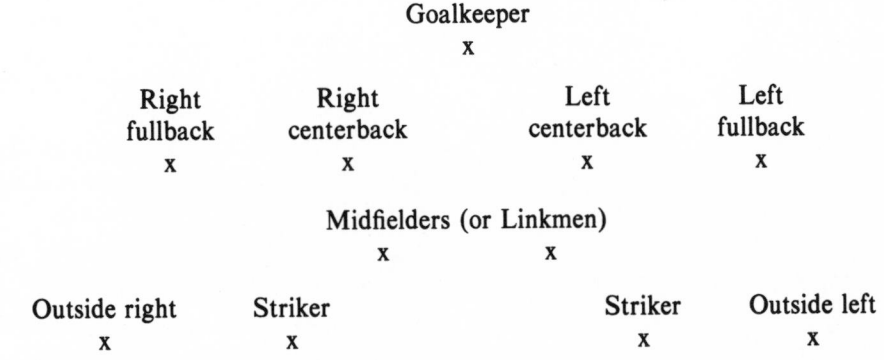

```
                         Goalkeeper
                             x

        Right           Right           Left            Left
      fullback        centerback      centerback       fullback
         x                x               x               x

                  Midfielders (or Linkmen)
                       x          x

  Outside right    Striker              Striker     Outside left
       x              x                    x             x
```

is an extremely fluid game and that during a game a team may be constantly changing its formations—playing 4-3-3 one minute, switching to 4-2-4 the next.

TARGETMAN: A tall, strong forward who plays a rather lonely role as the spearhead of the attack in certain modern formations. The ball is fed to him—usually a long pass out of defense, in the air—and his task is to control it or to head it down to his teammates running up to support him.

THROW-IN: When the ball goes over the touchline, it is put back into play by means of a throw-in taken by the team that did not kick the ball out. There are rules defining the exact way in which the ball must be thrown. Both feet must be on the ground outside the field of play or on the touchline; the ball must be thrown over the head using both hands equally. The thrower may not play the ball a second time until another player has played it. If the throw is taken improperly, the ball is given to the opposing team to throw in.

TIME: Under international rules, a soccer game consists of two forty-five-minute halves, with a five-minute interval. The referee is the official timekeeper. There are no time-outs called by players or coaches. Apart from small variations, for example, thirty-five-minute halves for schoolboy games, these are the rules that are followed throughout the world. The one exception is American high schools, where the rules recommend that the game be played in four quarters of eighteen minutes with a halftime interval of ten minutes. In college and high school games, an official timekeeper, and not the referee, keeps the time.

TIME-OUT: Time-outs cannot be called by players or coaches in soccer. The referee is the only one who can stop the clock, which he will do as little as possible—usually to allow an injured player to be treated or if he feels that a team is deliberately wasting time.

TOE-END: To kick the ball with the front of the toe. Such kicks are rarely used because little real power or accuracy can be obtained by toe-ending the ball.

TOUCHLINE: The line at each side of the field. A ball going over the touchline is said to have gone into touch. Also called sideline.

TRANSFER(S): The buying and selling of players by clubs is known as the transfer market.

Unlike baseball, football, and basketball, where player-for-player swaps are the rule, soccer transfers are usually straight cash purchases. In England, and particularly in Italy and Spain, enormous sums of money are involved. The first four-figure transfer fee came in England in 1905 when a player was bought for 1,000 pounds (worth $5,000 in those days). In 1963, a Rome team paid $580,000 for a player, a world record that stood until 1968 when Juventus of Turin bought Pietro Anastasi for just over $1 million. The current record is $2.2 million paid by Barcelona to the Dutch club Ajax for their star forward Johann Cruyff. During the 1970s, professional soccer players' organizations in many countries started to press for "freedom of contract," under which a player, once his contract had expired, would be free to negotiate with any club he pleased. If freedom of contract is widely accepted, then clubs would no longer have to pay a player's former club, and the days of huge transfer fees would be over.

TRAP: To bring the ball under control. Since the ball is likely to arrive at any angle, at any height, and at any speed, there are many different ways of trapping it—with the sole, the inside or the outside of the foot, the thigh, or the chest.

TRIPPING: Any sort of tripping—or attempt to trip—is illegal in soccer. The offender will have a direct free kick given against his team.

UNGENTLEMANLY CONDUCT: Soccer's version of unsportsmanlike conduct. Examples are swearing, waving the arms about to interfere with opponents, and dancing about and gesticulating "in a way calculated to distract opponents." The referee will caution the ungentlemanly player and give an indirect free kick against his team.

UP-AND-UNDER: An example of primitive soccer. A long, high pass designed to come down in the opposing goalmouth as forwards rush in underneath it.

UPRIGHTS: The goalposts.

USSF: The United States Soccer Federation, the governing body of soccer within the U.S.

UTILITY PLAYER: A player with all-around ability who can be used in attacking, midfield, or defensive roles.

VOLLEY: To kick the ball on the fly before it hits the ground.

WALL: A maneuver for defending against free kicks within scoring range. A number of defenders, usually from three to six, will stand close together forming a wall ten yards from the ball. The idea is to block as much of the kicker's view of the goal as possible. The kicker is thus left with a much smaller area to shoot at, and the goal keeper's task is made correspondingly simpler.

WALL PASS: The give-and-go, so called because in soccer games played by boys in the streets the ball is bounced off a wall instead of being played to a teammate.

WING: An area of the field near the touchline.

WINGER: The right and left outside forwards. See Tactics.

WOODWORK: The wooden structure that makes up the goal, the two goalposts, and the crossbar.

WORLD CUP: The greatest of the international soccer competitions. Its official title is the Jules Rimet Cup, named after the Frenchman who founded it. It is open to any country that is affiliated with FIFA, and the finals are played every four years, between the years of the Olympic Games. It is a competition for national teams, either amateur or professional, but inevitably it is dominated by the pros.

YELLOW CARD: To administer an official caution to a player, the referee enters his name in his notebook, then holds a yellow card in the air as an indication that the player has been cautioned. The player's name is sent on to the appropriate disciplinary authorities. Under international rules, a player cannot receive two yellow cards in one game. The second time he must be shown the red card and ejected from the game. See also Red Card.

APPENDIX B
The Laws of the Game

The soccer rules of the Fédération Internationale de Football Association (FIFA) are used all over the world and on all levels of play. They are the result of the deliberations of the International Football Association Board which meets annually and is supreme authority for changes and revisions. In most countries there is one regulatory body for the sport, and differences from the international standard are rare.

In America there are many athletic regulatory bodies—college, secondary schools, women's, amateur, United States Soccer Federation, North American Soccer League, etc. All of these have marked the game with their particular thumbprint. To their credit, their changes have been well intentioned and, significantly, all tend strongly toward conformity with the international FIFA norm.

Broadly, the differences a spectator might note are the following:

• In the interest of getting more players into the game, colleges allow seven substitutes; the NASL allows three. In secondary school, women's play, and on some youth levels under USSF, substitution is unlimited.

• Colleges and schools employ two officials with equal authority on the field as opposed to one referee and two linesmen found regulating the amateur and professional game.

• College and school officials employ a system of whistle and arm signals to distinguish each infraction. FIFA referees whistle all fouls but are sparing with signals otherwise. They wave play to start after a stoppage; point the direction of free kicks; raise one arm overhead to indicate an indirect free kick; point to the corners, to the half of the goal area, and to the penalty spot when kicks are to be taken there; and they push both arms forward at waist level to indicate a "Play on!" when an infraction has been seen but not given because it would disadvantage the play.

• The High School Federation shortens playing periods to thirty-five minutes, while in women's play, the game is divided into four periods rather than the usual two. In addition, schools and colleges allow ten minutes between halves, FIFA only five.

• There are provisions for overtime to resolve drawn games in college and school play but not in women's and USSF games. The NASL employs both overtime periods and a series of penalty kicks if the former fails to bring in a winner.

• In college play, protective devices, properly padded—such as casts, masks, etc.—are permitted if both coaches agree, while the High School Federation bans protectors of any sort. The High School Federation is most careful, too, regarding length of boot studs, banning ground-grippers in excess of ½ inch protrusion. All other governing bodies allow cleats and studs of up to ¾ inch in height.

• Player numbers are required on both front and back of the uniform in college; on the back only in school and women's play. Colleges require the goalkeeper to be numbered; the High School Federation does not. Interestingly, FIFA requires

526

no numbers at all, though it is rare to find a team anywhere that does not number players for identification purposes.

• A peculiar divergence can be found in the case of a restart after a temporary suspension of play, for example, after a serious injury. Usually the ball is dropped by the referee between two opposing players at the point play ceased. But college rules demand that when this would occur within either penalty area, the ball must be taken to the nearest point outside the area for the drop. The High School Federation requires that play be restarted with an indirect free kick from the team that was in clear possession when play was stopped.

• Still another oddity occurs in the NASL. For these games, an additional field mark is drawn across the field thirty-five yards from each end line. Up to this point, offsides is not applicable for the team in possession. The change was made to enhance scoring, but results have been inconclusive.

• Finally, there are two digressions in soccer as played in the United States regarding personal fouls. Women are permitted to let the ball contact the arms when they are crossed over the chest for protection, and the High School Federation requires that sliding tackles, to be accounted legal, must be made within the peripheral vision of the man tackled.

Notwithstanding the differences noted, the soccer buff would recognize his game wherever played and on whatever level. If he were a student of the game, he would know too, that similarities far outnumber differences in the rules and give soccer a unique place among world sport.

The Laws of the Game that follow have been authorized by the International Football Association Board and published by the Fédération Internationale de Football Association.

LAWS OF THE GAME

LAW I.—THE FIELD OF PLAY

The Field of Play and appurtenances shall be as shown in the following plan:

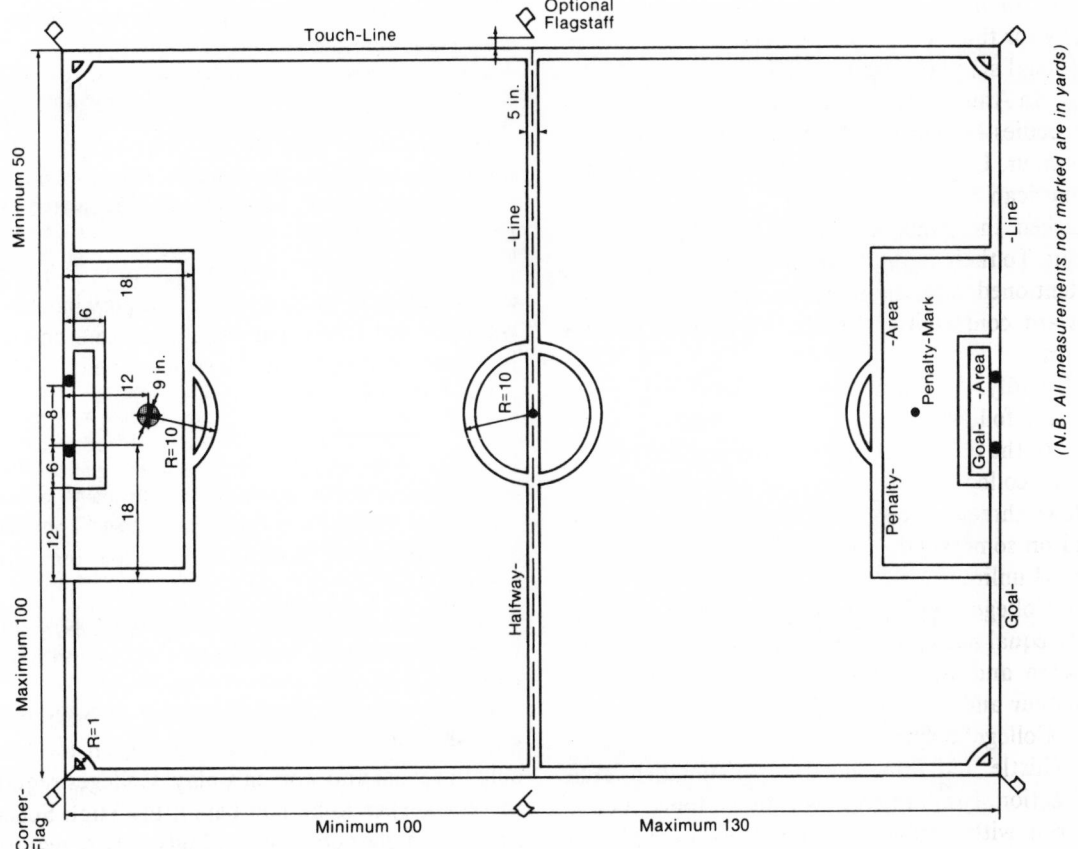

(1) **Dimensions.** The field of play shall be rectangular, its length being not more than 130 yards nor less than 100 yards and its breadth not more than 100 yards nor less than 50 yards. (In International Matches the length shall be not more than 120 yards nor less than 110 yards and the breadth not more than 80 yards nor less than 70 yards.) The length shall in all cases exceed the breadth.

(2) **Marking.** The field of play shall be marked with distinctive lines, not more than 5 inches in width, not by a V-shaped rut, in accordance with the plan, the longer boundary lines being called the touch-lines and the shorter the goal-lines. A flag on a post not less than 5 ft. high and having a non-pointed top shall be placed at each corner; a similar flag-post may be placed opposite the halfway line on each side of the field of play, not less than 1 yard outside the touch-line. A halfway-line shall be marked out across the field of play. The center of the field of play shall be indicated by a suitable mark and a circle with a 10 yards radius shall be marked round it.

(3) **The Goal-Area.** At each end of the field of play two lines shall be drawn at right-angles to the goal-line, 6 yards from each goal-post. These shall extend into the field of play for a distance of 6 yards and shall be joined by a line drawn parallel with the goal-line. Each of the spaces enclosed by these lines and the goal-line shall be called a goal-area.

(4) **The Penalty-Area.** At each end of the field of play two lines shall be drawn at right-angles to the goal-line, 18 yards from each goal-post. These shall extend into the field of play for a distance of 18 yards and shall be joined by a line drawn parallel with the goal-line. Each of the spaces enclosed by these lines and the goal-line shall be called a penalty-area. A suitable mark shall be made within each penalty-area, 12 yards from the mid-point of the goal-line, measured along an undrawn line at right-angles thereto. These shall be the penalty-kick marks. From each penalty-kick mark an arc of a circle, having a radius of 10 yards, shall be drawn outside the penalty-area.

(5) **The Corner-Area.** From each corner-flag-post a quarter circle, having a radius of 1 yard, shall be drawn inside the field of play.

(6) **The Goals.** The goals shall be placed on the center of each goal-line and shall consist of two upright posts, equidistant from the corner-flags and 8 yards apart (inside measurement), joined by a horizontal cross-bar the lower edge of which shall be 8 ft. from the ground. The width and depth of the goal-posts and the width and depth of the cross-bars shall not exceed 5 inches (12 cm). The goal-posts and the cross-bars shall have the same width.

Nets may be attached to the posts, cross-bars and ground behind the goals. They should be appropriately supported and be so placed as to allow the goal-keeper ample room.

Footnote:

Goal nets. The use of nets made of hemp, jute or nylon is permitted. The nylon strings may, however, not be thinner than those made of hemp or jute.

LAW II.—THE BALL

The ball shall be spherical; the outer casing shall be of leather or other approved materials. No material shall be used in its construction which might prove dangerous to the players.

The circumference of the ball shall not be more than 28 in. and not less than 27 in. The weight of the ball at the start of the game shall not be more than 16 oz. nor less than 14 oz. The pressure shall be equal to 0.6-0.7 atmosphere, which equals 9.0-10.5 lb./sq.in. ($=600$-700 gr/cm^2) at sea level. The ball shall not be changed during the game unless authorized by the Referee.

LAW III.—NUMBER OF PLAYERS

(1) A match shall be played by two teams, each consisting of not more than eleven players, one of whom shall be the goalkeeper.

(2) Substitutes may be used in any match played under the rules of an official competition at FIFA, Confederation or National Association level, subject to the following conditions:

(a) that the authority of the international association(s) or national association(s) concerned, has been obtained,

(b) that, subject to the restriction contained in the following paragraph (c) the rules of a competition shall state how many, if any, substitutes may be used, and

(c) that a team shall not be permitted to use more than two substitutes in any match.

(3) Substitutes may be used in any other match, provided that the two teams concerned reach agreement on a maximum number, not exceeding five, and that the terms of such agreement are intimated to the Referee, before the match. If the Referee is not informed, or if the teams fail to reach agreement, no more than two substitutes shall be permitted.

(4) Any of the other players may change places with the goalkeeper, provided that the Referee is informed before the change is made, and provided also, that the change is made during a stoppage in the game.

(5) When a goalkeeper or any other player is to be replaced by a substitute, the following conditions shall be observed:

(a) the Referee shall be informed of the proposed substitution, before it is made,

(b) the substitute shall not enter the field of play until the player he is replacing has left, and then only after having received a signal from the Referee,

(c) he shall enter the field during a stoppage in the game, and at the half-way line.

Punishment:

(a) Play shall not be stopped for an infringement of paragraph 4. The players concerned shall be cautioned immediately the ball goes out of play.

(b) For any other infringement of this law, the player concerned shall be cautioned, and if the game is stopped by the Referee, to administer the caution, it shall be re-started by an indirect free-kick, to be taken by a player of the opposing team, from the place where the ball was, when play was stopped. If the free-kick is awarded to a team within its own goal area, it may be taken from any point within that half of the goal area in which the ball was when play was stopped.

LAW IV.—PLAYERS' EQUIPMENT

(1) A player shall not wear anything which is dangerous to another player.

(2) Footwear (boots or shoes) must conform to the following standard:

(a) Bars shall be made of leather or rubber and shall be transverse and flat, not less than half an inch in width and shall extend the total width of the sole and be rounded at the corners.

(b) Studs which are independently mounted on the sole and are replaceable shall be made of leather, rubber, aluminium, plastic or similar material and shall be solid. With the exception of that part of the stud forming the base, which shall not protrude from the sole more than one quarter of an inch, studs shall be round in plan and not less than half an inch in diameter. Where studs are tapered, the minimum diameter of any section of the stud must not be less than half an inch. Where metal seating for the screw type is used, this seating must be embedded in the sole of the footwear and any attachment screw shall be part of the stud. Other than the metal seating for the screw type of stud, no metal plates even though covered with leather or rubber shall be worn, neither studs which are threaded to allow them to be screwed on to a base screw that is fixed by nails or otherwise to the soles of footwear, nor studs which, apart from the base, have any form of protruding edge rim or relief marking or ornament, should be allowed.

(c) Studs which are moulded as an integral part of the sole and are not replaceable shall be made of rubber, plastic, polyurethene or similar soft materials. Provided that there are no fewer than ten studs on the sole, they shall have a minimum diameter of three eights of an inch (10 mm.). Additional supporting material to stabilize studs of soft materials, and ridges which shall not protrude more than 5 mm. from the sole and moulded to strengthen it, shall be permitted provided that they are in no way dangerous to other players. In all other respects they shall conform to the general requirements of this Law.

(d) Combined bars and studs may be worn, provided the whole conforms to the general requirements of this Law. Neither bars nor studs on the soles shall project more than three-quarters of an inch. If nails are used they shall be driven in flush with the surface.

(3) The goalkeeper shall wear colors which distinguish him from the other players and from the referee.

Punishment: For any infringement of this Law, the player at fault shall be sent off the field of play to adjust his equipment and he shall not return without first reporting to the Referee, who shall satisfy himself that the player's equipment is in order; the player shall only re-enter the game at a moment when the ball has ceased to be in play.

LAW V.—REFEREES

A Referee shall be appointed to officiate in each game. His authority and the exercise of the powers granted to him by the Laws of the Game commence as soon as he enters the field of play.

His power of penalizing shall extend to offences committed when play has been temporarily suspended, or when the ball is out of play. His decision on points of fact connected with the play shall be final, so far as the result of the game is concerned. He shall:

(a) Enforce the Laws.

(b) Refrain from penalizing in cases where he is satisfied that, by doing so, he would be giving an advantage to the offending team.

(c) Keep a record of the game; act as timekeeper and allow the full or agreed time, adding thereto all time lost through accident or other cause.

(d) Have discretionary power to stop the game for any infringement of the Laws and to suspend or terminate the game whenever, by reason of the elements, interference by spectators, or other cause, he deems such stoppage necessary. In such a case he shall submit a detailed report to the competent authority, within the stipulated time, and in accordance with the provisions set up by the National Association under whose jurisdiction the match was played. Reports will be deemed to be made when received in the ordinary course of mail.

(e) From the time he enters the field of play, caution any player guilty of misconduct or ungentlemanly behaviour and, if he persists, suspend him from further participation in the game. In such cases the Referee shall send the name of the offender to the competent authority, within the stipulated time, and in accordance with the provisions set up by the National Association under whose jurisdiction the match was played. Reports will be deemed to be made when received in the ordinary course of mail.

(f) Allow no person other than the players and linesmen to enter the field of play without his permission.

(g) Stop the game if, in his opinion, a player has been seriously injured; have the player removed as soon as possible from the field of play, and immediately resume the game. If a player is slightly injured, the game shall not be stopped until the ball has ceased to be in play. A player who is able to go to the touch or goal-line for attention of any kind, shall not be treated on the field of play.

(h) Send off the field of play, any player who, in his opinion, is guilty of violent conduct, serious foul play, or the use of foul or abusive language.

(i) Signal for recommencement of the game after all stoppages.

REFEREES' SIGNALS (NASL)

Offsides
(Arm moving across body indicating team offside)

Indirect Free Kick

Time Allowance

Directional Signal
(Foul—indicates position accompanied by whistle)

Pushing

Retire 10 Yards

Unfair Tackle From Behind

Striking
(Clenched fist)

Caution/Ejection
(Caution—Yellow card; Ejection—Red card)

Handling

Play On/Advantage

Stop the Clock

Restart Clock
(Circular motion)

Goal After Shootout

Goal Not Allowed in Shootout

Foul Throw
(Ball not thrown in properly with both hands and delivered from behind and over head)

(j) Decide that the ball provided for a match meets with the requirements of Law II.

LAW VI.—LINESMEN

Two Linesmen shall be appointed, whose duty (subject to the decision of the Referee) shall be to indicate when the ball is out of play and which side is entitled to the corner-kick, goal-kick or throw-in. They shall also assist the Referee to control the game in accordance with the Laws. In the event of undue interference or improper conduct by a Linesman, the Referee shall dispense with his services and arrange for a substitute to be appointed. (The matter shall be reported by the Referee to the competent authority.) The Linesmen should be equipped with flags by the Club on whose ground the match is played.

LAW VIII.—DURATION OF THE GAME

The duration of the game shall be two equal periods of 45 minutes, unless otherwise mutually agreed upon, subject to the following: (a) Allowance shall be made in either period for all time lost through accident or other cause, the amount of which shall be a matter for the discretion of the Referee; (b) Time shall be extended to permit a penalty-kick being taken at or after the expiration of the normal period in either half.

At half-time the interval shall not exceed five minutes except by consent of the Referee.

LAW VIII.—THE START OF PLAY

(a) **At the beginning of the game,** choice of ends and the kick-off shall be decided by the toss of a coin. The team winning the toss shall have the option of choice of ends or the kick-off. The Referee having given a signal, the game shall be started by a player taking a place-kick (i.e., a kick at the ball while it is stationary on the ground in the center of the field of play) into his opponents' half of the field of play. Every player shall be in his own half of the field and every player of the team opposing that of the kicker shall remain not less than 10 yards from the ball until it is kicked-off; it shall not be deemed in play until it has travelled the distance of its own circumference. The kicker shall not play the ball a second time until it has been touched or played by another player.

(b) **After a goal has scored,** the game shall be restarted in like manner by a player of the team yielding the goal.

(c) **After half-time;** when restarting after half-time, ends shall be changed and the kick-off shall be taken by a player of the opposite team to that of the player who started the game.

Punishment. For any infringement of this Law, the kick-off shall be retaken, except in the case of the kicker playing the ball again before it has been touched or played by another player; for this offence, an indirect free-kick shall be taken by a player of the opposing team from the place where the infringement occurred, unless the offence is committed by a player in his oppo-nents' goal area, in which case, the free-kick shall be taken from a point anywhere within that half of the goal area in which the offence occurred.

A goal shall not be scored direct from a kick-off.

(d) **After any other temporary suspension;** when re-starting the game after a temporary suspension of play from any cause not mentioned elsewhere in these Laws, provided that immediately prior to the suspension the ball has not passed over the touch or goal-lines, the Referee shall drop the ball at the place where it was when play was suspended and it shall be deemed in play when it has touched the ground; if, however, it goes over the touch or goal-lines after it has been dropped by the Referee, but before it is touched by a player, the Referee shall again drop it. A player shall not play the ball until it has touched the ground. If this section of the Law is not complied with the Referee shall again drop the ball.

LAW IX.—BALL IN AND OUT OF PLAY

The ball is out of play:

(a) When it has wholly crossed the goal-line or touch-line, whether on the ground or in the air.

(b) When the game has been stopped by the Referee.

The ball is in play at all other times from the start of the match to the finish including:

(a) If it rebounds from a goal-post, cross-bar or corner-flag post into the field of play.

(b) If it rebounds off either the Referee or Linesmen when they are in the field of play.

(c) In the event of a supposed infringement of the Laws, until a decision is given.

LAW X.—METHOD OF SCORING

Except as otherwise provided by these Laws, a goal is scored when the whole of the ball has passed over the goal-line, between the goal-posts and under the cross-bar, provided it has not been thrown, carried or intentionally propelled by hand or arm, by a player of the attacking side, except in the case of a goalkeeper, who is within his own penalty-area.

The team scoring the greater number of goals during a game shall be the winner; if no goals, or an equal number of goals are scored, the game shall be termed a "draw"

LAW XI.—OFF-SIDE

1. A player is in an off-side position if he is nearer to his opponents' goal-line than the ball, unless:

(a) he is in his own half of the field of play, or

(b) there are at least two of his opponents nearer their own goal-line than he is.

2. A player shall only be declared off-side and penalised for being in an off-side position, if, at the moment the ball touches, or is played by, one of his team, he is, in the opinion of the Referee

(a) interfering with play or with an opponent, or

(b) seeking to gain an advantage by being in that position.

3. A player shall not be declared off-side by the Referee

(a) merely because of his being in an off-side position, or

(b) if he receives the ball, direct, from a goal-kick, a corner-kick, a throw-in, or when it has been dropped by the Referee.

4. If a player is declared off-side, the Referee shall award an indirect free-kick, which shall be taken by a player of the opposing team from the place where the infringement occurred, unless the offence is commited by a player in his opponents' goal area, in which case, the free-kick shall be taken from a point anywhere within that half of the goal area in which the offence occurred.

LAW XII.—FOULS AND MISCONDUCT

A player who intentionally commits any of the following nine offences:

(a) Kicks or attempts to kick an opponent;

(b) Trips an opponent, i.e., throwing or attempting to throw him by the use of the legs or by stooping in front of or behind him;

(c) Jumps at an opponent;

(d) Charges an opponent in a violent or dangerous manner;

(e) Charges an opponent from behind unless the latter is obstructing;

(f) Strikes or attempts to strike an opponent;

(g) Holds an opponent;

(h) Pushes an opponent;

(i) Handles the ball, i.e., carries, strikes or propels the ball with his hand or arm. (This does not apply to the goalkeeper within his own penalty-area);

shall be penalized by the award of a **direct free-kick** to be taken by the opposing team from the place where the offence occurred, unless the offence is committed by a player in his opponents' goal area, in which case, the free-kick shall be taken from a point anywhere within that half of the goal area in which the offence occurred.

Should a player of the defending team intentionally commit one of the above nine offences within the penalty-area he shall be penalized by a **penalty-kick.**

A penalty-kick can be awarded irrespective of the position of the ball, if in play, at the time an offence within the penalty-area is committed.

A player committing any of the five following offences:

1. Playing in a manner considered by the Referee to be dangerous, e.g., attempting to kick the ball while held by the goalkeeper;

2. Charging fairly, i.e., with the shoulder, when the ball is not within playing distance of the players concerned and they are definitely not trying to play it;

3. When not playing the ball, intentionally obstructing an opponent, i.e., running between the opponent and the ball, or interposing the body so as to form an obstacle to an opponent;

4. Charging the goalkeeper except when he

(a) is holding the ball;

(b) is obstructing an opponent;

(c) has passed outside his goal-area;

5. When playing as goalkeeper,

(a) takes more than 4 steps while holding, bouncing or throwing the ball in the air and catching it again without releasing it so that it is played by another player, or

(b) indulges in tactics which, in the opinion of the Referee, are designed merely to hold up the game and thus waste time and so give an unfair advantage to his own team

shall be penalized by the award of an *indirect free-kick* to be taken by the opposing team from the place where the infringement occurred, unless the offence is committed by a player in his opponents' goal area, in which case, the free-kick shall be taken from a point anywhere within that half of the goal area in which the offence occurred.

A player shall be **cautioned** if:

(j) he enters or re-enters the field of play to join or rejoin his team after the game has commenced, or leaves the field of play during the progress of the game (except through accident) without, in either case, first having received a signal from the Referee showing him that he may do so. If the Referee stops the game to administer the caution the game shall be restarted by an indirect free-kick taken by a player of the opposing team from the place where the ball was when the Referee stopped the game. If the free-kick is awarded to a team within its own goal area it may be taken from any point within the half of the goal area in which the ball was when play was stopped. If, however, the offending player has committed a more serious offence he shall be penalized according to that section of the law he infringed;

(k) he persistently infringes the Laws of the Game;

(l) he shows by word or action, dissent from any decision given by the Referee;

(m) he is guilty of ungentlemanly conduct.

For any of these last three offences, in addition to the caution, an **indirect free-kick** shall also be awarded to the opposing team from the place where the offence occurred unless a more serious infringement of the Laws of the Game was committed. If the offence is committed by a player in his opponents' goal area, a free-kick shall be taken from a point anywhere within that half of the goal area in which the offence occurred.

A player shall be *sent off* the field of play, if:

(n) in the opinion of the Referee he is guilty of violent conduct or serious foul play;

(o) he uses foul or abusive language;

(p) he persists in misconduct after having received a caution.

If play be stopped by reason of a player being ordered from the field for an offence without a separate breach of the Law having been committed, the game shall be resumed by an **indirect free-kick** awarded to the opposing team from the place where the infringement occurred, unless the offence is committed by a player in his opponents' goal area, in which case, the free-kick shall be taken from a point anywhere within that half of the goal area in which the offence occurred.

LAW XIII.—FREE-KICK

Free-kicks shall be classified under two headings: "Direct" (from which a goal can be scored direct against the offending side), and "Indirect" (from which a goal cannot be scored unless the ball has been played or touched by a player other than the kicker before passing through the goal).

When a player is taking a direct or an indirect free-kick inside his own penalty-area, all of the opposing players shall remain outside the area, and shall be at least ten yards from the ball while the kick is being taken. The ball shall be in play once it has travelled the distance of its own circumference and is beyond the penalty-area. The goalkeeper shall not receive the ball into his hands, in order that he may thereafter kick it into play. If the ball is not kicked direct into play, beyond the penalty-area, the kick shall be retaken.

When a player is taking a direct or an indirect free-kick outside his own penalty-area, all of the opposing players shall be at least ten yards from the ball, until it is in play, unless they are standing on their own goal-line, between the goal-posts. The ball shall be in play when it has travelled the distance of its own circumference.

If a player of the opposing side encroaches into the penalty-area, or within ten yards of the ball, as the case may be, before a free-kick is taken, the Referee shall delay the taking of the kick, until the Law is complied with.

The ball must be stationary when a free-kick is taken, and the kicker shall not play the ball a second time, until it has been touched or played by another player.

Notwithstanding any other reference in these Laws to the point from which a free-kick is to be taken, any free-kick awarded to the defending team, within its own goal area, may be taken from any point within that half of the goal area in which the free-kick has been awarded.

Punishment: If the kicker, after taking the free-kick, plays the ball a second time before it has been touched or played by another player an indirect free-kick shall be taken by a player of the opposing team from the spot where the infringement occurred, unless the offence is committed by a player in his opponents' goal area, in which case, the free-kick shall be taken from a point anywhere within that half of the goal area in which the offence occurred.

LAW XIV.—PENALTY-KICK

A penalty-kick shall be taken from the penalty-mark and, when it is being taken, all players with the exception of the player taking the kick, and the opposing goalkeeper, shall be within the field of play but outside the penalty-area, and at least 10 yards from the penalty-mark. The opposing goalkeeper must stand (without moving his feet) on his own goal-line, between the goal-posts, until the ball is kicked. The player taking the kick must kick the ball forward; he shall not play the ball a second time until it has been touched or played by another player. The ball shall be deemed in play as soon as it is kicked, i.e., when it has travelled the distance of its circumference, and a goal may be scored direct from such a penalty-kick. If the ball touches the goalkeeper before passing between the posts, when a penalty-kick is being taken at or after the expiration of half-time or full-time it does not nullify a goal. If necessary, time of play shall be extended at half-time or full-time to allow a penalty-kick to be taken.

Punishment:

For any infringement of this Law:

(a) by the defending team, the kick shall be retaken if a goal has not resulted.

(b) by the attacking team other than by the player taking the kick, if a goal is scored it shall be disallowed and the kick retaken.

(c) by the player taking the penalty-kick, committed after the ball is in play, a player of the opposing team shall take an indirect free-kick from the spot where the infringement occurred.

If, in the case of paragraph (c), the offence is committed by the player in his opponents' goal area, the free-kick shall be taken from a point anywhere within that half of the goal area in which the offence occurred.

LAW XV.—THROW-IN

When the whole of the ball passes over a touch-line, either on the ground or in the air, it shall be thrown in from the point where it crossed the line, in any direction, by a player of the team opposite to that of the player who last touched it. The thrower at the moment of delivering the ball must face the field of play and part of each foot shall be either on the touch-line or on the ground outside the touch-line. The thrower shall use both hands and shall deliver the ball from behind and over his head. The ball shall be in play as soon as it enters the field of play, but the thrower shall not again play the ball until it has been touched or played by another player. A goal shall not be scored direct from a throw-in.

Punishment:

(a) If the ball is improperly thrown in the throw-in shall be taken by a player of the opposing team.

(b) If the thrower plays the ball a second time before it has been touched or played by another player, an indirect free-kick shall be taken by a player of the opposing team from the place where the infringement occurred, unless the offence is committed by a player in his opponents' goal area, in which case, the free-kick shall be taken from a point anywhere within that half of the goal area in which the offence occurred.

LAW XVI.—GOAL-KICK

When the whole of the ball passes over the goal-line excluding that portion between the goal-posts, either in the air or on the ground, having last been played by one of the attacking team, it shall be kicked direct into play beyond the penalty-area from a point within that half of the goal-area nearest to where it crossed the line, by a player of the defending team. A goalkeeper shall not receive the ball into his hands from a goal-kick in order that he may thereafter kick it into play. If the ball is not kicked beyond the penalty-area, i.e., direct into play, the kick shall be retaken. The kicker shall not play the ball a second time until it has touched—or been played by—another player. A goal shall not be scored direct from such a kick. Players of the team opposing that of the player taking the goal-kick shall remain outside the penalty-area while the kick is being taken.

Punishment: If a player taking a goal-kick plays the ball a second time after it has passed beyond the penalty-area, but before it has touched or been played by another player, an indirect free-kick shall be awarded to the opposing team, to be taken from the place where the infringement occurred, unless the offence is committed by a player in his opponents' goal area, in which case, the free-kick shall be taken from a point anywhere within that half of the goal area in which the offence occurred.

LAW XVII.—CORNER-KICK

When the whole of the ball passes over the goal-line, excluding that portion between the goal-posts, either in the air or on the ground, having last been played by one of the defending team, a member of the attacking team shall take a corner-kick, i.e., the whole of the ball shall be placed within the quarter circle at the nearest corner-flag-post, which must not be moved, and it shall be kicked from that position. A goal may be scored direct from such a kick. Players of the team opposing that of the player taking the corner-kick shall not approach within 10 yards of the ball until it is in play, i.e., it has travelled the distance of its own circumference, nor shall the kicker play the ball a second time until it has been touched or played by another player.

Punishment:

(a) If the player who takes the kick plays the ball a second time before it has been touched or played by another player, the Referee shall award an indirect free-kick to the opposing team, to be taken from the place where the infringement occurred, unless the offence is committed by a player in his opponents' goal area, in which case, the free-kick shall be taken from a point anywhere within that half of the goal area in which the offence occurred.

(b) For any other infringement the kick shall be retaken.

INDEX

This index includes all persons, associations, clubs, leagues, teams (college and professional) appearing in the encyclopedia except those that are listed *only* in the college, ASL and NASL record sections, the All-Time NASL Player Register, World Cup summaries, and any other tabular material. Boldface numerals denote page references to photo captions.

A

Aandahl, Loren, 114, 116
Abadi, Henry, 116–17
Abel, Frank, **151**
Aberdeen (Scotland), 283
Adams, Francis, 68
Adams, Graham, 293
Adams, John Weston, 282
Adedeji, Felix, 109, **117**
Adelphi College (Panthers), 80, 103, 116, 119, 132
Ademir, 481
ADO (Holland), 283
Adolph, Bob, **73**
Aga Khan, 75, **75**
Agonafer, Shoa, 105, 113
Air Force Academy, United States (Falcons), 73, 75, 78, 81, 82, 87, 88, 92, 99, 129
Aja, Jose, 265
Akintunde, Key, **258**
Akron, University of (Zips), 70, 75, 78, 82, 85, 92, 94, 98, 127
Akuffo, Fred, **84**
Alabama A & M University (Bulldogs), 129, 132
Alabama, University of at Huntsville, 132
Alachua, 46
Alamu, Tekeda, 113, 116
Albany State University (Great Danes), 67
Albers, Yank, 96
Alberto, Carlos, 313, **315**, 324, 325, 489, 492
Albertosi, 490
Albino, Jerry, **223**
Alexis, Winston, 86, **199**
Alfano, Pete, 7
Ali, Muhammad, **315**
All-Americans, College, 58–59, 61, 63, 141–49

Allegheny College (Gators), 58, 67
Allen, Marvin, **221**
Allen, Rick, 109
All-Intercollegiate Team, 38
Allison, Malcolm, 285, 318
All-Stars (NASL), 289–90
Allyn, John, 282
Alon, Benny, **308**
Alonso, Julius G., 7, 266, 267, 269, 513
Alozie, Sydney, 87
Altoona (Pa.) Railroad Shops team, 43
Amarildo, 485, 486
Amateur Athletic Union (AAU), 507
American Football Association, 38
American Soccer League, 7, 263–279, 505, 507
American Soccer League News, 265, 267, 270, 271
American University (Eagles), 65, **154**
Amherst College (Lord Jeffs), 20, 34, 49, 60, 61, 96
Andersen, Roar, **130**
Anderson, Aly, **127**, 129
Anderson, Willy, 305
Andreadis, George, 61, 63
Angeliotti, Mike, **275**
Antoni, Irv, 57
Apostolidis, Kirk, 289
Appalachian State University, 121, 131
Aqui, Keith, 105, **110**
Araujo, Americo, 114
Arbelaez, Vic, 119
Archibald, Warren, 282, 289, 290, 295, 300
Arena, Bruce, 113
Army (Cadets), 45, 46, 57, 60, 63, 65, 67, 68, 84, 87, 88, 98, 113, 132
Arnautoff, Pete, 125
Ash, Mick, 290
Aston, Ken, 485
Astros (Mass.), 273
Atanasio, Ron, 120
Athey, Ed, 100
Athey, Ron, 103
Atlanta Apollos, 295, 299
Atlanta Chiefs, 282, 285, 286, 288, 290
Atlante (Mexico), 267
Atlantic Coast Conference, 67, 68, 70, 73, 75, 85, 87, 88, 94, 103, 117, 132
Atlantic Coast NCAA Tournament, 87, 94, 99, 109

Atuegbu, Fidelus (Andy), 119, 125, **128**
Aubuchon, Don, 117, **199**
Auguste, Arsene, 305
Austin, Ed, 109
Austin, Herb, 109

B

Babbit, James, 32, 35
Babson College (Beavers), 119, 120, 121, 125, 129
Bachman, Fred, 276
Bagley, Thomas, 32
Bahr, Casey, 100, 109, 127, 513
Bahr, Chris, 109, 117, 119, **126**, 127, **304**, 305, 513
Bahr, Matt, 119, **126**, 127, 513
Bahr, Walt, 8, 57, 70, **126**, 266, 269, 270, 273, 513
Bain, Ian, 107, 113, 119
Baker, Donald C., 43
Bakum, Myron, **219**
Balassi, Gerry, 79, 81
Baldwin, Merritt, **49**
Baldwin-Wallace College, 35, 38
Ball, Alan, 325, 328, 488
Ball State University (Cardinals), **157**
Ballantyne, Archie, 269
Baltimore Bays, 282, 284, 285, 288, 299
Baltimore St. Gerard's, 273
Baltimore, University of (Super Bees), 57, 60, 63, 65, 68, 70, 72, 75, 80, 85, 99, 120
Bamiro, Ayomi, 117
Bangu (Brazil), 79, 283
Banks, Gordon, 312, **313**, **487**
Baptista, Dick, 59
Baptista, Robert, 7, **73**, **255**
Barber, Eric, **287**
Barbosa, 482
Barrington, 92
Barriskill, Joseph J., 263, 512
Bartholomy, Bill, 282
Barto, Barry, 102
Bass, Clarence, **61**
Bates College (Bobcats), 96
Batie, Don, 309
Battle of Bern, The, 482
Baum, Joe, 8
Baumann, Jim, 120
Baumann, Steve, 109